THE BURNS ENCYCLOPEDIA

The
BURNS
Encyclopedia

MAURICE LINDSAY

HUTCHINSON OF LONDON

HUTCHINSON & CO (Publishers) LTD
178–202 Great Portland Street, London W1

London Melbourne Sydney
Auckland Johannesburg Cape Town
and agencies throughout the world

First published 1959
Second edition (revised and enlarged) 1970

This book has been set in Bembo type, printed in Great Britain
on antique wove paper by Anchor Press, and
bound by Wm. Brendon, both of Tiptree, Essex
ISBN 0 09 101430 1

INTRODUCTION

The idea of compiling this book occurred to me when I was first writing *Robert Burns: the Man; his Work; the Legend* (1954, 2nd Edition 1968). At that time, I thought a book of this kind would be useful to the general reader of Burns's poems whose difficulties with the Scots tongue could be overcome by looking up the glossaries attached to every edition of the poet's works, but whose lack of background information could not be remedied without recourse to the Chambers-Wallace or Henley and Henderson editions, both enormously bulky, hard to come by, and, in any case, inevitably out of date so far as some of the biographical information is concerned. So I began to make a few notes. Before I had got very far, other projects claimed my attention, and *The Burns Encyclopedia* lay, so to say, in arrested embryo; until, in the Spring of 1958, Mr Iain Hamilton, then Editor-in-Chief for Messrs Hutchinson, invited me to compile and write precisely the kind of volume I had originally meditated.

Time, however, was limited, since part of Mr Hamilton's intention was that *The Burns Encyclopedia* should form part of the Burns Bi-Centenary celebrations in January, 1959. With considerable assistance from my wife, the work was put together during the summer months of 1958. So rapid was its compilation and subsequent production that the first edition inevitably contained a number of errors. These have now been corrected, every entry in the book has been revised, a number have been extended, and many new entries have been added. It is therefore perhaps misleading to call this a second edition, since very few entries still appear as they originally did.

The book was, and is, designed to be of interest in several ways. First and foremost, of course, it is meant to provide a handrail for the ordinary reader of Burns anxious to explore the temper of the age in which the poet lived and wrote. In the second place, it is designed to attract readers interested in eighteenth-century Scotland, for whom the approach may well be that of the anthology-taster, browsing and savouring for leisure and pleasure. Those who find themselves periodically forced to their feet, by custom dubious and strange, to deliver Burns Supper orations should find it a convenient quarry.

The sources from which I have drawn my information are too numerous to mention individually. Whenever possible, I have used Burns's own works. Where the letters are concerned, the text I have followed is that of Professor de Lancey Ferguson's definitive edition. The text used for the poems in the first edition was that of Chambers-Wallace. Between editions, Professor James Kinsley's magnificent three-volume definitive text was published. I have used Professor Kinsley's text where it differs in word or line from the Chambers-Wallace text, but ignored minor variations of spelling, preferring the Chambers-

Wallace usually more modern versions to the archaic spelling of some originals to be found in Kinsley's edition.

James Currie was once thought to have distorted the story of Burns's life in order to use the poet as a Dreadful Warning against the evils of drink. Professor R. D. Thornton's *James Currie: The Entire Stranger and Robert Burns* (1963) has shown that this was probably an unfair interpretation of Currie's behaviour. In his youth, Currie was himself so intemperate that the unexpected respectability of his middle-age made it virtually impossible for him publicly to avoid condemning one whose sins he deemed to have been so similar to his discarded own. As is well known, the reformed rake often ends up the narrowest and most intolerant of puritans.

Currie's incompetence as an Editor may now thus be more or less satisfactorily explained. His processing of Burns's reputation, however, can hardly be condoned.

When cheese is processed, richness of flavour and tang of texture disappear. What is left is a smooth, tasteless substance, which may be easily spread and which could not possibly offend the dullest palate. The object of most of Burns's nineteenth-century editors and commentators was to turn the rich Dunlop of his life and work into a processed product acceptable to Church and State, and sufficiently characterless and colourless to enable him to occupy with absolute decorum the niche of National Bard prepared for him.

Reputations and cheeses differ in that while cheese cannot be unprocessed, reputations can. We owe the emergence of the real Burns first and foremost to Catherine Carswell and Franklin Bliss Snyder. Mrs Carswell's *The Life of Robert Burns* (1931) though written in the manner of a novel, creates a warm and convincing portrait of the poet. Snyder, in his book *The Life of Robert Burns* (1932), cuts away the pious falsifications of more than a century and brings the clear light of impartial scholarship and an awareness of international literary standards to bear on Burns's achievements. Since then, there have been Hans Hecht's *Robert Burns* (1936), J. de Lancey Ferguson's wholly admirable study *Pride and Passion* (1939), David Daiches' *Robert Burns* (1950), principally a piece of literary criticism, Thomas Crawford's *Burns: A Study of the Poems and Songs* (1960), and, to name only one other, Cyril Pearl's *Bawdy Burns* (1958), a witty but devastating attack on the so-called Christian virtues upon which Scotland's post-Reformation society was, and to some extent still is, based and against which Burns was so strenuous a rebel. Some further details of Agnes M'Lehose's life have been uncovered by Raymond Lamont Brown in *Clarinda: The Intimate Story of Robert Burns and Agnes MacLehose* (1968). Other aspects of Burns treated with scholarship and integrity by J. C. Dick in *The Songs of Robert Burns* (1903), and by J. de Lancey Ferguson, James Barke and Sydney Goodsir Smith in the Auk Society edition of *The Merry Muses* (1959). So greatly has our honesty of attitude to sexual peccadilloes altered that *The Merry Muses* can now be bought as a paperback on railway station bookstalls. Dick's collection has been re-issued along with a copy of *Burns's Notes on*

Scottish Song interleaved in the *Scots Musical Museum*, by Folklore Associates, Hatboro', Pennsylvania (1962). The same press has also put out a two volume reprint of the *Museum* itself (1962). Burns scholarship has otherwise been well served by Professor J. W. Egerer's *A Bibliography of Robert Burns* (1964).

It seems unlikely that any of the riddles ably examined by Hilton Brown in *There Was a Lad* (1949) will now be unravelled, though 'lost' Burns manuscripts will no doubt turn up from time to time. Discoveries, significant and insignificant, are annually reported in the pages of the Burns Chronicle. With kind help from the former Keeper of the Records of Scotland, Sir James Fergusson, and the Archivist to the Marquess of Bute, Miss Catherine Armet, I have been able to present some hitherto unknown facts about John Arnot of Dalquhatswood.

For the first edition of this book, the then President of the Burns Federation, Mr J. B. Hardie, wrote:

'Many people are mentioned in Burns's poems and letters. Reference to the Encyclopedia will immediately bring a much closer and personal acquaintance with any particular individual. Similarly, with places and anecdotes. The Encyclopedia is brimful with knowledge and information, and the reader who carefully studies it will not only get a clearer idea of Burns's attitude to people and to life generally, but will also get a new and better idea of Burns himself.

'Mr Lindsay's work makes most interesting and enlightening reading for the ordinary reader. Many may not have in their possession the complete letters of Burns. The Encyclopedia gives a remarkably extensive selection of the more noteworthy and revealing examples of his correspondence. A study of the Encyclopedia is a generous education in itself. Many of the entries contain the most vivid word-pictures, and the amount of detail in them should be an ideal aid to speakers on Burns, teachers and members of Scottish Societies.

'Maurice Lindsay has to be complimented on producing a book which should be in great demand, not only for its value as a work of reference, but for the sheer enjoyment it will give to its readers.'

The purpose of this book revised and enlarged, remains the furtherance of the enjoyment of Burns's poems and letters by readers who share my own pleasure and delight in them. To all such readers, therefore, this second edition of the Burns Encyclopedia is dedicated.

MAURICE LINDSAY

11 Great Western Terrace,
Glasgow, W.2

ACKNOWLEDGEMENTS

I should again like to acknowledge assistance from Sir James Fergusson of Kilkerran, formerly Keeper of the Records of Scotland; Miss Catherine Armet, Mr David Bruce, the Town Clerk of Inverness, who facilitated the reproduction of the picture of Provost Inglis who, as a Bailie, Burns met during his Highland Tour; Mr Archibald Stirling, whose photographic skill enabled the picture to be reproduced under difficult circumstances; and Mr C. W. Black and his staff at the Mitchell Library, Glasgow, who have helped me in many directions. My warmest thanks are due to Mr Alexander MacMillan, the Rector of Ravenspark Academy, Irvine, who generously put his skill as a proof reader and his detailed local knowledge of Burns in his contemporary setting at my disposal. I should also like to thank Miss Edith M. Horsley, whose interest, editorial skill and patience seemed marvellously inexhaustible during the months when this book was in course of preparation.

If anyone else feels that they should have been specifically included in this list of acknowledgements, I apologise for not naming them. They have not been overlooked knowingly, for I am deeply grateful to all those who have helped to make this book possible.

ILLUSTRATIONS

See also notes on the illustrations p. 395

A

Aberdeen
Burns arrived at Aberdeen on Sunday, 9th September 1787 during his Highland Tour. He recorded his impressions in his *Journal* the following day:

'—meet with Mr Chalmers, Printer, a facetious fellow—Mr Ross, a fine fellow, like Professor Tytler—Mr Marshall, one of the *poetae minores*—Mr Sheriffs, author of "Jamie and Bess", a little decrepid body, with some abilities—Bishop Skinner, a non-juror, son of the author of "Tullochgorum", a man whose mild, venerable manner is the most marked of any in so young a man—Professor Gordon, a good-natured, jolly-looking professor—Aberdeen a lazy town.'

The Burns statue in Aberdeen is the work of Henry Bain Smith, a local sculptor, and was unveiled on 15th September 1892.

Abraham, or Abram
The battle ground in front of Quebec where General Wolfe fell victorious in 1759. It was called after Maître Abraham, a local pilot. Burns mentioned it in the soldier's song from 'The Jolly Beggars' Cantata:

'When the bloody die was cast on the heights of Abram.'

Adair, Dr James M'Kittrick (1765-1802)
The son of an Ayr doctor, related to Mrs Dunlop.

James Adair studied in Geneva and at Edinburgh University, where he graduated in medicine. The Reverend Dr George Lawrie, minister of Loudon, introduced him to Burns, and he accompanied the poet on his tour to Harvieston in October 1787. He married Charlotte Hamilton, half-sister of Gavin Hamilton, on 11th November 1789. Adair practised in the Pleasance, Edinburgh, then moved to Harrogate, where he died.

After Burns's death, Adair provided Currie with an account of this tour, on which Burns himself kept no journal. Though inaccurate in some of its dates, Adair's account has been generally accepted as being 'substantially correct in other respects', to quote Snyder.

Adam, Dr Alexander (1741-1809)
Youngest son of a farmer, he was headmaster of George Watson's Hospital from 1760 to 1768. He then became Rector of the High School of Edinburgh, and held this position for the rest of his life. He died while teaching his class. He had a reputation as a fine teacher, and wrote philological books. Sir Walter Scott said: 'It was from this respectable man that I first learned the value of the knowledge I had hitherto considered only as a burdensome task.' Lord Brougham maintained that Adam was: 'one of the very best teachers he ever heard of, and by far the best he ever knew'. And Lord Cockburn said of Adam: 'He was born to teach Latin, some Greek, and all virtue.'

Burns, writing to Cruikshank, classical master of the High School, from Ellisland in December 1788, took a different view of Adam. The two masters had had a quarrel; Cruikshank had given his side of the affair and Burns reported: 'It gave me a very heavy heart to read such accounts of the consequence of your quarrel with that puritanic, rotten-hearted, hell-commissioned scoundrel, Adam. If, notwithstanding your unprecedented industry in public, and your irreproachable conduct in private life, he still has you so much in his power, what ruin may he not bring on some others I could name?'

Adam, Robert (1728-92)
The great Scottish 'classical' architect, whose public buildings include Register

House, Edinburgh. He was the second son of William Adam of Maryburgh, in Fife. His four brothers were also architects. He was born in Kirkcaldy and educated at Edinburgh University. When he died, after endowing Britain with many splendid buildings, he was buried in Westminster Abbey. Evidently, from the Ayr burgh accounts, he was paid for a plan of a bridge he had given them. His plan was not used. There was a local tradition that the mason who built the new bridge, Alexander Steven, was also its architect.

'Adam Armour's Prayer'

Adam Armour (b. 1771) was probably Jean Armour's brother, who, along with some other lads, 'stanged', or carried, Agnes Wilson, a female fornicator, astride a pole through the streets of Mauchline. He became involved in a breach of the peace, and while evading arrest, met Burns, whose advice he sought. The poet is supposed to have suggested that Armour should find someone to pray for him, and Armour to have replied: 'Just do't yoursel, Burns, I know no one so fit.'

The authority for this story is the unreliable and frequently inventive Allan Cunningham. Adam Armour is said to have become a mason, and to have visited Burns at Ellisland.

Adamhill

A farm in the parish of Craigie, two miles or so from Lochlea, occupied by John Rankine, Burns's:

'rough, rude, ready-witted Rankine,
   The wale o' cocks for fun an' drinking!'

Rankine's daughter, Anne, claimed to have been the subject of the song 'Corn Riggs'.

'Address to the Deil'

Scottish poets from Dunbar onwards have adopted a tone of bantering familiarity with the Devil. Of Burns's essay in this

genre, Gilbert Burns recorded: 'It was, I think, in the winter of 1784, as we were going with carts for coals to the family fire (and I could yet point out the particular spot) that Robert first repeated to me the "Address to the Deil". The curious idea of such an address was suggested to him by running over in his mind the many ludicrous accounts and representations we have from various quarters of this august personage.' (Gilbert was wrong about the date, since Burns told Richmond that it had been written in 1785-6.)

Obviously, neither Dunbar nor Burns really believed in the Devil. But whereas the older poet painted 'Mahoun', as he called him in 'The Dance of the Seven Deidly Sins', ruling a realistic, colourful Catholic Hell (provoked, however, beyond endurance by the Scottish bagpipes!), Burns used him to poke fun, not only at Scots superstition, but also at the credulity implied by Auld Licht notions on predestination.

'Hear me, *auld Hangie* for a wee,
An' let poor *damnèd bodies* be;
I'm sure sma pleasure it can gie,
   E'en to a *deil*,
To skelp an' scaud poor dogs like me,
   An' hear us squeal.'

'Ae Fond Kiss'

When Burns's affair with Mrs Agnes M'Lehose ('Clarinda') came to an end, and he settled down to married life with Jean Armour, he still retained a strong affection for 'Clarinda'. They met in Edinburgh for the last time on 6th December 1791. She was then about to set sail for Jamaica in the hope of achieving reconciliation with her husband (a hope that was not to be realised). On 27th December, Burns sent her 'Ae Fond Kiss' from Dumfries, a song so genuine in its resigned passion that it makes the drawing-room songs of 'sensibility' he had previously written for her seem artificial and insignificant. Sir Walter Scott thought that 'Ae Fond

Kiss' contained 'the essence of a thousand love tales'.

It appeared in the *Scots Musical Museum* in 1792, to the tune 'Rory Dall's port', which had first been published in the *Caledonian pocket Companion*, *c.* 1756 (bearing no relation to a tune of the same name in *Straloch's MS*, 1629). Rory Dall was the 'cognomen' of the harpers attached to the McLeods of Sky (so the tune is probably much older), while 'port' is Gaelic for 'air'. As with so many of Burns's loveliest songs, Victorian balladists also matched this one to settings utterly unworthy of the original air.

Afton Manuscript
A collection of his later poems presented by Burns to Mrs Alexander Stewart of Stair in 1791. It consisted of thirteen then unpublished poems, including 'Tam o' Shanter', 'Elegy on Captain Matthew Henderson', 'The Lament of Mary Queen of Scots', and both versions of 'Lines in Friar's Carse Hermitage'. In view of the inclusion of 'Tam o' Shanter' it is strange to find Burns writing in his Preface: 'Many Verses on which an Author would by no means rest his reputation in print, may yet amuse an idle moment in manuscript; and many Poems, from the locality of the subject, may be unentertaining or unintelligible to those who are strangers to that locality. Most, if not all, the following Poems are in one or other of these predicaments; and the Author begs whoever into whose hands they may fall not to publish what he himself thought proper to suppress.'

Mrs Stewart afterwards built a house on the Enterkine estate, which she called Afton Lodge, after her father's estate.

The small quarto volume of sixty-eight pages, sewn in limp boards, is now in the Cottage Museum, Alloway, gifted by Mrs Stewart's grandson, William Allason Cunninghame, in 1880. *See* **Stair Manuscript.**

'Afton Water'
One of Burns's most popular songs, it first appeared in the *Scots Musical Museum* in 1792. Currie stated that it was written in praise of Afton Water, and as a compliment to Mrs Stewart of Stair, who certainly received a copy from the poet in 1791. Gilbert Burns claimed that Mary Campbell was the heroine. Scott-Douglas agreed with Gilbert. Henley and Henderson, however, also stated that the song was written as a compliment to the River Afton, which flows into the Nith near New Cumnock. From a letter to Mrs Dunlop accompanying the verses, and dated 5th February 1789, it is clear that their interpretation is the correct one, since in this letter Burns speaks of the Afton as having 'some charming, wild, romantic scenery on its banks. I have a particular pleasure in those little pieces of poetry such as our Scots songs, etc., where the names and landskip-features of rivers, lakes, or woodlands, that one knows, are introduced. I attempted a compliment of that kind to Afton as follows: I mean it for Johnson's *Musical Museum*.'

The gently rippling tune, which Burns is believed to have sent to the *Museum*, matches the lyric exquisitely. Unfortunately, one or two Victorian balladists provided alternative settings that achieved greater popularity, but which would certainly have woken up the poet's Mary in some alarm.

Aiken, Andrew Hunter (d. 1831)
The dedicatee of the 'Epistle to a Young Friend'. Andrew was the eldest son of Robert Aiken. Having been first a merchant in Liverpool, Andrew settled in Riga, where he acted as British Consul and subsequently died. Andrew's eldest son, Peter, once possessed the original manuscript of 'The Cotter's Saturday Night'. *See* **Niven, William.**

Aiken, Robert (1739-1807)
The son of an Ayr sea-captain, John

Aiken, Robert Aiken (Orator Bob) became a prosperous and convivial lawyer
in his native town. After meeting Burns
about 1783, Aiken became impressed by
the merit of the poet's work. Burns
himself later declared that he had never
fully appreciated his own work until
Aiken read it aloud. The poet described
Aiken as his 'first poetic patron' in a
letter to John Ballantine of 20th November
1786, and, a few weeks later, in another
letter to Ballantine dated 13th December,
as his 'first kind Patron'. A similar reference occurs in a letter to Gavin Hamilton
of 7th December 1786, and in a further
letter to Ballantine written in January
1788. Aiken collected the names of a
hundred and forty-five subscribers for
the Kilmarnock Edition, almost a quarter
of the total. Burns dedicated 'The Cotter's
Saturday Night' to Aiken, and wrote the
'Epistle to a Young Friend' to the lawyer's
son, Andrew Hunter Aiken. Robert
Aiken successfully defended Gavin Hamilton before the Presbytery of Ayr in the
summer of 1785, as a result of which
Burns conceived the idea of 'Holy
Willie's Prayer'.

Robert Aiken was the recipient of
many letters from Burns. One, dated 16th
December 1786, begins: 'Dear Patron of
my Virgin Muse'. Another, placed by
Ferguson about 8th October 1786, is the
famous letter which mentions the poet's
first thoughts on the possibility of entering the Excise service, and contains the
confession that 'even in the hour of
social mirth, my gaiety is the madness of
an intoxicated criminal under the hands of
the executioner'. The note of hysteria, and
the suggestion that it might be best for
him to go abroad, have led some biographers to connect this letter with remorse over the death of 'Highland Mary'.
It was probably Aiken—his part in the
affair has never been proved—who mutilated the promissory paper Burns gave
to Jean Armour, by cutting out their
names, possibly to placate James Armour.

This led to a temporary coolness between
the lawyer and the poet.

Burns's letters to Aiken were probably
among the most revealing he ever wrote.
Unfortunately, most of them have been
destroyed; according to Aiken's daughter,
through the dishonesty of a clerk in his
father's office, though possibly just through
sheer carelessness.

Ailsa Craig

A rocky, conical-shaped island in the
Firth of Clyde, ten miles west by north
of Girvan. Two miles in circumference,
it is eleven hundred and twenty-nine
feet high. Its perpendicular cliffs have
long been a haunt of sea birds, and
until the eighteenth century its solan
geese and their eggs were considered a
delicacy. Curling stones have for long
been manufactured from its rock. Popularly nicknamed 'Paddy's Milestone' because of its efficiency as a landmark to
Irish travellers, it has had a lighthouse on
it since 1883. In the second version of
'Duncan Gray cam' here to woo', Burns
refers to the island:

'Duncan fleech'd and Duncan pray'd
  (Ha, ha, the wooing o't!).
Meg was deaf as Ailsa Craig
  (Ha, ha, the wooing o't!) . . .'

Ainslie, Douglas (1771-1850)

Brother of the poet's friend Robert
Ainslie. He succeeded his father as writer
and land steward on Lord Douglas's
estates in Berwickshire, and made a
considerable fortune. He later bought
Cairnbank, in Berwickshire. He died at
Eden Bank, near Banff.

Burns described him in his *Journal* of
his Border tour as: 'a clever, fine, promising young fellow', and in a letter of 23rd
July 1787, to Robert Ainslie, asked after
'that strapping chield your brother
Douglas'.

Ainslie, Mr

Robert Ainslie's father who lived at

Berrywell and was the poet's host on his Border tour. Burns described him in his *Journal* as: 'an uncommon character; his hobbies, agriculture, natural philosophy and politics. In the first he is unexceptionally the clearest-headed, best-informed man I ever met with; in the other two, very intelligent.'

Mr Ainslie presented Burns, when he was leaving, with a copy of the *Letters of Junius*, 'in testimony of the most sincere friendship and esteem'.

Ainslie, Mrs

Mother of Robert Ainslie. Burns described her in his *Journal* of the Border tour as: 'an excellent, sensible, cheerful, amiable old woman'.

Ainslie, Miss Rachel (b. 1768)

'Charming' sister of Robert Ainslie. Burns met her and her family when on the Border tour with her brother Robert. He described her in his *Journal*: 'Her person a little *embonpoint*, but handsome; her face, particularly her eyes, full of sweetness and good humour—she unites three qualities rarely to be found together—keen, solid penetration; sly, witty observation and remark; and the gentlest, most unaffected female modesty.'

When in church, she was hunting for a text, which was on obstinate sinners, Burns presented the following spontaneous lines to her:

'Fair maid, you need not take the hint,
    Nor idle texts pursue:
'Twas *guilty sinners* that he meant,
    Not *Angels* such as you!'

Writing to Robert Ainslie from Mauchline on 23rd July 1787, Burns asked after: 'my friend Rachel, who is as far before Rachel of old, as she was before her blear-eyed sister Leah'.

Ainslie, Robert (1766–1838)

The son of the land-steward of Lord Douglas's Berwickshire estates, Ainslie

was born at Berrywell, near Duns. He was a law student in the Edinburgh office of Samuel Mitchelson when Burns met him early in 1787. His carefree disposition and his zestful pleasure in wine, women and the poet's song, endeared him to Burns, and Ainslie accompanied the poet on the first part of the Border tour of May 1787. At Eyemouth they were both made 'Royal Arch Masons' of the local lodge, Ainslie on payment of a guinea fee, Burns without fee. Continuing the tour alone, Burns wrote to him regretting the laughter his presence had ensured. On 23rd July 1787, writing from Mauchline, Burns told Ainslie: 'There is one thing for which I set great store by you as a friend, and it is this—that I have not a friend upon earth, besides yourself, to whom I can talk nonsense without forfeiting some degree of his esteem.'

Ainslie matched Burns's moods: 'You assume a proper length of face in my bitter hours of blue-devilism.' Burns wrote to him from Edinburgh on 23rd November 1787, 'and you laugh fully up to my highest wishes at my good things'. For that reason, Burns really valued Ainslie's friendship. The poet introduced Ainslie to Mrs M'Lehose, and made him an early confidant in his affair with her, and in his final farming transaction. The 'horse-litter' letter, in which Burns describes having intercourse with Jean Armour when she was far advanced in pregnancy, was written to Ainslie from Mauchline on 3rd March 1788. It was therefore naturally to Ainslie that Burns wrote from Dumfries on 1st June 1788, asking him to call on May Cameron, an Edinburgh servant girl whom the poet had seduced, and 'give her ten or twelve shillings', adding the significant injunction, 'but don't for Heaven's sake meddle with her as a *Piece*'.

Ainslie married Jane Cunningham in 1798, by whom he had a son and several daughters. He divided his time between his office in Hill Street, Edinburgh, and his estate at Edingham, in the Stewartry of Kirkcudbright. He wrote several papers on agricultural subjects and legal and financial matters affecting landowners. In his later years he turned religious, and became the author of two works: *A Father's Gift to his Children* and *Reasons for the Hope that is in us.*

See Plate 8.

Albany, Duchess of. *See* Stuart, Charlotte

Alexander, Claud (1753–1809)

As paymaster-general of the East India Company's troops in Bengal, Alexander amassed a fortune and bought the estate of Ballochmyle from the Whiteefoord family in 1783. In 1788 he married Helenora, daughter of Sir William Maxwell of Springkell. Alexander was himself the son of a West of Scotland landed proprietor, and the brother of Wilhelmina, the 'Bonnie Lass of Ballochmyle'. He established a cotton-mill nearby, in partnership with David Dale.

Alexander, Wilhelmina (1756–1843)

Born at Paisley, fourth daughter of Claud Alexander of Newtoun and sister of Claud Alexander, laird of Ballochmyle estate on the Ayr, near Mauchline. Burns saw her while out walking, and on returning to Mossgiel, composed his song, 'The Bonnie Lass of Ballochmyle'. This he sent her with a high-flown letter of compliment, dated 18th November 1786. He requested permission to publish the song in 'a second edition of my poems'.

Miss Alexander ignored his letter. She never married, and in later life Burns's letter and love-song became her most cherished possession. She died in Glasgow.

As for Burns, he copied the letter into the Glenriddell Manuscript, and added a scathing comment about Miss Alexander being 'too fine a lady *to notice* so plain a compliment'. Of such men as her 'great brother', Burns opined: 'When Fate swore that their purses should be full, Nature was equally positive that their minds should be empty.'

Burns matched this song to the tune 'Ettrick Banks', first published in *Orpheus Caledonius*; but it is often sung to a somewhat indifferent setting by the music-hall accompanist and ballad writer William Jackson (1828–1876).

Alison, The Reverend Archibald (1757–1839)

An Edinburgh man educated at Glasgow University and Balliol College, Oxford, he took Anglican orders in 1784 and in the same year married a daughter of Dr John Gregory (originator of Gregory's Powder) of Edinburgh. After holding a number of English pluralities, he became senior minister of the Episcopal Chapel in Edinburgh in 1800, a position he held until his retirement in 1831.

He met Burns in Edinburgh during February 1789. The following year Alison published *Essays on the Nature and Principles of Taste*, a copy of which he sent to the poet. After some delay in acknowledging the book, Burns wrote Alison an enthusiastic letter from Ellisland dated 14th February 1791. One wonders how the worthy minister reacted to being told by the poet that, except for Euclid's *Elements of Geometry*, 'I never read a book which gave me such a quantum of information and added so much to my stock of ideas as your *Essays on the Principles of Taste*.'

Alison, Peggy

The supposed heroine of the song 'Bonnie Peggy Alison'. Burns's brother Gilbert claimed, however, that the heroine of 'Mary Morrison' also inspired this poem. She was probably Alison Begbie.

Burns himself told Thomson that this song was a juvenile production. Part of the song appeared in the *Scots Musical Museum* to one of Burns's favourite reels, 'The Braes o' Balquidder', which he probably found in Bremner's *Reels*, 1758. *See* **Begbie, Alison.**

Allan, David (1744–96)

The 'Scottish Hogarth' and illustrator of Burns's work, he was born in Alloa, son of the Shoremaster, also David Allan. The artist's mother, Janet Gullan, died two days after he was born. Educated at the parish school, through the influence of Lord Cathcart the young David entered the 'first officially recognised Academy of Art of the whole country', which had been started by Robert Foulis in 1754 at Glasgow University and which came to an end, bankrupt, in 1775. Robert Foulis and his brother, Andrew, were also responsible for producing fine editions of the classics, at their printing presses in Glasgow.

Allan's wealthy patrons, who included Lord Cathcart, Lady Frances Erskine, Lady Charlotte Erskine and Mrs Abercrombie of Tullibody, then combined to raise the money to send the young artist to Rome to study. In return, Allan painted various pictures for presenting to his patrons. He also did portraits of many aristocratic families.

But it was with his illustrations to Ramsay's *The Gentle Shepherd* that Allan's name became a household word throughout Scotland. In a letter to Alexander Cunningham, dated by Ferguson 3rd March 1794, Burns expressed his admiration for the artist: 'By the bye, do you know Allan? He must be a man of very great genius. Why is he not more known? Has he no Patrons; or do "Poverty's cold wind and crushing rain beat keen and heavy" on him? I once, and but once, got a glance of that noble edition of the noblest Pastoral in the world, and dear as it was; I mean, dear as to my pocket, I would have bought it; but I was told that it was printed and engraved for Subscribers only.

'He is the *only* Artist who has hit *genuine* Pastoral costume. . . .' And again

Burns wrote to Thomson: 'I look on Mr Allen [*sic*] and Mr Burns to be the only genuine and real Painters of Scottish Costume in the world.'

Burns, indeed, was right, for it was in his handling of peasant life and costume that the 'Scottish Hogarth' excelled.

In 1786, David Allan was appointed Director of the Trustees Academy of Art in Edinburgh, and it was in this capacity that he came into contact with the Principal Clerk, George Thomson, the Scottish folk-song collector. Thomson, of course, had approached Burns to write the words for his airs, and realised that he would need an illustrator. Not unnaturally, he turned to Allan, who besides illustrating *The Gentle Shepherd*, had also done the illustrations for an edition of James Thomson's *Seasons*. Allan's two best-known engravings of Burns's work are 'Tam o' Shanter' and 'The Cotter's Saturday Night' (a painting of which Thomson sent to the poet). In it the eldest son bears a striking resemblance to Burns. Allan never met Burns, but he copied the features from Nasmyth's portrait. Both pictures reflect Allan's characteristic humour—in 'The Cotter's Saturday Night' the small boy (who struck Burns as resembling William Nicol Burns) is about to cut the cat's tail and in 'Tam o' Shanter' there is Burns's shadowy figure presiding over the party. Allan's other well-known work was 'The Penny Wedding' which again shows his colloquial humour.

In all, Allan did twenty etchings for Thomson's collections, but they were never published in their entirety. The health of both artist and poet was rapidly deteriorating.

Burns died on 21st July, and was closely followed by Allan, on 6th August 1796.

Allan is buried in the Old Calton Cemetery, Edinburgh, not far from the grave of David Hume. By his wife, Shirley Welsh, herself a keen art student, and a great admirer of her husband's

work, he had five children, only one of whom, Barbara, reached adult life.
See Plate 13.

Allan, James
Was employed as carpenter or joiner on the estate of Fairlie in 1786, where Burns's father had been employed as a gardener during his first two years in Ayrshire. His wife Jean was a half-sister of Burns's mother. See **Allan, Jean**.

Allan, Jean, née Brown or Broun
A half-sister of Burns's mother. The poet stayed with her and her husband when James Armour took out a warrant to ensure that Burns supported his anticipated child by Jean. As the poet had no money, he expected imprisonment, and therefore sought shelter from the Allans. He wrote to Richmond from their house, which Burns called Old Room Foord—'room' or 'rome' meant a small farm, and Foord is possibly a corruption of 'Forest' or even 'Fairlie'—on 30th July 1786, telling him that he expected to sail on the *Nancy* for Jamaica within three weeks at 'farthest'. See **Old Rome Forest**.

Allan, River
A tributary of the Forth which flows through Perthshire and Stirlingshire for about twenty miles, and joins the Forth near Bridge of Allan. To the tune 'Allan Water' Burns wrote the love song beginning:

'By Allan-side I chanc'd to rove,
  While Phoebus sank beyond Benledi;
The winds were whispering thro' the
                                    grove,
  The yellow corn was waving
                              ready...'

The song appeared in Thomson's *Scottish Airs*. Burns told Thomson that he wrote his words for the air because the words to it in the *Museum* seemed unworthy. He added: 'I may be wrong, but I think it is not in my worst style.'

The air first appeared in *Blaikie's Manuscript*, 1692, and first seems to have been printed in *Original Scotch Tunes*, 1700.

Alloway Kirk
Built about 1516. First pointed in style, 'Alloway's auld haunted kirk' was last used for worship in 1756, by which time it had fallen into a state of disrepair. It became roofless very soon afterwards. When the parishes of Ayr and Alloway were joined in 1891 by the Boundary Commissioners, a proposal to remove the bell was mooted; but the villagers successfully protested against any such desecration.

William Burnes, the poet's father, lies buried in the churchyard; not, however, under his original stone, which was carried away in pieces by souvenir hunters. Alloway Kirk was, of course, the setting for Burns's poem 'Tam o' Shanter', based on legends which the poet transmitted to the antiquarian Francis Grose in a letter written probably in early June 1790.
See Plate 2.

Alloway Monument
Built on the banks of the River Doon, it was designed by Thomas Hamilton. The foundation stone was laid on 25th January 1820, by Mr (afterwards Sir) Alexander Boswell, with full masonic honours. It was opened on 4th July 1823. The cost—just over three thousand, three hundred and fifty pounds—was met by public subscription. The monument consists of 'a three-sided basement storey supporting a Greek peristyle'. The three-sided nature of the base was designed to symbolise the three divisions of Ayrshire: Cunningham, Kyle and Carrick. The influence is predominantly Greek. The bust of the poet on the terrace on the southern part of the monument was presented by the sculptor Patric Park, in 1847. The surrounding garden

contains Thom's statues of 'Tam o' Shanter' and 'Souter Johnnie'.

About fifty thousand people visit the memorial every year.

Anderson, Dr James (1739–1808)

Born at Hermiston, Midlothian, Anderson received his Doctorate in Law from Aberdeen University in 1780. He was interested in the advancement of agriculture, and an industrious journalist on this and other topics. Between 22nd December 1790 and 21st January 1794, he edited a literary and scientific magazine, *The Bee*, which achieved considerable distinction. Anderson invited Burns to contribute to *The Bee*, but although the poet thought of sending him his 'Lament for the Earl of Glencairn', he never contributed anything. *The Bee* did publish a letter by Burns to the Earl of Buchan, but it is supposed by Ferguson to have been sent in by the Earl himself, or by one of Burns's friends. Burns wrote to Anderson from Ellisland on 1st November 1790, asking to be 'set down' as a subscriber, and listing eleven other subscribers he had collected. He also requested two further copies of Anderson's prospectus for the magazine.

Anderson, Dr Robert (1750–1830)

Born at Carnwath, Lanarkshire, Anderson's father, a small-feuar, died when his son was ten, leaving the family in difficult circumstances. The boy went to school at Carnwath, Liberton and Lanark, then entered Edinburgh University as a theology student, though he soon deserted theology for medicine, ultimately graduating as a doctor. Soon after, he married and settled in Edinburgh, abandoning medicine for literature. He set about editing *A Complete Edition of the Poets of Great Britain* in fourteen volumes, which appeared between 1792 and 1795, with his own critical and biographical notices. He became friendly with Bishop Percy, of *Reliques* fame, and, as 'good old Dr Anderson', earned Southey's praise for having republished the earlier poets. Among his many literary labours was an edition, with a memoir of the author, of *The Works of John Moore, M.D.*, Burns's friend.

Anderson met Burns in Edinburgh, and recollected his impressions of the poet in a letter to Dr Currie, published in the *Burns Chronicle*, 1925:

'I saw Burns for the first time in the house of my friend Mr David Ramsay, printer of the Edinburgh Courant, who had invited a large company to dinner, on purpose to see him, in the first violence of the popular rage that prevailed during the winter he spent in Town, soliciting subscriptions for the new edition of his Poems. I was struck with his appearance, so different from what I had expected in an uneducated rustic. His person, though neither robust nor elegant, was manly and pleasing; and his countenance, though dark and coarse, uncommonly expressive and interesting. With an air of keen penetration and calm thoughtfulness approaching to melancholy, the usual attendant on genius, there was a kind of stern pride and supercilious elevation about him not incompatible with openness and affability, which might perhaps be properly termed a strong consciousness of intellectual excellence. His dress was plain, but genteel, like that of a farmer of the better sort: a dark-coloured coat, light figured waistcoat, shirt with ruffles at the breast, and boots, in which he constantly visited and walked about the Town. He wore his hair, which was black and thin, in a queue, without powder. Such was Burns, as he stood before me on the floor when I entered the drawing-room. His behaviour was suitable to his appearance: neither awkward, arrogant, nor affected, but decent, dignified and simple. In the midst of a large company of ladies and gentlemen assembled to see him, and attentive to his every look, word, and motion, he was in no way disconcerted, but seemed perfectly easy, un-embarrassed, and unassuming. He received me with particular attention, as the editor of the *Poems of Graeme,* a friend of mine who died young, whom as an elegiac writer he much admired, preferring him to Shenstone. We immediately entered into conversation, and in five minutes conversed as familiarly as if we had been acquainted five years. No words can do justice to the captivating charms of his conversation. It was even more fascinating than his poetry. He was truly a great orator. Though his knowledge in many instances was superficial, yet he conversed on every subject in a manner that evinced the strongest marks of genius, and acute-ness, combined with the most powerful sallies of wit, sarcasm, and satire. With acuteness of intellect, which might some-times be termed shrewdness, he possessed a still more useful talent, Good Sense, which enabled him instantly to discern which was right or wrong in literature, morality, and the general affairs of the world. He affected to despise those branches of knowledge which he had not cultivated, particularly abstract sciences. "I know nothing of logic or mathematics," I have heard him say, with great emphasis, "I profess only poetry." He was eager to assert the dignity and importance of poetry, which he termed the gift of heaven, though he frequently debased and degraded it by the misapplication of his own great powers to mean and unworthy purposes. He spoke of his own productions with great complacency, and justified the faults imputed to them by loud and vehement appeals from criticism to commonsense. He recited his own beautiful Songs very readily, and with peculiar animation and feeling, though he affected to be ignorant of the principles of music. In his intercourse with persons in high stations he was no syco-phant; but he was always the slave of his own passions, which were powerful, ardent, and irritable in such an excessive

degree as to unfit him for the commerce of life. Pride was most frequently pre-dominant, appearing sometimes in the form of insolence and sometimes in that of resentment, Accustomed to dog-matise among his familiar associates he would not condescend to practise the graces and respectful attentions required in the conversions of polite persons. Jealous of the independence of his mind, which was a prominent feature of his character, he spoke in a peremptory and decisive tone upon almost every subject of discussion. The pride of genius or the affection of singularity often led him wan-tonly to oppose received opinions, and pertinaciously to maintain the most unreasonable positions. His prejudices, personal, political, and religious, were strong, and misguided the rectitude of his judgment; and his temper was uncertain and capricious, being influenced by the impulse of passion or the whim of the moment. His opinions of persons and things were of little value, his praise and his censure being often bestowed without a proper regard to truth, justice, or modera-tion. His poetical enthusiasm, which inspires virtue, was no preservatice from the contagion of vice and the occasional excesses of passion. His morality with regard to women was lax. He transgressed the rules of sobriety openly; he was accused of ingratitude—perhaps justly, for he could not bear to conceive himself under an obligation; but his integrity in business was never questioned. Though proud and revengeful, he was naturally generous and compassionate; zealous in serving those he loved, and always ready to perform offices of kindness and human-ity. Though he was accustomed to admit impure and profane thoughts into his mind, yet I never heard him utter a word offensive to decency in the company of ladies; and though addicted to convivial excesses, yet I never heard that he violated the rules of sobriety in private families.

'Such is the impression which my mind

retains of this extraordinary man at this distance of time.

'He visited me frequently during the winter, and treated me with apparent confidence, in regard to his poems, patrons, &c. which I returned by a free communication of my sentiments on every subject and occurrence. In our habits and sentiments we differed widely, yet he endured me, though I never accompanied him to the tavern nor flattered his vanity. Political disputes then ran high. I was a Whig, attached to the principles upon which the Revolution was affected. He was a Tory, an idolator of monarchy, and a Jacobite as much as he could be. I was on the side of Fox and the parliament; He adhered to Pitt and the King. Such was his nationality that I could not shake his sentiments respecting the degradation of the imperial dignity of Scotland by the Union, and such was his monarchic enthusiasm that I could not prevail upon him to withdraw from his poems the vulgar abuse of Fox, founded on party misrepresentation and newspaper calumny. The progress of his sentiments from Jacobitism to Republicanism I am unable to trace, for I never saw him nor had any intercourse with him after he became a farmer and an exciseman. He spent most of the time of his residence in Edinburgh in visits and taverns, and wrote only a few occasional verses, of little value. Being decidedly of the opinion that an author is the best judge of his own writings, he steadily resisted the attempts of emendatory criticism. While the subscription was going on he suffered Dr Blair and Mr Mackenzie to believe that his poems should be altered and corrected according to their suggestions; but he secretly resolved to preserve the exceptionable passages, and finally rejected their suggestions, the result, he thought, of fastidious delicacy. He was not so much elated by the distinction he obtained in Edinburgh as might be expected. He knew that it would be transient, and he neglected not the means of turning it to his advantage. Mr Ramsay once, in his presence, shewed me a copy of Verses addressed to Burns, transmitted to him for publication. I objected to his printing them as they were bad, and proceeded from the mistaken idea of the Poet's character as to learning. Burns admitted the mistake, and acknowledged the verses were mean, but thought the printing them might do him service, by spreading the "wonder" and increasing his popularity. They were accordingly printed, expressly to oblige him.

'The vanity which led many women of rank and character to seek his acquaintance and correspondence is remarkable.'

Anderson, Robert
A tradesman in Dumfries from whom the poet sometimes bought boots.

Argyll, fifth Duke of. *See* Campbell, John.

Armorial Bearings
Writing to Alexander Cunningham on 3rd March 1794, Burns asked him to find out the expense of having a seal cut with his armorial bearings on a highland pebble to replace one lost. Burns explained: 'I do not know that my name is matriculated, as the Heralds call it, at all; but I have invented one for myself; so, you know, I will be chief of the Name; and by courtesy of Scotland, will likewise be entitled to Supporters.—These, however, I do not intend having on my Seal.—I am a bit of a Herald, and shall give you, Secundum artem, my ARMS.—On a field, azure, a holly-bush, seeded, proper, in base; a Shepherd's pipe and crook, Saltier-wise, also proper, in chief.—On a wreath of the colours, a woodlark perching on a sprig of bay-tree, proper, for Crest—"Woodnotes Wild"—At the bottom of the Shield, in the usual place—"Better a wee bush than nae bield".—By the Shepherd's pipe and crook, I do not mean the non-

sence of Painters of Arcadia; but a Stock-and-horn, and a Club; such as you see at the head of Allan Ramsay, in (David) Allen's quarto Edition of the Gentle Shepherd.'

Armour, James (d. 1798)

Burns's father-in-law was a master mason —hardly the 'architect' Burns claimed, when he wanted to impress his patrons— who also did some business as a contractor. He seems to have been a rather dour, churchy kind of man, though his initial dislike of Burns was probably based on the poet's radical leanings and lack of worldly prospects rather than on his morals.

When Armour, in March 1786, was told by his wife of Jean's pregnancy, he fainted, and his wife had to 'run for a cordial'. After Jean and Robert had both 'compeared' before the tyrannical Kirk Session of the day, the Armours persuaded her to go to relatives at Paisley, where they appear to have hoped that a prospective suitor, a weaver, Robert Wilson, might still take her, Burns's child and all. Burns held this to be desertion, since, either just before or after Jean became pregnant, he gave her a document (which he afterwards referred to as 'the unlucky paper') which may or may not have been witnessed by his friend James Smith, but which was apparently either a promise of marriage or a declaration of it. Armour persuaded someone, perhaps the lawyer Robert Aiken, to cut the two names out of the paper (which has long since disappeared), an act the news of which, Burns said, 'cut my very veins', and would not in any case have affected the legality of a marriage by declaration under the Scots Law of the day.

Jean bore twins on 3rd September 1786. In the early summer of 1787, Burns, fresh from his Edinburgh triumph, turned up at Mauchline again, to find the Armours now quite anxious to ensnare him. He described himself as disgusted at

their 'new servility', but nevertheless left Jean pregnant once more.

This time the Armours' fury was redoubled. They refused to shelter their daughter during this second mismanaged disgrace. Burns heard of her plight, but an injury to his leg and the charms of 'Clarinda' combined to delay his departure from Edinburgh. Eventually he reached Mauchline on 23rd February 1788, arranged accommodation for Jean, and had intercourse with her.

On the very day the luckless short-lived second set of twins were born, he wrote the 'horse-litter' letter to Ainslie. By the end of April, after a puzzling *volte-face*, he acknowledged Jean as his legal wife. Soon after, old Armour became reconciled to his son-in-law. Two of Burns's last letters were addressed to Armour, begging Mrs Armour to be sent for from Fife to come to Dumfries to look after Jean, then in the last stages of her final pregnancy. The letter, dated 10th July 1796, is signed: 'Your most affectionate son, R. Burns.'

Armour, Jean. *See* Burns, Jean Armour

Armstrong, John (1771-97)

A journalist and poet born at Leith. He went to Edinburgh University, studied for the Church, then got a job on a newspaper in London. His health failed, and he retired back to Leith. As a student, he published, with Peter Hill in 1789, a book with the unusual title, *Juvenile Poems, with remarks on poetry, and a dissertation on the best method of punishing and preventing crimes.*

He admired the poetry of Burns, who referred to him in a letter to Peter Hill, from Ellisland, on 2nd February 1790: 'Mr Armstrong, the young poet who does me the honour to mention me so kindly in his works, please give him my best thanks for the copy of his book. I shall write him my first leisure hour. I like his poetry much, but I think his style in prose quite astonishing.'

Arnot, John (c. 1738–c. 1789)

A subscriber to the first Edinburgh edition of Burns's poems, and the recipient of one of Burns's letters. When Burns transcribed that letter into the Glenriddell Manuscript, he called him John Arnot of Dalquhatswood in Ayrshire, 'One of the most accomplished of the sons of men that I ever met with—alas! had he been equally prudent!'

The Arnots of Dalquhatswood, in the parish of Loudoun, near Galston, Ayrshire, were a family who might well have been engulfed in obscurity but for Burns's friendship with John, and the connections of John's father and grand-father with the Loudoun family. William Arnot apparently lent money to the Earl of Loudoun on the strength of land securities. James, his son, who became factor to John, fourth Earl of Loudoun, had seven children: Margaret, Elizabeth, Hugh (born 1732: he joined the Army but became insane), James junior (died 1763), Thomas, John and William. Thomas became a surgeon with the East India Company in Canton, China, but died 26th June 1767, aboard the ship *Duke of Kingston* off the Western Isles, on his way home, predeceasing his father, and apparently leaving a movable estate which was shared between his father and his brothers and sisters. James, the father, also lent considerable sums of money to the Earl of Loudoun—£4,314 on one occasion and £1,600 on another (the documents relating to these transactions are in Register House, Edinburgh).

In a letter dated 20th February 1760, from James Arnot to Lord Loudoun, which seems to refer to John, Arnot writes: 'I acknowledge I have been too precipitent in sending him to London, was told there would be no difficulty in getting him to the East Indies and thought if he could get to his Brother he might put him in a way of earning a bitt of bread. Poor man he has lost some years of his youth. God grant he may see the folly of it.'

John was certainly in Macao, the Portuguese colony in China, in January 1766, for both he and Thomas wrote to Lord Loudoun, Thomas asking His Lordship to intercede with 'the court of Portugal . . . so as to procure liberty for him (John) to reside there as long as he pleases, and be more indulged in Trade'. John, however, seems to have remained in Canton, sending Lord Loudoun numerous packets of seeds of Chinese plants. In October 1769, he sent from Dalquhatswood 'a pott containing the stones of the fruit called Leechee' and 'a book of Chinese paintings'. John explained that 'the top of the pott was broke in coming down from London', suggesting that he had brought these gifts with him on his homecoming.

In 1770, John appears to have married, and in a letter to Lord Loudoun dated 28th February 1771, referring to John's affairs, James says: 'Poor Mrs. Arnot is in a bad state of health at present from a miscarriage.'

In 1783, John took out an overdraft from the Ayrshire Bank of Hunter and Company on the security of three other people, the year after he had borrowed £300, in conjunction with another man, from Mrs Rachel Hamilton, the widow of an Edinburgh wine merchant.

John Arnot's exact dates of birth, marriage and death have not yet been discovered. The name of Arnot does not appear in the Newmilns or Galston Parish Registers, except for an entry dated May 1760 in the Newmilns Register, which records the church baptism of an illegitimate daughter to John Arnot and Janet Little. There is nothing to connect Burns's John Arnot with the Arnot who fathered this little girl. And yet Burns's letter to Arnot, post-dated by Burns 'about the latter end of 1785' (and dated by Ferguson about 1786), describes in amusing but bawdy literary terms, full of sexual boastfulness, how the poet had successfully besieged and captured Jean

Armour, and subsequently was prevented from making her his wife by Jean's father. In it, Burns also called himself, 'One of the rueful-looking, long-visaged sons of Disappointment . . . I rarely hit where I aim, and if I want anything, I am almost sure never to find it where I seek it'.

By April 1791, when Burns completed the copying out of the Glenriddell Manuscript, and the introductory note to this letter, he wrote of Arnot as if he were already dead—'Alas! had he been equally prudent!'—and furthermore had died in dishonour, his death making Burns reflect:

'It is a damning circumstance in human-life, that Prudence, insular & alone, without earthly virtue, will conduct a man to the most envied eminences in life, while having every other good quality & wanting that one, which at best is itself but a half virtue, will not save a man from the world's contempt, & real misery, perhaps perdition.'

Arnot's fate is of little enough account to us now. And yet I confess to a curious desire to know what fearful folly Burns's friend, this 'accomplished' man, committed to earn 'the world's contempt'! What is here set forth is at least an advance on Ferguson's comment that 'no facts about Arnot are recorded beyond what Burns himself tells'.

Athole, fourth Duke of. *See* **Murray, John**

Auchincruive
An estate in the parish of St Quivox, Ayrshire, the ancient seat of the Cathcarts, bought in 1764 by Richard Oswald, a London merchant and a commissioner in Paris for peace negotiations with the Americans. After his death in 1784, his widow (*née* Mary Ramsay) remained in occupation. She, however, died in London in December 1788. Her body was brought back to St Quivox for burial beside her

husband. Dead, the poor woman provoked Burns to one of his most savage outbursts of ill nature. He recounted the circumstances in a letter to Dr Moore, dated 23rd March 1789: 'In January last, on my road to Ayrshire, I had put up at Bailie Whigham's, in Sanquhar, the only tolerable inn in the place. . . . My horse and I were both much fatigued with the labors of the day, and just as my friend the Bailie and I were bidding defiance to the storm over a smoking bowl, in wheels the funeral pageantry of the late great Mrs Oswald, and poor I am forced to brave all the horrors of the tempestuous night, and jade my horse . . . twelve miles further on.' Undoubtedly exasperating. But the dead woman could not be blamed, and, although detested by servants and tenants 'with the most heartfelt cordiality', as Burns told Moore, could hardly be said to have deserved a Pindaric ode containing venomous lines like:

'View the wither'd beldam's face—
Can thy keen inspection trace
Aught of Humanity's sweet, melting
grace?
Note that eye, 'tis rheum o'erflows,
Pity's flood there never rose . . .'

Auchincruive passed to Mrs Oswald's son, Richard Alexander Oswald, a government contractor during the American War, and to Burns a 'plunderer of armies'. It is now a teaching farm, owned by the West of Scotland Agricultural College.

'Auld Lang Syne'
The dismissory song now used throughout the English-speaking world. In Scotland, it gradually displaced the century-old 'Good-night and joy be wi' you a'.' In spite of the popularity of 'Auld Lang Syne', it has aptly been described as 'the song that nobody knows'. Even in Scotland, hardly a gathering sings it correctly, without some members of

the party introducing the spurious line: 'We'll meet again some ither nicht' for the line which Burns actually wrote: 'And we'll tak' a cup o' kindness yet', to say nothing of adding 'the days of' to the line 'For auld lang syne'!

On 17th December 1788, Burns said in a letter to Mrs Dunlop: 'Your meeting which you so well describe with your old schoolfellow and friend, was truly interesting. Out upon the ways of the world! they spoil these "social offsprings of the heart". Two veterans of the "men of the world" would have met with little more heart-workings than two old hacks worn out on the road. Apropos, is not the Scotch phrase *Auld lang syne* exceedingly expressive? There is an old song and tune which has often thrilled through my soul. You know I am an enthusiast in old Scotch songs. I shall give you the verses on the other sheet. . . . Light be the turf on the breast of the heaven-inspired poet who composed this glorious fragment! There is more of the fire of native genius in it than in half a dozen of modern English Bacchanalians.' The song 'on the other sheet' was Burns's first version of 'Auld Lang Syne'.

With slight emendations, the poet sent a copy of the song to Johnson, who delayed publishing it, possibly because the air to which it went had already appeared in the *Museum* with words by Ramsay, beginning: 'Should auld acquaintance be forgot'. But Johnson changed his mind and put the song into the fifth volume of the *Museum*, which appeared about six months after Burns's death, but which there is plenty of evidence in Burns's letters to suggest he had seen in proof stage. The tune to which it was matched in the *Museum* first appeared in Playford's *Original Scotch Tunes*, 1700, though doubtless it was then at least half a century old, for it was the tune to which the antecedents of Burns's poem were written.

The 'exceedingly expressive' germ-phrase has been traced back to an anonymous ballad in the *Bannatyne Manuscript* of 1568, 'Auld Kyndnes foryett'. The last of the eight stanzas goes:

'They wald me hals with hude and hatt,
Quhyle I wes rich and had anewch,
About me friendis anew I gatt,
Rycht blythlie on me they lewch;
But now they mak it wondir tewch,
And lattis me stand befoir the yett;
Thairfoir this warld is very frewch,
And auld kyndnes is quyt foryett.'

From that anonymous old poet's complaint of man's ingratitude, we move on to a slightly later ballad, probably by the courtly poet Sir Robert Ayton (1570–1638) who accompanied James VI and I to England, though sometimes attributed, on little evidence, to Francis Sempill of Beltrees (d. 1683?). First published in Watson's *Choice Collection of Scots Poems*, 1711, the anthology upon which the whole of the eighteenth-century Scots Revival was based, Ayton's poem begins:

'Should auld acquaintance be forgot,
    And never thought upon,
The flames of love extinguished,
    And freely past and gone?
Is thy kind heart now grown so cold
    In that loving breast of thine,
That thou canst never once reflect
    On old-long-syne?'

Chronologically, the next reference is a prose one: to a scurrilous work, *Scotch Presbyterian Eloquence Display'd*, published in London in 1694. The author quotes a sermon: 'Did you ever hear tell of a good God, and a cappet [pettish] prophet, Sirs? The good God said, Jonah, now billy Jonah, wilt thou go to Nineveh, for Auld lang syne? [old kindness].'

Henley and Henderson refer to a street song, dating from the end of the seventeenth century, which had the refrain:

'On old long syne,
    On old long syne, my jo,
On old long syne:
    That thou canst never once reflect
On old long syne.'

This, attributed to Francis Sempill, appeared in Watson's *Choice Collection*, but clearly derives from Ayton.

The song which Ramsay wrote to the tune, printed with his words in the *Museum*, was published in his *Scots Songs*, 1720. The first eight lines establish the connexion, and at the same time demonstrate that the poem represents Ramsay at his least inspired:

'Should auld acquaintance be forgot,
    Tho' they return with scars?
These are the noble hero's lot,
    Obtain'd in glorious wars:
Welcome, my Varo, to my breast,
    Thy arms about me twine.
And make me once again as blest,
    As I was lang syne.'

At least two other political ballads of the period exist which exhibit turns of phrase, the echo of which sounds in Burns's version: and in 'The Old Minister's Song', 'Tullochgorum' Skinner came nearer than most:

'Should auld acquaintance be forgot,
    Or friendship e'er grow cauld?
Should we nae tighter draw the knot
    Aye as we're growing auld?

How comes it, then, my worthy friend,
    Wha used to be sae kin',
We dinna for ilk ither spier
    As we did lang syne?'

Was Burns, in fact, aware of these older poems? Almost certainly he was. But if his claim to Mrs Dunlop was correct, and the forces of Nature have honoured his request, the turf must by lying lightly upon the breast of an unknown poet of whose intermediary version not a trace can be found.

Cromek alleged evidence that the two best stanzas were by Burns. William Stenhouse, the editor of an early nineteenth-century reissue of the *Museum*, stated that Burns admitted to Johnson that only three stanzas were old, the other two being written by himself. George Thomson was certainly suspicious of the supposed old originals. In September 1793, Burns forwarded him the third known manuscript of the song, with some minor changes, the most important of which is the substitution of 'my dear' for 'my jo' in the chorus. In the accompanying letter Burns remarked: 'One song more, and I have done, "Auld lang syne". The air is but mediocre; but the following song—the old song of the olden times, and which has never been in print, nor even in manuscript, until I took it down from an old man's singing —is enough to recommend any air.'

Some time later, after Thomson had discovered from Stephen Clarke that Johnson had a copy of 'Auld Lang Syne', and had noticed that the air was already in the *Museum* to Ramsay's words, he must have written to Burns, who replied in November 1794: 'The two songs you saw in Clarke's are neither of them worth your attention. The words of "Auld lang syne" are good, but the music is an old air, the rudiments of the modern tune of that name. The other tune you may hear as a common Scots country dance.'

What was 'the other tune'? Probably the tune which we know today, and to which Thomson published the words in *Scottish Airs*, 1799, claiming them to be 'From an old MS. in the editor's possession'. In the meantime, the song became popular. When Thomson issued his *Select Melodies* in 1822, he altered the source-note to 'From a MS. in the editors' possession', which was at least slightly more honest.

The first strain of the familiar tune appears in 'The Duke of Buccleugh's Tune', in *Apollo's Banquet*, 1690, though

I am inclined to think this establishes nothing beyond yet another interesting example of melodic coincidence. Its 'common Scots country dance' version appeared first in Bremner's *Scots Reels*, 1759, under the title 'The Miller's Wedding' and in Cumming's *Strathspeys*, 1780, as well as in McGlashan's *Strathspey Reels*, also published in 1780, in which it was called 'The Miller's Daughter'. Its 'commonness' is attested by the fact that it appeared in at least a further five similar publications within the next thirty years; was used twice to different words in the *Museum*; and was employed in a slightly pruned version in William Shield's ballad-opera *Rosina* in 1783. It is also closely related to the melodies of 'O can you labor lea' and 'Comin thro' the rye', which appear to derive basically from the same strathspey as 'Auld Lang Syne'.

Although Thomson's version of the words are usually to be met with in popular editions of Burns's poems, the Johnson version is probably the better. Both versions contain the line 'And we'll take a right gude-willy waught', which once occasioned a needless controversy. The term 'gude-willy waught' means 'a draught of good fellowship', 'gude-willy' being an Old English term, like Lydgate's (c. 1375–1462) 'A! faire lady! Welwilly found at al,' from the *Complaint of the Black Knight*, instanced by Dick.

'Auld Lichts' and 'New Lichts'
The Act of Union of 1707, protected the polity of the Presbyterian Kirk, but the Patronage Act of 1712 restored the right of lay patrons who were heirs of the original donors of ecclesiastical properties to present ministers of their own choice to vacant parishes. Patronage was accepted by the 'Moderate' core of the Kirk, but an Act of Assembly in 1732, giving the power of election to heritors and elders when a patron did not exercise his rights under the 1712 Act, brought

about a secession. A further secession occurred in 1747 over the Burgher's Oath, which required holders of public offices to affirm the religion 'presently professed in this kingdom'. Ramsay of Ochtertyre thought that: 'To a sober Presbyterian, no proposition seemed more self-evident', adding: 'Yet by means of perverse ingenuity in torturing words, did these wrong-headed men insist that it was inconsistent with their principles and professions.'

The two parties formed independent synods, which bitterly hated each other.

The Burghers later divided on the issue of civil compulsion in religious affairs, those who held to the obligations of the Solemn League and Covenant seceding as 'Auld Lichts', while the majority, willing to modify that commitment, were known as 'New Lichts'.

Apart from organisational differences however, the 'Auld Lichts' were more orthodox Calvinists, enthusiastic for original sin, election and predestination, while the 'New Lichts' tended to be more 'liberal in their theology and moralistic in their preaching'. Burns, of course, was on the side of the 'New Lichts'.

Auld, Walter
A saddler in Dumfries, who took delivery of parcels. Burns directed Peter Hill, the Edinburgh bookseller, to send his books through Auld.

Auld, The Reverend William (1709–91)
The younger son of the Laird of Ellanton, in Symington, Auld studied at the universities of Edinburgh and Glasgow, then, like so many Scots scholars in the eighteenth century, completed his training at the University of Leyden, in Holland. After being tutor in the family of the Laird of Schawfield, Auld was ordained at Mauchline in 1742. A zealous, hardworking man, though opinionative, he seems to have lacked ambition, and to have been quite content to remain a

parish minister. Although he was a rigid Whig and an upholder of the Auld Lichts, his attitude was probably old-fashioned rather than bigoted, and he is said by Chambers to have been 'kindly and courteous'.

Thus, in 1791, when he wrote of his parishioners for Sir John Sinclair's *Statistical Account*, his observations read like those of a kindly man lamenting 'the good old days'. Said Auld: 'The manner of living and dress is much altered from what it was about 50 years ago. At that period, and for some time after, there were only two or three families in this parish who made use of tea daily; now it is done by at least one half of the parish, and almost the whole use it occasionally. At that period good twopenny strong ale and home-spirits were in vogue; but now even people in the middling and lower stations of life deal much in foreign spirits, rum-punch and wine. . . . As to dress, about 50 years ago there were few females who wore scarlet or silks. But now nothing is more common than silk capes and silk cloaks. Women in a middling station are as fine as ladies of quality were formerly.' In 'The Kirk's Alarm', Burns called him 'Daddy Auld', and in the prefatory note to 'Holy Willie's Prayer', 'Father Auld', which suggests that in spite of the reprimands for fornication with Jean which Auld had to administer, Burns regarded Auld with a respect which was probably mutual. The severest satire Burns exercised on Auld was in a letter written from Edinburgh in December 1787, when he tells Gavin Hamilton: '. . . as I understand you are now in habits of intimacy with that Boanerges of Gospel Power, Father Auld, be earnest with him that he will wrestle in prayer for you, that you may see the vanity of vanities in trusting to, or even practising, the carnal moral works of charity, humanity, generosity, and forgiveness, things which you practised so flagrantly, that it was evident you

delighted in them, neglecting, or perhaps profanely despising the wholesome doctrine of faith without works, the only anchor of salvation.

At all events, when Jean and Robert had to make their three appearances before Auld, the poet was allowed to stand in his own pew instead of in the 'place of repentance', although Jean—with whom he had quarrelled over her parentally-enforced 'desertion' of him—and her friends, probably wanted him to stand by her side; but Auld would not agree to this, which, the poet revealed, 'bred a great trouble'. By keeping silent about his verbal vows, Burns then got from Auld his certificate as a blameless single man.

Auld baptised Jean's first set of twins, Jean and Robert.

So much for the charitable interpretation of Auld's character. On the other hand, it has to be admitted that the full story of the proceedings against Gavin Hamilton suggest a vindictiveness which it is hard to account for merely by assuming a clash of personalities.

Aumous Dish
The wooden vessel, between bowl and platter in shape, which professional mendicants carried and proffered for their alms. It is mentioned in the first stanza of 'The Jolly Beggars'.

Autobiography, Burns's
The name sometimes given to the Autobiographical Letter, dated from Mauchline on 2nd August 1787, which Burns sent to Dr John Moore. Burns venerated Moore far beyond that literary-minded medico's worth, and from time to time sent him later letters bringing the life-story given in the Autobiographical Letter up to date. In return, Moore gave Burns much bad advice, the gist of which was that he should abandon Scots and write in English, aiming at producing a livelier version of Thomson's *Seasons*

(*see* **Moore, Dr John**). The Autobiographical Letter, which necessarily forms the basis of all studies of the poet's life, is given in full in J. de Lancey Ferguson's *Letters of Robert Burns*. The manuscript was brought at Sotheby's as Lot 145 in the sale of *objets d'art* owned by one P. Cunningham, on 26th February 1855. It is now in the British Museum.

Ayr

The county town of Ayrshire, at the mouth River Ayr, and the 'capital' of the of the Burns country. It became a Royal Burgh in 1202. It was in Ayr that Wallace struck his first blow for the independence of Scotland, and in the castle of nearby Turnberry that Bruce began the struggle which ended in Bannockburn.

'Auld Ayr, wham ne'er a town surpasses,
For honest men and bonnie lasses',

as Burns called it, is today a thriving market town, centre of the county's administration and a holiday resort. Its features include the Wallace Tower (an early nineteenth-century erection), the Tam o' Shanter Inn, now a museum, the Old Tolbooth, a Burns statue by G. A. Lawson, put up in 1891, the Auld Kirk with its Kirkyard and Martyrs Monument, the Kirk Port, and the Auld Brig, the subject of Burns's poem 'The Brigs of Ayr'. *See* **Brigs of Ayr, The.**

See Plate 5.

Ayr, River

Rises on the eastern border of Ayrshire, near Sorn, and follows a meandering course of thirty-three miles eastward to Ayr Bay. Burns, who mentions it in several poems and songs, called it: 'Just one long lengthened, tumbling sea'.

B

Bachelors' Club, Tarbolton

A debating club founded on 11th November 1780, by Burns, Gilbert Burns, Hugh Reid, Alexander Brown, Thomas Wright, William M'Gavin and Walter Mitchell, all young men of Tarbolton parish. At this first meeting, in the house of John Richard, Burns was unanimously elected president for the night. Rules were drawn up, the tenth and most significant of which read: 'Every man proper for a member of this Society, must have a frank, honest, open heart; above anything dirty or mean; and must be a professed lover of one or more of the female sex. No haughty, self-conceited person, who looks upon himself as superior to the rest of the Club, and especially no mean-spirited, worldly mortal, whose only will is to heap up money shall upon any pretence whatever be admitted.' The subjects included: 'Whether do we derive more happiness from Love or Friendship?'; 'Whether is the savage man or the peasant of a civilised country in the most happy situation?'; 'Suppose a young man, bred a farmer, but without any future, had it in his power to marry either of two women, the one a girl of large fortune, but neither handsome in person or agreeable in conversation but who can manage the household affairs of a farm well enough; the other of them a girl every way agreeable in person, conversation and behaviour, but without any fortune, which of them shall he choose?' The poet, of course, was for the fortune-less lass!

Members' names added to the list of founders included that of David Sillar. The Club remained active for some years after Burns left the district. Its meeting-place is now preserved as a museum.

Bacon, Mr (d. 1825)

Landlord of Brownhill Inn, in Dumfriesshire, he married Catherine Stewart, sister of William Stewart, factor to the estate of Closeburn. An English commercial traveller called Ladyman arrived at the Inn, and was told by Bacon that he would be dining with Burns and his friends (Chambers says that this anecdote was quoted by Ladyman in 1824). One of the items on the menu was bacon. Burns and some of the company would have preferred to do without the presence of Mr Bacon, and when the landlord went out to see about fresh supplies of toddy, Burns's friends asked him to make up a spontaneous verse, to prove that it was really the poet himself whom Ladyman was meeting. With hardly a moment's thought, Burns produced:

'At Brownhill we always get dainty
good cheer
And plenty of bacon each day in the
year;
We've a' thing that's nice, and mostly
in season—
But why always *Bacon*?—come, tell
me the reason?'

In a rhymed letter to William Stewart, written at Brownhill, probably in January 1793, Burns begins:

'In honest Bacon's ingle-neuk,
Here maun I sit and think;
Sick o' the warld and warld's fock,
And sick, d-amn'd sick o' drink . . .'

The *Ayrshire Monthly News-Letter* of 5th April 1844 contained the following paragraph:

'At the sale of the effects of Mr Bacon, Brownhill Inn, after his death in 1825, his snuff-box, being found to bear the inscription:

Robert Burns
Officer
of
The Excise

—although only a horn mounted with silver, brought £5. It was understood to have been presented by Burns to Bacon, with whom he had spent many a merry night.'

Baillie, Lesley (d. 1843)

The daughter of Robert Baillie of Mayfield, Ayrshire. She married Robert Cumming of Logie in 1799. She passed through Burns's life in circumstances which the poet related to Mrs Dunlop in a letter written from 'Annan Waterfoot' on 22nd August 1792. After declaring himself to be 'in love, souse! over head and ears, deep as the most unfathomable abyss of the boundless ocean', Burns explained that, 'Mr Bailie with his two daughters . . . passing through Dumfries a few days ago, on their way to England, did me the honour of calling on me, on which I took my horse (tho' God knows I could ill spare the time) and convoyed them fourteen or fifteen miles and dined and spent the day with them. 'Twas about nine, I think, when I left them; and riding home I composed the following ballad. . . . You must know that there is an old ballad beginning with

My bonie Lizie Bailie,
I'll rowe thee in my plaidie etc.—

so I parodied it as follows . . .'
Then follows the poem beginning:

'The bonie Lesley Bailie,
O she's gaen o'er the Border;
She's gaen, like Alexander,
To spread her conquests farther . . .'

On 8th November 1792 he sent the song to George Thomson with a comment on how it should go to the tune 'The Collier's Bony Dochter'. Thomson replied, making suggestions for altering certain things. Burns, however, wrote from Dumfries on 1st December, saying, 'I must not, cannot alter, Bonie Lesley'. He added the revealing comment: 'that species of Stanza is the most difficult that

I have ever tried'.

As for Miss Baillie, 'the most beautiful, elegant woman in the world', he never saw her again. But he wrote to her from Dumfries towards the end of May 1793, enclosing 'Blythe hae I been on yon hill', a song he had composed for her. He thought highly of this song, sending it to Thomson matched to a slowed-down reel, 'The Quaker's Wife', which came from Bremner's *Reels*, 1759.

In a letter to another young woman, Deborah Duff Davies, written in June 1793, Burns remarked: 'When I sing of Miss Davies or Miss Lesley Baillie, I have only to feign the passion—the charms are real', a revealing comment on his ability to imagine himself in love with any woman on the slightest pretext.

Baird, The Reverend George Husband (1761-1840)

Baird was ordained minister of Dunkeld in 1787, and appointed minister of Greyfriars Kirk, Edinburgh, in 1792. In the same year he became Joint Professor of Oriental Languages in Edinburgh University. The following year, he became Principal, and in 1800 he was chosen as Moderator of the General Assembly of the Church of Scotland.

Early in 1791, Baird wrote to Burns telling him that he was preparing an edition of the poems of Michael Bruce, the proceeds to be used to alleviate the condition of Bruce's elderly mother. Baird wanted Burns to consider Bruce's manuscripts, and to supply some memorial couplets for Bruce's tombstone. Burns replied asking: 'Why did you, my dear Sir, write to me in such a hesitating style on the business of poor Bruce? Don't I know, and have I not felt the many ills, the peculiar ills, that Poetic Flesh is heir to?' He then offered the choice of 'all the unpublished poems' he had, among them, apparently, 'Tam o' Shanter'. News of this offer leaked out among Bruce's admirers, and Baird was prevailed upon not to use Burns's masterpiece in a context which, to the admirers of Bruce's religious poems, seemed inappropriate. Bruce's poems were published in 1799.

Ballantine, John (1743–1812)

A merchant and banker in Ayr, and an early patron and good friend of Burns. In 1786, Ballantine, as Dean of Guild, played a leading part in bringing about the building of the new Brig, and in the following year became Provost. He remained a bachelor.

Ballantine, like Aiken and Hamilton, opened up for Burns the world of Ayrshire's bourgeoisie and small gentry. Indeed, in 1791 Burns was thanking Ballantine for having helped to haul him 'up to the Court of the Gentiles, in the temple of Fame'. It was as a literary admirer, however, that Ballantine perhaps played his most valuable role. According to Gilbert Burns, Ballantine offered to lend the poet the money needed to pay Wilson for the printing of a second Kilmarnock Edition, though at the same time advising him this time to go to Edinburgh for a publisher. Burns took the advice, though not the money. He dedicated 'The Brigs of Ayr' to Ballantine, and favoured the banker with many of his most intimate confidences.

While Burns was in Edinburgh, he kept Ballantine informed of his doings and of the people he was meeting, in a number of letters. Ballantine got a parcel of subscription bills for the Second Edition, and, on 14th January 1787, first news of Burns's hankering to go back to farming, and of the suggestion of Patrick Miller that the poet might lease a farm on Miller's estate of Dalswinton. Ballantine was also kept informed of the progress through the press of the Second Edition, being told when the book was expected in ten days' time, and, on 18th April 1787 (the ten days having been somewhat exceeded) being asked to

find an agent who would market the hundred copies of the book which accompanied the letter, at less than the unconscionable 'Jewish tax of 25 per cent'. (What would Burns have thought of the modern bookseller's rate of thirty-three and a third per cent?)

Early in January 1788, Burns, crippled temporarily in one of his legs, 'owing to a fall by the drunken stupidity of a coachman', wrote to Ballantine from Edinburgh asking him to give brother Gilbert some money out of the proceeds of the copies of the Second Edition which Ballantine had disposed of, the first of several acts of assistance which the poet made to his brother.

At odd moments throughout his career, Burns wrote notes to Ballantine enclosing drafts of new poems. From a letter dated September 1791, written at Ellisland, it would appear that Ballantine may well have been one of his sponsors in the 'Excise matter', which had by then loomed large in the poet's life.

During the poet's last years, however, their correspondence came to an end, probably because of the increasing pressures on Burns's time and health, and the distance between Ayr and Dumfries.

See Plate 10.

Ballochmyle

A district in Ayrshire, near Mauchline, mentioned in 'The Lass of Ballochmyle', and in 'Farewell to Ballochmyle'. Burns said that this latter poem was written when Sir John Whitefoord and his family had to sell the Ballochmyle estate to Claud Alexander. Whitefoord, a partner in the banking establishment of Douglas, Heron & Co., Ayr, lost his fortune when the bank failed in 1772. The Maria of this poem was Whitefoord's daughter, Mary Anne.

Bannatine, The Rev. George (d. 1769)

A mutual friend of Burns and Dr Moore, he was minister of Craigie Parish Church in Ayrshire, from 1744 to 1764. From then until his death, he had the West Parish (later St George's) Church in Glasgow.

Bannockburn

A village near Stirling on the river Forth, and the scene of Robert the Bruce's victory over the English army of King Edward II, in 1314. Burns in company with Nicol, visited Bannockburn on Sunday, 26th August 1787. The entry in Burns's *Journal* reads: 'Came on to Bannockburn —shown the old house where James IIIrd was murdered—the field of Bannock-burn—the hole where glorious Bruce set his standard.'

Cunningham fabricated a fervent piece of romantic day-dreaming, wholly out of style with the rest of the *Journal*, but which is sometimes printed as if genuine. Cunningham apparently took his text from the remark in Burns's letter to Robert Muir, dated 26th August 1787: 'This morning I knelt at the tomb of Sir John the Graham, the gallant friend of the immortal Wallace; and two hours ago I said a fervent prayer for Old Caledonia over the hole in a blue whinstone, where Robert de Bruce fixed his royal standard on the banks of Bannockburn.'

Sir John the Graham is buried at Falkirk.

Barleycorn, John

The pseudonym used by Burns in his 'Address of the Scottish Distillers to the Right Honble. William Pitt' which appeared in the *Gazatteer and New Daily Advertiser*.

The letter arose out of the dissatis-faction expressed by the Scottish Distillers who had 'been lately ruined by a positive breach of the Public Faith, in a most partial tax laid on by the House of Com-mons, to favour a few opulent English Distillers, who, it seems, were of vast Electioneering consequence'.

Burns also wrote 'John Barleycorn—a Ballad', praising whisky, the product of barley:

> 'John Barleycorn was a hero bold,
>   Of noble enterprise;
> For if you do but taste his blood,
>   'Twill make your courage rise.

> 'Twill make a man forget his woe;
>   'Twill heighten all his joy:
> 'Twill make the widow's heart to sing,
>   'Tho the tear were in her eye.

> Then let us toast John Barleycorn,
>   Each man a glass in hand;
> And may his great posterity
>   Ne'er fail in old Scotland!'

Barskimming

Barskimming, the 'wild romantic grove' of 'The Vision', was the seat of Sir Thomas Miller of Glenlee, who was appointed Lord Chief Justice of the Court of Session with the title of Lord Barskimming in 1766. He became Lord President in 1788. His estate was next to Ballochmyle, near Mauchline, and was well known to Burns.

Bath, Earl of. *See* Pulteney, William.

Beattie, Dr James (1735–1803)

Born at Laurencekirk, Kincardinshire, Beattie was educated at the parish school, and at Marischal College, Aberdeen, where he was the best scholar in the Greek class. For five years he was a schoolmaster in Aberdeen Grammar School. In 1760, the year he published his *Original Poems and Translations*, he became Professor of Moral Philosophy in Marischal College. He achieved his literary reputation with his poem 'The Minstrel', published in two parts in 1771 and 1774, and much ad-mired in his day. In May 1770, Beattie published his *Essay on the Nature and Immutability of Truth in opposition to Sophistry and Scepticism*, which was an attempted refutation of Hume's doctrines. Beattie was one of a group of late eighteenth-century Scots who deliberately strove to rid their speech of Scotticisms.

Burns made several references to Beattie and his work. He told Dr Moore in January 1787: 'I am very willing to admit that I have some poetical abilities; and as few, if any Writers, either moral or poetical, are intimately acquainted with the classes of Mankind among whom I have chiefly mingled, I may have seen men and manners in a different phasis, which may assist originality of thought. Still I know very well, the novelty of my character has by far the greatest share in the learned and polite notice I have lately got; and in a language where Pope and Churchill have raised the laugh, and Shenstone and Gray drawn the tear; where Thomson and Beattie have painted the landskip, and Littleton and Collins described the heart; I am not vain enough to hope for distinguished Poetic fame.'

Telling his friends about Johnson's *Museum* Burns explained that 'Drs Beattie and Blacklock are lending a hand'. Thomson also sought, on Burns's recommendation, to get Beattie to devote some time 'in extending a little and adapting for our purpose the observations on Scottish pastoral music, contained in the third section of your Essay on Music and Poetry'. By 1792, however, when Thomson wrote, Beattie's health was failing, and nothing came of this suggestion.

Begbie, Alison (or Ellison)

The most important of the early friends of the opposite sex with whom the poet associated, Alison, or Ellison, Begbie is a somewhat shadowy figure. She is said to have been born in the parish of Galston, the daughter of a small farmer, and at the time she was being courted by Burns to have been a servant employed in a house near the river Cessnock, about two miles from Loudon. Burns was then at Lochlea.

Five letters from Burns were claimed by

Dr Currie to have been sent to Alison Begbie. Of these, only the manuscript of one—the first, in which Burns hopes the recipient will not despise him because he is 'ignorant of the flattering arts of courtship'—has been traced. The others were found by Dr Currie in draft form among Burns's papers.

In language of copy-book stiltedness, Burns leads up to a proposal of marriage in the fourth letter: 'If you will be so good and so generous as to admit me for your partner, your companion, your bosom friend through life, there is nothing on this side of eternity shall give me greater transport.' The only evidence to suggest that the letters were ever sent is the fact that the fifth draft takes the form of a brave acknowledgement of refusal.

The initial used in the one authentic letter is 'My dear E.'. In the autobiographical letter to Moore, Burns said that in his twenty-third year, somebody, 'a belle-fille whom I adored', jilted or refused him 'with peculiar circumstances of mortification'. The fifth letter in the series, supposedly to Begbie, gives no indication of the existence of any such circumstances, and, indeed, it was Burns's sister Isabella who first said that Alison Begbie was the person her brother referred to. Ferguson goes so far as to suggest that the letters may not have been 'personal letters of Burns's at all, since we have his own testimony that he often acted as go-between for his shyer and less literate friends'.

Miss Begbie is said to have married another a few years after her alleged 'jilting' of Burns—though to refuse a man's offer of marriage is not normally referred to as jilting!—and to have settled in Glasgow.

She is probably the 'lass of Cessnock Banks' who inspired 'On Cessnock banks a lassie dwells', and the Peggy Alison of 'Ilk care and fear, when thou art near', both of which appeared in the *Scots Musical Museum* to the tunes 'The Butcher Boy' and 'Braes o' Balquidder' respectively.

But her main claim to our grateful remembrance is that, according to some Burns scholars, she seems much more likely to have been the inspiration of that exquisite love-song 'O Mary at thy window be' than the actual Mary Morison who lies buried in the churchyard at Mauchline, and whom the poet is thought to have met only once. This song was marked by Burns to go to the tune 'Duncan Davidson', as printed by Dick in *The Songs of Burns*. Thomson published it with the tune, 'Bide ye yet'. It was matched to 'The Glasgow lasses'. in a collection, *Scotch Airs* published in 1818, but since then is usually published with the tune 'The Miller' (in the second volume of the *Museum*), one of the few unauthorised airs that suit the words better than the air chosen by the poet.

Begbie's

A tavern in Market Street, Kilmarnock, across the Marnock Water from the Laigh Kirk. It later became the Angel Hotel. Burns refers to it in 'The Ordination'. The bridge over the Marnock was so narrow that churchgoers were forced to walk in a row on their way to the tavern after their devotions. The poet alleged that the Laigh Kirk worshippers were accustomed to go:

'Aff to Begbie's in a raw,
An' pour divine libations
For joy this day.'

In the 'Rob Rhymer' manuscript, 'Crookes's' appears instead of 'Begbie's'. This may also have been a tavern, or perhaps an allusion to a member of the Crookes or Crox family in Kilmarnock, who were connected with the leather trade—Burns refers in the poem to 'ye wha leather rax an' draw'—and who may have invited friends in for a drink after church.

Belles of Mauchline, the

Six Mauchline girls mentioned in the song 'O leave novels, ye Mauchline belles'. They were Betty Miller, Jean Markland, Jean Smith, Helen Miller, Christina Morton and Jean Armour (*see* under each name).

The song warned the belles to beware of the amatory arts of 'Rob Mossgiel', but at least one of the belles failed to heed the warning.

The song was first published in part by Currie in 1800, and appeared in the *Scots Musical Museum* in 1803. Burns's title for the tune was 'Donald Blue', which Dick failed to trace. The tune in the *Museum* is described by Dick as 'evidently a pipe-tune of good Scottish type'.

'To a Louse' was reputed to have been written about one of the Belles.

Benson, Anna Dorothea Bridget (1773?-1856)

The daughter of James Benson, a new York wine merchant and a friend of the Craiks of Arbigland, in whose house Burns met her. She married twice, and by her first husband, Thomas Skepper, a barrister at York, she had a daughter who married Bryan Waller Procter, the author 'Barry Cornwall'. Her second husband was Basil Montague of London, whose third wife she became, in 1808.

From the role which she occupied in the correspondence between Thomas Carlyle and Jane Welsh, we learn that the lady was meddling, self-opinionated and sentimental. Burns sent her a stilted, fulsome letter of praise from Dumfries, dated 21st March 1793, accompanying a hitherto untraced sonnet—'though to tell you the real truth, the sonnet is a mere pretence, that I may have the opportunity of declaring with how much respectful esteem I have the honour to be, etc. . . .'

Allan Cunningham ascribed a statement to her that Burns drank 'as other men drank'. In a letter of 25th February 1834 she protested against the ascription, saying that Burns had been incapable of rudeness or vulgarity . . . well bred and gentlemanly in all the courtesies of life'. Even during the meeting of the Caledonian hunt, she 'never saw Burns once intoxicated, though the worthy Member for Dumfries and the good Laird of Arbigland and twenty more . . . were brought home in a state of glorious insensibility'.

Bentinck, William Henry Cavendish, third Duke of Portland (1738–1809)

Prime Minister of Great Britain. Under Rockingham, he was Lord Chamberlain from 1765 till 1766. In 1782, when Rockingham was again in power, the Duke became Lord Lieutenant of Ireland. Fox and North chose him as a 'convenient cypher' to head their coalition government. He held office as Prime Minister from then until the defeat of the British India Bill forced his dismissal. Under Pitt, he was Secretary of State for the Home Department from 1794 till 1801, when he became President of the Council.

In 1807, he was Prime Minister for the second time and First Lord of the Treasury.

His political influence was largely due to 'his rank, his mild disposition, and his personal integrity'.

Burns referred to 'the triumph of the Portland Band' in his 'Ode to the Departed Regency-Bill, 1789'. This was a Bill proposing power for the Prince of Wales because of the King's illness, favoured by Fox and opposed by Pitt. The Bill was withdrawn when it was announced that the King was recovering.

Berrywell

The home of Robert Ainslie's family, near Duns. Burns and Ainslie stayed there on their Border tour of 1787.

Beugo, John (1759–1841)

Beugo was born in Edinburgh, and in due course apprenticed to an engraver. Eventually he set up in business for himself. He met Burns when Creech employed him to engrave the Nasmyth portrait for the Second Edition of Burns's *Poems* (known as the First Edinburgh Edition). Like Nasmyth, he made no charge for his share of the work.

Writing to Ballantine on 24th February 1787, Burns tells him: 'I am getting my phiz done, by an eminent engraver, and if it can be ready in time, I will appear in my book, looking like all other *fools*, to my title-page.' Burns sent several copies of this engraving to his friends as gifts.

Probably as a result of additional sittings he gave, he became friendly with Beugo, who seems to have been a widely-read man, and who even tried his engraver's hand occasionally at verse-writing. He and Burns together studied French with a well-known Edinburgh French teacher, M. Louis Cauvin. An amusing note to Beugo from Burns, written probably in December 1787, but simply dated 'St James's Square, Tuesday even.' says: 'A certain sour-faced old acquaintance called Glauber's salts, hinders me from my lesson to-night. Tomorrow night I will not fail.'

The warmest letter to Beugo was written at Ellisland on 9th September 1788. It contains Burns's praise of Alexander Ross's 'The Fortunate Shepherdess' and gives Beugo some advice should he be intending to get married: 'Depend upon it, if you do not make some damned foolish choice, it will be a very great improvement on the Dish of Life.'

Beugo himself published a book of verse, *Poetry, Miscellaneous and Dramatic, by an Artist*, in 1797. Most of the contents are in frigid Augustan English couplets. although his poem 'Esk Water' has felicitous touches:

'To him alone, who with industrious
                                              aim,
Pursues an useful art, and honest fame;
To him who seeks his fellow's wants to
                                              know,

Who feels a brother's bliss, a brother's
woe;
To him alone does nature bounteous
reign
And smile eternal o'er the wide cham-
paign;
And thus in grotto, as in green abode,
To relish nature is to walk with God.'

Later, he was Secretary to the first exhibition of paintings held in Sir Henry
Raeburn's rooms in York Place, Edinburgh.
Beugo became the leading Scottish
engraver of the day, his work including
not only several of Raeburn's most
famous paintings, but notes for both
the Commercial and the British Linen
Banks.

He married Elizabeth McDowall of
Edinburgh, by whom he had a daughter.
Four portraits of Beugo have come down
to us, three of which are in the Scottish
National Portrait Gallery. He was buried
in Greyfriars Churchyard.

Beurnonville, Pierre de (1752–1821)
Born at Champignolle (Département
Aube), he was a general in the French
Republican army under the revolutionaries, and Minister of War in 1793. It
must be assumed that he changed his
opinions, because after Waterloo and
the restoration of Louis XVIII, he was
Marshal of France.

He is mentioned by Burns in his verses
'An Address to General Dumouriez':

'How does Dampierre do?
Aye, and Beurnonville too?
Why did they not come along with
you, Dumouriez?'

Bibles
Four Bibles associated with Burns have
been preserved:
(1) *The Armour Family Bible*, which
contains the record of the marriage of
James Armour and Mary Smith, 7th
December 1761, and the register of the
birth of their children, is in the Burns

House, Mauchline. The imprint on the
title page is: 'Edinburgh, printed by
Adrian Watkins, 1756'.
(2) *The 'Big Ha' Bible*, which belonged
to William Burns, and is mentioned in
'The Cotter's Saturday Night', is in the
Cottage Museum, Alloway. It was bought
at Sotheby's on 12 July 1921, for £450.
It carries the imprint: 'Edinburgh: Printed
by Alexander Kincaid, MDCCLXII'. A
'Ha' Bible' was the one kept in the hall
of a mansion, from where it was carried
into the room where the servants had
assembled for household worship.
(3) *The Poet's Family Bible*, which, on
the reverse of the title of the New Testament, contains an entry in Burns's own
hand recording his birth date and that of
his wife, as well as of his first seven
children by her. There are also entries
by James Glencairn Burns and William
Nicol Burns, sons of the poet.

This Bible passed from Jean Armour
Burns to the eldest son, Robert, and from
him to William Nicol Burns. He gave it
to his niece, Mrs S. E. M. T. Burns
Hutchinson, on whose death it was sold
at Quaritch's for £1,700. It is now in
the Cottage Museum, Alloway. It bears
the imprint: 'Edinburgh: Printed by
John Reid, 1766'.
(4) *Highland Mary's Bible*. A two-
volume copy bearing the date on the
title page, 1782, and the price, five
shillings and sixpence, marked on volume
one. (For the story of Burns's exchange
of Bibles with Mary, *see* **Campbell,
'Highland' Mary**.) On the fly-leaf on
volume one is written in Burns's hand:
' "And ye shall not swear by My Name
falsely: I am the Lord"—Levit. xix. 12'.

In the second volume, also in Burns's
hand, there is: ' "Thou shall not forswear
thyself but shall perform unto the Lord
thine oaths"—Math. V. 33.'
The names inscribed on the fly-leaves
of both volumes have been mutilated,
apparently by smudging. Mary's name
is inscribed in volume one—the 'M' and

part of the 'a' remain—and Robert's in volume two—the 'Robert' and the 's' of 'Burns' remain, together with 'Mossgaville', the old spelling of Mossgiel, and his mason's mark.

This Bible—incidentally, no trace has ever been found of the Bible Burns is supposed to have received from Highland Mary—passed from Mary's mother to her grandson, William Anderson, a mason from Renton, Dunbartonshire, who took it to Canada with him in 1834. There, he was forced to sell it. It was bought by a group of Burns lovers in Montreal for twenty-five pounds, and sent to the Provost of Ayr, who handed it over on 25th January 1841 to the Custodian of the Alloway Monument, where it still is. A lock of Highland Mary's hair has been pressed in volume one.

Biggar, The Misses

The four daughters of the Reverend Matthew Biggar, minister of Kirkoswald, whom Burns met occasionally. They were:

Margaret (1755–1843).
Janet (1756– 1814).
Elizabeth (1757–1838), who married John Graham, a farmer at Dalwhat, near Kirkoswald, and nephew of Douglas Graham, who was the model for 'Tam o' Shanter'.
Louisa (1761–1846), who married her father's successor at Kirkoswald, the Rev. James Inglis.

Biggar, The Rev. Matthew (d. 1806)

Minister of Kirkoswald (see **Biggar, The Misses**) from 1752 until his death. He Married Margaret, daughter of Robert Wodrow, minister of Eastwood and a somewhat biased Presbyterian historian.

Birtwhistle, Alexander

A Kirkcudbright merchant, and Provost of the burgh. He is supposed to have carried on a substantial foreign trade from the town.

Burns referred to him in his 'Election Ballad for Westerha' ';

'To end the work, here's Whistlebirk,
    Long may his whistle blaw, Jamie'.

In his 'Second Ballad on Mr Heron's Election' he called him 'roaring Birtwhistle'.

Bishop, John

Husband of Elizabeth Burns, child of Robert Burns and Elizabeth Paton. He was Baillie of Polkemmet's land steward. He had seven children.

Bishop, Mrs John

See **Burns, Elizabeth**.

Black, Mrs Betsy

Burns mentions her in a letter, dated 21st June, 1783, from Lochlea, to his cousin, James Burness in Montrose, in connexion with taking 'a small present of cheese' to him. There is also a note in the memorandum of Miss Isabella Begg, Burns's niece: 'My mother's recollections of Betsy Black are quite fresh. She belonged to Kilmarnock, had gone to the neighbourhood of Montrose to act as housekeeper in some gentleman's family, and had got acquainted with Mrs Burness, who sent messages and letters by her when she returned to see her relations in Ayrshire. The Lochlea folk sent letters by her back again to the Burnesses in Montrose, and the cheese which Burns mentions in a letter to his cousin, my mother thinks, was also sent by her. But they lost all trace of her after going to Mossgiel.'

Black Bonnet

A nickname for the elder stationed beside the collection plate at the church door to receive the congregation's offering. In the 'Epistle to John M'Math' Burns refers to his muse being

'. . . tir'd wi' mony a sonnet,
    On gown an' ban' an' douce black bonnet'.

Black Bull Hotel

An inn in Argyle Street, Glasgow, from which a 'fly on steel springs' left at eight o'clock in the morning, three times a week for Edinburgh, where it arrived the same evening. This hotel, which had thirty-two bedrooms, was built for the Highland Society in 1758. It closed down in 1849, and part of it became incorporated in a warehouse. A plaque on the front wall of the building registered the fact that: 'Robert Burns lodged here when this building was the Black Bull Inn. He visited Glasgow June, 1787, February and March 1788.' In 1958 the warehouse was demolished. The plaque was removed, to be affixed to the next building to go up on the site. Burns met his brother William at the Black Bull, as well as his friend Richard Brown.

The word 'Inn' has caused some confusion, for there was an old Black Bull Inn on the other side of the road. Its landlord became the first landlord of the new hotel. In Burns's day, the landlord was one George Durie.

Black Monday

Writing to Gavin Hamilton on 7th December 1786, Burns, remarking on his growing fame, told him: 'You may expect henceforth to see my birthday inserted among the wonderful events, in the Poor Robin's and Aberdeen Almanacks, along with the black Monday and the battle of Bothwel bridge.'

Black Monday—Easter Monday, 14th April 1360—was the day on which an English army, besieging Paris, suffered heavy losses as the result of a great storm.

Blacklock, Dr Thomas (1721–91)

A minor poet whose enthusiasm for Burns's work played an important part in Burns's career. Blacklock was born at Annan, Dumfriesshire, the son of a brick-layer, and lost his sight as a result of small-pox during his first year. Largely self-educated, he studied divinity at Edinburgh, and was ordained minister of Kirkcud-bright in 1762. But his parishioners complained that his blindness made him incapable of carrying out his parish duties, and in 1765 he retired to Edinburgh on a small annuity. This he augmented by writing, tutoring and running a small boarding establishment for scholars and students. A man of broad culture and keen intellectual power, Blacklock was befriended by both Dr. Johnson and Benjamin Franklin. Throughout his life he took a generous interest in the work of young writers.

John Home, the author of Douglas ('Whaur's your Wullie Shakespeare noo?'), called Blacklock 'a small, weakly, under thing—a chilly bloodless animal, that shivers at every breeze. But if nature has cheated him in one respect, by assigning to his share, forceless sinews, and a ragged form, she has made him ample compensation on the other, by giving him a mind endued with the most exquisite feelings. . . . He is the most flagrant enthusiast I ever saw'. Dr. Johnson, however, received Blacklock in 1773 with 'a most humane complacency' and 'looked on him with reverence', while David Hume found him 'a very elegant genius, of a modest backward temper, accompanied with that delicate pride which so naturally attends virtue in distress'.

Blacklock entered Burns's life unexpectedly and dramatically. In the autumn of 1786, though the success of the Kilmarnock volume was assured, Burns was in a state of emotional turmoil, partly as a result of the threatened legal action by Jean Armour's parents, and possibly also because of amatory complications with the unfortunate Mary Campbell. He thought, or at any rate wrote and talked a great deal, about emigrating to Jamaica, and even got the length of making preliminary negotiations for a passage. It is clear from his correspondence, however, that flight to Jamaica was never regarded by him as anything other than a last resort.

A letter from Dr Blacklock dated 4th September 1786, delivered through the Reverend George Lawrie of Loudon, from whom Blacklock had received a copy of the Kilmarnock Edition, played a major part in making Burns change his mind over the Jamaican business, and instead, go to Edinburgh, from whence Blacklock's letter of encouragement had come.

In the autobiographical letter to Dr Moore, Burns said: 'I had taken the last farewel of my few friends; my chest was on the road to Greenock; I had composed my last song I should ever measure in Caledonia . . . when a letter from Dr Blacklock to a friend of mine overthrew all my schemes by rousing my poetic ambition. The Doctor belonged to a set of Critics for whose applause I had not even dared to hope. His idea that I would meet with every encouragement for a second edition fired me so much that away I posted to Edinburgh without a single acquaintance in town.'

Blacklock had found in Burns's serious poems 'a pathos and delicacy' and 'a vein of wit and humour in those of a more festive turn which cannot be too much admired nor too warmly approved'. He thought he would 'never open the book without feeling my astonishment renewed and increased'. Blacklock mentioned that he had been told the first edition was already exhausted. 'It were therefore much to be wished', he went on, 'for the sake of the young man that a second edition, more numerous than the former, could immediately be printed.' He prophesied, 'a more universal circulation than anything of the kind which has been published within my memory'.

Once in Edinburgh, however, Burns delayed calling on Blacklock for two weeks. Blacklock wrote to Lawrie to say he had heard 'Mr Burns is, and has been some time, in Edinburgh. This news I am sorry to have had at second hand; they would have come much more welcome from the bard's own mouth.' Lawrie then wrote to Burns again, and on 5th February 1787 Burns was able to report to Lawrie that he had been to call on Blacklock, and found him to have 'a clear head and an excellent heart'.

Thereafter, a sincere friendship sprang up between the young major poet and the old minor one. Blacklock gave a breakfast in honour of Burns and the two men kept in touch, exchanging rhyming epistles in 1789. Blacklock's light jingle includes these lines:

'Most anxiously I wish to know
With thee of late how matters go;
How keeps thy much-loved Jean her
                                         health?
What promises thy farm of wealth?'

Perhaps it is hardly surprising that Burns's 'To Dr Blacklock' is not one of his most interesting rhymed epistles.

On 1st September 1790, Blacklock asked Burns, in another rhymed epistle, to contribute to Dr Anderson's magazine, *The Bee*, but Burns was busy with other matters and nothing came of the request. Blacklock, however, contributed ten songs to the *Scots Musical Museum*, at least four of them—'My love has forsaken me', 'Ye river so limpid and clear', 'Forbear, gentle youth, to pursue one in vain' and 'When, dear Evanthe, we were young'—matched to airs of his own composition. Writing to Johnson from Ellisland on 28th July 1788 (dated by Ferguson), however, Burns remarked, 'I have still a good number of Dr Blacklock's Songs among my hands, but they take sad hacking and hewing.'

Blacklock's first book of poems appeared in 1746, and other books in 1754 and 1756. Though he produced verse for about forty years, he remained quite uninfluenced by the vernacular work of Burns. His other works included an *Essay towards Universal Etymology*, and some theological papers. In his closing years he became deaf as well as blind, and suffered long periods of dejection, which he strove to conceal from his wife. James Beattie composed the Latin epitaph for his tombstone in St Cuthbert's Chapel of Ease.

See Plate 10.

Blair, Alexander

On 3rd April 1788, Burns addressed a letter from Mauchline to one Alexander Blair of Catrine House, Catrine. He regretted that he could not at the moment 'accede' to Mr Blair's request, farming at that moment not being 'propitious to poetry'. He promised, if he had the opportunity, to report upon his progress in a few weeks.

Nothing whatever is known of Alexander Blair. He may have been a friend or a pupil of the philosopher Dugald Stewart, the owner of Catrine Bank. On the other hand, the stiffness of style and the vagueness of content suggest that the letter may be a forgery. The original of the letter has not been traced since the 1890s. Ferguson suggests that it may be the work of the forger 'Antique' Smith, rather than by Burns.

Blair, David (1755?-1814)

Possibly a member of the firm of Blair and Lea, gun-makers, which was set up in Navigation Street, Birmingham, in 1783. A David Blair, gunmaker—St Paul's Square—the address to which Burns wrote Blair, first appears in Pye's Directory of Birmingham for 1787. According to Ferguson (who got his information from the City Librarian of Birmingham) Blair was a 'substantial' citizen whose name appears in subscription lists for the relief of the poor in 1812 and 1813, in which latter year he was among the founders of Birmingham Chamber of Manufacturers and Commerce. He lost two sons within two weeks of each other in May 1812, and died himself the following May.

Burns wrote to Blair from Ellisland on 23rd January 1789, apparently acknowledging the receipt of a gun. This letter suggests it was not his first communication. Thereafter, Burns sent him copies of his poems from time to time, a copy of the 1793 edition of his Poems, and, from Dumfries on 25th August 1795, a letter containing the history of 'Lord Balmerino's durk' which was then in Blair's possession, and the story of which Burns says he got from a friend who once owned it.

Pistols, presumably carried by Burns on his Excise duties and which he later presented to Dr W. Maxwell, were probably supplied by Blair. They are now in the National Museum of Antiquities in Edinburgh.

Blair, David

Nothing is known of this 'gentleman of a tolerable decent estate in the neighbourhood' whose unfulfilled engagement Burns mentions in a letter to Alexander Dalziel, written at Ellisland on 5th October 1790.

Obviously this Blair cannot have been the same person as the Birmingham gunsmith of the same name with whom Burns corresponded.

Blair, The Reverend Dr Hugh (1718-1800)

Burns's Edinburgh admirer, the Reverend Dr Hugh Blair, has been somewhat harshly treated by most of the poet's biographers, but he was a man of genuine intellectual substance in his day. He was born the only child of John Blair, a merchant who lost his money in the Darien Scheme.

The poet Robert Blair, who wrote The Grave, was his kinsman. Hugh Blair went to Edinburgh High School and Edinburgh University, graduating Master of Arts in 1739. He was licensed to preach in 1741, and soon after became tutor in the family of Simon, Master of Lovat.

Through the Earl of Leven, he gained his first pastorate, at Collessie, in Fife. From there, he went as junior minister to the Canongate Church, Edinburgh. In 1754 he was called to Lady Yester's and in 1760 to the High Kirk, St Giles. In religion, he was a 'moderate', attending and supporting the cause of the theatre, and playing a leading part as defender in the attacks on Lord Kames and David Hume from the narrower section of the Church. From 1762 onwards Blair also held the Chair of Rhetoric in Edinburgh University. His lectures on taste won him wide fame. It was Blair who encouraged James Macpherson to proceed with the collection of his Ossianic Fragments, and Blair who wrote the introduction to the first edition which appeared in 1760. He became the acknowledged arbitrator of rather conservative 'good taste', and as such was on the side of those who, like Adam Smith, were constantly trying to 'un-Scotch' themselves. His sermons were widely read when they appeared, and, although Gosse later referred to them as 'Blair's bucket of warm water' and Leslie Stephen wrote of Blair 'mouthing his sham rhetoric', they reveal a greater degree of liberal humanism than is to be found in the sermons of his less moderate contemporaries.

When Burns arrived in Edinburgh, Blair was two years off seventy. In spite of the disparity between their ages and temperaments, Blair was in the forefront of those who promoted the 'child of nature'. Josiah Walker reports an incident in which Burns unwittingly gave Blair, then his host, some pain. Burns, in answer to a question, said that of all the public places he had seen in Edinburgh, the High Church gave him 'the greatest gratification'. He then 'gave the preference as preacher to the Rev. Mr William Greenfield'—the colleague of his host. It was a thoughtless lapse which seems to have caused Burns as much pain as Blair, though it reflects the common view that in spite of his literary gifts, Blair was no great preacher.

In his *Second Commonplace Book,* Burns left a shrewd portrait of Blair.

'I never respect him with humble veneration; but when he kindly interests himself in my welfare, or, still more, when he descends from his pinnacle and meets me on equal ground, my heart overflows with what is called *liking*: when he neglects me for the mere carcase of greatness, or when his eye measures the difference of our points of elevation, I say to myself with scarcely an emotion, what do I care for him or his pomp either? . . . In my opinion Dr Blair is merely an astonishing proof of what industry and application can do. Natural parts like his are frequently to be met with; his vanity is proverbially known among his acquaintants; but he is justly at the head of what may be called fine writing. . . . He has a heart, not of the finest water, but far from being an ordinary one. In short, he is truly a worthy and most respectable character.'

So worthy, indeed, did Burns think him that the poet wrote to Blair on his departure from Edinburgh, a letter dated 3rd May 1787, thanking him for 'the kindness, patronage and friendship' Blair had shown him, and enclosing a proof of the Beugo engraving.

Burns's alteration of 'tidings of salvation' to 'damnation' in 'The Holy Fair' was made on Blair's suggestion. Blair was at least partly responsible for the exclusion of 'The Jolly Beggars' from the Edinburgh edition, as well as of a poem, now lost, called 'The Prophet and God's Complaint'. Blair always thought of Burns as a great and noble poet who had 'the words of the stable and the politics of the smithy'. (Schmitz—*Hugh Blair*). He therefore advised Dr Currie in 1797 not to publish too much about Burns's character, and to make the selection of his poems 'with much delicacy and caution', advice, however, which Currie hardly needed.

Blair married his cousin, Katherine Bannatine, in 1748. His son died in infancy, his daughter in her twenty-first year. His wife died in 1795.

Blair, Sir James Hunter (1741–87)

Born John Hunter, the son of an Ayr merchant, he became a banker in the banking company of Sir William Forbes, and acquired the estate of Robertland. On marrying the heiress of John Blair of Dunskey in 1770, he added Blair to his name. He was Member of Parliament for Edinburgh from 1780 to 1784, and Lord Provost of the City in 1784'. He was created a baronet in 1786. As Lord Provost, he carried through various reforms, including the beginning of work on rebuilding the University and the construction of the bridge over the Cowgate. The foundation stone of this bridge was laid by Lord Haddo, as Grand Master Mason of Scotland in 1785, after Parliament had passed an Act giving permission for the plans to be executed. Blair was knighted the following year.

Burns was cordially received by him when he arrived in Edinburgh. On Blair's death, the poet drafted a somewhat stilted elegy, beginning: 'The lamp of day, with ill-presaging glare', which extols, rather laboriously. Blair's public virtues. Burns called it 'just mediocre', but Ferguson describes it justifiably, as 'the disastrous Elegy on the Death of Sir James Hunter Blair'.

Blair was an enthusiastic Freemason. Hunter Square and Blair Street in Edinburgh were both named after him.

Blane, John

A farm servant to Burns at Mossgiel. When James Grierson recorded a conversation he had with Blane at Glasgow on 15th June 1814, Blane was then driver of the Lord Nelson Coach from Kilmarnock to Cumnock. Grierson's notes of Blane's conversation are not without

interest, and are therefore appended, but perhaps savour slightly of 'improved' gossip recollected years later of a man since become famous.

'J. B. sat beside Burns in church on the day when the Incident occured [sic] wh gave occasion to the Poem of the Louse, & was surprized when Burns awakened him, the middle of the same night, & repeated to him all the stanzas, requesting his opinion of them,—this was the most surprizing Proofs of the facility with which Burns composed, that Came within J. B.'s Knowledge—

'In the laborious employment of husbandry, the Peculiarities of Burns's [sic] mind were easily discernable—While engaged in Thrashing, it was evident that his mind was particularly occupied, from the varied alternations from slow to quick wh rendered it dangerous & even impossible for another to Keep time with him but in an hour or two he was quite exhausted & gave in altogether.—

'A simple occurrence commented on by Burns in his own commanding way, has never since failed to Impress this persons [sic] mind, in regard to Cruelty to animals. When walking together, J. B. having a whip in his hand, gave a slight touch of it at a sparrow, & deprived it of some of its feathers—Upon this occasion Burns made so solemn an appeal to his Conscience, upon the unnecessary & wanton barbarity of the action that he has Ever since been Influenced by his admonition to resist similar Temtations [sic]—Burns uniformly digested & arranged his Compositions mentally, before he committed them to paper-'

Boconnock

The reference 'tell yon guid bluid o' auld Boconnock's' in 'The Author's Earnest Cry and Prayer' is to The Earl of Chatham, William Pitt the Elder (1708–1778). He was the second son of Robert Pitt of Boconnock in Cornwall, and father of William Pitt the Younger, the 'guid bluid' referred to by the poet.

Bone, William

He married Nelly Kilpatrick, whom Burns met at the age of fifteen when harvesting. Bone was coachman to the Laird of Newark.

'Bonie Wee Thing'
See **Davies, Miss Deborah Duff.**

Boswell, James (1740–95)

Son of Alexander Boswell of Auchinleck, who was raised to the Bench as Lord Auchinleck. James Boswell was born at Edinburgh. He studied law at Glasgow University and in Utrecht, Holland, and became an advocate in 1766. He acted for the winning side in the Douglas case. He married Margaret Montgomerie in 1769. He met Samuel Johnson in London in 1763, and persuaded him to visit Scotland. Boswell accompanied Johnson on the tour of the Hebrides ten years later. In 1785, he published his *Tour of the Hebrides.*

Lord Auchinleck died in 1782. Thereafter, Boswell tried to get into Parliament, indulged in unlucky speculations, got 'not drunk, but intoxicated', to use his own phrase, and in 1788 moved to London, leaving his wife at Auchinleck for long spells, where she died. He bitterly reproached himself for having left her on the day of her death, on the orders of Lord Lonsdale, for whom Boswell was Recorder for Carlisle, until Lonsdale's crude bullying became too much even for Boswell. Though he contemplated a second marriage, it did not materialise. In 1791, he published his supreme achievement, his *Life of Samuel Johnson*, the best biography in the English language. Worn out by the intensity and frequency of his earlier pleasures, he died in London in 1795.

The Malahide papers have revealed a Boswell whose industry and honesty must be unsurpassed in English letters. Quite early in his career, he painted his own character in some lines of doggerel verse:

'Boswell is pleasant and gay,
For frolic by nature design'd;
He heedlessly rattles away
When the company is to his mind.
"This maxim", he says, "you may see,
We never have corn without chaff"
So not a bent sixpence cares he,
Whether *with* him or *at* him you
laugh.'

Though they were both Ayrshiremen, Burns and Boswell never met. That Burns hoped for such a meeting is shown by the letter he wrote to Bruce Campbell on 13th November 1788:

'I inclose you, for Mr Boswell, the Ballad you mentioned; and as I hate sending waste paper or mutilating a sheet, I have filled it up with one or two of my fugitive Pieces that occurred. Should they procure me the honor of being introduced to Mr Boswell, I shall think they have great merit. There are few pleasures my late will-o'-wisp character has given me, equal to that of having seen many of the extraordinary men, the Heroes of Wit & Literature in my Country; & as I had the honor of drawing my first breath almost in the same Parish with Mr Boswell, my Pride plumes itself on the connection. To crouch in the train of meer stupid Wealth & Greatness, except where the commercial interests of worldly Prudence find their account in it, I hold to be Prostitution in any one that is not born a Slave; but to have been acquainted with such a man as Mr Boswell, I would hand down to my Posterity as one of the honors of their Ancestor.'

In 'The Author's Earnest Cry and Prayer', Burns wrote:

'Alas! I'm but a nameless wight,
Trode i' the mirè out o' sight!
But could I like Montgomeries fight,
Or gab like Boswell,

There's some sark-necks I wad draw
                                    tight,
    An' tie some hose well.'

In 'The Fête Champêtre', Burns, listing the possible people to send to St Stephen's House, asked:

'Or will we send a man o' law?
    Or will we send a sodger?
Or him wha led o'er Scotland a'
    The meikle Ursa-Major?'

The allusion in the last line is to the well-known joke of the elder Boswell who, hearing his son speak of Johnson as a great luminary, quite a constellation, said, 'Yes, *Ursa Major!*'

Bowmaker, The Reverend Dr Robert (1731-97)

Ordained to the parish of Dunse (later Duns) in 1769. Burns attended his service when he stayed with the Ainslies on his Border tour. He described the doctor in his *Journal* as 'a man of strong lungs and pretty judicious remark; but ill-skilled in propriety, and altogether unconscious of his want of it'.

Boyd, Thomas

A mason and contractor in Dumfries. He built Burns's farmhouse at Ellisland. As may be seen from two of the poet's three letters to him, he took his time over the operation. Writing from his temporary home, Isle, on 8th February 1789, Burns begs him to 'set as many hands to work as possible' as he is 'distressed with the want' of his house in 'a most provoking manner'.

From the same address on 1st March, Burns protested he was 'a good deal surprised at finding my house still lying like Babylon in the prophecies of Isiah'. The house, when more or less finished in June 1790, was the first real home to which Burns was able to take his wife and family. The same year, Boyd was employed as architect for the new bridge over the Nith at Dumfries.

Boyd, The Reverend William (1748-1828)

Burns refers in 'The Ordination' to the public scene provoked by Boyd's induction at the parish Church of Fenwick in 1780. The trouble arose over Boyd's moderate principles

'Lang Patronage, with rod o' airn,
    Has shor'd the Kirk's undoin;
As lately Fenwick, sair forfairn,
    Has proven to its ruin:'

Boyd was finally ordained in the Council Chamber of Irvine on 25th June 1782. He eventually became popular, and remained in Fenwick until he died.

Breadalbane, fourth Earl of. *See* Campbell, John.

Breckenridge, Jean (1764-1841)

A Kilmarnock girl, she became Gilbert Burns's wife on 21 June 1791. She bore him six sons and five daughters. She died at Erskine, in the home of her son James.

Brice, David

A Mauchline man who became a shoe-maker in Glasgow, but about whom little else is known. Burns twice wrote to Brice from Mossgiel, on 12th June and 17th July 1786. The first letter tells Brice about 'poor ill-advised, ungrateful Armour', and was obviously written in some emotional turmoil. The second letter is also about Jean—'poor, foolish Armour', as he calls her. It tells Brice that Burns 'is now fixed to go to the West Indies in October', and relates that when doing his public penance for his fornication: 'Jean and her friends insisted much that she should stand along with me in the kirk, but the minister would not allow it, which bred a great trouble, I assure you, and I am blamed as the cause of it, tho' I am sure I am innocent.' The minister was, of course, Daddy Auld.

Brigs of Ayr', 'The
In the autumn of 1786, a new bridge over the Ayr was begun, the old one, which possibly dates from about 1232, being regarded as dangerous. While the work was in progress, under the direction of the mason Alexander Steven and Dean of Guild John Ballantine, Burns's friend and patron, Burns wrote his poem 'The Brigs of Ayr', a dialogue between the two bridges modelled on Robert Fergusson's 'Mutual Complaint of Plainstanes and Causey'. Burns's poem first appeared in the Edinburgh Edition of 1787. Robert Adam designed a new bridge, and was paid for the design by the Town Council. His plans were not used. A local tradition says that the design as well as the work was by Alexander Steven.

In the course of the 'flyting', the Auld Brig prophesies to the New: 'I'll be a brig when you're a shapeless cairn'. And in 1877, the New Brig collapsed, the arch at the south end having been damaged by floods. It was replaced by the present structure. In 1910, the Auld Brig was extensively restored.

Brodie, James of Brodie (1744-1824)
A naturalist and botanist whose wife had been burned to death accidentally, in Brodie House, near Nairn, the year before Burns stayed a night with Brodie on his Highland tour during September 1787. The poet described the botanist in his *Journal* as 'truly polite, but not just the Highland cordiality'.

Broun, Agnes (1732-1820)
The poet's mother. Daughter of Gilbert Broun, tenant of the three-hundred-acre farm of Craigenton, in Kirkoswald parish, she was the eldest of six children. She was ten when her mother died. For two years, she looked after the family, until her father remarried—he was married, in all, three times—and she was sent to live with a grandmother, Mrs Rennie, in Maybole, whose recollections went back to Covenanting times, and whose mind was a storehouse of old songs and ballads.

Agnes Broun was first of all engaged to a ploughman, William Nelson, but broke in off after seven years, allegedly because of some impropriety on her fiancé's part. She may have met William Burnes at the Maybole Fair of 1756. They were married on 15th December 1757. Robert, born on 25th January 1759, was the eldest of their seven children.

After William Burnes's death in 1784, his widow, who survived him for thirty-six years, lived most of the time with her son, Gilbert. She enjoyed an annuity of £5 which Robert had settled on her out of the loan he made to Gilbert. She died at Gilbert's home, Grant's Braes, East Lothian, and was buried in the churchyard of Bolton.

Mrs Begg, the poet's sister, wrote of her mother: 'She was rather under the average height; inclined to plumpness, but neat, shapely, and full of energy; having a beautiful pink-and-white complexion, a fine square forehead, pale red hair, but dark eyebrows, and dark eyes often ablaze with a temper difficult of control. Her disposition was naturally cheerful; her manner, easy and collected; her address, simple and unpresuming; and her judgement uncommonly sound and good. She possessed a fine musical ear, and sang well.'

Broun or Brown, Samuel (1739-1811)
The poet's maternal uncle, Samuel Broun of Kirkoswald, was the third son of Gilbert Broun of Craigenton and Agnes Rennie, his wife. It is sometimes claimed that it was to Broun's house that Burns went to stay while studying surveying at Kirkoswald in 1775, but it seems more probable that the poet lodged with the Nivens.

Broun was probably a man after Burns's own heart, for Broun married Margaret Niven, the daughter of Robert Niven, farmer and miller, at

Ballochniel, after they had both done penance before the Kirk Session for fornication. Three months later, in July 1765, their only child was born, a daughter, Jenny, mentioned by Burns in 'Hallow-een'. Broun was a farm worker at Balloch-niel.

Locally, the tradition has it that Broun was involved in smuggling, then something of a trade because of the wide range of goods on which Excise duty was levelled. Only one of Burns's letters to his uncle has survived. Dated Mossgiel, 4th May 1788, it asks Broun for '3 or 4 stones of feathers' from the Ailsa fowling season. (Solan geese and their eggs were presum-ably still considered a traditional Scottish delicacy, though the taste died soon after.) Burns goes on: 'It would be a vain attempt for me to enumerate the various transactions I have been engaged in since I saw you last, but this I know, I engaged in the *smuggling trade*, and God knows if ever any poor man experienced better returns—two for one!—but as freight and delivery has turned out so dear, I am thinking of taking out a licence and beginning in fair trade.'

This, of course, refers to his second experience of Jean's twin-bearing faculty, and to his newly-taken decision, which he announced in the closing paragraph, about 'a farm on the banks of Nith'.

Brow

A lonely hamlet on the shores of the Sol-way Firth, a few miles from Dumfries, where there is a saline well which was once supposed to have medicinal proper-ties. About 3rd July 1796, Burns, in the last stages of emaciation and debility and in the grip of an incurable heart disease, went there on the advice of his medical adviser, Dr William Maxwell. Part of the recommended cure consisted of wading up to the armpits into the Sol-way, almost the worst possible treatment for a man suffering from Burns's com-plaint. (At that time, of course, there was

no way of diagnosing endocarditis.)

Maria Riddell paid Burns a farewell visit at Brow and was horrified at the change in him. He returned to Dumfries on 18th July and died three days later.

Brown, Clockie

One of Burns's Mauchline friends arraign-ed in the *Libel Summons* to local fornicators. Evidently a watch-or clockmaker.

Brown, Hugh (bapt. 1720)

Related to Burns on the maternal side. Son of William Brown, Hugh was tenant of Ardlochan Mill, near Shanter farm. He was the prototype of The Miller in 'Tam o' Shanter'. He died unmarried.

Brown, Richard (1753–1833)

Brown was born in Irvine, where Burns met him in the autumn of 1781. Burns had gone to Irvine to learn flax-dressing, and the romantic figure of the young seaman, who afterwards became the master of a West Indiaman, seems to have fixed the poet's imagination. At any rate, Brown and Burns became fast friends, the sailor exercising an important influence on the poet, both in so far as women and poetry were concerned. In the Autobio-graphical Letter, Burns says of this inti-mate friendship: 'I formed a bosom friendship with a young fellow, the first created being I had ever seen, but a hapless son of misfortune. He was the son of a plain mechanic; but a great Man in the neighbourhood taking him under his patronage gave him a genteel education with a view to bettering his situation in life. The Patron dieing just as he was ready to launch forth into the world, the poor fellow in despair went to sea; where after a variety of good and bad fortune, a little before I was acquainted with him, he had been set ashore by an American Privateer on the wild coast of Connaught, stript of everything. I cannot quit this poor fellow's story without adding that he is at this moment Captain of a large west indiaman, belonging to the Thames.

'This gentleman's mind was fraught with courage, independence, Magnanimity, and every noble manly virtue. I loved him, I admired him, to a degree of enthusiasm; and I strove to imitate him. In some measure I succeeded: I had the pride before, but he taught it to flow in proper channels. His knowledge of the world was vastly superiour to mine, and I was all attention to learn. He was the only man I ever saw who was a greater fool than myself when WOMAN was the presiding star; but he spoke of a certain fashionable failing with levity, which hitherto I had regarded with horror. Here his friendship did me a mischief, and the consequence was, that soon after I resumed the plough, I wrote the WELCOME inclosed.' The poem referred to is, 'A poet's Welcome to his Lovebegotten Daughter', which is addressed to Elizabeth Paton's child, 'Dear bought Bess'.

In a letter written to Brown from Edinburgh on 30th December 1787, Burns says: 'Do you recollect a sunday we spent in Eglinton woods? you told me, on my repeating some verses to you, that you wondered I could resist the temptation of sending verses of such merit to a magazine: 'twas actually this that gave me an idea of my own pieces which encouraged me to endeavour at the character of a Poet.'

In the same letter, Burns also tells Brown: 'Almighty Love still "reigns and revels" in my bosom; and I am at this moment ready to hang myself for a young Edinr. widow.' The widow was Clarinda.

One other important revelation was made to Brown, whose ship, the *Mary and Jean,* was then lying at Greenock. In a letter dated Mauchline, 7th March 1788, Burns relates how he found Jean, on his return from Edinburgh, pregnant by him for a second time, and cast out by her family: 'I found Jean—with her cargo

very well laid in; but unfortunately moor'd, almost at the mercy of wind and tide: I have towed her into convenient harbour where she may lie snug till she unload; and have taken the command myself—not ostensibly, but for a time, in secret.'

This last apparent admission of marriage provides a link in the insoluble puzzle of the time and place of Burns's regular marriage to Jean.

Brown himself married late in 1787, or early in 1788, and settled in Port Glasgow. In his later years, he became respectable, and quarrelled violently with Burns after reputedly hearing the poet's allegations that he had taught Burns the art of seduction.

Brown received from Burns one of the very few signed presentation copies of the Kilmarnock Edition.

Bruar Water

Burns visited Bruar Falls during his Highland tour in 1787. The Bruar, a tributary of the Garry, flows a few miles west of Blair Atholl, near the main Perth to Inverness road. Burns noted: 'In Athole. Exceedingly picturesque and beautiful, but the effect is much impaired by the want of trees and shrubs.' When he reached Inverness, Burns addressed the Duke of Atholl, through whose estate the Bruar flowed, with 'The Humble Petition of Bruar Water':

'Let lofty firs, and ashes cool,
    My lowly banks o'erspread,
And view, deep-bending in the pool,
    Their shadows' wat'ry bed:
Let fragrant birks, in woodbines drest,
    My craggy cliffs adorn;
And, for the little songster's nest
    The close embow'ring thorn.'

The Duke later acted upon the poet's suggestion.

Bruce, Mrs Catherine (1696–1791)

During the autumn tour of 1787 which he

made with Dr James Adair, Burns called on an old Jacobite lady, Mrs Bruce of Clackmannan. She traced her ancestors back to King Robert the Bruce, but claimed that he was sprung from her family, and not vice versa, a claim, however, founded purely on family legend. She possessed a helmet and two-handed sword which she believed had once belonged to the Bruce. With the sword she conferred a knighthood on Burns and remarked, as Adair recorded, that she 'had a better right to confer that title than some people'. She conferred a similar honour on Dr Jamieson, Editor of the *Scots Dictionary*, a few months later. On her death, the sword and helmet came to the Earl of Elgin.

She was the daughter of Alexander Bruce of the Newton branch of the family, and married Henry Bruce of Clackmannan.

John Ramsay of Ochtertyre recorded that at the age of eighty, 'she used to rise at six in the morning to see that everything was in order'.

She lived in the old tower of the family, now a ruin, at the west end of Clackmannan village.

See Plate 11.

Bruce, James 'Abyssinian' (1730–94)

Born at Kinnaird House in Stirlingshire, he became a man of immense stature, and a famous traveller and explorer. He travelled on foot to the source of the Blue Nile (which he mistook for the Nile itself) and into the heart of then unknown Abyssinia. His contemporaries at first refused to believe him until, in 1790, on the insistence of Daines Barrington (the English jurist who produced a paper after examining the prodigious talents of the boy Mozart), Bruce wrote an account of his experiences.

Thereafter, scunnered at the literary world which failed to give him the recognition he thought he deserved, he retired to his estate. There, having grown 'ex-ceedingly heavy and lusty', he would ride slowly over his estate to his collieries, 'mounted on a charger of great power and size'. Now and again, he would dress himself up in his Abyssinian costume, and sit musing on past adventures.

He married, first, Adriana Allen, a Portuguese wine-merchant's daughter, who died in 1754; second, Mary Dundas of Carronhall, who died in 1784.

The manner of his death was gallant. Hurrying to hand a lady to her carriage, he missed his footing and pitched down the stairs of his own house, striking his head in the fall.

On Sunday, 26th August 1787, Burns and Nicol, at the beginning of the Highland tour, stopped at Larbert to admire: 'a fine monument of cast-iron erected by Mr Bruce, the African traveller, to his second wife. N.B. He used her very ill, and I suppose he meant it as much out of gratitude to Heaven as anything else.'

Bruce, The Reverend John (1758–1817)

Minister of Forfar parish church from 1782 to 1817, having been the assistant there for the two previous years. Burns met him on his Highland tour, describing him in his *Journal* as 'pleasant, agreeable and engaging'.

Brydges, Sir Samuel Egerton, Bt. (1762–1837)

Born at the manor-house of Wooton, between Canterbury and Dover, the second son of Edward Brydges, he was educated at Maidstone School, Canterbury, and Queens' College, Cambridge. He then entered the Middle Temple and was called to the bar in November 1787, but never practised. He bought himself a country seat, Denton Court, near his birthplace and retired there in 1792 to gratify his boyhood passion of 'giving himself up to English poetry'. He published volumes of his own poems, in 1785 and 1807, which were not well received, though his novels *Mary de*

Clifford (1792) and *Arthur Fitz-Albini* (1798) were fairly popular. His mistaken belief in what he considered his genius, and his dislike of his neighbour 'book-hating squires' caused him some unhappiness. In spite of some useful work as a bibliographer, however, he was left further dissatisfied after his failure before the House of Lords to establish his claim to the title Baron Chandos.

In 1810, Brydges moved to Lee Priory, near Canterbury, and in 1812 was elected M.P. for Maidstone. From 1813 to 1822, Brydges was concerned in the running of the Lee Priory Press, which put out fine editions of Elizabethan and other works, many of them rare and interesting.

From 1818, except for a visit of two years' duration to England, Brydges lived abroad, principally at Geneva. Twice married, he had by both wives large families. He published his autobiography in 1834.

The following reminiscence of his meeting with Burns was first published in the *Metropolitan Magazine*, and is of interest in that Brydges was very much a bookman from the South.

'I had always been a great admirer of his genius and of many traits in his character; and I was aware that he was a person moody and somewhat difficult to deal with. I was resolved to keep in full consideration the irritability of his position in society. About a mile from his residence, on a bench, under a tree, I passed a figure, which from the engraved portraits of him I did not doubt was the poet; but I did not venture to address him. On arriving at his humble cottage, Mrs Burns opened the door; she was the plain sort of humble woman she has been described: she ushered me into a neat apartment, and said that she would send for Burns, who was gone for a walk. In about half an hour he came, and my conjecture proved right: he was the person I had seen on the bench by the roadside. At first I was not entirely pleased with his countenance. I thought it had a sort of capricious jealousy, as if he was half inclined to treat me as an intruder. I resolved to bear it, and try if I could humour him. I let him choose his turn of conversation, but said a few words about the friend whose letter I had brought to him. It was now about four in the afternoon of an autumn day. While we were talking, Mrs Burns, as if accustomed to entertain visitors in this way, brought in a bottle of Scotch Whisky, and set the table. I accepted this hospitality. I could not help observing the curious glance with which he watched me at the entrance of this signal of homely entertainment. He was satisfied; he filled our glasses: "Here's a health to auld Caledonia!" The fire sparkled in his eye, and mine sympathetically met his. He shook my hand with warmth, and we were friends at once. Then he drank "Erin for ever!" and the tear of delight burst from his eye. The fountain of his mind and his heart now opened at once, and flowed with abundant force almost till midnight.

'He had amazing acuteness of intellect as well as glow of sentiment. I do not deny that he said some absurd things, and many coarse ones, and that his knowledge was very irregular, and sometimes too presumptuous, and that he did not endure contradiction with sufficient patience. His pride, and perhaps his vanity, was even morbid. I carefully avoided topics in which he could not take an active part. Of literary gossip he knew nothing, and therefore I kept aloof from it: in the technical parts of literature his opinions were crude and uninformed; but whenever he spoke of a great writer whom he had read, his taste was generally sound. To a few minor writers he gave more credit than they deserved. His great beauty was his manly strength, and his energy and elevation of thought and feeling. He had always a full mind, and all flowed from a genuine spring. I never conversed with a man who appeared to be more warmly impressed with the beauties of nature; and visions of female beauty and tenderness seemed to transport him. He did not merely appear to be a poet at casual intervals; but at every moment a poetical enthusiasm seemed to beat in his veins, and he lived all his days the inward if not the outward life of a poet. I thought I perceived in Burns's cheek the symptoms of an energy which had been pushed too far; and he had this feeling himself. Every now and then he spoke of the grave as soon about to close over him. His dark eye had at first a character of sternness; but as he became warmed, though this did not entirely melt away, it was mingled with changes of extreme softness.'

Brydone, Mrs
Wife of the traveller and author, Patrick Brydone. Burns said in his Border *Journal* that she was 'a daughter of Dr. Robertson, the historian, a most elegant woman in her person and manners; the tones of her voice remarkably sweet'.

Brydone, Patrick (c. 1741–1818)
Traveller and author whom Burns met at his home, Lennel House, when on his Border tour. Brydone had travelled extensively through Switzerland and Sicily. His book, *A Tour of Sicily and Malta* (1773), went through nine editions, and was translated into French and German. He chaperoned William Fullarton during that young man's European tour. Latterly he became Comptroller of the Stamp Office.

Burns recorded of him in his *Journal*: 'a most excellent heart, kind, joyous and benevolent; but a good deal of the French indiscriminate complaisance—from his situation past and present, an admirer of everything that bears a splendid title, or that possesses a large estate'.

Buchan, eleventh Earl of. *See* **Erskine, David Stewart**

Buchan, Mrs Elspat (c. 1738–91)
See **Buchanites, The**

Buchan, Dr William (1729–1805)
Author of Buchan's *Domestic Medicine*, a popular home encyclopedia published in 1769, which ran through many editions and sold 80,000 copies. In 'Death and Dr Hornbook', Burns remarked that the Doctor had grown 'weel acquaint wi' Buchan'.

Dr Buchan, who was a native of Roxburghshire, practised first in Edinburgh, but later had a large practice in London, and was well thought of. He is buried in the West Cloister of Westminster Abbey.

Buchanites, The
Burns referred to the arrival of the Buchanites in the south-west of Scotland in a letter to James Burness in Montrose, dated 3rd August 1784: 'We have been surprized with one of the most extraordinary Phenomena in the moral world, which, I dare say, has happened in the course of this Century. We have had a party of the Presbytry Relief as they call themselves, for some time in this country. A pretty thriving society of them has been in the Burgh of Irvine for some years past, till about two years ago, a Mrs Buchan from Glasgow came among them, and began to spread some fanatical notions of religion among them, and in a short time, made many converts among them, and among others their Preacher, one Mr. Whyte, who upon that account has been suspended and formally deposed by his brethren. . . . in Spring last the Populace rose and mobbed the old leader Buchan, and put her out of the town; on which, all her followers voluntarily quitted the place likewise, and with such precipitation, that many of them never shut their doors behind them; one left a washing on the green, another a cow bellowing at the crib without meat or anybody to mind her,

and after several stages, they are fixed at present in the neighbourhood of Dumfries. Their tenets are a strange jumble of enthusiastic jargon, among others, she pretends to give them the Holy Ghost by breathing on them, which she does with postures and practices that are scandalously indecent; they have likewise disposed of all their effects and hold a community of goods, and live nearly an idle life, carrying on a great farce of pretended devotion in barns, and woods, where they lodge and lye all together, and hold likewise a community of women, as it is another of their tenets that they can commit no moral sin. I am personally acquainted with most of them, and I can assure you the above mentioned are facts.'

Burns commented: 'This my Dr Sir, is one of the many instances of the folly of leaving the guidance of sound reason, and common sense in matters of Religion.'

According to the antiquarian, Joseph Train, author of the *History of the Buchanites from First to Last*, Mrs Elspat Buchan was the daughter, born about 1738, of John Simpson and Margaret Gordon, who kept a public-house at Fatmacken, between Banff and Portsoy. She contracted a regular or irregular marriage with a working potter called Robert Buchan, who removed to Glasgow, followed by his wife and three children. He was a member of the 'Presbytery Relief' sect, and he and his wife then met the preacher Hugh White (mentioned in Burns's letter to his cousin). At a meeting in Irvine, Mrs Buchan 'gave herself out to be the Third Person in the Godhead, and pretended to confer immortality on whomsoever she breathed; and promised eventually to translate direct to heaven in a body, without their tasting death, all who put unlimited faith in her divine mission'. She also claimed to 'have brought forth the man child' who was 'to rule all the nations with a rod of iron', in the shape of White. She was

familiarly called 'Luckie' Buchan, and she gained complete control over the minds of White and his wife and the other converts. Such was the Buchanites' behaviour that Mrs Buchan was mobbed and nearly killed by the Irvine rabble. She was formally expelled from the town by the magistrates. The society came to an end when Mrs Buchan shattered the illusions of her followers in 1791 by dying a natural death. *See also* **White, The Reverend Hugh; Hunter, Peter** and **Gardner, Jean.**

The Scots novelist John Galt relates in his autobiography that, when the Buchanites left Irvine, he 'with many other children also accompanied her, but my mother in a state of distraction pursued, and drew me back by the lug and the horn. I have not the slightest recollection of Mrs Buchan's heresies—how could I?—but the scene, and more than once the enthusiasm of the psalm-singing, has risen in my remembrance, especially in describing the Covenanters in *Ringan Gilhaize*.' As Galt was born in Irvine in 1779, he can only have been four years old when this event took place.

Buff and Blue

The colours of the Whig party, in Burns's day particularly associated with Charles James Fox. In 'Here's a Health to them that's awa' ' Burns wrote:

'It's guid to support Caledonia's cause
And bide by the Buff and the Blue.'

Burgess Tickets

Burns was six times made an honorary burgess: four times in 1787, once while he was at Ellisland, and once in 1794. (For details *see* **Jedburgh, Dumfries, Dumbarton, Linlithgow, Lochmaben** and **Sanquhar.**)

Honours of this sort were pretty freely given in the late eighteenth century, which is possibly why Burns made little reference to them.

Burke, Edmund (1729-97)

Irish-born politician who became a British statesman, and one of the most influential of writers both on politics and aesthetics. His *Philosophical Inquiry into the Origin of Our Ideas on the Sublime and Beautiful* was the most ambitious study of its kind undertaken up to 1756. Burke supported England's war against France, but had been consistently opposed to the Government's American policy. He is referred to as 'Paddy Burke' in 'When Guilford good our Pilot stood'.

Burnes and Burns

The poet used the old version of the family name until April 1786, when it last appears in his signature to a letter. Thereafter he adopted the spelling without the 'e'.

Burnes, Robert (1719-89)

Uncle to the poet, he left Kincardineshire, along with his brother William (Burns's father), to seek his fortune in the south. To begin with, he lived at Titwood, in Dreghorn parish, and earned his living in summer at the lime quarries at Lochridge, near Stewarton. He was supposed to have been afflicted by rheumatism which kept him indoors in the winter. He therefore started a small school in his home for the sons of local farmers. When completely crippled by his rheumatism, he moved to Stewarton, where he stayed in the Buck's Head Close, and then at another house in the town. Burns used to visit him on his journeys to and from Dunlop House, nearby. On his uncle's death, the poet did everything to ensure that the children found employment. Writing to his cousin, James Burness in Montrose, from Ellisland, on 9th February 1789, Burns said: 'We have lost poor uncle Robert this winter. . . . His Son William, has been with me this winter, and goes in May to bind himself to be a Mason with my fatherinlaw who is a pretty considerable Architect in Ayrshire. His other Son,

the eldest, John, comes to me, I expect in Summer. . . . His only daughter, Fanny, has been with me ever since her father's death and I purpose keeping her in my family till she be quite woman grown, and be fit for better service. She is one of the cleverest girls, and has one of the most amiable dispositions, that I have ever seen.'

Fanny eventually married a brother of Mrs Burns.

Burnes of Clochnahill, Robert

Grandfather of the poet, he rented Clochnahill farm in Dunnottar parish, on the estate of the Earl Marischal. His financial ruin was brought about by bad crops, low prices and a disastrous frost in 1740. He eventually gave up Clochnahill, and renounced his lease in 1745. After further disappointments, he retired to Denside Dunnottar.

He married Isabella, daughter of Alexander Keith, tenant farmer at Criggie in Dunnottar parish, and had a large family.

His eldest son, James, settled in Montrose, where Burns visited his son, also James, and to whom the poet wrote frequently.

The second son, William, was the poet's father.

The third son was Robert Burns's 'uncle Robert'.

Burnes, William (1721-84)

The poet's father was born at Clochnahill Farm, Dunnottar, Kincardineshire, and trained as a gardener, like Robert Burnes, his father before him, who had been employed as gardener at Inverugie Castle, Aberdeenshire, by the Earl Marischal. Tradition has it that Robert Burnes had Jacobite sympathies. At any rate, in 1748, William thought it prudent to get a certificate from three Kincardineshire landlords, testifying that he was 'a very well-inclined lad'. But in this year, Robert Burnes, who had ambitions as a farmer, was ruined by the economic consequences which followed the Rising of 1745, and the family broke up, William taking his certificate to Edinburgh where there was then a demand for gardeners. For two years he was employed 'landscaping' in the city, part of his work being in The Meadows. Then, in 1750, he moved west to Ayrshire, working first for the Laird of Fairlie, then for the Crawfords of Doonside. But he was ambitious to set up as a nurseryman for himself, so he feued, from Dr Alexander Campbell of Ayr, seven and a half acres of land at Alloway. But he was unable to make a living in this way alone, so he accepted employment as head gardener at Doonholm, the estate of a retired London doctor, Provost William Fergusson of Ayr. In the summer and autumn of 1757, Burnes began building a but and ben (two-roomed cottage) on the nursery land at Alloway, and on 15th December married Agnes Broun, or Brown, a farmer's daughter. The poet, their first child, was born on 25th January 1759, Gilbert in 1760, Agnes in 1762, Annabella in 1764, William in 1767, John in 1769, and Isabella in 1771. According to Gilbert, when Robert was nine or ten days old, the 'clay biggin' suffered damage by storm, and the poet and his mother had to be taken to the house of a neighbour until a tumbled gable was repaired.

By 1765, the cottage was becoming too small, and Burnes approached Provost Fergusson with a proposal to lease the farm of Mount Oliphant, two miles south-east of Alloway.

Fergusson gave him a twelve-year lease, with the option of a break at six, and lent him a hundred pounds to buy stock. But the farm proved unproductive and wearying.

The struggles which William Burnes had at Mount Oliphant from 1766 to 1777, and at Lochlea from 1777 until his death, prematurely worn out, are touched upon in the poet's Autobiographical Letter. Burns tells of the closing days at Mount Oliphant: 'My father was

advanced in life when he married; I was the eldest of seven children, and he, worn out by hardship, was unfit for labour. My father's spirit was soon irritated but not easily broken. There was a freedom in his lease in two years more and to weather these two years we retrenched expenses. We lived very poorly.' At Lochlea, things went no better. Burnes fell into arrears with his rent, and David M'Lure, the Landlord of Lochlea, put two petitions before the Sheriff of Ayrshire over alleged arrears of rent. Litigation threatened, and although Burnes won his appeal to the Court of Session on 27th January 1784, and paid in the balance of the rent which had been set against his own expenses in liming, fencing and erecting new buildings, he died on 13th February, of 'a phthiscal consumption', worn out beyond his years.

Burns also tells of his father's dislike of the Tarbolton dancing class. 'In my seventeenth year, to give my manners a brush, I went to a country dancing school. My father had an unaccountable antipathy against these meetings; and my going was, what to this hour I repent, in absolute defiance of his commands. My father, as I said before, was the sport of strong passions; from that instance of rebellion he took a kind of dislike to me. . . .'

The only letter of Burns's to his father, written from Irvine on 27th December 1781, begins: 'Honored Sir'. In spite of the old man's Calvinistic strictness, Burns afterwards spoke of his father with affectionate respect: 'The best of friends and the ablest of instructors' he described him to James Burness in a letter of 17th February 1784; and he sketched him as the devout and religious guidman in 'The Cotter's Saturday Night'.

It was certainly William Burnes's typically dour Scottish determination to make sure that his children received the best possible education available to them in the difficult curcumstances of the time which provided Burns with the intellectual background that enabled him to develop into the major poet and letter-writer he did, in fact, become. No doubt the poet also got his proud independence of spirit from his father.

Burness, James (1717–61)

The poet's uncle. He left his father's farm at Clochnahill to settle in Montrose. His second surviving son, James, a lawyer, met Burns in Stonehaven in 1787 and corresponded with him.

Burness, James (1750–1837)

Although a number of letters from the poet to his first cousin, James Burness, have survived, Burness, a Montrose lawyer, remains a shadowy figure in the background of the Burns story. In Edinburgh City Museum there is a letter, written in 1781, in which William Burnes, Burns's father, tells James in Montrose the family news in a manner which suggests the two families had been long out of touch. On 21st June 1783, Burns wrote on his father's behalf because old William Burnes was too ill to write himself and, indeed, was: 'in his own opinion, and indeed in almost everybody else's, in a dying condition'. On 17th February, 1784 he wrote again to tell his cousin of William Burnes's death, 'that melancholy event which for some time past we have from day to day expected'.

On 3rd August, writing from Mossgiel, Burns devotes most of his letter to telling Cousin James about the arrival in the district of 'the Presbytry Relief', or Buchanites. On 4th September 1787, Burns writes from Inverness asking James to meet him at the Inn, 'Stonehive'. They duly met on 10th September in Stonehaven.

Burns does not seem to have written to his cousin again until 9th February 1789, when he writes from Ellisland giving James news of his farm and

announcing his marriage to Jean. There is then a long gap in the surviving correspondence, until 12th July 1796, when Burns, in the agony of anxiety over debts, real and imaginary, which troubled him in his last days, wrote begging his cousin to send him ten pounds: 'O, James! did you know the pride of my heart, you would feel doubly for me! Alas! I am not used to beg! . . . Forgive me for once more mentioning by return of post. Save me from the horrors of a jail!' James sent the money, and after Burns's death a further five pounds to Jean with an offer to take young Robert and educate the boy with his own children, a generous offer since James does not seem to have been a rich man. Jean, however, did not want to part with any of her children.

Burnett, Eliza (1766–90)

Lord Monboddo's youngest daughter, a clever woman and something of a poetess, she was referred to by Burns in his 'Address to Edinburgh' as 'Fair Burnet'. On her death from consumption at Braid Farm, near Edinburgh, she became the subject of his 'Elegy on the late Miss Burnet of Monboddo', which begins:

'Life ne'er exulted in so rich a prize
As Burnet, lovely from her native
                                                    skies:
Nor envious death so triumph'd in a
                                                    blow
As that which laid the accomplished
                                                    Burnet low.'

When Burns sent a copy of his 'Address to Edinburgh' to William Chalmers of Ayr on 27th December 1786, he said of Elizabeth Burnett: 'There has not been anything nearly like her in all the combinations of Beauty, Grace and Goodness the great Creator has formed, since Milton's Eve on the first day of her existence.' In reply to Dr John Geddes, whom Burns met at Lord Monboddo's, and who is said to have asked the poet if he admired Miss Burnett, Burns is supposed to have remarked: 'I admire God Almighty more than ever, Miss Burnet is the most heavenly of all His works.'

Gossip-loving Mrs Alison Cockburn gave a third-party view of Burns and Miss Burnett in a letter to a friend dated 30th December 1786. She wrote: 'The town is at present agog with the ploughman poet, who receives adulation with native dignity, and is the very figure of his profession—strong and coarse—but has a most enthusiastic heart of LOVE. He has seen dutchess Gordon and all the gay world. His favrite for looks and manners is Bess Burnet—no bad judge indeed!'

Alexander Young, a prim Tory Writer to the Signet, while agreeing that Burns justly admired Miss Burnett, added: 'She had one great personal defect however—her teeth were much decayed and discoloured, but fortunately she had a very small mouth, and took care not to open it much in mixed company.' Somewhat ungallantly, the Right Honorable Charles Hope added: 'She had very thick, clumsy ancles, which She was at pains to conceal by wearing her petticoats uncommonly long—and she was not a good Dancer—but take her in all she was a beautiful creature.'

She was much attached to her father and, according to an anonymous contemporary: 'It was her chief delight to be the nurse and companion of his declining age.' She was, indeed, supposed to have rejected 'the most flattering opportunities of settlement in marriage, that she might amuse a father's loneliness, nurse the sickly infirmity of his age, and cheer him with all the tender cares of filial affection'.

She is buried in Greyfriars Churchyard, Edinburgh.

See Plate 7.

Burnett, James, Lord Monboddo (1714–99)

James Burnett was educated at Marischal College, Aberdeen, Edinburgh University and the University of Gröningen. He studied, first, Greek philosophy, and, later, law. He was admitted to the Scottish Bar in 1737. Thirty years later, he became a Lord of Session, taking this title from his father's estate, Monboddo, in Kincardineshire. He was a considerable scholar, though also a notable eccentric. His book *The Origin and Progress of Language* demonstrated how mankind had come to shed their primeval tails, and thus anticipated in conclusion, if not in argument, Darwin's evolutionary theories. Another aspect of Monboddo's learning was reflected in his philosophical conspectus, *Antient Metaphysics*.

His second daughter, Elizabeth Burnett, was a celebrated Edinburgh beauty, whose death from consumption at the age of twenty-five drew an elegy from Burns.

Burns visited Monboddo's house on several occasions, no doubt enjoying the judge's whimsicalities. One of these relates to his coming out of Court and finding the rain on. He is reported to have put his wig into his sedan chair, and walked home himself in the rain.

At his house in St John Street, Monboddo for many years held 'learned suppers'. These were convened at an early hour, and the cream of the intelligentsia were invited to partake of Attic repasts. The table was strewn with roses, after the practice of Horace at his home in the Sabine hills, and the wine-flasks were garlanded, after the manner of Anacreon's, at the Court of Polycrates of Samos.

Burns, Agnes (1762–1834)

Burns's eldest sister. She was baptised, according to the parish register of Ayr, by the Reverend William Dalrymple.

She married, in 1804, William Galt, a servant of her brother Gilbert's, and afterwards land-steward on the Irish estate of Mr Matthew Fortescue. She died without issue in Stephenstown,

County Louth, and is buried in St Nicholas Presbyterian churchyard at Dundalk.

Burns, Annabella (1764–1832)

Burns's second eldest sister, she was born in Alloway, and died, unmarried, at Grant's Braes, Haddingtonshire. She is buried in Bolton churchyard.

Burns, Elizabeth (1784–1817)

'Dear-bought Bess', as Burns called his first illegitimate daughter, was born to the servant-girl in the Burns household, Elizabeth Paton. Her birth was celebrated in 'A Poet's Welcome to his Love-Begotten Daughter' (or, as the poet more pithily put it, 'his Bastart Wean'). The poet asked:

'Lord grant that thou may ay inherit
Thy mither's looks an' gracefu' merit;
An' thy poor, worthless daddy's spirit,
    Without his failins,
'Twill please me mair to see thee heir it,
    Than stocket mailens. . . .'

'Dear-bought Bess' was baptised when two days old.

When Burns meditated flight to Jamaica in July 1786, he made out a Deed of Assignment, binding Gilbert Burns to 'ailiment, clothe and educate her . . . as if she was his own . . . until she arrive at the age of fifteen years'. To enable his brother to honour this engagement, the poet left all his movable effects and the profits from 'the publication of my Poems presently in the Press'. When Elizabeth Paton reached the age of twenty-one, she received £200 from the fund which had been set up to support the poet's family.

She married John Bishop, factor to Baillie of Polkemmet. Some claim she died in childbirth. She is buried in Whitburn Churchyard.

Burns, Elizabeth Riddell (1792–95)

Burns's only legitimate daughter to survive infancy, and whose early death caused him much heartbreak. She died at Mauchline, and is buried in the Armour lair of Mauchline Churchyard. She was named in honour of Mrs Riddell of Glenriddell.

Writing to Mrs Dunlop from Dumfries on 31st January 1796, Burns described his anguish at his daughter's death: 'I have lately drank deep of the cup of affliction. The Autumn robbed me of my only daughter and darling child, and that at a distance too, and so rapidly as to put it out of my power to pay the last duties to her. . . .'

He also told Mrs Walter Riddell in a letter from Dumfries, conjectured by Ferguson to have been written in October or November, dated September 1795, that: 'a severe domestic misfortune has put all literary business out of my head for some time past'.

Burns, Francis Wallace (1789–1803)

Second son of the poet named in honour of Mrs Dunlop. He was born at Ellisland and is buried in the Mausoleum at Dumfries.

Writing to Mrs Dunlop from Ellisland on 6th September 1789, Burns told her of the birth of little Frank: '. . . who, by the bye, I trust will be no discredit to the honorable name of Wallace, as he has a fine manly countenance, and a figure that might do credit to a little fellow two months older; and likewise an excellent good temper, though when he pleases he has a pipe, only not quite so loud as the horn that his immortal namesake blew as a signal to take out the pin of Stirling bridge'.

Burns, Gilbert (1760–1827)

The poet's brother and his partner at Mossgiel farm from Martinmas 1783. A quiet, rather timid man who deceived the Alloway schoolmaster John Murdoch into thinking that he was the cleverer of the brothers. Gilbert, as Ferguson puts it, 'never was able to shake off the mental attitude of the tenant farmer and the factor, whose ruling purpose in life is to do nothing that will offend "the gentry" '. Gilbert moved into Mossgiel farm, along with the rest of the family, after their father's death in 1784. Gilbert remained at Mossgiel until 1798, but he was only able to do so because of the generosity of his brother. Writing to Dr John Moore on 4th January 1789, Burns said: 'I have a younger brother, who supports my aged mother, another still younger brother, and three sisters, in a farm. On my last return from Edinburgh, it cost me about £180 to save them from ruin. Not that I have lost so much; I only interposed between my brother and his impending fate by the loan of so much. I give myself no airs on this, for it was mere selfishness on my part: I was conscious that the wrong scale of the balance was pretty heavily charged, and I thought that throwing a little filial piety and fraternal affection into the scale in my favor might help to smooth matters at the *grand reckoning*.' By turning over almost half the profits of his Edinburgh volume, Burns gave his brother the necessary capital to enable him to carry on.

According to Snyder, Gilbert was probably loaned about £200. Compound interest was to be paid at five per cent per year, and out of interest Gilbert was to deduct five pounds per year as an 'annuity to my mother allowed by my brother to be paid her out of the interest of his money in my hands', and the seven or eight pounds a year which was the cost of supporting 'Dear-bought Bess'. The actual date of the loan is not clear. Burns wrote to James Johnson on 25th May 1788, expressing unease over money owed him by Creech, saying: 'I want it much at present, as I am engaging in business pretty deeply both for myself and my brother', so presumably the transaction was then at least contemplated.

Writing to Mrs Dunlop in September 1794, Burns reveals his concern over the money: 'You know that my brother, poor fellow! was on the brink of ruin, when my good fortune threw a little money among my hands which saved him for a while. Still his ruinous farm threatens to beggar him, and though, a bad debt of ten pounds excepted, he has every shilling I am worth in the world among his hands, I am nearly certain that I have done with it for ever. This loss, as to my individual self, I could hold it very light; but my little flock would have been better for a couple of hundred pounds; for *their* sakes, it wrings my heart!' Though Burns did once think he might have to 'cut' Gilbert 'up' (bankrupt him), to relieve his own position, he never did.

Gilbert provided a home for 'Dear-bought Bess'—when Burns intended flight to Jamaica, he had a document drawn up leaving the profit of the Kilmarnock Edition and the proceeds from the sale of his estate to Gilbert on condition that the child was brought up as if his own— and for his mother, until her death at the age of eighty-eight in 1820. He also kept his sister Agnes until her marriage at the advanced age of forty-two, and his unmarried sister Annabella, who survived him by five years. In 1791, Gilbert himself married and, by his wife Jean Breckenridge of Kilmarnock, he had eleven children.

After leaving Mossgiel, Gilbert spent two years farming at Dinning, in Niths-dale. In 1800, he became manager of Captain John Dunlop's farm Morham, West Mains, East Lothian. Four years later he became factor on the East Lothian Estates of Lady Katherine Blantyre. Here, living at Grant's Braes, near Haddington, he ended his days.

In 1820, Gilbert Burns was given £250 for additional material to the eighth edition of Currie's *The Works of Robert Burns*. But the publishers, Cadell and Davies, warned him that he must not cast doubts upon the general accuracy of

Currie's portrait. The timid Gilbert therefore missed this chance to defend his brother's reputation. But out of his cheque he repaid his dead brother's loan.

Some of Gilbert's other writings about his brother are of particular value, especially the letter to Mrs Dunlop known as 'Gilbert's Narrative', printed in the appendix, **Burns Documents,** p. 387.

See Plate 1.

Burns, Isabella (Mrs Begg) (1771–1858)
Burns's youngest sister and baby of the family. She married John Begg, described in Mauchline marriage register as 'quarrier in Mossgiel'.

Begg took over the management of Gilbert's farm at Dinning, in Closeburn parish, when his brother-in-law became factor of the estate in Morham Muir in East Lothian.

Begg later became land-steward on the estate of Blackwood in Lanarkshire, which belonged to Mr James Hope Vere.

On her husband's death in 1813, after he had been thrown from his horse, Isabella went first to Ormiston in East Lothian, then to a cottage in Tranent, and finally settled at Bridge House, Alloway, where she died, and in the churchyard of which she is buried.

She supplied various Burns enthusiasts with her recollections of her life with her famous brother.

She had six sons and three daughters.

Burns, Lieut.-Colonel James Glencairn (1794–1865)
Third surviving son of the poet.

Like his elder brothers he was educated at Dumfries Grammar School, and later at Christ's Hospital, London. He went out to India as a cadet in the East India Company's Service and rose to the rank of Major.

After a visit home, he returned to India in 1833, where he was appointed Judge and Collector at Cahar. On his retiral in 1839, he lived in London, but later, when a

widower, stayed with his brother William Nicol, also a widower, at Cheltenham.

He married his first wife, Sarah Robinson, in 1818. She died three years later, just after the birth of their daughter, Sarah, who became the wife of Dr B. W. Hutchinson. Another daughter and son had died in infancy.

In 1828, James Glencairn married his second wife, Mary Becket, who died in 1844. They had one daughter, Ann. He was made Lieut.-Colonel in 1855.

James Glencairn is buried in the Mausoleum.

Sarah Hutchinson, daughter of James Glencairn's first wife, writing from Cheltenham on 27th October 1893, to D. M'Naught (the letters are reprinted in the *Burns Chronicle* for 1894) said: 'I was only twelve years old at my grandmother's death (i.e. Jean Armour's) consequently I have little recollection of incidents or anecdotes about my grandfather. . . . My father often said it was disgraceful the statements made out by people who lived in the Poet's time, containing, as they did, so much falsehood and exaggeration of the events of his life. Dr Currie had all the letters and papers sent to him by my grandfather when he wrote the Poet's life, but he never returned them to her, and her sons were too young then to ask for them; so other people became possessed of letters and poems of the Poet which ought to have been given back to the family. The copyright of Currie's *Life of Burns* ought to have been conferred upon his widow, but it was not'—an interesting comment on the methods employed by Dr Currie.

Mrs Hutchinson possessed David Allan's water-colour of 'The Cotter's Saturday Night', which she said the artist gave to Burns, as well as her grandfather's desk and the family Bible. Scott Douglas also asserts that the picture was a water-colour; Thomson refers to 'Allan's pencil', and Allan's latest biographer, T. Grouther Gordon, asserts that there is an oil-painting of this scene in the Blunt Collection. Presumably, however, Mrs Hutchinson knew what she had in the house.

Mrs Hutchinson's son, Robert Burns Hutchinson, was the only direct male descendant of the poet's. He lived in America, where he was a clerk in a shipping office.

See Plate 3.

Burns, Jean Armour (1767–1834)

The girl who became Burns's wife was one of the eleven children of James Armour, a master mason of Mauchline. Burns seems to have met her early in 1784, soon after he moved to Mossgiel, and was in a mood of emancipation following his father's death. She was one of the 'Mauchline Belles'.

The version of the first meeting of the two accepted by the hagiologists (though it has no basis in verifiable fact) is that when Burns was at a dance during Race Week, April 1784, where he was something of a wall-flower, his collie dog arrived. As he sent the dog home he was heard to remark that he wished he could find a lass who would love him as faithfully as his dog did. Crossing the village green a few days later, he was asked by a shapely brunette if he had found his lass yet. If this story is true—Jean, not surprisingly, gave a different account years later—it suggests that she sought out the poet. The association was not hurried—there was still Elizabeth Paton and 'Dear-bought Bess' on Burns's mind—but by early 1786, Jean was pregnant. She also had in her possession a paper signed by Burns, which, under the Scots law of the day, probably constituted a marriage contract. In March 1786, Mrs Armour had to run for a cordial for her husband, who fainted on being told the news. Mrs Armour first tried to conceal the sad fact, sending her daughter off to Paisley to stay with her uncle. Possibly Mrs Armour hoped that her daughter might perhaps still capture the weaver, Robert Wilson,

who had once been interested in her. But Holy Willie Fisher was soon on the scent. The Minutes of Mauchline Kirk Session for 10th June 1786 show that Jean Armour was 'called, compeared not, but sent a letter directed to the minister, the tenor whereof follows: "I am heartily sorry that I have given and must give your Session trouble on my account. I acknowledge I am with child, and Robert Burns in Mossgiel is the father. I am, with great respect, your most humble servant. . . ." '

Between March and June, however, Burns's own attitude had changed. His first impulse on realising that Jean was to bear his child seems to have been to marry her. He suggested as much in a letter to Gavin Hamilton, dated 15th April, and the same month told Arnot of Dalquhatswood: 'I would gladly have covered my Inamorata from the darts of Calumny with the conjugal Shield, nay, had actually made up some sort of Wedlock; but I was at that time deep in the guilt of being unfortunate, for which good and lawful objection, the Lady's friends broke all our measures, and drove me au desespoir.'

What happened was that old Armour, revived by his wife's cordial, forced Jean to yield up what Burns later referred to as 'the unlucky paper', but which 'made up some sort of wedlock', and took it to the lawyer Robert Aiken in Ayr, who cut out the names of the two parties, a mutilation which could have had no point other than to appease an unreasonable and irascible client, marriage by declaration alone being then valid.

Meanwhile, Burns regarded Jean's yielding up the paper to her father and her own departure to Paisley as 'desertion'. His greatest wish now was to get a certificate from the Kirk Session testifying that he was a single man. On 25th June he appeared before the Session and acknowledged his share in the affair. During July and August he made the necessary three appearances, and got his certificate from 'Daddy Auld'.

During the summer months, however, an hysterical note creeps into Burns's letters. There were possibly two causes for this. Burns, who had told Arnot in April 1786 that he was looking for 'another wife', and on 12th June 1786, had confessed to David Brice that he had been guilty of 'dissipation and riot... and other mischief', may very well have compromised himself with 'Highland' Mary Campbell, to the extent that she was also carrying a child of his. Burns, who had allowed his desperate thoughts to turn to Jamaica, that haven of refuge for unfortunate Scots in the eighteenth century, also found that James Armour had invoked civil law against him. Learning of the Jamaica project and that Burns was thinking of publishing a book from which there might be profit, Armour forced Jean to sign a complaint, with the result that a warrant was issued against Burns. Anticipating this, however, Burns had got the lawyer Chalmers to draw up a deed of trust making over all his property and profits to his brother Gilbert, who was to use them to bring up 'Dear-bought Bess'. Burns then virtually went into hiding, and was still full of apprehension when the Kilmarnock Edition came out on 31st July 1786.

Old Armour, however, seems to have been impressed by the obvious change which was coming over Burns's fortunes. By 1st September, Burns was able to tell Richard Brown: 'I am under little apprehension now about Armour. The warrant is still in existence, but some of the first Gentlemen in the county have offered to befriend me; and besides, Jean will not take any step against me, without letting me know, as nothing but the most violent menaces could have forced her to sign the petition. . . . She would gladly now embrace that offer she once rejected, but it shall never more be in her power.'

On 3rd September, a brother of Jean's came up to Mossgiel to tell Burns that Jean had borne him twins, Robert and Jean. In October, Mary Campbell, whom Burns had promised to marry and possibly take with him to Jamaica, died of 'malignant fever' at Greenock, but in circumstances which have suggested to some writers premature childbirth (*see* **Campbell, 'Highland' Mary**). On 27th November, Burns set out, bound, not for the West Indies, but for Edinburgh. With Mary out of the way, Burns could not resist the temptation of impressing Jean with his new-found fame at the close of one of his tours in the summer of 1787. The inevitable result was that Jean became pregnant again. This time, now that Burns was a man of fame, the attitude of the Armours was different. Possibly they 'threw' Jean at Burns, hopefully assuming she would have the wit to make him marry her before giving her body to him once more. In any case, when they found out that poor Jean had muffed things again, they were furious and refused to allow her to remain under their roof.

Burns, dallying with Clarinda in Edinburgh, heard about Jean's misfortunes shortly before Christmas. He was suffering from an injured leg as the result of a carriage accident, so he begged Willie Muir of Tarbolton to give her shelter. Tardily, Burns left Edinburgh for Mauchline where he arrived on 23rd February 1788. He took a room for Jean in Mauchline and arranged for a doctor to attend her. To Clarinda he wrote comparing Jean to a 'farthing taper'. To Ainslie on 3rd March, the day of Jean's confinement, he wrote: 'Jean I found banished like a martyr—forlorn, destitute and friendless; all for the good old cause: I have reconciled her to her fate: I have reconciled her to her mother: I have taken her a room: I have taken her to my arms: I have given her a mahogany bed: I have given her a guinea; and I have f——d her till she rejoiced with joy unspeakable and full of glory. But—as I always am on every occasion—I have been prudent and cautious to an astounding degree; I swore her, privately and solemnly, never to attempt any claim on me as a husband, even though anybody should persuade her she had such a claim, which she has not, neither during my life nor after my death. She did all this like a good girl, and I took the opportunity of some dry horse-litter, and gave her such a thundering scalade that electrified the very marrow of her bones.'

Hardly surprisingly, the second set of twins both died within a few weeks.

On 7th March, four days after Jean was made to swear she would never try to claim him as husband, Burns told Brown that he had 'towed her into convenient harbour where she may lie snug till she unload; and have taken command myself not ostensibly, but for a time, in secret. . . .'

Writing to Smith on 28th April, Burns said: 'To let you a little into the secrets of my pericranium, there is, you must know, a certain clean-limbed, handsome, bewitching young hussy of your acquaintance, to whom I have lately and privately given a matrimonial title to my corpus.' Burns's uncle, Samuel Brown, got a letter hinting marriage, dated 4th May, and on 25th May, Burns wrote to James Johnson: 'I am so enamoured with a certain girl's prolific twin-bearing merit, that I have given her a *legal* title to the best blood in my body; and so farewell Rakery!' On 28th May the surprised Ainslie was told: 'I have been extremely fortunate in all my buyings and bargainings hitherto; Mrs Burns not excepted, which title I now avow to the world. . . .' None of these references suggested the enraptured lover some of Burns's more romantic biographers would have us believe him!

The mystery with which Burns sought to disguise his marriage to Jean has never been satisfactorily unravelled. But in the Train manuscript, the note occurs: 'Jean Armour and Rob Burns were privately married in the writing office of Gavin Hamilton, Mauchline, by John Farquhar Esq., of Gilmilnscroft, J.P.' As Train's father had been land steward at Gilmilnscroft, his account has at least an air of probability (*see* **Gray of Gilmilnscroft, John Farquhar**).

Jean bore Burns nine children, the last on the day of her husband's funeral. Only three of them survived her. She seems to have been a generous, compliant woman, with a clear singing voice, though in no way her husband's intellectual equal, and willing to put up with his wildest extravagancies, even to the extent of taking in his bastard daughter by Anna Park with the remark, 'Our Robbie should have had twa wives.'

Jean outlived her husband by thirty-eight years, answering the questions of the early hagiologists with patient good-nature. Latterly she suffered from high blood pressure, and endured a series of strokes, the second of which left her partly paralysed and dependent on her favourite grand-daughter, Sara.

No portrait of her is known until she became a grandmother. Three of her in later years exist. Of the verbal portraits, that of Mrs Grant of Laggan is perhaps the best. Mrs Grant found her, at fifty-five, 'a very comely woman with plain sound sense and very good manners'.

Burns wrote in all fourteen songs commonly associated with Jean. Of these, by far the greatest is 'Of a' the Airts the Wind can Blaw', of which Burns said: 'The air is by Marshall; the song I composed out of compliment to Mrs Burns.' The song first appeared in 1790 in the *Scots Musical Museum*. The air first appeared as 'Miss Admiral Gordon's Strathspey' in William Marshall's *Collection of Reels*, 1781.

Among the other songs inspired by Jean Armour is that confident outburst of marital satisfaction, 'I hae a wife o' my ain', framed on an old model, though entirely original, and set to a tune taken from James Oswald's *Curious Collection of Scots Tunes*, 1740. It also appeared in the *Museum*. Schumann set the poem under the German title, 'Niemand', as he did also 'Out over the Forth, I looked to the north', originally set to a Gow tune. 'O were I on Parnassus' Hill', to another of Oswald's airs, appeared in Thomson's *Scottish Airs*, 1798.

Writing to Peggy Chalmers on 16th September 1788, Burns told her that his marriage 'was not in consequence of the attachment of romance perhaps; but I had a long and much-loved fellow creature's happiness or misery in my determination, and I durst not trifle with so important a deposit. Nor have I any cause to repent it. If I have not got polite tattle, modish manners, and fashionable dress, I am not sickened and disgusted with the multiform curse of boarding-school affectation; and I have got the handsomest figure, the sweetest temper, the soundest constitution, and kindest heart in the county. Mrs Burns believes, as firmly as her creed, that I am *le plus bel esprit, et le plus honnête homme* in the universe; although she [Jean] scarcely ever in her life, except the Scriptures of the Old and New Testament and the Psalms of David in metre, spent five minutes together on either prose or verse. I must except also from this last a certain late publication of Scots poems, which she has perused very devoutly; and all the ballads in the country, as she has (Oh, the partial lover! you will cry) the finest "wood-note wild" I ever heard.'

See Plate 3.

Burns, John (1769–83)
Burns's youngest brother. He is buried in Mauchline Churchyard.

Burns, John (d. 1844)
Cousin of the poet and son of Robert Burnes, his uncle. After his father's death, he worked for Burns at Ellisland. He was latterly employed to guard Stewarton

graveyard from invasion by the Resurrectionists.

Burns, Margaret (d. 1792)
The poet's 'poor namesake', and an Edinburgh prostitute.

Margaret's real name was Matthews. She was young, beautiful and lived in Rose Street. To quote Chambers: 'In August of the year 1789 some of her neighbours (in Rose Street) lodged a complaint that "since Whitsunday last, she and a Miss Sally Sanderson, who were persons of bad character, had kept a very irregular and disorderly house, into which they admit and entertain licentious and profligate persons of both sexes to the great annoyance of their neighbours and breach of the public peace. . . ." The case caused a considerable sensation, and more so when the two defendants were "banished forth of the city and liberties for ever". Miss Burns entered an appeal to the Court of Session by presenting a petition to the Lord Ordinary (Dreghorn): this was refused; she reclaimed to the Inner House, and the case was decided in her favour (22nd December, 1789).'

Shortly after, her health failed and she died in Rosslyn.

Prior to the success of her appeal, Burns wrote from Ellisland on 2nd February 1790, to the Edinburgh bookseller, Peter Hill:

'. . . how is the fate of my poor Namesake Mademoiselle Burns, decided? Which of their grave LORDSHIPS can lay his hand on his heart and say that he has not taken advantage of such frailty; nay, if we may judge by near six thousand years experience, can the World do without such frailty? O Man! but for thee, & thy selfish appetites & dishonest artifices, that beauteous form, & that once innocent & still ingenuous mind, might have shone conspicuous and lovely in the faithful wife and the affectionate mother; and shall the unfortunate sacrifice to thy pleasures have no claim on thy

c

humanity? As for those flinty-bosomed, puritannic Prosecutors of Female Frailty, & Persecutors of Female Charms—I am quite sober—I am dispassionate—to shew you that I am so I shall mend my pen ere I proceed—It is written, "Thou shalt not take the name of the Lord thy God in vain", so I shall neither say, G—— curse them! nor G—— blast them! nor G—— damn them! but may Woman curse them! May Woman blast them! May Woman damn them! May her lovely hand inexorably shut the Portal of Rapture to their most earnest Prayers & fondest essays for entrance! And when many years and much port and great business have delivered them over to Vulture Gouts and Aspen Palsies, *then* may the dear bewitching Charmer in derision throw open the blissful Gate to tantalise their impotent desires which like ghosts haunt their bosoms when all their powers to give or receive enjoyment, are for ever asleep in the sepulchre of their fathers! ! !'

At the time of the case, Burns's Publisher, Creech, was then a Bailie of the City and on the Bench when Miss Burns's case was heard. He was very annoyed at the final decision. A London Journal reported that 'Bailie Creech, of literary celebrity in Edinburgh, was about to lead the beautiful and accomplished Miss Burns to the hymeneal altar!' Creech was furious and was only persuaded not to sue by the promise of a counter-statement. This he got, and the statement ran thus:

'In a former number we noticed the intended marriage between Bailie Creech of Edinburgh and the beautiful Miss Burns of the same place. We now have the authority of that gentleman to say that the proposed marriage is not to take place, matters having been otherwise arranged to the mutual satisfaction of both parties and their respective friends.'

Burns wrote an epigram, 'Under the Portrait of Miss Burns':

'Cease, ye prudes, your envious railings,
    Lovely Burns has charms: confess!
True it is she had one failing:
    Had a woman ever less?'

Burns, Maxwell (1796–99)

Burns's youngest child, born on the day of his father's funeral, and called Maxwell, after the doctor who had attended both his father and mother. He is buried in the Mausoleum.

Burns, Robert (1759–96)

Robert Burns, Scotland's greatest poet, was born on 25th January 1759 in a two-roomed thatched cottage at Alloway, near Ayr, where his father, William Burnes, ran a small market garden. Old Burnes—the poet was the first to drop the 'e' from the spelling of the family name—had come out of the north-east the descendant of a long line of more or less unsuccessful farmers. But eighteenth-century Ayrshire, lying along the southern shores of the Firth of Clyde, in which he ultimately settled, though today one of the most fertile and economically best-balanced counties in Scotland, was then scarcely less backward than Kincardine-shire, from which he came.

The underlying trouble was the short-lease system by which farmers held their farms. A farmer who spent money improving his land was liable to find his rent had been put up when the lease came to be renewed, because the value of the landlord's property had been increased. So small farmers did their best to scrape as good a living out of the impoverished soil as they could, the members of their families labouring for the common weal.

Old Burnes was one of these struggling unsuccessful farmers. When Robert was seven, William found that his nursery and his gardening could no longer support his growing family. So he and his wife Agnes set up home in the farm of Mount Oliphant, a few miles from Alloway. It was while the family was at Mount Oliphant that Robert got much of his schooling—William had the traditional Scots respect for education, and saw to it that his children got the best that was available to them in the limited circumstances of the time—at Alloway, Dalrymple and Kirkoswald. By Whitsun 1777, however, when William Burnes freed himself from the sterile burden of Mount Oliphant, just in time to escape total ruin, Robert had started to labour with his father in the fields, had gained his first insight into the problems of the peasantry, and had probably already done that damage to his heart which resulted in his early death.

The farm of Lochlea, to which William Burnes next moved, lies midway between Tarbolton and Mauchline. The adolescent Burns attended a young man's debating society and a dancing class in Tarbolton, the latter 'in absolute defiance' of his stern, Calvinistic father's wishes. So long as he lived, however, the old man managed to hold in check the ardently-expanding temperament of his most gifted son. But in February 1784, worn older than his years, William Burnes died, after victoriously concluding a long-drawn-out dispute with his landlord which went the length of the Court of Session. Robert and his brother Gilbert then became partners in the farm of Mossgiel, which they rented from the Ayr lawyer Gavin Hamilton when it became obvious that their father was unlikely to live much longer.

Gilbert Burns remained at Mossgiel during the remainder of his brother's days, though he was only able to weather one particularly severe crisis with the aid of a loan from Robert. But the poet spent less and less time over farm concerns and more and more on literature and the lasses. In the series of great satires which he produced during 1786, he thundered against the hypocrisy of the extreme narrow 'Auld Licht' sect of the kirk, using their purely local squabbles to reflect his humanity and concern for universal values. He also started a series of ardent philanderings. Over the years, Burns's pre-marital and extra-marital affairs resulted in a fairly numerous brood of illegitimate children; but also in the warmest, richest, most tender and most sensuous love-songs that any poet has given to the world.

His seduction of Jean Armour, a Mauchline mason's daughter, and the repudiation of him which her outraged parents insisted upon, threw him into an emotional tangle which it is now impossible to sort out with any certainty. He may well have married her by declaration —valid under Scots Law until 1939— before her parents moved her to Paisley, away from him. At any rate, his entanglement with 'Highland' Mary Campbell, whom he invited (in verse) to flee with him to Jamaica—that unsavoury haven of eighteenth-century Scots in trouble!— ended with her mysterious death at Greenock in 1786. Jean Armour thereafter bore twins, and Robert rode off to Edinburgh to be lionised, the triumph of his 'Kilmarnock Poems', published earlier that year, having made him a celebrity, the so-called 'ploughman poet' without whom a smart party in the capital was not considered complete. In Edinburgh, he had his affair with Agnes ('Clarinda') Maclehose, summed up so poignantly in the song 'Ae fond kiss'. There, too, he met the engraver James Johnson, then planning to publish his Scots Musical Museum as a permanent repository for Scots folk-song. Fortunately, Johnson invited Burns's aid. Burns soon became virtually editor of the Museum, and during the last ten years of his life, 'Tam o' Shanter' apart, he poured all his rich genius into the moulds of songwriting and song-repairing prepared for him by Johnson and, later, by another editor, the dilettante clerk, George Thomson, with his Select Scottish Airs.

But after a while, Edinburgh soon

grew tired of Burns and left him with the problem of earning a living unsolved. In April 1788—after having seduced her once again, and wrapped his intentions and actions in further epistolary mystifications to his friends—Burns suddenly acknowledged his marriage to Jean Armour. From June 1788 until November 1791, Burns farmed Ellisland in Dumfriesshire, latterly holding at the same time an Excise appointment. Thereafter, until his death in July 1796, Burns lived in Dumfries, working as an officer in the Dumfries Port Division of the Excise. He died, not as his unctuous nineteenth-century biographers tried to make out, from excesses either of wine or of women, but from some form of endocarditis, established at Lochlea when the boy had to perform the labours of a man.

Burns was acquainted with the work of his Scottish predecessors, Barbour and Blind Harry, Dunbar, Henryson and Lyndsay, the Makars of the fourteenth to the sixteenth century. But it was the work of the poets of the eighteenth-century Scots Revival, notably Allan Ramsay and Robert Fergusson, which most strongly influenced Burns technically. He reached maturity when the verse forms and colloquial temper of the Ramsay-Fergusson school were both to hand and already popular. He established himself as a poet to be reckoned with just before the old agrarian way of life of Scotland, which had lasted more or less unchanged since medieval times, began to recede before the double pressure of the Industrial Revolution and the advance of Englishry. Thus, before it was too late, Burns in his poetry caught and fixed the old Scotland for all time.

His best poems, the satires and epistles, are those firmly rooted in the Scottish vernacular tradition; his poorest, those in which he strove to imitate the English Augustans. As a song-writer, his lyric gift was unsurpassed. The peasant obscenities of an earlier, coarser age he excised (pre-serving them, however, in his private collection of bawdry, *The Merry Muses of Caledonia**); the banalities of less gifted songsters he warmed into life. His sensitive ear was keen to detect the potentialities and possibilities of the national airs sent to him by Johnson and Thomson. His song-work kept him constantly occupied until a few days before his death.

Because he has preserved so much of the richness of Scotland's past, and because he possessed the gift of stating the commonplaces of life in a way which makes them significantly memorable, Burns has been all but idolised in Scotland. Much of the idolatry is foolish in the extreme, and is bestowed on him by people totally unable to appreciate the fine qualities of his work, or, indeed, literature of any kind, but who see him either as a sort of emotionally-charged national symbol, or an excuse for a good annual 'binge'. Burns Nights, held round about 25th January all over the world, are notable perhaps only occasionally for the wisdom of the speeches or the abilities of the performers: but they help to keep interest in Burns, and, indeed, the Scots tongue, alive.

But in spite of the stupidities and the platitudes they produce, at least they help periodically to focus attention for a little while on Burns, the poet. Some of those who are thus induced to investigate Burns's poems, having had their interest awakened at a Burns Supper, may read on, and read again often for sheer disinterested pleasure. In the long run, the poetry is what really matters.

Burns, Robert (1786–1857)
Eldest son of the poet. He was educated at Dumfries Grammar School, then had two sessions at Edinburgh and one at Glasgow University, where he was a prize-winner. He obtained a position in

* Professor Egerer claims that only six of these poems are by Burns, which may or may not be so, but he obviously rejoiced in the *genre*.

the Stamp Office in London, which had been offered to him by the Prime Minister, and from which he retired in 1833 with a small pension, to Dumfries, where he died. A letter from the Treasury Chambers of 16th August 1832, printed in the 1859 *Illustrated London News*, authorised the Commissioners of Stamps at Somerset House, 'to place him on the superannuation list of your department, at the allowance of £120 per annum'. The money was granted because of 'the great literary talents' of his father.

In his poem 'Nature's Law', the poet hinted at his hopes for his eldest son:

'Auld cantie Coil may count the day,
    As annual it returns,
The third of Libra's equal sway,
    That gave another Burns,*
With future rhymes an' other times,
    To emulate his sire;
To sing auld Coil in nobler style,
    With more poetic fire.'

Though he did write verse, however, he did not fulfil his father's hopes in this respect.

Burns was, from the start, proud of his son's intellectual abilities. Writing to Mrs Dunlop from Dumfries on 24th September 1792, he said:

'Your little godson is thriving charmingly, (Francis Wallace) but is a very devil. He, though two years younger, has completely mastered his brother. Robert is indeed the mildest, gentlest creature I ever saw. He has a most surprising memory, and is quite the pride of his schoolmaster.'

Robert Burns II married Anne Sherwood when he was twenty-two. They had one daughter, Eliza, who went out to India with her uncle, Colonel James Glencairn Burns, where she married a Dr Everitt of the East India Company. She died in 1878.

Both in London and in Dumfries,

* September was the birth month of Robert Burns II.

Robert Burns II augmented his income by teaching the classics and mathematics.

Burns, William (1767–90)

The poet's youngest brother, whom Burns took under his personal care when William was a youth of eighteen, something of a problem and urgently in need of a vocation. Burns first of all tried to get Ainslie to find William a job as a saddler's apprentice in Edinburgh, but Ainslie apparently failed to do so. William then boarded himself upon the poet in Nithsdale. Some months later, however, William was duly apprenticed to a saddler in Longtown. From there, he moved to Newcastle, where he worked with Messrs. Walker and Robson, saddlers. When William found a job in London as journeyman saddler with William T. Barber, in the Strand, the poet wrote from Ellisland on 10th February 1790, warning the youth of the perils of that city (where Burns himself had never been!), particularly 'that universal vice, Bad Women'. Yet when William had announced that he was in love, the poet had previously told his young brother in May, 1789: 'I am, you know, a veteran in these campaigns, so let me advise you always to pay your particular assiduities and try for intimacy as soon as you feel the first symptoms of the passion; this is not only best, as making the most of the little entertainment which the sportabilities of distant addresses always gives, but is the best preservative for one's peace. I need not caution you against guilty amours—they are bad everywhere, but in England they are the very devil.' 'Intimacy' in Burns's day, did not mean sexual intercourse, as it does in ours.

Several letters between the brothers survive to show Robert's concern for William's welfare, even to the point of giving him money, and William's respect for his elder brother's advice. There is also the suggestion that William was an easy giver-up, since the poet had frequently to counsel him: 'I beg you will endeavour to pluck up a *little* more of the man than you used to have'; and again: 'In a word, if ever you be, as perhaps you may be, in a strait for a little ready cash, you know my direction; I shall not see you bent while you fight like a man.'

On 16th July 1790, Burns told his brother that John Murdoch, the family tutor of their Alloway days, would get in touch with him. Murdoch did see William once before the unfortunate youth died on 24th July. On 14th September, Murdoch, after a delay of nearly two months, wrote a long letter to Burns explaining how, on receipt of the poet's letter of 16th July, which he received: 'on the 26th in the afternoon per favour of my friend Mr Kennedy, and at the same time was informed that your brother was ill. Being engaged in business till late that evening, I set out next morning to see him, and had three or four medical gentlemen of my acquaintance, to one or other of whom I might apply for advice, provided it should be necessary. But when I went to Mr Barber's, to my great astonishment and heart-felt grief, I found that my young friend had, on Saturday, bid an everlasting farewell to all sublunary things.'

Death was supposed to have been caused by a 'putrid fever'. Burns despatched a draft in payment of all bills incurred by his brother's last illness and funeral, the receipt for which is dated 8th October. Robert's relationship with William, Snyder says, was: 'affectionate, loyal, serious, never over-bearing or dictatorial, and always frank in his counsel. He treated William as he might have treated one of his own sons had he lived long enough to see him in the years of his young manhood.'

Burns, Colonel William Nicol (1791–1872)

Second surviving son of the poet, named after William Nicol, the schoolmaster of the Edinburgh High School. He was educated at Dumfries Grammar School and in London. He married Catherine, daughter of R. Crone, Esq., of Dublin. They had no family. Having sailed to India as a young man, he ultimately became a Lieut.-Colonel in the East India Company's service. He was made a Colonel at home in 1855. When he retired, he returned to England to Cheltenham, where he stayed with his younger brother. He is buried in the Mausoleum.

Writing to George Thomson in a letter dated by Ferguson May 1795, Burns explained why he had called his third son after the schoolmaster. It was because: '. . . of that propensity to witty wickedness and manfu' mischief, which even at twa days auld I foresaw would form the striking feature of his disposition.'

See Plate 3.

Burns Cottage, Alloway

The 'Auld Cley Biggin', as the poet himself described his birthplace, was put up by his father, William Burnes, on seven-and-a-half acres of ground purchased from Dr Alexander Campbell of Ayr in 1756. In it, Robert Burns was born on 25th January 1759. A few days later, an alarming incident befell the baby and his mother: an incident best described in a letter by Gilbert Burns first printed in Dr Currie's Edition of 1803:

'When my father built his "clay biggin"—Robert spelt it "cley"—he put in two stone jambs, as they are called, and a lintel, carrying up the chimney in his clay-gable. The consequence was, that as the gable subsided, the jambs remaining firm, threw it off its centre; and, one very stormy morning, when my brother was nine or ten days old, a little before daylight, a part of the gable fell out, and the rest appeared so shattered, that my mother, with the young poet, had to be carried through the storm to a neighbour's house, where they remained a week till their own dwelling was adjusted.'

Robert himself, in his song, 'There was a lad was born in Kyle', refers to the incident:

'Our Monarch's hindmost year but ane
Was five-and-twenty days begun,
'Twas then a blast o' Janwar win'
Blew hansel in on Robin. . . .'

Burns spent the first seven years of his life in this 'but and ben', which the worthy schoolmaster John Murdoch described as 'with the exception of a little straw, literally a tabernacle of clay', until the family moved to Mount Oliphant in 1766. Murdoch, who was writing retrospectively, added: 'In this cottage, of which I myself was at times an inhabitant, I really believe there dwelt a larger portion of content than in any Palace in Europe. "The Cotter's Saturday Night" will give some idea of the temper and manners that prevailed there.'

Old Burnes thereafter let the cottage to various tenants until 1781, when it and the ground were bought by the Incorporation of Shoemakers in Ayr for a hundred and sixty pounds. That body let both land and buildings, and shortly before 1800, their first tenant turned the place into an ale-house. It remained an ale-house until 1881, when it was acquired by the Alloway Burns Monument Trustees, who pulled down the additional buildings added by the Incorporation of Shoemakers, and restored the 'Auld Cley Biggin' to its original proportions.

It is now the most important of the Burns Museums and contains not only many domestic relics of the poet's life, but virtually a complete collection of all editions of his work.

See Plate 2.

Burns Federation
Founded at Kilmarnock in 1885, its objects being:
(1) To strengthen and consolidate by universal affiliation the bond of fellowship existing amongst the members of Burns Clubs and kindred societies.
(2) To purchase and preserve manuscripts and other relics connected with the poet.
(3) To repair, renew, or mark with suitable inscriptions, any buildings, tombstones, etc., interesting from their association with Burns.
(4) To encourage and arrange School Competitions in order to stimulate the teaching of Scottish History and Literature.
The Federation also produces every year the *Burns Chronicle*.

Burnside, Anne (1759–1838)
See **Burnside, Dr William.**

Burnside, Dr William (1751–1806)
Minister of the New Church in Dumfries, he moved to St Michael's in the same town in 1794. He wrote a history of Dumfries, part of which was incorporated in Sir John Sinclair's *Statistical Account*.

Burns, in a letter to William Nicol from Mauchline, dated 18th June 1787, described the minister as: 'a man whom I shall ever gratefully remember'. Burns then goes into eulogies over Anne, the minister's wife; 'and his wife, Gude forgie me! I had almost broke the tenth commandment on her account. Simplicity, elegance, good sense, sweetness of disposition, good humour, kind hospitality, are the constituents of her manner and heart: in short—but if I say one word more about her, I shall be directly in love with her.'

Bushby, John (d. 1802)
Dumfries lawyer, and, according to the *Edinburgh Almanac* of 1799, sheriff elect of Dumfries. He factored several estates and was owner of a private bank. A North of England man who retained something of his North Country dialect he made two prosperous marriages and bought Tinwald Downs, a country mansion near Dumfries. We know little

of the relationship between Bushby and
Burns. Tradition has it that the two
men were friendly at one time but
quarrelled when Burns was scalded by a
very hot pudding, which, Bushby had
humorously claimed, was ice cold. The
poet thereafter lashed out satirically at
Bushby and his relations, notably in the
ballad 'John Bushby's Lamentation' and
in the 'Epitaph':

> 'Here lies John Bushby, honest man!
> Cheat him, devil—if you can.'

A comment in the Young manuscript,
however, puts a different complexion on
the Bushby-Burns relationship. (Incidentally, Young's copy of the epitaph has
'Catch' at the beginning of the second
line instead of 'Cheat'.) Young says that
Bushby was Sheriff Clerk of the County
when Burns came to Dumfries. It seems
unlikely that one in such a position would
indulge in a prank so silly as that traditionally alleged and recorded by Chambers. Young claims to have got a copy of
the 'Epitaph' from Syme. Young goes
on: 'I put it into the hands of Mr Bushby
as soon as it was received, and he merely
laughed at it, seeming to think it rather
complimentary, and said he would ask
the fellow to dine with him some day at
Tinwald Downs, where I heard he went
with his friend Mr Syme, who was
intimate with Mr Bushby.'

In *Letters of John Ramsay, 1799–1821*,
addressed to his cousin Mrs Dundas,
Ramsay of Ochtertyre writes, on 21st
September, 1802:

'Heard you of old Bushby's dream the
penult night of his life? when he thought
he had fallen into a deep pit and after
many efforts, got thro a gate which
precipitated him lower and lower, till
he awakened and behold it was a hideous
Phantasma; and after eating a *Dives*
dinner he breathed his last, "unhouselled,
unanointed, unaneeled"*; not more than
well prepared for his great change. He
was one of the few men who could lead
counties by the nose with the mask of
honesty; to him bankruptcy proved the
road to wealth and luxury.'

Bushby, Maitland (b. 1767)
The son of John Bushby of Tinwald
Downs. He became an advocate and
Sheriff of Wigtownshire. In the second
of the Heron Election Ballads, Burns
refers to him as having the heart but
not the head of his father. The same
gibe occurs in his 'Epistle from Esopus to
Maria'.

Bushby of Kempleton, William
A brother of John Bushby of Tinwald
Downs, and referred to in the second
Heron Election Ballad as: 'Kempleton's
birkie, a chiel no sae black at the bane'.
He was ruined by the failure of the Douglas, Heron and Co., Bank, and as a result
went to the East Indies, where he made a
'fine Nabob fortune'.

* Ramsay misquotes Shakespeare's 'unhousel'd,
disappointed, unaneal'd', *Hamlet* I, v.

C

Cadie

Errand runners in Edinburgh, referred to in relation to Fox's notorious gambling habits in 'The Author's Earnest Cry and Prayer'. The traveller Edward Burt called 'The *Cawdys*, a very useful Black-guard, who attends the Coffee-Houses and pub-lick Places to go Errands; and though they are wretches, that in Rags lye upon the Stairs, and in the Streets at Night, yet are they often considerably trusted . . .'

'Ça Ira'

A song promising to hang, burn or break 'les aristocrates' which became popular in France during the Revolution, and was sung in 1789 by the insurgents as they marched on Versailles.

Because of the oppressive nature of the Tory Government in Britain in its attitude to any kind of liberal reform, the Revolution at first awakened strong sympathies in many British hearts; sympathies, however, which were altered when the idealism of the earlier days gave place to the 'Reign of Terror'.

'Ça Ira' was called for one night in the theatre at Dumfries when Burns happened to be present. A hubbub followed, and Burns feared that his loyalty, which had already been called in question once by the Excise Commission, might again be doubted. So he thought it necessary to explain the incident away in a letter of 5th January 1793 to Graham of Fintry, who was one of the Excise Commissioners: 'I was in the playhouse one night, when "Ça Ira" was called for. I was in the middle of the Pit, and from the Pit the clamour arose. One or two individuals with whom I occasionally associate were of the party, but I neither knew of the Plot, nor joined in the Plot; nor ever opened my lips to hiss or huzza, that, or any other Political tune whatever. I looked on myself as far too obscure a man to have any weight in quelling a Riot; and at the same time as a character of higher respec-tability, than to yell in the howlings of a rabble. This was the conduct of all the first Characters in this place; and these Characters know, and will avow, that such was my conduct.'

But to Mrs Dunlop, on 6th December 1792, he had confessed:

'. . . we are a good deal in commotion ourselves, and in our Theatre here, "God save the King" has met with some groans and hisses, while "Ça ira" has been repeatedly called for. For me, "I am a *Placeman*, you know, a very humble one indeed, Heaven knows", but still so much so as to gag me from joining in the cry. What my private sentiments are, you will find out without an Interpreter.'

'Ca' the Yowes'

This very lovely song, with its modal tune, first appeared in the *Scots Musical Museum* in 1790. The manuscript, con-taining the opening bars of the tune, is in the British Museum. In the inter-leaved *Museum* Burns noted: 'This beauti-ful song is in the true old Scotch taste, yet I do not know that ever either air or words were in print before.'

The last two stanzas are Burns's, according to Dick, while the first two were 'made out of the original first stanza.'

Writing to Thomson in September, 1794, Burns said: 'I am flattered at your adopting "Ca' the Yowes," as it was owing to me that ever it saw the light. About seven years ago, I was well acquain-ted with a worthy little fellow of a clergyman, a Mr Clunzie, who sang it charmingly; and, at my request, Mr Clarke took it down from his singing. When I gave it to Johnston, I added some stanzas to the song, and mended others. . . .'

The author of the original stanzas was said to have been Tibbie Pagan, an eccentric old woman who sold whisky without a licence, and accompanied its dispensation to her customers with a fund of broad stories. However, a collection of her pieces was published in Glasgow in 1805, and 'Ca' the Yowes' was not of their number.

Caledonian Hunt, the

An association of noblemen and country gentlemen who shared a common interest in field sports, races, balls and social assemblies. Burns dedicated the first Edinburgh Edition of his *Poems* to the Hunt, some of whose members had befriended or patronised him in Edinburgh. The dedication is couched in his fullest-blown prose style:

'Though much indebted to your goodness, I do not approach you, my Lords and Gentlemen, in the usual stile of dedication, to thank you for past favours; that path is so hackneyed by prostituted Learning, that honest Rusticity is ashamed of it. Nor do I present this "Address" with the venal soul of a servile Author, looking for a continuation of those favors. I was bred to the Plough and am independent. I come to claim the common Scottish name with you, my illustrious Countrymen; and to tell the world that I glory in the title. I come to congratulate my Country, that the blood of her ancient heroes still runs uncontaminated; and that from your courage, knowledge, and public spirit, she may expect protection, wealth and liberty. . . .'

Included in the Minutes of the Meeting of the Caledonian Hunt at Edinburgh on 10th January 1787, is an acknowledgement of this dedication:

'A motion being made by the Earl of Glencairn, and seconded by Sir John Whitefoord in favour of Mr Burns, Ayrshire, who had dedicated the new edition of his poems to the Caledonian Hunt, the meeting was of the opinion that in consideration of his superior merit, as well as of the compliment paid to them, Mr Hogart should be directed to subscribe for one hundred copies in their name, for which he should pay Mr Burns twenty-five pounds, upon the publication of his book.'

Burns himself was enrolled as a member of the Caledonian Hunt on 10th April 1792.

'Caledonian Pocket Companion, The'

This *Favourite Collection of Scotch Tunes with Variations for the German Flute or Violin* was published in London by James Oswald in 1759. The entire work extended to twelve parts, and in spite of its name, it was the largest collection of its kind to be published.

James Oswald (1711–69) began life as a dancing master at Dunfermline, but having won attention by a *Collection of Minuets* published two years before, moved to Edinburgh in 1736. He found it difficult to earn a living there, however, and in 1741 emigrated to London. His departure drew a poetic lament from Allan Ramsay, alleging that Edinburgh's loss was London's gain. In London, Oswald wrote music for a number of plays, and published, among other works, *Twelve Songs* (c. 1742), *Six Pastoral Solos for a Violin and Violoncello* (c. 1745), airs for *Spring, Summer, Autumn and Winter* (c. 1747) and *Twelve Seranantas [sic] for two Violins and a Violoncello* (c. 1765).

Burns took seven airs from the *Caledonian Pocket Companion* and from Oswald's *Curious Collection* of Scots Songs (1740): for 'It is na, Jean, thy bonny face'; 'Anna, thy charms my bosom fire'; 'You wild, mossy mountains'; 'If thou should ask my love'; 'O were I on Parnassus' Hill'; 'The lovely lass o' Inverness'; and 'Go, fetch to me a pint o' wine'. He thus fulfilled his prophecy made in a letter to James Johnson from Ellisland, probably written in the early summer of 1791: '. . . I was so lucky lately as to pick up an entire copy of Oswald's Scots music and I think I shall make glorious work out of it.'

He added: 'I want much Anderson's Collection of strathspeys, and then I think I will have all the music of the country.'

Cambusdoon Manuscript

A collection of twenty pages, the first sixteen of which are in Burns's handwriting. The pages in Burns's hand contain, 'The Birks of Aberfeldy', 'Written in the Hermitage at Taymouth', 'Written at the Falls of Foyers', 'The Humble Petition of Bruar Water', 'Elegy on Sir John Hunter Blair', 'Andrew and his Cutty Gun, composed at Auchtertyre on Miss Euphemia Murray of Lentrose', 'On Scaring some Waterfowl in Loch Turit', and a poem not composed by Burns, 'Here's to the King, Sir'. This last poem, according to Chambers, was probably written about 1718, in view of the allusion it contains to Charles XII of Sweden. At the top of the page containing it, but now nearly obliterated, are the words, 'from the mind' in Burns's handwriting, suggesting either that he wrote it down from memory, or touched up the Jacobite song. Some of the other poems contain earlier variants of the text which appeared in the 1793 edition.

The last four pages contain a poem to the memory of Burns by a Mrs Allardyce, wife of the minister of Forgue, Aberdeenshire, and dated 1818. She may once have owned the collection, which also contains a short catalogue, not in Burns's handwriting, of some of his poems to Clarinda and other pieces.

Cameron, May

A servant girl in Edinburgh, who bore Burns a child which he admitted was his. It was probably early in June 1787, when he was in Dumfries receiving the freedon of the burgh, that May Cameron's letter —probably written for her by a friend, and dated 26th May—reached him: 'I beg, for God sake, you will write and let me know how I am to do. You can write to any person you can trust to get me a place to stay till such time as you come to town yourself.' Burns immediately wrote an undated note to Ainslie (who was in the same paternal predicament himself), asking him to: 'send for the wench and give her ten or twelve shillings . . . and advise her out to some country (friends). . . . Call immediately, or at least as soon as it is dark, for God sake, lest the poor soul be starving.—Ask her for a letter I wrote her just now, by way of token—it is unsigned.' (Ferguson dates this letter 'about 1st June 1788, which for obvious reasons must be incorrect.)

Ainslie evidently complied with this request, but the girl cannot have been satisfied, because she later had served on Burns a writ *in meditatione fugae*: 15th August 1787, however, was the date of a document freeing him from the writ and its unpleasant implications of arrest. Burns kept this document, which carries two verses of an 'old and broadly humorous song', according to Chambers. Chambers said further that 'the terms of this writ must have been merely used formally, in order to force him to grant the required security'.

Campbell, Betty

In Chambers' day it was believed locally that she had been a servant at Stair House whom Burns had courted. But John McVie, in *Burns and Stair*, maintained that there was no record of her having been a servant at Stair, and suggested that her so-called flirtation with Burns was a figment of 'Mrs Grundy's' imagination, 'first recorded by Chambers'.

Campbell, Bruce (1734-1813)

He owned the estate of Mayfield and Milrig, in the parish of Galston, Ayrshire, and married Annabella, the daughter of James Wilson of Kilmarnock, whom Ferguson says was 'perhaps a relative of

Burns's printer'. One of his sons, Alexander, became a favourite of General Wellesley, the future Duke of Wellington, but died of wounds received at the Battle of Assaye.

Burns sent Campbell some copies of the subscription sheets for the Kilmarnock Edition. Only one letter from Burns to Campbell survives. Dated Mauchline, 13th November 1788, it accompanied copies of poems designed for 'Mr Boswell'. Burns writes: 'Should they procure me the honor of being introduced to Mr Boswell, I shall think they have great merit. There are few pleasures my late will-o'-wisp character has given me, equal to that of having seen many of the extraordinary men, the Heroes of Wit and Literature in my country; and as I had the honor of drawing my first breath almost in the same Parish with Mr Boswell, my Pride plumes itself on the connection ... to have been acquainted with such a man as Mr Boswell, I would hand down to posterity as one of the honors of their ancestor.' So far as is known, Burns and James Boswell never met.

Campbell, Lord Frederick (1736–1816)
Third son of the fourth Duke of Argyll. In Parliament he represented the Glasgow and Ayr burghs from 1761 to 1780, and Argyll from 1780 to 1799.

Burns calls him a 'true Campbell' in The Author's Earnest Cry and Prayer', along with Sir Ilay Campbell. In 1774 Lord Frederick laid the foundation-stone of the new Register House in Edinburgh, which had been designed by Robert Adam.

Campbell, 'Highland' Mary (1763–86)
Burns's 'Highland' Mary was born to Archibald Campbell of Daling, a seaman, and Agnes Campbell of Auchamore, by Dunoon, who had married in 1762. She was the eldest of a family of four. She lived with her parents, first, near Dunoon, then at Campbeltown, and finally at

Greenock. In her early 'teens, she went to Ayrshire and became a nursemaid in Gavin Hamilton's house in Mauchline. Hamilton's married daughter, Mrs Todd, remembered Mary Campbell coming to look after her brother Alexander in 1785. Mrs Todd described her as 'very pleasant and winning', though not a beauty. From there, she moved to Coilsfield (Burns's 'Castle o' Montgomery'), where she was employed as a dairymaid. According to Grierson, who met Mary's sister, Mrs Anderson, in 1817, Mary was 'tall, fair haired with blue eyes'.

The firm facts of her early life are sketchy enough; but the facts of her relationship with Burns are even more sketchy. According to Burns's mother and his sister, Isabella, Burns turned seriously to Mary Campbell after he had been 'deserted' by Jean Armour. She, of course, was despatched to Paisley in March 1786.

In the spring of 1786, Burns wrote a song, 'The Highland Lassie, O'. On a note in the interleaved *Museum* (once thought to be a forgery by Cromek, but shown by Ferguson in an article in the *Philological Quarterly*, July 1930, to be genuine), Burns wrote: 'This was a composition of mine in very early life, before I was known at all in the world. My Highland lassie was a warm-hearted, charming young creature as ever blessed a man with generous love. After a pretty long tract of the most ardent reciprocal attachment, we met by appointment, on the second Sunday of May, in a sequestered spot by the Banks of Ayr, where we spent the day in taking farewell, before she should embark for the West Highlands to arrange matters among her friends for our projected change of life. At the close of Autumn following she crossed the sea to meet me at Greenock, where she had scarce landed when she was seized with a malignant fever, which hurried my dear girl to the grave in a few days, before I could even hear of her illness.' Another song, apparently inspired by Mary Campbell, begins:

'Will ye go to the Indies my Mary,
    And leave auld Scotia's shore?
Will ye go to the Indies, my Mary,
    Across th' Atlantic roar?'

This suggests that Burns may have asked Mary to go with him to Jamaica; that she consented, but died at Greenock before the plan could be put into action. We also learn, however, that on that May Sunday Burns and Mary Campbell exchanged Bibles, and possibly some sort of matrimonial vows. The Bible Mary gave Burns has never been seen; the little two-volume Bible Burns gave Mary is in the Monument at Alloway (*see* **Bibles**).

The song 'The Highland Lassie, O', on which the inserted comment, already quoted, was made, states quite specifically:

'She has my heart, she had my hand,
    By secret troth and honor's band!
Till the mortal stroke shall lay me low,
    I'm thine, my Highland Lassie, O.'

When Mary Campbell died, possibly from a fever contracted when nursing her brother Robert, possibly as a result of premature childbirth, she was buried in the old West Highland Churchyard at Greenock, in a lair owned by her host and relation Peter Macpherson. On 23rd February 1803, Greenock Burns Club minuted their resolution to ask Mr Macpherson 'to allow the Club to add a tablet to the memory of Mary Campbell to his lairs', a resolution which took forty years to be translated into reality.

A hundred and thirty-four years after her death, the West Churchyard was needed for industrial expansion, and on 5th November 1920, Mary Campbell's grave was opened. Among the remains was found the bottom board of an infant's coffin. This aroused speculation, based on Burns's self-confessed belief in trying at once for intimacy where women were concerned, about the real cause of Mary's death, particularly in view of the already-mentioned hints that he may have contracted a Scots marriage by declaration with her.

The facts are examined at length by Snyder in *The Life of Robert Burns* (1932); by Hilton Brown in *There Was a Lad* (1949); and by the present writer in *Robert Burns: The Man; His Work; The Legend* (1954; 2nd edition 1968).

What does seem beyond dispute is that Mary Campbell, long after she was dead, in some way troubled Burns's conscience.

Writing to Brice on 12th June 1786, while Mary was still alive, Burns had confessed to 'dissipation and riot . . . and other mischief'.

Writing to Aiken in October 1786, after her death, Burns burst out: 'I have been for some time pining under secret wretchedness, from causes which you pretty well know—the pang of disappointment, the sting of pride, with some wandering stabs of remorse, which never fail to settle on my vitals like vultures, when attention is not called away by the calls of society or the vagaries of the Muse. Even in the hour of social mirth, my gaiety is the madness of an intoxicated criminal under the hands of the executioner.'

Writing to Mrs Dunlop, after a quarrel, on 7th July 1789, Burns said: 'Yours . . . has given me more pain than any letter, one excepted, that I ever received.'

Mrs Begg told Chambers that one afternoon at Mossgiel, during the autumn of 1786: 'a letter for Robert was handed in. He went to the window to open and read it, and she was struck by the look of agony which was the consequence. He went out without uttering a word.' Could this have been the 'one excepted' letter; the letter, written perhaps by one of her brothers, telling Burns of Mary's death?

Under cover of a letter dated 8th November 1789, Burns sent Mrs Dunlop the poem now called 'To Mary in Heaven', though it was never so called by Burns. On this poem, Scott Douglas commented: 'When we find Burns, after eighteen months' experience of loving wedlock with his own Jean, suddenly appealing to the shade of Mary in these words:

"See'st thou thy lover lowly laid?
Hear'st thou the groans that rend his
                                  brest?"

we feel constrained to say, "If this is not the language of remorse, what is it?" '

There was again a reference to 'my ever dear Mary' to Mrs Dunlop in a letter of 13th December 1789, speculating on the prospects of 'another life'.

According to Wallace, Mary's father burned the poet's letters to his daughter, and forbade his name to be mentioned in the family circle.

This is not the place to speculate on whether Burns was bigamously married to Mary, or whether she died bearing his child. But the absurd 'official' view of her as an 'ideal maiden', an emblem of spiritual purity, is clearly nonsense, and part of the deliberate falsification begun by Currie and assiduously carried on throughout the nineteenth century, until Snyder finally challenged the sentimental pseudo-scholarship of almost all Burns's earlier biographers.

The two songs and the poem 'To Mary in Heaven' do not represent Burns even at his second best. It is thus nonsense to claim, as Allan Bayne has done, that ' "Highland Mary" for ever remains as the inspirer of Burns at his best . . . and whoever seeks to defile this ideal maiden deserves the reprobation of all pure-minded men and women!' (One smiles, in passing, at the Victorian pretence that virginity is woman's 'pure' or 'ideal' state!) Without seeking to belittle this girl whom sentimentality has elevated to the absurd role of Burns's 'Beatrice', the contemporary, or near contemporary

comment of John Richmond for the Train Manuscript may be quoted, with the caution that while gossip remains gossi it is often inspired by at least a small degr of basic truthfulness. Said Richmond:

'Her character was loose in the extreme. She was *kept* for some time by a brother of Lord Eglinton's, and even while a servant with Gavin Hamilton, and during the period of Burns' attachment it was well known that her meetings with Montgomery were open and frequent. The friends of Burns represented to him the impropriety of his devotedness to her, but without producing any change in his sentiments. Richmond told Mr Grierson that Montgomery and Highland Mary frequently met in a small ale-house called the Elbow, and upon one occasion he and some of Burns's friends—knowing they were actually together in the Elbow and having often in vain tried to convince Robert of her infidelity—upon this occasion they promised to give ocular proof of their assertions. The party retired to the Elbow. Richmond, (Mr Grierson's informant) was one, and they took their seats in the kitchin [sic] from which two rooms branched off to the right and left—being all the accommodation the house contained. . . . After waiting long, and when Burns was beginning to ridicule their suspicions, Mary Campbell appeared from one of the rooms—was jeered by the party, in a general way—blushed and retired. Another long interval elapsed and Burns began to rally his spirits, which were very much sunk. Montgomery walked out of the same room. Burns coloured deeply—compressed his lip—and muttered "*damn* it". After enduring considerable bantering from his friends, he soon gave way to the general hilarity of the evening, and his friends thought he had seen enough of Highland Mary, but in a few days after, he returned "like the dog to its vomit".'

It must be observed in passing, however,

that there was no pub in Mauchline called The Elbow, so far as is known.

Campbell, Sir Ilay (1734–1823)

The eldest son of Archibald Campbell of Succoth, he became Lord Advocate in 1784, succeeding Henry Erskine. He represented the Glasgow burghs in Parliament from 1784 to 1789, in which year he became Lord President of the Court of Session, in succession to Sir Thomas Miller. He was created a baronet in 1808.

In 'The Author's Earnest Cry and Prayer', Burns referred to him and Lord Frederick Campbell as 'true Campbells'. There is also a reference to him as Lord Advocate in the poem 'Extempore in The Court of Session'.

Lord Cockburn, in *Memorials of his Time*, described Sir Ilay as having 'great experience and great reputation in every legal sphere'. His forensic writing was 'admirable', though 'his speaking, always admirable in matter, was the reverse of attractive. His voice was low and dull, his face sedate and hard'.

Sir Ilay's reports on the state of the courts of law in Scotland, which he compiled over a period of fifteen years, are still valuable works of reference. Glasgow University conferred on him the degree of Doctor of Laws. He was Lord Rector of the University from 1799 to 1801.

Campbell, James Mure, fifth Earl of Loudon (1726–86)

Before succeeding to the title on the death of his cousin, the fourth Earl, in 1782, he was Colonel James Mure Campbell of Rowallan, husband of Flora McLeod of Raasay (*see* **McLeod, Isabella**), and only son of Sir James Campbell of Lawers. He had a military career and was Member of Parliament for Ayr from 1754 to 1761. He shot himself on 28th April 1786, according to Burns 'out of sheer heartbreak at some mortifications he suffered, owing to the deranged state of his finan-

ces'. Burns composed his song 'Raving winds around her blowing' on the death of Loudon and his lady within a few weeks of each other, dedicating them to Lady Loudon's sister, Miss Isabella McLeod of Raasay.

Campbell, John, fifth Duke of Argyll (1723–1806)

He succeeded his father in 1770, became the first President of the Highland Society of Scotland and married a celebrated beauty, Elizabeth Gunning, widow of the sixth Duke of Hamilton in 1759. Both Duke and Duchess were subscribers to Burns's *Poems*.

Burns arrived at Inverary in June 1787, when the Duke of Argyll had a large house-party. The inn-keeper was too busy attending to the Duke's guests to have time for passing travellers. Burns is supposed to have scrawled his 'On Incivility shown him at Inverary' on one of the inn windows:

> 'Whoe'er he be that sojourns here,
>   I pity much his case—
> Unless he come to wait upon
>   The Lord *their* God, "His Grace . . .

Campbell, John, fourth Earl of Breadalbane (1762–1834)

The fourth Earl of Breadalbane was one of the sixteen Scottish representative peers from 1784 to 1802. He was made Baron Breadalbane of Taymouth Castle in 1806, and Marquis in 1831. In 1786, the Highland Society met in London to discuss the encouragement of Scottish projects, among them, fishing. The Marquis of Breadalbane told the Meeting that one hundred people from Macdonald of Glengarry's estates had raised money to emigrate. The meeting agreed that they should try to move the Government to frustrate this wholesale emigration by helping Scottish fishing, agriculture and industry, and by raising money to achieve this end. Their announcement appeared in *The Edinburgh Advertiser* of 30th May.

Burns wrote his 'Address of Beelzebub' on this subject, prefacing it with the satiric comment: 'To The Rt Hon. the Earl of Breadalbane, President of The Rt Honorable and Honorable The Highland Society, which met on the 23rd of May last, at The Shakespeare, Covent Garden, to concert ways and means to frustrate the designs of FIVE HUNDRED HIGHLANDERS who, as The Society were informed by Mr M'Kenzie of Applecross, were so audacious as to attempt an escape from their lawful lords and masters whose property they were, by emigrating from the lands of Mr M'Donald of Glengarry to the lands of Canada, in search of that fantastic thing—LIBERTY.' Dr Johnson commented: 'The great business of insular policy is now to keep the people in their own country. As the world has been let in upon them they have heard of happier climates and less arbitrary government . . . all that go may be considered lost to the British crown.' Johnson, notoriously anti-Scottish, failed to see that political and sociological events stemming from the Union of 1707 had reduced the Highlanders, one of whom, at Anoch, had once reminded the Doctor that 'no man willingly left his native country'.

Even so, it is wryly amusing to find Burns supporting a cause which, within half a century, had become transformed into the tragic, compulsory evacuations of the Clearances!

Campbell of Netherplace, William, (d. 1786)

His estate lay between Mossgiel and Mauchline. He seems to have been a gentleman much ruled by his wife—Lilias Neilson (d. 1826), daughter of a Glasgow merchant —because Burns wrote three epitaphs on 'A Hen-pecked Country Squire'. The nastiest one is:

'One Queen Artemisia, as old stories tell,

When deprived of her husband she
                    lovèd so well,
In respect for the love and affection
                    he shewed her,
She reduced him to dust, and she
                    drank off the powder.
But Queen Netherplace, of a different
                    complexion,
When called on to order the funeral
                    direction
Would have ate her dead lord, on a
                    slender pretence,
Not to shew her respect, but—to save
                    the expense!'

Campbell, Thomas

A note of farewell from Burns to Campbell, dated, 'Mr J. Merry's, New Cumnock, Saturday morn: 19th Aug., 1786' is the only record of friendship between the two men, to survive. Burns says: 'I have met with few men in my life whom I more wished to see again than you, and Chance seems industrious to disappoint me of that pleasure. I came here yesterday fully resolved to see you . . . but a conjuncture of circumstances conspired against me. Having an opportunity of sending you a line, I joyfully embraced it. It is perhaps the last mark of our friendship you can receive from me on this side of the Atlantic. Farewell! May you be happy up to the wishes of parting Friendship!'

Campbell owned the small estate of Pencloe, in Glen Afton, about two miles from New Cumnock kirk.

Campbells

The reference in 'The Vision' to 'the Campbells, chiefs of fame', is to the Loudon branch of the clan, who owned Mossgiel and its neighbouring ground. Gavin Hamilton was their factor.

Candlish, James (1759–1806)

Born McCandlish, he was a boyhood neighbour and schoolmate of Burns. He studied medicine at Glasgow University, and in 1794 married Jean Smith, the sister of Burns's friend James Smith, linen-draper, and one of the Mauchline Belles. They had four children. About 1788, he settled in Edinburgh as a lecturer in medicine. In 1787 Burns sought his help in getting a song they had sung together at school, 'Pompey's Ghost', for the *Museum*. Candlish, in due course, did as he was asked, saying: 'Being myself unskilled in music as a science, I made an attempt to get the song you mentioned set by some other hand; but, as I could not accomplish this, I must send you the words without the music.'

In a letter to Peter Hill, dated March 1791, from Ellisland, Burns refers to Candlish as: 'the earliest friend except my only brother that I have on earth, and one of the worthiest fellows that ever any man called by the name of Friend'.

Capillaire Club

An Edinburgh Club whose membership was 'composed of all who inclined to be witty and joyous'. Captain Matthew Henderson was a member.

Capillaire was a syrup flavoured with Maidenhair fern—*Capillus veneris*.

Cardonnel, Adam de (d. 1820)

Afterwards Cardonnel-Lawson, he had studied medicine, but gave it up to concentrate on his love of antiquities and numismatics. He met Captain Grose when he came to Scotland in 1789, and helped him in his investigations. Shortly afterwards he left Scotland for Northumberland. His principal work was *Numismata Scotiae*.

When Burns did not know Grose's whereabouts, and wanted to effect an introduction between the Captain and Professor Dugald Stewart, he sent his letter to Grose care of Adam de Cardonnel, who lived in Edinburgh at the time. He also enclosed a copy of the humorous 'Verses on Captain Grose'.

Carfrae, Mrs

Burns's and Richmond's landlady at Edinburgh in Baxter's Close. According to Main, Mrs Carfrae charged Richmond two and sixpence a week for the rent of his room, increasing the charge to three shillings a week when Burns arrived.

Carfrae, The Reverend Patrick (1742–1822)

Educated at Edinburgh University, he was ordained minister of Morham in 1766, and translated to Dunbar in 1795, in which year he received the degree of Doctor of Divinity. He remained in Dunbar until he retired in 1820. He wrote the account of Morham in Sir John Sinclair's *Statistical Account of Scotland*, and took a leading part in preparing for the press James Mylne's *Poems, consisting of Miscellaneous Pieces and Two Tragedies*, about which he exchanged letters with Burns (see **Mylne, James**). Morham was the parish in which Mrs Dunlop lived. Because of his habit of preaching from manuscripts, Mr Carfrae was nicknamed 'Paper Pate'.

Carlins', 'The Five

The Election Ballad Burns wrote when Sir James Johnstone and Patrick Miller junior were contesting the seat of the Dumfries burghs. The burghs are represented as figurative characters.

'Maggy by the banks o' Nith, a dame wi' pride enough' was Dumfries; 'Marjory o' the mony Lochs, a carlin auld and teugh' was Lochmaben; 'Blinkin Bess of Annandale' was Annan; 'Whisky Jean that took her gill, in Galloway sae wide' was Kirkcudbright; and 'Black Joan frae Crichton-Peel, o' gipsy kith and kin' was Sanquhar.

Miller won the election.

Carlisle

The county town of Cumberland, England. While on his Border Tour, Burn stayed at the Malt Shovel Inn, Rickergate. From there, on 1st June 1787—'or I believe the 39th o' May rather'—Burns wrote a letter entirely in Scots—the only example of its kind to survive—addressed to 'Kind Honest-Hearted Willie' Nicol. It recounts the hardship of the day's journey, and the virtues of his mare. It goes on: 'I hae dander'd owre a' the kintra frae Dumbar to Selcraig, and hae forgather'd wi' monie a guid fallow, and monie a weel-far'd hizzie, I met wi' twa dink quines in particular, ane o' them a sonsie, fine fodgel lass, baith braw and bonie; the tither was a clean-shankit, straught, tight, weel-far'd winch, as blythe's a lintwhite on a flowerie thorn, and as sweet and modest's a new blawn plumrose in a hazle shaw. They were baith bred to mainers by the beuk, and onie ane o' them has as muckle smeddum and rumblegumtion as the half o' some Presbytries that you and I baith ken. They play'd me sik a deevil o' a shavie that I dair say if my harigals were turn'd out, ye wad see twa nicks i' the heart o' me like the mark o' a kail-whittle in a castock.'

In the *Journal of the Border Tour*, edited by Professor Fitzhugh, part of Burns's entry (taken, however, from Cunningham, this portion of the original manuscript having apparently disappeared) for Thursday, 31st May, reads:

'I came to Carlisle. (Meet a strange enough romantic adventure by the way in falling in with a girl and her married sister—the girl, after some overtures of gallantry on my side, sees me a little cut with the bottle, and offers to take me in for a Gretna-green affair. I, not being quite such a gull as she imagines, make an appointment with her, by way of vive la bagatelle, to hold a conference on it when we reach town. I meet her in town and give her a brush of caressing and a bottle of cyder; but finding herself un peu trompée in her man, she sheers off.) Next day I meet my good friend Mr Mitchell and walk with him round the town and its environs, and through his printing works, etc—four or five hundred people employed, many of them women and children. Dine with Mr Mitchell, and leave Carlisle.'

The printing works Burns visited may well have been the printfield of Messrs Mitchell, Ellwood and Co., one of four then in the city, and his host the partner in the firm.

Carmichael, Rebekah

A young poetess whose *Poems* appeared in 1790 and were sold by Peter Hill. Burns's name appears for two copies on the subscription list. On 2nd August 1791, Mrs M'Lehose asked him in a letter: 'Pray have you seen Greenfield's Poems? Or Miss Carmichael's? The last are very poor, I think.' Burns sent Miss Carmichael his own copy of the works of Robert Fergusson, with two lines written above and the following verse written under the portrait which served as a frontispiece:

'Curse on ungrateful man, that can be
                                        pleas'd
And yet can starve the author of the
                                        pleasure.
O thou, my elder brother in
                                        misfortune,
By far my elder brother in the muse,
With tears I pity thy unhappy fate!
Why is the bard unfitted for the
                                        world,
Yet has so keen a relish of its pleasures?'

Miss Carmichael later married a Mr Hay.

Carron

On Sunday, 26th August 1787, Burns and Nicol, embarked on their Highland tour, called at the Carron Iron Works, apparently with the somewhat surprising hope of being admitted. With a diamond he recently acquired, and which he used also on the windows of inns in Stirling and Falkirk, Burns wrote on a window of the inn at Carron:

'We cam na here to view your works,
  In hopes to be mair wise,
But only, lest we gang to hell,
  It may be nae surprise:
But when we tirl'd at your door,
  Your porter dought na hear us;
Sae may, shou'd we to hell's yetts
                                come,
  Your billy Satan sair us!'

The Carron Ironworks, some three
miles south of Falkirk, were founded
by Dr Roebuck of Sheffield in 1760.
During the Napoleonic wars, the Iron-
works turned out a useful piece of artillery
known as the Carronade.

Cassilis, Earls of. *See* Kennedy Family.

Catrine

Catrine House, a mile south-west of
Catrine town, was the seat of Professor
Dugald Stewart, the philosopher, and
of his father before him, Burns's 'learned
sire and son'. The small town of Catrine
lies in the parish of Sorn, on the river
Ayr, about two and a half miles from
Mauchline. Here in 1787, Claud Alex-
ander of Ballochmyle, brother of Burns's
'Bonnie lass o' Ballochmyle', established
a cotton factory in partnership with
David Dale. They also set up a cotton-
mill village, the growth of which drove
Professor Dugald Stewart to dispose of
Catrine House.

Burns dined with Stewart at Catrine
House on 23rd October 1786, and there met
Lord Daer, son of the Earl of Selkirk, the
outcome of which was the 'Lines on
Meeting Lord Daer'. Stewart was the
first of the Edinburgh intellectuals to
take Burns up socially. The poet sent
him copies of new poems on several
occasions.

A monument to Stewart by Playfair
stands on the Calton Hill, Edinburgh.

Cauvin, Louis (c. 1754-1825)

Taught Burns French in Edinburgh,
along with Beugo, the engraver. He said
that the poet made as much progress in
three months as any of his ordinary pupils
did in three years.

He retired latterly to a farm at Duddingston, and left his fortune to the parish
for the endowment of a hospital. His
father also taught French in Edinburgh.

Chalmers, Mrs Euphemia

Second daughter of Thomas Murdoch of
Cumloden, she married John Chalmers of
Fingland, and had two daughters, of
whom the younger was Margaret Chalmers. Mrs Chalmers lived with her
brother-in-law John Tait, W.S., at
Harvieston, where Burns met her.

Chalmers, James (1742-1810)

In the Journal of his Highland Tour of
1787, Burns's entry for Monday, 10th
September, reads: 'Meet with Mr Chalmers, Printer, a facetious fellow.' James
Chalmers was the son of D. Chalmers,
founder of the *Aberdeen Journal*. James
passed through Marischal College, studied
printing at London and Cambridge,
and on his father's death became editor
as well as printer of the *Aberdeen Journal*.

Chalmers, Margaret (1763?-1843)

The daughter of a farmer, her mother was
a sister of Gavin Hamilton's stepmother.
Margaret Chalmers was born at Fingland,
Kirkcudbrightshire. Her father was later
forced to sell his estates and took a farm
near Mauchline, where Burns may have
met her. Most recent biographers of Burns
agree that Peggy Chalmers was probably
the recipient of the undated latter, placed
by Ferguson in January 1787, which
begins: 'My dear Countrywoman' and
confesses love: 'I know you will laugh at
it, when I tell you that your Pianoforte
and you together have play'd the deuce
somehow, about my heart. I was once a
zealous Devotee to your Sex, but you
know the black story at home. My
breast has been widowed these many

months, and I thought myself proof against the fascinating witchcraft; but I am afraid you will "feelingly convince me what I am". I say, I am afraid, because I am not sure what is the matter with me, I have one miserable bad symptom, which I doubt threatens ill: when you whisper, or look kindly to another, it gives me a draught of damnation.'

Clearly, this is lover's language. Margaret Chalmers, when in Edinburgh, often played and sang for blind Dr Blacklock, and Burns probably met her again there.

In November, Burns addressed two love-songs to Margaret Chalmers: 'Where, braving angry winter's storms' (to the tune 'Neil Gow's Lamentation for Abercairney' it appeared in the *Museum* in 1788) and 'My Peggy's Face, my Peggy's Form' (which appeared in Thomson's *Scottish Airs* to an unauthorised air, in 1801, and in the *Museum*, 1803, to the air 'My Peggy's Face'). The second song begins:

'My Peggy's face, my Peggy's form,
The frost of Hermit age might warm;
My Peggy's worth, my Peggy's mind,
Might charm the first of human kind.
I love my Peggy's angel air,
Her face so truly, heavenly fair,
Her native grace so void of art,
But I adore my Peggy's heart.'

Burns followed this up with a letter from Edinburgh, dated December 1787, by Chambers, and (rather surprisingly) 6th November by Ferguson, which begins: 'I just now have read yours. The poetic compliments I pay cannot be misunderstood. They are neither of them so particular as to point *you* out to the world at large; and the circle of your acquaintances will allow all I have said. Besides I have complimented you chiefly, almost solely, on your mental charms. Shall I be plain with you? I will; so look to it. Personal attractions, madam, you have much above par; wit, understanding and

worth, you possess in the first class. This is a cursed flat way of telling you these truths, but let me hear no more of your timidity.'

Her 'timidity' was over Burns's proposed publication of the songs he had written to her. 'My Peggy's Face, my Peggy's Form' was, in fact, delayed for nearly fifteen years, and then divorced from the Gaelic air, 'Ha a chaillich air mo Dheith', which Burns originally intended for it.

On the third Highland tour, made in October 1787, Burns went to Harvieston and spent eight happy days in Peggy Chalmers's company. Years later, she told the poet Thomas Campbell, that Burns had proposed to her, but that she had refused him. She must have done so in a kindly manner, for she remained a confidante who received letters from him (sprinkled with French tags) almost up to the date of her marriage in December 1788 to a banker, Lewis Hay, of Sir William Forbes's bank in Edinburgh.

Writing to her from Ellisland on 16th September 1788, and remembering that Harvieston visit, Burns burst out: '... when I think I have met with you, and have lived more of real life with you in eight days than I can do with almost anybody I meet with in eight years— when I think on the improbability of meeting you in this world again—I could sit down and cry like a child!'

Peggy Chalmers was undoubtedly one of the only two intellectually able women with whom Burns became friendly (the other was Maria Riddell). That he loved her is obvious, not only from her own story of his proposal, but from his remark in a letter of 10th January 1788, to Mrs M'Lehose, that he registered a female friend 'in my heart's core by Peggy Chalmers'.

That she seemed an obvious choice as a wife for Burns from Mrs M'Lehose's standpoint is clear from her question in a letter of 31st January 1788: 'Miss Chalmers' letters are charming. Why did not such a woman secure your heart? O the caprice of human nature, to fix on impossibilities.'

Miss Chalmers's letters to Burns have disappeared. According to Cromek, Mrs Adair (*née* Charlotte Hamilton) threw Burns's letters to Peggy Chalmers into the fire. Certainly, the series is incomplete; but one wonders how those which have survived did so if Cromek's story was entirely true. (Burns did not normally date his drafts, and a number of the Margaret Chalmers letters which have been traced are dated.)

In the *Burns Chronicle* for 1944, Margaret Chalmers's obituary notice from *The Scotsman* of 1st April 1843, is printed. The obituary was reprinted from the *Inverness Courier*, where it first appeared. It reads: 'Died at Pau, in Bearn (Berne), on the 3rd inst. Mrs Lewis Hay, daughter of James Chalmers, Esq., of Fingland, and widow of Lewis Hay, Esq., one of the partners of the Banking House of Sir William Forbes, J. Hunter and Co. Ed'. She settled in Berne after the death of her husband in 1800. She had three sons and three daughters.

See Plate 7.

Chalmers, William

A Writer and Notary Public in Ayr, who drew up the notarial intimation of the assignation of Burns's property in favour of Gilbert, his brother, when the poet meditated flight to Jamaica. At the same time, Chalmers asked Burns to write a poem for him to present to his young lady. The result was the poem, 'To Willie Chalmers' Sweetheart', in which Burns humorously advances the merits of his friend's amorous cause and gives the girl this advice:

'Some gapin, glowrin countra laird
  May warsle for your favour;
May claw his lug, and straik his beard,
  And hoast up some palaver:

My bonie maid, before ye wed
  Sic clumsy-witted hammers,
Seek Heaven for help, and barefit skelp
  Awa wi' Willie Chalmers.'

In November 1786, Chalmers was called upon by Burns in a humorous mock-mandate ('In the name of the NINE. Amen!') to burn an enclosed 'bawdy, nefarious, abominable and wicked song or ballad'. He sent Chalmers copies of some of his poems, including the 'Address to Edinburgh'.

Chapman, Dr

Headmaster of Banff Grammar School when Burns and Nicol breakfasted with him on their Highland tour. Nicol had been a junior master at Dumfries Academy under Chapman, when Chapman was headmaster there.

Charteris, the younger, of Amisfield, Francis, (1749–1808)

Thirty-sixth Grand Mastermason of Scotland from 1786 to 1787. He was a member of Lodge Harrington St John, and an affiliated member of Canongate Kilwinning. His father succeeded to the Earldom of Wemyss in 1787, when Charteris became Lord Elcho. He himself never succeeded to the title, as he predeceased his father by ten months. He subscribed for four copies of the Edinburgh Edition.

In a letter to John Ballantine, dated 14th January 1787, Burns referred to a masonic meeting, where 'the Most Worshipful Grand Master Charters, and all the Grand Lodge of Scotland visited. The meeting was most numerous and elegant; all the different Lodges about town were present, in all their pomp. The Grand Master who presided with great solemnity, and honor to himself as a Gentleman and Mason, among other general toasts gave, "Caledonia, and Caledonia's Bard, brother B—", which rung through the whole Assembly with multiplied honors and repeated acclamations.' The poet had no idea that this was to happen, and: 'downright thunderstruck, and trembling in every nerve, made the best return in my power. Just as I finished, some of the Grand Officers said so loud as I could hear, with a most comforting accent, "Very well indeed!" which set me something to rights again.'

Chesterfield, fourth Earl of. *See* **Stanhope**.

Chloris. *See* **Lorimer, Jean**.

Christison, Alexander (c. 1753–1820)
A master at Edinburgh High School who later became Professor of Humanity at Edinburgh University. Sir Robert Christison, physician and professor of Medical Jurisprudence and Materia Medica, was his son.

It was at the Christisons' house in Edinburgh that Burns, according to Cromek, said to a minister who was criticising Gray's 'Elegy' in general and inaccurate terms: 'Sir, I now perceive a man may be an excellent judge of poetry by square and rule, and after all, be a d— blockhead!' The minister is said to have been the Reverend William Robb of Tongland, Kirkcudbrightshire, who died in 1797.

Clarinda. *See* **M'Lehose, Agnes**.

Clark, Samuel, Jun. (1769–1814)
A solicitor in Dumfries and, according to his tombstone in St Michael's kirkyard, Conjunct Commissary Clerk and Clerk of the Peace for the County. He married Mary Wight in 1798, and had fourteen children. He was a friend of Burns and it was in Clark's company that the poet gave the toast in January 1794 at the time of the French Revolution: 'May our success in our present war be equal to the justice of our cause', a toast which

Burns later claimed 'the most outrageous frenzy of loyalty' could not object to. But a certain Captain Dods did take exception to the toast, and words were exchanged: 'such as generally . . . end up in a brace of pistols'. Burns was afraid that news of this affair might damage his reputation with the Excise Commissioners, and wrote two frenzied, undated letters to Clark, appealing for his support in seeing that the incident was not misrepresented to the Supervisor General, William Corbet, and that 'every gentleman who was present' should be assured of the poet's regrets.

Clark, William
Provost of Dumfries in 1787, when Burns received the freedom of the burgh on 4th June.

Clark, William
Burns's servant at Ellisland, during the winter half-year of 1789–90. Clark gave the following recollection of Burns to Chambers for his *Life and Works of Burns*:

'Soon after Burns became tenant of Ellisland, William Clark lived with him as servant during the winter half-year, he thinks, of 1789–90. . . .

'Burns kept two men and two women servants; but he invariably, when at home, took his meals with his wife and family in the little parlour. Clark thought he was as good a manager of land as the generality of the farmers in the neighbourhood. The farm of Ellisland was said to be moderately rented, and was susceptible of much improvement, had improvement been in repute. Burns sometimes visited the neighbouring farmers, and they returned the compliment; but that way of spending time and exchanging civilities was not so common then as now, and, besides, the most of the people thereabouts had no expectation that Burns's conduct and writings would be so much noticed afterwards. Burns kept nine or ten milch cows, some young cattle, four horses, and several pet sheep: of the latter he was very fond. During the winter and spring time, when he was not engaged with the Excise business, he occasionally held the plough for an hour or so for him (William Clark), and was a fair workman, though the mode of ploughing now-a-days is much superior in many respects. During seed-time, Burns might be frequently seen, at an early hour, in the fields with his sowing-sheet; but as business often required his attention from home, he did not sow the whole of the grain. He was a kind and indulgent master, and spoke familiarly to his servants, both in the house and out of it, though, if anything put him out of humour, he was gey gul-dersome for a wee while: the storm was soon over, and there was never a word of upcast afterwards. Clark never saw him really angry but once, and it was occasioned by the carelessness of one of the woman-servants who had not cut potatoes small enough, which brought one of the cows into danger of being choked. His looks, gestures, and voice on that occasion were terrible: W.C. was glad to be out of his sight, and when they met again Burns was perfectly calm. If any extra work was to be done, the men sometimes got a dram; but Clark had lived with masters who were more flush in that way to their servants. Clark, during the six months he spent at Ellisland, never once saw his master intoxicated or incapable of managing his own business . . . Burns, when at home, usually wore a broad blue bonnet, a blue or drab long-tailed coat, corduroy breeches, dark-blue stock-ings, and cootikens, and in cold weather a black-and-white-checked plaid wrapped round his shoulders. Mrs Burns was a good and prudent housewife, kept every-thing in neat and tidy order, was well liked by the servants, for whom she provided abundance of wholesome food. At parting, Burns gave Clark a certificate of character, and, besides paying his wages in full, gave him a shilling for a fairing.'

Clarke, James (1761?–1825)

Born at Closeburn, Dumfriesshire, he became a schoolmaster at Moffat Grammar school in 1786, and first librarian of the Subscription Library there.

About 1790 he married Jane Simpson, a native of Cumberland. They had three daughters. In 1791 he was charged with cruelty to his pupils by the authorities of Moffat, who, with Lord Hopetoun behind them, did all they could to have him discredited. Burns took up his cause, writing to Alexander Cunningham on 11th June 1791, on Clarke's behalf. Burns also drafted a letter for Clarke to send to the Lord Provost of Edinburgh, one of the patrons of the school, asking for a fair hearing; and in 1792, when the row was at its worst, Burns tried to get Clarke another position through the good offices of Robert Riddell. Clarke remained at Moffat, vindicated, until he was appointed, in 1794, master of the Burgh School at Forfar. There he re-mained, apparently successful and respec-ted, until 1802, when he became rector at the grammar school in Cupar, Fife. He finally retired to Dollar, where he kept a boarding-house and had as a neighbour William Tennant, the author of 'Anster Fair'. Clarke was apparently a good musician and fiddler. Though at the time of Clarke's trouble, Burns himself was hard-pressed, he seems to have lent the schoolmaster a considerable sum of money, which the schoolmaster was still paying back in small sums at the time of the poet's death. Burns's last letter to him, written on 26th June 1796, from Dumfries, is an acknow-ledgement of one such repayment, and an appeal for another 'by return of post'.

Clarke, Stephen (d. 1797)

Clarke was an Edinburgh musician and music teacher whom James Johnson had brought in to harmonise the airs for his Scots Musical Museum. In 1787, when

Burns became involved in the project, Clarke was organist of the Episcopal Chapel in the Cowgate, Edinburgh. After his death, his son William continued the work.

Clarke seems to have been somewhat indolent, even careless. Burns's letters abound in expressions of exasperation at him. To begin with, it was 'Clarke, the well-known Musician, presides over the musical arrangement' when Burns was writing to James Hoy on 20th October 1787, announcing his involvement in the *Museum*. Writing from Ellisland on 19th June 1789, Burns told Johnson: 'Mr Clarke and I have frequent meetings and consultations on your work.' In July 1792, Burns undertook to get Clarke to come to Drumlanrig to give singing lessons to two of the M'Murdo girls. Clarke seems to have ignored the first request, and on 16th July Burns followed it up with a humorous letter: 'Mr Burns begs leave to present his most respectful Compliments to Mr Clarke. Mr B— some time ago did himself the honor of writing Mr C— respecting coming out to the country to give a little Musical instruction in a highly respectable family, where Mr C— may have his own terms, amd may be as happy as Indolence, the Devil, and the Gout will permit him. Mr B— knows well that Mr C— is engaged so long with another family; but cannot Mr C— find two or three weeks to spare to each of them? Mr B— is deeply impressed with, and awefully conscious of, the high importance of Mr. C—'s time, whether in the winged moments of symphonious exhibition at the keys of Harmony, while listening Seraphs cease from their own less delightful strains; or in the drowsy hours of slumbrous repose, in the arms of his dearly beloved elbow-chair, where the frowsy but potent Power of Indolence, circumfuses her vapours round, and sheds her dews on the head of her DARLING SON— but half a line conveying half a meaning from Mr C— would make Mr B— the very happiest of mortals.'

Burns's quippery had its effect, and Clarke went to the M'Murdos. The visit resulted in some songs for the M'Murdo girls, including, 'There was a lass and she was fair'. Burns told George Thomson in July 1793; 'Mr Clarke, who wrote down the air from Mrs Burns's woodnote wild, is very fond of it; and has given it a celebrity by teaching it to some young ladies of the first fashion here.' Thomson, however, disliked the air, which was subsequently lost! From a foot-note to another letter to Thomson in the same month, it would seem that Clarke was now also teaching in the family of Patrick Miller of Dalswinton.

In later letters to both Johnson and Thomson, references to Clarke's indolence abound. Once, he even went so far as to lose a song-packet altogether, not all of which Burns could replace from memory.

Today, Clarke's harmonisations in the *Museum* seem rudimentary. But they are at least more lastingly acceptable than the florid accompaniments Thomson got out of Beethoven, Haydn, Pleyel and the others, which delight us now solely as period pieces. Furthermore, Clarke's treatment conforms to the criterion of taste in such matters laid down by the eighteenth-century musical historian Hugo Arnot: 'The proper accompaniment of a Scots song is a plain dropping bass, on the harpsichord or guitar. The full chords of a thorough bass should be used sparingly and with judgment, not to overpower but to support and raise the voice at proper pauses.'

Clarke's other publications included a set of *Sonatas based on Scots Airs*. Burns passed on his copy to Maria Riddell, saying they were 'of no use to me'.

Cleghorn, Robert (d. 1798?)

Born at Corstorphine, near Edinburgh,

Cleghorn came of an Episcopalian family, whose birth and death dates therefore do not appear in the register of the Parish Kirk.

He farmed at Saughton Mills, near Edinburgh, and was a keen supporter of the 'Crochallan Fencibles'. He married a widow named Allen. Their son, John, was a friend of Byron, and upset the puritanical streak in the make-up of the rakish 'Milord' by showing him Burns's letters to his grandfather.

When he was in Edinburgh, Burns was a frequent visitor to Saughton Mills. Besides being a skilful farmer, Cleghorn had a good voice, and Burns sent him songs on several occasions, including his 'Chevalier's Lament' to the air Captain O'Kean'. In August 1795, Cleghorn and his brother-in-law and stepson visited Burns at Dumfries. After the poet's death, Cleghorn was a handsome contributor to the Subscription raised for his widow and family.

It is quite clear from the surviving letters between Burns and Cleghorn that the poet regarded him as the most appreciative recipient of his bawdy verse, some of it original, some of it traditional, passed down verbally from one male generation to another. These pieces eventually appeared in the collection known as *The Merry Muses of Caledonia* (*see* **Merry Muses**).

Writing to Cleghorn on 25th October 1793, Burns says: 'There is, there must be, some truth in original sin. My violent propensity to B—dy convinces me of it. Lack a day! if that species of Composition be the Sin against the Holy Ghaist, I am the most offending soul alive.'

Clinton, Sir Henry (1738?–95)

Only son of Admiral, the Honourable George Clinton, Governor of Newfoundland and later of New York. He quickly rose to the rank of Major-General, and having accompanied Generals Howe and Burgoyne to America during the War of Independence, distinguished himself at Bunker's Hill. He became Howe's Second-in-Command, and finally took over the command of the British Forces in America from Howe. When his own Second-in-Command, Lord Cornwallis, capitulated at Yorktown in 1781, thereby finally losing the American colonies, Clinton resigned and returned to England.

He was voted M.P. for Boroughbridge in 1772 through the influence of his cousin, the second Duke of Newcastle. In 1790 he entered Parliament again, this time as representative for Launceston. He died at Gibraltar, where he was Governor.

He and General Howe are both praised for their generalship by Burns in his 'Address of Beelzebub'.

Clow, Jenny

A girl with whom Burns had a purely physical liaison in Edinburgh, while engaged in his unconsummated affair with Clarinda. Jenny bore him a son, whom Burns was willing to take into his home, but she would not part with him. In November 1791, as Burns arrived in Dumfries, he received a letter from 'Clarinda', informing him that Jenny Clow 'to all appearances is at this moment dying. Obliged, from all the symptoms of a rapid decay, to quit her service, she is gone to a room almost without common necessaries, untended and unmourned. In circumstances so distressing, to whom can she so naturally look for aid as to the father of her child. . . .' Burns asked Mrs M'Lehose to get a porter to take five shillings from the poet to Jenny.

The complete text of a letter to Ainslie from Ellisland, dated 6th January 1789, makes it clear that Burns intended to see Jenny in Edinburgh, 'settle that matter with her, and free her hand of the process'. Apparently she had served the poet with a writ, as did May Cameron under similar circumstances.

Cockburn, Mrs Alison (1712–94)

Authoress of one of the versions of 'The Flowers of the Forest', and for sixty years one of the 'queens of Edinburgh society'. The daughter of Robert Rutherford of Fairnilee, in Selkirkshire, she married Patrick Cockburn, an advocate, in 1731. Nine years before she met Burns she had described Walter Scott as 'the most extraordinary genius of a boy'.

In one of her letters she recorded her opinion of Burns: 'The town is at present (December 1786) agog with the ploughman poet, who receives adulation with native dignity, and is the figure of his profession, strong and coarse, but has a most enthusiastick heart of LOVE. He has seen dutchess Gordon and all the gay world: his favrite for looks and manners is Bess Burnett—no bad judge indeed.' In another letter she wrote: 'The man will be spoiled if he can spoil, but he keeps his simple manners, and is quite sober.'

Mrs Cockburn's niece was Elizabeth Scott (1729–89), wife of Walter Scott of Wauchope, near Jedburgh. Mrs Cockburn lent her niece a copy of the Kilmarnock Poems.

Cochrane, Lady Elizabeth (1745–1811)

The daughter of the eighth Earl of Dundonald, she married Patrick Heron. She was the composer of an air, 'The Banks of Cree', for which Burns wrote the song beginning 'Here is the glen and here the bower'. In 1794, he sent both air and words to George Thomson, who, however, disliked the air, and despite Burns's orders to the contrary, published the song to the tune of 'The Flowers of Edinburgh'. There is now no trace of Lady Elizabeth's air.

Coil, River

A tributary of the River Ayr, mentioned in 'The Brigs of Ayr'.

Coilsfield

Burns's 'Castle o' Montgomerie' was, in his day, the home of Colonel Hugh Montgomerie, later Earl of Eglinton. The estate was almost six miles from Ayr, on the Ayr to Mauchline road, and on the right bank of the Faile Burn. Mary Campbell is supposed to have worked at Coilsfield as a dairy-maid. The name is said to derive from the belief that Coilus, or Coel Hen, King of the Picts, was buried nearby. Burns wrote:

'Ye banks and braes and streams
                                          around
   The castle o' Montgomerie,
Green be your woods, and fair your
                                          flours,
   Your waters never drumlie!
There simmer first unfauld her robes,
   And there the langest tarry;
For there I took the last farewell
   O' my sweet Highland Mary.'

Coilus or Coila

Coilus or Coel Hen, was a King of the Picts, from whose name the Ayrshire district of Kyle derives. He is also said to be the original of the nursery rhyme 'Old King Cole'. Tradition has it that he is buried near the family seat of the Montgomeries of Coilsfield, where the place is said to be a small mound marked by a few trees. When it was opened up in 1837, two urns were revealed containing ashes, but whose they were was, naturally, not discoverable! In 'The Vision', the reference to Coilus is:

'There, where a sceptr'd Pictish shade
Stalk'd round his ashes lowly laid.'

Burns took the name Coila for his muse (see 'The Vision': 'Coila my name; and this district as mine I claim').

When Mrs Dunlop informed the poet that a woman painter was engaged in painting Coila, Burns replied, writing from Mossgiel on 7th March 1788: 'I an highly flattered by the news you tell me of Coila. I may say to the fair painter who does me so much honor, as Dr

Beattie says to Ross, the poet of his muse Scota, from which, by the by, I took the idea of Coila ('tis a poem of Beattie's in the Scottish dialect, which perhaps you have never seen)—

> "Ye shake your head, but o' my fegs,
> Ye've set auld Scota on her legs;
> Lang had she been in beffs and flegs,
>   Bumbaz'd and dizzie,
> Her fiddle wanted strings and pegs,
>   Wae's me, poor hizzie." '

The poem, Dr James Beattie's only excursion into Scots, is titled 'To Mr. Alexander Ross at Lochlee, author of The Fortunate Shepherdess and other poems in the broad Scottish dialect.'

'Comin' Thro' the Rye'

Burns's popular song, set to the strathspey 'The Miller's Wedding', appeared in The Scots Musical Museum in 1796. A broader version exists in 'The Merry Muses'. The tune is related to those of 'Auld Lang Syne', and 'O can ye labour lea, young man'.

Commonplace Books

Burns left two Commonplace Books. The first, which was clearly not intended for publication, was begun in April 1783 and abruptly terminated in October 1785. It contained a number of his earlier poems, and numerous reflections on life and poetry.

The second Commonplace Book was begun in Edinburgh in April 1787 and seems much more of a rough draft of ideas and observations intended for later use. The estimates of Blair and Greenfield, quoted in the articles upon these divines, are an example. The second Commonplace Book is sometimes loosely referred to as the Edinburgh Journal.

Concordance

A Burns concordance, compiled and edited by J. B. Reid, was published in Glasgow in 1889. Its full title is: A Complete Word and Phrase Concordance to the Poems and Songs of Robert Burns, incorporating a glossary of Scotch words, with notes, index, and appendix of readings.

Connel, James

A Mauchline carrier, of whom Burns sometimes made use.

Constable, Lady Winifred Maxwell (1736–1801)

The only surviving child of the sixth and last Earl of Nithsdale, who forfeited his lands for his share in the 1715 rising. Herself a staunch Jacobite, she married William Haggerston Constable of Everingham in 1758, who assumed the name and arms of Maxwell.

Lady Winifred, on her return to Scotland after a protracted absence, rebuilt her ancestral home, Terreagles, in the Stewartry of Kirkcudbright. Burns occasionally visited her there, and his 'Nithsdale's Welcome Hame' was written for her return. In a letter to her from Ellisland, dated 16th December 1789, he remarks: '. . . with your Ladyship I have the honor to be connected by one of the strongest and most endearing ties in the whole Moral World— Common Sufferers in a Cause where even to be unfortunate is glorious, the Cause of Heroic Loyalty.' Burns then repeated his cherished belief that his ancestors were 'out' in the Jacobite risings: 'Though my Fathers had not illustrious Honors and vast Properties to hazard in the contest; though they left only their humble cottages only to add so many units more to the unnoted croud that followed their Leaders; yet, what they could they did, and what they had they lost: with unshaken firmness and unconcealed Political Attachment, they shook hands with Ruin for what they esteemed the cause of their King and their Country.' With this letter, Burns sent a copy of his verses, 'To William Tytler Esq. of Woodhouselee.'

'Revered defender of beauteous Stuart
Of Stuart, a name once respected;
A name which to love was the mark
                    of a true hert,
But now 'tis despised and neglected. . .'

(Incidentally, the second stanza begins
with what was surely Burns's worst line:

'Tho' something like moisture
                conglobes in my eye!')

When Burns was laid up with a broken
right arm in the spring of 1791, he received
from Lady Winifred the present of a
snuff-box containing on the lid an inlaid
miniature of Queen Mary. (Chambers
wrote that: 'Many years after, one of the
poet's sons, having taken this box with
him to India, had the misfortune to
damage the portrait irreparably in leaping
on board a vessel.') Burns replied to Lady
Winifred on 25th April 1791, thanking
her for the gift: 'I assure your Ladyship,
I shall set it apart: the symbols of Religion
shall only be more sacred. In the moment
of Poetic composition, the Box shall be
my inspiring Genius.'

Copland of Collieston, William
Advocate and Kirkcudbrightshire land-
owner. His 'whiskers' are mentioned
in Burns's second Heron Election Ballad.

Corbet, William (1755–1811)
A senior officer of the Excise whose
influence was of assistance to Burns in his
own Excise career.

According to Joseph Farington, R.A.,
who met Burns at Friar's Carse in 1792, and
who, when he revisited Scotland in
1801 had dinner in Glasgow with Corbet's
brother, Corbet: 'was the officer who
succeeded to the command of the
troops engaged in the Island of Jersey
after Major Peirson was killed. His
portrait is in the picture printed by Copley
of that subject.' Unfortunately, Farington
did not identify Corbet in Copley's
picture, which is now in the National

Gallery, London. The Battle of Jersey was
a French raid upon the island in 1781.

If Farington's reminiscence was accurate, Corbet must have been promoted
in the Excise service with some rapidity,
for in 1784 he is listed as being a Supervisor at Linlithgow. In 1786 and 1787 he
was Supervisor-General at Stirling, and
from 1789 to 1791, Acting Supervisor-
General at Edinburgh, a post he held permanently thereafter until 1797, when he
became Collector of the Excise at Glasgow.
At Glasgow, he was a member of the
convivial club called the Board of Green
Cloth. He married Jean McAdam of
Kirkcudbright, by whom he had several
children. His Glasgow address was 14
Miller Street. He died at Meadowside, Par-
tick, and was buried in the cemetery of
Ramshorn Church.

He first appears in the Burns story in
February 1790, when Mrs Dunlop asked
Burns if a Mr Corbet in the Excise
'could be of any use' in getting him on.
If so, she could perhaps renew an old
friendship with Mrs Corbet on his behalf.

Burns replied in March 1790: 'You
formerly wrote me, if a Mr Corbet in
the Excise could be of use to me. If it is a
Corbet who is what we call one of our
General Supervisors, of which we have
just two in Scotland, he can do everything
for me. Were he to interest himself
properly for me, he could easily, by
Martinmas 1791, transport me to Port
Glasgow, port Division, which would
be the ultimatum of my present Excise
hopes.' ('A Port Division,' Burns explained
to Mrs Dunlop on 3rd February 1792, 'is
twenty pounds a year more than any
other Division, besides as much rum and
brandy as will easily supply an ordinary
family.')

Mrs Dunlop wrote to Mrs Corbet,
and after an unnecessary setback of despair
because rumour had promoted Corbet
Collector seven years ahead of fact, she
managed to interest him in Burns. At
any rate, towards the end of 1790, Corbet

apparently asked Findlater, Dumfries Supervisor and Burns's immediate superior, to let him have an assessment of the poet's character and ability.

Two days before Christmas 1790, Findlater wrote to Corbet, describing Burns as 'an active, faithful and zealous officer' who 'gives the most unremitting attention to the duties of his office . . . and, tho' his experience must be as yet small, he is capable, as you may well suppose, of achieving [sic] a much more arduous task than any difficulty that the theory or practice of our business can exhibit'.

Corbet, one infers from Burns's own references to him, did actually visit Dumfries and meet the poet, late in 1791 or early in 1792. He may have been responsible for getting Burns transferred to a 'foot-walk' in Dumfries—'Dumfries third division'—just before the poet left Ellisland, instead of the laborious rural district—'Dumfries first itinerary'—which often involved riding 200 miles a week. He certainly stood by Burns when, in December 1792, the poet's radical opinions and utterances led someone to denounce him to the Excise Board as unpatriotic. The usual routine enquiry in such cases was ordered and Burns drove himself frantic with worry and fright over the threat to his livelihood. Corbet came to Dumfries to conduct the inquiry, along with Mitchell and Findlater; but Findlater testified that Burns was 'exact, vigilant, and sober, that, in fact, he was one of the best officers in the district'.

No stain on Burns's character was put on record, but Corbet probably gave him some friendly, plain-spoken advice, making it clear that 'whatever might be Men or Measures', it was for the poet 'to be silent and obedient'.

Cornwallis, Charles (1738–1805)
Later first Marquis, Cornwallis fought with distinction at Philadelphia, and was appointed British commander in Carolina. He defeated Gates in August 1780, and

Nathaniel Greene in March 1781. He surrendered at Yorktown 18th October 1781. He is mentioned in Burns's 'Fragment' of 1784, 'When Guilford good,' which inspired Blair to remark that 'Burns's politics always smell of the smithy'.

Corri, Domenico (1746–1825)
An Italian composer, conductor and music publisher. Born in Rome, he became a pupil of Porpora at Naples.

On Dr Burney's recommendation, Corri and his wife, a singer, were invited to Edinburgh in 1781, where he became conductor of the Musical Society, a position he retained for eighteen years. He lived for part of each year in Edinburgh, and part in London. About 1790, his 'piano manufacturing' and music selling business failed, and he settled permanently in London, where he went into partnership with the pianist and composer Dussek, who married his daughter.

He died at Hampstead. His son, Natale, also settled in Edinburgh, and ran Corri's Concert Room, at the top of Leith Walk, among his other musical activities.

Corri's works included the operas *Alessandro Nell Indie* and *The Travellers.* He wrote *Six Canzones dedicated to Scots Ladies.* More important was his *New and Complete Collection of the most favourite Scots Songs including a few English and Irish* which he published in 1783, and which had a title page designed by David Allan. Burns made several references to Corri's Scots songs in his letters to Thomson, revealing his knowledge of these, as of all such collections of the period.

George Thomson said it was Corri's singing of old Scots songs which first led him to begin to make his own collection.

Corsincon
A hill 1,547 feet high, in New Cumnock parish, about 25 miles from Ellisland. It is mentioned in the song 'O, were I on

Parnassus Hill' and in 'Does Haughty Gaul Invasion Threat?'

'O, were I on Parnassus hill,
Or had o' Helicon my fill,
That I might catch poetic skill
    To sing how dear I love thee!
But Nith maun be my Muse's well,
My Muse maun be thy bonie sel',
On Corsincon I'll glow'r and spell,
    And write how dear I love thee.'

Cotter's Saturday Night', 'The

The poem by which, a handful of songs apart, Burns is probably best known, was written in the autumn of 1785, or early in the winter of 1785-6. Gilbert Burns recorded his recollections of its origin: 'Robert had frequently remarked to me that he thought there was something peculiarly venerable in the phase, "Let us worship God!" used by a decent, sober head of a family, introducing family worship. To this sentiment of the author, the world is indebted for "The Cotter's Saturday Night". When Robert had not some pleasure in view in which I was not thought fit to participate, we used frequently to walk together, when the weather was favourable, on the Sunday afternoons—those precious breathing times to the labouring part of the community—and enjoyed such Sundays as would make one regret to see their number abridged. It was on one of these walks that I first had the pleasure of hearing the author repeat "The Cotter's Saturday Night". I do not recollect to have read or heard anything by which I was more highly electrified. The fifth and sixth stanzas and the eighteenth thrilled with peculiar ecstasy through my soul. The cotter in the "Saturday Night" is an exact copy of my father in his manners, his family devotion, and exhortations; yet the other parts of the description do not apply to our family. None of us were "at service out among the farmer's men". Instead of our depositing our "sair-won penny-fee" with our parents, my father laboured hard, and lived with the most rigid economy, that he might be able to keep his children at home, thereby having an opportunity of watching the progress of our young minds, and forming in them early habits of piety and virtue; and from this motive alone did he engage in farming, the source of all his difficulties and distresses.'

The poem was first published in the Kilmarnock Edition, although manuscript copies were given to some of Burns's friends, notably John Kennedy. Henry Mackenzie saw in the poem a description of 'one of the happiest and most affecting scenes to be found in a country life . . . a domestic picture of rustic simplicity, natural tenderness, and innocent passion that must please the reader whose feelings are not perverted'.

Later critics, with more detachment, have, however, drawn attention to the dichotomy between the English Augustan style in which some of the stanzas are couched, and the Scots vernacular style of the purely descriptive stanzas, modelled on Fergusson's 'The Farmer's Ingle'. David Allan, 'The Scottish Hogarth,' illustrated the poem. In a letter to George Thomson, dated May 1795, Burns sent his grateful compliments to Allan, 'that he has honored my rustic Muse so much with his masterly pencil'.

See Plate 13.

Court of Equity, The

The title of a secret bachelors' association, whose members met sporadically at the Whitefoord Arms Inn, Mauchline. The purpose of the association was 'to search out, report, and discuss the merits and demerits of the many scandals that crop up from time to time in the village', and to determine what punishment should be meted out to the offenders. Burns was 'Perpetual President'; John Richmond 'Clerk of the Court'; James Smith 'Procurator Fiscal'; and William

Hunter 'Messenger at Arms'. The association became defunct when Burns left the Mauchline district.

Its meetings were commemorated in a humorously bawdy poem, 'The Court of Equity,' which has hitherto been excluded from collected editions of the poet's work, but which is printed in full as an appendix to Catherine Carswell's excellently human study, *The Life of Robert Burns* (1930), in Cyril Pearl's *Bawdy Burns* (1958), and in James Kinsley's *The Poems and Songs of Robert Burns* (1968) as 'Libel Summons—'

Coutts, Alexander

A Whitehaven man, hitherto unidentified, who apparently sent Burns two rhyming 'elegant epistles'. A short note from Ellisland, dated 28th April 1791, begs time to answer them 'in kind'. So far as we know, they were never so answered.

Craig, Andrew (d. 1782)

Son of Andrew C. Craig, a Glasgow Merchant, and father of Agnes, who became Burns's 'Clarinda'. Craig had been elected to the Faculty of Physicians and Surgeons in 1745, and the following year was made Town Surgeon at a salary of £10 per annum. Most of his income, of course, came from his private patients. Agnes, born at the Craig home in the Saltmarket, was the Craig's fifth child, though only one other, Margaret, survived. Craig's wife died in 1767.

Craig disapproved of the proposed marriage of his daughter to the young lawyer James M'Lehose, and forbade M'Lehose his house, then as now a sure way of cementing rather than breaking an undesirable relationship. But his daughter prevailed, and her father gave her away at her wedding on 25th June 1776, when she was not yet seventeen. Very probably the marriage took place in St Andrew's Church, St Andrew's Square, Glasgow, where her uncle, the Reverend William Craig, ministered.

By 1780, Agnes had returned to her father's house, where she had her fourth child. But her father died on 13th May 1782, whereupon Agnes M'Lehose moved to Edinburgh.

Craig, who had been in poor health for some time before his death, left her the rents on some property in Glasgow (which was sold to provide her with an annuity), and fifty pounds in the bank. Craig stipulated in his will that none of his effects must come into the hands of M'Lehose.

Craig, William, Lord (1745-1813)

Son of William Craig, a minister in Glasgow, and cousin-german of Burns's 'Clarinda'. He was raised to the bench as Lord Craig in 1792, and in 1795 became a judge of the Court of Justiciary. According to an article in the *Burns Chronicle* of 1924, the author had gone over a manuscript of Lord Craig's poems, which were 'of the *Man of Feeling* order'. The manuscript is prefaced by the following notes:

'These poems from the pen of Lord Craig, better known as a contributor to the *Mirror* and the *Lounger* than as a lawyer, have never been printed.

'Lord Craig was Cousin of Burns's Clarinda and these MSS. were given to her son (Andrew M'Lehose, W.S.) by him. To this gentleman Lord Craig left a considerable sum of money and his library, on his decease. The Library was sold shortly before the death of the beneficiare, who had become impoverished.'

Craig, and some other advocates, belonged to the literary society called the 'Tabernacle', who met and discussed and read essays in a tavern. Craig suggested they publish their essays. The society's name was accordingly changed to the 'Mirror Club', and the publication was called *The Mirror*. It was published by Creech on Tuesdays and Saturdays, the first issue appearing on Saturday 23rd January 1779. The 110th and last issue appeared on 27th May 1780.

Henry Mackenzie and Lord Craig made the most numerous contributions, the latter bringing into notice the poems of the gifted young Michael Bruce.

See Plate 9.

Craigieburn

A locality near Moffat, Dumfriesshire, where the parents of Jean ('Chloris') Lorimer lived, and where she was born in 1775. The Craigie is a burn which joins the River Moffat nearby. Burns writes of the district in his song 'Craigieburn Wood'.

Craik, Helen (1750?-1825)

The spinster daughter of the head of the family of Craik of Arbigland in Kirkbean parish, about twelve miles south of Dumfries. Burns may have been introduced to her by Captain Riddell or by Captain Hamilton. At any rate, he paid a visit to Arbigland. A versifier herself, Helen Craik was deeply steeped in *Werther*, and other sentimental favourites of the day. She was the authoress of the lines, written in a hand other than Burns's, on the title-page of the Glenriddell Manuscript of his poems. She published five anonymous novels between 1796 and 1805.

Two of Burns's letters to Miss Craik have survived. The first, dated 9th August 1790, and written from Ellisland, accompanied manuscript copies of two of Burns's 'late Pieces' and is of importance because, having thanked her for the loan of a book, Burns then goes on to give his views on the poet's dilemma: 'It is often a reverie of mine, when I am disposed to be melancholy, the characters and fates of the Rhyming tribe. There is not among all the Martyrologies that ever were penned, so rueful a narrative as Johnson's Lives of the Poets. In the comparative view of Wretches, the criterion is not, what they are doomed to suffer, but how they are formed to bear. Take a being of our kind; give him a stronger imagination and more delicate sensibility, which will ever between them engender a more ungovernable set of Passions, than the usual lot of man: implant in him an irresistible impulse to some idle vagary, such as, arranging wild-flowers in fantastical nosegays, tracing the grasshopper to his haunt by his chirping song, watching the frisks of the little minnows in the sunny pool, or hunting after the intrigues of wanton butterflies—in short, send him adrift after some wayward pursuit which shall eternally mislead him from the paths of Lucre; yet, curse him with a keener relish than any man living for the pleasures that only Lucre can bestow; lastly, fill up the measure of his woes by bestowing on him a spurning sense of his own dignity; and you have created a wight nearly as miserable as a Poet.'

Miss Craik died at Flimby Lodge, Cumberland.

Cranstoun, Helen D'Arcy (1765-1838)

The sister of Henry Kerr Cranstoun, husband of Mary Anne Whitefoord. Helen D'Arcy became the second wife of Professor Dugald Stewart, and author of a one-time popular song, 'The Tears I Shed'. Burns added the first four lines of the last stanza, and published her song in the *Scots Musical Museum*.

Crawford of Cartsburn, Thomas (1741-91)

A country gentleman, whose estate lay near Greenock. He travelled a good deal on the Continent and was a warm admirer of Burns. They had a common friend in Richard Brown. Crawford wrote the poet a cheerful letter from Cartsburn on 16th March 1788, inviting Burns to stay with him and offering to send a servant and horse for him. Burns, however, seems to have had too much on his mind—his taking of the lease of Ellisland, and the death of his and Jean Armour's second set of twins—to have any inclination for making new friends at that particular moment.

Creech, William (1745–1815)

That 'upright, pert, tart, tripping wight' William Creech was the son of the Reverend William Creech, minister of Newbattle, where the future publisher was born. The father died four months after the birth of his son, and the boy was brought up by his mother at Dalkeith and Perth. Later, she moved to Edinburgh, where young William was designed for the University, but she became friendly with the wife of His Majesty's Printer for Scotland, Alexander Kincaid, as a result of which her son was offered, and accepted, a job in the bookselling side of Kincaid's business. After a period of travel on the Continent with his former schoolfellow at Dalkeith Lord Kilmaurs, the son of the Earl of Glencairn, Creech was taken into partnership in a new bookselling firm founded by Kincaid. In 1773, Kincaid retired from the business, devoting his full attention to his printing, leaving Creech free to transact business both as publisher and bookseller from his premises in the centre of the High Street of Edinburgh, in his own name. He remained in his High Street premises for forty-four years, where he became friendly with members of the 'literati' like Lord Kames, Dr Hugh Blair, Dr James Beattie, Henry ('Man of Feeling') Mackenzie and Professor Dugald Stewart.

Burns was introduced to Creech by Lord Glencairn soon after his arrival from Ayrshire in 1786. His Lordship asked Creech whether he would undertake to produce a second and enlarged edition of Mr Burns's poems. Creech, however, recommended a subscription edition, for which he undertook to subscribe 500 copies.

Burns thereafter saw a good deal of Creech while in Edinburgh, and sketched him in the Second Commonplace Book: 'My worthy bookseller, Mr Creech, is a strange, multiform character. His ruling passions of the left hand are an extreme vanity and something of the more harm-

less modifications of selfishness. The one, mixed as it often is with great goodness of heart, makes him rush into all public matters and take every instance of unprotected merit by the hand, provided it is in his power to hand it into public notice; the other quality makes him, amid all the embarrassment in which his vanity entangles him, now and then to cast half a squint at his own interest. His parts as a man, his deportment as a gentleman, and his abilities as a scholar, are above mediocrity. Of all the Edinburgh literati, he writes most like a gentleman. He does not awe you with the profoundness of the philosopher, or strike your eye with the soarings of genius; but he pleases you with the handsome turn of his expression and the polite ease of his paragraph. His social demeanour and powers, particularly at his own table, are the most engaging I have ever met with.'

On 17th April 1787, at the house of Henry Mackenzie, Burns and Creech drew up a 'Memorandum of Agreement' whereby on Mackenzie's advice, Burns received 100 guineas for the 'property' of his poems in addition to his subscription money: an agreement which, in the light of Burns's posthumous fame, seems ridiculous, but at the time must have seemed fair, even generous! Creech tried to get Cadell of London to take up some of the edition of about 3,000 copies. Cadell, however, delayed replying, and on 23rd April Creech agreed 'to take the whole upon himself.'

Creech was, however, an uncommonly mean man, and in the event, delayed not only in paying Burns's subscription money, but both in issuing and honouring the promissory note for the 100 guineas. It was in part to try to settle with Creech that Burns came back to Edinburgh in the autumn of 1787. On 22nd January, Burns told Margaret Chalmers: 'I have broke measures with Creech, and last week I wrote him a keen, frosty letter. He replied in forms of chastisement, and promised me upon his honor that I should have the account on Monday; but this is Tuesday, and yet I have heard not a word from him.' On 4th January 1789, Burns told Dr Moore that Creech 'kept me hanging about Edinburgh from the 7th of August 1787, until the 13th April 1788, before he would condescend to give me a statement of affairs; nor had I got it even then but for an angry letter I wrote him, which irritated his pride'.

Burns did, however, change his verdict; for when writing to Moore on 23rd March, he said: 'I was at Edinburgh lately, and finally settled with Mr Creech; and I retract some ill-natured surmises in my last letter, and own that at last, he has been amicable and fair with me.'

Burns later co-operated with Creech in finding extra material for the two-volume edition which appeared in November 1793, though he repaid the business of the delayed settlement by himself delaying the correcting of the copy of the earlier edition, which Creech had sent to him for that purpose. So Creech simply went ahead without waiting for Burns's comments!

Creech became a member of the Town Council in 1780, a magistrate of Edinburgh in 1788, and in 1811, Lord Provost. He remained famous for his supper parties, at which the company was large and the provision made for them small. Of his own writings his *Edinburgh Fugitive Pieces* preserve a good deal of their interest and their author's charm of style.

Burns commemorated Creech in two poems. One the 'Lament for the Absence of William Creech, publisher' written on the Border Tour, reflects their relationship before the quarrel over the delayed payment. Creech was then in London on business and Burns laments the fact that the levées are suspended:

'Now worthy Greg'ry's Latin face,
Tytler's and Greenfield's modest grace;

M'Kenzie, Stewart, such a brace
    As Rome ne'er saw;
They a' maun meet some ither place
    Willie's awa!'

'On William Creech', written after the quarrel, enumerates Creech's vices. In 'The Poet's Progress', these are said to be:

'Much specious lore, but little
                        understood,
(Veneering oft outshines the solid
                        wood),
His solid sense, by inches you must tell,
But mete his cunning by the Scottish
                        ell!'

Yet Creech was not without a sharp wit of his own. To one who made him an April Fool, he quipped:

'I pardon, sir, the trick you've played
                        me
When an April fool you made me;
Since one day only I appear
What you, alas, do all the year.'

Creech died unmarried.

Cririe, James (1752–1835)
A minor Scottish poet whose 'Address to Loch Lomond' led Burns to describe him as 'a Poet of Nature's Making'. He became Rector of the High School at Leith in 1788, and succeeded William Cruikshank in the High School of Edinburgh in 1795. He finished his days as minister of Dalton Parish, Dumfriesshire. His *Scottish Scenery, or Sketches in Verse* was published in London in 1803.

Crochallan Fencibles
In eighteenth-century Edinburgh there were numerous convivial clubs each with its own designation to describe the character of its proceedings. One such club was the Crochallan Fencibles. Its name was derived from two sources. Daniel Douglas, proprietor of the tavern in Anchor Close, off the High Street, where the club met, was known for his

singing of the Gaelic song 'Crodh Chail-ein', or 'Colin's Cattle'. This was taken as the first part of the Club's name. The other half arose from the voluntary arming which was taking place because of the alarms caused by the American War of Independence. The wits, among whom was the printer William Smellie, the founder of the Club (*see* **Smellie, William**), took the name of the Crochallan Fencibles, the office-bearers having pseudo-military rank. The President, or Colonel of the Club, was a writer to the signet, William Dunbar, whom Burns called 'rattling roaring Willie', after the musician celebrated in the *Border Minstrelsy*. He it was who first introduced Burns to the works of Spenser.

The Club members were noted for the conviviality of their meetings, and the 'gude companie' they kept. It is probable that many of the pieces which make up *The Merry Muses* were presented by Burns at meetings of the Fencibles.

Crombie, Alexander

A Dalswinton builder, who put up the farm buildings at Ellisland, and whom Burns once lent twenty pounds, which Crombie was dilatory in repaying.

Cromek, Robert Hartley (1770–1812)

The author of *Reliques of Robert Burns* was an engraver to trade. Born at Hull, he trained as a lawyer, but abandoned law to follow artistic pursuits. He studied engraving with Bartolozzi and afterwards met Blake, whose drawings illustrating Blair's poem 'The Grave' Cromek acquired for twenty guineas. In 1808, he published an edition of this poem with etchings after Blake by Schiavonetti, which led to a rupture with Blake, who had expected to be employed on the engraving him-self. Cromek's attempts to make money out of Blake, Schiavonetti and Stothard brought him into some opprobrium, and resulted in Blake calling him 'a petty, sneaking thief I knew'.

In 1808, Cromek came to Scotland to collect information about Burns. This he published the same year in his *Reliques of Burns, consisting of Original Letters, Poems and Critical Observations on Scottish Songs*. The finding of a manuscript in Burns's hand in 1922, proved that the song notes, for long suspected of being Cromek forgeries, are mostly by Burns himself, and are thus particularly valuable. But although Cromek put in a lot of scholar-ship and hard work, his habit of making 'portmanteau' versions of Burns's letters led to suspicion being cast on everything he did.

Cromek made a second tour in 1809, during which he met Allan Cunningham, who supplied him with 'old songs' of his own fabrication. Cromek made use of Cunningham's not always accurate know-ledge, without acknowledgement, in *Memoirs of Nithsdale and Galloway Songs, with Historical and Traditional Notices relative to the Manners and Customs of the Peasantry*, published in 1810.

He died of consumption on 14th March 1812.

Cruikshank, William (d. 1795)

He was schooled by his uncle and name-sake at Duns, Berwickshire, and later became an M.A. of Edinburgh University. In 1770, he became Rector of the High School in the Canongate, and two years later, Latin master at Edinburgh High School, where Burns met him through William Nicol. On his return from his northern tour, Burns lived with the Cruikshank family in No. 2 St James's Square from autumn 1787 until his departure from the capital in February 1788. Their twelve-year-old daughter Jane, or Jeany, caught Burns's affection, and for her he wrote 'The Rosebud', and 'Beauteous Rosebud, young and gay'. Despite her years, she was a good musician able to sing Burns's airs and accompany herself.

Burns wrote a kindly epitaph on Cruikshank:

> . . . 'His fau'ts they a' in Latin lay,
> In English nane e'er kent them.'

Cullie, David

The outgoing tenant of the farm at
Ellisland. Burns lodged with him and
his wife until he could arrange accomo-
dation at Ellisland for his family. The
house, near the tower of the Isle, seems to
have been little better than a hut. Burns
described it in a letter to Margaret Chalmers, dated 16th September 1788: 'This
hovel that I shelter in, while occasionally
here, is pervious to every blast that blows,
and every shower that falls; and I am
only preserved from being chilled to
death by being suffocated with smoke.'
And again in the lines 'To Hugh Parker':

> 'Here, ambush'd by the chimla cheek,
> Hid in an atmosphere of reek,
> I hear a wheel thrum i' the neuk,
> I hear it—for in vain I leuk:
> The red peat gleams, a fiery kernel,
> Enhusk'd by a fog infernal.
> Here, for my wonted rhyming raptures
> I sit and count my sins by chapters;
> For life and spunk like ither Christians,
> I'm dwindled down to mere existence;
> Wi' nae converse but Gallowa' bodies,
> Wi' nae kend face but Jenny Geddes.'

Jenny Geddes was Burns's horse.

Culloden

The scene of Prince Charles Edward Stuart's
defeat at the hands of the Duke of Cumberland on 16th April 1746, on a part of
the country-side called Drummossie Moor.
Burns visited the spot on 6th September
1787, while on his Highland tour with
Nicol. Surprisingly, in view of his
strong Jacobite leanings, Burns's only
reaction, in his *Journal*, to the scene of the
final defeat of the House of Stuart was:
'Came over Culloden Muir—reflections
on the field of battle.'

Cunningham, Alexander (d. 1812)

A nephew of Principal William Robertson, the historian, Alexander Cunningham
was the eldest son of James Cunningham of
Hyndhope. When Burns arrived in Edinburgh, Cunningham was practising law. It
is not known exactly when or where
they met, but it may well have been at a
meeting of the Crochallan Fencibles.
Cunningham's chambers were in St
James's Square, where the poet lodged
for a time with William Cruikshank, so
that neighbourly proximity may equally
possibly have given rise to the friendship.

Before he met Burns, Cunningham had
been wooing Anne, the daughter of John
Stewart of East Craigs. Writing from
Ellisland on 27th July 1788, Burns
enclosed some verses, asking:

> 'And is thy ardour still the same?
> And kindled still at Anna?
> Others may boast a pastoral flame,
> But thou art a volcano.'

Volcano or no, Anne Stewart turned
down Cunningham in favour of an Edinburgh surgeon, Forrest Dewar, to whom
she bore a son and three daughters. On
24th January 1789, Burns wrote to console
his friend:

'When I saw in my last Newspaper that a
Surgeon in Edin^r was married to a certain
amiable and accomplished young lady
whose name begins with, Ann; a lady
with whom I fancy I have the honor of
being a little acquainted, I sincerely felt
for a worthy much-esteemed friend of
mine. As you are the single only instance
that ever came within the sphere of my
observation of human nature, of a young
fellow, dissipated but not debauched, a
circumstance that has ever given me the
highest idea of the native qualities of your
heart, I am certain that a disappointment
in the tender passion must, to you, be
a very serious matter. To the hopeful
youth, keen on the badger-foot of Mammon, or listed under the gaudy banners of
Ambition, a love-disappointment, as such,
is an easy business; nay, perhaps he hugs
himself on his escape; but to your scanty

tribe of mankind, whose souls bear, on the richest materials, the most elegant impress of the Great Creator, Love enters deeply into their existence, and is entwined with their very thread of life. I myself can affirm, both from bachelor and wedlock experience, that Love is the Alpha and the Omega of human enjoyment. All the pleasures, all the happiness of my humble Compeers, flow immediately and directly from this delicious source. It is that spark of celestial fire which lights up the wintry hut of Poverty, and makes the chearless mansion, warm, comfortable and gay. It is the emanation of Divinity that preserves the Sons and Daughters of rustic labour from degenerating into the brutes with which they daily hold converse. Without it, life to the poor inmates of the Cottage would be a damning gift.'

As there seems to have been no formal engagement between Cunningham and Anne Stewart, Burns's reference to her as having prostituted her character merely by changing her mind, seems somewhat absurd. Cunningham is alleged by tradition to have been permanently prostrated by the loss; but in fact, on 10th April 1792, he married Agnes, younger daughter of the Reverend Henry Moir of Auchtertool, by whom he had two sons.

Writing on 4th May 1789, Burns revealed his feelings towards blood sports: 'I have just put the last hand to a little Poem, which I think will be something to your taste. One morning lately as I was out pretty early in the fields sowing some grass-seeds, I heard the burst of a shot from a neighbouring Plantation, and presently a poor little wounded hare came crippling by me. You will guess my indignation at the inhuman fellow, who could shoot a hare at this season when they all of them have young ones; and it gave me no little gloomy satisfaction to see the poor injured creature escape him. Indeed there is something in all that multiform business of destroying for

our sport individuals in the animal creation that do not injure us materially, that I could never reconcile to my ideas of native Virtue and eternal Right.' The poem was: 'On Seeing a Fellow Wound a Hare with a Shot,' dated April 1789:

'Inhuman man! curse on thy barb'rous
                                         art,
   And blasted be thy murder-aiming
                                         eye;
   May never pity soothe thee with a
                                         sigh,
Nor ever pleasure glad thy cruel
                                         heart!

Go live, poor wanderer of the wood
                          and field,
   The bitter little that of life remains!
No more the thickening brakes and
                          verdant plains
To thee shall home, or food, or
                          pastime yield.

Seek, mangled wretch, some place of
                          wonted rest,
   No more of rest, but now thy
                          dying bed!
   The sheltering rushes whistling o'er
                          thy head,
The cold earth with thy bloody
                          bosom prest. . . .'

Incidentally, the marksman was supposed to have been John Thomson, son of a farmer near Ellisland, and Burns is supposed to have threatened to throw him into the Nith.

The friendship between Burns and Cunningham was warm and frank. Writing to the poet from Edinburgh on 25th September 1789, with a gift copy of Johnson's *Lives of the Poets*, Cunningham said:

'Accept this copy of the *Lives of the Poets*. In addition to your value as my friend, it is a small tribute of the sincerity with which I admire you as one of their number. Let me indulge every wish of my heart for your prosperity and happiness, which, by the way, has not always been the concomitant or realised in the lives of those who have written for the instruction and entertainment of mankind.'

The way of life and the prospects of an after-life were both themes in the long letters begun by Burns in December 1789, but not finished and despatched until 16th February 1790:

'. . . . What strange beings we are! Since we have a portion of conscious existence, equally capable of enjoying Pleasure, Happiness & Rapture, or of suffering Pain, Wretchedness, & Misery, it is surely worthy of enquiry whether there be not such a thing as a Science of life; whether Method, Economy and Fertility of expedients, be not applicable to Enjoyment; and whether there be not a want of dexterity in Pleasure which renders our little scantling of happiness still less, and a profuseness, an intoxication in bliss, which leads to Satiety, Disgust and Self-abhorrence.

'There is not a doubt but that health, talents, character, decent competency, respectable friends, are real and substantial blessings, and yet do we not daily see those who enjoy many or all of these good things, and notwithstanding, contrive to be as unhappy as others to whose lot few of them have fallen. I believe one great source of this mistake or misconduct is owing to a certain stimulus with us called Ambition, which goads us up the hill of life, not as we ascend other eminences, for the laudible curiosity of viewing an extended landscape, but rather for the dishonest pride of looking down on others of our fellow-creatures seemingly diminutive in humbler stations. . . .

'All my fears & cares are of this world: if there is Another, an honest man has nothing to fear from it. I hate a man that wishes to be a Deist, but I fear, every fair, unprejudiced Enquirer must in some degree be a Sceptic. It is not that there are any very staggering arguments against the Immortality of Man; but, that like Electricity, Phlogiston, &c. the subject is so involved in darkness that we want Data to go upon. One thing frightens me much: that we are to live forever, seems too good news to be true. That we are to enter into a new scene of existence, where exempt from want & pain we shall enjoy ourselves & our friends without satiety or separation—how much would I be indebted to any one who could fully assure me that this were certain fact! . . .'

Enclosing the first version of 'The Banks of Doon' on 11th March 1791, Burns invited Cunningham's 'strictures' on it, adding his own views on a poet's partiality for what he has just created:

'. . . For my own part, a thing that I have just composed, always appears through a double portion of that partial medium in which an Author will ever view his own Works. I believe in general, Novelty has something in it that inebriates the fancy; & not unfrequently dissipates & fumes away like other intoxication, & leaves the poor Patient as usual with an aching heart. A striking instance of this might be adduced in the revolution of many a Hymeneal honeymoon.'

On 5th February 1792, Burns wrote to his 'ever dear Cunningham', invoking his assistance in the affair of James Clarke, the Moffat schoolmaster threatened with dismissal for alleged cruelty to his pupils.

On 10th September 1792, Cunningham got a long fanciful letter, touching once again upon religion, and giving Burns's considered view of marriage:

'. . . you must know, I have set a nipperkin of Toddy by me, just by way of Spell to keep away the meikle horned Deil, or any of his subaltern Imps who may be on their nightly rounds.

'But what shall I write to you? "The Voice said, Cry: & I said, What shall I cry!" O thou Spirit! whatever thou art, or wherever thou makest thyself visible. Be thou a Bogle by the eerie side of an auld thorn, in the dreary glen through which the herd-callan maun bicker in his gloamin route frae the fauld! Be thou a Brownie, set, at dead of night, to thy task by the blazing ingle, or in the solitary barn, where the repercussions of thy iron flail half affright thyself, as thou performest the work of twenty of the sons of men ere the cockcrowing summon thee to thy ample cog of substantial brose! Be thou a Kelpie, haunting the ford, or ferry, in the starless night, mixing thy laughing yell with the howling of the storm, & the roaring of the flood, as thou viewest the perils & miseries of Man on the foundering horse, or in the tumbling boat! Or, lastly, be thou a Ghost, paying thy nocturnal visits to the hoary ruins of decayed Grandeur; or performing thy mystic rites in the shadow of the time-worn Church, while the Moon looks, without a cloud, on the silent, ghastly dwellings of the dead around thee; or, taking thy stand by the bed-side of the Villian, or the Murderer, pourtraying on his dreaming fancy, pictures, dreadful as the horrors of unveiled Hell, & terrible as the wrath of incensed Deity! ! ! Come, thou Spirit, but not in these horrid forms; come with the milder, gentle, easy inspirations which thou breathest round the wig of a prating Advocate, or the tête of a tea-bibing Gossip, while their tongues run at the light-horse gallop of clish-maclaiver for ever & ever—come, & assist a poor devil who is quite jaded in the attempt to share half an idea among half a hundred words; to fill up four quarto pages, while he has not got one single sentence of recollection, information, or remark, worth putting pen to paper for.

'I feel, I feel the presence of Super-natural assistance! Circled in the embrace of my elbow-chair, my breast labors like the bloated Sybil on her three-footed stool, & like her too, labors with Nonsense. Nonsense, auspicious name! ! ! Tutor, Friend, & Finger-post in the mystic mazes of Law; the cadaverous paths of Physic; & particularly in the sightless soarings of School Divinity, who, leaving Common Sense confounded at his strength of pinion, Reason delirious with eyeing his giddy flight & Truth creeping back into the bottom of her well, cursing the hour that ever she offered her scorned alliance to the wizard Power of Theologic Vision —raves abroad on all the winds, "On Earth, Discord! A gloomy Heaven above, opening her jealous gates to the nineteen thousandth part of the tithe of mankind! And below, an inescapable & inexorable Hell, expanding its leviathan jaws for the vast residue of Mortals! ! !" O doctrine comfortable & healing to the weary wounded soul of man! Ye sons & daughters of affliction, ye pauvres Miserables, to whom day brings no pleasure, & night yields no rest, be comforted! "'Tis but one, to nineteen hundred thousand, that your situation will mend in this world; so, alas, the Experience of the Poor & the Needy too truly affirms; & 'tis nineteen hundred thousand to one, by the dogmas of Theology, that you will be damned eternally in the World to come!"

'But of all Nonsense, Religious Nonsense is the most nonsensical; so enough, & more than enough of it—Only, by the bye, will you, or can you tell me, my dear Cunningham, why a religioso turn of mind has always a tendency to narrow & illiberalise the heart? They are orderly; they may be just; nay, I have known them merciful: but still your children of Sanctity move among their fellow-creatures with a nostril snuffing putrescence, & a foot spurning filth, in short, with that conceited dignity which your titled Douglasses, Hamiltons, Gordons, or any other of your Scots Lordlings of seven centuries standing, display when they accidentally mix among the many-aproned Sons of Mechanical life. I remember, in my Plough-boy days, I could not conceive it possible that a noble Lord could be a Fool, or that a Godly man could be a Knave. How ignorant are Plough-boys! Nay, I have since discovered that a *godly woman* may be a—!—But hold—Here's t'ye again—this Rum is damn'd generous Antigua, so a very unfit menstruum for scandal.

'Apropos, how do you like, I mean *really* like, the Married Life? Ah, my Friend! Matrimony is quite a different thing from what your love-sick youths & sighing girls take it to be! But Marriage, we are told, is appointed by G— & I shall never quarrel with any of HIS Institutions. I am a Husband of older standing than you, & I shall give you *my* ideas of the Conjugal State—(En passant, you know I am no Latin, is not 'Conjugal' derived from 'Jugum' a yoke?)—Well then, the scale of Goodwifeship I divide into ten parts—Good-nature, four; Good-sense two; Wit, one; Personal Charms, viz. a sweet face, eloquent eyes, fine limbs, graceful carriage (I would add a fine waist too, but that is so soon spoilt you know), all these one: as for the other qualities belonging to, or attending on, a Wife, such as fortune, connections, education (I mean, education extraordinary), family blood, &c. divide the two remaining degrees among them as you please; only, remember that all these minor properties must be expressed by *fractions*; for there is not any one of them in the aforesaid scale, entitled to the dignity of an Integer.'

On 20th February 1793, Burns included a political catechism in his letter:

'Quere, What is Politics?

Answer, Politics is a science wherewith, by means of nefarious cunning, & hypocritical pretence, we govern civil Polities for the emolument of ourselves & our adherents.

Quere, What is a Minister?

Answer, A Minister is an unprincipled fellow, who by the influence of hereditary, or acquired wealth; by superior abilities; or by a lucky conjuncture of circumstances, obtains a principal place in the administration of the affairs of government.

Q. What is a Patriot?

A. An individual exactly of the same description as a Minister, only, out of place.'

On 25th February 1794, recovering from an illness Burns wrote in depression:

'. . . Are you deep in the language of consolation? I have exhausted in reflection every topic of comfort. *A heart at ease* would have been charmed with my sentiments and reasonings; but as to myself, I was like Judas Iscariot preaching the Gospel: he might melt and mould the hearts of those around him, but his own kept its native incorrigibility.

'Still there are two great pillars that bear us up, amid the wreck of misfortune and misery. The ONE is composed of the different modifications of a certain noble, stubborn something in man, known by the names of courage, fortitude, magnanimity. The OTHER is made up of those feelings and sentiments which, however the sceptic may deny them or the enthusiast disfigure them, are yet, I am convinced, original and component parts of the human soul; those *senses of the mind*, if I may be allowed the expression, which connect us with, and link us to, those awful obscure realities—an all-powerful and equally beneficent God, and a world to come, beyond death and the grave. The first gives the nerve of combat, while a ray of hope beams on the field; the last pours the balm of comfort into the wound which time can never cure.

'I do not remember, my dear Cunningham, that you and I ever talked on the subject of religion at all. I know some who laugh at it, as the trick of the crafty FEW to lead the undiscerning MANY; or at most as an uncertain obscurity, which mankind can never know anything of, and with which they are fools if they give themselves much to do. Nor would I quarrel with a man for his irreligion, any more than I would for his want of musical ear. I would regret that he was shut out from what, to me and to others, were such superlative sources of enjoyment.'

It was Cunningham to whom 'The Red, Red Rose' was sent, in the autumn of 1794. From 'Brow-Sea-bathing quarters' on 7th July 1796, Burns wrote to him:

'. . . Alas! my friend, I fear the voice of the Bard will soon be heard among you no more! For these eight or ten months I have been ailing, sometimes bed-fast & sometimes not; but these last three months I have been tortured with an excruciating rheumatism which has reduced me to nearly the last stage. You actually would not know me if you saw me. Pale, emaciated, & so feeble as occasionally to need help from my chair—my spirits fled! fled!—but I can no more on the subject—only the Medical folks tell me that my last & only chance is bathing & country quarters & riding. The deuce of the matter is this: when an Excise-man is off duty, his salary is reduced to 35£ instead of 50£. What way, in the name of thrift, shall I maintain myself & keep a horse in Country-quarters—with a wife & five children at home, on 35£? I mention this, because I had intended to beg your utmost interest & all friends you can muster, to move our Commiss^rs of Excise to grant me the full salary. I dare say you know them all personally. If they do not grant it me, I must lay my account with an exit truly en poëte, If I die not of disease I must perish with hunger. . .'

As late as 12th July, Burns sent Cunningham a song 'Here's a Health to Ane I lo'e dear', with a mention of his plan to get Excise promotion, an event, as we know, which was only frustrated by his death.

Having acquired part of an estate in South Carolina through his wife, Cunningham became a Writer to the Signet in 1798. But by 1806 he had gone into partnership with his uncle, Patrick Robertson, as a jeweller. He was the moving spirit in the raising of money for the poet's

family. His correspondence with Syme may be seen in the *Burns Chronicle*. Raeburn painted his portrait.

See Plate 11.

Cunningham, Allan (1784–1842)

A Scottish poet and man of letters who was born at Keir, Dumfriesshire. His father was a neighbour of Burns at Ellisland. In later life, Allan claimed to remember hearing Burns recite 'Tam o' Shanter' to his father in 1790, a feat of memory surely unparalleled in one so young.

Cunningham began life as a stonemason's apprentice. He and his brother James became friendly with James Hogg, from whom doubtless Allan gained some of his interest in balladry. In 1807, Cunningham contributed some songs to Roche's *Literary Recreations*, and in 1809 collected old ballads for Robert Hartley Cromek's *Remains of Nithsdale and Galloway Song*. Many of these were, however, Cunningham's own work, a fact of which Cromek has been accused of being perfectly well aware.

Cunningham went to London in 1810, and in 1814 became clerk of works to the sculptor Francis Chantrey, retaining this position until Chantrey's death in 1841. Cunningham's two best original songs are 'My Ain Countree', popular with the Scots, and, 'A Wet Sheet and a Flowing Sea', which has become one of the best known among British sea songs. Cunningham had five sons—all of whom wrote books or edited the works of others, though none were full-time authors—and one daughter.

In 1834, Cunningham, by then a well-established editor, poet and journalist in London, brought out, with Lockhart's blessing, *The Works of Robert Burns, with his Life*, in eight volumes. The *Life* abounds in falsifications, many of them so fantastic as to raise doubts even as one reads. Snyder's verdict was: 'This biography certainly pictures Burns more or less as he actually was, but is absolutely unreliable as regards specific facts. Anything that Cunningham says may be true: nothing that he says should be believed without contributary testimony.'

Cunningham, Elizabeth, Countess of Glencairn (1725-1801)

The daughter of Hugh McGuire, a musician and carpenter in Ayr, she received a large dowry from Governor Macrae of Madras, whom her father had befriended in earlier years. She married William, thirteenth Earl of Glencairn in 1744, and was widowed in 1775. Her second son became the fourteenth Earl, and her third son the fifteenth and last Earl. When Burns met her, she was living with her unmarried daughter, Lady Elizabeth, at Coates House, near Edinburgh.

Cunningham, Lady Elizabeth 'Betty' (d. 1804)

The younger sister of James, Earl of Glencairn. She lived with her mother, the Dowager Countess, at Coates House, near Edinburgh, She never married.

It was to Lady Cunningham that Burns wrote from Ellisland on 22nd January 1789, indicating his poetic plans. After describing his situation—the prospects of farming with his Excise Commission in reserve—Burns went on: 'I muse and rhyme, morning, noon and night; and have a hundred different Poetic plans, pastoral, georgic, dramatic, and etc., floating in the regions of fancy somewhere between Purpose and resolve.' Many of them, particularly the 'dramatic', were, alas, doomed to remain there.

It was to Lady Cunningham that Burns first sent a copy of his 'Lament for James, Earl of Glencairn', on her brother's death. In the accompanying letter, undated, he wrote: 'If, among my children, I shall have a son that has a heart, he shall hand it down to his child as a family honor, and a family debt, that my dearest existence I owe to the noble house of Glencairn!'

When the 1793 edition of his *Poems* appeared, Burns sent a copy to Lady Cunningham, with this note: 'But for the generous patronage of the late James, Earl of Glencairn to the Author, these volumes had never been. In memory of the obligations he conferred on me; and in gratitude to your Ladyship for your goodness, do me the honor to accept these volumes.'

Cunningham, James, fourteenth Earl of Glencairn (1749-91)

He was born at Finlayston, the second son of the thirteenth Earl. For a time he served as a Captain in the West Fencible Regiment. His elder brother having predeceased him, James Cunningham succeeded his father as fourteenth Earl in 1775. Fron 1780 to 1784, he was one of the Representative Scots Peers in the House of Lords. While there, he supported Fox's India Bill. In 1785, Glencairn, as patron of Kilmarnock parish, presented a staunch Conservative, the Reverend William Mackinlay, to fill the vacancy, though Glencairn himself was not apparently an Auld Licht supporter, his desire being to fulfil the wishes of the majority of the parishioners. The appointment, however, produced Burns's satire 'The Ordination'. Glencairn's factor, Alexander Dalziel, drew the Earl's attention to the Kilmarnock Edition, by which he was much impressed. When Burns arrived in Edinburgh in 1786, armed with a letter of introduction from Dalrymple of Orangefield (who was married to Lady Glencairn's sister), the Earl received the poet warmly in his home and introduced him to his friends. One of these was the Dean of the Faculty of Advocates, Henry Erskine, who, in his turn introduced Burns to the Duchess of Gordon. Another was the publisher, William Creech, who had once been Glencairn's tutor and travelling companion. Burns afterwards described Glencairn as his 'titular Protector'. He told Mrs Dunlop, in a letter of 22nd March 1787: 'The noble Earl of Glencairn, to whom I owe more than any man of earth, does me the honor of giving me his strictures; his hints, with respect to impropriety or indelicacy, I follow implicitly.' Clearly, Glencairn was able to extend to Burns the benefits of his patronage without upsetting the poet's sensibility. In fact, he was to Burns in Edinburgh pretty much what Gavin Hamilton had been to Burns in Ayrshire. When the subscription list for the 1787 edition of Burns's *Poems* was opened, Glencairn and his mother took twenty-four copies. As a result of the Earl's influence, within ten days of the poet's arrival in Edinburgh, the Caledonian Hunt subscribed 'universally, one and all', accounting for one hundred copies. When the book was about to appear, Burns asked the Earl's permission to publish in an Edinburgh newspaper his 'Verses Intended to be written below a Noble Earl's Picture'. Glencairn did not give his permission, however, possibly feeling that such advertising would be too blatant.

On 4th May 1787, when Burns was leaving Edinburgh, he sent Glencairn a somewhat stilted but obviously sincere letter thanking him for 'all that patronage, that benevolence, and that friendship with which you have honored me'.

In January 1788, when Burns had decided that he must enter the Excise service, he wrote to Glencairn asking his assistance in getting him an appointment.

Glencairn never married and never enjoyed good health. In the autumn of 1790 his health began to fail, and he went to Lisbon in search of relief. He returned to England and died at Falmouth soon after landing, on 30th January 1791.

In the letter accompanying his 'Lament for James, Earl of Glencairn', which Burns sent to Dalziel on 10th March, he says: 'God knows what I have suffered at the loss of my best Friend, my first my dearest Patron and Benefactor; the man to whom I owe all that I am and have!'

Cunningham, John, fifteenth Earl of Glencairn (1750–96)

He succeeded his brother, Burns's patron, to the estate. He was an officer in the 14th Regiment of Dragoons, but later took orders in the Church of England.

When the 1793 edition of Burns's *Poems* was published, the poet presented the fifteenth Earl with a copy. He married Lady Isabella Erskine, daughter of the Earl of Buchan, but they were childless and the title died with him.

Cunningham of Robertland, Lady

She was reputed to be the 'Mrs C. mentioned by Burns in a letter to Robert Aiken, dated 3rd April 1786, and written at the time the proposals for the Kilmarnock Edition were going to press. Her husband was one of the first Ayrshire lairds to recognise Burns's genius.

Cunninghame of Annbank and Enterkin, William, (1757–?)

He provided the subject of Burns's ballad 'The Fête Champêtre'—written to the tune 'Killiecrankie'—which Cunninghame gave when he attained his majority and inherited his grandfather's estates, the two mansion houses of which were both in a ruinous state. Gilbert Burns recorded the reasons for the fête, which was held in the summer of 1788, the year Burns began farming at Ellisland: 'Wishing to introduce himself with some *éclat* to the country, he got temporary erections made on the banks of the Ayr, tastefully decorated with shrubs and flowers for a supper and ball, to which most of the respectable families in the county were invited. It was a novelty in the county and attracted much notice. A dissolution of Parliament was soon expected, and this festivity was thought to be an introduction to a canvas for representing the county. Several others candidates were

spoken of, particularly Sir John Whitefoord, then residing at Cloncaird, commonly pronounced Glencaird, and Mr
Boswell, the well-known biographer of
Dr Johnson'—who is referred to as 'the
meikle Ursa Major' in the first stanza of
the poem—'The political views of this
festive assemblage which are alluded to
in the ballad, if they ever existed, were,
however, laid aside, as Mr Cunninghame
did not canvas the county.'
As Burns put it:

'When Love and Beauty heard the
news,
The gay green-woods amang, man;
Where, gathering flowers and busking
bowers,
They heard the blackbird's sang,
man;
A vow, they seal'd it with a kiss,
Sir Politics to fetter;
As theirs alone, the potent bliss
To hold a Fête Champêtre.'

The 'ether-stone', or adder-stone, referred to in the concluding stanza, was
used by the Druids as an amulet. There
was a Druid superstition that adders
formed little streaky coloured stones
from their slough, which were believed
to act as charms. These stones, of course,
were simply beads made by primitive
man.

As to the location of the 'Fête Champêtre', John McVie has written: 'As
Annbank was a comparatively small
house in those days, and as Cunninghame
ultimately took up his residence in
Enterkin, it is very probable that the func-
tion was held in the holm on the banks
of the river immediately below Enterkin House.'

Cunninghame married Catherine,
daughter of Stewart of Afton, in 1794.
They had one son.

Cunninghame, Sir William Augustus (d. 1828)

He owned the estates of Milncraig

(Coylton) in Ayrshire and Livingston in
West Lothian. He was Member of
Parliament for Linlithgow from 1774–90.
Burns called him 'The bauld Sir Willie'
in 'The Author's Earnest Cry and Prayer'.
Sir William was son-in-law to Sir Robert
Myreton of Gogar, called by Mackenzie
'the most inveterate swearer in Scotland'.

Currie, Dr James (1756–1805)

Burns's first editor and major biographer
was born on 31st May 1756, at Kirkpatrick Fleming, Dumfriesshire, where
his father was minister. Schooled at Dumfries, he emigrated to Virginia in 1771,
settling as a merchant on the James River.
He suffered from endemic fever and many
setbacks, and in 1776 sailed for Greenock,
intending to study medicine at Edinburgh
and return to practise it in America. But
three days out, the ship in which he was
sailing was seized by the Revolutionaries,
and he was captured and made to serve
in the Colonial Army. He bought his
freedom, set sail again, and was captured
a second time. To gain his freedom on
this occasion he had to sail a hundred and
fifty miles in an open boat. Illness and
other misfortunes continued to try him,
but he at last reached Deptford, England,
on 2nd May 1777. Whilst in his first
year at Edinburgh University, he bathed
imprudently at the end of a thirty-two
mile walk, and took rheumatic fever, a
disease which eventually helped to kill
him. He graduated in 1780, and settled
ten months later in Liverpool. In 1792,
he was able to buy himself a small estate
in Dumfriesshire. He met Burns once,
briefly, in Dumfries. The following
year, under the pseudonym 'John Wilson',
Currie published a letter to Pitt urging
him not to go to war with France. His
main contribution to medicine was his
*Medical Reports on the Effects of Water,
Cold and Warm, as a Remedy in Fever and
Febrile Diseases, whether applied to the
Surface of the Body, or used as a Drink, with
observations on the Nature of Fever and on*

the Effects of Opium, Alcohol and Inanition, published in 1797, which ran through four editions. He died of heart failure on 31st August 1805, at Sidmouth, where he is buried.

After Burns's death, Currie, as an admirer of Burns's poetry, was chosen to edit the poet's work, the others considered being Maria Riddell, Maxwell, Syme and Dugald Stewart, none of whom was able to undertake it. Currie himself was ill-equipped for the task. As a young man Currie was intemperate both in drink and in speech. The respectability he unexpectedly gained in middle life had to be lived up to. He thus felt he could not publicly condone what seemed to him the drunken bouts of a poetic rake, even if there was a good and painful reason. Consequently, although never a strict teetotaller himself, except while suffering from his consumptive bouts, he deplored Burns's fondness for drink, and started what was to become the accepted legend for more than a century, that Burns was a confirmed alcoholic. Currie openly stated his intention of avoiding controversial topics, and took fantastic liberties with Burns's documents, and with other facts, to achieve his aim.

In his defence, however, it should be said that no one else appeared able or willing to undertake the task at the time; that he had had no training in editorial scholarship, even according to the lax standards of the day; and that his primary aim was to help to raise money in aid of the poet's family. His four volume edition appeared in 1800, and cost one pound eleven and sixpence the set. Two thousand copies were printed. A second edition, revised, was published in 1801, a third in 1802, and a fourth in 1803. An eighth edition in 1820, published by Cadell and Davies in London, had added 'Some Further Particulars of the Author's Life' by Gilbert Burns. But Gilbert was warned by the Publishers not to impugn Currie's accuracy, and so

allowed the chance to vindicate his brother's reputation to go for nothing.

An interesting and very full study of Currie and his times, *James Currie the Entire Stranger and Robert Burns* by R. D. Thornton, appeared in 1963.

Currie, John

A miller in Carse-mill and a neighbour of Burns at Ellisland. Burns described him in a letter to John Tennant of Auchenbay, dated 22nd December 1788, as 'a good man', a 'very good man, even for a £500 bargain'.

Currie had been much impressed with Burns's whisky, and wanted to know if Tennant could supply him 'with liquor of an equal quality' for his public house. Currie and his wife sold 'foreign spirits but all along thought that whisky would have degraded their house'. Burns converted them to a more reasonable viewpoint.

Curtis, Rear Admiral Sir Roger (1746–1816)

Son of Roger Curtis of Downton, Wiltshire, and said to be descended from the Roger Curtis who served aboard the *Swiftsure*, and was killed at Algiers in 1662. Curtis entered the Navy in 1762, and became involved in a controversy arising out of his action in fleeing before the French towards the end of 1780. But thereafter, for more than eighteen months he played an important part in the succour and relief of Gibraltar, particularly in the destruction of the Spanish floating batteries on 13th September 1782.

Burns mentioned him in the soldier's song from 'The Jolly Beggars' Cantata:

'I lastly was with Curtis, among the
floating batt'ries.'

Curtis was president of the court martial which tried and acquitted Lord Gambier on a charge of excess of caution. By his wife Sarah Brady, Curtis had a daughter and two sons, one of whom became an admiral.

D

Daer, Lord. *See* **Douglas-Hamilton.**

Dalgarnock

Referred to in the song 'Last May a braw Wooer'. The temporarily refused wooer complains that, having put off her man, he thereupon wooed her 'black cousin Bess', and:

'But a' the neist week, as I petted wi'
care,
I gaed to the tryst o' Dalgarnock,
And wha but my fine fickle lover was
there?'

Set to the tune 'The Lothian Lassie' (Burns modelled his original song on an older poem of the same name), it first appeared in Thomson's *Scottish Airs*, 1799, and had an immediate success.

According to Burns, Dalgarnock was 'a romantic spot near the Nith, where are still a ruined church and a burial ground'.

Dalhousie Manuscript

A collection of letters and songs in holograph sent by Burns to George Thomson. Formerly at Brechin Castle, it is now in the Pierpont Morgan Library, New York.

Dalrymple

A village about four miles from Ayr, by the River Doon. Burns, when almost fourteen, attended school at Dalrymple for a short while. A Free Church was later built on the site of the former school.

Dalrymple, James (1752?–95)

The son of Charles Dalrymple of Ayr, James Dalrymple married Miss Macrae M'Guire in 1750. She was the heiress to the estate of Orangefield, in Monkton Parish, and the sister of Elizabeth, Countess of Glencairn. James Dalrymple succeeded to the estate in 1785. When, the following year, Burns rode to Edinburgh, Dalrymple, together with John Samson of Kilmarnock, seems to have guaranteed George Reid of Barquharie the safe return of the 'pownie' he lent the poet for the journey.

Dalrymple also gave Burns a letter of introduction to the Earl of Glencairn, who exerted himself most generously on the poet's behalf. 'I have found a worthy warm friend in Mr Dalrymple of Orange-field,' the poet wrote John Ballantine from Edinburgh on 13th December 1786, 'who introduced me to Lord Glencairn, a man whose worth and brotherly kindness to me I shall remember when time will be no more.' And in one of the suppressed stanzas of 'The Vision', Burns described Dalrymple as:

'The owner of a pleasant spot
Near sandy wilds, I last did note
A heart too warm, a pulse too hot
At times o'er ran;
But large in every feature wrote,
Appeared the man.'

On 7th December 1786, Dalrymple introduced the poet at a meeting of Canongate Kilwinning Lodge of Freemasons, but after February 1787 he disappears from Burns's correspondence.

The 'pulse too hot' proved his undoing. A keen hunter, he dissipated his fortune and was declared bankrupt in 1791, his trustees being the Reverend William Dalrymple, Robert Aiken and John Ballantine.

The house of Orangefield for some years formed part of the terminal hotel buildings at Prestwick Airport, but has since been demolished.

Dalrymple, The Reverend William (1723–1814)

William Dalrymple was the younger son of the Sheriff-Clerk of Ayr, James Dalrymple. He was licensed to preach in 1745, and became junior minister of Ayr Parish in 1746, where he remained so for ten years. In June 1756, however, he was preferred to the first Ministry. Burns's father, William Burnes, sat under Dalrymple, no doubt approving of the mild flavour of liberalism which modified the minister's Calvinism, though never brought him into conflict with the orthodox. Dalrymple baptised Robert Burns when the poet was one day old. In 1779, St Andrews University conferred the degree of Doctor of Divinity on Dalrymple, and in 1781 he became Moderator of the General Assembly. Dalrymple at one time owned the estate of Mount Charles, and was an uncle of Burns's lawyer friend Robert Aiken.

In 'The Twa Herds', Burns depicted Dalrymple as having been 'lang' the 'fae' of the Auld Licht faction, and in 'The Kirk's Alarm,' Burns called him, 'D'rymple mild, D'rymple mild'.

Dalrymple contributed the article on Ayr Parish to Sir John Sinclair's *Statistical Account*.

Dalswinton

A mansion which belonged to Burns's landlord at Ellisland, Patrick Miller. It lay on the other side of the River Nith, on the former site of the Red Comyn's castle. On Dalswinton Loch the first steam boat, designed by William Symington, was launched by Miller on 14th October 1788, and tradition alleges that Burns was one of the passengers.

Dalziel, Alexander (d. 1819)

Son of the innkeeper at Noblehouse, in Newlands parish. A friend of Robert Fergusson's, Dalziel was one of Burns's ablest correspondents.

He became factor of the Earl of Glencairn's estate of Finlayston, in the parish of Kilmalcolm, Renfrewshire. Cromek alleged that Dalziel was the person who brought the Kilmarnock Edition to Glencairn's notice, and encouraged the Earl to persuade Burns to produce a second edition in Edinburgh, a claim which has

also been made for Dalrymple of Orangefield. (Ferguson points out that the one claim does not necessarily invalidate the other!)

When Glencairn died at Falmouth, Burns wrote on 10th March 1791 to Dalziel: 'I can easily guess from my own heart what you have felt on a late most melancholy event. God knows what I have suffered at the loss of my best Friend, my first, my dearest Patron and Benefactor; the man to whom I owe all that I am and have! I am gone into mourning for him, and with more sincerity of grief that I fear some will, who by Nature's ties ought to feel on the occasion.

'I will be exceedingly oblidged to you indeed, to let me know the news of the Noble Family, how the poor Mother and the two sisters support their loss. I had a packet of Poetic bagatelles ready to send to Lady Betty, when I saw the fatal tidings in the Newspaper. I see by the same channel that the honored Remains of my noble Patron are designed to be brought to the Family Burial place. Dare I trouble you to let me know privately before the day of interment, that I may cross the country and steal among the croud, to pay a tear to the last sight of my ever-revered Benefactor? It will oblidge me beyond expression.'

Dalziel was clearly a good friend of the poet's. After Burns's death, Dalziel became one of the founder members of Greenock Burns Club.

Dalziel, Professor Andrew (1742–1806)

Professor of Greek in Edinburgh University. Burns referred to the 'delicacy' of his 'taste' in a letter written from Ellisland on 20th January 1789, to Professor Dugald Stewart. Burns presented a volume of Fergusson's poems to Mrs Dalziel inscribed on the fly-leaf with the lines beginning:

'Ah, woe is me, my mother dear'.

In a letter to Sir Robert Liston, dated

25th January 1787, the professor described Burns: '. . . We have got a poet in town just now, whom everybody is taking notice of—a ploughman from Ayrshire—a man of unquestionable genius, who has produced admirable verses, mostly in the Scottish dialect, though some of them are nearly in English. He is a fellow of strong common sense, and by his own industry has read a good deal of English, both prose and verse. . . . He behaves wonderfully well; very independent in his sentiments, and has none of the *mauvaise honte* about him, though he is not forward.'

Andrew Dalziel was a native of West Lothian. He held his chair for thirty-four years, from 1772 to 1806. In 1785 he was appointed librarian of the University. He began to write a history of Edinburgh University, but died before he could complete the work.

Dalzell of Barncroch, John

His estate lay near Kirkcudbright, and he dined with Burns and Syme at the inn in the town when they were on their Galloway tour. Dalzell was a man who liked humour and good company, and the three had 'a very agreeable party'.

Dalzell was a close friend of Gordon of Kenmure (with whom Burns and Syme stayed), who sent him a snuff-mull. Dalzell acknowledged the gift, according to Chambers, with a verse:

'Your present I received, and letter;
No compliment could please me better,
Ex dono Kenmure I'll put on it
And crown it wi' a silver bonnet,—
In spite of a' the deils in——
　　　　　　　Your humble servant,
　　　　　　　John Dalzell.'

Burns gave Syme a copy of 'Scots Wha Hae' to give to Dalzell.

Dampierre, Auguste-Henri-Marie Picot, Marquis de (1756–95)

A French general of aristocratic family, born in Paris. He distinguished himself under Dumouriez at the battle of Jemmapes, but was killed under the walls of Valenciennes.

He is mentioned by Burns in his poem 'An Address to General Dumouriez':

'How does Dampierre do?
Aye, and Beurnonville too?
Why did they not come along with
　　　　　　　　　　　you,
　　Dumouriez?'

Davidson, Betty

The widow of a cousin of Burns's mother, who frequently stayed with the family, helping with the household chores. She had a fund of stories and songs to entertain the Burns children. Burns said in his Autobiographical Letter that she had 'the largest collection in the country of tales and songs concerning devils, ghosts, fairies, brownies, witches, warlocks, spunkies, kelpies, elf-candles, dead-lights, wraiths, apparitions, cantraips, inchanted towers, giants, dragons, and other trumpery'; which, as Snyder remarks, could well have been localised in the nearby churchyard of 'Alloway's auld haunted kirk'.

Davidson, John (1728–1806)

He is generally supposed to have been the prototype of 'Souter Johnnie' in 'Tam o' Shanter'. He lived at Glenfoot of Ardlochan, near the farm called Shanter. Latterly he lived in Kirkoswald, where he was buried. A shoe-maker to trade, he was a man known for his wit and jests. He married Anne Gillespie in 1763, who at one time had been in service to Gilbert Broun or Brown, Burns's maternal grandfather. The poet was a frequent visitor at their home. Davidson's mull (for snuff) is preserved in the Burns Monument in Edinburgh.

Davies, Deborah Duff

The daughter of Dr Daniel Davies of Tenby, in Pembrokeshire, and a relative of the Riddell family. Burns met her when he was at Ellisland, and made her the heroine of some songs and epigrams. Small of stature, she was nevertheless a beauty. She went abroad for her health, but soon afterwards died of consumption at an early age. Cunningham alleges, probably fancifully, that she was jilted by one Captain Delaney, and as a result 'went into a decline'. As Ferguson puts it: 'Any one who cares to believe Cunningham is free to do so.'

Burns's first letter to her has never been accurately placed, August 1789, '91, or '92 all being suggested by Ferguson. They appear to have accompanied the somewhat stilted lines, 'The charms of lovely Davies'. Miss Davies's social position put her into the category of the 'untouchables', so far as Burns was concerned, and although a cheerful letter from her to him, sent from Fontainebleau in 1792, survives, Burns's letters to her were all couched in his most artificial style, obviously designed to impress.

In a particularly turgid letter, written on 6th April 1793, Burns rants about the inequalities which allow 'misbegotten chance' to put foolish men in high places. What was perhaps really in his mind, however, is revealed in a later paragraph, and by the tenderly passionate song enclosed with the letter. The paragraph reads: 'Still the inequalities of life are, among Men, comparatively tolerable: but there is a delicacy, a tenderness, accompanying every view in which one can place a lovely WOMAN, that are grated and shocked at the rude, capricious distinctions of Fortune. Woman is the blood-royal of life: let there be slight degrees of precedency among them, but let them all be sacred.' The song was the exquisite 'Bonie Wee Thing', 'composed on my little idol, the charming lovely Davies', as Burns himself recorded. It first appeared in the *Museum*, 1792. The air goes back to an original in the *Straloch Manuscript*, 1627.

Writing to Mrs Dunlop in June 1793, Burns compared Miss Davies, 'positively the least creature ever I saw, to be at the same time unexceptionably, and indeed uncommonly, handsome and beautiful', with a Mrs S——, 'a huge, bony, masculine, cowp-carl, horse-godmother, he-termagant, of a six-feet figure, who might have been bride to Og, King of Bashan: a Goliah of Goth.' He added an epigram:

'Ask why God made the GEM so
                                    small,
    And why so huge the granite?
Because, God meant mankind should
                                    set
    That higher value on it.'

In a letter to Miss Davies, probably written in June 1793, Burns revealed yet another aspect of his process of putting himself in the regimen of admiring a fine woman. 'Bye the bye,' he told her, 'I am a good deal luckier than most poets. When I sing of Miss Davies or Miss Lesley Baillie, I have only to feign the passion—the charms are real.'

So, however, is the passion in 'Bonie Wee Thing'.

Dawson, Mrs
An old lady from Paisley whom Burns met in West Lothian at the start of his Highland tour. He described her in his *Journal* as: 'Like old Lady W[auchope] and still more like Mrs C——, her conversation is pregnant with strong sense and just remark, but, like them a certain air of self-important and a *duresse* in the eye, seem to indicate, as the Ayrshire wife observed of her cow, that "she had a mind o' her ain".'

'Death and Dr Hornbook'. See Wilson, John.

Death of Burns
Few great men have been cursed with a biographer as unscrupulous and cruel as Burns in the person of James Currie.

The unhappiest aspect of the prose picture of Burns's character which Currie drew, was that the good man thought he was acting out of the best Christian motives.

Currie's account of the death of Burns accuses the poet of continuous drunkenness, and hints at venereal disease:

'Perpetually stimulated by alcohol in one or other of its various forms . . . in his moments of thought he reflected with the deepest regret on his fatal progress, clearly foreseeing the goal towards which he was hastening, without the strength of mind necessary to stop, or even to slacken his course. His temper became more irritable and gloomy; he fled from himself into society, often of the lowest kind. And in such company, that part of the convivial scene in which wine increases sensibility and excites benevolence, was hurried over, to reach the succeeding part, over which uncontrolled passion generally presides. He who suffers the pollution of inebriation, how shall he escape other pollution? But let us refrain from the mention of errors over which delicacy and humanity draw the veil.'

Such proposterous impertinence is hard to stomach, even after the lapse of a century and a half! Currie's picture of Burns as a besotted whore-chaser—there has never been a single shred of evidence to support the 'other pollution' smear—was passed down the nineteenth century. In 1815, Alexander Peterkin made some attempt to correct it by publishing testimonies as to Burns's sobriety from, among others, Alexander Findlater, James Gray and Gilbert Burns. But Lockhart and Cunningham kept up the sorry legend of Currie's telling.

Chambers gives the least fancifully garnished account of a mishap which apparently overtook the poet in January 1796, and which has been much magnified by Lockhart and others: 'Early in the month of January, when his health was in the course of improvement, Burns tarried to a late hour at a jovial party in the Globe Tavern. Before returning home, he unluckily remained for some time in the open air, and, overpowered by the effects of the liquor he had drunk, fell alseep. In these circumstances, and in the peculiar condition to which a severe medicine had reduced his constitution, a fatal chill penetrated to his bones; he reached home with the seeds of a rheumatic fever already in possession of his weakened frame.'

Unfortunately for this story, Burns's letters indicate that he was confined to his room during almost the whole of January. The Globe Inn being less than a quarter of a mile from Burns's home, it is, as Snyder put it: 'altogether improbable that he would have been so reckless as to drink himself into insensibility, or that his friends would have allowed him to fall asleep in the snow on the way home.' Snyder therefore advises—and who would not agree with him?—the branding of the entire story as fiction, and recommends that it should be disregarded.

The truth of the matter seems to be that Currie, at least during his consumptive attacks an upholder of that campaign against alcohol so ineptly named the temperance cause, deliberately encouraged the notion that Burns's Dumfries days were one long debauch, and that the poet drank himself to death. This view was acceptable at the high table of Victorian morality, and therefore glibly echoed by all the nineteenth-century biographers, culminating in the blunt censures of W. E. Henley. True, there was the testimony of the friends and eye-witnesses of Burns who knew the man intimately; but Victorian prudishness could not be overcome by mere eye-witness testimonies.

In 1926, however, the legend of Burns the drunkard, was, at long last, finally nailed to the mast by one of the most eminent medical men of his day, Sir James Crichton-Browne. In *Burns from a New Point of View*, he concluded: 'Burns's death was not an accidental event, but the natural consequence of a long series of events that had preceded it . . . Burns died of endocarditis, a disease of the substance and lining membrane of the heart, with the origination of which alcohol had nothing to do, though it is possible that an injudicious use of alcohol may have hastened its progress. It was rheumatism that was the undoing of Burns. It attacked him in early years, damaged his heart, embittered his life, and cut short his career.'

Well justified, indeed, was Sir James in calling Currie 'the arch calumniator' who 'has tainted the pages of all who have written about Burns since his time'.

Later examinations of Burns's symptoms by other medical men have largely confirmed Sir James's findings. In particular, Snyder quotes Dr Harry B. Anderson of Toronto:

'The case was an ordinary one of rheumatism with heart complications, shortness of breath, faintness, weakness, rapid, irregular pulse (auricular fibrillation), and towards the end, fever, parched tongue, and delirium, presumably due to a bacteriological endocarditis which developed as a terminal infection.'

Deil's awa wi' the Exciseman', 'The

Lockhart, in his *Life of Burns*, published in 1828, states that on the authority of one of Burns's brother Excise officers, it was written as Burns tramped the wet sands of the Solway, keeping watch on the movements of the crew of a stranded smuggler while his companion went to get help so that the vessel could be boarded. It made its bow in an undated letter, conjectured by Ferguson to belong to March 1792, to the General Supervisor of the Excise in Edinburgh, John Leven, which mostly relates to tax permits, but adds:

'Mr Mitchell mentioned to you a ballad which I composed, and sung at one of his Excise Court dinners: here it is—

The deil's awa wi' th' Exciseman,
     Tune—"Madam Cossy".

If you honor my ballad by making it one of your charming bon vivant effusions, it will secure it undoubted celebrity.'

Dick thought the tune 'Madam Cossy' was 'The Quaker's Wife', which derives from a Gaelic air, though gives no reason for this supposition. The fact is that the song was first published in the *Scots Musical Museum* in 1792, with Burns's approval, to a tune called 'The Hempdresser', an English tune, which nevertheless found its way, titleless, into the *Caledonian Pocket Companion*, c. 1756, which is doubtless where Burns found it.

Dempster, George (1732–1818)

A parliamentary orator famous in his day, and a Scottish patriot who was known as 'Honest George'. His parliamentary career as a member for Forfar burghs lasted from 1761–90. Burns makes several references to him; one in the 'Epistle to James Smith' ('A title, Dempster merits it'); another in 'The Vision' ('Hence, Dempster's zeal—inspirèd tongue'); and a third in 'The Author's Earnest Cry and Prayer' ('Dempster, a true blue Scot I'se warran' ').

Dempster was a native of Dundee, where his father and grandfather amassed considerable wealth by trading, and which he inherited while still young. He was educated at Dundee Grammar School, St Andrews University, and Edinburgh, where he became a member of the Faculty of Advocates. While in Parliament he supported the Rockingham Party and Pitt's financial plans. He also supported Fox's India Bill.

In 1786 he purchased the estate of Skibo in Sutherland, where he turned his attention to Scottish fishing and agriculture. He promoted the formation of a Society for the extension and protection of Scottish Fisheries. The Company bought large acres of land and built harbours, quays and storehouses, but was ruined by the outbreak of war with France in 1793. Dempster taught his countrymen how to pack their salmon in ice for transit to London and other large cities. He was a model landlord, resigning most of his feudal rights, and draining and improving the land and conditions of the peasantry. He spent the latter part of his life at his estate of Dunichen, near St Andrews, where his old friend Dr Adam Ferguson, founder of the Poker Club, lived.

Devon, River

The Devon rises in the Ochil Hills, and takes a rugged course to join the River Forth at Alloa. The Falls of Devon, near Crook of Devon, form a famous beauty spot. It was as a result of Burns's visit to Harvieston, Clackmannanshire, near the Devon, in 1787, that he wrote the song 'The Banks of the Devon', inspired by Charlotte Hamilton (see **Hamilton, Charlotte**), who also inspired his last song of all, 'Fairest Maid on Devon Banks', written a few days before his death.

Dinning

The farm near Ellisland which Burns's brother Gilbert occupied when he left Mossgiel. (*See* **Burns, Gilbert.**)

Dods, Captain

An officer stationed at Dumfries. One evening, at a private gathering in July 1794, Burns gave as a toast: 'May our success in the present war be equal to the justice of our cause.' Captain Dods interpreted the toast as an innuendo against the Government, and took offence.

Burns had already had his loyalty to the Government questioned by the Board of Excise. He had been exonerated, but thought this contretemps with Dods might result in fresh trouble with the Board. Accordingly, he wrote next morning to Samuel Clark, junior, the clerk of the Peace for Dumfries-shire, acknowledging that he had been 'drunk last night', and appealing for his assistance:

'. . . you know that the report of certain Political opinions being mine, has already once before brought me to the brink of destruction. I dread lest last night's business may be misrepresented in the same way. You, I beg, will take care to prevent it. I tax your wish for Mr Burns's welfare with the task of waiting as soon as possible, on every gentleman who was present, and state this to him, and as you please, shew him this letter. What after all was the obnoxious toast? "May our success in the present war be equal to the justice of our cause"—a toast that the most outrageous frenzy of loyalty cannot object to. I request and beg that this morning you will wait on the parties present at the foolish dispute. The least delay may be of unlucky consequence to me. I shall only add, that I am truly sorry that a man who stood so high in my estimation as Mr Dods, should use me in the manner in which I conceive he has done.'

Doig, David (1719–1800)

Rector of Stirling Grammar School, when Burns had supper with him and some others on his Highland tour. Doig had been educated for the Church before becoming a teacher. He contributed articles on classical and oriental literature to the *Encyclopaedia Britannica*, and had a long controversy over the origin of civilisation with Lord Kames.

Burns described him in his *Journal* of the tour as: 'a queerish figure, and something of a Pedant'.

Don, Sir Alexander (d. 1815)

Married the 'divine' Lady Harriet, sister of the Earl of Glencairn. Burns dined with them in Kelso on his Border tour.

Don, Lady Henrietta (1752–1801)

Elder daughter of the thirteenth Earl of

Glencairn and sister to Earl James, Burns's patron. In 1778, she married Sir Alexander Don, Bart., of Newton-Don, Berwickshire. Her daughters, Elizabeth and Mary—one of whom Burns referred to as 'Lady Harriet's little angel whose epithalamium I am pledged to write'—were accidentally drowned in 1793. Her only son succeeded to the title when he was twenty-six, on his father's death in 1815.

On 26th March 1787, Burns sent Lady Don: 'a parcel of my epistolary performances', which had obviously been asked for. He added: 'I might have altered or omitted some things in these letters; perhaps I ought to have done so; but I wished to show you the Bard and his style in their native colors.' Burns dined with Lady Harriet at her home on 12th May 1787, while on his Border tour.

Writing from Ellisland, on 23rd October 1791, Burns sent Lady Don his 'Lament for James, Earl of Glencairn'. Underneath it he wrote: 'To Lady Hariot Don, this Poem, not the fictitious creation of poetic fancy, but the breathings of real woe from a bleeding heart, is respectfully presented by

The Author.'

The parcel of 'epistolary performances' makes up the Don Manuscript, which is now in the Library of the University of Edinburgh.

Don Manuscript

A collection of Burns's letters which he made in 1787 for Lady Henrietta Don, elder daughter of the thirteenth Earl of Glencairn, and sister of the poet's patron, James, the fourteenth Earl. It was forwarded to Lady Don under cover of a letter dated 26th March 1787: 'I have here sent you a parcel of my epistolary performances. . . . I might have altered or omitted some things in these letters; perhaps I ought to have done so; but I wished to show you the Bard and his style in their native colors.'

The letters are, of course, all examples of his early style, but the fact that he made the collection shows that even in his Edinburgh days he took his letter-writing seriously. It is now in the library of Edinburgh University, and known as the Laing MSS.

Doon, River

Flows from Loch Doon, on the borders of Ayrshire and Kirkcudbrightshire, to the Firth of Clyde, which it enters about ten miles west of Ayr. It divides the Ayrshire districts, Carrick and Kyle.

Burns mentions it many times, notably in 'Tam o' Shanter', and in the song 'Ye banks and Braes o' Bonie Doon'. This—possibly the most popular of all Burns's songs—first appeared in the *Scots Musical Museum* in 1792. It also appeared in Thomson's *Scottish Airs*. In a letter to Thomson, dated November 1794, Burns asked: 'Do you know the history of the air? It is curious enough. A good man years ago, a Mr Jas Miller, Writer in your good town, a gentleman whom, possibly, you know—was in company with our friend, Clarke; and talking of Scots music, Miller expresses an ardent ambition to be able to compose a Scots air. Mr Clarke, partly by way of a joke, told him to keep to the black keys of the harpsichord, and preserve some kind of rhythm; and he would infallibly compose a Scots air. Certain it is, that within a few days, Mr Miller produced the rudiments of an air, which Mr Clarke, with some touches and corrections, fashioned into the tune in question.' Thus, using the pentatonic scale, one of the world's loveliest airs was fashioned! A copy was given to Neil Gow, who called it 'The Caledonian Hunt's Delight' and printed it in his *Strathspey Reels*, 1788, four years before it appeared with Burns's words in the *Museum*. The manuscript of the song, in the British Museum, has Gow's title crossed out.

See Plate 6.

Douglas, Charles

Brother of Dr Patrick Douglas of Garallan, whose Jamaican estate, near Port Antonio, he managed. He offered Burns the position of book-keeper when the poet meditated emigration.

Douglas, Daniel or Dawnie

A highlander who kept a tavern in Anchor Close, off the High Street, Edinburgh, where the Crochallan Fencibles met. His singing of the Gaelic air 'Crodh Chailein', or 'Colin's Cattle' gave the Club the first part of their name. *See* **Crochallan Fencibles.**

Douglas, Dunbar, fourth Earl of Selkirk (1722–1799)

Dunbar Douglas, fourth Earl of Selkirk, succeeded to the earldom in 1744. He was Lord Lieutenant of the Stewartry of Kirkcudbright. The Earl supported the Government during the rebellion of 1745, and in 1770 took a prominent part in resisting ministerial influence in the election of Scottish representative peers.

Between late July and 2nd August 1793, Burns, in company with John Syme, toured Galloway. They spent 'a most happy evening' at St. Mary's Isle, during which the poet was asked to recite his poem 'Lord Gregory'. Syme later told Currie: 'Such was the effect, that a dead silence ensued. It was such a silence as a mind of feeling naturally preserves. . . . The fastidious critic may perhaps say some of these sentiments are of too elevated a kind for such a style of composition. . . . But this is a cold-blooded objection, which will be *said* rather than *felt*.' Stenhouse described the air as 'a very ancient Gallowegian melody'. What Kinsley calls 'a grudging tribute' was paid by Burns to the Earl in the Heron ballad ('Wham will we send to London Town').

> 'Tho wit and worth, in either sex,
> Saint Mary's Isle can show that;
> Wi' Lords and Dukes let Selkirk mix,
> For weel does Selkirk fa' that.'

It was, indeed, grudging because, Syme tells us, Burns arrived at St Mary's Isle in a bad temper, recalling that he was making for 'the seat of a Lord, yet that Lord was not an aristocrat, at least in his sense of the world'.

Douglas, Earl of Ormond
See **Wallace, Laird of Craigie.**

Douglas of Garallan, Dr Patrick (d. 1819)

A medical doctor whose estate was in the parish of Old Cumnock. He was one of those involved in the Douglas-Heron Bank collapse. Burns visited him in Ayr, and it was through Dr Douglas, who had bought an estate in Jamaica which his brother, Charles, managed, that Burns was offered the post of book-keeper to Charles in Port Antonio. The Rev. Hamilton Paul listed him as one of those present at the first meeting in 1801 in the Cottage at Alloway held to celebrate the poet's birth. Dr Douglas was for a time a surgeon in the West Lowland Fencible Regiment.

Douglas, William, third Earl of March and fourth Duke of Queensberry—'Old Q'—(1724–1810)

Only son of William, second Earl of March, and his wife, Lady Anne Hamilton. He succeeded his father to the Earldom of March in 1731, and his cousin to the Dukedom in 1786. An inveterate speculator, he was notorious for his behaviour on the Turf. As an early mentor of Fox, he was blamed for teaching the future politican his extravagant gambling habits.

Queensberry was Lord of the Bedchamber to George III from 1760 to 1789. During the King's illness, Queensberry went to extraordinary lengths to assess the probability of recovery. However, he made a wrong decision, supported the Prince of Wales's claim to full sovereign powers, and, on the King's recovery, was dismissed on the instance of the Queen and Pitt.

Queensberry was the most considerable landlord in Nithsdale, and although Burns sent him a copy of 'The Whistle' with a fulsome letter dated 24th September 1791, the poet loathed him, as is shown by these lines:

'All hail, Drumlanrig's haughty Grace—
Discarded remnant of a race
    Once godlike,—great in story!
His forbears' virtues all contrasted—
The very name of Douglas blasted—
    His that inverted glory!

'Hate, envy, oft the Douglas bore;
But he has superadded more
    And sunk them in contempt!
Follies and crimes have stained the
                                    name,
But, Queensberry, thine the virgin
                                    claim,
    From aught that's good exempt!'

The Duke's dislike of the King, of whom Burns himself, it should be said, was in his heart no ardent supporter, drew from Burns further lines on the Duke of Queensberry, which conclude:

'The turn-coat Duke his King forsook
    When his back was at the wa', man:
The rattan ran wi' a' his clan
    For fear the hoose should fa', man.

'The lads about the banks o' Nith,
    They trust his Grace wi' a', man:
But he'll sair them as he sair'd the
                                    King—
Turn tail and rin awa, man.'

A paragraph appeared in the *Star* of 22nd February 1790, with which Burns was credited: 'The agents of his (Sir James Johnstone's) Ducal Opponent are perfectly on a par with their degraded Master, whom they are a-kin to in everything but that Nobility which he has so long debased by his apostasy from the best of Kings, in the moment of distress. . . .

'When Old Q was last amongst us,

Scorn and execration followed wherever he went; and it is a notorious fact that he was obliged, in more places than one, to collect his vassals to protect him from insult.'

On that occasion, Burns was engaged in electioneering; but, more dispassionately, he had written of the Duke to Graham of Fintry on 9th December 1789: 'Were you to know his sins, as well of Omission as Commission to this outraged land, you would club your curse with the execrating voice of the Country.'

In 1795, the Duke stripped the woodlands around Drumlanrig Castle and Neidpath Castle in Peebleshire, to find money for a dowry for Maria Fagniani, whom he fancied was his daughter, when she married the Earl of Yarmouth. (Incidentally, George Selwyn, a well-known wit of the day, also left this lady a fortune, under the impression that she was *his* daughter!) This action incurred the immediate wrath of Burns, and the later wrath of Wordsworth. Burns was said to have inscribed his 'Verses on the Destruction of the Woods near Drumlanrig' on the back of a window-shutter in an inn or toll-house near the scene of the devastations. In this poem, the wandering poet meets the 'genius of the stream', and asks if the destruction has been caused by some 'bitter Eastern blasts', but is told:

' "Nae eastlin blast", the sprite replied,
    "It blew na here sae fierce and fell,
And on my dry and halesome banks
    Nae canker-worms get leave to
                                    dwell:
Man! cruel man!" the genius sighed—
    As through the cliffs he sank him
                                    down—
"The worm that gnawed my bonny
                                    trees,
    That reptile wears a ducal crown".'

In the *Burns Chronicle* for 1919, however, the Burns scholar J. C. Ewing, demonstrated conclusively that these verses are by Henry Mackenzie and not

Burns, his authority being a letter from Mackenzie to Dr Currie dated 22nd October 1802, and explaining that Mackenzie, viewing the destruction of the woods with his daughter, wrote them in the manner of Burns as a *jeu d'esprit*, pretending that he had copied them from 'the Window-Shutter of a little inn'.

Nevertheless, Mackenzie's indignation sounds genuine enough.

After his visit of 18th September 1803, Wordsworth burst out:

'Degenerate Douglas! oh, the unworthy
                                          Lord!
Whom mere despite of heart could
                                  so far please,
And love of havoc (for with such
                                      disease
Fame taxes him) that he could send
                                  forth word
To level with the dust a noble horde,
A brotherhood of venerable Trees,
Leaving an ancient Dome, and
                          towers like these,
Beggared and outraged! Many hearts
                                  deplored
The fate of those old Trees: and oft
                              with pain
The traveller, at this day, will stop
                              and gaze
On wrongs, which Nature scarcely
                          seems to heed;
For sheltered places, bosoms, nooks
                              and bays
And the pure mountains, and the
                          gentle Tweed,
And the green silent pastures, yet
                              remain.'

Queensberry was a liberal patron of Italian opera, although, it was said, more out of interest in the prima donnas and dancers than in the music.

In later years he sold his house at Newmarket and lived at Richmond, where he collected pictures and *objets d'art*.

Finally, he was largely confined to his house in Piccadilly. In his last infirmity,

he employed the former physician to Louis XV, Père Elisée, who was to be paid a large sum for every day his patient was kept alive, but nothing from the moment he died.

Raikes, in his *Journal*, said of 'Old Q': 'He was a little sharp-looking man, very irritable, and swore like ten thousand troopers.' Mackenzie, in *Anecdotes and Egotisms*, claimed that he was 'a disciple of Epicurus but without the virtue of the Epicurean system; and he had none of the hypocrisy of pretending to virtue or disinterestedness'. Although he had a number of illegitimate children, he never married, and his titles were dispersed on his death. The dukedom of Queensberry, with some other titles and Drumlanrig Castle, passed to the third Duke of Buccleuch, in whose family they remain.

Douglas, Sir William, and James

Brothers of Carlinwark. Sir William had the name of the town changed to Castle Douglas by Royal warrant. They also owned Orchardton.

Burns mentions them in his Second Heron Election Ballad:

'An' there'll be Douglasses doughty,
    New christening towns far and
                          near . . .'

Douglas, Heron & Company

Douglas, Heron & Company, with its head office at Ayr, was opened in 1769. It traded as the Ayr Bank. Soon afterwards, branches were opened in Edinburgh and Dumfries, and agencies were established at Glasgow, Inverness, Kelso, Montrose and Campbeltown, among other places. The branches operated separately under their own boards. The original shareholders included eminent men like the Governor, the Duke of Queensberry, the Duke of Buccleuch, the Earl of Dumfries, the Earl of March, Sir Adam Fergusson of Kilkerran, Patrick

Heron of Heron, and the Honourable Archibald Douglas. But there were no bankers on any of the boards.

Almost from the beginning, the bank emptied their coffers by giving privileged customers excessive loans, later striving to make good the position by making paper money.

In May 1772, the directors, realising their error, tried to retrench; but in June of that year, the London Banking House of Neale, James, Fordyce and Doune, failed, putting several Scottish Banks in difficulties. The Ayr Bank struggled for just over a year to retain confidence, but the Bank of Scotland, the Royal and the British Linen Company refused to accept the Ayr Bank's notes. In August 1773 a general meeting of the partners resolved on liquidation. The total loss to the partners, of whom there were 225, was £663,396 18s. 6d., and the shock was felt throughout Scotland.

According to Kerr's *History of Banking*, the downfall of the Ayr Bank was brought about by: 'trading beyond their means; divided control by permitting branches to act independently; forcing the circulation of their notes; giving credit too easily; ignorance of the principles of business; and carelessness or iniquity of officers.'

Douglas-Hamilton, Basil William, Lord Daer (1763-94)

The second son of the fourth Earl of Selkirk whose elder brother, Sholto, died in infancy. While attending Edinburgh University, Lord Daer lived with Professor Dugald Stewart, with whom he also stayed at the Professor's country home, Catrine, in Ayrshire. It was here that Burns met him when he dined with Stewart on 23rd October 1786, the meeting being the poet's first with a member of the nobility. But Lord Daer was liberal-minded. Later, through having friends in France who were concerned in the Revolution, Lord Daer became a warm admirer of it, and was a member of 'The

Friends of the People', and an advocate of Parliamentary reform.

In the 'Lines on meeting with Lord Daer', Burns said of him:

'Nae honest, worthy man need care
To meet with noble, youthful Daer,
  For he but meets a brother.'

Of a delicate constitution, Lord Daer died in France, predeceasing his father.

Dove (or Dow), John

Burns's 'Johnie Pigeon' was Innkeeper of the Whitefoord Arms, Mauchline, which was frequented by the Poet, whose 'Epitaph on John Dove' immortalises him. Scott Douglas and Chambers claim it probable that Dove originated from Paisley, and that he is the 'Paisley John' of another poem.

Burns was a member of a Bachelors Club which, in 1785, met at the Whitefoord Arms.

Dowie, John (d. 1817)

Owner of a much frequented tavern in Libberton's Wynd. He always wore his cocked hat and buckles at his knees and on his shoes. *See below.*

Dowie's Tavern

A tavern in Libberton's Wynd, Edinburgh, kept by Johnnie Dowie. It was a favourite haunt of Burns, Masterton, Nicol and their friends. In a small room known, because of its size, as 'The Coffin', Burns is supposed to have written some of his songs, among them 'O Poortith Cauld'.

Dowie's customers were mostly lawyers and writers who liked good food, and his tavern had a reputation for respectability. He refused to open a bottle after midnight. When he died, in 1817, he left his fortune to his son, a Major in the Army.

Dowie's was demolished in 1834.

Drama, Burns and the

Burns never wrote a play, the cantata 'The Jolly Beggars' being his nearest approach to the stage. It, of course, could hardly have been meant to be acted, although Cedric Thorpe Davie's stylised version for four singers and a chamber group of instrumentalists (made in 1953 for the Scottish Festival at Braemar, and subsequently broadcast, televised, recorded in part, and played all over Scotland) provides one solution to the problem inherent in a piece where each character is allowed only one major utterance.

Burns did, however, have in mind, from 1787 onwards, the idea of writing a play. He told Graham of Fintry on 10th September 1788, that if he were in the Excise service: '. . . it would likewise favor my Poetical schemes. I am thinking of something in the rural way of the Drama-kind. Originality of character is, I think, the most striking beauty in that Species of Composition, and my wanderings in the way of my business would be vastly favorable to my picking up original traits of Human nature.'

The poet discussed a Highland folk-subject with Ramsay of Ochtertyre, and came away with a letter of introduction to an expert in Highland music, the Reverend Walter Young of Erskine.

The tale which, Ramsay claimed, had impressed Burns hardly seems promising dramatic material:

'Its hero was a Highlander named Omeron Cameron, who received the Earl of Mar in his humble cottage, when the earl had to skulk from his enemies. Being himself forced into exile on this account by his own clan, he went to Kildrummy Castle with his wife and children, to claim a requital from the earl, who had bidden him to do so if ever misfortune should befall him. Upon hearing who it was, the earl started from his seat with a joyful exclamation, and caused Omeron to be conducted with all possible respect into the hall. He afterwards conferred on him a four-merk land, near the castle.'

Even more unpromising is the subject possibly referred to in January 1789, when he told Lady Cunningham that he had: '. . . a hundred different Poetic plans, pastoral, georgic, dramatic and etc. floating in the regions of fancy, somewhere between Purpose and resolve.'

Currie is our only authority for the story that Burns had actually resolved on a plot and title for a play, *Rob Mac-Quechan's Elshon*, based on the almost certainly apocryphal incident in which MacQuechan, Bruce's cobbler, accidentally drove his awl into that leader's foot while repairing a shoe damaged in a lost battle.

Henry Mackenzie, who had urged the poet to write a pastoral play, regretted that Burns had never fulfilled his plans to write a drama, and many commentators have echoed his regrets. Yet the only sort of drama Burns appears to have contemplated writing seems to have been of the parochial *genre* kind which later appeared as Scots kitchen comedy.

Burns was undoubtedly a brilliant master of the dramatic monologue. But, as Professor de Lancey Ferguson says in his splendid and perceptive study, *Pride and Passion*: '. . . his triumph in the dramatic monologue is the best reason for believing that the attempt would have failed. His numerous references to the drama and dramatic writing never so much as hint that Burns had grasped the elements of theatrical technique. For him a play was merely a vehicle for declamatory speeches and the expression of "sentiments" which would make neat quotations; a cobbling together of purple patches and of scattered episodes supposed to depict "originality of character". If it ever occurred to him that a good play is a unified structure in which a single impression is built up through a series of artfully contrived climaxes, he never put the idea on paper.'

Drumlanrig Castle
The seat of the Dukes of Queensberry.

built in 1679 by William Lukup, though the main front may be by Sir William Bruce. It overlooks the Nith on the right bank of which it stands, near the village of Thornhill. In Burns's day it was the home of William, the fourth Duke, to whom Burns was bitterly opposed, as is shown by such poems as the 'Verses on the Destruction of the Woods near Drumlanrig'. *See* **Douglas, William, fourth Duke of Queensberry**.

The poet was, however, extremely friendly with the Duke's Chamberlain, John M'Murdo.

Drummond, William, fourth Viscount Strathallan (d. 1746)

Killed at Culloden, his name and that of his eldest son, James, were included in the Bill of Attainder passed in 1746. Burns's 'Strathallan's Lament' is probably put into the mouth of the son James, fifth Viscount Strathallan, who died in France in 1765. The 'Lament' appears in the second volume of Johnson's *Museum*.

Ducat-Stream

Mentioned in 'The Brigs of Ayr'. Burns noted that it was 'a noted ford just above the Auld Brig'. Before the old Bridge was built, the ford was the only means of entry to the town, and many people lost their lives there during winter storms and spring tides.

Dudgeon, William (c. 1753–1813)

Born at Tyningham, a Berwickshire poet of local reputation whose song 'Up among yon cliffy rocks,' enjoyed contemporary popularity. The Ainslies invited him to Berrywell when Burns was their guest. Burns called Dudgeon 'a Poet at times', and thought him to have 'a worthy, remarkable character, a good deal of penetration, a great deal of information, some genius, and extreme Modesty'. All his life a farmer, he died at Newmains, Whitekirk.

Dudhope, third Viscount. *See* Scrimgeour, John.

Dumbarton

A royal burgh on the Clyde, and formerly the ancient capital of Strathclyde. At the end of his short West Highland tour, made during the summer of 1787, Burns visited Dumbarton. On 29th June, he was presented with his Burgess ticket, made out and signed by the Town Clerk, John McAulay, who entertained the poet at his home, Levengrove House, where Burns may possibly have stayed.

The Burgess ticket, which now hangs in the Municipal Buildings, declares that Mr Burns, of Ayrshire, compeared and was 'admitted and received a Burgess and guild brother with power to use and enjoy the privilegs and immunities thereto belonging'. On the reverse side is the burgh coat of arms. The Burgess ticket was presented to Dumbarton in 1923 by Mrs Burns Gowring, a great-granddaughter of the poet.

According to a nineteenth-century tradition, Burns's name does not appear in the Burgh Roll because of the opposition of the parish minister, the Reverend James Oliphant, formerly of Kilmarnock, to his acceptance as a freeman.

Dumfries

The county town of Dumfriesshire, on the River Nith. It was made a royal burgh by William the Lion in 1186, and it was in the chapel of the Minorite Convent, which stood near the corner of the present Castle Street and Friar's Vennel, that the Bruce slew the Red Comyn in 1305. In the thirteenth century, Lady Devorgilla, wife of the founder of Balliol College, built the first stone bridge over the Nith. In 1746, Prince Charles Edward Stuart, retreating from Derby, set up his headquarters for a night in the County Hotel. The room is still preserved. Dumfries, in the early eighteenth century, considered itself a future rival port to Glasgow. 'Queen of the South', it called itself, though Burns called it, 'Maggie by the banks o' Nith'.

It was a busy, bustling, thriving little town when Burns took up residence in it towards the end of 1791. He had often visited it before, of course, his first visit being on 4th June 1787, when he was made a Burgess, according to a list of Honorary Burgesses kept by the Town Council. The Dumfries ticket disappeared for many years, but turned up at an exhibition in Edinburgh's Music Hall in 1859. It was sold at Sotheby's in 1904 for fifty-five pounds, and was later that year acquired by John Thomson, a private collector and owner of the Hole-i'-th'-Wa' Inn at Dumfries. According to Andrew McCallum in the *Burns Chronicle* for 1942, the text reads: 'At Dumfries the fourth day of June one thousand seven hundred and eighty-seven years: the said day Mr Robert Burns, Ayrshire, was admitted Burgess of this Burgh with liberty to him to exerce and enjoy the whole immunities and privileges thereof as amply and freely as any other does, may, or can enjoy. Who being present accepted the same, and gave his oath of Burgess-ship to His Majesty and the Burgh in common form.'

One of the 'immunities and privileges' was that children of Dumfries's Honorary Burgesses could be educated for ten marks Scots as against the eighty pounds Scots (£6 13s. 4d.) demanded for the children of other people. Burns successfully claimed this privilege for his sons in 1793.

Burns's first home in Dumfries, rented from Captain John Hamilton of Allershaw, was a three-room-and-kitchen second-floor flat in Wee Vennel, now Bank Street. John Syme had his office on the ground floor. On the top storey a blacksmith, George Haugh, lived. On 19th May 1793 the Burns family moved into the self-contained house in Mill Street, now Burns Street, which is preserved as a museum. It, too, was rented—at eight pounds a year—from Captain Hamilton.

Burns seems to have entered fully into the life of the town. He had many friends and became a member of the Dumfries Volunteers. He described his own early days in Dumfries as: 'Hurry of business, grinding the faces of the publican and sinner on the merciless wheels of the Excise, making ballads, and then drinking and singing them; and, above all, correcting the press of two different publications.' The two publications were Johnson's *Scots Musical Museum* and Thomson's *Select Scottish Airs*.

Mrs Burns later recalled her husband's domestic habits at Dumfries for John McDiarmid: 'Burns was not an early riser, excepting when he had anything particular to do in the way of his profession. Even tho' he had dined out, he never lay after nine o'clock. The family breakfasted at nine. If he lay long in bed awake he was always reading. At all meals he had a book beside him on the table. He did his work in the forenoon, and was seldom engaged professionally in the evening. Dined at two o'clock when he dined at home. Was fond of plain things, and hated tarts, pies and puddings. When at home in the evening, he employed his time in writing and reading, with the children playing about him. Their prattle never disturbed him.'

And of life in the second Dumfries home, Robert Burns junior told Chambers that: '. . . the house in Mill Street was of a good order, such as were occupied at that time by the better class of burgesses; and his father and mother led a life that was comparatively genteel. They always had a maid-servant, and sat in their parlour. That apartment, together with two bedrooms, was well furnished and carpeted; and when good company assembled, which was often the case, the hospitable board which they surrounded was of a patrician mahogany. There was much rough comfort in the house, not to have been found in those of ordinary citizens; for the poet received many presents of jam and country produce from the rural gentlefolk, besides occasional barrels of oysters from Hill, Cunningham, and other friends in town; so that he possibly was as much envied by some of his neighbours as he has since been pitied by the general body of his countrymen.'

Burns died in Dumfries on 21st July 1796. He was given a military funeral on 25th July, his body being carried to St Michael's Churchyard to the 'Dead March' from Handel's *Saul*. The whole town turned out to honour his memory, and the Volunteers fired a volley on his grave. Nineteen years later, Burns was reinterred in the Mausoleum built by public subscription, at a cost of about one thousand five hundred pounds, to plans by T. F. Hunt.

See Plate 15.

Dumouriez, Charles Francois (1739–1823)

Born at Cambrai, he entered the French army before the Revolution, although he later fought for it. He won the battle of Valmy, that decisive victory against the German and Austrian armies who were intent on restoring the monarchy. He also won the battle of Jemmapes, and conquered Belgium. Thereafter he deserted the army of the Republic on 5th April 1793, and was only prevented by accident from betraying his troops into the hands of the enemy. He went back to the Royalists. He ultimately settled in England, where he died. Burns, in common with most British people, anglicised his name to Dumourier.

Burns wrote his poem, 'An Address to General Dumouriez', and included the lines:

'How does Dampierre do?
Aye, and Beurnonville too?
Why did they not come along with
                                        you,
        Dumouriez?'

Dampierre was one of the generals whom Dumouriez thought were going to desert with him, but who did not, in fact, do so. Nor did Beurnonville, an emissary of the Convention.

Dunbar, William (d. 1807)

The third son of Alexander Dunbar of Boath, Nairnshire, who claimed descent from the tenth Earl of Dunbar, through Lady Agnes Randolph, his wife. William Dunbar was a Writer to the Signet in Edinburgh, and 'Colonel' of the Crochallan Fencibles, a convivial club which he helped to found, each of whose members assumed a military title. He was Depute-Master of the Canongate Kilwinning Lodge at the time Burns visited it. Dunbar presented the poet with an edition of Spenser's works, which Burns much appreciated. Writing from his lodgings in the Lawnmarket, Edinburgh, on 30th April 1787, Burns told Dunbar: 'The time is approaching when I shall return to my shades; and I am afraid my numerous Edinburgh friendships are of so tender a construction that they will not bear carriage with me, Yours is one of the few that I could wish of a more robust constitution.'

Burns celebrated Dunbar's rumbustious good humour by adapting the Border Ballad 'Rattling, Rovin' Willie':

'As I cam by Crochallan
    I cannilie keekit ben,
Rattlin', roarin' Willie
    Was sittin' at yon boord-en';
Sittin' at yon boord-en',
    And amang gude companie;
Rattlin', roarin' Willie,
    You're welcome hame to me.'

Several letters passed between Burns and Dunbar, from which it may be inferred that the lawyer wrote less frequently than Burns hoped he might. But Burns sent him drafts of new poems from time to time, inviting Dunbar's return: 'Before an Author gets his Piece finished, he has viewed and reviewed it so often—he has brought it so near the mental eye, that it is within the sphere of vision, and he is no longer a judge of its merits. A judicious candid friend is then all he has to trust to. . . .'

This piece of wisdom, which might be called 'what every poet knows', accompanied a draft of both versions of 'Written in Friar's Carse Hermitage', and dates from February 1789.

From Ellisland, on 14th January 1790, after another hint that Dunbar was a tardy correspondent, Burns explained why he had decided to go into the Excise. This letter remained unfinished until 2nd February, when Burns began a long postscript: 'I have not for sheer hurry of business been able to spare five minutes to finish my letter.

'Besides my farm business, I ride on my Excise matters at least 200 miles every week. . . .'

Latterly, the correspondence seems to have languished, though Burns periodically exhorted friends like Peter Hill, the bookseller, to give his good wishes to his 'old friend' Dunbar.

Dunbar finally became Inspector-General of Stamp Duties for Scotland. He never married.

'Duncan Gray'

This song was written for Thomson's *Scottish Airs*, and appeared in 1798. Burns called it 'that kind of light-horse gallop of an old air which precludes sentiment. The ludicrous is the leading feature.'

The tune is in the *Caledonian Pocket Companion*, 1751. It appeared in the *Scots Musical Museum*, 1788 to an older version of the words.

Burns wrote a version of his song for the *Merry Muses*, 'Can ye play me, Duncan Gray?'

Duncan, The Reverend Dr Robert (1753–1815)

Son of a Boston colonist, a sergeant in the army, assistant minister at Irvine, and finally minister at Dundonald, where he was ordained in 1783. He was the author of a sermon on infidelity apparently widely read in Burns's day. He was described by Burns in 'The Twa Herds' as 'Duncan Deep'. Glasgow University made him a Doctor of Divinity in 1806.

Duncan, William

A friend of Burns who trained as lawyer. Burns wrote Craufurd Tait, an Edinburgh lawyer, on Duncan's behalf, asking him if he could find a place for the young man. Burns described Duncan as 'a young lad of your own profession, and a gentleman of much modesty and great worth'.

Dundas, Henry (1742–1811)

Son of Robert Dundas of Arniston, Lord President of the Court of Session, member of Parliament for Midlothian 1774–90, Lord Advocate 1775, Treasurer of the Navy 1782, Home Secretary 1791, created Viscount Melville 1802. Burns referred to him in 'The Author's Earnest Cry and Prayer' as 'a chap that's d-mn'd auldfarran. Dundas his name'.

For nearly thirty years he was the most powerful man in Scotland, and as the government election agent, controlled the election of nearly all the Scottish members of the House of Commons. He was a close and trusted friend and colleague of Pitt. Lord Cockburn, who was related to Dundas by marriage, described him as: 'the Pharos of Scotland. Who steered upon him was safe; who disregarded his light was wrecked. It was to his nod that every man owed what he got, and looked for what he wished.' Henry Mackenzie said that he had 'very little general knowledge . . . but . . . a great deal of invention and acuteness' and 'spoke broad Scotch'.

During the brief Whig administration, Dundas was impeached for having allegedly improperly appropriated public money. However, he was acquitted. Scott attended the public dinner in honour of the acquittal held in Edinburgh on 27th June 1806. But one result of the trial was that, as Cockburn put it, 'the mainspring of the Scottish pro-consular system' was weakened.

Romney, Reynolds and Raeburn all painted Dundas.

Dundas, Robert, Lord Arniston (1713-87)

Lord Advocate 1754, and Lord President of the Court of Session from 1760. Burns wrote a poem, 'On the Death of Lord President Dundas', which he described as:

'O heavy loss, thy country ill could
                                bear!
A loss these evil days can ne'er repair!'

Lord Cockburn said of him: 'Robert Dundas of Arniston, the son of one Lord President and the grandson of another, was in public affairs the most important person in this country. For he was Lord Advocate in the most alarming times, and at a period when extravagant and arbitrary powers were ascribed to that office. I knew him well; and lived many autumns with him, at Arniston, in my youth. His abilities and acquirements were moderate: and owing to the accident of his birth which placed him above all risk of failure in life, he was never in a situation where he was compelled to improve either. Hence, with all the advantages of his position, all the favour of agents, and all the partiality of courts, he never commanded any independent private practice. . . . He was a little, alert, handsome, gentlemanlike man, with a countenance and air beaming with sprightliness and gaiety, and dignified by considerable fire: altogether inexpressibly pleasing. It was impossible not to like the owner of that look.'

Burns's dislike of the Dundas family, however, is explained in a letter dated 11th March 1791, to Alexander Cunningham: 'I have two or three times in my life composed from the wish, rather than from the impulse, but I never succeeded to any purpose. One of these times I shall ever remember with gnashing of teeth. 'Twas on the death of the late Lord President Dundas. My very worthy and most respected friend, Mr Alexr. Wood, Surgeon, urged me to pay a compliment in the way of my trade to his Lordship's memory. Well, to work I went, and produced a copy of Elegiac verses, some of them I own rather commonplace, and others rather hide-bound, but on the whole, though they were far from being in my best manner, they were tolerable: and had they been the production of a Lord or a Baronet, they would have been thought very clever. I wrote a letter, which however was in my very best manner, and inclosing my Poem, Mr Wood carried all together to Mr Solicitor Dundas that then was, and not finding him at home, left the parcel for him. His Solicitorship never took the smallest notice of the Letter, the Poem, or the Poet. From that time, highly as I respect the talents of their Family, I never see the name, Dundas, in the column of a newspaper, but my heart seems straitened for room in my bosom; and if I am obliged to read aloud a paragraph relating to one of them, I feel my forehead flush, and my lip quivers. Had I been an obscure Scribbler, as I was then in the hey-day of my fame; or had I been a dependent Hanger-on for favor or pay; or had the bearer of the letter been any other than a gentleman who has done honor to the city in which he lives, to the Country that produced him, and to the God that created him, Mr Solicitor might have had some apology.

'But enough of this ungracious subject.'

Dundas of Arniston, Robert (1758-1819)

Lord Advocate 1789, member of Parliament for Midlothian 1790-1801. When Dundas was elected Dean of the Faculty over Burns's friend Henry Erskine, the poet produced the song 'The Dean of Faculty' about 'pious Bob . . . simple Bob.' He was the son of Lord Arniston.

Dunfermline

A royal burgh in Fife, sixteen miles north-west of Edinburgh, and once a Royal seat. In its Abbey, founded in 1072 by Queen Margaret, wife of King Malcolm Ceann-mor, Robert the Bruce lies buried. It was at Dunfermline in 1581 that James VI signed the first National Covenant, and where, in 1650, Charles II signed the Dun-fermline Declaration, reaffirming his oath to adhere to the Covenant.

The town was the birth-place of the American railroad millionaire, Andrew Carnegie. It possesses the Murison Collec-tion of Burns's books and manuscripts, presented to the Carnegie Library by Sir Alexander Gibb. Its main industry today is the making of damask linen.

Burns visited Dunfermline with Dr. Adair during his tour of Clackmannan-shire in October 1787. Adair recorded: 'At Dunfermline we visited the Abbey Church now consecrated to Presbyterian Worship. Here I mounted the cutty stool, or stool of repentance, while Burns addressed to me a ludicrous reproof and exhortation, parodied from one that had been delivered at one time in Ayrshire. In the church, two broad flagstones marked the grave of Robert Bruce, for whose memory Burns had more than common veneration. He knelt and kissed the stone with sacred fervour, and heartily execrated the worse than Gothic neglect of the first of Scottish heroes.'

Dungeon-clock, Ayr

In 'The Brigs of Ayr', there is an allusion to 'the drowsy Dungeon-Clock'. This clock was on the Tolbooth steeple, or Old Jail of Ayr, which was in the middle of the Sandgate. Because it was obstructing the traffic, the entire building was taken away in 1826.

Dunlop, Andrew (d. 1804)

Mrs Dunlop's fourth son. He served in the army during the American Revo-lution, and retired with the rank of major. He was managing the family estate of Dunlop, near Stewarton, in succession to his father, when Burns knew him. During the French Revolution he raised and commanded the Ayrshire Fencible Cavalry. He did not marry.

Burns wrote to him on 31st May 1788, mainly about his own marriage:

'I mentioned to your Mother in a letter I wrote to her yesterday, which is the third or fourth I have wrote her to Haddington, that my Philosophy was gravelled to account for that Partiality from the house of Dunlop of which I have the honor to be so much the Object. Do you know that except from your Mother and the good family, my existence or non-existence is now of as little im-portance to the Great World I lately left, as the satelites of the Georgium Sidus is to a parcel of your Ditchers. I foresaw this from the beginning. Ambition could not form a higher wish than to be wedded to Novelty; but I retired to my shades with a little comfortable pride and a few com-fortable pounds; and even there I enjoy the peculiar happiness of Mrs Dunlop's friendship and Correspondence, a happi-ness I shall ever gratefully prize next to the dearest ties that wind about my heart, so in my Ploughman Compliment I bid the World—Gude Speed.

'Your Mother never hinted at the report of my late change in life, and I did not know how to tell her. I am afraid that perhaps she will not entirely enter into the motives of my conduct, so I have kept aloof from the affair altogether. I saw, Sir, that I had a once, & still much-lov'd fellow-creature's happiness or misery among my hands; and I could not dally with such a matter. Pride & seeming Justice like true murderous King's Advo-cates talked much of injuries & wrongs; but Generosity, Humanity & Forgiveness were such irresistible Counsel for the poor Pannel, that a Jury of old Attachments & new Endearments brought in a verdict—NOT GUILTY!'

Dunlop, Anthony (1775-1828)

Seventh son of Burns's friend, Mrs Dunlop. He went to sea when he was twelve, in 1787. In a letter of 10th April 1790, Burns suggested to Anthony's mother that the boy possessed: 'a purity, a tenderness, a dignity, an elegance of soul, which are of no use, nay, in some degree, absolutely disqualifying, for the truly important business of making a man's way into life.'

Anthony Dunlop spent the earlier part of his life in the merchant navy, married Ann Cunningham, daughter of the Collector of Customs in Irvine, in 1803, and after a time, settled as a tenant farmer in the Isle of Man. There, he bought a small estate, which he named Ellerslie, after the birth-place of Sir William Wallace. He became involved in litigation, however, and got himself heavily into debt. On 29th June 1828, he committed suicide in an Edinburgh hotel.

Dunlop, Mrs Frances Anna (1730-1815)

She was born Frances Anna Wallace, eldest daughter of Sir Thomas Wallace of Craigie—who claimed descent from Sir Richard, cousin to the great Sir William Wallace—and Dame Eleanora Agnew. In 1748, Frances Anna Wallace married John Dunlop of Dunlop (1707-85); according to a tradition quoted by Wallace, she made a run-away match from Dunskey House. She seems to have lived happily with her elderly husband, bearing him seven sons and six daughters. In 1761, on her mother's death, she fell heiress to the estate of Lochryan. When her father died in 1774, the estate of Craigie went to her eldest surviving son, Thomas Wallace, who took his father's surname; but owing to 'heavy encumbrances' and mismanagement, Craigie had

to be sold in 1785, which caused her considerable distress. On 5th June 1785, too, Mrs Dunlop's husband died. The double blow resulted in 'a long and severe illness, which reduced her mind to the most distressing state of depression'. Then Miss Betty M'Adam gave her 'The Cotter's Saturday Night' to read. It led Mrs Dunlop to communicate with its author, and resulted in a friendship, which, except for a break towards the end of the poet's life, gave her a new and absorbing interest.

As Gilbert Burns recorded: 'Mrs Dunlop sent off a person express to Mossgiel, distant fifteen or sixteen miles, with a very obliging letter to my brother, desiring him to send her half-a-dozen copies of his *Poems*, if he had them to spare, and begging he would do her the pleasure of calling at Dunlop House as soon as convenient. This was the beginning of a correspondence which ended only with the poet's life (nearly); the last use he made of his pen was writing a short letter to this lady a few days before his death.'

Burns replied to Mrs Dunlop's note from Mossgiel on 15th November 1786, in autobiographical vein, adding: 'I have only been able to send you five Copies: they are all I can command. I am thinking to go to Edinburgh in a week or two at farthest, to throw off a second Impression of my book; but on my return, I shall certainly do myself the honor to wait on you. . . .' Burns visited Mrs Dunlop at least five times—June 1787; February 1788, when he stayed for two days; May 1789, another two-day visit; 21st June 1791, a call on the occasion of Gilbert's marriage; and December 1792, when, with Dr Adair, he stayed four days.

She herself stated the relationship she wished to establish when she told Burns: 'I have been told Voltaire read all his manuscripts to an old woman and printed nothing but what she would have ap-

E

proved. I wish you would name me to her office.' Burns never so named her, so she named herself. She gossiped; she criticised him; she treated him like a son whose affection a mother craves, whose achievements she feels pride in, but whose passions she fears and half-resents, particularly where sex is concerned. On 30th December 1786, she was already trying to cure him of what she called his 'undecency': 'I can wish you catch no one thing from Thomson, unless it were the resolution with which he plucked up every one of those luxuriant weeds that will be rising in too rich a soil, and from which I would be glad to see you wholly exempt.'

She gave a copy of the *Poems* to Dr Moore, and urged Burns to write to Moore himself. He was somewhat tardy in doing so, but when he did, there was established that curious exaggerated regard which the man of genius had for the man of talent, but which led to Burns sending Moore his Autobiographical Letter. While Mrs Dunlop's first flush of praise must have warmed his heart, he cautioned her on 15th January 1787, as he had cautioned others:

'You are afraid I shall grow intoxicated with my prosperity as a Poet: alas! Madam, I know myself and the world too well. I do not mean any airs of affected modesty; I am willing to believe that my abilities deserve some notice; but in a most enlightened, informed age and nation, when poetry is and has been the study of men of the first natural genius, aided with all the powers of polite learning, polite books, and polite company—to be dragged forth to the full glare of learned and polite observation, with all my imperfections of aukward rusticity and crude unpolished ideas on my head—I assure you, Madam, I do not dissemble when I tell you I tremble for the consequences. The novelty of a Poet in my obscure station, without any of those advantages which are reckoned necessary for that character, at least at

this time of day, has raised a partial tide of public notice which has borne me to a height, where I am absolutely, feelingly certain my abilities are inadequate to support me; and too surely do I see that time when the same tide will leave me, and recede, perhaps, as far below the mark or truth. . . .

'Your patronising me and interesting yourself in my fame and character as a Poet, I rejoice in; it exalts me in my own idea; and whether you can or cannot aid me in my subscription is a trifle. Has a paltry subscription-bill any charms to the heart of a bard, compared with the patronage of the descendant of the immortal Wallace? . . .'

Her criticism, though womanly, was frank enough: 'You ought to take off a few patches which consummate beauty has no use for, which in a polite and enlightened age are seldom wore, and which a delicate, manly mind cannot regret the want of. Forgive my saying that every undecency is below you, and sinks the voice of your fame by putting to silence your female admirers.'

Mrs Dunlop gave him her views on possible future careers. On 29th March 1787, having heard of Burns's notion to buy a commission, she told him that 'a military line wears several attractions, not wholly to be slighted', though she advised him never to give way to his hankering after militaristic glamour unless he could 'command at least £250 more than the £400 which is the regulated price. . . . At any rate, the pomp of war is more for poetry than practice, and although warriors may be heroes, peace soldiers are mostly powdered monkies.'

She also told Burns of Adam Smith's suggestion that he should become a Salt Officer, a plan which came to nothing, probably because of Smith's illness in 1786 and 1787. Later, she even talked of Burns becoming a Professor of Agriculture!

When her copies of the first Edinburgh Edition reached her, she was angry with the poet for failing to bowdlerise some of his reprinted pieces, as she had suggested. Burns replied from Edinburgh on 30th April 1787: 'Your criticisms, Madam, I understand very well, and could have wished to have pleased you better. You are right in your guess that I am not very amenable to counsel. Poets, much my superiors, have so flattered those who possessed the adventitious qualities of wealth and power that I am determined to flatter no created being, either in prose or verse, so help me God!'

Soon after 9th June, when Burns made his 'éclatant return' to Mauchline after his Border tour, he called on Mrs Dunlop for the first time. In August, he sent her the original copy of his Autobiographical Letter, intended for Doctor Moore, which she read with 'more pleasure than Richardson or Fielding could have afforded me'.

Their correspondence went on, in spite of the offence which Burns sometimes gave the old lady when she suspected that he was not reading her letters properly —they were written in a cramped, rather illegible hand—people, affairs and books being discussed with friendliness and freedom. Burns valued her intelligent and kindly interest in him, even when he discreetly chose to overlook her well-meant but frequently unsound, literary advice. She, for her part said: 'Take my honest word; I consider your correspondence as an acquisition for which mine can make no return, as a commerce in which I alone am the gainer; the sight of your hand gives me inexpressible pleasure. . . .'

Burns wrote more letters to her than to any other correspondent. Her family troubles—the death of her son-in-law, Henri, followed, not long afterwards by the death of her daughter, Mrs Henri, the illness of Agnes Eleanor, another daughter married to Joseph Elias Perochon,

a French Royalist, and the instability of her son, Anthony—aroused Burns's deepest sympathies.

The correspondence, which meant so much to both of them, ran into difficulties late in 1794. As far back as November 1792, Mrs Dunlop had expressed fears at the spread of the revolutionary spirit in her part of the country, but Burns did not take the hint. In a letter of 5th January 1793, just after his loyalty had been called in question, Burns poured imprecations on the 'miscreant wretch' who would turn over a man's 'faithful wife and prattling innocents' to 'Beggary and Ruin', continuing: 'Can such things be? Oui! Telles choses se font! Je viens d'en faire une epreuve maudite. (By the way, I don't know whether that is French; and much would it go against my soul, to mar anything belonging to that gallant people; though my real sentiments of them shall be confined alone in my correspondence with you.)'

Ten weeks passed before Mrs Dunlop replied, on 16th March. Her letter was full of reproof: ''Tis not enough, my dr. Sir, never to write improperly but to one; that one cannot wish you as well as I do and encourage it.' When Burns wrote to her, from a 'solitary inn' at Castle Douglas on 25th June 1794, he sent her his 'Ode for General Washington's Birthday'. On 8th September she replied, noting that he was: 'enthusiastically fond of the theme. So was I once, but your Goddess has behaved in such a way as to injure her reputation, and acquire so very bad a name, that I find it no longer fit to acknowledge my favour for her, since her company is not now profuse of bliss nor pregnant with delight; and she is too much attached of late to the society of butchers. . . .' Burns failed to take this second warning, and on 20th December 1794—part of the letter was not finished until 12th January 1795— wrote strongly in criticism of Dr. Moore's *Journal During A Residence in France.*

(Mrs Dunlop, incidentally, considered Moore something of a radical!)

'He has paid me a pretty compliment, by quoting me, in his last Publication, though I must beg leave to say, that he has not written this last work in his usual happy manner. Entre nous, you know my Politics; & I cannot approve of the honest Doctor's whining over the deserved fate of a certain pair of Personages. What is there in the delivering over a perjured Blockhead & an un-principled Prostitute to the hands of the hangman, that it should arrest for a moment, attention, in an eventful hour, when, as my friend Roscoe in Liverpool gloriously expresses it—

"When the welfare of Millions is hung
                             in the scale
And the balance yet trembles with
                                  fate!"

But our friend is already indebted to People in power, & still looks forward for his Family, so I can apologise for him; for at bottom I am sure he is a staunch friend to liberty. Thank God, these London trials have given us a little more breath, & I imagine that the time is not far distant when a man may freely blame Billy Pit, without being called an enemy to his Country.'

Two of Mrs Dunlop's daughters had married French royalist refugees, and four of her sons and one grandson had Army connections. She naturally took deep offence at this apparently deliberate attack on her views; offence so deep, indeed, that she ignored two letters, one written during the summer of 1795; the second, the pathetic letter of 31st January 1796:

'These many months you have been two packets in my debt. What sin of ig-norance I have committed against so highly a valued friend I am utterly at a loss to guess. Your son, John, whom I had the pleasure of seeing here, told me that you had gotten an ugly accident of a fall, but told me also the comfortable news that you were gotten pretty well again. Will you be so obliging, dear Madam, as to condescend on that my offence which you seem determined to punish with a deprivation of that friend-ship which once was the source of my highest enjoyments? Alas! Madam, ill can I afford, at this time, to be deprived of any of the small remnant of my pleasures. I have lately drank deep of the cup of affliction. The Autumn robbed me of my only daughter & darling child, & that at a distance too & so rapidly as to put it out of my power to pay the last duties to her. I had scarcely began to recover from that shock, when I became myself the victim of a most severe Rheu-matic fever, & long the die spun doubtful; until after many weeks of a sick-bed it seems to have turned up more life, & I am beginning to crawl across my room, & once indeed have been before my own door in the street.'

Within a few days of his death, Burns wrote her his last letter:
'Madam

I have written you so often without rec.g any answer, that I would not trouble you again but for the circum-stances in which I am. An illness which has long hung about me in all probability will speedily send me beyond that bourne whence no traveller returns. Your friend-ship with which for many years you honored me was a friendship dearest to my soul. Your conversation & especially your correspondence were at once highly entertaining & instructive. With what pleasure did I use to break up the seal! The remembrance yet adds one pulse more to my poor palpitating heart!

Farewell ! ! !'

At that pathetic cry she relented. A letter from John Lewars to her, written just after Burns's death confirms Currie's statement that almost the last line the poet was able to read on his death-bed was a reconcilatory message from her. She herself survived the poet by nineteen years. When she died, her total movable estate was worth £800.

Both sides of the Burns/Mrs Dunlop correspondence were published in 1898, by William Wallace, under the title: *Robert Burns and Mrs Dunlop*. Several of her letters, discovered later, were printed in the *Burns Chronicle* for 1904. It was from Wallace's book that a few lines from her own verse-picture, part caricature of Burns, are taken:

'Genius and humour sparkle in the
                                                                eyes,
Frank independence native ease supplys.
Good sense and manly spirit mark the
                                                                air,
And mirth and obstinacy too were
                                                                there.
A peering glance sarcastic wit confest,
The milk of human kindness fill'd the
                                                                brest.
While pride and parts the features
                                                        thus control,
Good-nature lurk'd an inmate of the
                                                                soul.
So the green nut's sweet, milky juice
                                                        comprest
In a hard shell and acid husk is
                                                        drest. . . .'

See Plate 11.

Dunlop, Sir Thomas (d. 1786)
Eldest son of Mrs Dunlop, he married Eglintoune Maxwell, sister of the Duchess of Gordon, in 1783, in which year his debts forced him to sell Craigie estate, which he had inherited in 1771. He went to live in England, where he died.

Dunlop and Wilson, Messrs.
The leading booksellers and printers in Burns's day in the West of Scotland. Their Premises were in Glasgow. An unverifiable tradition alleges that Burns asked them to publish his poems in 1786, but that they declined.

Dunn, David, or Dun (d. 1810)
Maybole parish schoolmaster and a magistrate of the town. Writing to William Niven from Mossgiel on 30th April 1786, Burns wished to be remembered to Dunn 'in the most respectful manner'.

Dunn, Jean
Joseph Train related an incident in which Jean Dunn was said to be involved with Burns in his capacity as an officer of the Excise. When Burns and his fellow officer Robertson entered Jean's house, suspecting her of illicit trading in Kirkpatrick-Durham, Jean stepped out, leaving only the servant and her own little daughter in the house. When asked if there had been any brewing done, the servant answered to the contrary, saying they had no licence to brew. Whereupon the child exclaimed, 'That's no true, the muckle black kist is fou' o' the bottles o' y'll that my mother sat up a' night brewing for the fair.' 'Does that bird speak?' said Robertson, pointing to one hanging in a cage. 'There is no use for another speaking-bird in this house,' said Burns, 'while that little lassie is to the fore. We are in a hurry just now; but as we return from the fair, we'll examine the muckle black kist.'

On their return, needless to say, the kist was empty.

Train was, of course, an enthusiastic gossip. It is up to the reader to put his own value on his stories.

Duns
Duns, formerly Dunse—the spelling was officially altered in 1882—in Berwickshire, was visited by Burns while on his Border tour in 1787. In his *Journal*, he wrote: 'Sunday, May 6th, went to Church at Dunse.' He called at the town a second time: 'Wednesday, May 10th, Dine at Dunse with the Farmers' Club company.'

The town, which was founded in 1588, takes its name from the nearby hill, Duns Law. Berrywell, the family home of Burns's friend Robert Ainslie, was nearby.

E

Earnock Manuscript

The correspondence between Gilbert Burns and the publishers, Messrs Cadell and Davis, over Gilbert's edition of *Burns's Life and Work*. It also includes correspondence about Dr Currie's edition, Cromek's *Reliques*, and letters from, among others, George Thomson.

The manuscripts were bound by Sir John Watson Bart., of Earnock, after whose death in 1889, they were sold by auction and taken to America. Volumes 7 and 8 of the *Burns Chronicle* contain details of the collection and reprint the Gilbert Burns/Cadell and Davis letters.

Easton, Esther

The wife of a working gardener in Jedburgh who had a remarkable memory for poetry. Burns met her with Isabella Lindsay in Jedburgh when on his Border Tour, recording the visit thus: 'Miss Lindsay and myself go to see *Esther*, a very remarkable woman for reciting poetry of all kinds.'

Ecclefechan

A small village in Dumfriesshire which became the birthplace of Thomas Carlyle.

Burns twice visited the village. On the second visit, 7th February 1795, he wrote to Thomson: 'You cannot have any idea of the predicament in which I write you. In the course of my duty as Supervisor (in which capacity I have acted of late) I came yesternight to this unfortunate, wicked, little village. I have gone forward—but snows of ten feet deep have impeded my progress: I have tried to "gae back the gate I cam again", but the same obstacle has shut me up within insuperable bars. To add to my misfortune; since dinner, a Scraper has been torturing Catgut, in sounds that would have insulted the dying agonies of a Sow under the hands of a Butcher—and thinks himself, *on that very account*, exceeding good company. In fact, I have been in a dilemma, either to get drunk, to forget the miseries; or to hang myself, to get rid of these miseries: like a prudent man (a character congenial to my every thought, word and deed), I, of two evils have chosen the least, and am very drunk—at your service!'

Edgar, John (d. 1816?)

An accountant to the Board of Excise and Salt Duties in Edinburgh. His name does not appear on the almanac list of Excise officers after 1816.

Burns wrote to him from Dumfries on 25th April 1795, protesting against incurring censure over 'the Wine-Account of this district not being sent in'. He explained the reason for the delay—his handing back of the District to Findlater, for whom he had been acting while Findlater was indisposed—and finished:

'This, Sir, is a plain state of Fact; and if I must still be thought censureable, I hope it will be considered that this Officiating Job being my first, I cannot be supposed to be completely master of all the etiquette of the business.

'If my supposed neglect is to be laid before the Honourable BOARD, I beg you will have the goodness to accompany the complaint with this letter.'

Edina

A poetic name for Edinburgh, first used by the Latin poet and tutor to Mary, Queen of Scots, George Buchanan (1506–82) and later by Burns in his 'Address to Edinburgh', and by Byron in his *English Bards and Scotch Reviewers*.

Burns's opening line, 'Edina, Scotia's darling seat', gave the cue to a firm of bathroom manufacturers to apply the name 'Edina' to one of their necessary products.

Editions Published in Burns's Lifetime

1. Kilmarnock Edition—Printed and issued by John Wilson, Kilmarnock, on 31st July 1786. It cost three shillings. Six hundred copies were printed. The volume was dedicated to Gavin Hamilton.
2. First Edinburgh Edition—Printed by William Smellie, published by William Creech, by subscription 'for the sole benefit of the author', on 21st April 1787.

This edition, however, was re-set and reprinted more or less simultaneously, since it was over-subscribed. Three thousand copies in all were published.

After the first batch had been printed, the type had to be re-set. An error crept into a line in the 'Address to a Haggis', whereby 'Auld Scotland wants nae skinking ware', became 'Auld Scotland wants nae stinking ware'. The second form of the 1787 edition has thus become known as the 'Stinking Burns'. The price to subscribers was five shillings, to other purchasers six. As with the Kilmarnock Edition, Burns assumed all personal responsibility.

On 23rd April, Burns disposed of the property of his poems for one hundred guineas to Creech in a 'memorandum of Agreement' (*see* **Creech, William**). Thereafter, Creech put out the:

3. Second Edinburgh Edition—Published by Creech, in 18th February 1793, in two volumes 'greatly enlarged with New Poems'. One of the 'New Poems' in the extra fifty pages was 'Tam o' Shanter'.

This edition was re-issued in 1794.

Burns probably cleared just over £50 from the Kilmarnock volume and about £855 from the First Edinburgh Edition together with the sale of the copyright, which resulted in his receiving only a few complimentary copies from Creech for the Second Edinburgh Edition.

Eglinton, eleventh Earl of. *See* **Montgomerie, Archibald.**

Elliot, Dr

Burns met him in Jedburgh on his Border tour. He described him in his Journal as 'an agreeable, good-hearted, climate-beaten, old veteran, in the medical line; now retired to a romantic, but rather moorish place, on the banks of the Roole'.

Elliot, George Augustus (1717–90)

Made Lord Heathfield in recognition of his services in defending Gibraltar in 1782, after it had been laid siege to for three years by the Spaniards. Burns makes the old soldier mention him in the song, 'I am a son of Mars', in 'The Jolly Beggars' Cantata:

'Yet let my country need me, with
Elliot to head me,
I'd clatter on my stumps at the sound
of a drum.'

Ellisland

The farm of Ellisland stands on the banks of the River Nith, six and a half miles north-west of Dumfries. It was bought by Patrick Miller of Dalswinton (*see* **Miller, Patrick**) in 1777, an enthusiast for agriculture experiment, who offered it to Burns in 1787. Burns took it from 11th June 1788, but, as he had to build a farmhouse, did not occupy it until the following summer. Miller allowed Burns three hundred pounds towards the cost of the new farmhouse, and for other repair work and fencing. The lease was for seventy-six years, at a rent of fifty pounds a year for the first three years, and thereafter, seventy pounds a year.

When Burns took on Ellisland, as in the case of most farms in eighteenth-century Scotland, the soil was exhausted. It was also stony. Neither crop growing nor dairy farming, to which Burns turned, paid, and Burns was soon thoroughly disillusioned. His first biographer, Robert Heron, said: '. . . a lease was granted to the poetical farmer at the annual rent which his own friends declared that the due cultivation of his farm might easily enable him to pay. But these friends, being Ayrshiremen, were little acquainted with the soil, with the manures, with the markets, with the dairies, with the modes of improvement in Dumfries-shire; they had estimated his rental at Ayrshire rates, so that contrary to his Landlord's intentions, he must pay more for Ellisland than Ellisland was worth.' By the end of 1790 Burns had decided that Ellisland was 'altogether a ruinous business'. He might have had some difficulty in getting free of his lease, had not a neighbouring proprietor, John Morin, offered to buy the farm for nineteen hundred pounds, an offer Miller accepted. Burns and his family left Ellisland for Dumfries in November 1791. *See p. 383.*

Ellisland was farmed until 1921, when it was bought by a former President of Edinburgh Burns Club, George Williamson, who gifted it to the nation. The place where Burns wrote, among other things, 'Tam o' Shanter', 'Of a' the airts the wind can blaw', 'O were I on Parnassus hill', 'I hae a wife o' my ain' and 'Willie brewed a peck o' maut', is now preserved as a working farm, open to visitors.

See Plate 4.

Elphinston, James (1721–1809)
Born in Edinburgh, he kept a boarding school in Kensington, London, described by Alexander Carlyle as 'a Jacobite seminary'. He was a friend of Samuel Johnson. Elphinston made a translation of the Latin poet Martial's *Epigrams*, of which Johnson said 'there are in these verses too much folly for madness, I think, and too much madness for folly.' Burns mentioned him in a letter to 'Clarinda', dated 14th January 1788: 'The poetry of Elphinstone can only equal his prose-notes.'

Burns wrote an epigram on Elphinstone on a copy of Elphinston's *The Epigrams of M. Val Martial, in twelve books, with a comment*, while he was waiting for somebody 'in a merchant's shop of my acquaintance'. Burns enclosed the epigram in his letter to Clarinda:

'O thou whom Poesy abhors,
Whom Prose has turned out of doors!
Heard'st thou yon groan? proceed no
                                       further;
'Twas laurell'd Martial calling,
                                       Murther!

Erskine, Captain Andrew (d. 1793)
Youngest son of the fifth Earl of Kellie. He served for a time in the Army, then settled in Edinburgh, where he helped George Thomson with his *Scottish Airs*. He had published his correspondence with James Boswell in 1763. Finally, oppressed by debt, he drowned himself in the River Forth. He was a friend of Henry Erskine, in a letter to whom Burns described the Captain as a 'Son of Parnassus' and 'my much valued friend'.

Erskine, David Stewart, eleventh Earl of Buchan (1742–1829)
The Earl succeeded to the title in 1767. He fancied himself as a patron of the arts, and dabbled in writing. In 1780, he was one of the founders of the Scottish Society of Antiquaries. He wrote to Burns on 1st February 1787, in patronising terms which no doubt he considered his rank entitled him to use: 'I have redd with great pleasure several of your poems, and I have subscribed in Lady Glencairn's list for six copies of your book for myself, and two for Lady Buchan.

'These little doric pieces of yours in our provincial dialect are very beautiful, but you will soon be able to diversify your language, your rhyme and your subject, and then you will have it in your power to show the extent of your genius, and to attempt works of greater magnitude, variety and importance.' Buchan then advised Burns to keep his 'Eye upon Parnassus, and drink deep of the fountains of Helicon, but beware of the Joys that is dedicated to the Jolly God of wine', and to renew his inspiration by visiting the classic scenes of Scottish literature and history. Burns replied on 7th February: 'Your Lordship touches the darling chord of my heart when you advise me to fire my muse at Scottish story and Scottish scenes. I wish for nothing more than to make a leisurely Pilgrimage through my native country; to sit and muse on those once hard-contended fields, where Caledonia, rejoicing, saw her bloody lion borne through broken ranks to victory and fame; and catching the inspiration, to pour the deathless Names in Song.' But, Burns reminded the dilettante Earl, he had to live, and for that reason: 'must return to my rustic station, and, in my wonted way woo my rustic Muse at the Plough-tail'.

In August 1791, the Earl invited Burns to the crowning of a bust of the poet Thomson, and suggested that Burns might write an appropriate poem. Burns replied that he could not attend because of the harvest. However, he sent the stanzas 'Address to the Shade of Thomson, on Crowning his Bust at Ednam, Roxburghshire, with a Wreath of Bays'. In the event, the bust was smashed in a drunken frolic before the ceremony could take place, and the Earl had to lay the wreath on a volume of Thomson's poems! Burns sent him a copy of 'Scots Wha Hae' in January 1794. The Earl unveiled an enormous statue of Wallace on the river bank of Tweed, near Dryburgh, in 1814. At the same time he crowned a bust of Burns, speaking twelve lines of verse he had composed in memory of the poet. His most audacious performance was his intrusion into Scott's family when Sir Walter was ill in 1819. Buchan had plans for the funeral ceremony!

Scott later described Buchan as 'a person whose immense vanity, bordering upon insanity, obscured, or rather eclipsed, very considerable talents . . .'

Most of Buchan's cultural eccentricities betrayed a strong love of self-advertisement. At Kirtland, West Lothian, where he had a mansion, he built a model solar system, $12,183\frac{28}{100}$ miles to an inch in scale, only one stone relic of which remains today. He also erected a memorial to his ancestors in the grounds of Dryburgh Abbey, a figure of James 1, which is still to be seen.

The Reverend George William Hay Drummond, in *A Town Eclogue* (1804) satirises Buchan thus:

'His brain with ill-assorted fancies
                                              stor'd,
Like shreds and patches on a tailor's
                                              Board,
Women, and whigs, and poetry and
                                              pelf,
And ev'ry corner stuffed with mighty
                                              self.'

Erskine, The Hon. Henry (1746–1817)

Second son of the tenth Earl of Buchan. He became an advocate, and was elected Dean of the Faculty in 1786. He twice held the office of Lord Advocate; in 1783 and in 1806–7. He was noted for his legal skill, his vigorous pleading and his humour.

In his 'Extempore in the Court of Session' Burns humorously compares Erskine's style with that of Sir Ilay Campbell, the Lord Advocate, who was a poor orator:

'Collected, Harry stood awee,
    Then open'd out his arm, man;
His lordship sat wi' ruefu' e'e,
    And ey'd the gathering storm, man;
Like wind-driv'n hail it did assail,
    Or torrents owre a lin', man;
The BENCH sae wise lift up their
                                              eyes,
    Half-wauken'd wi' the din, man.'

Burns first met him at a meeting of the Canongate Kilwinning Lodge, when Dalrymple of Orangefield introduced the poet to Erskine as the Past-Master.

In his *Life of Lord Jeffrey*, Lord Cockburn referred to Erskine's popularity: 'nothing was so sour as not to be sweetened by the glance, the voice, the gaiety, the beauty of Henry Erskine.' On a tablet later affixed to his birthplace, there are the words: 'No poor man wanted a friend while Harry Erskine lived.'

Erskine, John Francis (1701–1825)

Afterwards 27th Earl of Mar and 12th Lord Erskine. He and Burns never met, but when a rumour reached Erskine's notice that the poet had been dismissed from his Excise post because of his radicalism, Erskine wrote to Robert Riddell offering to lead a subscription on Burns's behalf. Burns was deeply moved by the gesture and wrote to thank Erskine on 13th April 1793.

Erskine, Thomas (1750–1823)

The third son of the tenth Earl of Buchan, and a younger brother of Henry Erskine, Thomas Erskine became an early admirer of Burns's work. Erskine was called to the English bar in 1779 when he 'came into the first practice in the Kingdom', according to Henry Mackenzie; became Member of Parliament for Portsmouth in 1783; and Lord Chancellor in 1806. His decisions in this office are said to have been styled 'Apocrypha'. He defended Tom Paine in 1792.

Burns referred to him as 'Erskine, a spunkie Norland billie', in 'The Author's Earnest Cry and Prayer'. Lord Cockburn, in *Memorials of his Time*, described the return of the Lord Chancellor to Edinburgh in 1820 as an old man. 'The Whigs,' said Cockburn, 'gave him a public dinner on 21st February, at which about 300 attended . . . the largest convocation of the party that had yet taken place. Erskine, though old and feeble, spoke several times, always elegantly, gently and with liveliness, and once or twice disclosed gleams of his better days.'

His chief characteristic was great vanity, but his wit was proverbial, especially his epigrams and puns. 'He was an honourable politician, an enthusiast for liberty and an incomparable advocate and orator,' according to the Dictionary of National Biography. He acted for the defence in several political trials with considerable success.

Excise

For Burns's Excise Commission, see p. 385.

F

Faile, River

A tributary of the Ayr, which bounded part of the Coilsfield estate. The Reverend Hamilton Paul thought it was where, or near where, the Faile joined the Ayr, that Burns and Mary Campbell parted. The exact spot is unknown, though there is a memorial at the conjectured place.

Falconer, William (1732–69)

The son of a barber in Edinburgh's Netherbow, he was the author of the poem *The Shipwreck*, much admired by Mrs Dunlop. On 24th December 1789, she wrote to Burns: 'I would go twenty miles, if I had it in my power to do it with decency, to see William Falconer. . . . What a warmth of soul must he have originally possest when the ocean was not able to quench it! . . . Do write me what you think of this volume. Is my estimation fantastical, or does your judgment second mine? I hope it does, for I resolve, if I can find *The Shipwreck*, it shall be placed close by your side on my shelf, at least for one month, my inseparable friend and companion. I will turn to it when the tempest howls, and pray for the poor wanderers of the wave with double hope and double fervour.'

Replying to her letter from Ellisland on 25th January 1790, Burns told her of Falconer's fate: 'Falconer, the poor unfortunate Author of the Shipwreck, that glorious Poem which you so much admire, is no more. After weathering that dreadful catastrophe he so feelingly describes in his Poem, and after weathering many hard gales of Fortune, he went to the bottom with the Aurora frigate! I forget what part of Scotland had the honor of giving him birth, but he was the son of obscurity and misfortune. He was one of those daring adventurous spirits which old Caledonia beyond any other nation is remarkable for producing.'

But the literary historian J. H. Millar wrote of *The Shipwreck*: 'It is difficult even to counterfeit interest in the fortunes of Palemon, and Albert, and Anna; and if the reading of the poem once begun is not soon desisted from, it is because of the peculiar fascination which arises from the mingling of two such incongruous elements as the poetical diction of the eighteenth century and the terms of the seaman's art.' In view of such differing opinions, a sample may not be out of place:

'A lowering squall obscures the
                              southern sky,
Before whose sweeping breath the
                              waters fly;
Its weight the topsails can no more
                              sustain—
Reef topsails, reef! the master calls
                              again.
The halyards and top bow-lines soon
                              are gone,
To clue lines and reef tackles next
                              they run:
The shivering sails descend: the yards
                              are square:
Then quick aloft the ready crew
                              repair. . . .'

Fall, Robert (d. 1796)

Member of a wealthy merchant family, and Provost of Dunbar at the time Burns dined with him, during his Border tour. He was alleged to have been of gipsy, or 'Fa', origin.

Burns described the Provost in his *Journal* as 'an eminent merchant, and most respectable character, but undescribable, as he exhibits no marked traits'. His wife was: 'a genius in painting; fully more clever in the fine arts and sciences than my friend Lady Wauchope, without her consummate assurances of her own abilities'.

Provost Fall's house at Dunbar, once a town house of the Earl of Lauderdale, still stands, part of a barracks, though no longer used for military purposes.

Farington, Joseph (1747–1828)

Born at Leigh, Lancashire, he was the elder brother of the historical painter George Farington. Joseph was a pupil of Richard Wilson, and from 1778 to 1813 he exhibited constantly at the Royal Academy where he was elected an Associate in 1783, and an Academician in 1785. He was also a member of the Incorporated Society of Artists. He painted many landscapes of Cumberland and Westmorland. He made a tour of Scotland and left a diary, which was edited by James Greig in 1923, and in Volume I of which this dinner-party list is noted:

'July 20 (1792)—At dinner there came Mr Hamilton . . . Captain Gordon . . . Captain Patrick Millar . . . Mr Burns the Scottish Poet, at present an Exciseman in Dumfries, on 70£ a year. He is married and has a family. He is a middle-sized man abt 36, black complexioned, and his general appearance that of a tradesman or mechanick. He has a strong expressive manner of delivering himself in conversation. He is not acquainted with the Latin language.'

Ferguson, Dr Adam (1723–1816)

Born at Logierait in Perthshire, he was appointed Professor of Natural Philosophy at Edinburgh University in 1759, and Professor of Moral Philosophy in 1764. He published his *Essay on Civil Society* in 1767, and a *History of the Roman Republic* in 1783.

His house was in a street called *The Sheens*, or Sciennes (which derived its name from its nearness to the ruins of an ancient monastery dedicated to St Catherine of Sienna), and was the meeting-place of the Edinburgh literati. Sir Walter Scott described Dr Ferguson's house in Edinburgh as: 'a general point of reunion among his friends, particularly of a Sunday, where there generally met, at a hospitable dinner party, the most distinguished literati of the old time who still remained, with such young persons as were thought worthy to approach their circle, and listen to their conversation'

One 'such young person' was Scott himself, who, as a lad of sixteen, was keenly eager to meet Burns. This he did (the only recorded meeting) at Adam Ferguson's house. Burns had been very much affected by a picture on the wall of a dead soldier, with his widow, child and dog beside him in the snow. Underneath, was a verse. Burns turned to the assembled distinguished company, and asked if anyone knew the author. No one did, until the young Scott remarked: 'They're written by one Langhorne.' Whereupon Burns, said Scott, in a letter to Lockhart in 1827, 'rewarded me with a look and a word, which, though in mere civility, I then received, and still recollect, with great pleasure'.

Ferguson, Sir Adam (1771–1854)

Eldest son of Professor Adam Ferguson, he was an intimate friend of Sir Walter Scott. He entered the army, serving with Wellington in the Peninsular War. He was taken prisoner in 1812 for six years. On his release he settled near Abbotsford at Huntly Burn. He became the deputy-keeper of the Scottish regalia, and was knighted by George IV in 1822. He gave a similar account of the meeting between Burns and Scott to that given by Scott himself. *See* **Ferguson, Dr Adam.**

Fergusson, Alexander (1746?–96)

A descendant of Annie Laurie, and the Laird of Craigdarroch. He was a lawyer, and a Justice of the Peace for Dumfries. A letter from Burns, written in the Globe Inn, October 1789, appeals to Fergusson to do something for 'poor Robie Gordon'. 'The hour is at hand when I must assume the execrable office of whipper-in to the blood-hounds of Justice, and must, must let loose the ravenous rage of the carrion sons of b—tches on poor Robie. I think

you can do something to save the unfortunate man, and I am sure, if you
can, you will.' Burns's concern for Gordon
contrasts with his attitude to Johnston of
Mirecleugh under apparently similar circumstances. *See* **Mitchell, John.**

Fergusson married Deborah, daughter
of Robert Cutlar, a merchant in Dumfries,
through her inheriting the lands of
Arroland, in Kirkcudbright. Fergusson was
with the Grand Master Mason of Scotland
on the occasion when the health of 'Caledonia, and Caledonia's Bard, brother
B——' was toasted.

Fergusson, who was noted for his
convivial habits, was the winner of the
contest which gave rise to Burns's racy
ballad, 'The Whistle'.

This was a drinking contest that took
place at Friar's Carse on 16th October
1789. 'The little ebony whistle' itself,
according to Burns, was supposed to have
been brought over to Scotland by a 'match-
less champion of Bacchus', who accompanied Anne, James VI's Danish queen.
It was laid on the table before the start
of a drinking orgy, and whoever was able
to blow it after his companions were
below the table, retained it as a trophy.
The Dane lost it to Sir Robert Lawrie of
Maxwelton, the Member of Parliament
for Dumfriesshire, who in turn lost it
to a member of the Riddell family. The
competitors during the bout at which
Burns was present were Sir Robert
Lawrie, Robert Riddell and Fergusson
of Craigdarroch, who blew the winning
blast. John M'Murdo of Drumlanrig was
the judge. The poet describes how the
first two contestants withdrew:

'Next uprose our Bard, like a prophet
                            in drink—
'Craigdarroch, thou'lt soar when
                    creation shall sink!
But if thou would flourish immortal
                            in rhyme,
Come—one bottle more—and have at
                        the sublime!" '

Craigdarroch drank 'upwards of five
bottles of claret'.

William Hunter, one of the servants at
Friar's Carse, later testified that: 'When the
gentlemen were put to bed, Burns walked
home, without any assistance, not being
the worse of drink': yet one more piece
of evidence that Burns, in an age when
excessive drinking was common, was
not himself a heavy drinker. Chambers
points out that in James VI's reign there
was no Sir Robert Lawrie of Maxwelton.
However, he says: 'The story had probably some such foundation as that described, though Burns's dates are wrong.'

Fergusson of Craigdarroch, Mrs Alexander

Burns wrote a lament for her son, who
died at the age of eighteen or nineteen,
'Mrs Fergusson of Craigdarroch's Lamentation for the death of her Son'.

But the poet made double use of this
poem, having also sent it to his early
patroness, Mrs Alexander Stewart of
Afton, on the death of her only son,
Alexander Gordon Stewart, who died
at a Military Academy at Strasburg in
December 1787, aged sixteen.

Allan Cunningham claimed that he
possessed a copy of the 'Lament' with a
note by Burns, saying: 'The Mother's
Lament was composed, partly with a
view to Mrs Fergusson of Craigdarroch,
and partly to the worthy patroness of
my early unknown muse, Mrs Stewart of
Afton.'

Fergusson of Kilkerran, Sir Adam, (1733–1813)

The third Baronet, he was Member
of Parliament for Ayrshire 1774–1780
and 1790–96. Johnson called him 'a
vile Whig', but Boswell observed 'that
there were few people but were mixed
characters, like a candle: half wax, half
tallow. But Sir Adam Fergusson was all
wax, a pure taper, whom you may
light and set upon any lady's table.'

In 'The Author's Earnest Cry and Prayer', Burns refers to 'aith-detesting, chaste Kilkerran'. According to Kinsley, Sir James Fergusson has related a family story about Sir Adam's rebuke to his children: 'Dinna think that because I'm no swearin' I'm no angry'.

Fergusson, Robert (1750–74)

Second son of William Fergusson, accountant in the British Linen Company's Bank, Edinburgh, and his wife Margaret Forbes, like her husband, of Aberdeenshire descent. Robert was born in the Cap-and-Feather Close, Edinburgh, now partly occupied by North Bridge Street. He was educated at the High School, from where he went on a bursary to the Grammar School at Dundee. Two years later, he proceeded, on a Fergusson bursary, to the Universary of St Andrews, where his career was cut short by his father's death. He returned to Edinburgh and took an ill-paid job as a copyist in a legal office. His first Scots poem to be published appeared on 2nd January 1772, in Ruddiman's *Weekly Magazine, or Edinburgh Amusement*, where the majority of his best poems thereafter first appeared, until his early death in a mad-house less than three years later. From the press of Walter and Thomas Ruddiman, in 1773, came *Poems* by Robert Fergusson.

Although Fergusson's prentice pieces were in somewhat stilted English, in 'The Daft-Days', his first Scots piece, he showed himself the fitting recipient of the vernacular mantle laid aside by Allan Ramsay fourteen years before. In quick-moving Scots, Fergusson wrote of Edinburgh scenes and Edinburgh people. Even more than his predecessor, Ramsay, he had a considerable influence on his successor, Robert Burns.

Burns used several of the staves adapted to Scots use by Ramsay and Fergusson. He inherited the form of the Verse Epistle, popularised, but not actually 'invented', by Ramsay. Most important

of all, Burns developed the temper of Fergusson's colloquial comment, vastly increasing its range and pointedness. From the number of stanza and subject matter parallels, it is quite obvious that Burns, before writing his own satires and epistles, had deeply steeped himself in Fergusson's work. Thus, Fergusson's 'Caller Water' was the starting point for Burns's 'Scotch Drink': Fergusson's 'Mutual Complaint of Plainstanes and Causey', the model for 'The Twa Dogs': 'Leith Races' for 'The Holy Fair', and so on. Without in any way disparaging Fergusson's achievement, it would be true to say that Burns, with one exception, usually far out-stripped Fergusson in range and power. The exception is Fergusson's 'Farmer's Ingle', which is, as David Daiches says, 'both in inspiration and in integrity of feeling superior to Burns's 'Cotter's Saturday Night'.

But Burns was uncommonly generous in acknowledging his debts, both in prose and in verse. In the 'Epistle to William Simson', for instance, he said:

'My senses wad be in a creel, [*my head would be turned*
Should I but dare a hope to speel,
                                        [*climb*
Wi' Allan, or wi' Gilbertfield
        The braes o' fame;
Or Fergusson, the writer-chiel,
        A deathless name.'

'Allan' was, of course, Allan Ramsay, and 'Gilbertfield' William Hamilton of Gilbertfield. Burns then went on:

'O Fergusson! thy glorious parts
Ill suited law's dry, musty arts!
My curse upon your whunstane hearts,
        Ye Enbrugh Gentry! [*Edinburgh*
The tythe o' what ye waste at cartes
        Wad stow'd his pantry!' [*would have filled*

There is also the 'Apostrophe to Fergusson, Inscribed Above and Below His Portrait':

'Curse on ungrateful man, that can be
                                    pleas'd
And yet can starve the author of the
                                    pleasure.
'O thou, my elder brother in
                                    misfortune,
By far my elder brother in the muse,
With tears I pity thy unhappy fate!
Why is the Bard unfitted for the world,
Yet has so keen a relish of its pleasures?'

These lines were inscribed in Burns's
hand in a copy of the Second Edition of
Fergusson's *Poems*, 1782, given by Burns
to Rebekah Carmichael, on 19th March
1787. (In the dedication, Burns describes
her as a 'poetess'. She published a book of
verse in 1790). Henley and Henderson
consider the dedication to have been
written later than the lines of verse, the
inference being that Burns gave Miss
Carmichael his own copy. Edinburgh
Central Library possesses Burns's copy of
the 1785 edition of Fergusson, with Burns's
signature and a three-stanza poem, the
first of which also appears on the head-
stone over Fergusson's grave in the
Canongate Kirk.

On 6th February 1787, Burns wrote to
the Bailies of the Canongate—who passed
on his request to the authorities in charge
of the Cemetery—for permission to
put a stone on Fergusson's unmarked
grave. Permission given, Burns commissioned an architect, Robert Burn, to erect
the stone, on which appeared the lines:

'No sculptur'd Marble here, nor
                                pompous lay,
No storied Urn nor animated Bust;
This simple stone directs pale Scotia's
                                    way
To pour her sorrows o'er the Poet's
                                    dust.'

The two additional stanzas were written in
the *Second Commonplace Book*.

Five years later, Burns paid the bill.
Enclosing the money to Hill, Burns
wrote on 5th February 1792: 'I send you
by the bearer, Mr Clarke, a particular
friend of mine . . . £5 10 per acct. I owe
to Mr Robt Burn, Architect, for erecting
the stone over poor Fergusson. He was
two years in erecting it, after I commissioned him for it; and I have been two
years paying him, after he sent me his
account; so he and I are quits. He had the
hardiesse to ask me interest on the sum;
but considering that the money was due
by one Poet, for putting a tombstone
over another, he may, with grateful
surprise, thank Heaven that ever he saw a
farthing of it.'

Ferintosh
See **Forbes of Culloden.**

Ferrier, James (1744–1829)
Father of Susan Edmonstone Ferrier, the
novelist, and Jane Ferrier *See* **Ferrier,
Jane.** A Writer to the Signet and, from
1802–26, principal Clerk of the Court of
Session. He was one of the poet's circle
of friends in Edinburgh. He built a house
in George Street, near St Andrew's
Church. In its day, it was the most westerly
house in that district, and his fellow
lawyers considered that it would injure
his business to live so far out.

Ferrier, Jane (1767–1846)
Eldest daughter of James Ferrier, Writer
to the Signet, and sister of the novelist
Susan Ferrier. She married General
Samuel Graham, Deputy-Governor of
Stirling Castle. Burns sent her some
verses, 'To Miss Ferrier', along with a
copy of his 'Elegy on Sir James Hunter
Blair'. She was a celebrated beauty when
Burns met her, as well as a clever artist.
With Edward Blore, she made drawings
of the carvings in Stirling Palace, which
were engraved and published under the
name of *Lacunar Strevelinense* (*1817*).

Fête Champêtre, The
See **Cunningham of Annbank and
Enterkine, William**

Findlater, Alexander (1754-1839)

Son of the Reverend Thomas Findlater, Minister of Linton, Peebleshire. He joined the Excise in 1774, was appointed Examiner on 1st June 1790, and in April 1791 became Supervisor at Dumfries. He went to Edinburgh as General Supervisor in 1797, and succeeded William Corbet at Glasgow as Collector in 1811, where he remained until he retired in 1825. His first wife, who died in 1810, was Susan Forrester of Falkirk; his second wife, Catherine Anderson.

Findlater had been supervisor at Dumfries for about six months, when Burns moved into the town. There, he became the poet's immediate superior. But, as Findlater afterwards put it: 'My connection with Robert Burns commenced immediately after his admission into the Excise, and continued to the hour of his death. In all that time the superintendence of his behaviour as an officer of the revenue, was a branch of my especial province, and it may be supposed I would not be an inattentive observer of the general conduct of a man and a poet so celebrated by his countrymen.'

A friendship quickly sprang up between the two men. In February 1790 (if Ferguson's dating is correct) there is a note from Burns to Findlater accompanying some new-laid eggs from Ellisland 'all of them couch, not thirty hours out'. Burns put Findlater on the list of Dumfries people on the subscription list for Dr Anderson's magazine The Bee. Yet friendship did not result in any slackening of Findlater's scrutiny of Burns's work. A letter of June 1791, in which Burns explains himself, shows this clearly enough: 'I am both much surprised and vexed at that accident of Lorimer's Stock. The last survey I made prior to Mr Lorimer's going to Edir. I was very particular in my inspection and the quantity was certainly in his possession as I stated it. The surveys I have made during his absence might as well have been marked "key absent", as I never found any body but

the lady, who I know is not mistress of keys, & etc. to know anything of it, and one of the times, it would have rejoiced all Hell to have seen her so drunk. I have not surveyed there since his return. I know the gentleman's ways are, like the grace of G——, past all comprehension; but I shall give the house a severe scrutiny tomorrow morning, and send you in the naked facts.

'I know, Sir, and regret deeply that this business glances with a malign aspect on my character as an Officer; but as I am really innocent in the affair, and as the gentleman is known to be an illicit Dealer, and particularly as this is the single instance of the least shadow of carelessness or impropriety in my conduct as an Officer. I shall be peculiarly unfortunate if my character shall fall a sacrifice to the dark manoeuvres [sic] of a Smuggler.' The 'Smuggler', incidentally, was the father of 'Chloris' Lorimer.

During the illness of Findlater for some months from December 1794, Burns was appointed Acting Supervisor in his place.

Findlater defended Burns's loyalty and efficiency at the inquiry into the charges of disloyalty levelled against the poet in December 1792, and defended the dead poet in Alexander Peterkin's edition of 1815 against the calumnies of Heron, Currie, and those others who sought to paint Burns in his Dumfries days as 'a hopeless drunkard'.

See Plate 12.

Findlay, James
See Markland, Jean.

Fisher, William (1737-1809)

The prototype of 'Holy Willie' was the son of Andrew Fisher, farmer at Montgarswood, Mauchline. William Fisher farmed with his father, and at the age of thirty-five was chosen elder of the parish. He was, it seems, assiduous in his duties so far as visiting the sick and the aged went, but he lacked what has been called 'a sense of Christian forbearance'. At any-rate, it was thought to be on his instigation that the minister and kirk session of Mauchline instituted proceedings against Gavin Hamilton for an alleged failure to observe the Sabbath in what the kirk session deemed a proper manner. As Gavin Hamilton was a much valued friend of Burns, the poet turned his satirical powers against Fisher in 'Holy Willie's Prayer', the 'Epitaph on Holy Willie' and 'The Kirk's Alarm'.

In a note which Burns later prefixed to 'Holy Willie's Prayer', for Glenriddell, the poet described him as: 'a rather oldish bachelor elder in the parish of Mauchline, and much and justly famed for that polemical chattering which ends in tippling orthodoxy, and for that spiritualised bawdry which refines to liquorish devotion.'

He was, in fact, husband to Jean Hewatson, who bore him several children. But of his narrowness, the persecution of the liberal-minded Hamilton is abundant evidence. As Snyder put it: 'When men like Fisher represented the temporal power of orthodox Calvinism, it was small wonder that rebels against the establishment were easy to find; or that a rebel like Burns, embittered by personal humiliation and the treatment of his friend Hamilton, should have broken forth in derisive mockery.'

In spite of Burns's feelings on the Hamilton case, however, the remarkable thing is that 'Holy Willie's Prayer' never descends to abuse, or softens to farce. The character-drawing is firm and consistent, and the self-important, insignificant little church elder of Mauchline becomes the prototype of hypocrisy itself in what is perhaps the greatest satire against that vice written in any European tongue.

Fisher himself, however, fell from grace. On 14th October 1790, he stood before the eighty-one-year-old 'Daddy' Auld to receive a rebuke for drunkenness, a harangue which the minister preserved in his book of rebukes, and which ended:

'Be upon your guard in all time coming against this bewitching sin, shun bad company, avoid taverns as much as possible, and abhor the character of a tippler. Abstain carefully from strong drink, and from everything that may intoxicate and injure you; and withal seek wisdom from heaven to guide you, and grace to enable you to walk stedfastly in ways of sobriety and holiness all your days.'

Posterity has doubted whether or not Fisher was, in fact, granted either of these lines of wisdom. In 'The Kirk's Alarm', which appeared in 1790, Burns makes a clear accusation of embezzlement:

'Holy Will, Holy Will,
There was wit i' your skull,
When ye pilfered the alms o' the poor;
The timmer is scant,
When ye're ta'en for a saunt,
Wha should swing in a rape for an
hour.'

In 1834, when Fisher had been twenty-one years dead, the somewhat unreliable Allan Cunningham made a definite accusation of pilfering from an alms-box out of Burns's stanza. Other biographers, including Chambers, followed suit. No evidence to support such a charge has ever been found.

However, Fisher froze to death in a ditch on a snowy night in February 1809.

Fleming, Agnes (b. 1765)

The daughter of John Fleming, who, according to Cunningham, farmed Calcothill, half a mile north of Lochlea. She has been thought by some to be the heroine of the song 'My Nanie O', one of the few poems Burns's father knew and approved. Her surname was said by Burns's brother Gilbert, to be Fleming, but the Reverend Hamilton Paul gave her name as Sheriff—perhaps her married name or the name of another possible subject of the song, Agnes Sherriff of Kilmarnock—when writing to Dr Robert

Chambers. According to Cunningham 'Nannie Fleming' died unmarried at an advanced age. For reasons of euphony, Burns later changed 'Stinchar' to 'Lugar' in the first line of his song.

The words first appeared in the Edinburgh Edition of 1787; the song, with its tune, 'My Nanie O', in Thomson's *Scottish Airs*, 1793. Thomson wanted to change the air, but Burns disapproved, and had his own way. The song later appeared in the *Museum* in 1803, to an air by a Durham musician, Thomas Ebdon. But the title air, which goes back in origin to the *Graham Manuscript*, 1694, and was first published in *Orpheus Caledonius*, 1725, has always been the more popular version.

Flint, Mrs Christian or Kirstie Kirkpatrick (1765–1836)

A mason's wife in Closeburn, Dumfries. According to Chambers, Burns used to give her his newest songs to sing over, and if any word sounded harsh or grating, he would change it in favour of a better.

Professor Gillespie of St Andrews University recorded in 1829 in the *Edinburgh Literary Journal* that he used to see Burns's horse tethered outside her door, and listen to the songs she was singing for him. He continued: 'The songstress was a Mrs Flint. She was neither pretty nor witty, but had a pipe of the most overpowering pitch, and a fine taste for song.'

Fontenelle, Louisa (d. 1800)

An actress popular in Scotland in Burns's day. Genest says in his *Some Account of the English Stage* that her first appearance on any stage was at Covent Garden, on 6th November 1788. She took the role of 'Moggy' in the first representation of *The Highland Reel*, by O'Keefe, according to the *Thespian Dictionary*. She took the same role at Edinburgh's Theatre Royal on her first Scottish appearance on 17th

October 1789. In the summer seasons of 1790–91–92, Louisa Fontenelle acted at the Theatre Royal, Haymarket, London, but by January 1793, she was back in Edinburgh to join Mrs Esten's company for the season, playing Lucy in *The Beggars' Opera*, and other roles. She also played in Glasgow at the theatre in Dunlop Street. In the winter of 1792, Sutherland's company, playing at Dumfries, included Louisa Fontenelle.

She must have been a woman of great charm and culture. Burns greatly admired her acting and wrote for her 'The Rights of Woman', an address to be given by her on her Benefit Night of 26th November 1792. With the Prologue, he sent a letter to her: 'In such a bad world as ours, those who add to the scanty sum of our pleasures, are positively our benefactors. To you, Madam, on our humble Dumfries boards, I have been more indebted for entertainment, than ever I was in prouder Theatres. Your charms as a woman would insure applause to the most indifferent Actress, and your theatrical talents would secure admiration to the plainest figure.' He also wrote a poem 'To Miss Fontenelle, on Seeing her in a Favorite Character':

'Sweet naïveté of feature,
  Simple, wild, enchanting elf,
Not to thee, but thanks to nature,
  Thou art acting but thyself.

Wert thou awkward, stiff, affected,
  Spurning nature, torturing art;
Loves and graces all rejected,
  Then indeed thou'dst act a part.'

For her Benefit Night in December the following year, Burns wrote another Address, 'Still anxious to secure your partial favour', declaring in the accompanying letter: 'God knows I am a powerless individual. And, when I thought on my Friends, many a heart-ache it has given me! But if Miss Fontenelle will accept this honest compliment to her personal charms, amiable manners, and gentle heart, from a man, too proud to flatter, though too poor to have his compliments of any consequence, it will sincerely oblige her *anxious* Friend, and most devoted humble Servt. . . .'

She later married an actor, James Williamson, and at some unknown date they went to America where they both died, Louisa of yellow fever in Charleston, S.C.

Jackson in his memoirs includes Louisa Fontenelle along with Mrs Yates, Mrs Esten, Mrs Jordan and Mrs Siddons, in a list of 'the most capital performers that could be had', while he was manager of the Theatre Royal, Edinburgh.

Forbes of Culloden, Duncan (1644?–1704)

In 1690 the Scottish Parliament passed an Act permitting Forbes perpetually to distil whisky free of duty on his estate of Ferintosh in Cromarty, in recognition of his services at the Revolution which expelled James VII and II. As a result he accrued considerable wealth, and *Ferintosh* came to be known as a synonym for whisky.

In 1785 an Act was passed abolishing this right, and stating that the Forbes of the day was to be compensated adequately. If he did not agree, the case was to be tried by jury before the Scottish Court of Exchequer. He did not agree, and the case duly came up. His defence proved that the privilege was justly his, and although it could have been made to yield £7,000 a year, in fact the profit was just over £1,000; and further that the late Lord President, Mr Duncan Forbes (1685–1747), had provided £20,000 of his own money in suppressing the 1745 Rebellion. The jury surprised their Lordships by awarding Forbes £21,580.

The Scottish distillers complained at the severity of the Excise laws, and many went out of business, with the result that the price of barley began to be affected. Also,

there was a decided increase in illicit distilling.

As a consequence of the outcry, the Government discontinued the tax on low wines and spirits, and an annual tax was put on the stills according to their size. Burns alluded to this act in a note to his poem 'The Author's Earnest Cry and Prayer', which deals with the previous oppressive Excise laws.

Foreman, Mr

Out-argued by Burns in 'a dispute about Voltaire' when the poet visited Coldstream with Ainslie on his Border tour.

Fox, Charles James (1749–1806)

A politician regarded in Burns's day as the supporter of liberty for the people, and the opponent of Tory junta oppression. Fox enjoyed periods of immense popularity, which he lost again owing to his coalition with North, his support of the India Bill, and, on its rejection, his attempts to prevent an appeal to the country.

Burns mentions him in 'A Dream', a satire based upon a pompous official birthday 'Laureate's Ode' by the then Poet Laureate, Thomas Warton. Burns addresses the future George IV:

> 'For you, young Potentate o' Wales,
>   I tell your Highness fairly,
> Down Pleasure's stream, wi' swelling
>   sails,
>   I'm tauld ye're driving rarely:
>   [*rapidly*
> But some day ye may gnaw your
>   nails,
>   An' curse your folly sairly,
> That e'er ye brak Diana's pales, [*broke
>   the bounds of chastity*
>   Or rattl'd dice wi' Charlie
>   By night or day.'

'Charlie' was the third son of Henry Fox, later Baron Holland of Foxley. While at Eton, his father took him to the Continent, teaching him gambling habits which he never lost, and which sometimes reduced him to poverty. He had a wide knowledge of world literature and art, and was a man of taste whose critical faculty was always acute. Despite his stoutness, he never lost his interest in energetic sports. A distinguished orator, he was an even more vigorous debater, although he lacked some of the qualities necessary for a great statesman. The violence of his language constantly stood in the way of his career.

Most of his time in Parliament was necessarily spent in opposition to the Government. He was returned for Midhurst, Sussex, before he was twenty, the seat being bought by his father and uncle. On his father's instructions, he supported the policies of the Duke of Grafton. Shortly afterwards, he joined Lord North's administration as a Lord of the Admiralty, and as a result of his zealousness for privilege and his efforts against the freedom of the Press, he became very unpopular. He was attacked and rolled in the mud by the mob, who, however, reversed their views of him when he left the Tory party and joined Rockingham and the Whigs. His later misjudgments of the political scene practically ruined the Whig party.

He was strongly opposed to the American War of Independence, which was favoured by Lord North; he applauded the revolt of the French soldiers against their officers at the time of the Revolution, to join the people in their struggle for liberty; he was strongly in favour of abolishing the slave trade; attacked the maladministration of the Navy; and wanted shorter Parliaments to limit the Crown's influence, to which he attributed most of the country's misfortunes. He was a close friend of the Prince of Wales, and this was one of the reasons why he was so hated by George III, who blamed Fox for teaching his son the gambling habit. Despite his position of *enfant terrible*, he had great charm and wit.

During Pitt's administration, Lord Cockburn recorded in his *Memorials*, Fox's birthday was: 'generally celebrated by a dinner every year. But only a very few of the best Whigs could be got to attend, or were wished for. It was not safe to have many, especially as great prudence was necessary in speaking and toasting. Yet even the select, through rarely exceeding a dozen or two, were seldom allowed to assemble without Sheriff's Officers being sent down the names of those who entered.'

On Pitt's death in 1806, Fox became Foreign Secretary in Grenville's administration, but died of dropsy before his vigorous opposition to Napoleon could be translated into action. He is buried in Westminster Abbey, near Pitt.

Dr Johnson said of Fox: 'Fox divided the Kingdom with Caesar, so that it was a doubt whether the nation should be ruled by the sceptre of George III or the tongue of Fox.'

Franklin, Benjamin (1706–90)

A brilliant American, born of British parents, he was the first printer and bookseller in Philadelphia. His scientific experiments led to the invention of the lightning conductor in 1749, and he did some valuable work on the study of electricity. He discovered the Gulf Stream and helped to draw up the American Declaration of Independence. Burns refers to him in his 'Address of Beelzebub' as the kind of leader some Highlanders, who had been prevented from emigrating, needed:

'Some daring Hancock, or a Franklin,
May set their Highland bluid
                                a-ranklin.'

Franklin was elected President of the Commonwealth of Pennsylvania, and re-elected three times.

In 1757, Franklin came to England to appeal to the British Government to settle the dispute between the Assembly and the proprietors over taxation. (The 'proprietors' were the descendants of William Penn, who lived in England, and by the Charter were privileged to appoint and instruct the governors of Pennsylvania'.) He remained for five years. In 1760, a Bill of the Assembly taxing the proprietors' estates, except unsurveyed waste land, was allowed by the King.

Franklin corresponded at this time with Lord Kames, David Hume, and Dr Johnson. He visited Edinburgh University, and received the degree of D.D. in 1759 from St Andrews University. In 1762, he received the degree of D.C.L. from Oxford.

Fraser, Thomas (c. 1770–1825)

Born in Edinburgh, he was an oboist and composer. He went to Dumfries in 1793, where he instructed 'a band of Music for a Fencible Corps quartered in this country'. Burns heard him play, and was much taken with one of his airs. Burns said, writing to George Thomson in June 1793: 'Mr Fraser plays it slow and with an expression that quite charms me. I got such an enthusiast in it that I made a song for it, which I here subjoin and inclose Fraser's set of the tune.' The song was, 'Blythe hae I been on Yon Hill' to the air of a reel called, 'The Quaker's Wife'. Burns had heard a grand-aunt sing it to the name of 'Liggeram cosh, my bonnie wee lass'. Lesley Baillie was the subject of Burns's song.

The Reverend Archibald Lawrie recorded in his *Journal*, that when he visited Burns in Dumfries: 'after dinner we had some charming music from a Mr Fraser, master of a band of soldiers raised by and belonging to Lord Breadalbane; having drunk tea, we went to a wood upon the banks of the River Nith, when Mr Fraser took out his hautboy and played a few tunes delightfully, which had a very pleasing effect in the wood.'

Freemasonry, Burns and

During the last quarter of the eighteenth century, Freemasonry was at the height of its popularity. To the Age of Enlightenment, its tenets seemed to promise brotherhood and intellectual equality. Scholars, philosophers, gentlemen, farmers and tradesmen were Masons in Scotland.

Burns was a Mason from 1781 until his death. He was initiated on 4th July 1781, in St David's Lodge, No. 174, Tarbolton. He was passed and raised in the same Lodge on 1st October 1781. Less than a year later, the old members of St James's Kilwinning Lodge—which had amalgamated with St David's—broke away, seized the effects of the St James's Lodge, and reopened it. Burns was among those concerned in the disruption who went over to St James's. He was elected Depute Master of St James's on 27th July 1784, a position he held for four years.

It was partly because of his Masonic connections that Burns was so widely received when he arrived in Edinburgh in 1786. For among his fellow-masons in Ayrshire were Sir John Whitefoord, James Dalrymple of Orangefield, Sheriff Wallace of Ayr, Gavin Hamilton, the Provost of Ayr, John Ballantine, Professor Dugald Stewart, Dr John Mackenzie of Mauchline, William Parker of Kilmarnock and many others; among the less exalted brothers were the tailor, Alexander Wood, James Humphry, the 'noisy polemic', and John Wilson, the schoolmaster.

When he reached the capital, Burns was made a member of Canongate Kilwinning Lodge No. 2 Edinburgh. An apparently quite baseless tradition alleges that members also made him their Poet Laureate. Among the members of this Lodge were Lord Elcho, Lord Torphichen, the Earl of Eglinton, the Earl of Glencairn, Patrick Miller of Dalswinton, Lord Pitsligo, Alexander Cunningham the lawyer, William Nicol the schoolmaster, William Creech the publisher, Henry Mackenzie the lawyer and author, and Alexander Nasmyth the painter.

Burns received honorary membership from Loudoun Kilwinning, at Newmilns, on 27th March 1786, and from St John's Kilwinning, Kilmarnock, on 26th October 1786. In company with Ainslie, Burns received the Royal Arch degree from St Abb's Lodge No. 70, on 19th May 1787, at Eyemouth. On 27th December 1791, when he had moved to Dumfries, Burns became a member of St Andrews Lodge No. 179. He was elected Senior Warden in 1792. He last visited this lodge three months before his death.

See Plate 5.

Friar's Carse

A beautiful estate on the River Nith, once owned by Captain Robert Riddell of Glenriddell. The house was built on the former site of a small monastic establishment. This particularly fertile part of Nithsdale had once been owned by the monks of Melrose. The Carse, which extended eastwards, was bordered by shrubberies, which reached almost to Ellisland. Riddell had given Burns a key to the grounds, and the poet frequently wandered through the estate, meditating in a little house, or hermitage, which the Captain had built. On 28th June 1788, Burns produced the first version of his lines, 'Written in Friar's Carse Hermitage'. The first version and the altered one both appear in Burns's *Second Common-Place Book*.

'Thou whom chance may hither lead,
Be thou clad in russet weed,
Be thou deckt in silken stole,
Grave these counsels on thy soul.

Life is but a day at most,
Sprung from night,—in darkness lost;
Hope not sunshine ev'ry hour,
Fear not clouds will always lour.'

On Robert Riddell's death in 1794, his widow could have allowed the property to go to her brother-in-law, Walter Riddell, who, under the terms of his brother's will, would have had to pay the widow an annuity. But the widow so hated Walter Riddell that she refused to exercise this option, and the property was sold.

See Plate 14.

Fullarton, Colonel William (1754–1808)

Son of a botanist, William Fullarton of Fullarton, Dundonald, Ayrshire, Fullarton was educated at Edinburgh University, and travelled extensively. He made a European tour in the care of Patrick Brydone. Later, Fullarton entered the army, and became a colonel in the 98th Regiment. With the outbreak of the Dutch War, the regiment was sent to the Cape of Good Hope, and then to India, where he also served as a diplomat. At the beginning of the French War in 1793, he raised the Regiment of the 23rd Light Dragoons, known as 'Fullarton's Light Horse'. He became Governor of Trinidad in 1802. He published in 1793 an *Account of Agriculture in Ayrshire*, and a *View of English Interests in India*. Burns made a complimentary reference to him in 'The Vision'. Together with a friend, the Colonel visited Burns at Ellisland in 1791. In a letter which Burns sent to him from Ellisland on 3rd October 1791, along with some poems, Burns told Fullarton: 'I am ambitious, covetously ambitious of being known to a gentleman whom I am proud to call my Countryman: a gentleman who was a Foreign Embassador [sic] as soon as he was a Man; and a Leader of Armies as soon as he was a Soldier; and that with an eclat unknown to the usual minions of a Court. . . . If the gentleman who accompanied you when you did me the honor of calling on me is with you, I beg to be respectfully remembered to him.' Burns signed himself Fullarton's 'highly obliged and most devoted servant'.

Fullerton married the elder daughter of the fifth Lord Reay in 1792, and had one daughter,

Fyffe, Dr M

The recipient of a letter from Burns written on 'Saturday morn: six o'clock', on the day he set out on his Border Tour, therefore on 5th May 1787. Nothing whatever is known of this Fyffe, nor can any doctor or surgeon of this name be traced in Edinburgh at this time. But the letter contains a valedictory jingly stanza on Edinburgh:

'Now, God in Heaven bless REEKIE's
                                       town
  With plenty, joy and peace!
And may her wealth and fair renown
  To latest times increase!!! Amen.'

G

Gage, General Thomas (1721–87)
Governor of Massachusetts, he held Boston somewhat unaggressively against the rebels in 1775, and was reinforced by Sir William Howe, John Burgoyne and Sir Henry Clinton. The main credit for the Bunker Hill victory went to Howe, who succeeded Gage as Commander-in-Chief in October, hence Burns's reference to 'Poor Tommy Gage' in 'A Fragment' ('When Guilford good').

Galloway, seventh Earl of. *See* **Stewart, John.**

Gardner, Jean (d. 1793?)
Burns's sister, Mrs Begg, maintained that the poet was for a time fond of Jean Gardner, a member of the Buchanites. She was the daughter of an Irvine butcher, in whose house the preacher Hugh White was supposed to have lodged. Train alleged that she was the 'darling Jean' of Burns's 'Epistle to Davie', but there is no evidence to support this notion. Chambers, and most writers since, have considered the reference to be to Jean Armour.

Train quoted a fanatical member of the Sect, Andrew Innes: 'When I was sent back from Thornhill for Mr Hunter, Jean Gardner came with me from Irvine to Closeburn, and when we were in the neighbourhood of Tarbolton, she seemed to be in fear, and in a rather discomposed condition; when I inquired the cause, she said it was lest Burns, the poet, should see her, for if he did, he would be sure to interrupt her, for they had been on terms of intimacy, but we proceeded on our journey without meeting any obstruction.'

Jean Gardner, whom Chambers had been told was 'a young woman of very surpassing beauty', married another member of the Sect, George Hill, and emigrated with him to America. She is said to have died of fever in Philadelphia.

Garland, The
The original name for 'The Kirk's Alarm'.

Garlies, George, Lord
Eldest surviving son of the Earl of Galloway. Member of Parliament for Saltash from 1790 to 1795, when he resigned the seat in his brother's favour. He is 'Our King's L—L—' in 'The Election', and Burns's reference to his 'grateful return' is to the official calling in question of Garlies' writ in the election of 1795.

Garpal Water
Burns called it 'haunted Garpal' in 'The Brigs of Ayr', and noted that 'the banks of Garpal Water is one of the few places in the West of Scotland, where those fancy scaring beings, known by the name of GHAISTS, still continue pertinaciously to inhabit'. It is a tributary of the Ayr.

Gates, General Horatio (c. 1729–1806)
The colonist commander who forced the surrender of General Burgoyne's army at Saratoga on 17th October 1777. Reference is made to Burgoyne losing his way (and his Brigadier, Simon Fraser) at Saratoga in 'A Fragment' ('When Guilford good').

Ged, Johnie
Commemorated in 'Death and Dr Hornbook', he was the parish gravedigger.

Geddes Burns
Bishop John Geddes's copy of the interleaved 1787 Edinburgh Edition of Burns's poems, in which the poet wrote additional poems. It was printed in a facsimile edition of 473 copies for distribution to the Bibliophile Society of Boston in 1908. The preface erroneously gives the name

of the original owner of the work as Alexander Geddes, instead of John Geddes, his elder brother, to whom the copy in fact belonged. *See* **Geddes, Dr John**. The original is now in the Henry E. Huntingdon Library, San Marino.

Geddes, Jenny

The name Burns gave to his mare, on which he rode on his Border and Highland tours. He bought her in Edinburgh for 'over £4 Sterling'. In a letter to William Nicol from Carlisle, dated 1st June 1787, Burns described his journey on Jenny Geddes during the Border tour, at great length and in Scots. Among other things, she was: 'a yauld, poutherie Girran for a' that; and has a stomach like Willie Stalker's meere that wad hae digested tumbler-wheels'.

Writing to James Smith on 30th June, Burns related how, at the end of his short West Highland tour a few days before, by the shores of Loch Lomond: 'by came a Highlandman at the gallop, on a tolerably good horse, but which had never known the ornaments of iron or leather. We scorned to be out-galloped by a Highlandman, so off we started, whip and spur. My companions, though seemingly gaily mounted, fell sadly astern; but my old mare, Jenny Geddes, one of the Rosinante family, strained past the Highlandman in spite of all his efforts with the hair halter; just as I was passing him, Donald wheeled his horse, as if to cross before me to mar my progress, when down came his horse, and threw his rider's breekless a—e in a clipt hedge; and down came Jenny Geddes over all, and my Bardship between her and the Highlandman's horse. Jenny Geddes trode over me with such cautious reverence that matters were not so bad as might well have been expected; so I came off with a few cuts and bruises, and a thorough resolution to be a pattern of sobriety for the future.'

An abbreviated account of this race was given to John Richmond from Mossgiel in a letter of 7th July 1787.

For the Highland tour, Burns and Nicol left Edinburgh in a chaise, and on 23rd August 1787, Burns told Ainslie of this, adding: '. . . so Jenny Geddes goes home to Ayr-shire, to use a phrase of my Mother's, "wi' her finger in her mouth".'

Writing to Mrs Dunlop from Ellisland on 13th June 1788, Burns said: 'This is the second day, my honored friend, that I have been on my farm. A solitary Inmate of an old smoky "SPENCE"; far from every Object I love or by whom I am belov'd, nor any acquaintance older than yesterday except Jenny Geddes, the old mare I ride on.'

Jenny Geddes is the name tradition has given to the woman who, on 23rd August 1637, in St Giles Cathedral, Edinburgh, is said to have thrown a stool at the Bishop of Edinburgh, who, on the authority of Charles I, was trying to force into use in the Scottish Church *The Book of Common Prayer, and Administration of the Sacraments; And other Parts of Divine Service for the Use of the Church of Scotland. Edinburgh: Printed by Robert Young.*

Geddes, Dr John (1735–99)

He was Roman Catholic Bishop of Dunkeld and elder brother of the biblical critic Bishop Alexander Geddes. Burns first met Dr John Geddes at the house of Lord Monboddo in Edinburgh, during the winter of 1786–7. Geddes took an interest in the poet's work, and was responsible for getting five Catholic Seminaries, including that of the Scots College at Valladolid, of which he had once been Rector, to subscribe to the Edinburgh Edition of 1787. Burns took Geddes's own copy, bound with blank sheets at both ends, with him on his Highland tour, and delayed returning it for almost two years. Writing to Geddes from Ellisland on 3rd February 1789, the poet apologised for having kept the book so long: 'You will see in your book, which I beg your pardon for detaining so long, that I have been tuning my lyre on the banks of Nith. Some larger poetic plans that are floating in my imagination, or partly put in execution, I shall impart to you when I have the pleasure of meeting with you. . . .'

On the death of Dr Geddes, the book passed into the hands of his sister, Margaret Geddes, who was married to John Hyslop, a Scots surgeon, and lived in Finsbury Square, London. On Hyslop's death, the book passed to their daughter, also Margaret Hyslop, who gave it to the English anatomist, Dr Henry Goadly, when he left England for America in 1838.

In 1863, a Nairn man, James Black, who had settled in Detroit, and who had become friendly with Dr Goadly, bought the book from the Doctor's widow. It then passed into the hands of the American collector W. K. Bixby, President of the Burns Club of St Louis, who, in 1908, had it photographed and 'reproduced by lithographic and gelatine process' in a limited edition of 473 copies, distributed only to the members of the Bibliophile Society of Boston. Unfortunately, however, Bixby erroneously attributed the original ownership of the book of Alexander, instead of to John Geddes. This facsimile has become known as *The Geddes Burns*.

George III (1738–1820)

Affectionately called 'Farmer George' because of his homely interest in his people's affairs, he was on the throne during Burns's lifetime. His reign was marked by the loss of the American colonies, by periods of insanity, and by a fecund domesticity, in striking contrast to that of his son, the Prince of Wales.

Burns, a periodic Jacobite, indicated his views on this sovereign in the lines scratched on the window of the inn at Stirling where he was staying:

'Here Stewarts once in glory reigned.
And laws for Scotland's weal
                    ordained;
But now unroofed their palace stands,
Their sceptre's swayed by other hands;
Fallen indeed, and to the earth
Whence grovelling reptiles take their
                                    birth,
The injured Stewart line is gone,
A race outlandish fills their throne;
An idiot race, to honour lost;
Who know them best despise them
                                    most.'

When the king recovered from his first attack of insanity and the Regency Bill (on the 'departure' of which Burns wrote an ode) had been thrown out, Thursday, 23rd April 1789, was set aside as a day of public thanksgiving for the King's recovery. Burns regarded the 'whole business as a solemn farce or pageant mummery' and accordingly wrote his 'Stanzas of Psalmody', which he sent to Stuart of *The Star*, signed Duncan M'Leerie. See **M'Leerie, Duncan.**

George IV (1762–1830)

As Prince of Wales he was referred to by Burns in 'The Bonnie Lass of Albanie' as 'a witless youth' who was usurping Albany's place. Soon after attaining his majority, the Prince had accumulated debts to the amount of half a million pounds.

He secretly married his mistress, Mrs Fitzherbert, in 1785, whom he later repudiated. Because of his profligate behaviour and increasing debts, he was forced to marry his cousin, Caroline of Brunswick, but they formally separated after the birth of their only child, Charlotte.

In 1811, when his father finally became incurably insane, he became Regent. He came to the throne on his father's death in 1820.

As George IV, he was the first sovereign to come to Scotland since the visit of

Charles II in 1650. Sir Walter Scott stage-managed his enthusiastic reception. This visit, in 1822, included the appearance of the stout monarch in a kilt.

Gibson, Mrs Agnes
See **Poosie Nansie.**

Gibson, George
Husband of Poosie Nansie.

Burns, in 'Adam Armour's Prayer', called him 'black-bearded Geordie'.

Gibson, Janet (d. 1813)
'Poosie Nansie's' (Mrs Agnes Gibson's) half-witted daughter, nicknamed 'Racer Jess' as the result of her willingness to run errands or races for wagers. She is mentioned in 'The Holy Fair' and as 'Jenny' in 'Adam Armour's Prayer'.

Gillespie, John
An Excise Officer who was stationed for some time at Dumfries. He was an unsuccessful suitor of Jean Lorimer, Burns's 'Chloris'. As late as 1791, Burns was trying to persuade Gillespie that he still had a chance with Jean. Gillespie, then at Portpatrick, was sent one of the poet's 'Chloris' songs, and told: 'I drank tea with the young lady at her home yesternight; and on my whispering her that I was to write you, she begged me to inclose you her compliments. In fact, the lady, to my certain knowledge, is down on her marrow bones of repentance respecting her usage of a certain gentleman.'

For once, however, Burns was wrong in the matter of reading a female heart. Soon afterwards, Jean Lorimer married a man called Whelpdale, a marriage which ended disastrously. See **Lorimer, Jean.**

Glenbuck
The source of the River Ayr. Burns mentioned it in 'The Brigs of Ayr'. Glenbuck village lies in the hills of Muirkirk parish, in East Ayrshire, not quite half a mile from the Lanarkshire border.

Glencairn, Countess of
See **Cunningham, Elizabeth.**

Glencairn, fourteenth and fifteenth Earls of
See **Cunningham.**

Glenriddell Manuscript
This most famous collection of Burns's manuscripts was made for his friend Captain Robert Riddell, Laird of Friar's Carse, near Dumfries, at Riddell's request. These were two calf-bound volumes, one containing verse and one containing a selection of twenty-seven of the poet's letters, though Burns and Riddell quarrelled and Riddell died soon afterwards without the letter volume ever having been presented. At the end of the volume of poems, Burns wrote: 'Let these be regarded as the genuine sentiments of a man who seldom flattered any, and never those he loved'. The copying seems to have been completed on 27th April 1791.

The book contained fifty-three unpublished poems, among them 'In Mauchline there dwells six proper young belles', the 'Epistle to John Goldie', the 'Elegy on the Death of Sir John Hunter Blair', 'Holy Willie's Prayer', 'Tam o' Shanter', and the 'Lament for James, Earl of Glencairn'.

Included also were some foot-notes by Burns, and a transcript of the Autobiographical Letter to Dr Moore; partly in Burns's own hand and partly in the hand of an amanuensis.

On Riddell's death, Burns showed considerable anxiety to get the volume back. In a letter from Dumfries, undated, though probably written in May 1794, beginning 'Madam' (though according to Ferguson, addressed to Miss Sophy or Elinor Riddell, Robert Riddell's sister), Burns wrote: 'I have a favor to request of you, Madam; and of your sister, Mrs Riddell, through your means. You know that at the wish of my late friend, I made a collection of all my trifles in verse which I had ever written. They are many of them local, some of them puerile and silly, and all of them unfit for the public eye. As I have some little fame at stake—a fame that I trust may live when the hate of those who "watch for my halting", and the contumelious sneer of those whom accident has made my superiors, will, with themselves, be gone to the regions of oblivion; I am uneasy now for the fate of those manuscripts. Will Mrs Riddell have the goodness to destroy them, or return with them to me?'

After Burns's own death, the two Riddell quarto volumes, along with the poet's other manuscripts—even down to 'the sweepings of his desk'—were sent to his biographer, Dr Currie. Currie retained them, as did his son, Wallace Currie. On his death in 1853, his widow presented them to the Liverpool Athenaeum, where they remained in a box, except during an exhibition, when they were brought out and put in a show case. After a somewhat sordid secret transaction, the Athenaeum sold them to Quaritch of London for £4,500. In spite of Scots protests, they were then sold to an American Collector, John Gribbel of Philadelphia, who gifted them to the Scottish National Library under terms which ensure that they will remain in possession of 'the people of Scotland for ever'.

In 1914, before sending his purchase to its permanent home, Mr Gribbel caused to be published privately in Philadelphia a facsimile edition of the two famous volumes, whose history is traced in the introduction.

Globe Tavern

An inn in Dumfries, owned by Mr and Mrs Hyslop. Anna Park was barmaid there and was a niece of Mrs Hyslop. *See* **Park, Anna.** Burns described the Globe Tavern in a letter to George Thomson as 'for these many years my favourite Howff'. It is still an inn.

Glover, Jean (1758–1811)

Born at Kilmarnock, the daughter of a weaver, she developed uncommon good looks and a fine singing voice. She became stage-struck at an early age, and eloped from her parents' home with a sleight-of-hand performer called Richard. Thereafter, she performed with him at public houses and other small places of entertainment up and down the country. There is a record of her having performed at a public house in Muirkirk, where her brother worked in the iron-works, in 1795, and soon after at Irvine. A correspondent of James Paterson, author of *The Contemporaries of Burns* (1840) told him that she had seen Jean Glover 'playing on a tambourine at the mouth of a close, in which was the exhibition-room of her husband the conjurer,' and thought her 'the bravest woman I had ever seen step in leather shoon.' A final reference to her performing at Letterkenny, in Ireland, a few months before her death, was also noted by Paterson.

Burns, who printed her song 'O'er the moor amang the heather' in the *Scots Musical Museum* in 1792, to a tune which first appeared in Bremner's Reels, 1760, and was republished in several later eighteenth century collections, took a less kindly view of Jean Glover, explaining how he came to collect the piece.

'This song is the composition of a Jean Glover, a girl who was not only a w—— but also a thief; and in one or other character has visited most of the correction houses in the west. She was born, I believe, in Kilmarnock. I took the song down from her singing as she was strolling the country with a slight-of-hand blackguard.'

Goldie, John (1717–1809)

John Goldie (or Goudie) was the son of the miller at Craigmill, on Cessnock Water. When only fourteen, he made a working model of a mill. He moved to Kilmarnock, where he set up as a cabinet-maker. He later became a winemerchant, but continued his scientific and theological investigations. His *Essays on various Important Subjects, Moral and Divine*, popularly known as 'Goudie's Bible', was an attempt to distinguish 'true from false religion'. It appeared in 1780, and became widely popular. Six years later, he published *The Gospel Recovered from its Captive State*, which established him as the opponent of the Auld Licht order he had supported as a younger man.

In 1808 he published *Conclusive Evidence Against Atheism*. He lost money in mining speculations towards the close of his life.

Being in Mauchline, he called on Burns at Mossgiel, and invited the poet to visit him at Kilmarnock.

Goldie became one of the sureties to the printer, John Wilson, for the publication of the Kilmarnock Edition. In the 'Epistle to John Goldie', Burns begins:

'O Gowdie, terror o' the whigs,
Dread o' blackcoats and reverend wigs!
Sour Bigotry on his last legs
    Girns an' looks back,
Wishing the ten Egyptian plagues
    May seize you quick . . .'

Goldie, Colonel of Goldielea

Mentioned by name in Burns's second Heron election ballad. He owned the estate of Goldielea, which he sold, on a down payment, to Walter Riddell, who renamed it Woodley Park. When Riddell could not find the balance of the purchase money, Colonel Goldie repossessed the estate.

Gordon, Jane, Duchess of Gordon (1746–1812)

Second daughter of Sir William Maxwell, third baronet of Monreith, Wigtownshire, by his wife Magdalen Blair of Blair. She was born in Hyndford's Close, Edinburgh, where her mother had a second-floor flat. She was a boisterous girl, according to

tradition, on several occasions with her sister, Betty (who became Lady Wallace of Craigie, unconventional wife of Mrs Dunlop's estranged eldest son, Sir Thomas Wallace), riding on the back of pigs, turned loose from a neighbouring wynd, down the High Street. In 1767, she married Alexander, fourth duke of Gordon, to whom she bore two sons and five daughters. She herself was a beauty, as may be seen from her portrait by Sir Joshua Reynolds. She had ready business sense, a quick wit and a good nature, but 'singular coarseness of speech'. In London, her house in the Mall was the social centre of the Tory party. In Edinburgh, she was arbiter of fashion. Writing to John Ballantine on 13th December 1786, Burns listed her as one of his 'avowed Patrons and Patronesses'. Mrs Alison Cockburn, too, commented: 'The town is at present agog with the ploughman poet, who receives adulation with native dignity, and is the very figure of his profession, strong and coarse, but has a most enthusiastick heart of love. He has seen dutchess Gordon and all the gay world . . .'

'Dutchess Gordon' invited Burns to several of her drawing-room parties, and on one occasion told Scott that Burns was the only man whose conversation carried her off her feet.

Because of her forthrightness, many unpleasant and derogatory stories were spread about her. On 10th April 1789, Burns wrote an angry letter to the *Gazetteer*, which had copied a sneering stanza, allegedly by Burns, from *The Star*. To the Editor of the *Star*, he wrote on 13th April:

'Mr Printer,

I was much surprised last night on being told that some silly verses on the Duchess of Gordon, which had appeared in a late Paper of yours, were said to be my composition. As I am not a Reader of any *London Newspaper*, I have not yet been able to procure a sight of that paper. I know no more of the matter than what a friend of mine, from having slightly glanced over the paragraph, could recollect; but this I know, I am not the author of the verses in question. My friend told me that the Printer himself expressed a doubt whether the poem was mine: I thank you, Sir, for that doubt. A Conductor of another London paper was not so candid when he lately inserted a disrespectful stanza on the same highly respectable personage, which he, with unqualified assurance, asserted to be mine; though in fact, I never composed a line on the Duchess of Gordon in my life. I have such a sense of what I personally owe to her Grace's benevolent patronage, and such a respect for her exalted character, that I have never yet dared to mention her name in any composition of mine, from a despair of doing justice to my own feelings.

'I have been recollecting over the sins and trespasses, peccadilloes and backslidings of myself and my forefathers, to see if I can guess why I am visited and punished with this vile calamity,* to be, at one time, falsely accused of the two most damning crimes, of which, as a man and as a poet, I could have been guilty—INGRATITUDE and STUPIDITY.

'I beg of you, Sir, that in your very first paper, you will do justice to my injured character with respect to those verses, falsely said to be mine; and please mention farther that in the *Gazeteer and New Daily Advertiser*, of March 28, another forgery of the like nature was committed on me, in publishing a disrespectful stanza on the Duchess of Gordon. I have written to the Conductor of that Paper, remonstrating on the injury he has done me; but lest from some motive or other, he should decline giving me that redress I crave, if you will undeceive the Public, by letting them know through the channel of your universally known paper, that I am guiltless of either the

* Probably a misprint for 'calumny'.

one or the other miserable pieces of rhyme, you will much oblige,
        Sir, Your very humble servant, . . .'
The Duchess was regarded as a skilful matchmaker, three of her five daughters marrying dukes and the fourth a marquis.

Towards the end of her life she became estranged from her husband and most of her family, and led a wandering, aimless and homeless existence, her quarrel with her husband having lost her her former position in society.

She died at Pulteney's Hotel, Piccadilly and was buried at Kinrara, Inverness-shire, at her own request.

Gordon, John, seventh (but for the attainder, tenth) Viscount Kenmure (1750–1840)

Served as John Gordon in the 17th Regiment of Foot. After 1780, was Member of Parliament for Kirkcudbright for a time. Though he was forced to sell part of his estates to pay off debts, assistance from his mother enabled him retain Kells and Balmaclellan.

Burns stayed with him and his wife for three days at Kenmure Castle, from 27th July 1793, when the poet and his friend Syme were making a tour of Galloway. Syme related that when Mrs Gordon's lapdog 'Echo' died, she asked Burns for an epitaph. This Burns rather reluctantly gave her— 'In wood and wild, ye warbling throng', one of his feebler efforts. Burns referred to him in his second Heron Election Ballad as 'Kenmure sae gen'rous'.

Gordon was a grandson of the Jacobite Viscount Kenmure, who 'came out' in 1715 and lost his head in consequence, but became the subject of Burns's delightful song—or revision of an old song— 'O, Kenmure's on and awa, Willie,' which first appeared in the *Scots Musical Museum in* 1792. He became Vice-Lieutenant of the Stewartry in 1822. In 1824, the family title was restored to Gordon.

He was a subscriber to George Thomson's publications.

Gordon, Lord George (1751–93)

Born in London, third and youngest son of Cosmo George Gordon, Duke of Gordon. He was educated at Eton and entered the navy, but resigned shortly before the outbreak of the American War because the then head of the Admiralty, Lord Sandwich, would not promise him a commission. In 1774, he threatened to oppose General Fraser, who was standing for Inverness-shire, so Fraser bought him the pocket borough of Ludgershall. In 1779, Lord George organised and headed the Protestant Association, formed to have the Catholic Relief Act of 1778 repealed. On 2nd June 1780, he led a mob which marched on Parliament, carrying a monster petition. The mob destroyed Roman Catholic chapels, pillaged the homes of Catholics, set fire to Newgate, and attacked the Bank of England. Before the riots were quelled, 450 people had been killed. Gordon was tried for high treason, but thanks largely to the skill of Henry Erskine, was acquitted, on the grounds that his intentions had not been treasonable.

When Burns was in Edinburgh in 1786, interest had revived in Lord George, because of his refusal to come forward as a witness in court over an ecclesiastical dispute in which he had become involved, and his subsequent excommunication for contempt of court, by the Archbishop of Canterbury. The following year, he was convicted for writing a pamphlet which reflected on the laws and criminal justice in Britain, and for publishing a libel against Marie Antoinette, and the French Ambassador in London. He fled to Holland to escape imprisonment, but on French representations was ordered to return to England, where he was put into Newgate prison, There he lived in considerable style, and ultimately died.

Burns made passing reference to Lord George's anti-popery campaign in a letter to James Dalrymple of Orangefield, dated February 1787.

Gordon, Professor Thomas (c. 1714–97)

In the Journal of the Highland tour of 1787, Burns listed among the people he met in Aberdeen on Monday, 10th September: 'Professor Gordon, a good-natured, jolly-looking professor'. Thomas Gordon held in succession the professorships of Humanity and Philosophy in King's College, Aberdeen, for sixty-one years. He had the reputation of being a particularly able teacher. He was the author of manuscript collections illustrating the history of the college. The manuscripts have been preserved in the university library.

Gordon of Balmaghie, Thomas (d. 1806)

A son of William Gordon of Campbelton, he bought Balmaghie estate in 1786. He married Agnes Augusta Dempster, a daughter of John Dempster of Dunnichen, by whom he had a large family, some of whom had distinguished careers.

He was the Tory opponent of Patrick Heron of Kerroughtree when they contested the Stewartry of Kirkcudbright in February 1795. Gordon, himself a man of property, was supported by his uncle, Murray of Broughton, one of the wealthiest landowners in the South of Scotland. The Earl of Galloway was also favouring him.

Burns wrote several election ballads in favour of his friend Heron, whose political views agreed with his own.

In the first ballad, the poet refers to Gordon as:

'A beardless boy comes o'er the hills
Wi's uncle's purse an' a' that ...'

Gordon lost the election.

Gordon Castle

The Castle, in Burns's day a seat of George,

fourth Duke of Gordon and his beautiful and witty Duchess, Jane Maxwell, is situated near Fochabers, Morayshire. Burns visited the place during his Highland tour, and became friendly with the duke's librarian and companion, James Hoy. Burns commemorated the visit in his song, 'Castle Gordon', which ends:

'Wildly here, without control
Nature reigns and rules the whole;
In that sober pensive mood,
Dearest to the feeling soul,
She plants the forest, pours the flood,
Life's poor day I'll musing rave
And find at night a sheltering cave,
Where waters flow and wild woods
                   wave,
By bonie Castle Gordon.'

Like most of the poetic visiting cards Burns felt impelled to leave behind him in houses where he had been entertained during his tours, 'Castle Gordon' is not a particularly inspired production.

It was as a result of the visit to Castle Gordon that a temporary breach with his travelling companion, William Nicol, occurred. Burns, who had met the Duchess in Edinburgh and been invited to call, left Nicol at the inn in Fochabers. After drinking wine with his host and hostess, the poet rose to go, and on being pressed to stay, explained the position about Nicol. The Duke suggested sending a servant to fetch Nicol to join the company for dinner, but Burns insisted on going with the servant.

Nicol, however, was in a fury at being neglected, and had ordered the saddling of the horses, intending to go on alone. Nicol gave the poet the choice of accompanying him there and then, or waiting behind by himself. Burns had thus little choice but to go with his irascible companion.

Of the Duke and Duchess, Burns wrote in his *Journal*: '. . . the duke makes me happier than ever great man did—noble, princely; yet mild, condescending and affable, gay and kind—the Duchess charming, witty, and sensible—God bless them.'

Gow, Neil (1727–1807)

By far the best-known of the Scots fiddle composers, from whose dance tunes Burns drew many of the airs for his songs, Gow (the first of a family of Scots dance-music composers) was born at Inver, near Dunkeld, and was sixty when Burns met him on his Highland tour. In his *Journal*, Burns described Gow, who played for him, as 'a short, stout-built Highland figure, with his greyish hair shed on his honest social brow—an interesting face, marking strong sense, kind open-heartedness mixed with un-mistrusting simplicity'. Burns later visited Gow's house.

Gow's main publications were a *Collection of Strathspey Reels*, 1784, 1788 and 1792, and the *Complete Repository of Original Scots Slow Strathspeys and Dances*, 1799, 1808, 1822.

Neil Gow had his portrait painted several times by Raeburn.

See Plate 13.

Gracie, James (1756?–1814)

Born at New Abbey, Kirkcudbright, he became manager of the bank at Dumfries. A warm friendship grew up between him and Burns, who complimented him in an epigram on his becoming Dean of Guild of Dumfries:

'Gracie, thou art a man of worth,
  O, be thou Dean for ever!
May he be damn'd to Hell henceforth
  Who fauts thy weight or measure!'

He was for twenty years a magistrate of Dumfries, and a captain in the Dumfries Volunteers. Latterly his fortunes were reversed. He took up accountancy, but died bankrupt.

Burns wrote from Brow eight days before he died, thanking Gracie for the offer of an airing in his carriage.

Graham, Douglas (baptised 1738; died 1811)

Leased the farm of Shanter, between the Maidens rocks, in Carrick. Burns met him there when he was visiting John Davidson. Graham owned a boat, the *Tam O'Shanter*, which it was believed he used for contraband purposes. He was probably the prototype of 'Tam O'Shanter.' He is reputed to have been as fond of drink as his superstitious, irascible and rather eccentric wife (*née* Helen M'Taggart) was opposed to it.

Graham of Fintry, Robert (1749-1815)

Graham of Fintry, in Forfarshire, was a descendant of Sir Robert Graham of Strathcarron, ancestor of the Grahams of Claverhouse. In 1780, he sold his estate, of which he was the twelfth laird, but retained his designation. He married Margaret Elizabeth Mylne of Mylnefield, by whom he had four sons and ten daughters. Burns first met Graham at Athole House, on 31st August 1787, while on the Highland tour. Graham was appointed a Commissioner of the Scottish Board of Excise in 1787.

Burns is supposed to have first confided his desire to be appointed to the Excise to his Doctor in Edinburgh, 'Lang' Sandy Wood, who spoke on the poet's behalf to Graham.

Burns first mentioned Graham in a letter to Josiah Walker, sent to Blair Atholl (as it is now spelt) from Inverness, and dated 5th September 1787. In it, Burns enumerated the pleasures he had enjoyed while visiting Athole House, among them, 'Mr Graham of Fintrie's charms of conversation'. On 7th January 1788, Burns wrote to Graham: 'When I had the honour of being introduced to you at Athole-house, I did not think of putting that acquaintance so soon to the test. . . . You know, I daresay, of an application I lately made to your Board, to be admitted an Officer of Excise. I have, according to form, been examined by a Supervisor, and today I give in his Certificate with a request for an Order for instruction. In this affair, if I succeed, I am afraid I shall but too much need a patronising friend. . . .'

On 2nd August, Burns indicated to Mrs Dunlop that he proposed writing an Epistle to: 'the Gentleman on whose friendship my excise hopes depend—Mr Graham of Fintry, one of the worthiest and most accomplished Gentlemen, not only of this Country, but I will dare to say it, of this Age'. Burns wrote to Graham on 10th September 1788, telling him that Ellisland 'does by no means promise to be such a Pennyworth as I was taught to expect'. Graham also heard how the poet lent money to keep Gilbert and his sisters on 'a farm in Ayr-shire'. Then came the point of the letter: 'There is one way by which I might be enabled to extricate myself from this embarrassment, a scheme which I hope and am certain is in your power to effectuate. I live here, Sir, in the very centre of a country Excise-Division; the present Officer lately lived on a farm which he rented in my nearest neighbourhood; and as the gentleman, owing to some legacies, is quite opulent, a removal could do him no manner of injury; and on a month's warning, to give me a little time to look again over my Instructions, I would not be afraid to enter on business. I do not know the name of his Division, as I have not yet got acquainted with any of the Dumfries Excise People; but his own name is Leonard Smith. It would suit me to enter on it, beginning of next Summer. . . .'

With this somewhat unscrupulous letter went the 'First Epistle to Robert Graham of Fintry Esq.', in which Burns repeated his request for patronage in heroic couplets:

'Why shrinks my soul, half-blushing, half-afraid,
Backward abash'd to ask thy friendly aid?

I know my need, I know thy giving
                                hand,
I tax thy friendship at thy kind
                        command . . .

Burns seems to have thought highly of
the poem, too, for he sent copies of it to a
number of correspondents, among them
Professor Dugald Stewart and Henry
Erskine.

It was almost a year before Burns
got the favour he craved; not, apparently,
through any fault of Graham's, but, as
Burns told Mrs Dunlop on 25th March
1789: 'There are in the Excise Board
certain regulations' which, notwithstanding Mr Graham's warmest exertions,
baffle all my hopes.'

Graham's 'warmest exertions' were
repeatedly requested, and, in fact, considerably benefited Burns, as is testified
not only by the obviously heartfelt
gratitude of the poet's letters to him,
but from second and third verse Epistles,
of which Graham was the recipient.
Graham also took a keen interest in
Burns's poetry, and was sent manuscript
copies of many new songs and poems.
He was, indeed, in Burns's own words,
a true 'Friend of the Poet, Tried and
Leal'.

When Burns's loyalty was called in
question at the end of December 1792,
it was to Graham that he appealed for
help, writing on the last day of that
year: 'I believe, Sir, I may aver it, and in
the sight of Omnipotence, that I would
not tell a deliberate Falsehood . . . and I
say, that the allegation, whatever villain
has made it, is a LIE! To the British
Constitution, on Revolution principles,
next after my God, I am mosy devoutly
attached.' (By 'Revolution', of course,
Burns meant 1688.)

Graham apparently wrote back a kindly
letter, naming the specific charges that
had been levelled against Burns, to which
Burns replied at length on 5th January
1793:

'Now, to the charges which Malice &
Misrepresentation have brought against
me.

'It has been said, it seems, that I not only
belong to, but head a disaffected party
in this place. I know of no party in this
place, Republican o[r] Reform, except an
old party of Borough-Reform; with
which I never had anything to do.
Individuals, both Republican & Reform,
we have, though not many of either;
but if they have associated, it is more
than I have the least knowledge of: &
if there exists such an association, it
must consist of such obscure, nameless
beings, as precludes any possibility of
my being known to them, or they to me.

'I was in the playhouse one night, when
ÇA IRA was called for. I was in the middle
of the Pit, & from the Pit the clamour
arose. One or two individuals with whom
I occasionally associate were of the party,
but I neither knew of the Plot, nor
joined in the Plot; nor ever opened my
lips to hiss, or huzza, that, or any other
Political tune whatever. I looked on myself as far too obscure a man to have any
weight in quelling a Riot; at the same
time as a character of higher respectability, than to yell in the howlings of a
rabble. This was the conduct of all the
first Characters in this place; & these
Characters know, & will avow, that such
was my conduct.

'I never uttered any invectives against
the king. His private worth, it is altogether impossible that such a man as I,
can appreciate; and in his Public capacity, I
always revered, & ever will, with the
soundest loyalty, revere, the Monarch of
Great Britain, as, to speak in Masonic,
the sacred KEYSTONE OF OUR ROYAL ARCH
CONSTITUTION.

'As to REFORM PRINCIPLES, I look upon
the British Constitution, as settled at
the Revolution, to be the most glorious
Constitution on earth, or that perhaps
the wit of man can frame; at the same
time, I think, & you know what High

and distinguished Characters have for some time thought so, that we have a good deal deviated from the original principles of that Constitution; particularly, that an alarming System of Corruption has pervaded the connection between the Executive Power and the House of Commons. This is the Truth the Whole truth, of my Reform opinions; opinions which, before I was aware of the complection of these innovating times, I too unguardedly (now I see it) sported with: but henceforth, I seal up my lips. However, I never dictated to, corresponded with, or had the least connection with, any political association whatever—except, that when the Magistrates & principal inhabitants of this town, met to declare their attachment to the Constitution, & their abhorrence of Riot, which declaration you would see in the Papers, I, as I thought my duty as a Subject at large, & a Citizen in particular, called upon me, subscribed the same declaratory Creed.

'Of Johnston, the publisher of the Edinr. Gazetteer, I know nothing. One evening in company with four or five friends, we met with his prospectus which we thought manly & independant; & I wrote to him, ordering his paper for us. If you think that I act improperly in allowing his Paper to come addressed to me, I shall immediately countermand it. I never, so judge me, God! wrote a line of prose for the Gazetteer in my life. An occasional address, spoken by Miss Fontenelle on her benefit-night here, which I called the Rights of Woman, I sent to the Gazetteer; as also, some extempore stanzas on the Commemoration of Thomson: both of these I will subjoin for your perusal. You will see that they have nothing whatever to do with Politics. At one time when I sent Johnston one of these poems, but which one, I do not remember, I inclosed, at the request of my warm & worthy friend, Robᵗ Riddel Esq: of Glenriddel,

a prose essay signed Cato, written by him, & addressed to the delegates for the County Reform, of which he was one for this County. With the merits, or demerits, of that Essay, I have nothing to do, farther than transmitting it in the same Frank, which Frank he had procured me.

'As to France, I was her enthusiastic votary in the beginning of the business. When she came to shew her old avidity for conquest, in annexing Savoy, &c. to her dominions, & invading the rights of Holland, I altered my sentiments. A tippling Ballad which I made on the Prince of Brunswick's breaking up his camp, & sung one convivial evening, I shall likewise send you, sealed up, as it is not every body's reading. This last is not worth your perusal; but lest Mrs FAME should, as she has already done, use, & even abuse, her old privilege of lying, you shall be the master of everything, le pour et le contre, of my political writings & conduct.

'This, my honored Patron, is all. To this statement I challenge disquisition. Mistaken Prejudice, or unguarded Passion, may mislead, & often have misled me; but when called on to answer for my mistakes, though, I will say it, no man can feel keener compunction for his errors, yet, I trust, no man can be more superior to evasion or disguise.'

The storm blew over, however, no doubt partly as a result of Graham's influence. But writing to Erskine of Mar—who erroneously believed that Burns had actually been dismissed, and who had written to Captain Riddell offering to start a subscription fund for the poet—on 13th April 1793, Burns related his belief that: 'there existed a system of corruption between the Executive Power and the Representative part of the Legislature which boded no good to our glorious Constitution; and which every patriotic Briton must wish to see amended. Some such Sentiments as these I stated in a letter to my generous Patron, Mr Graham, which he laid before the Board at large, where it seems my las[t] remark gave great offence; and one of our Supervisors General, a Mr Corbet, was instructed to enquire on the spot, into my conduct, and to document me—"that *my* business was to *act*, not to think; and that whatever might be Men or Measures, it was for me to be silent and obedient". Mr Corbet was likewise my steady friend; so between Mr Graham and him, I have been partly forgiven.'

On 7th January 1794, Burns laid before Graham a scheme whereby there could be: 'an officer's appointment saved to the public'.

The last surviving letter from Burns to Graham, again urging promotion, and sent in the autumn of 1794, finishes: 'Should the Chapter of Chances and Changes, which God forbid! ever place a Child of yours in the situation to need a Friend, as I have done; may they likewise find that Generous Friend that I have found in you!'

See Plate 12.

Graham, James, later third Duke of Montrose (1755–1836)

Succeeded his father, the second Duke in 1790. He was member of Parliament for Richmond in 1780, and in 1794 for Great Bedwin, in Wiltshire, when Burns wrote 'The Author's Earnest Cry and Prayer' in which he described Graham as 'that glib-gabbet Highland baron'. During Pitt's office, Graham held the posts of President of the Board of Trade, Postmaster General, Paymaster of the Forces, and Lord Justice General. He was Chancellor of Glasgow University from 1780 until his death. The *Greville Memoirs* contain a disparaging estimate of his character and abilities. But he obtained for the Highlanders permission to wear their national dress, which had been prohibited by law as a consequence of the Rising of 1745. He was also astute enough to 'only affect to complain' of the Scottish climate when he met Dr Johnson, lest, as Boswell tells us, 'if he had spoken as favourably of his country as he really thought, Dr Johnson might have attacked it'.

Grant

An actor whom Burns knew well in Dumfries. He wrote a letter to a lady (possibly Mrs Riddell) asking her to attend Mr Grant's benefit night. He described the actor as having 'genius and worth which would do honour to patronage: he is a poor and modest man . . .'

He is possibly the actor referred to by William Charles Macready in his *Reminiscences*, as the one whose sudden illness gave the younger Macready his understudy's chance in Glasgow in 1810, as Count Villars, a French refugee, in Morton's play *Education*.

Chambers alleged that Burns gave Grant the masonic apron which the poet had received from Sharpe of Hoddam. In his turn, Grant was reputed to have given the apron to a Whitehaven solicitor, Edwin Holwell Heywood, while he was acting there in 1810. Edwin Heywood was the nephew of Peter Heywood, of *Mutiny on the Bounty* fame.

Grant, The Reverend David (d. 1791)

Minister at Ettrick in 1786, translated the same year to Ochiltree where he remained until his death. Burns called him 'Davie Bluster' in 'The Kirk's Alarm':

'Davie Bluster, Davie Bluster, for a
        saunt if ye muster,
  It's a sign they're no nice o' recruits;
  Yet to worth let's be just, Royal
        Blood ye might boast—
If the Ass were the king o' the
        brutes,
Davie Bluster! If the Ass were the
      king o' the brutes.'

In the Don MS text used by Professor Kinsley, the stanza runs:

'Davie Rant, Davie Rant, wi' a face
　　　　　　　　　　like a saunt,
And a heart that wad poison a hog;
Raise an impudent roar, like a breaker
　　　　　　　　　　lee-shore,
Or the kirk will be tint in a bog.'

Writing to Lady Elizabeth Cunningham, Burns called Grant 'a designing, rotten-hearted Puritan'.

Gray of Gilmilnscroft, John Farquhar- (1751–c. 1801)

Son of the Reverend James Gray, minister at Strathblane. He owned the estate of Kilmerdinny. In 1777, he married Jane Farquhar, heiress of Gilmilnscroft, only child of Alexander Farquhar of Gil-milnscroft, who died in 1779. Gray changed his name to Farquhar-Gray on his marriage. He was a Justice of the Peace and, as such, according to one tradition quoted by Train, married Burns and Jean Armour in 'the writing office of Gavin Hamilton', Mauchline. This seems the most likely of the various traditions concerning Burns's marriage.

Gray, The Reverend James (1770–1830)

After having been apprenticed to a shoe-maker, Gray educated himself to become a schoolmaster. When Burns arrived in Dumfries, Gray was Latin master and *ipso facto* headmaster, of Dumfries Academy. He taught Burns's children.

In 1801 he moved to the High School of Edinburgh. In the capital, his home was a rendezvous of the literati, among them James Hogg, the Ettrick Shepherd, who married Gray's sister-in-law, Margaret Phillips. Gray was made the fifteenth bard in 'The Queen's Wake', the passage beginning 'The next was bred on southern shore' referring to him. In 1822, Gray became Principal of Belfast Academy. Soon afterwards, he decided to take orders, and was admitted a deacon of the Church of Ireland in 1823. In 1826 he went to India, and became chaplain

at the station of Bhooj, in Cutch. Whilst there, he made the first written vocabu-lary of Cutchee, and translated parts of the Bible into that language. His other writings were works on classical topics, and two collections of poems, *Cora, or the Vale of Clwyd and other Poems* and *Sabbath Among the Mountains*, which described his recollections of Roseneath.

Gray's main importance in the Burns story, however, is that in 1815 he wrote a defence of the poet for the biographer Alexander Peterkin. In this, Gray pointed out the vast quantity of poetry written by Burns during his Dumfries days: 'Not many days passed . . . in which he did not compose some piece of poetry or some song designed to delight the imagination and soften the heart.' Gray then described Burns as: 'A kind and attentive father who took great delight in cultivating the minds of his children'. He added: 'I would ask any person of common candour if employments like these are consistent with habitual drunken-ness?' Gray was thus the first person to challenge the Currie legend of Burns as a drunken debauchee.

Gray, Simon

A retired London business man in Duns who considered himself a poet. When Burns was at Berrywell, on his Border tour, he received on 5th May 1787 some of Gray's work for his views on it. He sent it back with the comment:

'Symon Gray,
You're dull to-day.'

Undaunted, Gray sent another lot, to which Burns replied:

'Dullness with redoubled sway,
Has seized the wits of Symon Gray.'

Not content with this, Gray sent yet a third lot of his pieces.

Burns sent back his views, this time at length. The nature of them can be readily appreciated from the following lines:

'Such damned bombast no age that's
past
Will shew, or time to come.'

Gray left annuities and a bread fund to
Duns, and according to Kinsley 'is
commemorated in a local literary society'.

Greenfield, The Reverend William (d. 1827)

Professor of Rhetoric and Minister of
St. Andrew's Church when Burns came
to Edinburgh. Three months later he
became Blair's associate-preacher at the
High Church. Burns had a regard for
him as a man, and preferred his preaching
to that of Blair. In his second *Commonplace
Book*, he said of him:

'Mr Greenfield is of a superior order.
The bleedings of humanity, the generous
resolve, a manly disregard of the paltry
subjects of vanity, virgin modesty, the
truest taste, and a very sound judgment,
characterise him. His being the first
Speaker I ever heard is perhaps half owing
to industry. He certainly possesses no
small share of poetic abilities; he is a
steady, most disinterested friend, without
the least affectation, of seeming so; and,
as a companion, his good sense, his
joyous hilarity, his sweetness of manners
and modesty, are most engagingly charming.'

Writing to Greenfield in December
1786, Burns unburdened to him his
doubts about his sudden fame, and his
expectations for the future:

'Never did Saul's armour sit so heavy
on David when going to encounter
Goliah, as does the encumbering robe of
public notice with which the friendship
and patronage of some "names dear to
fame" have invested me. . . . I am willing
to believe that my abilities deserved a
better fate than the veriest shades of
life; but to be dragged forth, with all
my imperfections on my head, to the
full glare of learned and polite observation, is what, I am afraid, I shall have

bitter reason to repent. . . . "When
proud Fortune's ebbing tide recedes",
you may bear me witness when my
bubble of fame was at the highest, I
stood, unintoxicated, with the inebriating
cup in my hand, looking forward, with
rueful resolve, to the hastening time when
the stroke of envious Calumny, with
all the eagerness of vengeful triumph,
should dash it to the ground.'

At the height of his career in 1796,
Greenfield became Moderator of the
General Assembly, and the University
of Edinburgh conferred on him the
degree of Honorary Doctorate of Divinity.

But two years later, for some unknown
reason—possibly, Ferguson suggests, because of some sexual scandal—he found
himself in such difficulties that he fled
to the North of England, stripped of
his academic honours by the university,
and excommunicated by the Church. He
remained in England under the assumed
name of Rutherford.

The records of the Presbytery of Edinburgh merely state that because of
'certain flagrant reports concerning his
conduct . . . they laid him under a sentence of excommunication'.

Greenfield thereafter supported himself by teaching and writing. He was
the author of several works, the most
important being *Essays on the Sources of
the Pleasures received from Literary Compositions*, which he published in 1809. In
the same year, Sir Walter Scott introduced him to the publisher, John Murray.
Greenfield thereafter contributed to the
Quarterly Review under the name of
Richardson.

Greenock, River

A tributary of the river Ayr, mentioned
in 'The Brigs of Ayr'.

Gregory, Dr James (1753–1821)

Son of the Professor of Medicine at
Aberdeen and Edinburgh and great-
grandson of the seventeenth-century

mathematician and astronomer. Gregory was educated at Aberdeen, Edinburgh and Oxford. In 1776 he became Professor of Physick in Edinburgh University, and in 1790 he succeeded Cullen as Professor of the Practice of Medicine. His *Conspectus Medicinae Theoreticae* (widely read in its day) was published in 1780. He disliked 'meddlesome medicine', believed in fresh air and exercise, and was an able lecturer. He was the inventor of 'Gregory's Powder', long prescribed as a laxative.

George William Hay Drummond, in *A Town Eclogue* (1804), deals thus with Gregory's book:

'Some style this jumble of satyric
                                    strokes
"An Hospital for invalided jokes,"
And others in a higher rank to class
                                    'em
"The classic surgeon's Gradus ad
                            Parnassum."'

The *Dictionary of Natural Biography* states that Gregory 'wasted his great powers on temporary and irritating controversies'. He was fined for defamation in a row with a Dr Hamilton, which ended with Hamilton being given a beating with a stick by Gregory. Another of his rows resulted in his expulsion from the Edinburgh College of Physicians, for breaking his oath not to divulge its proceedings, and for making false statements. But Lord Cockburn thought him 'a curious and excellent man, a great physician, a great Lecturer, a great Latin scholar and a great talker, vigorous and generous, large of stature and with a strikingly powerful countenance'.

He married twice. By his second wife, a Miss McLeod, he had eleven children. Their fourth son, William, was later to hold his father's old chair in Edinburgh.

Burns had a great respect for Gregory, whom he described in a letter to Clarinda, of 28th December 1787, as: 'A gentleman for whose character, abilities and critical knowledge I have the highest veneration'.

Gregory gave Burns a copy of an English translation of Cicero, and the poet wrote on the fly-leaf:

'Edin. April 23d, 1787—This book, a present from the truly worthy and learned Dr Gregory, I shall preserve to my latest hour, as a mark of gratitude, esteem and veneration I bear the Donor. So help me God!'

Burns submitted his poem 'The Wounded Hare' to Dr Gregory for criticism, which he gave freely, complaining both of the stanza form and the 'coarseness' of the language. Burns seems to have been quite taken aback by his strictures.

In one of Burns's letters to Dugald Stewart from Ellisland, 20th January 1789, the poet mentioned 'the justness (iron justice, for he has no bowels of compassion for a poor poetic sinner) of Dr Gregory's remarks'.

In 'Willie's Awa', Burns listed 'worthy Gregory's Latin Face' as one of those to be seen habitually at Creech's levees. *See Plate 8.*

Grenville, Lord. *See* **Wyndham, William**

Grierson, Dr George
A Glasgow friend of Burns, and a fellow mason.

Grierson of Dalgoner, James (1753–1843)
A local laird whom Burns knew when he lived at Ellisland. Grierson had an interest in literature, and in 1805 became an enthusiastic collector of Burns Material. It was he who stated that Burns's friend James Smith 'went to St Lucia and died there'. Grierson's ancestor, Sir Robert Grierson, is buried in Dunscore Churchyard, near Ellisland. In Covenanting times, Sir Robert's name was more feared and hated in Galloway than even that of John Graham himself.

Grieve, James

Laird of Boghead, Tarbolton, an estate which lay west from Lochlea farm.

Burns lampooned him in one of his mock epitaphs:

'Here lies Boghead amang the dead,
    In hopes to get salvation;
But if such as he in Heav'n may be,
    Then welcome—hail! damnation.'

Grieve, Miss Patty

Wife of a farmer called Thomson. Burns rode over to meet them when he was at Berrywell. According to his *Border Journal*, she was 'formerly a flame of Mr Robert Ainslie's'.

Grieve, William

One of the freemasons who made Burns and Ainslie Royal Arch Masons of St Abb's Lodge. Burns was admitted 'gratis', and they 'considered themselves honoured by having a man of such shining abilities for one of their companions'. Ainslie had to pay a guinea.

Burns described Grieve in his *Journal of the Border Tour* as: 'a joyous, warmhearted, clever fellow—takes a hearty glass, and sings a good song'. His brother Robert was described as his 'partner in trade, a good fellow, but says little'. William Grieve's attachment to his family was such that when he was out 'which by the bye is often the case, he cannot go to bed till he sees if all his sisters are sleeping well'.

Grose, Captain Francis (1731–91)

His father came from Switzerland and set up as a jeweller in London, where he fashioned George II's coronation crown. Francis, who was probably his eldest son, served in the Army, and retired with the rank of captain. He also studied art, was at one time Richmond Herald in the College of Arms, but resigned his tabard to Henry Pugolas for 600 guineas. Next he became Paymaster and Adjutant of the

Surrey Militia, a position he was equally unsuited for, since he kept no books and gave no receipts, with the result that the private fortune he had inherited from his father had to be used to make up deficits. He published his *Antiquities of England and Wales* in six volumes between 1773–87, and *The Antiquities of Scotland* in two volumes, in 1789 and 1791. Burns met him while he was in Scotland collecting material for his Scottish work.

Writing to Mrs Dunlop from Ellisland on 17th July 1789, Burns told her: 'Captn Grose, the well-known Author of the Antiquities of England and Wales has been through Annandale, Nithsdale and Galloway, in the view of commencing another Publication, The Antiquities of Scotland. As he has made his headquarters with Captn Riddel, my nearest neighbour, for these two months, I am intimately acquainted with him; and I have never seen a man of more original observation, anecdote and remark. Thrown into the army from the Nursery, and now that he is the father of a numerous family who are all settled in respectable situations in life, he has mingled in all societies and known everybody. His delight is to steal thro' the country almost unknown, both as most favorable to his humor and his business. . . . If you discover a cheerful-looking grig of an old, fat fellow, the precise figure of Dr Slop, wheeling about your avenue in his own carriage with a pencil and paper in his hand, you may conclude: "Thou art the man"!'

Burns took to this fat, jovial man with an inexhaustible fund of stories, and suggested to him that he should include Alloway Kirk in his forthcoming volume. Grose agreed, but, Gilbert Burns recorded, on condition that Burns provided a witch tale to go with his drawing. In June 1790, Burns sent Grose a prose witch tale with a variant in a letter to Grose, following it up with a rhymed version, the superb 'Tam o' Shanter'. Grose naturally preferred the poetic version, and 'Tam o' Shanter' was published in the second volume of Grose's *The Antiquities of Scotland*. It had, however, already appeared in the *Edinburgh Magazine* for March 1791. Grose also inspired Burns to write the witty lines 'On Captain Grose's Peregrinations through Scotland':

'Hear, Land o' Cakes, and brither
                                    Scots,
Frae Maidenkirk to Johnny Groat's—
If there's a hole in a' your coats,
    I rede you tent it:
A chield's amang you takin' notes,
    And faith he'll prent it!

If in your bounds ye chance to light
Upon a fine, fat, fodgel wight,
O' stature short but genius bright,
    That's he, mark weel—
And wow! he has an unco sleight
    O' cauk and keel . . .'

Grose also inspired 'On Captain Grose' and the epigram, 'On Captain Francis Grose'.

Grose left Scotland to visit Ireland to continue his work there, but died soon afterwards of an apoplectic fit. He is buried near Dublin.

Grose's works were certainly well in advance of their kind at the time they were published, and are still of considerable interest. His *A Classical Dictionary of the Vulgar Tongue* (1785) was of some importance in the development of lexicography.

See Plate 8.

Guilford, Frederick, Lord North (1732–92)

Son of the first Earl of Guilford, educated at Eton and Christchurch. At twenty-two he was elected Member of Parliament for Banbury. After holding several offices, he followed Grafton as George III's chief minister in 1770, holding office throughout the American War. He counselled peace, but was persuaded by the king to retain office although he knew the war to be hopeless. He insisted on resigning, however, on the news of Cornwallis's surrender at Yorktown in 1782. In April the following year he formed a coalition with Fox under the nominal premiership of the Duke of Portland, but the Coalition Ministry went out of office on Fox's India Bill the following December, and North gave up politics. He is 'Guilford good' in Burns's 'A Fragment'.

H

Haggis', 'To a

Apparently written by Burns soon after his arrival in Edinburgh in 1786, possibly for a dinner at the house of Andrew Bruce, a merchant friend. This seems more probable than the legend that it was composed extempore during a dinner at the house of John Morrison, a Mauchline cabinet-maker. It was the first of Burns's poems to be published in an Edinburgh periodical. For a contemporary recipe, see **MacIver, Susanna**.

Hall of Dunglass, Sir James, fourth Baronet (1761–1832)

A chemist and geologist. He wrote some papers in support of the Huttonian theory of the earth, and was President of the Royal Society of Edinburgh for some years. His son, Captain Basil Hall, was a friend of Sir Walter Scott.

Burns had breakfast with Sir James when on his Border tour.

Halliday, James

The man who made Burns's drain at Ellisland.

Writing on 7th November 1789, to the Dumfries lawyer, David Newall (at whose house, Isle, Burns stayed while Ellisland was being completed), Burns said: 'The bearer, James Halliday, is the lad who executed the drain between Isle and Ellisland. It is now finished, at least four or five days work more will conclude it; and these few days' work must, I doubt, stand over until next Spring, as the business is impractible in wintry weather. . . . I have not taken an accurrate [sic] measure of the drain, but by a pretty near guess, I take it to be about 80 Roods in length. Seventeen pence per rood was the bargain, which, taking 85 roods as the just length, makes the whole amount

£6-0-5—but at this rate the poor fellows will scarce have 1/- per day... and between you and me, they very well deserve 14 or 15d per day, as they wrought both hard and dirty and kept no stated hours, but from sun to sun almost.'

Writing again to Newall in the spring of 1790, Burns said: 'Inclosed is a state of the account between you and me and James Halliday respecting the drain. I have stated it at 20d per rood, as in fact, even at that, they have not the wages they ought to have had, and I cannot for the soul of me see a poor devil a loser at my hand. Humanity, I hope, as well as Charity, will cover a multitude of sins, a mantle, of which—between you and me—I have some little need.'

Halloween

All Hallows E'en, the last day of October, and a night when witches and warlocks were supposed to reign in Scotland. It is the title of one of the poems in the Kilmarnock Edition, couched in the old Scots stanza form used in 'The Holy Fair'. Daiches very properly says that it is: 'of more interest to the expert in folklore than to the general reader; its accumulation of descriptions of Halloween folk customs, couched in a language containing a higher percentage of rustic Scots words than is found in any other of Burns's poems, becomes tedious in spite of the lively movement and the skilfully manipulated verse'.

Hamilton, Dr

An acquaintance of Burns when the poet was living in Irvine. Hamilton was one of those who stood security to the printer for the Kilmarnock Edition. His father, Hamilton of Craighlaw, was Provost of Irvine.

Hamilton, Charlotte (1763–1806)

She was the elder daughter of John Hamilton of Kype, a Mauchline lawyer, by his second wife. On the death of her father, she and the second family moved to Harvieston, near Dollar, the home of the writer John Tait, husband of her maternal aunt. She was a half-sister of Gavin Hamilton of Mauchline. Burns first met her when he made a day's visit to Harvieston on 27th August 1787, and was much struck by her beauty. When he wrote to Gavin Hamilton to describe Charlotte and her brothers and sisters at Harvieston, the poet called her: 'not only beautiful, but lovely. Her form is elegant; her features not regular, but they have the smile of sweetness, and the settled complacency of good nature in the highest degree. . . . Her eyes are fascinating; at once expressive of good sense, tenderness and a noble mind'. Together, they rode to see the Falls of Devon. Burns's second visit to Harvieston was with Dr James Adair, who accompanied him on his tour of October 1787. Burns celebrated Charlotte's beauty with 'The Banks of the Devon', which appeared in the *Scots Musical Museum* the following year.

Dr Adair also admired Charlotte, who, indeed, became his wife in 1789. They had five children. Charlotte returned to Edinburgh after her husband's death, and died there.

Hamilton, Gavin (1751–1805)

The dedicatee of the Kilmarnock Edition was the fifth son of John Hamilton of Kype by his first wife, Jacobina Young. His father was a lawyer, clerk to the regality of Mauchline. He bought the tower known as the Castle of Mauchline, but later sold it and leased it back from the Earl of Loudon. Gavin entered his father's office, but soon set up in practice on his own. When, in 1771, the Kirk Session made a move to suppress begging by discontinuing the giving of alms to travelling professional beggars, they set up a special fund to relieve the genuine poor, which was to be a stent of a penny in the pound of the valued rent. Four years later, Gavin Hamilton was appointed

collector of stent. By 1778, however, Daddy Auld was finding it inconvenient to his Auld Licht conscience to have a New Licht official functioning for him, and there followed one of those sordid kirk intrigues particularly rife in Scotland at this time. Auld persuaded the kirk session to stigmatise Hamilton as having been in default by six pounds, two shillings and twopence halfpenny whilst stent collector. Hamilton ignored this move, so Auld stopped the parochial distribution of money to the poor on the grounds that the necessary money was being fraudulently retained by Hamilton. Hamilton's case was that it had never been collected, because those from whom it was due could not pay. Legal action followed, and the Kirk Session apparently lost. So Auld altered the line of his attack. He convened the Kirk Session meeting to examine the communion roll two weeks earlier than usual. The customary warning to non-attenders was issued, among others, to Hamilton. But the recorded minutes of the meeting show beyond doubt that Hamilton was the target of their aggression. He, however, got sight of the minutes, and struck back sharply with a protest. The row developed, and Hamilton appealed to the Presbytery of Ayr. He appeared before them on 25th June 1785, charged with:

(1) Unnecessary absences from church two Sabbaths in December and three Sabbaths in January together.

(2) Setting out on a journey to Carrick on the third Sabbath of January.

(3) Habitual if not total neglect of family worship.

(4) Abusive letter to session dated 13th November 1784.

The Presbytery found in Hamilton's favour, and Auld and his Session then appealed to the Synod of Glasgow and Ayr. They, too, upheld Hamilton.

This was the dispute in which Burns so exulted, and which produced the dedicatory poem in the Kilmarnock

Edition, 'Holy Willie's Prayer' and some smaller poems. Burns had been introduced to Hamilton by Aiken in the autumn of 1783, when the Burns family was still at Lochlea. Hamilton's education, warmth and common sense endeared him to the poet, who set out his character in the 'Epistle to John M'Math'.

'There's Gau'n, misca'd waur than a
                                        beast,
Wha has mair honor in his breast
Than mony scores as guid's the priest
    Wha sae abus't him;
An' may a bard no crack his jest
    What way they've use't him?

See him, the poor man's friend in
                                        need,
The gentleman in word an' deed—
An' shall his fame an' honor bleed
    By worthless skellums,
An' not a muse erect her head
    To cowe the blellums?'   [babblers

Hamilton became factor to the Earl of Loudon, from whom he leased Mossgiel, intending to make it a place of summer retreat. But Hamilton's wife, Helen Kennedy, had other views, so Hamilton accepted Burns's offer to sub-lease it from Martinmas, 1784.

Hamilton interested himself enthusiastically in Burns's affairs, and disposed of quite a number of the proposals for the Kilmarnock Edition. When in August, 1787, Burns reached Harvieston, near Dollar, where Hamilton's half-brothers and sisters were staying, he sent a detailed description of them back to Hamilton at Ayr, since he had been 'told you have not seen them these several years'.

About March 1788, however, Hamilton apparently suggested to Burns that he should become a guarantor to Gilbert Burns for a considerable sum. Burns replied: 'The language of refusal is to me the most difficult language on earth, and you are the man of the world . . . to whom it gives me the greatest pain to hold such language. My brother has al-

ready got money, and shall want nothing in my power to enable him to fulfil his engagement with you; but to be security on so large a scale even for a brother, is what I dare not do, except I were in such circumstances of life as that the worst that might happen could not greatly injure me. I never wrote a letter which gave me so much pain in my life, as I know the unhappy consequences: I shall incur the displeasure of a Gentleman for whom I have the highest respect, and to whom I am deeply obliged.'

The friendship survived, however, though not perhaps with quite its earlier ardour. The last letter Burns wrote to Hamilton, dated 16th July 1793, from Dumfries, invoked Hamilton's assistance on behalf of Mrs Muir, who was in trouble over the settlement of the affairs of her husband, William Muir, miller of Tarbolton. It contains some amusing reflections on marriage.

Gavin Hamilton lived in a house adjoining the Castle at Mauchline. He had eight children. The poem 'The Calf' resulted from a wager between Burns and Hamilton.

Hamilton, The Reverend George (d. 1832)

Minister of Gladsmuir from 1790 until his death, and Moderator of the General Assembly in 1805. Burns had written some defamatory verse about the King on the window of his room in Stirling, which included the lines:

'The injured Stewart line is gone,
A race outlandish fills their throne;
An idiot race, to honor lost;
Who know them best despise them
                                        most'.

Hamilton is alleged to have added his own lines to those of Burns. They conclude:

'These few rash lines will damn thy
                                        name,
And blast thy hopes of future fame.'

In the Glenriddell Manuscript, under the title of 'The Poet's Reply to the Threat of a Censorious Critic', Burns referred to this matter: 'My impudent lines were answered, very petulantly, by *somebody*, I believe a Rev. Mr Hamilton. In an MS., where I met the answer, I wrote below:

'With Aesop's lion, Burns says, sore I feel
Each other blow, but d—n that ass's heel.'

Hamilton, James

A Glasgow grocer with whom Burns was in correspondence over the purchase of copies of the poems of his 'brother Poet, Mr Turnbull'. James Hamilton and Company had their premises at 86 Trongate in 1787, as Ferguson discovered from Jones's Directory of Glasgow for that year. The firm's name is missing from the same reference book for 1789. As in the second of the two surviving letters to Hamilton, dated 26th May 1789, Burns consoled the grocer for his misfortunes. It has been supposed by some writers, notably J. C. Ewing, that these were of a business nature. Presumably, Hamilton failed.

Writing from Ellisland on 27th April the same year, Burns observed: 'This country has nothing new. Mankind are the same everywhere. In this place, as in Glasgow I suppose too, of the men talled honest, and the women called chaste, a number supposed to be near the full half of them are not what they pretend to be; and of the remaining half, many of them are thought to have still worse faults.'

Hamilton, John

John Hamilton of Sundrum, a few miles north-east of Alloway, was a merchant and agricultural improver. He acquired the estate of Sundrum from Lord Cathcart about 1750, and married Lillias, sister

of Hugh Montgomerie of Coylfield, who later became twelfth Earl of Eglinton. He was appointed 'Oversman' or referee in William Burnes's dispute with his landlord David M'Lure. Hamilton decided that of the £775 claimed by M'Lure, £543 was offset by credits for improvements made by Burnes, part payments on rent, and other matters.

Hamilton of Allershaw, Capt. John

Burns rented three small rooms and a kitchen in a second floor tenement from Hamilton in Wee Vennel, now Bank Street, when he and his family first came to Dumfries. Shortly after his daughter Elizabeth's birth, Burns rented, again from Hamilton, a bigger detached house near the southern end of Mill Vennel, now Burns Street. He moved in on 19th May 1793. Because of his generosity to a friend called Crombie, in 1791, when he endorsed a note for him, and now, in 1795, had to pay upon it, Burns found that he was in arrears to Hamilton for rent. This caused him undue embarrassment. When the poet paid three guineas towards his rent, the Captain wrote asking if he had in any way offended the poet. To this, Burns replied on 31st January 1795, that his 'backwardness' had arisen 'not from his taking offence,' but 'from the abashing consciousness of obscure station in the ranks of life'. More probably it came from the bitter memories of the humiliation debt had brought to his father.

Hamilton was a Captain in the Dumfries Volunteers.

Hamilton of Gilbertfield, William (1665?–1751)

A minor Scots poet, remembered mainly because of the song 'Willie was a Wanton Wag', which appeared in Ramsay's *Tea-Table Miscellany*, and the mock elegy 'The Last Dying Words of Bonny Heck'.

Hamilton, born at Ladyland, Ayrshire,

was the second son of Captain William Hamilton. The poet entered the army, saw service on the Continent, then spent the remainder of his life as a country gentleman, living first at Gilbertfield in Lanarkshire, and, afterwards, at Latvick on the other side of Dechmont Hill. He became friendly with Allan Ramsay, and the two poets exchanged their 'Familiar Epistles'. Hamilton's Epistles showed considerable dexterity in the handling of the 'standard Habbie' stanza. Indeed, Burns, in his 'Epistle to William Simson', mentions Ramsay, Gilbertfield and Fergusson, as the poets in whose company he hoped 'to speel' the braes of fame.

In 1722 Hamilton published an abridged and modernised version of Blind Harry's *Wallace*, which, though in every sense an artistic failure, aroused Burns's boyhood interest and enthusiasm and, as he recorded in the Autobiographical Letter: 'poured a Scottish prejudice in my veins which will boil along there till the flood-gates of life shut in eternal rest'.

Hancock, John (1737–93)

President of the Congress of Philadelphia, he is supposed to have been the first to sign the Declaration of Independence. Burns described him as 'daring Hancock' in his 'Address of Beelzebub'.

Hastie MSS

A collection of eleven letters between Johnson and Burns and portions of the *Museum* in holograph, now in the British Museum.

Haugh, George

A blacksmith who lived on the floor above Burns when he moved to the Wee Vennel in Dumfries. When the Burns family removed from the Wee Vennel to the Mill Vennel, Haugh supplied them with a grate and fender and other articles, to the amount of £1 7s. 4d.

Hay, Charles (1747–1811)

The son of James Hay of Cocklaw, he was admitted to the Bar at the age of twenty-one. When raised to the Bench in 1806, he took the title of Lord Newton. He held the office of major and muster-master-general in the Crochallan Fencibles. Lord Cockburn said that Hay was famed for 'law, paunch, whist, claret, and worth', though he had no taste for literature. His friendship with Burns was presumably social, although on 24th December 1787 Burns sent him a copy of 'On the death of the late Lord President', with the comment: 'These kind of subjects are much hackneyed; and besides, the wailings of the rhyming tribe over the ashes of the Great, are damnably suspicious, and out of all character for sincerity. These ideas damp'd my Muse's fire; however, I have done the best I could . . .'

Hay, Lewis (d. 1800)

A clerk in Sir William Forbes's banking house in Edinburgh. He married Burns's close friend Margaret Chalmers in 1788, having become a partner in the business the same year. His connection with the firm in the first place was through Sir James Hunter Blair, with whom he had been at school in Ayr.

In a contemporary biography, he was described as 'son of Captain John Hay, of the *Princess Anne* yacht'.

Henderson, Captain Matthew (1737–88)

The son of David Henderson of Tannoch in Ayrshire and Tannochside in Lanarkshire. One his father's death, Henderson inherited both properties, which he later had to sell to pay for his convivial life in Edinburgh. He was connected by marriage with James Boswell. A well-known 'society' figure in Edinburgh, Henderson was a member of the Poker and Capillaire Clubs. Burns got to know him while lodging in St James Square, Edinburgh, where Henderson also stayed, and they became friendly. On Henderson's death,

Burns wrote his 'Elegy on Captain Matthew Henderson', subtitled 'A Gentleman who Held the Patent for His Honours immediately from Almighty God!' In a letter accompanying the poem, which the poet sent to Professor Dugald Stewart, dated 30th July 1790, Burns described Henderson as: 'an intimate acquaintance of mine; and, of all mankind I ever knew, he was one of the first for a nice sense of honor, a generous contempt of the adventitious distinctions of Men, and sterling tho' sometimes outré wit'.

The composition of the 'Elegy', however, was accomplished in two stages, for Burns told Cleghorn on 23rd July: 'At the time of his death I composed an elegiac Stanza or two, as he was a man I much regarded; but something came in my way so that the design of an Elegy to his memory gave up. Meeting with the fragment the other day among some old waste papers I tried to finish the Piece, and have this moment put the last hand to it.'

It was perhaps the fact that Henderson's enjoyment of life had been the cause of his poverty which endeared him to Burns, who burst out to Graham of Fintry on 4th September 1790 (from the Globe Inn, Dumfries):

'Poor Matthew! I can forgive Poverty for hiding Virtue and Piety. They are not only plants that flourish best in the shade, but they also produce their sacred fruits more especially for another world. But when the haggard Beldam throws her insidious veil over Wit, Spirit, & etc., but I trust another world will cast light on the subject.'

The 'Elegy' is an exercise in the medieval catalogue poem, in which all creatures in turn, even the sun and moon, are instructed by the poet to mourn the deceased.

Burns's attitude to obituary pieces of this sort is to be found in a letter to Dr Moore, dated 28th February 1791: 'Poets have in this the same advantage as Roman Catholics: they can be of service to their Friends after they have passed that bourne where all other kindness ceases to be of any avail. Whether after all, either the one or the other be of any real service to the Dead is, I fear, very problematical; but I am sure they are highly gratifying to the Living: and as a very orthodox text, I forget where, in Scripture, says "Whatsoever is not of faith, is sin"; so, say I, Whatsoever is not detrimental to Society and is of positive Enjoyment, is of God the Giver of all good things, and ought to be received and enjoyed by his creatures with thankful delight. As almost all my Religious tenets originate from my heart, I am wonderfully pleased with the idea that I can still keep up a tender intercourse with the dearly beloved Friend, or still more dearly beloved Mistress, who is gone to the world of Spirits.'

Henri, Mrs James (d. 1792)

Susan, the second daughter of Mrs Dunlop, married in 1788 James Henri of Bernaldean, a French refugee. They rented Loudon Castle in Ayrshire. Henri died there on 22nd June the following year, leaving his wife four months pregnant. A son was born, celebrated by Burns's lines 'On the Birth of a Posthumous Child'. In 1792, Mrs Henri went to France with him, presumably to establish her claim to the family estates, but died at Muges, Aigullon, near Bordeaux, while on the visit. Her son did heir the Henri estate.

Writing to Mrs Dunlop from Ellisland on 6th December 1790, Burns reproved that lady for not letting him know 'how poor Mrs Henri recovers. There is something so interesting in her situation that I cannot get her out of my head, morning, noon or night. The first tragedy I ever saw performed, was "Douglas"; and Mrs Henri eternally puts me in mind of the horrors I felt for Lady Randolph's distresses'. When Burns heard of her death, he wrote to Mrs Dunlop in October: 'What shall I say to comfort you, my much-valued friend? I can but grieve with you; consolation I have none to offer, except that which religion holds out to the children of affliction. . . .

'Alas Madam! who would wish for many years? What is it but to drag existence until our joys gradually expire, and leave us in a night of misery: like the gloom which blots out the stars one by one from the face of night, and leaves us, without a ray of comfort, in the howling waste!'

Herd, David (1732–1810)

A native of St Cyrus in Kincardineshire, whose collection, *Ancient and Modern Scottish Songs, Heroic Ballads, etc.,* appeared in 1776. The one-volume 1769 edition, it is surmised from a letter of Bishop Percy to Paton, was entirely or in part edited by Paton. Otherwise Herd is always alluded to as the editor.

Herd became the clerk of an accountant in Edinburgh, a Mr David Russell.

Scott said Herd: 'was known and generally esteemed for his shrewd, manly common sense, and antiquarian science, mixed with much good-nature and great modesty. His hardy and antique mould of countenance, and his venerable grizzled locks, procured him, amongst his acquaintances, the name of Graysteil.' Scott called Herd's collection 'the first classical collection of Scottish songs and Ballads'.

Ritson (*see* **Ritson, Joseph**) was 'bound in gratitude to acknowledge indebtedness to it' for 'a number of excellent and genuine compositions, never before printed'.

Burns was, of course, familiar with Herd's collection.

Heron, Lady Elizabeth (1745–1811)

Daughter of Thomas Cochrane, eighth Earl of Dundonald, she married Patrick Heron of Heron in 1775, and bore him two daughters. She sent Burns an air which she had composed, 'The Banks o' Cree', for which he wrote the verses

beginning 'Here is the glen and here the bower'. Thomson, however, did not like the air and, despite Burns's express orders to the contrary, published the song to the tune 'The Flowers of Edinburgh' in 1798, when Burns was no longer alive to protest.

Heron of Heron, Patrick (1736?–1803)
See **Douglas, Heron & Company**

A member of a Lincolnshire family, he was one of the founders of the Douglas, Heron & Company's bank, which was established in Ayr in 1769, and had numerous branches in other towns. It failed in 1773, and caused heavy financial losses to depositors and shareholders.

Burns met Heron at Kerroughtree, his Galloway estate, when the poet visited Kirkcudbright in June 1794 with David McCulloch and John Syme. Heron stood for the Stewartry as Whig candidate in 1795, and Burns helped his campaign by writing satirical Election Ballads.

Burns seems to have felt a little uneasy about the propriety of his action, for he found it necessary to indulge in self-justification when he wrote to Heron from Dumfries in March 1795:

'To pillory on Parnassus the rank reprobation of character, the utter dereliction of all principle, in a profligate junto, which has not only outraged virtue, but violated common decency; which, spurring even hypocrisy as paltry iniquity below their daring; to unmask their flagitiousness to the broadest day—to deliver such over to their merited fate—is surely not merely innocent, but laudable; is not only propriety, but virtue. You have already, as your auxiliary, the sober detestation of mankind on the heads of your opponents; and I swear by the lyre of Thalia to muster on your side all the votaries of honest laughter and fair, candid ridicule!'

In 1796, Parliament was dissolved, but Heron was re-elected and held his seat until 1802. Burns, although ill, again wrote an Election Ballad for him, but did not live to see his re-election.

Heron won again at the General Election in 1802, but was unseated in May 1803, and his name was erased from the rolls by order of the House. He died at Grantham on his way home to Scotland. He married Lady Elizabeth Cochrane.

Patrick's brother Basil, 'the auld major' of the 'Election Ballad', subscribed to the Museum.

Heron, Robert (1764–1807)

Born in Creehead, New Galloway, the son of a weaver, Heron became Burns's first biographer, and was partly responsible, along with Dr Currie, for the widely current, though erroneous, nineteenth-century view that Burns drank himself to an early grave. After studying at Edinburgh University, Heron became a licentiate of the Church in 1789. But he was really a professional man of letters, and was, in fact, finally imprisoned in Newgate Jail for debt. There he would have died, but because of the severity of his last illness, he was removed to the Fever Hospital in St Pancras, where he died a week after his admittance.

He wrote on a wide variety of subjects for a large number of periodicals and kept from time to time a Journal, characterised by a certain engaging frankness. For example, the entry for Saturday, 19th September 1789, reads: 'Prayed carelessly and hastily. At breakfast read my chapter, carelessly too, although it related the trial and last sufferings of my Saviour. . . .' The entry for 6th August 1791, reads: 'Mr Grierson dined with me and drank tea. He, Mr Bradefute, and Mr Burns supped. Left me at eleven.' Grierson later wrote the notes about Burns and his friends which are now known as the Grierson Manuscript.

Because it was the first biography of Burns to be written, Heron's *Memoir of the Life of the Late Robert Burns*—1797,

although it had appeared in *The Monthly Magazine and British Register*, Volume III, in two parts, a year earlier—is of greater interest than its intrinsic merits deserve.

However, as well as several errors and numerous references to the poet's excesses, apparently designed to blacken his character, the essay does contain a fairly shrewd tribute to Burns's achievement:

'It may be doubted whether he has not, by his writings, exercised a greater power over the minds of men, and, by consequence, on their conduct, upon their happiness and misery, upon the general system of life, than has been exercised by any half-dozen of the most eminent statesmen of the present age.'

When Heron visited Burns at Ellisland on his way to or from New Galloway, Burns gave him a letter to take to Blacklock, which Heron failed to deliver. Burns referred to this in his 'Epistle to Dr Blacklock':

'The ill-thief blaw the Heron south!
And never drink be near his drouth!
He tauld myself by word o' mouth,
    He'd tak my letter,
I lippened to the chief in trouth,
    And bade nae better.

But aiblins, honest Master Heron
Had, at the time, some dainty fair one,
To ware his theologic care on
    And holy study;
And tired o' souls to waste his lear on,
    E'en tried the body.'

Burns first met Heron at Dr Blacklock's house in Edinburgh.

Heron recorded an obviously spontaneous description of the reception the Kilmarnock Edition received: 'Old and young, high and low, grave and gay, learned or ignorant, all were alike delighted, agitated, transported. I was at that time resident in New Galloway, contiguous to Ayrshire; and I can well remember, how that even plough-boys and maid-servants would have gladly bestowed the wages which they earned the most hardly, and which they wanted to purchase necessary clothing, if they might but procure the works of Burns.'

Heron's *Journey through the Western Counties of Scotland*, published in 1793, is a social study still worth reading.

Catherine Carswell's essay *Heron: A Study in Failure*, which appeared in *The Scots Magazine* for October 1932, was based upon Heron's *Journal of my Conduct*, 1789–98, the manuscript of which is in the Laing Collection, Edinburgh University Library.

Heron, Robert—Memoir of the Life of the Late Robert Burns

'Biography is, in some instances, the most trifling and contemptible, in others, the most interesting and instructive of all the species of literary composition. It would be difficult to persuade one's self to agree with several late historians of the lives of poets, philosophers, and statesmen; that, the mere, industrious accumulation of dates, anecdotes, and witticisms, of transactions in which no peculiarities of genius and character were displayed, or of obscure events by which the habits of feeling, thought, or action, were in no way remarkably influenced; can deserve to be ambitiously studied, or admired, as the perfection of biographical writing. The following memoir of the life of one who was a GREAT MAN, *solely of* GOD ALMIGHTY's *making such;* has been composed under the direction of a very different, although perhaps not a more correct, critical principle. If, however, this principle be just; it is the proper business of the biographer; TO TRACE THE GRADUAL DEVELOPMENT OF THE CHARACTER AND TALENTS OF HIS HERO, WITH ALL THE CHANGES WHICH THESE UNDERGO FROM THE INFLUENCE OF EXTERNAL CIRCUMSTANCES, BETWEEN THE CRADLE AND THE GRAVE; AND AT THE SAME TIME, TO RECORD ALL THE EMINENT EFFECTS WHICH THE DISPLAY OF THAT CHARACTER, AND THE EXERCISE OF THOSE TALENTS, HAVE PRODUCED UPON NATURE AND ON HUMAN SOCIETY, IN THE SPHERE WITHIN WHICH THEY WERE EXHIBITED AND EMPLOYED. The writer's wishes will be amply gratified; if this TRIFLE shall be found to afford any exposition of the nicer laws of the formation and progress of human character, such as shall not be scorned as *data* by the moral philosopher, or as facts to enlighten his imitations, by the dramatist; if it shall be received by the world in general, as an honest though humble tribute to the merits of illustrious genius; and above all, if it shall be regarded by the candid and the good, as presenting some details and reflections, of which the direct tendency is, to recommend that steady VIRTUE, without which even genius in all its omnipotence is soon reduced to paralytic imbecility, or to maniac mischievousness.

'Robert Burns was a native of *Ayrshire*, one of the western counties of *Scotland*. He was the son of humble parents. His father passed through life in the condition of a hired labourer, or a small farmer. Even in this situation, it was not hard for him to send his children to the parish-school, to receive the ordinary instruction in reading, writing, arithmetic, and principles of religion. By such a course of education, young Robert profited to a degree that might have encouraged his friends to destine him to one of the liberal professions, had not his father's poverty made it necessary to remove him from the school, as soon as he had grown up, to earn for himself the means of support, as a ploughboy or a shepherd.

'The establishment of PARISH-SCHOOLS; but for which, perhaps, the infant energies of this young genius might never have received that first impulse by which alone they were to be excited into action; is one of the most beneficial that have been ever instituted in any country; and one that, I believe, is no where so firmly fixed, or extended so completely throughout a whole kingdom, as in Scotland. Every parish has, here, a schoolmaster, almost as invariably as it has a clergyman. For a sum rarely exceeding twenty pounds, in salary and fees, this person instructs the children of the parish in reading, writing, arithmetic, book-keeping, Latin, and Greek. The schoolmasters are generally students in philosphy or theology. Hence, the establishment of the parish-schools, beside its direct utilities, possesses also the accidental advantage of furnishing an excellent nursery of future candidates for the office of parochial clergymen. So small are the fees for teaching, that no parents, however poor, can want the means to give their children at least such education as young BURNS received. From the *spring* labours of a ploughboy, from the *summer* employment of a shepherd, the peasant-youth often returns, for a few months, eager to receive new instruction in the parish-school.

'It was so with BURNS. He returned from labour to learning, and from learning went again to labour; till his mind began to open to the charms of taste and knowledge; till he began to feel a passion for books and for the subjects of books, which was to give a colour to the whole thread of his future life. On nature, he soon began to gaze with new discernment, and with new enthusiasm. His mind's eye opened to perceive affecting beauty and sublimity, where, by the mere gross peasant, there was nought to be seen, but water, earth, and sky, but animals, plants, and soil: even as the eyes of the servant of Elisha were suddenly enlightened to behold his master and himself guarded from the Syrian bands, by horses and chariots of fire, to all but themselves, invisible.

'What might perhaps first contribute to dispose his mind to poetical efforts, is, a particular practice in the devotional piety of the Scottish peasantry. It is still common for them to make their children get by heart the psalms of David, in that version of homely rhymes, which is used in their churches. In the morning, and in the evening of every day; or, at least on the evening of every Saturday and Sunday; these psalms are sung in solemn family-devotion, a chapter of the bible is read, an extemporary prayer is fervently uttered. The whole books of the sacred scriptures are continually in the hands of almost every peasant. And it is impossible, that there should not be occasionally some souls among them, awakened to the divine emotions of genius, by that rich assemblage which these books present, of almost all that is interesting in incidents, or picturesque in imagery, or affectingly sublime or tender in sentiments and character. It is impossible that those rude rhymes, and the simple artless music with which they are accompanied, should not occasionally excite some ear to a fond perception of the melody of verse. That BURNS had felt these impulses, will appear undeniably certain to whoever shall carefully peruse his *Cottar's Saturday's Night;* or shall remark, with nice observation, the various fragments of *scripture* sentiment, of *scripture* imagery, of *scripture* language, which are scattered throughout his works.

'Still more interesting to the young peasantry, are those ancient ballads of love and war, of which a great number are yet popularly known and sung in Scotland. While the prevalence of the Gaelic language in the northern parts of this country, excluded from those regions the old Anglo-Saxon songs and minstrels: These songs and minstrels were, in the mean time, driven by the Norman conquests and establishments, out of the southern counties of England; and were forced to wander, in exile, towards its northern confines, or even into the southern districts of the Scottish kingdom.

Hence, in the old English songs, is every eminent bard still related to have been of the *north country;* but, on the contrary, in the old Scottish songs, it is always the *south country,* to which every favourite minstrel is said to belong. Both these expressions are intended to signify one district; a district comprehending precisely the southern counties of Scotland, with the most northern counties of England. In the south of Scotland, almost all the best of those ballads are still often sung by the rustic maid or matron at her spinning-wheel. They are listened to, with ravished ears, by old and young. Their rude melody; that mingled curiosity and awe, which are naturally excited by the very idea of their antiquity; the exquisitely tender and natural complaints sometimes poured forth in them; the gallant deeds of knightly heroism, which they sometimes celebrate; their wild tales of demons, ghosts and fairies, in whose existence superstition alone has believed; the manners which they represent; the obsolete, yet picturesque and expressive language in which they are often clothed; give them wonderful power to transport every imagination, and to agitate every heart. To the soul of BURNS, they were like a happy breeze touching the strings of an Æolian harp, and calling forth the most ravishing melody.

'Beside all this, the *Gentle Shepherd,* and the other poems of *Allan Ramsay,* have long been highly popular in Scotland. They fell early into the hands of BURNS. And while the fond applause which they received, drew his emulation; they presented to him likewise treasures of phraseology, and models of versification. *Ruddiman's Weekly Magazine* was, during this time, published; was supported chiefly by the original communications of correspondents; and found a very extensive sale. In it, BURNS read, particularly, the poetry of *Robert Ferguson,* written chiefly in the Scottish dialect, and exhibiting many specimens of uncommon

poetical excellence. The *Seasons* of *Thomson,* too, the *Grave* of *Blair,* the far-famed *Elegy* of *Gray,* the *Paradise Lost* of *Milton,* the wild strains of *Ossian,* perhaps the *Minstrel* of *Beattie,* were so commonly read, even among those with whom BURNS would naturally associate, that poetical curiosity, although less ardent than his, could, in such circumstances, have little difficulty in procuring them.

'With such means to give his imagination a poetical bias, and to favour the culture of his taste and genius, BURNS gradually became a poet. He was not one of those forward children, who, from a mistaken impulse, begin prematurely to write and to rhyme, and hence, never attain to excellence. Conversing familiarly for a long while, with the works of those poets who were known to him: Contemplating the aspect of nature, in a district which exhibits an uncommon assemblage of the beautiful and the ruggedly grand, of the cultivated and the wild: Looking upon human life with an eye quick and keen, to remark as well the stronger and leading, as the nicer and subordinate features of character: It was thus that he slowly and unconsciously acquired a poetical temper of soul, and a poetic cast of thought. He was distinguished among his fellows, for extraordinary intelligence, good sense, and penetration, long ere they suspected him to be capable of writing verses. His mind was mature, and well stored with such knowledge as lay within his reach; he had made himself master of powers of language, superior to those of almost any former writer in the Scottish dialect; before he conceived the idea of surpassing *Ramsay* and *Ferguson.*

'In the mean time, beside the studious bent of his genius, there were other features in his opening character, which might seem to mark him for a poet. He began early in life to regard with sullen disdain and aversion, all that was sordid in the pursuits and interests of the peasants among whom he was placed. He became discontented with the humble labours to which he saw himself confined, and with the poor subsistence that was all he could earn by them. He was excited to look upon the rich and great, whom he saw around him, with an emotion between envy and contempt; as if something had still whispered to his heart, that there was injustice in the exterior inequality between his fate and theirs. While such emotions arose in his mind, he conceived an inclination,—very common among the young men of the more uncultivated parts of Scotland,—to go abroad to *America* or the *West Indies*, in quest of a better fortune.—His heart was, at the same time, expanded with passionate ardour, to meet the impressions of love and *friendship*. With several of the young peasantry, who were his fellows in labour, he contracted an affectionate intimacy. He eagerly sought admission into the brotherhood of *Free Masons;* which is recommended to the young men of this country, by nothing so much as by its seeming to extend the sphere of agreeable acquaintance, and to knit closer the bonds of friendly endearment. In some *Mason Lodges* in his neighbourhood, BURNS had soon the fortune, whether good or bad, to gain the notice of several gentlemen who were better able than his fellow-peasants, to estimate the true value of such a mind as his. One or two of them might be men of convivial dispositions, and of religious notions rather licentious than narrow; who encouraged his talents, by occasionally inviting him to be the companion of their looser hours; and who were at times not ill pleased to direct the force of his wit and humour against those sacred things which they affected outwardly to despise as mere *bugbears*, while perhaps they could not help inwardly trembling before them as realities. For a while, the native rectitude of his understanding, and the excellent principles in which his

infancy had been educated, withstood every temptation to intemperance or impiety. Alas! it was not always so.— He was even in the first years of his rising youth, an ardent lover: feeling the passion, not affected, light, and sportive; but solemn, anxious, fervent, absorbing the whole soul; such as it is described by Thomson in his enrapturing poem on *Spring*. When his heart was first struck by the charms of village beauty; the *love* he felt was pure, tender, and sincere, as that of the youth and maiden in his own *Cottar's Saturday's Night*. If the ardour of his passion hurried him afterwards to triumph over the chastity of the maid he loved; the tenderness of his heart, the manly honesty of his soul, soon made him offer, with eager solicitude, to repair by marriage the injury of love.

'About this time in the progress of his life and character, did he first begin to be publicly distinguished as a POET. A *masonic* song, a satirical epigram, a rhyming epistle to a friend, attempted with success; taught him to know his own powers, and gave him confidence to try tasks more arduous, and which should command still higher applause. The annual celebration of the *Sacrament of the Lord's Supper*, in the rural parishes of Scotland, has much in it of those old *Popish* festivals, in which superstition, traffic, and amusement, used to be strangely intermingled. BURNS saw, and seized, in it, one of the happiest of all subjects, to afford scope for the display—of that strong and piercing sagacity by which he could almost intuitively distinguish the reasonable from the absurd, and the becoming from the ridiculous;—of that picturesque power of fancy, which enabled him to represent scenes, and persons, and groupes, and looks, attitudes, and gestures, in a manner almost as lively and impressive, even in words, as if all the artifices and energies of the pencil had been employed;—of that knowledge which he had necessarily acquired of the manners, passions, and prejudices of the rustics around him, of whatever was ridiculous, no less than of whatever was affectingly beautiful, in rural life. A thousand prejudices of *Popish*, and perhaps too of ruder *Pagan* superstition, have from time immemorial; been connected in the minds of the *Scottish* peasantry, with the annual recurrence of the *Eve of the Festival of all the Saints,* or *Hallowe'en*. These were all intimately known to BURNS, and had made a powerful impression upon his imagination and feelings. Choosing them for the subject of a poem, he produced a piece, which is, almost to frenzy, the delight of those who are best acquainted with its subject; and which will not fail to preserve the memory of the prejudices and usages which it describes, when they shall, perhaps, have ceased to give one merry evening in the year to the cottage fire-side. The simple joys, the honest love, the sincere friendship, the ardent devotion of the cottage; whatever in the more solemn part of the rustic's life is humble and artless, without being mean or unseemly; or tender and dignified, without aspiring to stilted grandeur, or to unnatural, buskined pathos; had deeply impressed the imagination of the rising poet; had in some sort wrought itself into the very texture of the fibres of his soul. He tried to express in verse what he most tenderly felt, what he most enthusiastically imagined; and composed the *Cottar's Saturday's Night*.

'These pieces, the true effusions of genius, informed by reading and observation, and prompted by its own native ardour, as well as by friendly applause; were soon communicated from one to another among the most discerning of BURNS's acquaintance; and were, by every new reader, perused and re-perused with an eagerness of delight and approbation, which would not suffer him long to withhold them from the press. A *subscription* was proposed; was earnestly

promoted by some gentlemen, who were glad to interest themselves in behalf of such signal poetical merit; was soon crowded with the names of a considerable number of the inhabitants of Ayrshire; who, in the proffered purchase, sought not less to gratify their own passion for *Scottish* poesy, than to encourage the wonderful ploughman. At the manufacturing village of KILMARNOCK were the poems of BURNS, for the first time, printed. The whole edition was quickly distributed over the country.

'They were every where received with eager admiration and delight. They eminently possessed all those qualities which never fail to render any literary work quickly and permanently popular. They were written in a phraseology, of which all the powers were universally felt; and which, being at once, *antique*, *familiar*, and now *rarely written*, was hence fitted for all the dignified and picturesque uses of poetry, without being disagreeably obscure. The imagery, and the sentiments, were, at once, faithfully natural, and irresistibly impressive and interesting. Those topics of satire and scandal in which the rustic delights; that *humorous* imitation of character, and that *witty* association of ideas familiar and striking but not naturally allied to one another, which have force to shake his sides with laughter; those fancies of superstition at which he still wonders and trembles; those affecting sentiments and images of true religion, which are at once dear and awful to his heart; were all represented by BURNS with all a poet's magic power. Old and young, high and low, grave and gay, learned or ignorant, all were alike delighted, agitated, transported. I was at that time resident in *Galloway*, contiguous to *Ayrshire*: and I can well remember, how that even plough-boys and maid-servants would have gladly bestowed the wages which they earned the most hardly, and which they wanted to purchase necessary clothing, if they might but procure the works of BURNS. A copy happened to be presented from a gentleman in Ayrshire to a friend in my neighbourhood. He put it into my hands, as a work containing some effusions of the most extraordinary genius. I took it, rather that I might not disoblige the lender, than from any ardour of curiosity or expectation. "An unlettered ploughman, a poet!" said I, with contemptuous incredulity. It was on a Saturday evening. I opened the volume, by accident, while I was undressing, to go to bed. I closed it not, till a late hour on the rising Sunday morn, after I had read over every syllable it contained. And,

'*Ex illo Corydon, Corydon est tempore nobis! Virg, Ec. 7.*

'In the mean time, some few copies of these fascinating poems found their way to Edinburgh: and one was communicated to the late amiable and ingenious Dr THOMAS BLACKLOCK. There was, perhaps, never one among all mankind whom you might more truly have called *an angel upon earth* than Dr BLACKLOCK! He was guileless and innocent as a child, yet endowed with manly sagacity and penetration. His heart was a perpetual spring of overflowing benignity. His feelings were all tremblingly alive to the sense of the sublime, the beautiful, the tender, the pious, the virtuous. Poetry was to him the dear solace of perpetual blindness. Cheerfulness, even to gaiety, was, notwithstanding that irremedial misfortune under which he laboured, long the predominant colour of his mind. In his latter years, when the gloom might otherwise have thickened around him, hope, faith, devotion the most fervent and sublime, exalted his mind to heaven, and made him still maintain much of his wonted cheerfulness in the expectation of a speedy dissolution.

'This amiable man of genius read the poems of BURNS with a nice perception, with a keenly impassioned feeling of all their beauties. Amid that tumult of emo-tions of benevolence, curiosity, and admiration, which were thus excited in his bosom; he eagerly addressed some encouraging verses to the rustic bard; which, conveying the praises of a poet, and a judge of poetical composition; were much more grateful to BURNS, than any applauses he had before received from others. It was BLACKLOCK's invitation that finally determined him to abandon his first intentions of going abroad to the West Indies; and rather to repair to Edinburgh, with his book, in hopes, there to find some powerful patron, and, perhaps, to make his fortune by his poetry.

'In the beginning of the winter 1786–87, BURNS came to Edinburgh. By Dr BLACKLOCK he was received with the most flattering kindness; and was earnestly introduced to every person of taste and generosity among the good old man's friends. It was little BLACKLOCK had in his power to do, for a brother poet. But that little he did with a fond alacrity, and with a modest grace, which made it ten times more pleasing, and more effectually useful to him, in whose favour it was exercised, than even the very same services would have been from almost any other benefactor. Others soon interposed, to share with BLACKLOCK in the honor of patronising BURNS. He had brought, from his Ayrshire friends, some letters of recommendation. Some of his rural acquaintances coming, as well as himself, to Edinburgh for the winter, did him what offices of kindness they conveniently could. Those very few, who possessed at once true taste and ardent philanthropy, were soon earnestly united in his praise. They who were disposed to favour any good thing belonging to Scotland, purely because it was Scottish, gladly joined the cry. Those who had hearts and understandings to be charmed, without knowing why, when they saw their native customs, manners, and language made the subjects and the materials of poesy, could not suppress that voice of feeling which struggled to declare itself for BURNS. For the dissipated, the licentious, the malignant wits, and the free-thinkers, he was so unfortunate as to have satire, and obscenity, and ridicule of things sacred, sufficient to captivate their fancies. Even for the pious, he had passages in which the inspired language of devotion might seem to come mended from his tongue. And then, to charm those whom naught can charm—but wonders; whose taste leads them to admire only such things as a juggler eating fire; a person who can converse as if his organs of speech were in his belly; a lame sailor writing with his toes, for want of fingers; a peer or a ploughman making verses; a small coal-man directing a concert;—why, to those people, the Ayrshire poet might seem precisely one of the most wonderful of the wonders after which they were wont to gape.—Thus did BURNS, ere he had been many weeks in Edinburgh, find himself the object of universal curiosity, favour, admiration, and fondness. He was sought after, courted with attentions the most respectful and assiduous, feasted, flattered, caressed by all ranks, as the first boast of our country; whom it was scarcely possible to honour and reward to a degree equal to his merits. In comparison with the general favour which now promised to more than crown his most sanguine hopes, it could hardly be called *praise* at all, which he had obtained in Ayrshire.

'In this posture of our poet's affairs, a new edition of his poems was earnestly called for. He sold the copy-right to Mr CREECH, for one hundred pounds. But his friends, at the same time, suggested, and actively promoted *a subscription* for an edition to be published for the benefit of the author, ere the bookseller's right should commence. Those gentlemen who had formerly entertained the public of Edinburgh with the periodical publi-

cation of the papers of the MIRROR; having again combined their talents in producing the LOUNGER; were, at this time, about to conclude this last series of papers. Yet, before the LOUNGER relinquished his pen, he dedicated *a number* to a commendatory criticism of the poems of the Ayrshire bard. That criticism is now known to have been composed by HENRY MACKENZIE, ESQ.; whose writings are universally admired for an *Addisonian* delicacy and felicity of wit and humour, by which the CLIO of the *Spectator* is more than rivalled; for a wildly tender pathos that excites the most exquisite vibrations of the finest chords of sympathy in the human heart; for a lofty, vehement, persuasive eloquence, by which the immortal *Junius* has been sometimes perhaps excelled, and often almost equalled! The subscription-papers were rapidly filled. The ladies, especially, vied with one another—who should be the first to subscribe, who should procure the greatest number of other subscribers, for the poems of a bard who was now, for some moments, the idol of fashion. The *Caledonian Hunt*, a gay *club*, composed of the most opulent and fashionable young men in Scotland, professed themselves the patrons of the Scottish poet, and eagerly encouraged the proposed republication of his poems. Six shillings were all the subscription-money demanded for each copy. But many voluntarily paid half-a-guinea, a guinea, or two guineas. And it was supposed that the poet might derive from the subscription, and the sale of his copy-right, a clear profit of, at least, seven hundred pounds; a sum that, to a man who had hitherto lived in his indigent circumstances, would be absolutely more than the vainly expected wealth of Sir Epicure Mammon!

'BURNS, in the mean time, led a life differing from that of his original condition in Ayrshire, almost as widely as differed the scenes and amusements of London, to which OMIAH was introduced, under the patronage of the Earl of SAND-WICH, from those to which he had been familiar in the Friendly Isles. The conversation of even the most eminent authors, is often found to be so unequal to the fame of their writings, that he who *read* with admiration, can *listen* with none but sentiments of the most profound contempt. But, the conversation of BURNS was, in comparison with the *formal* and *exterior* circumstances of his education, perhaps even more wonderful than his poetry. He affected no soft airs, no graceful motions of politeness, which might have ill accorded with the rustic plainness of his native manners. Conscious superiority of mind taught him to associate with the great, the learned, and the gay, without being over-awed into any such bashfulness as might have made him confused in thought, or hesitating in elocution. He possessed, withal, an extraordinary share of plain common sense, or *mother-wit*, which prevented him from obtruding upon persons, of whatever rank, with whom he was admitted to converse, any of those effusions of vanity, envy, or self-conceit, in which authors are exceedingly apt to indulge, who have lived remote from the general practice of life, and whose minds have been almost exclusively confined to contemplate their own studies and their own works. In conversation he displayed a kind of intuitive quickness and rectitude of judgment upon every subject that arose. The sensibility of his heart, and the vivacity of his fancy, gave a rich colouring to whatever reasoning he was disposed to advance: and his language in common discourse, was not at all less happy than in his writings. For these reasons, he did not cease to please immediately after he had been once seen. Those who had met and conversed with him once, were pleased to meet and converse with him again and again. I remember, that the late Dr ROBERTSON once observed to me, that he had scarcely ever met with any

man whose conversation discovered greater vigour and activity of mind than did that of Burns. Every one wondered that the rustic bard was not *spoiled* by so much caressing, favour, and flattery as he found; and every one went on to *spoil* him, by continually repeating all these, as if with an obstinate resolution that they should, in the end, produce their effect. Nothing, however, of change in his manners, appeared, at least for a while—to show that this was at all likely to happen. He, indeed, maintained himself with considerable spirit, upon a footing of equality with all with whom he had occasion to associate or converse. Yet he never arrogated any superiority, save what the fair and manly exertion of his powers, at the time, could undeniably command. Had he but been able to give a steady preference to the society of the virtuous, the learned, and the wise, rather than to that of the gay and the dissolute, it is probable that he could not have failed to rise to an exaltation of character and of talents fitted to do high honour to human nature.

'Unfortunately, however, that happened which was natural in those unaccustomed circumstances in which BURNS found himself placed. He could not assume enough of superciliousness, to reject the familiarity of all those who, without any sincere kindness for him, importunately pressed to obtain his acquaintance and intimacy. He was insensibly led to associate less with the learned, the austere, and the rigorously temperate, than with the young, with the votaries of intemperate joys, with persons to whom he was recommended chiefly by licentious wit, and with whom he could not long associate without sharing in the excesses of their debauchery. Even in the country, men of this sort had begun to fasten on him, and to seduce him to embellish the gross pleasures of their looser hours with the charms of his wit and fancy. And yet, I have been informed by Mr ARTHUR

BRUCE, a gentleman of great worth and discernment, to whom Burns was, in his earlier days, well known; that he had, in those times, seen the poet steadily resist such solicitations and allurements to excess in convivial enjoyment, as scarcely any other person could have withstood. But, the enticements of pleasure too often unman our virtuous resolution, even while we wear the air of rejecting them with a stern brow. We resist, and resist, and resist; but, at last, suddenly turn and passionately embrace the enchantress. The *bucks* of Edinburgh accomplished, in regard to BURNS, that in which the *boors* of Ayrshire had failed. After residing some months in Edinburgh, he began to estrange himself, not altogether, but in some measure, from the society of his graver friends. Too many of his hours were now spent at the tables of persons who delighted to urge conviviality to drunkenness, in the tavern, in the brothel, on the lap of the woman of pleasure. He *suffered* himself to be surrounded by a race of miserable beings who were proud to tell; that they had been in company with BURNS; and had seen BURNS as loose and as foolish as themselves. He was not yet irrecoverably lost to temperance and moderation: but he was already almost too much captivated with their wanton rivals, to be ever more won back to a faithful attachment to *their* more sober charms. He now also began to contract something of new arrogance in conversation. Accustomed to be, among his favourite associates, what is vulgarly but expressively called, *the cock of the company*; he could scarcely refrain from indulging in similar freedom and dictatorial decision of talk, even in the presence of persons who could less patiently endure his presumption.

'Thus passed two winters, and an intervening summer, of the life of BURNS. The subscription-edition of his poems, in the mean time, appeared; and, although not enlarged beyond that which came from the *Kilmarnock* press, by many new pieces of eminent merit, did not fail to give entire satisfaction to the subscribers. He at one time, during this period, accompanied, for a few weeks, into *Berwickshire, Robert Ainslie, Esq.,*—a gentleman of the purest and most correct manners, who was accustomed sometimes to soothe the toils of a laborious profession, by an occasional converse with polite literature, and with general science. At another time, he wandered on a jaunt of four or five weeks, through the *Highlands*, in company with the late Mr WILLIAM NICOL; a man who had been before the companion and friend of Dr GILBERT STUART; who in vigour of intellect, and in wild, yet generous, impetuosity of passion, remarkably resembled both STUART and BURNS; who, for his skill and facility of Latin composition, was perhaps without a rival in Europe; whose virtues and genius were clouded by habits of Bacchanalian excess; whose latter years were vexatiously embittered by a contest with a person of far meaner talents, and narrower intelligence; who by the most unwearied and extraordinary professional toil, in the midst of as persevering dissipation, by which alone it was at any time interrupted, won and accumulated an honourable and sufficient competence for his family; and, alas! who died, within these few weeks, of a jaundice, with a complication of other complaints, the effects of long-continued intemperance! So much did the zeal of friendship, and the ambition of honest fame, predominate in NICOL's mind, that he was, in his last hours, exceedingly pained by the thought that since he had survived BURNS, there remained none who might rescue his mixed character from misrepresentation, and might embalm his memory in never-dying verse!

'In their excursion, BURNS and his friend NICOL were naturally led to visit the interesting scenery adjacent to the duke of Athol's seat at *Dunkeld*, on the banks of the Tay. While they were in a contiguous inn, the duke, accidentally informed of Mr BURNS's arrival so near, invited him, by a polite message, to *Dunkeld-House*. BURNS did not fail to attend his obliging inviter; was received with flattering condescension; made himself sufficiently agreeable by his conversation and manners; was detained for a day or two by his Grace's kind hospitality; and, ere he departed, in a poetical petition, in the name of the river *Bruar*, which falls into the Tay, within the duke's pleasure-grounds at *Blair Athol*; suggested some new improvements of taste, which I believe to have been since happily made, in compliance with his advice. I relate this little incident, to do honour rather to the duke of Athol, than to BURNS: for, if I be not exceedingly mistaken, nothing that history can record of George the Third, will in future times, be accounted more honourable to his memory, than the circumstances and the conversation of his well known interview with Dr Johnson. The two congenial companions, BURNS and NICOL; after visiting many other of those romantic, picturesque, and sublime scenes, of which the fame attracts travellers of taste to the Highlands of Scotland; after fondly lingering here and there for a day or two at a favourite inn; returned at last to Edinburgh: and BURNS was now to close accompts with his bookseller, and to retire with his profits in his pocket to the country.

'Mr CREECH has obligingly informed me, that the whole sum paid to the poet for the copy-right, and for the subscription copies of his book, amounted to nearly eleven hundred pounds. Out of this sum, indeed, the expences of printing the edition for the subscribers, were to be deducted. I have likewise reason to believe, that he had consumed a much larger proportion of these gains, than prudence could approve; while he superintended the impression, paid his court to his patrons, and waited the full payment of the subscription-money.

'He was now at last to fix upon a plan for his future life. He talked loudly of independence of spirit, and simplicity of manners; and boasted his resolution to return to the plough. Yet, still he lingered in Edinburgh, week after week, and month after month; perhaps expecting that one or another of his noble patrons might procure him some permanent and competent annual income, which should set him above all necessity of future exertions to earn for himself the means of subsistence; perhaps unconsciously reluctant to quit the pleasures of that voluptuous town-life to which he had for some time too willingly accustomed himself. An accidental dislocation or fracture of an arm or a leg, confining him for some weeks to his apartment, left him, during this time, leisure for serious reflection: and he determined to retire from the town, without longer delay. None of all his patrons interposed to divert him from his purpose of returning to the plough, by the offer of any small pension, or any sinecure place of moderate emolument, such as might have given him competence without withdrawing him from his poetical studies. It seemed to be forgotten, that a ploughman thus exalted into a man of letters, was unfitted for his former toils, without being regularly qualified to enter the career of any new profession; and that it became incumbent upon those patrons who had called him from the plough, not merely to make him their companion in the hour of riot, not simply to fill his purse with gold for a few transient expences; but to secure him, as far as was possible, from being ever over-whelmed in distress, in consequence of the favour which they had shown him, and of the habits of life into which they had seduced him. Perhaps, indeed, the same delusion of fancy betrayed both BURNS and his patrons into the mistaken idea that, after all which had passed, it was still possible for him to return, in cheerful content, to the homely joys and simple toils of undissipated rural life.

'In this temper of BURNS's mind, in this state of his fortune, a *farm* and the *excise* were the objects upon which his choice ultimately fixed for future employment and support. Mr ALEXANDER WOOD, the surgeon who attended him during the illness occasioned by his hurt; no sooner understood his patient's wish, to seek a resource in the service of the *excise*; than he, with the usual activity of his benevolence, effectually recommended the poet to the commissioners of excise: and the name of BURNS was enrolled in the list of their *expectant-officers*. PETER MILLAR, Esq. of *Dalswinton*, deceived, like BURNS himself, and BURNS's other friends, into an idea, that the poet and exciseman might yet be respectable and happy as a farmer; generously proposed to establish him in a farm, upon conditions of lease, which prudence and industry might easily render exceedingly advantageous. BURNS eagerly accepted the offers of this benevolent patron. Two of the poet's friends from *Ayrshire* were invited to survey that farm in *Dumfriesshire*, which Mr MILLAR offered. A lease was granted to the poetical farmer, at the annual rent which his own friends declared, that the due cultivation of his farm might easily enable him to pay. What yet remained of the profits of his publication, was laid out in the purchase of farm-stock. And Mr MILLAR might, for some short time, please himself with the persuasion, that he had approved himself the liberal patron of genius; had acquired a good tenant upon his estate; and had placed a deserving man in the very situation in which alone he himself desired to be placed, in order to be happy to his wishes.

'BURNS, with his JANE, whom he now married, took up their residence upon his farm. The neighbouring farmers and gentlemen, pleased to obtain for an inmate among them, the poet by whose works they had been delighted; kindly sought his company, and invited him to their houses. He found an inexpressible charm in sitting down, beside his wife, at his own fire-side; in wandering over his own grounds; in once more putting his hand to the spade and the plough; in forming his inclosures, and managing his cattle. For some moments, he felt almost all that felicity which fancy had taught him to expect in his new situation. He had been, for a time, idle: but his muscles were not yet unbraced for rural toil. He had been admitted to flatter ladies of fashion; he had been occasionally seduced by the allurements of venal beauty: But, he now seemed to find a joy in being the husband of the mistress of his affections, in seeing himself the father of her children, such as might promise to attach him for ever to that modest, humble, domestic life in which alone he could hope to be permanently happy. Even his engagements in the service of the excise, did not at the very first, threaten necessarily to debase him by association with the mean, the gross, and the profligate, to contaminate the poet, or to ruin the farmer.

'But, it could not be. It was not possible for BURNS now to assume that soberness of fancy and passions, that sedateness of feeling, those habits of earnest attention to gross and vulgar cares, without which, success in his new situation was not to be expected. A thousand difficulties were to be encountered and overcome, much money was to be expended, much weary toil was to be exercised, before his farm could be brought into a state of cultivation, in which its produce might enrich the occupier. The prospect before him, was, in this respect, such as might well have discouraged the most stubbornly laborious peasant, the most sanguine projector in agriculture. Much more, therefore, was it likely, that this prospect should quickly dishearten BURNS; who had never loved labour; and who was, at this time, certainly not at all disposed to enter into agriculture with the enthusiasm of a projector. Beside all this, I have reason to believe, that the poet had made his bargain rashly, and had not duely availed himself of his patron's generosity. His friends from Ayrshire, were little acquainted with the soil, with the manures, with the markets, with the dairies, with the modes of improvement in Dumfries-shire. They had set upon his farm, rather such a value of rental, as might have borne in Ayrshire, than that which it could easily afford in the local circum-stances in which it was actually placed. He himself had inconsiderately submitted to their judgment, without once doubting whether they might not have erred against his interests, without the slightest wish to make a bargain artfully advantageous for himself. And the necessary consequence was, that he held his farm at too high a rent, contrary to his landlord's intention.— The business of the excise too, as he began to be more and more employed in it, distracted his mind from the care of his farm, led him into gross and vulgar society, and exposed him to many un-avoidable temptations to drunken excess, such as he had no longer sufficient forti-tude to resist. Amidst the anxieties, distractions, and seducements, which thus arose to him; home became in-sensibly less and less pleasing; even the endearments of his JANE's affection began to lose their hold on his heart; he became every day less and less unwilling to forget in riot those gathering sorrows which he knew not to subdue.

'Mr Millar, and some others of his friends, would gladly have exerted an influence over his mind, which might have preserved him, in this situation of his affairs, equally from despondency, and from dissipation. But BURNS's temper spurned all controul from his superiors in fortune. He resented, as an arrogant encroachment upon his independence, that tenor of conduct by which Mr

MILLAR wished to turn him from dissolute conviviality, to that steady attention to the business of his farm, without which it was impossible to thrive in it. In the neighbourhood were other gentlemen occasionally addicted, like BURNS, to convivial excess; who, while they ad-mired the poet's talents, and were charmed with his licentious wit; forgot the care of his real interests in the pleasure which they found in his company, and in the gratification which the plenty and fest-ivity of their tables appeared evidently to afford him. With these gentlemen, while disappointments and disgusts con-tinued to multiply upon him in his present situation, he persisted to associate every day more and more eagerly. His crosses and disappointments drove him every day more and more into dissipation; and his dissipation tended to enhance whatever was disagreeable and perplexing in the state of his affairs. He sank, by degrees, into the boon companion of mere excisemen: and almost every drunken fellow, who was willing to spend his money lavishly in the ale-house, could easily command the company of BURNS. The care of his farm was thus neglected: Waste and losses wholly consumed his little capital: He resigned his lease into the hands of his landlord; and retired, with his family, to the town of Dumfries: Determining to depend entirely for the means of future support upon his income as an excise-officer.

'Yet, during this unfortunate period of his life, which passed between his departure from Edinburgh to settle in Dumfriesshire, and his leaving the country in order to take up his residence in the town of Dumfries, the energy and activity of his intellectual powers appears to have been not at all impaired. He made a collection of Scottish songs, which were published, the words with the music, by a Mr JOHNSTONE, an engraver, in Edinburgh, in three small volumes, in octavo. In making this collection, he, in many instances, accommodated new verses to the old tunes, with admirable felicity and skill. He composed several other poems, such as the tale of *Tam o' Shanter*, the *Whistle, Verses on a wounded Hare*, the *Pathetic Address to R... G... of F...*, and some others which he afterwards permitted Mr CREECH to insert in the *fourth* and *fifth* editions of his poems. He assisted in the temporary institution of a small, subscription-library, for the use of a number of the well-disposed peasants in his neighbourhood. He readily aided, and by his knowledge of genuine Scottish phraseology and manners, greatly enlightened, the antiquarian researches of the late ingenious Captain GROSE. He still carried on an epistolary correspondence, sometimes gay, sportive, humorous, but always enlivened by bright flashes of genius, with a number of his old friends, and on a very wide diversity of topics. At times, as it should seem from his writings of this period he reflected, with inexpressible heart-bitterness, on the high hopes from which he had fallen; on the errors of moral conduct, into which he had been hurried, by the ardour of his soul, and, in some measure, by the very generosity of his nature; on the disgrace and wretchedness into which he saw himself rapidly sinking; on the sorrow with which his misconduct oppressed the heart of his JANE; on the want and destitute misery in which it seemed probable that he must leave her and their infants. Nor, amidst these agonising reflections, did he fail to look, with an indignation half invidious, half contemptuous, on those, who, with moral habits not more excellent than his, with powers of intellect far inferior, yet basked in the sun-shine of fortune, and were loaded with the wealth and honours of the world, while *his* follies could not obtain pardon, nor his wants an honourable supply. His wit became, from this time, more gloomily sarcastic; and his conversation and writings began to assume something of a tone

of misanthropical malignity, by which they had not been before, in any eminent degree, distinguished. But, with all these failings; he was still that exalted mind which had raised itself above the depression of its original condition, with all the energy of *the lion, pawing to set free his hinder limbs from the yet incumbering earth*: He still appeared *not less than archangel ruined!*

'What more remains there for me to relate? In Dumfries his dissipation became still more deeply habitual. He was here exposed more than in the country, to be solicited to share the riot of the dissolute and the idle. Foolish young men, such as writers' apprentices, young surgeons, merchants' clerks, and his brother excisemen, flocked eagerly about him, and from time to time pressed him to drink with them, that they might enjoy his wicked wit. His friend NICOL made one or two autumnal excursions to Dumfries, and when they met in Dumfries, friendship, and genius, and wanton wit, and good liquor could never fail to keep BURNS and NICOL together, till both the one and the other were as dead drunk as ever SILENUS was. The *Caledonian Club*, too, and the *Dumfriesshire and Galloway Hunt*, had occasional meetings in Dumfries, after BURNS came to reside here: and the poet was, of course, invited to share their conviviality, and hesitated not to accept the invitation. The morals of the town were, in consequence of its becoming so much the scene of public amusement, not a little corrupted: and, though a husband and a father, poor BURNS did not escape suffering by the general contamination, in a manner which I forbear to describe. In the intervals between his different fits of intemperance, he suffered still the keenest anguish of remorse and horribly afflictive foresight. His JANE still behaved with a degree of maternal and conjugal tenderness and prudence, which made him feel more bitterly the evil of his misconduct, although they could not reclaim him. At last, crippled, emaciated, having the very power of animation wasted by disease, quite broken-hearted by the sense of his errors, and of the hopeless miseries in which he saw himself and his family depressed; with his soul still tremblingly alive to the sense of shame, and to the love of virtue; yet even in the last feebleness, and amid the last agonies of expiring life, yielding readily to any temptation that offered the semblance of intemperate enjoyment; he died at Dumfries, in the summer of the year 1796, while he was yet three or four years under the age of forty.

'After his death, it quickly appeared that his failings had not effaced from the minds of his more respectable acquaintance, either the regard which had once been won by his social qualities, or the reverence due to his intellectual talents. The circumstances of want in which he left his family, were noticed by the gentlemen of Dumfries, with earnest commiseration. His funeral was celebrated, by the care of his friends, with a decent solemnity, and with a numerous attendance of mourners, sufficiently honourable to his memory. Several copies of verses, having, if *no other merit, at least that of a good subject*; were inserted in different newspapers, upon the occasion of his death. A contribution by subscription, was proposed, in order to raise a small fund, for the decent support of his widow, and the education of his infant children. This subscription has been very warmly promoted, and not without considerable success, by *John Syme* Esq. of Dumfries; by *Alexander Cunningham*, Esq. in Edinburgh; and by Dr *James Currie* and Mr *Roscoe* of Liverpool. Mr *Stephen Kemble*, manager of the theatre-royal at Edinburgh, with ready liberality, gave a benefit-night for this generous purpose. A publication of the poet's posthumous works is now in preparation, the profits of which are to be appropriated to the same pious use. It is hoped, that such a sum may be made

up, in all, as shall secure his widow from destitute want, and shall bestow upon his children the advantages of a liberal education. It will be rather a tribute to BURNS, than the mere dole of charity.

'I shall conclude this paper with a short estimate of what appear to me to have been BURNS's real merits, as a poet and as a man.

'The most remarkable quality he displayed, both in his writings and his conversation, was, certainly, an enlarged, vigorous, keenly discerning, COMPREHENSION OF MIND. Whatever be the subject of his verse; he seems still to grasp it with giant force; to wield and turn it with easy dexterity; to view it on all sides, with an eye which no turn of outline and no hue of colouring can elude; to mark all its relations to the group of surrounding objects; and then to select what he chooses to represent to our imaginations, with a skilful and happy propriety, which shows him to have been at the same time, master of all the rest. It will not be very easy for any other mind, however richly stored with various knowledge; for any other imagination, however elastic and inventive; to find any new and suitable topic that has been omitted by BURNS, in celebrating the subjects of all his greater and more elaborate poems. It is impossible to consider, without astonishment, that amazing fertility of invention which is displayed, under the regulation of a sound judgment, and a correct taste, in the pieces intituled *the Twa Dogs; the Address to the De'il; Scotch Drink; the Holy Fair; Hallowe'en; the Cottar's Saturday Night; To a Haggis; To a Louse; To a Mountain Daisy; Tam O'Shanter; on Captain Grose's Peregrinations; The humble Petition of Bruar water; The Bard's Epitaph.* Shoemakers, footmen, threshers, milk-maids, peers, stay-makers, have all written verses, such as deservedly attracted the notice of the world. But in the poetry of these people, while there was commonly some genuine effusion of the sentiments of agitated nature, some exhibition of such imagery as at once impressed itself upon the heart; there was also ever much to be excused in consideration of their ignorance, their want of taste, their extravagance of fancy, their want or abuse of the advantages of a liberal education. BURNS has no pardon to demand for defects of this sort. He might scorn every concession which we are ready to grant to his peculiar circumstances, without being, on this account, reduced to relinquish any part of his claims to the praise of poetical excellence. He touches his lyre, at all times, with the hand of a master. He demands to be ranked, not with the WOODHOUSES, the DUCKS, the RAMSAYS, but with the MILTONS, the POPES, the GRAYS. No poet was ever more largely endowed with that strong common sense which is necessarily the very source and principle of all fine writing.

'The next remarkable quality in this man's character, seems to have consisted in native strength, ARDOUR, and delicacy of FEELINGS, passions, and affections. *Si vis me flere; dolendum primum est ipsi tibi.* All that is valuable in poetry, and at the same time, peculiar to it, consists in the effusion of particular, not general, *sentiment*, and in the picturing out of particular *imagery*. But education, reading, a wide converse with men in society, the most extensive observation of external nature, however useful to improve, cannot, even all combined, confer, the power of comprehending either *imagery* or *sentiment* with such force and vivacity of conception, as may enable one to impress whatever he may choose upon the souls of others, with full, irresistible, electric energy. This is a power which naught can bestow save native soundness, delicacy, quickness, ardour, force of those parts of our bodily organisation, of those energies in the structure of our minds, on which depend all our sensations, emotions, appetites, passions, and affections. Who ever knew a

man of high original genius, whose senses were imperfect, his feelings dull and callous, his passions all languid and stagnant, his affections without ardour, and without constancy? Others may be artisans, speculatists, imitators in the fine arts. None but the man who is thus richly endowed by nature, can be a poet, an artist, an illustrious inventor in philosophy. Let any person *first* possess this original soundness, vigour, and delicacy of the primary energies of mind; and *then* let him receive some impression upon his imagination which shall excite a passion for this or that particular pursuit: he will scarcely fail to distinguish himself by illustrious efforts of exalted and original genius. Without having, *first*, those simple ideas which belong, respectively, to the different senses; no man can ever form for himself the complex notions, into the composition of which such simple ideas necessarily enter. Never could BURNS, without this delicacy, this strength, this vivacity of the powers of bodily sensation, and of mental feeling, which I would here claim as the indispensible native endowments of true genius; without these, never could he have poured forth those sentiments, or pourtrayed those images, which have so powerfully impressed every imagination, and penetrated every heart. Almost all the sentiments and images diffused throughout the poems of BURNS, are fresh from the mint of nature. He sings what he had himself beheld with interested attention,— what he had himself felt with keen emotions of pain or pleasure. You actually see what he describes: you more than sympathise with his joys: your bosom is inflamed with all his fire: your heart dies away within you, infected by the contagion of his despondency. He exalts, for a time, the genius of his reader to the elevation of his own; and, for the moment, confers upon him all the powers of a poet. Quotations were endless. But any person of discernment, taste, and feeling, who shall carefully read over

1 *The Burns portraits: drawing by Archibald Skirving (upper left), miniature by Alexander Reid (upper right), the Swinton portrait (lower left), painting by Peter Taylor, which is more probably of Gilbert Burns (lower right), and the likeness by Alexander Nasmyth (centre).*

2 *Lochlea (above), Alloway Kirk (centre), and Burns's birthplace.*

3 *Mrs Robert Burns with her favourite grandchild, Sara (upper left), Robert Burns the Younger (upper right), and his brothers Lieutenant Colonel James Burns (left) and Colonel William Burns.*

4 The birthplace in Alloway today (upper left); Mossgiel Farm (upper right), Ellisland Farm (lower left) and Mount Oliphant.

5 *Ayr (upper left),
Irvine (upper right),
Kilmarnock (lower left),
and the procession of
St James's Lodge,
Tarbolton.*

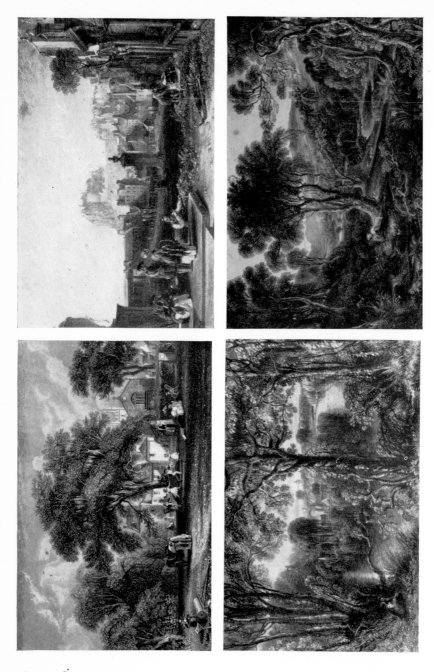

6 *Mauchline (upper left), Edinburgh Castle (upper right), the Banks of Doon (lower left), and Glenafton.*

7 *Euphemia Murray (upper left), Jessie Lewars, later Mrs James Thomson (upper right), Lucy Johnstone, later Mrs Lucy Oswald (lower left), Eliza Burnett (lower right), and Margaret Chalmers, later Mrs Lewis Hay (centre).*

8　The Rev. John Skinner (above), Dr John Moore (left centre), and Robert Ainslie (lower left), Captain Francis Grose (lower right), and a cartoon of Dr James Gregory (upper right).

9   *The Rev. John Kemp (left), Lord Craig (right), 'Clarinda'—Mrs Agnes M'Lehose—and Clarinda's lodging in General's Entry, Potter Row, Edinburgh.*

10 *William Inglis (above), James Cunningham, 14th Earl of Glencairn (upper left), John Ballantine (upper right), the Rev. Thomas Blacklock (lower left), and William Smellie.*

11   *Mrs Catherine Bruce of Clackmannan (upper left), Mrs Frances Dunlop of Dunlop (upper right), William Niven (lower left), Alexander Cunningham (lower right), and John Syme (centre).*

12   *Robert Graham of Fintry (above), Alexander Findlater (upper left),*
Patrick Miller of Dalswinton (upper right), the Rev. George Lawrie (lower left),
and George Thomson.

13   *Neil Gow by Sir Henry Raeburn, a silhouette of John Wilson, 'Dr Horn-book', and 'The Cotter's Saturday Night' by David Allan, in which Burns's head was used as a model for the eldest son, sitting next his father.*

14 *Maria Woodley, later Mrs Walter Riddell, by Sir Thomas Lawrence,*
Robert Riddell of Glenriddell, and Friar's Carse.

15 *Patrick Miller's pioneer steamboat of 1788, engined by William Symington, and Dumfries in the 1830s.*

I have sent you a proof impression of Beugo's work for me, done on Indian paper, as a trifling but sincere testimony with what heart-warm gratitude

I have the honor to be,
Revered Sir,
your much indebted humble servant.
Robt Burns

Lawn Market
Friday morn.

16 *An autograph letter, the room in Dumfries in which Burns died, and the Burns home in Mill Street, now a museum.*

BURNS's book, will not fail to discover, in its every page, abundance of those sentiments and images to which this observation relates.—It is originality of genius, it is soundness of perception, it is delicacy of passion, it is general vigour and impetuosity of the whole mind, by which such effects are produced. Others have sung, in the same Scottish dialect, and in similar rhymes, many of the same topics which are celebrated by BURNS. But, what with BURNS awes or fascinates; in the hands of others only disgusts by its deformity, or excites contempt by its meanness and uninteresting simplicity.

'A THIRD quality which the life and the writings of BURNS show to have belonged to his character, was, a quick and correct DISCERNMENT of the distinctions between RIGHT and WRONG, between TRUTH and FALSEHOOD; and this, accompanied with a passionate preference of whatever was *right* and *true*, with an indignant abhorrence of whatever was *alse* and morally *wrong*. It is true that he did not always steadily distinguish and eschew the evils of drunkenness and licentious love; it is true that these, at times, seem to obtain even the approbation of his muse. But there remains in his works enough to show, that his cooler reasons, and all his better feelings, earnestly rejected those gay vices, which he could sometimes, unhappily, allow himself to practise, and would sometimes recommend to others, by the charms which his imagination lent them. What was it but the clear and ardent discrimination of justice from injustice, which inspired that indignation with which his heart often burned, when he saw those exalted by fortune, who were not exalted by their merits? His *Cottar's Saturday Night*, and all his graver poems, breathe a rich vein of the most amiable, yet manly, and even delicately correct, morality. In his pieces of satire, and of lighter humour, it is still upon the accurate and passionate discernment of falsehood, and of moral

turpitude, that his ridicule turns. Other poets are often as remarkable for the incorrectness, or even the absurdity of their general truths; as for interesting sublimity or tenderness of sentiment, or for picturesque splendour of imagery. BURNS is not less happy in teaching general truths, than in that display of sentiment and imagery, which more peculiarly belongs to the province of the poet. BURNS's morality deserves this high praise; that is not a system merely of *discretion*; it is not founded upon any scheme of superstition; but seems to have always its source, and the test by which it is to be tried, in the most diffusive benevolence, and in a regard for the universal good.

'The only other leading feature of character that appears to be strikingly displayed in the life and writings of BURNS, is a *lofty-minded* CONSCIOUSNESS *of his own* TALENTS *and* MERITS. Hence, the fierce and contemptuous asperity of his satire; the sullen and gloomy dignity of his complaints, addressed, not so much to alarm the soul of pity, as to reproach injustice, and to make fortunate baseness shrink abashed; that general gravity and elevation of his sentiments, which admits no humbly insinuating sportiveness of wit, which scorns all compromise between the *right* and the *expedient*, which decides with the authoritative voice of a judge from whom there is no appeal, upon characters, principles, and events, whenever they present themselves to notice. From his works, as from his conversation and manners, *pride* seems to have excluded the effusion of *vanity*. In the composition, or correctness of his poetry, he never suffered the judgment, even of his most respectable friends, to dictate to him. This line in one of his poems, ("When I *look back* on *prospects drear*") was criticised; but he would not condescend either to reply to the criticism, or to alter the expression. Not a few of his smaller pieces are sufficiently trivial, vulgar, and hack-

G

neyed in the thought, are such as the pride of genius should have disdained to write, or, at least, to publish, But there is reason to believe that he despised such pieces, even while he wrote and published them; that it was rather in regard to the effects they had already produced upon hearers and readers, than from any overweening opinion of their intrinsic worth, he suffered them to be printed. His wit is always dignified. He is not a merry-andrew in a motley coat, sporting before you for your diversion: but a hero, or a philosopher, deigning to admit you to witness his relaxations; still exercising the great energies of his soul; and little caring, at the moment, whether you do, or do not, cordially sympathise with his feelings.

'His poems may be all distributed into the two classes of *pastorals* and *pieces upon common life and manners*. In the former class, I include all those in which rural imagery, and the manners and sentiments of rustics, are chiefly described. In the latter I would comprehend his epigrams, epistles, and, in short, all those pieces in which the imagery and sentiments are drawn from the condition and appearances of common life, without any particular reference to the country. It is in the first class, that the most excellent of his poems are certainly to be found. Those few pieces which he seems to have attempted in that miserable strain, called *the Della Crusca* style, appear to me to be the least commendable of all his writings. He usually employs those forms of *versification*, which have been used chiefly by the former writers of poetry in the Scottish dialect, and by some of the elder English poets. His *phraseology* is evidently drawn from those books of English poetry which were in his hands, from the writings of former Scottish poets, and from those unwritten stores of the Scottish dialect, which became known to him, in the conversation of his fellow-peasants. Some other late writers in the Scottish dialect seem to think, that not to write English; is certainly, to write Scottish. BURNS, avoiding this error, hardly ever transgressed the propriety of English grammar, except in compliance with the long-accustomed variations of the genuine Scottish dialect.

'From the preceding detail of the particulars of this poet's life, the reader will naturally and justly infer him to have been an honest, proud, warm-hearted man; of high passions, a sound understanding, a vigorous and excursive imagination. He was never known to descend to any act of deliberate meanness. In Dumfries, he retained many respectable friends, even to the last. It may be doubted whether he has not, by his writings, exercised a greater power over the minds of men, and by consequence, on their conduct, upon their happiness and misery, upon the general system of life, than has been exercised by any half dozen of the most eminent statesmen of the present age. The power of the statesman, is but shadowy, so far as it acts upon externals alone. The power of the writer of genius, subdues the heart and the understanding, and having thus made the very springs of action its own, through them moulds almost all life and nature at its pleasure. BURNS has not failed to command one remarkable sort of homage, such as is never paid but to great original genius. A crowd of poetasters started up to imitate him, by writing verses as he had done, in the Scottish dialect. But, O *imitatores! servum pecus!* To persons to whom the Scottish dialect, and the customs and manners of rural life in Scotland, have no charm; I shall possibly appear to have said too much about BURNS. By those who passionately admire him, I shall, perhaps, be blamed, as having said too little.'

Highland Harry

Burns said he picked up the chorus of this song—'My Harry was a gallant gay'—

'from an old woman in Dunblane; the rest of the song is mine'.

Peter Buchan states that: 'the original song related to a love attachment between Harry Lumsdale, the second son of a Highland gentleman, and Mrs Jeanie Gordon, daughter to the Laird of Knockespock, in Aberdeenshire. The lady was married to her cousin, Habichie Gordon, a son of the Laird of Rhynie; and some time after, her former lover having met her and shaken her hand, her husband drew his sword in anger, and lopped off several of Lumsdale's fingers, which Highland Harry took so much to heart that he soon after died.'

Burns gave the song a Jacobite slant in accordance with his personal views.

To the tune 'Highland Watch's Farewell to Ireland', from Stewart's *Reels* 1762, the song appeared in the *Scots Musical Museum* in 1790.

Hill, Peter (1754–1837)

Son of James Hill and his wife, Mary Russell, Peter Hill was born at Dysart, Fife. When Burns met him in 1787, he was still a clerk in Creech's bookshop, but in 1788, he set up his own bookselling business. His wife, Elizabeth Lindsay, whom he married in 1780, is said to have been socially his superior, and is supposed to have disapproved of her husband's friendship with Burns. Hill became Edinburgh's City Treasurer, and Treasurer of Heriot's Hospital. In 1814, he was appointed Collector of Cess.

Hill acted as a kind of Edinburgh banker for Burns, and a number of the poet's letters to him deal solely with business matters. Others deal in part with the ordering of books, either for Burns's own personal library, or for the Monkland Friendly Society, which Burns and Robert Riddell organised early in 1789. But there are many personal observations in Burns's side of the correspondence, and sometimes *double entendres*. Writing from Mauchline on 18th July 1788, when Hill had complained of Burns's neglect of him, the poet said: 'You injured me, my dear Sir, in your construction of the cause of my silence. From Ellisland in Nithsdale to Mauchline in Kyle, is forty and five miles; there, a house a-building, and farm enclosures and improvements to tend; here, a new—not so much indeed a *new* as a *young* wife—Good God, Sir, could my dearest Brother expect a regular correspondence from me! I who am busied with the sacred Pen of Nature, in the mystic Volume of Creation, can I dishonour my hand with a dirty goose feather, on a parcel of washed old rags? I who am "called as was Aaron" to offer in the Sanctum Sanctorum, not indeed the mysterious bloody types of future MURDER but the thrice-hallowed quintessence of future EXISTENCE; can I—but I have apologised enough. . . .'

It was to Hill that Burns wrote on 5th February 1792, about the paying of the bill for the erection of the tombstone over the grave of Robert Fergusson: 'I send you by the bearer, Mr Clarke, a particular friend of mine, six pounds and a shilling, which you will dispose of as follows: £5 10s., per acc^t I owe to Mr Robt Burn, Architect, for erecting the stone over poor Ferguson. He has been two years in erecting it, after I commissioned him for it; and I have been two years paying him, after he sent me his account; so he and I are quits. He had the hardiesse to ask me interest on the sum; but considering that the money was due by one Poet, for putting a tombstone over another, he may, with grateful surprise, thank Heaven that ever he saw a farthing of it.' The rest of the money was to buy more books.

Hill, in company with Cameron, a paper manufacturer, and Ramsay, printer of the *Edinburgh Evening Courant*, visited Burns at Dumfries. Their visit was referred to in a letter dealing with the 'annual kipper' or smoked salmon, which Burns apparently sent Hill. His last letter to the bookseller, dated 29th January

1796, when its writer had already entered his fatal decline, deals with the sending of the 'annual kipper'.

'Holy Willie's Prayer'

One of Burns's most telling poems, and perhaps the greatest satire in European literature. The model for the poet's godly hypocrite was William Fisher. See **Fisher, William**. It was first printed anonymously in an eight-page pamphlet in 1789, along with 'quotations from the Presbyterian Eloquence'. Burns uses a local character and a local incident—the affair of Gavin Hamilton and the Presbytery of Ayr—to produce a poem universal in its implications.

Hood, Thomas

Accompanied Burns and Ker into England, on the Border tour, after the poet had parted from Ainslie, who returned to Edinburgh.

Burns described Ker and Hood in a letter to Ainslie from Newcastle, 29th May 1787:

'Old Mr Thos Hood has been persuaded to join our Partie, and Mr Kerr and he do very well, but alas! I dare not talk nonsense lest I lose all the little dignity I have among the sober sons of wisdom and discretion, and I have not had one hearty mouthful of laughter since that merry-melancholy moment we parted.'

Hood, William, Senior

An elder in Tarbolton. Burns wrote a mock epitaph on him, which is inserted in the First Common-Place Book, under the title 'Epitaph on Wm. Hood, Senr. In Tarbolton':

'Here Souter Hood in death does
                                    sleep—
To hell, if he's gane thither,
Satan, gie him thy gear to keep,
He'll haud it weel thegither.'

Hornbook', 'Death and Dr

See **Wilson, John**.

Howden, Francis (d. 1848)

An Edinburgh jeweller who, in 1792, was appointed goldsmith and medallist for Scotland by the Prince of Wales.

Burns, from 'St James's Square Noon 2d Attic story', sent him 'a small shade to set', requesting that it be ready by the following evening, for a lover on the verge of matrimony: 'The Parties, one of them at least, is a very particular acquaintance of mine; the honest lover.... Let me conjure you, my friend, by the bended bow of Cupid; by the unloosed cestus of Venus; by the lighted torch of Hymen, that you will have the locket finished by the time mentioned.'

There is no other record of friendship between Burns and Howden, except this letter of December 1787.

Howe, General Sir William (1729–1814)

Educated at Eton, he had a distinguished Military career, succeeding General Gage as commander-in-chief of the British forces in the American War of Independence. He was successful at Bunker's Hill in 1775. This victory he followed with the capture of New York in 1776. The following month he defeated the Americans at White Plains, and again at Brandywine in 1777. Then he resigned because of lack of support at home. His resignation was accepted because of his failure to engage with Washington at Valley Forge. He was succeeded by Sir Henry Clinton. Howe rose to the rank of full general and was Governor of Berwick-on-Tweed, and later Plymouth, where he died. Before the American war, he had commanded a Light Infantry battalion under his friend Wolfe, at the capture of Quebec.

He also represented Nottingham for a time in Parliament on behalf of the Whigs.

Burns mentions his generalship in his 'Address of Beelzebub'.

Hoy, James (1747–1828)

Librarian to the Duke of Gordon at Castle Gordon. Chambers described him as: 'The Duke's librarian, companion and friend, a well-read man, who lived in the castle for forty-six years without ever losing the Dominie-Sampson-like purity of heart and simplicity of manners by which he was distinguished'.

Burns met Hoy at Castle Gordon during his Highland tour, on the occasion when, to placate Nicol, the poet had to forgo 'dining with the Duke and Duchess'. Burns referred to the incident when he wrote to Hoy from Edinburgh on 20th October 1787: 'I shall certainly, among my legacies, leave my latest curse to that unlucky predicament which hurried me, tore me away from Castle Gordon. May that obstinate son of Latin Prose be curst to Scotch-mile periods, and damn'd to seven league paragraphs; while Declension and Conjugation, Gender, Number, and Time, under the ragged banners of Dissonance and Disarrangement eternally rank against him in hostile array! ! ! ! ! !'

The main purpose of Burns's letter, however, was to acquaint Hoy with the *Scots Musical Museum*, and to make a request: 'My request is; "Cauld Kail in Aberdeen" is one intended for this Number; and I beg a copy of His Grace of Gordon's words to it, which you were so kind as to repeat to me. You may be sure we won't prefix the Author's name, except you like; tho' I look on it as no small merit to this work that the names of many of the Authors of our old Scotch Songs, names almost forgotten, will be inserted.'

Burns wrote to Hoy again on 6th November, when the librarian had complied with his request. Said Burns: 'The Duke's song, independent totally of his dukeship, charms me. . . . I could name half-a-dozen Dukes that I guess are a devilish deal worse employed; nay, I question if there are half-a-dozen better.'

Humphry, James (1755–1844)

A Mauchline mason supposed to be the subject of the epitaph 'On a Noisy Polemic'. Humphry was employed both at Lochlea and Mossgiel. He first brought himself to Burns's notice because he had some book knowledge, and spoke well. But he frequently engaged in arguments in which he rarely had enough knowledge to support himself, and so earned Burns's description:

'Below thir stanes lie Jamie's banes
                                                [these
       O Death, it's my opinion
Thou ne'er took such a bleth'ran bitch,
       Into thy dark dominion!'

Humphry, however, was reputed to have been pleased that he had been the subject of Burns's muse! According to Cunningham, he loved 'to talk of Burns and of the warm debates between them on Effectual Calling and Free Grace'. He died in an almshouse at Failford.

Hunter, née Home, Anne (1742–1821)

Wife of the surgeon John Hunter, and the authoress of, amongst others, the well-known song 'My Mother bids me bind my hair', set to music by Haydn, whom she got to know while the composer was in London. Dr Gregory sent Burns two of her pieces to let him see 'how much correctness and high polish enhance the value of such compositions'. The doctor was criticising Burns's 'On Seeing a Wounded Hare'.

Hunter, John

A Writer to the Signet who bought the estate of Doonholm, and probably the subject of Burns's 'Epitaph for J. H'.

Hunter, Peter

The Public Prosecutor of Irvine, who owned several ships trading from the town. He lived in the Glasgow Vennel, where Burns lodged when he was learning the flax trade. In all probability Burns knew Hunter, who became a member of the Buchanites. He left Irvine, along with Mrs Buchan and her followers, to go to Galloway.

Hunter, William
A Mauchline shoe-maker referred to in 'Libel Summons'.

Hutcheson, David
The 'wee Davock' of the poem 'The Inventory', subtitled 'In answer to a Mandate by the Surveyor of Taxes'.

'For men, I've three mischievous boys,
Run-deils for rantin' an' for noise;
                    [*regular devils*
A gaudsman ane, a thrasher t'other
                    [*the plough-driver*
Wee Davoc hauds the nowt in
            fother. . . .' [*cattle fodder*

Hutcheson, the orphan son of a Lochlea ploughman, lived with Burns at Lochlea farm. The poet was said to have been especially kind to this child, teaching him English, and sometimes carrying him home on his shoulder from the fields. He took care of Hutcheson until the boy was able to earn his own living.

Hutchinson, John
Lived in St Ann's, Jamaica, and corresponded with Burns. He congratulated the poet on not going to Jamaica, saying he had 'great reason to believe that Mr Douglas's employ would by no means have answered your expectations'.

Hyslop, Mrs 'Meg'
Landlady of the Globe Tavern in Dumfries which, Burns said in a letter to George Thomson in 1796, 'for these many years

has been my Howff'. Her niece was Anna Park, who bore Burns an illegitimate daughter, Elizabeth.

Burns referred to Mrs Hyslop always as 'Meg'. Her husband, William, was the landlord.

The story is told that, on one occasion, Burns forgot to order dinner for himself, Nicol and Masterton. Meg produced a tup's head, which she and her husband were going to have themselves. Nicol, it seems, 'fined' Burns for his fault by commanding a grace. Burns produced:

'O Lord, when hunger pinches sore,
    Do thou stand us in stead,
And send us from thy bounteous store,
    A tup—or wether—head. Amen.'

When they had eaten, Burns was 'ordered' to return thanks. This brought forth:

'O Lord, since we have feasted thus,
    Which we so little merit,
Let Meg now take away the flesh,
    And Jock bring in the spirit. Amen.'

A variant of this is to be found in the Wallace-Chambers edition, entitled 'Grace after Meat'.

'Lord, Thee we thank, and Thee alone
    For temporal gifts we little merit!
At present we will ask no more—
    Let William Hyslop bring the spirit.'

Hyslop, William 'Jock'
Husband, of 'Meg' Hyslop, and landlord of the Globe Inn, Dumfries. *See* above. Burns told Thomson in 1796 that the Globe 'has been my HOWFF, and where our friend Clarke and I have had many a merry squeeze'.

I

Inglis, William (1747–1801)

A Bailie on Inverness Town Council who entertained the poet during his Highland tour. In 1797, Inglis became Provost. He retired in 1800. He was reputed to be an able and public-spirited citizen. His portrait in his Provost's robes hangs in the Town Hall.

A note from Burns to Inglis, dated 4th September 1787, is extant. It asks the postponement of a meeting, because Burns was 'jaded to death with the fatigue of today's journey'. He was staying in Ettles Hotel.

See Plate 10.

Inglis, The Reverend William (1741–1826)

Until Burns got suitable accommodation for his family at Ellisland, he lodged with the outgoing tenant David Cullie or Kelly, who was a member of the Reverend William Inglis's congregation at Loreburn Street Church, Dumfries. Inglis and Burns met, and later Burns joined Inglis's Church. He attended the poet on his death-bed.

Inglis was born at Freuchie, in Fife, of Presbyterian dissenting parents. He was ordained minister of the Anti-burgher congregation at Leslie in 1765, and shortly afterwards was transferred to Dumfries.

On a monument erected in Dumfries by his congregation is printed the testimony: '... As a minister, he was a fearless reprover of vice, a faithful promoter of virtue, assiduous and punctual in the discharge of all his various duties.'

Irvine

An old town in Ayrshire at the mouth of the river Irvine, and part of a late twentieth-century New Town complex. Bruce confirmed it a royal burgh in 1308. It was at one time used as a seaport for Glasgow, but about 1620 the harbour began to silt up, and the Glasgow merchants eventually developed Port-Glasgow in place of Irvine.

In 1781, when Burns was twenty-two, he became dissatisfied with his prospects as a farmer. For several years, he and Gilbert had taken some land from their father at Lochlea, and as a speculation of their own, grown flax on it. At that time, flax was a paying crop. The poet even won a prize of three pounds for his linseed growing, as a notice in the *Glasgow Mercury* for 16th–23rd January 1783, reveals. Apparently, it struck Burns that their profit margin could be increased if they could heckle it themselves for the spinners. Accordingly, Burns went to Irvine probably in the spring of 1781 to learn the trade. The experiment was an unfortunate one, lasting only about six months, during which time he was often plunged deeply in a gloom which was reflected in: 'Winter—A Dirge' and 'Prayer Under the Pressure of Violent Anguish'.

Concern over his son's health brought William Burnes over to Irvine to see him.

The house in which he started this unpleasant work was in the Smiddy Bar, but its exact site is no longer known. The end of the experiment came with the New Year: 'My partner was a scoundrel of the first water, who made money by the mystery of thieving; and to finish the whole, while we were giving a welcome carousel to the new year, our shop burnt to ashes and left me, like a true poet, not worth a sixpence.'

The Scottish novelist John Galt was born in Irvine in 1779, in a house on the site of which the Bank of Scotland in High Street now stands.

The Burns statue in Irvine, the work of a sculptor who was himself a minor Scots poet, Pittendrigh MacGillivray, was unveiled on 18th July 1896, by the then Poet Laureate, Alfred Austin.

See plate 5

Irvine Manuscript
Thirty-four pages of the holograph printer's copy of *Poems* (1786). They are housed in the Burns Museum belonging to Irvine Burns Club.

J

Jaffray, The Reverend Andrew (1723-95)

Minister of Ruthwell parish church, and later of Lochmaben, in Dumfriesshire. He was the father of Jean Jaffray (q.v.), who was the 'Blue-Eyed Lassie' of 'I gaed a waefu' gate yestreen'. Burns sometimes stayed at the Manse at Lochmaben on his Excise excursions. In a letter to the Provost of Lochmaben, Robert Maxwell, dated 20th December 1789, Burns said: 'If you meet with that worthy old veteran in religion and good fellowship, Mr Jeffry, or any of his amiable Family, I beg you will give them my best compliments.'

Jaffray, Jean (1773-1850)

Only daughter of the Rev. Andrew Jaffray of Ruthwell and later Lochmaben, she was the 'Blue-Eyed Lassie' of the song 'I gaed a waefu' gate yestreen', which Burns wrote for her when she was about fifteen and which was published in *The Scots Musical Museum*, 1790. Unfortunately it was set to an air by Robert Riddell which spans two octaves, and is very nearly unsingable. She later spoke to George Thomson of Burns's 'manly, luminous observations and artless manners' when he visited the manse on his Excise rides. She married a Liverpool merchant, William Renwick, and settled with him in New York, where she enjoyed the friendship of the literati, including Washington Irving. A son of George Thomson visited her in 1822, by which time she was a widow. Her visitor recorded: 'She has told me that she often looks back with a melancholy satisfaction on the many evenings she spent in the company of the great bard, in the social circle of her father's fireside, listening to the brilliant sallies of his imagination and to his delightful conversation. "Many times,"

said she, "have I seen Burns enter my father's dwelling in a cold rainy night, after a long ride over the dreary moors. On such occasions, one of the family would help to disencumber him of his dreadnought and boots, while others brought him a pair of slippers and made him a warm dish of tea. It was during these visits that he felt himself perfectly happy, and opened his whole soul to us, repeated and even sang, many of his admirable songs, and enchanted all who had the good fortune to be present with his manly, luminous observations and artless manners. I never . . . could fancy that Burns had ever followed the rustic occupation of the plough, because everything he said or did had a gracefulness and charm that was in an extraordinary degree engaging." '

A collected volume of her writings was published after her death. Her son, James Renwick, LL.D., became Professor of Natural Philosophy and Chemistry in Columbia College.

Jedburgh

A border town on the Jed which has the ruins of a splendid Abbey, founded in 1118 by David I. Mary, Queen of Scots lodged in a house in the town when she came to open the Justice Aire, or Circuit Court, in October 1566. The house in which she stayed is preserved as a museum. Prince Charles Edward Stuart stayed in the Castlegate for a night in 1745. Wordsworth lodged at 5 Abbey Close in 1803.

Burns visited Jedburgh during his Border tour, and lodged in No. 27 Canongate, from the 8th to the 11th of May. In his *Journal* of the tour, he relates that he was: 'waited on by the Magistrates and presented with the freedom of the burgh'. He did not, however, sign the burgess roll, and until 1939 his burgess ticket was believed lost. In that year, however, it came up for sale. Unfortunately, Jedburgh was unable to raise the money to buy it back. According to Andrew McCallum, in the *Burns Chronicle*, 1942, the ticket records that on 11th May 1787; 'Robert Burns Esquire was entered and received into the Libertys of this Burgh, Create and made a free Burges and Guild Brother of the same, who gave his Oath with all Ceremonies used and wont. Whereupon He required Acts of Court and protested for an Extract of the same under the Common Seal of this Burgh.'

'John Anderson My Jo'

Burns's tribute to fidelity and life-long affection, first published in the Museum to a tune from the *Caledonian Pocket Companion* (1759). An old version of the song in the same stanza form substitutes complaint at a decline in sexual prowess, and is to be found in *The Merry Muses*. Percy's *Reliques* (1765) contain a still older version, communicated by Lord Hailes, in which a woman admits to mothering bastards.

Johnson, James (c. 1750–1811)

Johnson, who is believed to have been a native of Ettrick, after apprenticeship to James Reed became an engraver and music-seller in Edinburgh. When Burns arrived in the Capital, Johnson had devised, or had introduced to Scotland, a process 'to strike music upon pewter', which enabled a considerable saving to be achieved in music printing, though he himself gained little enough from his enterprise.

Sometime before 1787, this poorly educated man, whose spelling was atrocious, and whose engraving shop was in Bell's Wynd, conceived the idea of collecting the words and music of all the existing Scots songs, and publishing them from his music shop in the Lawn Market. By the time he met Burns, the first volume of his *Scots Musical Museum* containing the first hundred songs, was already in the press. Johnson invited Burns's collaboration, and the poet's enthusiasm eventually outdid even that of

Johnson. Thereafter, until his death, Burns was virtually the real editor of the *Museum*, contributing about 160 songs of his own, and mending and patching many others—his system of signature-letters still disguises how many! Three further volumes of the *Museum* were published during Burns's lifetime, and a fifth was ready for the press at the time of his death, in 1796. It took Johnson, on his own again, until 1803 to produce the sixth and last volume. The musical editorship was held, first by Stephen Clarke, and later by his son, William.

Throughout their association, Johnson —unlike George Thomson, with whom Burns also worked—always accepted Burns's superior taste, and never questioned his advice. On Burns's death, poor though he was, Johnson contributed £4 to the fund raised for the poet's widow and children.

Johnson's work, however, was largely neglected, and sneered at by many of Burns's editors and biographers. He himself died in poverty. His widow, left destitute, died in a workhouse in 1819. Yet the *Scots Musical Museum* was in its day, and has remained, by far the most important collection of Scots songs ever made.

The first letter from Burns to Johnson was written on 4th May 1787, by which time Burns, about to set out on his 'vacation tours', was as yet uncommitted: 'Farewel, my dear Sir! I wished to have seen you, but I have been dreadfully throng as I march tomorrow. Had my acquaintance w^t you been a little older, I would have asked the favor of your correspondence; as I have met w^t few people whose company and conversation gave me so much pleasure, because I have met w^t few whose sentiments are so congenial to my own.'

A month later, Burns was sending Johnson his first 'song cargoes'. On 20th October, Burns told the Duke of Gordon's librarian, James Hoy, of his personal interest in the project: 'An engraver, James

Johnson, in Edin^r has, not from mercenary views but from an honest Scotch enthusiasm, set about collecting all our native Songs and setting them to music; particularly those that have never been set before. Clarke, the well-known Musician, presides over the musical arangement; and Drs Beattie and Blacklock, M^r· Tytler, Woodhouselee, and your humble serv^t to the utmost of his small power, assist in collecting the old poetry, or sometimes to a fine air to make a stanza, when it has no words.'

Writing to James Candlish in February 1788, Burns reiterated his enthusiasm: 'At present I have time for nothing. Dissipation and business engross every moment. I am engaged in assisting an honest Scots Enthusiast, a friend of mine, who is an Engraver, and has taken it into his head to publish a collection of all our songs set to music, of which the words and music are done by Scotsmen. This, you will easily guess, is an undertaking exactly to my taste.'

The growing intimacy of the friendship between Johnson and Burns was reflected in a letter from Mauchline of 25th May 1788, announcing the poet's marriage: 'I am so enamoured with a certain girl's prolific twin-bearing merit, that I have given her a *legal* title to the best blood in my body; and so farewell Rakery!'

Now and again, Burns had to encourage the engraver. In a letter dated 15th November 1788, Burns consoled him: 'Perhaps you may not find your account, *lucratively*, in this business; but you are a Patriot for the Music of your Country; and I am certain, Posterity will look on themselves as highly indebted to your Publick spirit. Be not in a hurry; let us go on correctly; and your name shall be immortal.' Again the letter of 19th June 1789, sent from Ellisland: 'What are you doing, and what is the reason that you have sent me no proof sheet to correct? Though I have been rather remiss in writing you, as I have been hurried, puzzled, plagued and

confounded with some disagreeable matters, yet believe me, it is not owing to the smallest neglect or forget of you, my good Sir, or your patriotic work. Mr Clarke and I have frequent meetings and consultations on your work.'

Even as late as June 1796, within seven weeks of his death, Burns was still urging Johnson to keep going: 'You may probably think that for some time past I have neglected you and your work; but, Alas, the hand of pain, and sorrow, and care has these many months lain heavy on me! Personal and domestic affliction have almost entirely banished that alacrity and life with which I used to woo the rural Muse of Scotia. In the meantime, let us finish what we have so well begun. . . .

'Many a merry meeting this Publication has given us, and possibly it may give us more, though, alas! I fear it. This protracting, slow, consuming illness which hangs over me, will, I doubt much, my ever dear friend, arrest my sun before he has well reached his middle career, and will turn over the Poet to far other and more important concerns than studying the brilliancy of Wit or the pathos of Sentiment. . . . Your Work is a great one; and though, now that it is near finished, I see if we were to begin again, two or three things that might be mended, yet I will venture to prophesy, that to future ages your Publication will be the textbook and standard of Scottish Song and Music'— a prophecy which has come true.

The letter ends with the pathetic request for a 'spare copy . . . by the very first Fly' which Burns wanted to give to Jessy Lewars.

Johnson heard no more from the man who made him immortal. Yet, as Snyder has pointed out, the debt was not all on one side: 'Without the spur of Johnson's initial enthusiasm, and the opportunity for publication afforded by the *Museum*, Burns's lyric accomplishment could not have been as astonishing as it was. 'Hence any estimate of Burns as a writer of songs must take into account the fact that it was Johnson who opened the gates through which Burns poured the lyric flood at which the world still wonders.'

Johnston

Laird of Clackleith, and an acquaintance of Burns when he was living at Ellisland. He is called 'that trusty auld worthy' in 'The Kirk's Alarm'.

Johnston of Carnsalloch, Grace

Niece to Gordon of Balmaghie, she became the mistress of her uncle, Murray of Broughton, who deserted his wife on her behalf, and whose great wealth enabled him to get away with this outrage, not only with impunity but without forfeiting the alliance of his wife's relations, one of whom he was supporting in the election which called forth Burns's Heron Election Ballads of 1795, where there are references to both of them.

Johnston, Thomas

Farmer of Mirecleugh, or Muircleugh, in the parish of Durisdeer, and in September 1790, defendant in an Excise fraud case in which Burns's testimony against him —printed in De Lancey Ferguson's edition of his letters—has survived.

Johnston, Captain William

The founder of the *Gazetteer* newspaper in Edinburgh in November 1792, and a supporter of reform. A few months later, he was imprisoned by the authorities, an experience later also undergone by his editorial successor. Burns's lines 'On some Commemorations of Thomson' appeared in the *Gazetteer*. And on 13th November 1792, Burns wrote to Johnston begging leave to have his name inserted as a subscriber. Burns finished his note with an exhortation and a quotation from Pope's 'The Temple of Fame': 'Go on, Sir! Lay bare, with undaunted heart and steady hand, that horrid mass of corruption called Politics and State-Craft! Dare to draw in their native colors these "Calm, thinking VILLAINS whom no faith can fix!—" whatever be the Shibboleth of their pretended Party.'

Two months later, however, when someone complained to the Board of Excise about Burns's loyalty, one of the charges apparently levelled was friendship or sympathy with William Johnston. Writing to Graham of Fintry on 5th January 1793, Burns protested: 'Of Johnston, the publisher of the Edinr Gazetteer, I know nothing. One evening in company with four or five friends, we met with his prospectus which we thought manly and independent; and I wrote to him, ordering his paper for us. If you think that I act improperly in allowing his Paper to come addressed to me, I shall immediately countermand it. I never, so judge me, God! wrote a line of prose for the Gazetteer in my life. An occasional address, spoken by Miss Fontenelle on her benefit night here, which I called, the Rights of Woman, I sent to the Gazetteer; as also some extempore stanzas on the Commemorations of Thomson; both of these I will subjoin for your perusal. You will see that they have nothing whatever to do with Politics.

'At the time when I sent Johnston one of these poems, but which one, I do not remember, I inclosed, at the request of my warm and worthy friend, Robert Riddel Esq: of Glenriddel, a prose Essay signed Cato, written by him, and addressed to the delegates for the County Reform, of which he was one for this County. With the merits or demerits of that Essay, I have nothing to do, farther than transmitting it in the same Frank, which Frank he had procured me.'

Riddell's letter set forth, in reasonable terms, the case for extending the Franchise.

Johnstone of Westerhall, Sir James (1726–94)

The fourth baronet, he had been a lieu

tenant-colonel in the army. He represented the Dumfries Burghs in Parliament from 1784–89 and Weymouth from 1791–4. He lost his Dumfries seat to Patrick Miller junior, of Dalswinton.

Burns wrote an 'Election Ballad for Westerha'' (which was principally directed against the Duke of Queensberry, whom the poet intensely disliked, and who, in the manner of the time, had set up Miller as 'his' candidate for the 1789 election). Burns claimed:

'There's no a callant tents the kye
But kens o' Westerha' Jamie.'

Johnstone was also the 'belted Knight' of 'The Five Carlins', his opponent, Miller, 'A Soger boy, wha spak wi' modest grace'.

Johnstone, William (d. 1805)

Younger brother of Sir James Johnstone, and afterwards fifth Baronet of Westerhall. He married Frances Pulteney, heiress of her father William Pulteney, Earl of Bath, and an eminent statesman. Her husband at his death was reputed to be one of the richest men in the British Empire, since he had acquired, through his wife, the Earl of Bath's estates.

Burns referred to this great affluence in the 'Second Epistle' to Robert Graham on the Dumfries Burgh Elections: 'Not Pulteney's wealth can Pulteney save'.

Jolly Beggars', 'The

Burns's Cantata 'Love and Liberty', now known as 'The Jolly Beggars', had its origin, according to Chambers, in a chance late-night visit to Poosie Nansie's in Mauchline, when Burns had as companions Smith and Richmond. After 'witnessing much jollity' amongst a company who by day appeared as miserable beggars, Burns and his friends came away, the poet expressing much amusement, especially at the ongoings of an old maimed soldier. A few days later, Burns recited the first draft of the poem to Richmond, who later alleged that it originally contained songs for a sweep and a sailor which subsequently disappeared.

Burns let it be thought that he never contemplated publishing the Cantata, and indeed, laid it aside, until Thomson reminded him about it in 1793. In September of that year, Burns replied to him: 'I have forgot the Cantata you allude to, as I kept no copy, and indeed did not know that it was in existence; however, I remember that none of the songs pleased myself, except the last— something about,

"Courts for cowards were erected,
Churches built to please the priest"—'

Nevertheless, some notes of Dr Hugh Blair's, preserved in the Esty Collection, show that Blair was at least in part responsible for the exclusion of the Cantata from the First Edinburgh Edition (as well as for the exclusion of a poem, now lost, 'The Prophet and God's Complaint'). Burns made a fair copy of the cantata for Lady Don with minor modifications from the original Alloway manuscript. The Cantata was first printed in part as a chapbook in 1799 by Stewart and Meikle of Glasgow. It was first published complete in 1802 under the title 'The Jolly Beggars: or Tatterdemallions. A Cantata', by Thomas Stewart of Glasgow, who added the Merry Andrew fragment which he is thought to have got from Richmond in 1801.

Burns had as his immediate models a piece in Ramsay's *Tea-Table Miscellany*, 'Merry Beggars', and another, 'The Happy Beggars'. But Dr Daiches has pointed out that the Cantata is in the tradition of a 'long line of songs and poems in goliardic vein which goes far back into the Middle Ages'. Burns, of course, transcends all the earlier examples, achieving what Henley and Henderson described as: 'This irresistible presentation of humanity caught in the act and summarised for ever in the terms of art'. Matthew Arnold wrote of 'The Jolly Beggars': 'The world of Chaucer is fairer, richer, more significant than that of Burns; but when the largeness and freedom of Burns gets full sweep, as in "Tam o' Shanter", or still more in that puissant and splendid production, "The Jolly Beggars" there is more than hideousness and squalor, there is bestiality; yet the piece is a superb poetic success. It has a breadth, truth, and power which makes the famous scene in Auerbach's cellar, of Goethe's *Faust*, seem artificial and tame beside it, and which are only matched by Shakespeare and Aristophanes.'

'The Jolly Beggars' presents difficulties in staging, because each of the characters has only one song to sing. Arrangements popular in their day were those of Sir Henry Bishop (1786–1855) and John More Smieton (1857–1904), but by far the most successful realisation is probably the stylised arrangement for four voices and chamber instrumental ensemble which Cedric Thorpe Davie made for the Scottish Festival at Braemar in 1953, and which was subsequently staged at the Edinburgh International Festival, televised, broadcast, recorded, and performed in local halls throughout Scotland by the Saltire Singers and others.

K

Kelso

A border town on the river Tweed, at the meeting-place of the Tweed and the Teviot. It contains the ruins of the Tironesian Abbey, founded in 1428 by David I. Nearby Floors Castle is the seat of the Dukes of Roxburghe.

On 8th May 1787, during his Border tour, Burns visited Kelso, and recorded in his *Journal*: 'Breakfast at Kelso; charming situation of Kelso; fine bridge over Tweed; enchanting views and prospects on both sides of the river, particularly the Scotch side.'

The bridge which took Burns's fancy was swept away in the great Border flood of 26th October 1797, and was replaced by Rennie's five-arched bridge between 1800 and 1803.

Kemp, The Reverend Dr John (1744–1805)

'Clarinda's' minister. He went from Trinity Gask to the Tolbooth Church, Edinburgh, in 1779, and held this charge until his death. He received the degree of D.D. from Harvard University, U.S.A., in 1793. He married three times. His first wife was Beatrix, daughter of Andrew Simpson, an Edinburgh merchant. By her he had four children. His second wife was Lady Mary Ann Carnegie, youngest daughter of George, Earl of Northesk. He married her in 1797, and she died the following year. His third wife was Lady Elizabeth Hope, seventh daughter of John, Earl of Hopetoun. He married her in 1799. She died in 1801. Among Dr Kemp's publications was *Observations on the Islands of Shetland* (1801).

Towards the close of his life, this man, who had been so censorious of the affair between his most famous parishioner and Burns, was himself involved in a scandal which only his death saved from ruining him. He became a kind of father-confessor to Lady Colquhoun of Luss, whose daughter his son, David, a weaver, had married. Sir James Colquhoun, 24th of Colquhoun and 26th of Luss, took an action for divorce from his wife on the grounds of her association with Dr Kemp. But in April 1805 both Sir James and Dr Kemp died. The preliminary proceedings, however, excited the interest of John Ramsay of Ochtertyre, who kept asking his cousin, Mrs Dundas, for the latest news about the case from Edinburgh. He commented:

'An intrigue with a Lady that has been near 30 years married was never I suppose heard of in the commissary court. The love of the suitors for Penelope whose husband had been away for twenty years, appears incredible to us moderns. It would seem however they courted her for power and pelf, of which she had the disposal . . . father confessors were better suited to popery than to presbytery or semi-methodism.' And again: 'Lady Colquhoun might have made religion her darling luxury, without trusting too much to a protestant father confessor, whose son, under that guise, stole the heart of her fair amiable daughter! The popish ones had no sons bred wabsters to spread their nets.'

The Reverend George William Auriol Hay Drummond (1761–1807), in *A Town Eclogue* (Edinburgh, 1804), satirised Kemp, who was also Secretary of the Society in Scotland for Propagating Christian Knowledge, as Maskall:

'Pent in a close, stampt with religious
name,
Vile Maskall skulks in everlasting
shame. . . .
Seduce a daughter from her driv'ling sire
Doom to a weaver's arms the well-
born miss,
Then greet the mother with a holy kiss.

See Plate 9.

Kemp, Mrs (d. 1796)

In a letter from 'Clarinda' to Burns, she mentions being at a Mrs Kemp's house. This lady was probably Beatrix, the first wife of 'Clarinda's' minister. She was the daughter of Andrew Simpson, an Edinburgh merchant. She was married in 1780.

Kenmure, seventh Viscount. See Gordon, John.

Kennedy, Jean (b. 1738)

Daughter of Alexander Kennedy, she was born in Crossraguel, and with her sister Anne kept a small inn at the Kirk-town of Kirkoswald (any little village with a parish church was called 'The Kirkton' or 'Kirktown'). Her tavern was a respectable one, and she and her sister were known as 'The Leddies'. She is the 'Kirkton Jean' of 'Tam O' Shanter', but in the poem, instead of the inn being described as 'The Leddies' House', as it was in reality, Burns called it 'The Lord's House'.

Kennedy, John (1757–1812)

A kinsman of Mrs Gavin Hamilton, he was factor to the Earl of Dumfries at Dumfries House, near Cumnock, when Burns met him in 1786. Later, he became the Earl of Breadalbane's factor. After holding this post for eighteen years, he retired to Edinburgh. He is buried in the old Carlton burial ground. He was for a time a close friend of the poet, who sent him copies of several of his poems. He probably got the first glimpse of 'The Gowan', as 'To a Mountain Daisy' was originally called. On 3rd March 1786, Burns, in answer to Kennedy's request, seems to have sent it to him along with 'The Cotter's Saturday Night', and accompanied it with the lines 'To John Kennedy'. Of the 'Cottager', as Burns called it, the poet said in his covering note: 'If you have a leisure minute I should be glad if you would copy it,

and return me either the original or the transcript, as I have not a copy of it by me, and I have a friend who wishes to see it.' The enclosed lines 'To John Kennedy' invited the recipient to have a drink with the poet at Dow's, should he ever come in 'by Mauchlin Corse' (so called from the cross, or corse that stood there):

'Now if ye're ane o' warl's folk, [a
                              worldly person
Wha rate the wearer by the cloak,
An' sklent on poverty their joke
    Wi' bitter sneer,
Wi' you nae friendship I will troke,
    Nor cheap nor dear.

'But if, as I'm informèd weel,
Ye hate as ill's the vera deil
The flinty heart, that canna feel—
    Come, Sir, here's to you!
Hae, there's my haun, I wiss you weel,
    An' gude be wi' you.'

The following month, Kennedy wrote asking for subscription papers for the Kilmarnock Edition, and, in sending them, Burns said of 'The Gowan': 'I am a good deal pleased with some sentiments myself, as they are just the native querulous feelings of a heart which, as the elegantly melting Gray says, "melancholy has marked for her own".' A copy of the wholly successful 'To a Mouse', later critics have considered that it is just this contrived 'elegantly melting' Augustan element which makes 'To a Mountain Daisy' comparatively unsuccessful.

When Burns was on the point of going to Greenock to join the *Nancy* for Jamaica, he wrote a farewell note to Kennedy, dated August 1786, from Kilmarnock. It finishes with the stanza:

'Farewell, dear Friend! may gude luck
                              hit you
And 'mong her favourites admit you!
If e'er Detraction shore to smit you,
    May nane believe him!
And any deil that thinks to get you,
    Good Lord, deceive him.'

Kennedy may have been the 'Factor John' in 'The Kirk's Alarm', though either John M'Murdo, or John Tennant of Glenconner, may have been meant.

Kennedy, Margaret or Peggy (1766–95)

The daughter of the factor to the Earl of Cassilis, Robert Kennedy of Daljarrock, near Colmonel, and younger sister of Mrs Gavin Hamilton, at whose house Burns met her when she was eighteen. Being much impressed by her beauty and wit, he wrote the song, 'Young Peggy' in her honour, enclosing it in a letter to her. It was published in 1787 in Johnson's *Scots Musical Museum*.

The year previous to their meeting, Miss Kennedy had met Capt. (later Col.) Andrew M'Doual of Logan, Wigtonshire, who is mentioned in the second Heron Election Ballad as 'Sculdudd'ry', and in 1794 bore him a daughter. She tried to get him to declare that she had been married to him privately, but the Captain denied both his paternity and the marriage. An action was raised, but she died before it was concluded.

In 1798, the Consistorial Court declared in favour of the marriage and the child's legitimacy, but the legitimacy decision was reversed by the Court of Session, who, however, awarded damages of £3,000 to the dead woman, and alimentary provision for the child.

Kennedy, Thomas (d. 1846)

According to Chambers, Burns had known Kennedy when the poet was a boy. Burns later came upon him when Tam was a pedlar. In his old age, Kennedy knew William Cobbett who printed the following lines, either from manuscript or from recollection.

'As Tam the chapman on a day
Wi' Death forgather'd by the way,
                          [*had a meeting*]
Weel pleas'd he greets a wight sae
                          famous,

And Death was nae less pleas'd wi'
                          Thomas.
Wha cheerfully lays down his pack,
And there blaws up a hearty crack;
His social, friendly, honest heart
Sae tickled Death, they couldna part;
Sae, after viewing knives and garters,
Death taks him hame to gie him
                          quarters.'

Kennedy died in Homor, Courtland County, New York.

Kennedy Family

The Earls of Cassilis, whose family name was Kennedy, were the chief family in Carrick. Burns mentions them in his song 'My Lady's Gown there's Gairs upon't':

'My Lady's white, my Lady's red,
And the kith and kin o' Cassilis
                          blude . . .'

Ker, Mr

A friend of Mr Ainslie, Senior, whom Burns met at the Farmer's Club in Kelso, while on his Border tour. He described him in his *Journal* as: 'a most gentlemanly, clever, handsome fellow, a widower with some fine children, his mind and manner astonishingly like my dear old friend Robert Muir, in Kilmarnock; everything in Mr Ker's most elegant'.

He accompanied Burns into England, after Ainslie had returned to Edinburgh.

Ker, William

Postmaster of Edinburgh. He had the reputation of being willing to frank a letter for a friend. Burns made a reference to this habit in a letter to Mrs Dunlop from Ellisland on 17th December 1788: 'I shall give you the verses on the other sheet, as I suppose Mr Ker will save you the postage.' The 'Verses' were 'An old song and tune which [had] often thrilled my soul'—'Auld Lang Syne'.

Kilmarnock

A town in Ayrshire about sixteen miles from Ayr, created a Burgh of Barony under the Boyd family in 1591. In Burns's day, it had a population of almost 3,000, and was mainly a market town, although it was known for its 'Kilmarnock Cowls'. It has since become industrial, carpets, agricultural machinery and whisky being the among its wares. It was the birthplace of poet and essayist Alexander Smith, in 1830.

It was at Kilmarnock, from the press of John Wilson—his premises are marked by a plaque—that Burns's *Poems* were first published on 31st July 1786. Stitched in a blue-grey cover, the volume cost three shillings. A perfect copy today fetches over £2,000.

Burns described the circumstances preceding his decision to publish, in his Autobiographical Letter: 'I weighed my productions as impartially as in my power; I thought they had merit; and 'twas a delicious idea that I would be called a clever fellow, even though it should never reach my ears a poor Negro-driver, or perhaps a victim to that inhospitable clime gone to the world of Spirits. I can truly say that pauvre Inconnu as I then was, I had pretty nearly as high an idea of myself and my works as I have at the moment. It is ever my opinion that the great, unhappy mistakes and blunders, both in a rational and religious point of view, of which we see thousands daily guilty, are owing to their ignorance, or mistaken notions of themselves. To know myself had been all along my constant study. I weighed myself alone; I balanced myself with others; I watched every means of information how much ground I occupied both as a Man and as a Poet: I studied assiduously Nature's DESIGN where she seem'd to have intended the various LIGHTS and SHADES in my character. I was pretty sure my poems would meet with some applause; but at the worst, the roar of the Atlantic would deafen the voice of

Censure, and the novelty of west-Indian scenes make me forget Neglect.

'I threw off six hundred copies, of which I had got subscriptions for about three hundred and fifty. My vanity was highly gratified by the reception I met with from the Publick; besides pocketing, all expences deducted, near twenty pounds.'

See Plate 5

Kilmarnock Edition, Reviews of the

Burns's *Poems Chiefly In The Scottish Dialect*—The 'Kilmarnock Edition'—was published by John Wilson of Kilmarnock on 31st July 1786, at the cost of three shillings per copy. Six hundred and twelve copies were printed and the edition was sold out in just over a month after publication. The following reviews of the volume were published:

From *The Edinburgh Magazine*, October 1786 (by Dr Robert Anderson):

'When an author we know nothing of solicits our attention, we are but too apt to treat him with the same reluctant civility we show a person who has come unbidden into company. Yet talents and address will gradually diminish the distance of our behaviour, and when the first unfavourable impression has worn off, the author may become a favourite, and the stranger a friend. The poems we have just announced may probably have to struggle with the pride of learning and the partiality of refinement; yet they are entitled to particular indulgence. Who are you, Mr Burns? Will some surly critic say; at what university have you been educated? What languages do you understand? What authors have you particularly studied? Whether has Aristotle or Horace directed your taste? Who has praised your poems, and under whose patronage are they published? In short, what qualifications entitle you to instruct or entertain us? To the questions of such a catechism, perhaps, honest Robert Burns would make no satisfactory answer. My good sir, he might say, I am a poor country man. I was bred up at the School of Kilmarnock, I understand no languages but my own. I have studied Allan Ramsay and Fergusson. My poems have been praised at many a fireside, and I ask no patronage for them if they deserve none. I have not looked at mankind through the spectacles of books! "An ounce of mother wit you know, is worth a pound of clergy", and Homer and Ossian, for anything that I have heard, could neither read nor write. The author is indeed a striking example of native genius bursting through the obscurity of poverty and the obstructions of laborious life, and when we consider him in this light, we cannot help regretting that wayward fate has not placed him in a more favoured situation. Those who view him with the severity of lettered criticism, and judge him by the fastidious rules of art, will discover that he has not the doric simplicity of Ramsay, or the brilliant imagination of Fergusson, but those who admire the exertions of untutored fancy, and are blind to many faults for the sake of numberless beauties, his poems will afford singular gratification. His observations on human characters are acute and sagacious, and his descriptions are lively and just. Of rustic pleasantry he has a rich fund, and some of his softer scenes are touched with inimitable delicacy. He seems to be a boon companion, and often startles us with a dash of libertinism which will keep some readers at a distance. Some of his subjects are serious, but those of the humorous kind are the best. It is not meant, however, to enter into a minute investigation of his merits, as the copious extracts we have subjoined will enable our readers to judge for themselves. The character Horace gives to Ofellus is particularly applicable to him: *"Rusticus abnormis sapiens, crassaque Minerva".*'

(Here follows the 'Address to the Deil', and long quotations from the 'Epistle to

J. Lapraik', 'The Holy Fair', and 'Hallowe'en'.)

From *The Monthly Review*, December 1786:

'*Poeta nascitur non fit* is an old maxim, the truth of which has been generally admitted; and although it be certain that, in modern times, many verses are manufactured from the brain of their authors with as much labour as the iron is drawn into form under the hammer of the smith, and required to be afterwards smoothed by the file with as much care as the burnishers of Sheffield employ to give the last finish to their wares; yet, after all, these verses, though ever so smooth, are nothing but *verses*, and have no genuine title to the name of *Poems*. The humble bard, whose work now demands our attention, cannot claim a place among these polished versifiers. His simple strains, artless and unadorned, seem to flow without effort from the native feelings of the heart. They are always nervous, sometimes inelegant, often natural, simple and sublime. The objects that have obtained the attention of the author are humble; for he himself, born in a low station, and following a laborious employment, has had no opportunity of observing scenes in the higher walks of life; yet his verses are sometimes struck off with a delicacy and artless simplicity that charms like the bewitching though irregular touches of a Shakespeare. We regret that these poems are written in some measure in an unknown tongue, which must deprive most of our readers of the pleasure they would otherwise naturally create; being composed in the Scottish dialect, which contains words that are altogether unknown to an English reader: beside, they abound with allusions to modes of life, opinions, and ideas of the people in a remote corner of the country, which would render many passages obscure, and consequently uninteresting, to those who perceive not the forcible accuracy of the picture of the object to

which they allude. This work, therefore
can only be fully relished by the natives
of that part of the country where it was
produced, but by such of them as have a
taste sufficiently refined to be able to
relish the beauties of Nature, it cannot
fail to be prized.

'By what we can collect from the
poems themselves, and the short preface to
them, the author seems to be struggling
with poverty, though cheerfully supporting
the fatigues of a laborious employment.
He thus speaks of himself in one of the
poems:

"The star that rules my luckless lot,
Has fated me the russet coat,
And damn'd my fortune to the groat;
    But, in requit,
Has blest me wi' a random-shot
    O' country wit."

He afterwards adds:

"This life, sae far's I understand,
Is a' enchanted fairy-land,
Where Pleasure is the magic-wand,
    That, wielded right,
Maks hours like minutes, hand in hand
    Dance by fu'light.

"The magic wand then let us wield;
For, ance that five-and forty's speel'd,
See, crazy, weary, joyless Eild,
    Wi' wrinkled face,
Comes hostin', hirplin', owre the field,
    Wi' creepin' pace.

"When ance life's day draws near the
                        gloamin',
Then fareweel vacant careless roamin';
And fareweel cheerfu' tankards foamin',
    And social noise;
And fareweel, dear deluding woman!
    The joy of joys!"

'Fired with the subject, he then bursts
into a natural warm, and glowing description of youth:

"O Life! how pleasant is thy morning,
Young Fancy's rays the hills adorning!
Cold-pausing Caution's lesson scorning

We frisk away,
Like schoolboys, at the expected
                        warning,
    To joy and play.

"We wander there, we wander here,
We eye the rose upon the brier,
Unmindful that the thorn is near,
    Among the leaves;
And though the puny wound appear,
    Short while it grieves."

' "None of the following works"
(we are told in the Preface) "were ever
composed with a view to the press. To
amuse himself with the little creations of
his own fancy, among the toil and fatigues
of a laborious life; to transcribe the various
feelings, the loves, the griefs, the hopes, the
fears in his own breast; to find some kind
of counterpoise to the struggle of a world,
always an alien scene, a task uncouth to the
poetical mind—these were his motives for
courting the Muses, and in these he found
poetry its own reward."

'These poems are chiefly in the comic
strain. Some are of the descriptive cast,
particularly "Hallowe'en", which contains a lively picture of the magical tricks
that are still practised in the country at that
season. It is a valuable relic which, like
Virgil's Eighth Eclogue, will preserve the
memory of these simple incantations long
after they would otherwise have been
lost. It is very properly accompanied
with notes explaining the circumstances to
which the poem alludes. Sometimes the
poems are in the elegiac strain, among
which class the reader will find much of
Nature in the lines "To a Mouse",
on turning up her nest with the plough, in
November 1785, and those "To A Mountain Daisy", on turning one down with
the plough in April 1786. In these we
meet with a strain of that delicate tenderness which renders the Idylls of Madame
Deshouliers so peculiarly interesting. Some
of the poems are in a more serious strain;
and as these contain fewer words that
are not pure English than the others, we

shall select one as a specimen of our author's manner.

'The poem we have selected exhibits a beautiful picture of that simplicity of manners which still, we are assured on the best authority, prevails in those parts of the country where the author dwells. That it may be understood by our readers, it is accompanied by a Glossary and Notes, with which we have been favoured by a friend who thoroughly understands the language, and has often, he says, witnessed with his own eyes that pure simplicity of manners which are delineated with the most faithful accuracy in this little performance. We have used the freedom to modernise the orthography a little, wherever the measure would permit, to render it less disgusting to our readers south of the Tweed. [Here follows a copy of "The Cotter's Saturday Night", with a few minor changes in the orthography.]

'These stanzas are serious. But our author seems to be most in his element when in the sportive, humorous strain. The poems of this cast, as hath been already hinted, so much abound with provincial phrases and allusions to local circumstances, that no extract from them would be sufficiently intelligible to our English readers.

'The modern ear will be somewhat disgusted with the measure of many of these pieces, which is faithfully copied from that which was most in fashion among the ancient Scottish bards, but has been, we think with good reason, laid aside by the later poets. The versification is, in general, easy, and it seems to have been a matter of indifference to our author in what measure he wrote. But if ever he should think of offering anything more to the public, we are of opinion his performances would be more highly valued were they written in measures less antiquated. The few Songs, Odes, Dirges, etc. in this collection are very poor in comparison with the other pieces. The author's mind is not sufficiently stored

with brilliant ideas to succeed in that line.

'In justice to the reader, however, as well as the author, we must observe that this collection may be compared to a heap of wheat carelessly winnowed. Some grain of a most excellent quality is mixed with a little chaff and half-ripened corn. How many splendid volumes of poems come under our review, in which, though the mere chaff be carefully separated, not a single atom of perfect grain can be found, all being light and insipid! We never reckon our task fatiguing when we can find, even among a great heap, a single pearl of price; but how pitiable is our lot when we must toil and toil and can find nothing but tiresome uniformity, with neither fault to rouse nor beauty to animate the jaded spirits!'

From *The Lounger,* December 1786 (by Henry Mackenzie):

'To the feeling and susceptible there is something wonderfully pleasing in the contemplation of genius, of that supereminent reach of mind by which some men are distinguished. In the view of highly superior talents, as in that of great and stupendous natural objects, there is a sublimity which fills the soul with wonder and delight, which expands it, as it were, beyond its usual bounds, and which, investing our nature with extraordinary honours, interests our curiosity and flatters our pride.

'This divinity of genius, however, which admiration is fond to worship, is best arrayed in the darkness of distant and remote periods, and is not easily acknowledged in the present time, or in places with which we are perfectly acquainted. Exclusive of all the deductions which envy or jealousy may sometimes be supposed to make, there is a familiarity in the near approach of persons around us, not very consistent with the lofty ideas which we wish to form of him who has led captive our imagination in the triumph of his fancy, overpowered our feelings with the tide of passion, or enlightened our reason with the investigation of hidden truths. It may be that, "in the olden time", genius had some advantages which tended to its vigour and its growth, but it is not unlikely that, even in these degenerate days, it rises much oftener than it is observed; that in "the ignorant present time" our posterity may find names which they will dignify, though we neglected, and pay to their memory those honours which their contemporaries have denied them.

'There is, however, a natural and, indeed, a fortunate vanity in trying to redress this wrong which genius is exposed to suffer. In the discovery of talents generally unknown, men are apt to indulge the same fond partiality as in all other discoveries which they themselves have made; hence we have had repeated instances of painters and of poets, who have been drawn from obscure situations, and held forth to public notice and applause by the extravagant encomiums of their introducers, yet in a short time have sunk again to their former obscurity, whose merit, though perhaps somewhat neglected, did not appear much under-valued by the world, and could not support, by its own intrinsic excellence, the superior place which the enthusiasm of its patrons would have assigned it. I know not if I shall be accused of such enthusiasm and partiality when I introduce to the notice of my readers a poet of our own country, with whose writings I have lately become acquainted; but if I am not greatly deceived, I think I may safely pronounce him a genius of no ordinary rank. The person to whom I allude is Robert Burns, an Ayrshire ploughman, whose poems were some time ago published in a country town in the west of Scotland, with no other ambition, it would seem, than to circulate among the inhabitants of the country where he was born, to obtain a little fame from those who have heard of his talents. I hope I

shall not be thought to assume too much if I endeavour to place him in a higher point of view, to call for a verdict of his country on the merit of his works, and to claim for him those honours which their excellence appears to deserve.

'In mentioning the circumstances of his humble station, I mean not to rest his pretensions solely on that title or to urge the merits of his poetry when considered in relation to the lowness of his birth, and the little opportunity of improvement which his education could afford. These particulars, indeed, might excite our wonder at his productions; but his poetry, considered abstractedly, and without the apologies arising from his situation, seems to me fully entitled to command our feelings and to obtain our applause.

'One bar, indeed, his birth and education have opposed to his fame—the language in which most of his poems are written. Even in Scotland the provincial dialect which Ramsay and he have used is now read with a difficulty which greatly damps the pleasure of the reader; in England it cannot be read at all, without such a constant reference to a glossary as nearly to destroy the pleasure.

'Some of his productions, however, especially those of the grave style, are almost English. From one of these I shall first present my readers with an extract, in which I think, they will discover a high tone of feeling, a power and energy of expression, particularly and strongly characteristic of the mind and the voice of a poet. 'Tis from his poem entitled "The Vision", in which the genius of his native county, Ayrshire, is thus supposed to address him:

"With future hope, I oft would gaze
Fond, on thy little early ways.
Thy rudely caroll'd chiming phrase,
    In uncouth rhymes;
Fired at the simple artless lays
    Of other times.

"I saw thee seek the sounding shore,
Delighted with the dashing roar;
Or when the north his fleecy store
      Drove thro' the sky,
I saw, grim Nature's visage hoar
      Struck thy young eye.

"Or when the deep-green mantled
                                    earth
Warm cherish'd ev'ry flow'ret's birth,
And joy and music pouring forth
      In ev'ry grove,
I saw thee eye the general mirth
      With boundless love.

"When ripen'd fields, and azure skies,
Called forth the reaper's rustling noise,
I saw thee leave their ev'ning joys,
      And lonely stalk,
To vent thy bosom's swelling rise,
      In pensive walk.

"When youthful love, warm-
                              blushing, strong,
Keen-shivering shot thy nerves along,
Those accents, graceful to thy tongue,
      Th' adorèd *Name*,
I taught thee how to pour in song,
      To sooth thy flame.

"I saw thy pulse's maddening play,
Wild send thee Pleasure's devious way,
Misled by Fancy's meteor ray,
      By passion driven;
But yet the light that led astray
      Was light from heaven.

'Of strains like the above, solemn and
sublime, with that rapt and inspired
melancholy in which the Poet lifts his
eye "above this visible diurnal sphere",
the poems entitled "Despondency", "The
Lament", "Winter, a Dirge", and the
"Invocation to Ruin", afford no less
striking examples. Of the tender and the
moral specimens equally advantageous
might be drawn from the elegiac verses
entitled "Man was made to mourn",
from "The Cotter's Saturday Night", the
stanzas "To a Mouse", or those "To a
Mountain Daisy', on turning it down
with the plough in April 1786. This last

poem I shall insert entire, not from its
superior merit, but because its length
suits the bounds of my paper: [Here
follows 'To A Mountain Daisy'.]

'I have seldom met with an image more
truly pastoral than that of the lark in the
second stanza. Such strokes as these mark
the pencil of the poet, which delineates
Nature with the precision of intimacy, yet
with the delicate colouring of beauty and
of taste. The power of genius is not less
admirable in tracing the manners than in
painting the scenery of Nature. That
intuitive glance with which a writer like
Shakespeare discerns the characters of men,
with which he catches the many changing
lines of life, forms a sort of problem in
the science of mind, of which it is easier to
see the truth than to assign the cause.

'Though I am far from meaning to
compare our rustic bard to Shakespeare,
yet whoever will read his lighter and more
humorous poems, his "Dialogue of the
Dogs", his "Dedication to G—— H——
Esq.", his "Epistle to a Young Friend",
and "To W. S——n", will perceive with
what uncommon penetration and sagacity
this heaven-taught ploughman, from his
humble unlettered station, has looked
upon men and manners.

'Against some passages of these last
mentioned poems it has been objected
that they breathe a spirit of libertinism and
irreligion. But, if we consider the ignorance and fanaticism of the lower
class of the people in the country where
these poems were written, a fanaticism of
that pernicious sort which sets faith in
opposition to good works, the fallacy and
danger of which a mind so enlightened as
our poet's could not but perceive, we shall
not look upon his lighter muse as the
enemy of religion (of which in several
places he expresses the justest sentiments)
though she has been somewhat unguarded
in her ridicule of hypocrisy.

'In this, as in other respects, it must be
allowed that there are exceptional parts
of the volume he has given to the public,

which caution would have suppressed, or correction struck out; but poets are seldom cautious and our poet had, alas! no friends or companions from whom correction could be obtained. When we reflect on his rank in life, the habits to which he must have been subject, and the society in which he must have mixed, we regret perhaps more than wonder that delicacy should be so often offended in perusing a volume in which there is so much to interest and please us.

'Burns possesses the spirit as well as the fancy of a poet. That honest pride and independence of soul which are sometimes the muse's only dower, break forth on every occasion in his works. It may be then, I shall wrong his feelings while I indulge my own, in calling the attention of the public to his situation and circumstances. That condition, humble as it was, in which he found content, and wooed the muse, might not be deemed uncomfortable; but grief and misfortunes have reached him there; and one or two of his poems hint, what I have learned from some of his countrymen, that he has been obliged to form the resolution of leaving his native land, to seek under a West Indian clime, that shelter and support which Scotland has denied him. But I trust means may be found to prevent this resolution from taking place; and to do my country no more than justice when I suppose her ready to stretch out her hand to cherish and retain this native poet, whose 'wood-notes wild' possess so much excellence. To repair the wrongs of suffering or neglected merit, to call forth genius from the obscurity in which it had pined indignant, and place it where it may profit or delight the world; these are exertions which give to wealth an enviable superiority, to greatness and to patronage a laudable pride.'

From *The New London Magazine*, December 1786:

'We do not recollect to have ever met with a more signal instance of true and uncultivated genius than in the author of these poems. His occupation is that of a common ploughman, and his life has hitherto been spent in struggling with poverty. But all the rigours of fortune have not been able to repress the frequent efforts of his lively and vigorous imagination. Some of these poems are of a serious cast, but the strain which seems most natural to the author is the sportive and humorous. It is to be regretted that the Scottish dialect, in which these poems are written, must obscure the native beauties with which they appear to abound and renders the same unintelligible to an English reader. Should it, however, prove true that the author has been taken under the patronage of a great lady in Scotland, and that a celebrated professor has interested himself in the cultivation of his talents, there is reason to hope that his distinguished genius may yet be exerted in such a manner as to afford more generous delight. In the meantime we must admire the genuine enthusiasm of his untutored muse, and bestow the tribute of just applause on one whose name will be transmitted to posterity with honour.'

From *The New Town and Country Magazine*, August 1787:

'Robert Burns, we are informed, is a ploughman, but blessed by Nature with a powerful genius. His subjects are not, as might have been expected, confined to the objects which surrounded him; he is satirical as well as pastoral, and humorous as well as pathetic. These poems being "chiefly in the Scottish dialect" it must necessarily confine their beauties to a small circle of readers; however, the author has given good specimens of his skill in English. The following stanza is not only very elegant, but highly poetical.'

[Here follows the ninth stanza of 'The Cotter's Saturday Night', beginning:

'Oh happy love! where love like this is found'.]

It is marvellous that such true though somewhat stinted praise was given in that 'elegant' age to one like Burns, whose mission was to abolish the shamming and affected style of poetry then accepted as the only recognised standard.

From *The English Review*, February 1787:
'In an age that is satiated with literary pleasures, nothing is so grateful to the public taste as novelty. This ingredient will give a gust to very indifferent fare and lend a flavour to the produce of the home brewed vintage. Whatever excites the jaded appetite of an epicure will be prized, and a red herring from Greenock or Dunbar will be reckoned a *delice*. From this propensity in human nature a musical child, a rhyming milkwoman, a learned pig, or a Russian poet will "strut their hour upon the stage", and gain the applause of the moment. From this cause, and this alone, Stephen Duck, the thresher, and many other nameless names have glittered and disappeared like those bubbles of the atmosphere which are called falling stars.

'Robert Burns, the Ayrshire ploughman, whose poems are now before us, does not belong to this class of *obscurorum virorum*. Although he is by no means such a poetical prodigy as some of his *malicious* friends have represented, he has a genuine title to the attention and approbation of the public, as a natural, though not a legitimate, son of the muses.

'The first poems in this collection are of the humorous and satirical kind, and in these our author appears to be most at home. In his serious poems we can trace imitations of almost every English author of celebrity but his humour is entirely his own. His "Address to the Deil (Devil)", "The Holy Fair" (a country sacrament), and his "Epistle" in which he disguises an amour under the veil of partridge-shooting, are his masterpieces in this line; and happily in these instances his humour is neither local nor transient, for the devil, the world, and the flesh will always keep their ground. "The Vision" is perhaps the most poetical of all his performances. Revolving his obscure situation, in which there was nothing to animate pursuit or gratify ambition, comparing his humble lot with the more flourishing conditions of mercantile adventures, and vowing to renounce the unprofitable trade of verse for ever, there appeared to him a celestial figure: not one of the nine muses, celebrated in fiction, but the real muse of every inspired poet, the Genius of his native district and frequented scenes. This is an elegant and happy imagination. The form of Nature that first met his enamoured eyes is the muse of every inspired poet. The mountains, the forests, and the streams are the living volumes that impregnate his fancy and kindle the fire of genius. The address of this rural deity to him marks the character and describes the feelings of a poet:

"Of these am I—Coila my name:
And this district as mine I claim,
Where once the Campbells, chiefs of
                                    fame,
    Held ruling pow'r,
I mark'd thy embryo-tuneful flame,
    Thy natal hour.

"With future hope I oft would gaze
Fond, on thy little early ways,
Thy rudely-carroll'd, chiming phrase,
    In uncouth rhymes;
Fired at the simple, artless lays,
    Of other times.

"I saw thee seek the sounding shore,
Delighted with the dashing roar;
Or when the north his fleecy store
    Drove thro' the sky,
I saw grim Nature's visage hoar
    Struck thy young eye.

"Or when the deep green-mantled
                                    earth
Warm cherish'd every floweret's
                                    birth,
And joy and music pouring forth

In ev'ry grove;
I saw thee eye the general mirth
    With boundless love.

"When ripen'd fields, and azure skies,
Call'd forth the reaper's rustling noise,
I saw thee leave their evening joys,
    And lonely stalk,
To vent thy bosom's swelling rise
    In pensive walk.

"When youthful love, warm-blushing,
                                strong
Keen shivering shot thy nerves along
Those accents, grateful to thy tongue,
    Th' adorèd *Name*,
I taught thee how to pour in song
    To soothe thy flame."

'"Hallowe'en," or Even, gives a just and
literal account of the principal spells
and charms that are practised on that
anniversary among the peasants of Scotland, from the desire of prying into futurity,
but it is not happily executed. A mixture
of the solemn and burlesque can never
be agreeable.
    ' "The Cotter's (Cottager's) Saturday
Night" is, without exception, the best
poem in the collection. It is written in the
stanza of Spenser, which probably our
bard acquired from Thomson's "Castle
of Indolence" and Beattie's "Minstrel".
He describes one of the happiest and most
affecting scenes to be found in a country
life, and draws a domestic picture of
rustic simplicity, natural tenderness, and
innocent passion that must please every
reader whose feelings are not perverted.
    The odes "To a Mouse on turning up
her Nest" and "To a Mountain Daisy" are
of a similar nature, and will strike every
reader for the elegant fancy and the vein
of sentimental reflection that runs through
them. As the latter contains few provincial
phrases we shall present it to the reader.'
    [Here follows 'To A Mountain Daisy'.]
'The stanza of Mr Burns is generally
ill-chosen, and his provincial dialect
confines his beauties to one half of the

island. But he possesses the genuine characteristics of a poet; a vigorous mind, a
lively fancy, a surprising knowledge of
human nature, and an expression rich,
various, and abundant. In the plaintive
or pathetic he does not excel; his love-
poems (though he confesses, or rather
professes, a *penchant* to the *belle passion*)
are execrable; but in the midst of vulgarity
and commonplace, which occupy one
half of the volume, we meet with many
striking beauties that make ample compensation. One happy touch on the Eolian
harp from fairy fingers awakes emotions
in the soul that make us forget the ante-
cedent mediocrity or harshness of the
natural music.
    'The liberal patronage which Scotland
has extended to this self-taught bard
reflects honour on the country. If Mr
Burns has flourished in the shade of obscurity, his country will form higher
expectations from him when basking in
the sunshine of applause. His situation,
however, is critical. He seems to possess
too great a facility of composition and is
too easily satisfied with his own productions. Fame may be procured by novelty,
but it must be supported by merit. We
have thrown out these hints to our young
and ingenious author because we discern
faults in him which, if not corrected, like
the fly in the apothecary's ointment,
may give an unfortunate tincture and
colour to his future compositions.'
    Shorter notices also appeared within a
few months in the *New Annual Register*,
published in London, the *Northern Gazette*,
published in Aberdeen, and in the *Edinburgh Evening Courant* of 13th November
1787, which said of Burns two weeks
before he arrived in the Capital:
    'The county of Ayr is perhaps superior
to any in Scotland in number of Peers,
Nobles and wealthy Commoners; and
yet not one of them has upon this occasion
stepped forth as a patron to this man,
nor has any attempt been made to interest
the public in his favour. His poems are

read, his genius is applauded, and he is left to his fate.'

Kilpatrick, Nellie (1760–1820)

Burns's 'Handsome Nell', the poet's partner when he was harvesting in his fifteenth year. She was the daughter of Allan Kilpatrick, miller at Parclewan, near Dalrymple. She married the Laird of Newark's coachman, William Bone.

In the Autobiographical Letter, Burns tells how this 'bonie, sweet, sonsie lass', initiated him in 'a certain delicious Passion'. He 'looked and fingered over her hand, to pick out the nettle-stings and thistles.... Among her other love-inspiring qualifications, she sung sweetly; and 'twas her favourite reel to which I attempted giving an embodied vehicle in rhyme. I was so presumptive as to imagine that I could make verses like printed ones, composed by men who had Greek and Latin; but my girl sang a song which was said to be composed by a small country laird's son, on one of his father's maids, with whom he was in love; and I saw no reason why I might not rhyme as well as he ... Thus with me began Love and Poesy ...'

The tune to the song, 'O once I lov'd a bonny lass', has not come down to us.

Kirkpatrick, The Reverend Joseph (1750–1824)

Minister of Dunscore Parish (in which Ellisland is situated), from 1776 until 1806, when he removed to Wamphray. He married Anne M'Millan, daughter of the minister of Torthorwald. Burns attended Kirkpatrick's church, until he disagreed with Kirkpatrick's sermon on the centenary of the defeat of the Stuarts in 1688. This drew from Burns a letter, dated 8th November 1788, signed 'A Briton' and published in the *Evening Courant*. In it, Burns affirmed his loyalty to the Hanoverian line, but deplored the belittling of the Stuarts: 'The Stuarts have been condemned and laughed at for the folly and impracticability of their attempts in 1715 and 1745. That they failed, I bless my God most fervently; but cannot join in the ridicule against them. Who does not know that the abilities or defects of leaders and commanders are often hidden until put to the touchstone of exigence; and that there is a caprice of fortune, an omnipotence in particular accidents, and conjunctures of circumstances, which exalt us as heroes, or brand us as madmen, just as they are for or against us?'

Burns then went on to draw a modern parallel, in bold strokes: 'Man, Mr Printer, is a strange, weak, inconsistent being. Who would believe, Sir, that in this our Augustan age of liberality and refinement, while we seem so justly sensible and jealous of our rights and liberties, and animated with such indignation against the very memory of those who would have subverted them, who would suppose that a certain people, under our national protection, should complain, not against a Monarch and a few favorite advisers, but against our whole legislative body, of the very same imposition and oppression, the Romish religion not excepted, and almost in the very same terms as our forefathers did against the family of Stuart! I will not, I cannot, enter into the merits of the cause; but I dare say, the American Congress, in 1776, will be allowed to have been as able and as enlightened and, a whole Empire will say, as honest as the English Convention in 1688; and that the fourth of July will be as sacred to their posterity as the fifth of November is to us.'

But, the cause of freedom apart, Burns found Kirkpatrick hopelessly dull and narrow, as he told Alexander Cunningham on 11th March 1791: 'My Parish-priest ... is in himself one vast constellation of dullness, and from his weekly zenith rays out his contradictory stupidity to the no small edification and enlightening of the heavy and opaque pericraniums of his gaping Admirers.'

There is other testimony than that of Burns to Kirkpatrick's inadequacies. Robert Riddell, in certain *Addenda to the Statistical Account*, described Kirkpatrick's contribution to the original work as: 'the worst account yet printed, except the account of the parish of Terregles. Much more may be said of Dunscore, but the ignorance and stupidity of the minister is such, and so great a Mule is he, that no good can be done with him'.

Kirkpatrick, Thomas

A blacksmith in Stoop. Burns wrote a pithy mock epitaph on him:

'Here lies, 'mang ither useless matters, Auld Thomas wi' his endless clatters.'

Kirkwood, William

A horsedealer of Baillieston, who was supposed to have sold Burns a 'red-wud Kilburnie blastie' of a horse at Kilbirnie Fair. This beast is mentioned in 'The Inventory'.

L

Ladyman, Mr
See **Bacon, Mr**

Laigh Kirk
The parish church of Kilmarnock, which stands near the centre of the town. In Burns's day, the building dated from about the middle of the eighteenth century, though it stood on the site of a much older church. The Reverend William Lindsay was the first minister of the Moderate school to be inducted there. The church is mentioned in 'The Ordination'—'Swith to the Laigh Kirk, ane an' a''. Lindsay's induction was so much against popular sentiment, that a riot took place. The living belonged to the Earl of Glencairn. The church—rebuilt in 1802 after a fall of plaster caused a disaster which resulted in the death of twenty-nine people —stands on the other side of the Cross in Bank Street, into which the tower and its basement project. Tradition has it that the ground floor of the old church was once used as a prison.

Burns gives the internal history of the Laigh Kirk from the time of the Reverend William Lindsay to that of the Reverend James Mackinlay in 'The Ordination'.

The three people mentioned in the first verse of 'Tam Samson's Elegy—Mackinlay, Robertson and Tam Samson himself —are buried next each other, at the western angle of the north gable of the church.

Lambie, John
A Stevenston thatcher who, when interviewed by Grierson, claimed to have 'led the Plough when Burns turned up the mouse' at Lochlea. It had 'an uncommonly large nest'.

Lamie, James
An elder of Mauchline Church who was sent by the Kirk Session, along with William Fisher, to speak to Jean Armour's parents about their daughter being pregnant by Burns.

Land o' Cakes, The
Burns used this expression to describe Scotland in the opening line of his poem 'On the Late Captain Grose's Peregrinations Thro' Scotland':

'Hear, Land o' Cakes and brither Scots'.

Robert Fergusson had already used the expression in his poem 'The King's Birthday in Edinburgh':

'Oh, soldiers! for your ain dear sakes
For Scotland's, alias, Land o' Cakes.'

About the middle of the fourteenth century Froissart visited Scotland, and in his *Chronicles*, described the staple diet of the Scots soldier: 'Under the flap of his saddle, each man carries a broad plate of metal; behind the saddle, a little bag of oatmeal. When they have eaten too much . . . sodden flesh, and their stomach appears weak and empty, they place this plate over the fire, mix with water their oatmeal, and when the plate is heated, they put a little of the paste upon it, and make a thin cake, like a cracknel or biscuit, which they eat to warm their stomachs; it is therefore no wonder that they perform a longer day's march than other soldiers.'

This is the earliest recipe for, and tribute to, Scots oatcakes, known to me.

Lapraik, John (1727–1807)
An elderly farmer-bard who lived at Dalquhram, in the parish of Muirkirk, until he was ruined by the Ayr Bank failure of 1783, and forced to sell his property. He was at one time imprisoned for debt. Later, he moved, first to Muirkirk, where he leased a farm, and then to Muirsmill, where he became innkeeper and postmaster. He married, first, Margaret Rankine, sister of John Rankine of Adamhill, and second, Janet Anderson.

Lapraik was one of a number of local poets who provided Burns in his early days with a necessary literary environment. Lapraik had his poems put out by Wilson of Kilmarnock in 1788, with small success. One of them, which Lapraik apparently based on an anonymous piece in *Ruddiman's Weekly Magazine* for 14th October 1773, 'When I Upon Thy Bosom Lean', appeared in the *Scots Musical Museum*, possibly touched up by Burns.

Lapraik's real importance, however, is that his friendship with Burns stimulated the poet to write two of his best verse epistles to Lapraik. The first, dated 1st April 1785, follows the usual pattern of the eighteenth-century verse-epistle form —a scene-setting followed by a bouquet of fulsome compliment to the recipient, the main matter of the epistle, then a concluding section celebrating the pleasures of friendship and conviviality. In the 'First Epistle to John Lapraik', Burns sets out his poetic creed:

'I am nae poet, in a sense,
But just a rhymer, like, by chance,
An' ha'e to learning nae pretence;
    Yet, what the matter?
Whene'er my muse does on me glance,
    I jingle at her . . .

'Gi'e me ae spark o' Nature's fire,
That's a' the learning I desire;
Then, tho' I drudge thro' dub an' mire
    At pleugh or cart,
My Muse, tho' hamely in attire,
    May touch the heart.'

To this admirable outburst of perceptiveness, Lapraik duly replied in jauntier kind, sending his son to deliver it to Burns while he was sowing in a field at Mossgiel. So Burns sat down on 21st April to write again. The 'Second Epistle to John Lapraik' is mainly autobiographical in content. It details the bad luck which has been the writer's share, and leads to a declaration on the value of lowliness and contentment:

'Were this the charter of our state,
"On pain o' hell be rich an' great",
Damnation then would be our fate,
    Beyond remead;
But, thanks to heav'n, that's no the
                                        gate
    We learn our creed.

'For thus the royal mandate ran,
When first the human race began,
The social, friendly, honest man,
    Whate'er he be,
" 'Tis he fulfils great Nature's plan,
    An' none but he."

The 'Third Epistle to J. Lapraik.' dated 13th September 1785, poorer in quality than its predecessors, was first published in Cromek's *Reliques* in 1808.

Largs
A holiday resort on the Firth of Clyde. Burns refers to the battle of Largs in his poem 'Caledonia, A Ballad'. It took place in 1263, when Alexander III defeated King Haakon, thus breaking the Norse power in Scotland.

'But brave Caledonia in vain they
                                    assail'd,
    As Largs well can witness and
                                Loncartie tell.'

Lauder, Margaret (d. 1817)
Wife of the Reverend William Lindsay, minister of the Laigh Church, Kilmarnock, and once erroneously believed to have been the Earl of Glencairn's housekeeper. *See* **Lindsay, Reverend William.** Burns referred to her in 'The Ordination': 'Curst Common Sense, that imp o' hell, Cam' in wi' Maggie Lauder.'

There is a note in the Rob Rhymer Manuscript which says: 'I suppose the author here means Mrs Lindsay, wife to the late Rev. and worthy Mr Lindsay, as that was her maiden name, I am told. N.B.—He got the Laigh Kirk of Kilmarnock.'

Lauderdale, eighth Earl of. *See* **Maitland.**

Lawrie, The Reverend Dr Archibald (1768–1837)
Son of the Rev. George Lawrie, he was educated at Edinburgh University, where, as a student, he was friendly with Burns, whom he had previously met in the Manse at Newmilns. There is a note by Burns, dated 'Lawnmarket, Monday noon', which invites Lawrie to 'the Play'.

In 1799, he succeeded his father at Loudon Parish Church, Newmilns, to which, in 1793, he had been appointed as assistant. His first wife, Anne, was a sister of Dr James M'Kittrick Adair, who married one of Burns's heroines, Charlotte Hamilton. Archibald Lawrie remained at Loudon until his death. Under cover of a note from Mossgiel, dated 13th November 1786, Burns sent Lawrie two volumes of Ossian, which he had promised, and a collection of songs. On a previous visit to Newmilns, Archibald Lawrie apparently made a remark which Burns took as a rebuke to himself. When the parcel of books was opened, a slip of paper fell out; on it were the lines:

'Rusticity's ungainly form
    May cloud the highest mind;
But when the heart is nobly warm,
    The *good* excuse will find.

Propriety's cold, cautious rules
    Warm fervour may o'erlook;
But spare poor sensibility
    Th' ungentle, harsh rebuke.'

No letters to Lawrie survive after Burns's Edinburgh period. The lively Edinburgh student, to whom Burns lent books, accompanied to the theatre, and wrote in praise of port, had doubtless developed into a serious divine.

Lawrie, Christina or Christie (1766–1827)
A daughter of the Reverend George

Lawrie. When Burns was in Edinburgh, he enjoyed listening to her playing the spinet. Indeed, we have Gilbert's testimony that: 'The first time Robert heard the spinnet played upon was at the house of Dr Lawrie'. On 5th February 1787, Burns wrote to her father:

'By far the most agreeable hours I spend in Edinr must be placed to the account of Miss Lowrie and her Piano forte. I cannot help repeating to you and Mrs Lowrie a compliment that Mr M'kenzie, the celebrated 'Man of feeling', paid to Miss Christie the other night at the Concert. I had come in at an interlude, and sat down by him, till I saw Miss Lowrie in a seat not very far distant, and went up to pay my respects to her. On my return to Mr M'kenzie, he asked me who she was: I told him 'twas the daughter of a reverend friend of mine in the West country. He returned there was something very striking to his idea in her appearance. On my desiring to know what it was, he was pleased to say: "She has a great deal of the elegance of a well-bred Lady about her, with all the sweet simplicity of a Country girl".'

Christina Lawrie married a Glasgow bookseller, Alexander Wilson.

Lawrie, The Reverend Dr George (1727–99)
Son of a minister of Kirkmichael, George Lawrie was educated at Edinburgh University, ordained minister of Loudon, near Galston, in 1763. He remained there all his life. The following year, he married Mary Campbell, daughter of Archibald Campbell, Professor of Divinity at St Andrews University. Lawrie's eldest daughter, Christina (q.v.), was something of a musician. Lawrie's son, Archibald, born in 1768, married Dr Adair's sister Anne. In 1791, Glasgow University gave Lawrie a Doctorate of Divinity.

Lawrie occupies a place of importance in the Burns story because in 1786, impressed with the worth of the poems in the Kilmarnock Edition, he sent a copy to Dr Blacklock, then a figure of some influence in polite Edinburgh's quasi-literary society. On 4th September, Blacklock wrote enthusiastically to Lawrie, and expressed high praise for Burns's work. Lawrie showed Blacklock's letter to Gavin Hamilton, who in turn showed it to Burns. In the Autobiographical Letter to Dr Moore, Burns said: 'I had taken the last farewel of my few friends; my chest was on the road to Greenock; I had composed my last song I should ever measure in Caledonia, "The gloomy night is gathering fast", when a letter from Dr Blacklock to a friend of mine overthrew all my schemes by rousing my poetic ambition.'

There were probably deeper reasons why Burns finally decided that he need not flee the country, but the importance of Lawrie's interest in promoting the poet's reputation should not be minimised.

Burns was two weeks in Edinburgh before he visited Blacklock, by whose encouragement he set so much store. The blind old man wrote to Lawrie: 'By the by, I hear that Mr Burns is, and has been some time, in Edinburgh. The news I am sorry to have heard at second hand; they would have come much more welcome from the bard's own mouth.' Lawrie then wrote to Burns, who visited Blacklock, and after some delay, reported on 5th February 1787: 'In Dr Blacklock, whom I see very often, I have found what I would have expected in our friend, a clear head and an excellent heart.'

Lawrie apparently gave Burns some words of advice when taking him to task for his tardiness in calling on Blacklock; for in his reply, the poet makes plain the fact that even in the midst of 'hurried life and distracted attention', his peasant common sense did not desert him.

'I thank you, Sir, with all my soul for your friendly hints; though I do not need them so much as my friends are apt

to imagine. You are dazzled with newspaper accounts and distant reports, but in reality I have no great temptation to be intoxicated with the cup of Prosperity. Novelty may attract the attention of mankind a while; to it I owe my present eclat: but I see the time not distant far when the popular tide which has borne me to a height of which I am perhaps unworthy shall recede with silent celerity and leave me a barren waste of sand, to descend at my leisure to my former station. I do not say this in the affectation of modesty; I see the consequence is unavoidable, and am prepared for it.'

See Plate 12

Lawrie, Louisa (b. 1769)

Fourth and youngest daughter of the Rev. George Lawrie. She had in her possession for many years lines in Burns's handwriting, apparently part of a poem describing festivities at the Manse.

'The night was still, and o'er the hill
    The moon shone on the castle wa'
The mavis sang, while dew-drops hang
    Around her on the castle wa'.

Sae merrily they danced the ring
    Frae eenin till the cock did craw;
And aye the ower-word o' the spring
    Was Irvine's bairns are bonnie a'.'

The manse of Loudon parish church was on the River Irvine, and at that time the old castle of Newmills (now Newmilns) could be seen from it. See **Lawrie, Reverend Dr George** and **Lawrie, Reverend Dr Archibald**.

Like her sister, Christie, Louisa was also a keen musician, and earned Burns's praise for her spinet playing. She died unmarried.

Lawrie, Sir Robert (d. 1804)

Represented Dumfries in Parliament from 1774 until his death. The Lawrie baronetcy died with his son, Admiral Sir Robert Lawrie, in 1848, who left no heir.

The penultimate Sir Robert took part in the famous drinking bout celebrated in Burns's 'The Whistle' (*see* **Fergusson, Alexander**), but despite a gallant effort, could not stay the course:

'The gallant Sir Robert fought hard
to the end;
But who can with Fate and quart
bumpers contend?
Though Fate said, a hero should perish
in light;
So uprose bright Phoebus—and down
fell the knight.'

Lawrie of Redcastle, Walter Sloan

Figured in the second of Burns's Heron Election Ballads:

'But we winna mention Redcastle,
The body—e'en let him escape!
He'd venture the gallows for siller,
An' 'twere na the cost o' the
rape!'

His grandfather's name, according to Grierson, was 'Clautenpluck', and he changed it to 'Laurieston'. Grierson also tells us that Lawrie was 'a very little man— a landlady once made a bill reckoning one short of the number in company . . . she had missed Mr Laurie, pointing to him —"O" says she, "as for little master", clasping his hand, "I do not mind him!" ': which explains part of Burns reference to him.

Lawson

A local wine-merchant in Dumfries, whose 'port entrenchèd' the 'hold' of 'Maxwelton that baron Bold', Burns told Graham of Fintry in his 'Second Epistle' to him at the time of the Dumfries Burgh elections.

Lawson, Adam de Cardonnel

An antiquary and numismatist who assisted Grose and, according to a letter from Burns to Findlater, was 'acquainted with the Captain's motions'.

H

Lees, John

A shoemaker in Tarbolton, who as a lad, played 'blackfoot' to Burns in some of his courting expeditions. In 1837, when Lees was an old man, he told Chambers that when he had succeeded in bringing some girl out of doors, Burns would say 'Now, Jock, ye may gang hame'.

Leglen Wood

Leglen Wood, which stands on the banks of the Ayr about three miles from Auchencruive, was said by Blind Harry in his poem *Wallace* to be a favourite hiding place of the Scottish patriot. Burns came under the influence of this poem in Hamilton of Gilbertfield's abridged arrangement, in which we are told Wallace would go:

'Syne to the Leglen Wood, when it
was late,
To make a silent and a safe retreat.'

Writing to Mrs Dunlop from Mossgiel on 15th November 1786, Burns described his youthful pilgrimage to the spot:

'I chose a fine summer Sunday, the only day of the week in my power, and walked half a dozen of miles to pay my respects to the "Leglen Wood", with as much devout enthusiasm as ever pilgrim did to Loretto; and as I explored every den and dell where I could suppose my heroic Countryman to have sheltered, I recollect (for even then I was a Rhymer) that my heart glowed with a wish to be able to make a Song on him, equal to his merits.'

In 1929, a cairn was unveiled on a mound overlooking the River Ayr.

Leven, John (d. 1803?)

A Supervisor of Excise in Edinburgh, named in the almanac lists for 1801 as General Supervisor in Edinburgh, and so addressed by Burns, who wrote to him in March 1792 about a consignment of tin over which some irregularity had arisen. The important point about the letter, however, is that, business disposed of, Burns added: 'Mr Mitchell mentioned to you a ballad, which I composed and sung at one of his Excise Court dinners: here it is. . . . If you honor my ballad by making it one of your bon vivant effusions, it will secure it undoubted celebrity.'

The ballad was 'The Deil's awa wi' th' Exciseman'.

Lewars, Jessy (1778–1855)

The last of the poet's heroines, Jessy Lewars was the younger daughter of John Lewars, Supervisor of Excise at Dumfries. After her father's death in 1789, she lived with her brother John Lewars, the younger, who was a brother Excise officer of Burns. Their house was in Mill Vennel, now Burns Street, immediately opposite the Burns home. Jessy was friendly with both Robert and Jean. When in the Lewars' house, the poet heard Jessy singing a once popular song 'The Robin cam' to the Wren's Nest', and composed for the air his own words 'O wert thou in the cauld blast'.

During the illness which relentlessly wore the poet down during the last six months of his life, the eighteen-year-old Jessy helped to nurse him. Even on this, his last illness, and under the eyes of his wife, Burns whipped himself into a state of poetic passion over the kindly Jessy, fancying himself in love with her. 'O wert thou in the cauld blast', a splendid song, sounds the note of genuine passion. 'Talk not to me of savages', in which the poet takes 'Jessy's lovely hand' in his, 'a mutual faith to plight', does not. In 'Here's a health to ane I love dear', the second stanza admits the hopelessness of the poet's passion for Jessy:

'Altho' thou maun never be mine,
Altho' even hope is denied;
'Tis sweeter for thee despairing,
Than aught in the world beside—
                                    Jessy.'

In June 1796, Burns wrote to Johnson in Edinburgh: 'My wife has a very particular friend of hers, a young lady who sings well, to whom she wishes to present The Scots Musical Museum. If you have a spare copy, will you be so obliging as to send it by the very first Fly, as I am anxious to have it soon.' Johnson did as he was asked, and Burns inserted on the back of the title-page of the first volume, the lines beginning:

'Thine be the volumes, Jessy fair,
And with them take the Poet's
                                    prayer:—
That Fate may in her fairest page,
With every kindliest, best presage
Of future bliss, enrol thy name . . .'

Jessy Lewars looked after the poet's four small boys for a time after Burns's death. Robert, the eldest, remained with her for a year.

Long after Burns's death, Jessy Lewars gave Chambers her account of the poet. It testified to Burns's simple and temperate habits: 'as far as circumstances left Burns to his own inclinations. He was always anxious that his wife should have a neat and genteel appearance. In consequence, as she alleged, of the duties of nursing, and attending to her infants, she could not help being sometimes a little out of order. Burns disliked this, and not only remonstrated against it in a gentle way, but did the utmost that in him lay to counteract it by buying for her the best clothes he could afford. She was, for instance, one of the first persons in Dumfries who appeared in a dress of gingham—a stuff now common, but, as its first introduction, rather costly, and almost exclusively used by persons of superior conditions.'

Jessy Lewars married James Thomson, a writer in Dumfries, in June 1799, and had five sons and two daughters. She was buried in St Michael's Churchyard, Dumfries, not far from Burns's own grave.

See Plate 7

Liberty', 'Ode to

A lost poem by Burns. It is possible that the poems we now know as 'As I stood by yon roofless Tower' and 'Ode for General Washington's Birthday' constitute the two halves of the 'Ode to Liberty'.

Liberty', 'Tree of

A poem attributed to Burns, but about the genuineness of which there is some dispute. No original has come to light. Allan Cunningham rejected the poem. A manuscript of it was given to Chambers in 1838 by a Mr Duncan of Mosesfield, and Chambers printed it in the form given below. In 1867, Hately Waddell included it in his edition, remarking 'The poem is admitted to be in our Author's handwriting,' and stating that he does 'not doubt the genuineness of the authorship in this case', though he thinks it 'by no means in Burns's own style'. (Burns, of course, had several styles, ranging from his use of a thick and rich Lallans to a watery Augustan English!) Scott Douglas rejected the poem in 1877-9. The testimony of Gebbie in 1876 and Angellier in 1893 would appear to suggest that the manuscript was still in existence then. But until its restoration by Kinsley, the poem had not been included in British editions since Scott Douglas's Kilmarnock edition of 1876, although the Russian translator Marshak included it in his translated edition of Burns, without question.

Although internal evidence does suggest departure from Burns's usual practice in referring to England, and in the use of fewer Scots words than usual when he employed the 'Gilliecrankie' measure, Crawford has pointed out that 'thy England' refers to Alfred's England, so that 'Britain' would have been wholly inappropriate. Too much cannot be read into linguistic variances, for Burns used various consistencies of Scots on different occasions. Crawford suggests that the manuscript in Duncan of Mosesfield's

possession may have been a copy from an original, and that errors and misprints may have crept in. 'The Tree of Liberty' does seem to me likely to be the work of Burns, not only because its sentiments concur with his prose sentiments during the period of his life when it was written, and because no other poet known to have been writing in Scotland in the 1790s could possibly have produced it.

Trees of Liberty—'hung round with garlands of flowers, with emblems of freedom and various inscriptions', as Burns's friend Dr John Moore described them in *A Journal of a Residence in France*—were set up in many Scottish towns during the Reform agitation. No doubt there were religious overtones in the choice of the tree as the appropriate symbol, suggested by, amongst many other references, George Herbert's

'Man stole the fruit, but I must climb
                                    the Tree,
The Tree of Life, for all but only
                                    me.'

Since 'The Tree of Liberty' is now difficult to come by, the text is printed in full as it appeared in Chamber's edition of 1838:

'The Tree of Liberty'
(Here printed for the first time, from a manuscript in the possession of Mr James Duncan, Mossfield [sic], near Glasgow.)

'Heard ye o' the tree o' France,
   I watna what's the name o't;
Around it a' the patriots dance,
   Weel Europe kens the fame o't.
It stands where ance the Bastille stood,
   A prison built by kings, man,
When superstition's hellish brood
   Kept France in leading strings, man.

'Upo' this tree there grows sic fruit,
   Its virtues a' can tell, man,
It raises man aboon the brute,
   It maks him ken himsel, man.
Gif ance the peasant taste a bit,
   He's greater than a lord, man,

And wi' the beggar shares a mite
  O' a' he can afford, man.

'This fruit is worth a' Afric's wealth,
  To comfort us 'twas sent, man:
To gie the sweetest blush o' health,
  And mak us a' content, man.
It clears the een, it cheers the heart,
  Maks high and low gude friends,
                               man;
And he wha acts the traitor's part,
  It to perdition sends, man.

'My blessings aye attend the chiel,
  Wha pities Gallia's slaves, man,
And staw'd a branch, spite o' the deil,
  Frae yont the western waves, man.
Fair virtue water's it wi' care,
  And now she sees wi' pride, man,
How weel it buds and blossoms there,
  Its branches spreading wide, man.

'But vicious folk aye hate to see
  The works o' Virtue thrive, man;
The courtly vermin's banned the tree,
  And grat to see it thrive, man;
King Loui' thought to cut it down,
  When it was unco sma', man,
For this the watchman cracked his
                              crown,
Cut off his head and a', man.

'A wicked crew syne, on a time,
  Did tak a solemn aith, man,
It ne'er should flourish to its prime,
  I wat they pledged their faith, man,
Awa they gaed wi' mock parade,
  Like beagles hunting game, man,
But soon grew weary o' the trade,
  And wished they'd been at hame,
                               man.

'Fair freedom, standing by the tree,
  Her sons did loudly ca', man,
She sang a song o' liberty
  Which pleased them ane and a', man.
By her inspired, the new-born race
  Soon grew the avenging steel, man;
The hirelings ran—her foes gied chase
  And banged the despot weel, man.

'Let Britain boast her hardy oak,
  Her poplar and her pine, man,
Auld Britain ance could crack her joke,
  And o'er her neighbours shine, man,
But seek the forest round and round,
  And soon 'twill be agreed, man,
That sic a tree can not be found,
  Twixt London and the Tweed, man.

'Without this tree, alake this life
  Is but a vale o' woe, man;
A scene o' sorrow mixed wi' strife,
  Nae real joys we know, man,
We labour soon, we labour late,
  To feed the titled knave, man;
And a' the comfort we're to get
  Is that ayont the grave, man.

'Wi' plenty o' sic trees, I trow,
  The warld would live in peace, man;
The sword would help to mak a plough,
  The din o' war wad cease, man.
Like brethren wi' a common cause,
  We'd on each other smile, man;
And equal rights and equal laws
  Wad gladden every isle, man.

'Wae worth the loon wha wadna eat
  Sic halesome dainty cheer, man;
I'd gie my shoon frae aff my feet,
  To taste sic fruit, I swear, man.
Syne let us pray, auld England may
  Sure plant this far-famed tree, man;
And blythe we'll sing, and hail the day
  That gave us liberty, man.'

Lindsay, Isabella (b. 1764)

Daughter of a Jedburgh doctor, she
attracted the poet's attention when he
stopped there during his Border tour of
1787. He described her in his *Journal* as:
'. . . a good-humor'd amiable girl;
rather short *et embonpoint*, but handsome
and extremely graceful—beautiful hazle
eyes, full of spirit, and sparkling with
delicious moisture—an engaging face
and manner, un tout ensemble that speaks
her of the first order of female minds'.

She married Adam Armstrong twenty-
four days after having parted with Burns,

and in view of her engagement, was apparently much criticised locally for her 'easy manners' with the poet. Armstrong was employed by the Russian Government. On her marriage, she went with her husband to Russia, where she died without ever returning to Scotland.

Burns ended his description of his Jedburgh visit with another reference to Isabella: 'Sweet Isabella Lindsay, may Peace dwell in thy bosom, uninterrupted, except by the tumultuous throbbings of rapturous Love! That love-kindling eye must beam on another, not me; that graceful form must bless another's arms, not mine!'

Lindsay, The Reverend William (1725? -74)

The first New Licht minister to be inducted at the Laigh or Parish Church of Kilmarnock. Tradition has it that he received the living from the Earl of Glencairn through his wife Margaret Lauder, who was once thought to have been Glencairn's housekeeper, though this has now been disproved. She was the daughter of a Dalkeith writer.

Lindsay was inducted in 1764, much against popular sentiment; so much so that there was a riot at the ceremony. A shoemaker by the name of Hunter wrote a scoffing ballad about the occasion. Several people were sentenced to one month's imprisonment and whipped through the streets.

A curious anecdote was told by William Aiton of Hamilton about the affair. The minister of Fenwick fled on horseback from the scene. At the same time, an English commercial traveller, who asked the way to Glasgow, was told to follow the minister. This he did, to the terror of the minister, who thought he was being pursued by an outraged Calvinist. On finding his mistake when he halted at a farmer friend's house, traveller and minister laughed heartily, and the traveller stayed the night at the farmer's house.

Linkumdoddie

A locality, possibly imaginary, used by Burns in the song 'Willie Wastle dwalt on Tweed',

'The spot they ca'd it
                Linkumdoddie. . . .'

But the place where the singularly unprepossessing Mrs Wastle lived has been claimed to be 'five and a half miles from Broughton, on the road to Tweedsmuir and Moffat'. On the opposite bank of the Tweed, where Logan Water joins the river, there once stood a thatched cottage called Linkumdoddie. At the end of the eighteenth century, a weaver called Gideon Thomson lived there, but local history is silent about his wife. Burns stayed more than once at the Crook Inn, a few miles away from this place, when travelling between Dumfries and Edinburgh.

Dick points out that a popular seventeenth-century rhyme is quoted in *Scotch Presbyterian Eloquence Display'd* published in 1694. A Linton preacher remarks: 'Our bishops thought they were very secure this long time, like

"Willie Willie Wastle, I am in my
                                    castle;
A' the dogs in the town, dare not ding
                                    me down".'

Willie Wastle's Castle, Home, in the south-east corner of Roxburghshire, was besieged by Cromwell. The owner challenged Cromwell to do his worst. Cromwell did. The Castle was destroyed.

The tune 'Sic a wife as Willie had' goes back to *180 Loyal Songs* published in 1685, but bears no relation to Burns's tune: all of which suggests that Burns's brilliant comic song was inspired by some political seventeenth-century rant known to him but lost to us. Burns's song appeared in the *Scots Musical Museum*. The manuscript is in the British Museum.

Linlithgow

A royal burgh and the county town of West Lothian. The Palace of the Stewart kings, like St Michael's Kirk nearby, both replaced more ancient buildings on the same sites, yet are themselves very old. It was in the Palace of Linlithgow that Sir David Lyndsay's *Satire of the Three Estatis* was first performed in 1540 before James V; and earlier, in St Michael's Church that Sir David probably 'staged' the warning apparition, which, however, failed to persuade James IV not to set out upon the excursion which ended with his death on Flodden Field. Mary, Queen of Scots was born in Linlithgow Palace. The splendid building was burned by the carelessness of General Hawley's troops, fleeing from Prince Charles Edward Stewart's army on 3rd February 1746.

According to Dr William Wallace, Burns was made a freeman of Linlithgow on 16th November 1787. Wallace claimed that the burgess ticket had been preserved, and was worded: 'At Linlithgow, the sixteenth day of November, one thousand seven hundred and eighty seven years, the which day, in the presence of James Andrew, Esquire, Provost of the Burgh of Linlithgow; William Napier, James Walton, Stephen Mitchell, John Gibson, bailies: and Robert Speedie, Dean-of Guild, compeared Mr Robert Burns, Mossgiel Ayrshire, who was made and created Burgess and Guild Brother of the said Burgh, having given his oath of fidelity according to the form used thereanent.'

Burns did not sign the burgess roll. The alleged date of the ticket is a little puzzling in that there is no independent evidence to show that Burns was in Linlithgow on that day.

Burns visited Linlithgow during his Highland tour, in company with Nicol. On the first day of the trip, Saturday, 25th August 1787, Burns recorded: 'Linlithgow, the appearance of rude, decayed, idle grandeur—charmingly rural, retired situation—the old rough royal palace a tolerably fine, but melancholy ruin—sweetly situated on a small elevation on the brink of a Loch—shown the room where the beautiful injured Mary Queen of Scots was born—a pretty good old Gothic church—the infamous stool of repentance standing, in the old Romish way, in a lofty situation.

'What a poor, pimping business is a Presbyterian place of worship, dirty, narrow, squalid, stuck in a corner of old Popish grandeur such as Linlithgow and, much more, Melrose! ceremony and show, if judiciously thrown in, absolutely necessary for the bulk of mankind, both in religious and civil matters.'

Little, Janet (1759–1813)

Daughter of George Little, of Nether Bogside, Ecclefechan, Dumfriesshire. 'The Scottish Milkmaid' poet, in whose work Mrs Dunlop tried to interest Burns.

In December 1792, Burns spent four days at Dunlop House, when apparently Janet Little's poems, published in 1792, were discussed. Ten weeks later, Mrs Dunlop wrote reproving Burns for things he had said during the visit, some of them concerning the Milkmaid: 'Methinks I hear you ask me with an air that made me feel as I had got a slap in the face, if you must read all the few lines I had pointed out to your notice in poor Jenny's book. How did I upbraid my own conceited folly at that instant that had ever subjected one of mine to so haughty an imperious critic! I never liked so little in my life as at that moment the man whom at all others I delighted to honour. . . . I then felt for Mrs Richmond (Jenny Little), for you, and for myself, and not one of the sensations were such as I would wish to cherish in remembrance.'

Janet herself wrote to Burns, but it is not known if he ever replied to her 'part poetic and part prosaic' letter. At that time, she was in charge of the dairy at

Loudon Castle, where Mrs Dunlop's daughter, Mrs Henri, lived.

Later, Janet Little visited Ellisland in hopes of seeing the poet, but failed in her endeavour, as he was in bed with a broken arm.

She recorded in verse her disappointment in a piece beginning:

'Is't true? or does some magic spell
    My wond'ring eyes beguile?
Is this the place where deigns to dwell
    The honour of our isle?

'The charming Burns, the Muse's care,
    Of all her sons the pride.
This pleasure oft I've sought to share,
    But been of it denied.'

She was married to a labourer at Loudon Castle, John Richmond, a widower with five children, and twenty years older than Janet.

Lochlie

Lochlie, or Lochlea, to give it its modern spelling (Burns used both versions), lies two and a half miles north-east of Tarbolton, and just over three miles north-west of Mauchline. When William Burnes freed himself from his obligations at Mount Oliphant, and moved into David M'Lure's one hundred and thirty-acre farm of Lochlie, he agreed to pay the unduly high annual rental of a pound an acre. The farm stands about four hundred feet above sea-level, and looks south-west over a depression surrounded by low-hills. Though nowadays obviously fertile, it is not difficult to imagine how swampy it must have been at Whitsun, 1777, when it became William Burnes's last home. M'Lure, an Ayr Merchant, possibly lent Burnes some capital—'The nature of the bargain was such as to throw a little ready money in [my father's] hand at the commencement; otherwise the affair would have been impractical,' his son later recorded—but felt such confidence

in his new tenant that the exact terms of the lease were never set down in writing

It was while at Lochlie that Burns's need for companionship asserted itself, for Gilbert records that at this period Robert's 'attachment to [the society of women] became very strong, and he was constantly the victim of some fair enslaver'. During the winter of 1779, too, Burns attended a country dancing school 'to give my manners a brush', as he put it. His father profoundly disapproved. Robert also formed friendships with men, among them James Findlay, later the poet's instructor in the Exciseman's craft; John Wilson, schoolmaster, grocer, apothecary and subject of 'Death and Dr Hornbook'; and the local poetasters, David Sillar, Alexander 'Saunders' Tait, and John Rankine. Burns's rather formal love affair with Alison—or Ellison—Begbie, occurred while he was at Lochlie, probably in the early months of 1781. And, of course, he participated from Lochlie in the debates of the Tarbolton Bachelors' Club. From Lochlie, too, Burns set out for Irvine, probably early in the summer of 1781, to learn flax-dressing, a depressing experience which made him ill, and from which he returned to the family circle early in 1782.

The summer of 1782 was a cold season of exceptional storminess. Since 1779 Burnes had been in difficulties, probably paying no rent to M'Lure. The summer of 1782 was the last straw. In May 1783 a warrant of sequestration was operated against Burnes, by then a prematurely aged and dying man. Burnes took his case to the Court of Session in Edinburgh, and won: but this defence of his honour cost him all his savings. A few days later, he died, on 13th February 1784.

About four months before, Robert and his brother Gilbert, anticipating the inevitable, had secretly taken a lease from Gavin Hamilton on a farm of their own: Mossgiel.

The farm buildings which now stand at

Lochlie have no connection with those once lived in by Burns.

Lochmaben

'Marjory o' the many Lochs,
A Carlin auld and teugh.'

An ancient royal burgh in Annandale parish, Dumfriesshire. In the castle in the loch, Bruce's family once lived. Lochmaben, referred to in 'The Five Carlins', is about eight miles from Dumfries. Hallheaths, the home of the Walter Riddells at the time of Burns's death, lay to the east of Lochmaben.

Writing to Graham of Fintry from Ellisland on 9th December 1789, Burns, alluding to Lochmaben, remarked that he had 'the honor to be a Burgess of the town'. Neither record nor even mention of the conferring of this honour can now be found in the burgh records.

Lochryan Mss

Forty-two of Burns's letters to Mrs Dunlop, kept by the Dunlop family at Lochryan for almost a century, then owned by R. B. Adam of Buffalo, N.Y., and now in the Pierpont Morgan Library, New York. They were first published in 1898 in William Wallace's *Robert Burns and Mrs Dunlop*.

Lockhart, George

The name of Lockhart 'merchant and manufacturer', appeared in the first *Glasgow Directory*, 1787. Chambers conjectured that he lived at Miss Hanna Gray's lodgings 'above the post-office, Princes Street', referred to in the succeeding issue of the *Directory*, since Burns addressed his one surviving letter to Lockhart 'at Miss Gray's Glasgow'. Dated 18th July 1788, from Mauchline, it deals with the loveliness of 'the Miss Bailies I have seen in Edn^r', and promises copies of some 'rhyming things'. According to Chambers, Burns, on hearing Lockhart sing some of his songs for the

first time, is supposed to have remarked: 'I'll be hanged if I ever knew half their merit till now!'

Lockhart, John Gibson (1794–1854)

Scottish man of letters, editor and journalist, son-in-law and, later, biographer, of Sir Walter Scott. Lockhart was born in the manse of Cambusnethan, Lanarkshire, where his father, Dr John Lockhart, was minister. His mother, a woman of marked intellectual gifts, was the daughter of the Reverend John Gibson of Edinburgh. Lockhart went to Glasgow High School, until ill-health necessitated his removal. But at the age of twelve he was sent to Glasgow University, where his precocity, especially in Greek, won him a Snell exhibition at Oxford. Before his fourteenth birthday he had gained entry to Balliol College. His reading was wide, and he took a first in classics in 1813. He was called to the Scottish bar in 1816. The following year he met Goethe at Weimar, and soon after his return from Germany, joined the staff of *Blackwood's Magazine*. The brilliance of the criticism of Lockhart and John Wilson ('Christopher North') startled the Edinburgh world. But it was an aggressive, bitter brilliance, as is borne out by the reviews on Coleridge, Leigh Hunt and Keats, in which Lockhart is presumed to have had a share. In 1818 Lockhart met Scott, and in 1820, married Scott's eldest daughter, Sophia. The Lockharts wintered in Edinburgh, but spent the summers at Chiefswood, near Abbotsford. From 1818 to 1825, Lockhart worked prodigiously, his books including his best novel, *Reginald Dalton* (1823), and the perceptive *Peter's Letters to His Kinsfolk* (1819), which describes the Edinburgh scene, and has taken its place as a minor Scottish classic.

In 1825, Lockhart became editor of the *Quarterly Review*, though he continued to write for *Blackwood's*. His masterpiece was, of course, his great *Life of Sir Walter Scott*, published in seven volumes in 1837 and

1838. The revelation of Scott's transactions with the Ballantynes and Constable caused an outcry. In *The Ballantyne Humbug Handled*, that bitterness which seems to have eaten into Lockhart was again revealed. After Boswell's *Johnson*, Lockhart's *Scott* is the greatest biography in English. Its author made over the profits to Scott's creditors.

Lockhart's last years were clouded by misfortunes, which he bore stoically. His eldest boy (the 'Hugh Littlejohn' of Scott's *Tales of a Grandfather*) died in 1831; Scott himself the following year; Mrs Lockhart in 1837; and his surviving son, Walter, in 1852.

Lockhart resigned the editorship of the *Quarterly Review* in 1853, spent a winter in Rome, then was taken to Abbotsford by his daughter Charlotte (Mrs James Hope-Scott) where he died in the next room to that in which Scott had died. He lies in Dryburgh Abbey at Scott's feet.

Lockhart comes into the Burns story because in 1828, he produced his *Life of Robert Burns* as Volume XXIII of *Constable's Miscellany*. Because Lockhart was the only one of Burns's biographers to have been the author of a classic, his *Burns* has been treated with a respect and given a circulation which its merits, in spite of its graceful style, do not justify. For it is misleading and dishonest. As Snyder puts it: 'The best that one can say of it to-day . . . is that it occasioned Carlyle's review. It is inexcusably inaccurate from beginning to end, at times demonstrably mendacious, and should never be trusted in any respect or detail.'

Logan, Hugh (1739–1802)

Laird of Logan, Cumnock, and a local *bon viveur*. He is thought to be the subject of Burns's unpleasant mock-epitaph beginning 'Here lies Squire Hugh'.

Logan, Dr Hugh

For many years the only doctor in May-bole. According to one account, noted by Chambers: 'Spunkie Youthfu' Tammie', mentioned by Burns in a letter dated Mossgiel, 30th August 1786, to William Niven, was the younger brother of Dr Logan. The lad emigrated to, and died in, Jamaica.

Logan, of Afton and, later, Laight, John (d. 1816)

Proprietor of Knockshinnock in New Cumnock, he married Martha, the, daughter of Captain MacAdam of Laight, on the River Afton. When the Captain died, Logan lived at Laight, which marched with Knockshinnock. He was a friend of Gavin Hamilton, who introduced him to Burns. Logan subscribed to the Kilmarnock Edition, and Burns sent him twenty copies to distribute. He mentioned Logan in 'The Kirk's Alarm'. Logan received a copy of the poem from Burns with a letter dated 7th August 1789, along with the injunction not on any account 'to give, or permit to be taken, any copy of the Ballad'. The poet visited him several times on his journeys to and from Ayrshire, and during one of his visits is said to have written 'Afton Water'.

Logan, Miss Susan

Sister of Major Logan, 'thairm-inspirin', rattlin' Willie'. Burns sent her his poem, 'To Miss Logan, with Beattie's Poems for a New-Year's Gift, Jan. 1, 1787'.

Logan, Major William (d. 1819)

A retired army officer who lived at the house of Park, in Ayr. He was a convivial wit, and a keen violinist. Burns met him at Ayr. The Major lived with his mother and unmarried sister, Susan, for whom Burns had some admiration, sending her a copy of Beattie's poems on New Year's Day 1787, with the lines 'Again the silent wheels of time'. The poet called her father 'thairm-inspirin', rattlin' Willie' in the 'Epistle to Major Logan'.

The Major latterly suffered from the effects of over-indulgence. When his minister called to see him, that worthy remarked to Logan that it would take great fortitude to bear his sufferings. To which Logan retorted: 'Aye, it would take *fiftitude*.'

At one time in his career, when serving with the 80th Regiment of Foot (Royal Edinburgh Volunteers), he had been a prisoner in America. Describing this experience, he is supposed to have said: 'Plenty to eat and drink, and no parades.'

Loncartie

Mentioned by Burns in his 'Caledonia, a Ballad'. According to the historian Hector Boece, Kenneth III defeated the Danes at Luncarty, four miles from Perth, in A.D. 990, inflicting enormous casualties:

'But brave Caledonia in vain they
    assail'd
As Largs well can witness and
    Loncartie tell.'

Lonsdale, first Earl of. *See* Lowther.

Lorimer, Jean (1775–1831)

Daughter of William Lorimer, a merchant and farmer of Kemmishall, about two miles below Ellisland on the Nith, she was born at Craigieburn, near Moffat. Her good looks attracted several Excise people besides Burns: Lewis, Thomson, and particularly John Gillespie, a colleague of Burns in the Excise office. On behalf of Gillespie, Burns wrote several poems to Jean including 'Sweet closes the ev'ning on Craigieburn Wood', 'Come let me take thee to my breast' and 'Poortith Cauld', with its note of personal yearning.

Jean, however, would not have Gillespie, and eventually eloped to Gretna Green with a young spendthrift called Whelpdale, who, after three weeks of marriage, left his wife to escape from his creditors.

She returned to her father at Kemmishall, and reverted to her maiden name.

When her father's fortunes failed, they moved to Dumfries. She was a frequent visitor at the Burns home.

Much has been made of Burns's friendship with Jean Lorimer, whom he called by the artificial name of 'Chloris'. Writing to Thomson, about 'Craigieburn Wood', in October 1794, Burns referred to Chloris as a source of inspiration: 'The Lady on whom it was made, is one of the finest women in Scotland; and, in fact (entre nous), is in a manner to me what Sterne's Eliza was to him: a Mistress or Friend, or what you will, in the guileless simplicity of Platonic love.' Thomson was told not to put any of his 'squinting construction' on this; but, as Hilton Brown remarked: 'others have squinted pretty obliquely since'.

In the same letter, Burns revealed the way in which he whipped himself into an emotional state over a woman in order to make of her material for a song.

'Do you think that the sober gin-horse routine of existence could inspire a man with life, and love, and joy—could fire him with enthusiasm, or melt him with pathos, equal to the genius of your Book?—No! No!!!—When ever I want to be more than ordinary *in song*: to be in some degree equal to your divine airs; do you imagine I fast and pray for the celestial emanation? Tout au contraire! I have a glorious recipe, the very one that for his own use was invented by the Divinity of Healing and Poesy when erst he piped to the flocks of Admetus. I put myself on a regimen of admiring a fine woman; and in proportion to the adorability of her charms, in proportion you are delighted with my verses.'

Of the twenty-four songs certainly written to 'Chloris' Lorimer, whatever the state of her charms, none is among Burns's finest. She was, however, the inspiration of the poem, 'Lassie wi the lintwhite locks'.

Burns's friendship with the Lorimers

declined towards the end of his life. When her father finally lost his memory, Jean became a family governess. After enduring years of desertion, she visited her husband when he was in the debtor's prison at Carlisle, having squandered several fortunes. She died at Newington.

Lorimer, William
Father of Jean, Burns's 'Chloris'. *See* **Lorimer, Jean**. He was a farmer at Kemmishall, whom Burns introduced to John Somerville, in a letter from Ellisland 11th May 1791, as: 'a gentleman worth your knowing, both as a man and (what is case in point), as a man of property and consequence, who goes to town just now, to advise with and employ an Agent in some law-business'.

Presumably, at this time Burns did not know of Lorimer's 'dark manœuvres of a smuggler'. However, in a letter to Alexander Findlater, June 1791, Burns admitted that Lorimer himself had not been present during his last surveys at Kemmishall. As Lorimer was known to be 'an illicit dealer', the poet promised to 'give the house a severe scrutiny'. Lorimer finally went bankrupt.

Loudon, fifth Earl of. *See* **Campbell, James Mure**

'Love and Liberty'. *See* **'The Jolly Beggars'.**

Lowther, James, first Earl of (1736–1802)
Descended from Sir Christopher Lowther, the first earl was a member of Parliament from 1757 to 1784, using his wealth to dominate politics in the North of England. His nominees in the House were known as 'Sir James's ninepins'. Alexander Carlyle, in his *Autobiography*, summed him up as being 'more detested than any man alive . . . a shameless political sharper, a domestic bashaw, and an intolerable

tyrant over his tenants and dependants'. Carlyle concludes that he was 'truly a madman, though too rich to be confined'. He appointed Boswell Recorder of Carlisle, but humiliated him into resignation. If 'From Esopus to Maria' be genuine, Burns refers in it to Lonsdale's treatment of the Dumfries Players. *See* **Williamson**.

Loyal Natives Club, Dumfries
A collection of somewhat conservative citizens who, on 18th January 1793, formed themselves into a Club for 'Supporting the Laws and Constitution of the Country'.

Cromek wrote: 'At this period . . . when political animosity was made the ground for private quarrel, some foolish verses were circulated containing an attack on Burns and his friends for their political opinions. They were written by some members of a club styling themselves the "Loyal Natives" of Dumfries, or rather by the united genius of that Club, which was more distinguished for drunken loyalty, than either for respectability or poetical talent.' One of the pieces of jingle handed to Burns was:

'Ye sons of Sedition, give ear to my
                                    song,
Let Syme, Burns amd Maxwell
                        persuade every throng,
With Craken, the attorney, and
                        Maxwell the quack,
Send Willie, the monger, to hell with
                        a smack.'

'Willie the monger', was, of course, the Prime Minister, William Pitt. Burns replied:

'Ye true "Loyal Natives", attend to
                                    my song,
In uproar and riot rejoice the night
                                    long,
From envy and hatred your corps is
                                    exempt;
But where is your shield from the
                        darts of contempt?'

Luath

A favourite dog of Burns's, killed while wandering. The poet immortalised him in 'The Twa Dogs'. Luath was the name of Cuchullin's dog in Ossian's *Fingal*.

Burns described his Luath as 'a gash an' faithfu' tyke'.

Lugar, River

A tributary of the River Ayr, mentioned in 'The Brigs of Ayr'.

Lunardi, Vincenzo (1759–1806)

Said to have been born at Lucca, Italy, Lunardi prided himself on being 'the first aerial traveller in the English atmosphere', and in 1784 made balloon ascents from sites in and near London. He made ascents from Edinburgh and Glasgow the following year.

A Shetland minister, the Reverend John Mill, either saw, or read about, one of Lunardi's Scottish Ascents, and recorded in his Diary:

'A French man [*sic*] called Lunardi fled over the Firth of Forth in a Balloon, and lighted in Ceres parish, not far from Cupar, in Fife; and O! how much are the thoughtless multitude set on these and like foolish vanities to the neglect of the one thing needful. Afterwards, 'tis said, when soaring upwards in the foresaid machine, he was driven by the wind down the Firth of Forth, and tumbled down into the sea near the little Isle of May, where he had perished had not a boat been near who saved him and his machine.'

On the occasion of his first Edinburgh ascent, in October 1785, all business was suspended, and he got a tremendous send-off. *The Scots Magazine* reported: 'The beauty and grandeur of the spectacle could only be exceeded by the cool, intrepid manner in which the adventurer conducted himself; and indeed he seemed infinitely more at ease than the greater part of his spectators.'

Lunardi was secretary to the Neapolitan Ambassador in London, Prince Caramanico.

He published, in 1786, *An Account of Five Aerial Voyages in Scotland, in a Series of Letters to his Guardian, Gherardo Campagni.*

A bonnet, balloon-shaped, was named after him. Burns mentioned the bonnet in 'To a Louse': 'But Miss's fine Lunardi, fye.'

M

Mabane, Miss

An Edinburgh lady whom Burns visited, and to whom he wrote from St James's Square, on 1st December 1787, about a trinket. She married a Colonel Wright, and 'died in Edinburgh', according to Chambers.

Maggie

An old mare belonging to Burns, and the subject of his poem: 'The Auld Farmer's New-Year Morning Salutation to His Auld Mare, Maggie'. The poem says:

'It's now some nine-an'-twenty year,
Sin' thou was my guidfather's meere;
He gied me thee, o' tocher clear,
                              [dowry
An' fifty mark; [Scots coin worth
                              13s. 4d.
Tho' it was sma', 'twas weel-won gear,
                              [well earned money
An' thou was stark.' [strong

Having given the mare her ripp of corn, the poet, anticipating 'John Anderson, my jo', remembers the experiences man and animal have shared:

'We've worn to crazy years thegither;
We'll toyte about wi' ane anither;
                              [stagger
Wi' tentie care I'll flit thy tether
To some hain'd rig, [reserved piece
                              of ground
Whare ye may nobly rax your leather,
                              [stretch,
Wi' sma' fatigue.'

Mailie

Burns's pet sheep, who bade the herder, Hughoc, tell Burns of her death, in the poem 'The Death and Dying Words of poor Mailie, the Author's only pet

Yowe'. Burns also wrote her elegy in the poem 'Poor Mailie's Elegy'.

Gilbert Burns later recorded: 'The circumstances of the poor sheep were pretty much as Robert has described them. He had, partly by way of frolic, bought a ewe and two lambs from a neighbour, and she was tethered in a field adjoining the house at Lochlea. He and I were going out with our teams, and our two younger brothers to drive for us, at mid-day, when Hugh Wilson, a curious-looking awkward boy, clad in plaiding, came to us with much anxiety in his face, with the information that the ewe had entangled herself in the tether, and was lying in the ditch. Robert was much tickled with Hughoc's appearance and posture on the occasion. Poor Mailie was set to rights and when returned from the plough in the evening, he repeated to me her "Death and Dying Words", pretty much in the way they now stand.'

Maitland, James, eighth Earl of Lauderdale (1759–1839)

One of the sixteen Scottish peers elected to the Lords, and a founder of the 'Friends of the People'. At the time he met Burns in Edinburgh, Maitland represented the seat of Malmesbury for Fox in Parliament. He succeeded to the earldom in 1789, but still adhered to his liberal views. In the subsequent political trials instigated by the government of Pitt, Maitland could not be touched with impunity, so it was on humbler men like Thomas Muir that the government's fear was vented.

In 1806 Maitland was created a Baron of the United Kingdom. He was also Keeper of the Great Seal. He undertook an unsuccessful diplomatic mission to France to attempt a peace settlement.

Burns, writing to Dr John Mackenzie of Mauchline from Edinburgh on 11th January 1787, said that he had met Maitland and his brother at breakfast and found them 'exceedingly easy, accessible, agreeable fellows; and seemingly pretty clever'.

Mansfield, first Earl of. *See* **Murray, William.**

Manson, James
Manson's Inn, Tarbolton, was the meeting-place of St James Lodge from 1784. Manson had been its treasurer from 1774. He served his brother masons 'small beer of a very superior kind', hence the reference to 'Manson's barrels' in 'To Dr John MacKenzie'.

Manuscripts
During his lifetime, Burns made manu-script collections of some of his letters and poems for several of his friends. The Afton, Don, Glenriddell, Cambus-doon and Stair collections are noted separately.

Collections made by subsequent hands include the Dalhousie Manuscript of letters to George Thomson and the Lochryan Manuscript of letters to Mrs Dunlop, both in the Morgan Library, New York: the collection in the Cottage Museum, Alloway, which includes the series of letters to Robert Graham of Fintry, the Second Commonplace Book, and a number of poems in addition to the Afton Manuscript: about a hundred manuscripts in Edinburgh divided between the University Library (the Don Manu-script), the City Museum (the letters to James Burness), the Scottish National Library (the Glenriddell Manuscript), the Scottish National Portrait Gallery and the Scottish Museum of Antiquities; the British Museum, whose collection of letters include the Autobiographical Letter to Dr Moore, and, in the Hastie Manu-script, the greatest single collection of poems.

Other public institutions having Burns's manuscripts include the Huntington Lib-rary, San Marino, California, the Public Library, Dunfermline, the Burns Monu-ment, Kilmarnock, and the Burns Museum, Irvine.

Many Burns manuscripts are still in private collections, mainly in America. Most of these will presumably find their way into public collections in the course of time.

Markland, Jean (1765-1851)
One of the 'Mauchline belles'. She was the daughter of a Mauchline merchant, George Markland, and she and her parents were charged before the kirk-session for attributing witchcraft to the wife of another merchant. The charge was not proceeded with. She later married a Tarbolton excise officer, James Findlay, to whom, according to Chambers, she was introduced by the poet. Findlay is generally said to have instructed Burns in gauging and book-keeping for the Excise. Jean died in Greenock.

Marshall, William (1745-1818)
One of these experimenting agricultural-ists whose work in the eighteenth century did much to increase the productivity of the land. He was the author of *Rural Econ-omy of England* in twelve volumes, one of which dealt with Yorkshire. Burns listed the Yorkshire volume as one of the books he was reading when he wrote to Robert Graham of Fintry on 13th May 1789, from whom he had apparently borrowed it. He reported returning it 'by the Carrier' with another letter to Graham, dated 9th December 1789.

Marshall, William (1748-1833)
Born at Fochabers and trained as a clock-maker, he spent much of his life as butler to the Duke of Gordon. Burns, who adapted Marshall's dance tune, 'Miss Admiral Gordon's Strathspey', to his love song, 'Of a' the airts the wind can blow', described Marshall as 'the first composer of strathspeys of the age'.

The poet may well have met Marshall when he dined with the Duke of Gordon during the Highland tour of 1787. Marshall's melodic gift was stronger than that of any of the other composers of Scotland's 'music in the vernacular', except possibly, Nathaniel Gow, Neil's son

Marshall's publications were: a *Collection of Recls*, 1781; *Scottish Airs, Melodies, Strathspeys, Reels*, 1822; and the posthumous *Collection of Scottish Melodies*.

Masterton, Allan (d. 1799)

He came from a Linlithgowshire family. When Burns was in Edinburgh, Masterton was a writing master in Stevenlaw's Close, in the High Street. In 1795, he became writing master in the High School, along with his brother Dugald, and his nephew, also Dugald. He had a good knowledge of Scots song, and was by way of being a composer himself. William Nicol introduced him to Burns. They visited Nicol in the autumn of 1789 at lodgings he had taken near Moffat. The jollification resulted in that splendid drinking song, 'Willie brew'd a peck o' maut', for which Masterton wrote the music. The song appeared in the *Scots Musical Museum*, 1790. He also wrote the music for several other Burns songs, including the airs for 'Strathallan's Lament', 'The Braes o' Ballochmyle', 'The Bonnie Birks o' Ayr', 'On Hearing a Young Lady Sing', and 'Ye gallants bright, I rede ye right', the last of which Burns wrote for Masterton's daughter, Ann.

In a letter to Captain Riddell, dated 16th October 1789, Burns described Masterton as 'one of the worthiest men in the world, and a man of real genius'. Masterton became a sort of intermediary for Burns in Edinburgh when he wrote to Peter Hill and others buying books. None of Burns's letters to Masterton has survived.

Masterton, Miss Ann

Daughter of Allan Masterton. She married a Dr Derbishire, who practised first in Bath and then in London. They had one son.

Burns recorded in a note to the song 'Beware o' Bonie Ann' that he 'composed this song out of compliment to Miss Ann Masterton, the daughter of my friend Allan Masterton. . . .'

The song appeared in Johnson's *Museum*.

Mauchline Conversation Society

The minute book of the society shows it to have existed from 30th October 1786, until 20th November 1797. David Sillar was at the top of the list of the original members, and although Burns did not attend any of the meetings, his brother Gilbert was a leading conversationalist. If members did not attend, they were fined, and the money was used to buy books. These included Rousseau's *Emile*, Voltaire's *Peter the Great*, Mackenzie's *The Man of Feeling*, and sets of *The Mirror* and *The Lounger*.

Love and marriage, and the French Revolution, seem to have been subjects which interested the members. Two of Gilbert Burns's questions were: 'Whether, in a young man's looking out for a wife, he ought to have more regard to her fortune or her personal charms?' and: 'Whether it is probable, if a Republican form of Government were to take place, it would lead to more happiness for the present generation?'

Maule, William Ramsay, Lord Panmure of Brechin and Navar (1771-1852)

Second son of George Ramsay, eighth Earl of Dalhousie, Maule heired the Panmure lands under the will of his uncle William in 1787. He was a friend of Fox and seems popularly to have been considered a libertine; but the Government thought differently, for they conferred a baronetcy upon him, and he became Lord Panmure in 1831. He married twice. The title died with his son.

When Burns knew Maule, he was an officer in a regiment stationed at Dumfries. In a letter of 29th October 1794, Burns sent the epigram: 'To the Hon. Wm. R.

Maule of Panmure', to Mrs Dunlop with the comment: 'One of the Corps provoked my ire the other day which burst out as follows:

"Thou fool, in thy phaeton towering,
Art proud when that phaeton is
                              prais'd?
Tis the pride of a Thief's exhibition
When higher his pillory's rais'd." '

In spite of this attack, Panmure settled on Burns's widow an annuity of sixty pounds, but only had to disburse it for eighteen months, after which Burns's son, James, was able to relieve him of the charge.

Maxwell of Cardoness, David (d. 1825)

A Kircudbrightshire laird created a baronet in 1804. He figures in the second Heron Election ballad:

'An there'll be Cardoness, Esquire,
   Sae mighty in Cardoness' eyes . . .

Cardoness supported the Tory candidate, Gordon of Balmaghie. In a letter to Mrs Dunlop, Burns described him as a 'stupid, money-loving dunderpate'.

Burns also wrote of him as 'A Galloway Laird—Not quite so wise as Soloman':

'Bless Jesus Christ, O Cardoness,
   With grateful lifted eyes,
Who taught that not the soul alone,
   But body too shall rise;
For had he said "The soul alone,
   From death I will deliver,"
Alas! Alas! O Cardoness,
   Then thou hadst lain for ever!'

And again: 'On Being Shown a beautiful Country Seat':

'We grant they're thine, those beauties
                                    all,
   So lovely in our eye:
Keep them, thou eunuch, Cardoness,
   For others to enjoy!'

Maxwell, The Rev. George

Minister of Buittle (1762–1807). Burns

described him as 'mair o' the black than the blue' in the Second Heron Election Ballad.

Maxwell of Curruchan, George

Called 'Staunch Geordie' in Burns's Second Heron Election Ballad.

Maxwell, James (1720–1800)

A Paisley poet who, in 1773, published at Glasgow *A New Version of the Whole Book of Psalms in Metre*.

Writing to Graham of Fintry on 9th December 1789, Burns hoped that Graham would find time to read, among other books, 'The Paisley poet's version of the Psalms of David'.

Maxwell was a prolific rhymster, who signed himself 'Poet of Paisley', and sometimes also 'S.D.P.': Student of Divine Poetry!

Maxwell of Terraughty, John (1720–1814)

After being apprenticed to a joiner, Maxwell set up in business for himself, with the profits of which he bought back the family estate of Terraughty, previously sold because of financial difficulties. Later, he also bought Portrack, in the Parish of Holywood. By his second marriage, he came to own Munches. When Burns settled in Dumfriesshire, Maxwell was a well-known county figure. For his seventy-first birthday, Burns wrote him an epistle, beginning 'Health to the Maxwells' veteran Chief!'

In the second stanza Burns prophesied:

'This day thou metes threescore eleven,
And I can tell that bounteous Heaven.
(The second-sight, ye ken, is given
   To ilka Poet)
On thee a tack o' seven times seven,
   Will yet bestow it.'

Bounteous Heaven certainly went some way towards fulfilling the poet's prophecy for 'teugh Jockie', as Burns called Maxwell in the first of the Heron Election Ballads, lived to be ninety-four.

Maxwell, Robert (d. 1792)

Provost of Lochmaben, Dumfriesshire, from 13th September 1782, to 29th September 1790. Burns, in a letter to Graham of Fintry, dated 9th December 1789, described Maxwell as: 'one of the soundest headed, best hearted, whisky-drinking fellows in the south of Scotland'. The poet's one surviving letter to Maxwell is a covering note for the bawdy ballad, 'I'll tell you a tale of a Wife', which is to be found in *The Merry Muses*.

Maxwell, Wellwood

A first lieutenant in the Dumfriesshire Volunteers under Colonel de Peyster. Two companies of the volunteers were raised in 1795 as a defence force, deemed necessary because the Regular Army was engaged in the war with France. Maxwell is mentioned as 'Wattie' in the Second Heron Election Ballad.

Maxwell, Dr William (1760–1834)

Second son of James Maxwell of Kirkconnel, he was educated at the Jesuit College at Dinant in France, and became a doctor. While on the Continent, he developed Republican opinions, becoming a member of the National Guard. In this capacity, he was present at the execution of Louis XVI, dipping his handkerchief in that unfortunate monarch's blood. In 1794 he returned to Scotland and settled in Dumfries, where he met Burns. Because of his Jacobin leanings, he was viewed with some suspicion by the authorities, but his professional skill overcame these difficulties, and he eventually became a much respected practitioner. Maxwell attended Burns during his last illness, diagnosing the stabbing agonies of endocarditis as 'flying gout', and prescribing sea-bathing in country quarters and horse-riding; 'cures' which probably hastened Burns's end. Shortly before his death,

the poet presented Maxwell with his pair of Excise pistols, which are now in the Museum of the Scottish Society of Antiquaries. Jean Armour Burns called the son born to her on the day of her husband's funeral Maxwell, after the doctor, who attended her.

Together with Cunningham and Syme, Maxwell became one of the Trustees who collected money for a fund to ensure that Burns's widow and children did not want.

Maxwell, Winifred. *See* Constable.

Mayne, John (1759?–1836)

Born in either 1759 or 1761 at Dumfries, he became a printer there, having studied at the Foulis Brothers' Academy in Glasgow. Latterly he went to London, where he became part-owner and editor of *The Star*, and where he died.

Three of his poems have survived; the picturesque 'Glasgow', 'The Siller Gun', and the song 'Logan Braes'.

While still a printer with *The Dumfries Journal*, he published 'The Siller Gun' in its first form in Ruddiman's *Magazine* of November 1780. Scott said of his later version of the same poem that it 'surpassed the efforts of Ferguson, and came near to those of Burns'.

It is very probable that Burns knew of Mayne's poem, because there are obvious similarities between 'The Siller Gun', which describes a traditional shooting contest, and 'Hallowe'en'.

Meikle, Andrew (1719–1811)

A millwright at Houston Mill, near Dunbar. He invented the Threshing Mill in 1784, and patented it in 1788. Burns met him at Duns while on his Border tour.

Menagerie Handbill

This handbill was found just prior to 1940 in Cambridge, the property of Jessy Lewars's great-grand-daughter, Mrs Jessy Lewars Dove, along with a manuscript copy of 'The blue-eyed Lassie'. *See* **Lewars, Jessy.**

When Burns was being nursed by Jessy on his deathbed, the handbill advertising 'A Grand Menagerie of Wild Beasts Alive', to be seen in the Market Place, Dumfries, was handed in to the poet's room. Burns took it, and on the reverse side wrote down the following impromptu verses:

'Talk not to me of savages
　From Afric's burning sun;
No savage e'er can rend my heart,
　As Jessy, thou hast done.

'But Jessy's lovely hand in mine,
　A mutual faith to plight,
Not even to view the Heavenly choir
　Would be so blest a sight.'

The *Burns Chronicle* of 1940 contains a reproduction of the handbill.

Menteath, The Reverend James Stuart (d. 1802)

Rector of Barrowby in Lincolnshire. He assumed the name of Stuart in 1770. He purchased Closeburn estate from Sir Thomas Kirkpatrick in 1783. His factor was William Stewart. Burns and Captain Riddell started a parish library, the Monkland Friendly Society. In a letter to the Edinburgh bookseller Peter Hill from Ellisland, 2nd April 1789, Burns mentioned this project and added, 'There is another, in emulation of it, going on at Closeburn, under the auspices of Mr Menteath of Closeburn, which will be on a greater scale than ours. I have likewise secured it for you.'

Menteath's son, Charles, was created a Baronet in 1838.

Merry, John

The husband of Anne Rankine, who claimed to be the Annie of 'The Rigs o' Barley'.

Merry was an innkeeper in Cumnock.

Merry Muses of Caledonia, The

In December 1793, Burns wrote to John M'Murdo, chamberlain to the Duke of Queensberry: 'I think I once mentioned something of a collection of Scots songs I have for some years been making: I send you a perusal of what I have got together. I could not conveniently spare them above five or six days, and five or six glances at them will probably more than suffice you. When you are tired of them, please leave them with Mr Clint, of the King's Arms. There is not another copy of the collection in the world; and I should be sorry that unfortunate negligence should deprive me of what has cost me a good deal of pains. . . .'

The collection referred to, which Burns also seems to have circulated among others of his friends—Cleghorn, M'Adam, Smellie, and Robert Maxwell among them—was an anthology of bawdy songs and poems, some of them obviously by Burns himself. Rebel that he was against the absurdities and artificial restraints upon sex which Presbyterian divines had sought to impose since the Reformation (and the Catholic Church since the preachings of Paul!), Burns thoroughly enjoyed collecting the bawdy folk-songs that were the ultimate evidence of the failure of the Kirk's doctrines of distortion. He also enjoyed writing his own, and, in his Edinburgh days, presenting them to the Crochallan Fencibles.

When the dishonest Currie first published the above-quoted letter to M'Murdo, he inserted the sentence 'A very few of them are my own'. On this piece of deception, the poet's apologists have based their self-elected defence of him. The fact is that Burns probably wrote, or 'improved', a substantial number of the bawdy poems in *The Merry Muses*, and by far the best. Sometimes he combined social satire and literary criticism with bawdry. Always, his bawdy poems are infused with laughter. In them, Burns looks at sex as the basic, levelling element in the human situation, laughs, and invites us to laugh with him. Burns's bawdy poems can thus in no way be compared with pornographic writings, the sole object of which is secret, prurient titillation; a distinction which the apologists have, unhappily for themselves, overlooked.

Since Burns's bawdy poems are still relatively inaccessible, two examples are quoted to illustrate the point. In 'For a' that' or 'The Bonniest Lass that ye Meet', Burns takes a devastating swipe at the absurd hypocrisy of the Kirk.

'The bonniest lass that ye meet neist,
    Gie her a kiss an' a' that,
In spite o' ilka parish priest,
    Repentin' stool, an' a' that.
        For a' that, an' a' that,
            Their mim-mou'd sangs an' a'
                                    that,
        In time and place convenient
            They'll do't themselves for a'
                                    that.

'Your patriarchs, in days o' yore,
    Had their handmaids an' a' that;
O' bastard gets, some had a score,
    And some had mair than a' that.
        For a' that an' a' that,
            Your langsyne saunts, an' a'
                                    that,
        Were fonder o' a bonnie lass,
            Than you or I, for a' that.

'King Davie, when he waxed auld,
    An's bluid ran thin an' a' that,
An' fand his c—s were growin' cauld,
    Could not refrain, for a' that.
        For a' that an' a' that,
            To keep him warm, an' a' that,
        The daughters o' Jerusalem
            Were waled for him, an' a' that.

'Who wadna pity thae sweet dames
    He fumbled at, an' a' that,
An' raised their bluid up into flames,
    He couldna drown for a' that.
        For a' that an' a' that;
            He wanted pith, an' a' that;

For, as to what we shall not name,
    What could he do, but claw
                                    that.

'King Solomon, prince o' divines,
    Wha proverbs made, an' a' that,
Baith mistresses an' concubines
    In hunders had, for a' that.
        For a' that an' a' that,
            Tho' a preacher wise, an' a' that,
        The smuttiest sang that e'er was
                                    sung,
            His "Sang o' Sangs" is a' that.

'Then still I swear, a clever chiel
    Should kiss a lass, an' a' that,
Though priests consign him to the deil,
    As reprobate, an' a' that.
        For a' that, an a' that,
            Their canting stuff, an' a' that,
        They ken nae mair wha's
                                    reprobate,
            Than you or I, for a' that.'

In 'Wha'll Mow me Now?' the social comment is equally obvious.

'O wha'll mow me now, my jo,
    And wha'll mow me now?
A sodger with his bandeleers,
    Has bang'd my belly fu'.

'O I hae tint my rosy cheek,
    Likewise my waist sae sma',
O wae gae wi' the sodger loon,
    The sodger did it a'!

'O wha'll mow me now, my jo, etc.

'For I maun thole the scornfu' sneer,
    O mony a saucy queen,
When, curse upon her godly face,
    Her c—t's as merry's mine.

'O wha'll mow me now, my jo, etc.

'Our dame holds up her wanton tail,
    As oft as down she lies,
And yet misca's a young thing,
    The trade if she but tries.

'O wha'll mow me now, my jo, etc.

'Our dame has aye her ain gudeman,
  And mows for glutton greed,
And yet misca's a poor thing,
  That mows but for its bread.

'O wha'll mow me now, my jo, etc.

'Alack! sae sweet a tree as love,
  Sae bitter fruit should bear,
Alas that e'er a merry c—t
  Should draw so many a tear.

'O wha'll mow me now, my jo, etc.

'But devil tak' the lousy loon,
  Denies the bairn he got;
Or leaves the merry lass he lo'ed,
  To wear a ragged coat.

'O wha'll mow me now, my jo, etc.'

According to one tradition, the manuscript of *The Merry Muses* is supposed to have been stolen shortly after Burns's death, either from his wife, or from Dr Currie.

The first edition was published anonymously, probably in 1800 (the paper is so water-marked) and probably in Edinburgh for the Crochallan Fencibles (according to the title page), a drinking club of which Burns was a member. Only one copy is known to have survived. It was at one time in the possession of Scott Douglas, but has been in the Rosebery collection for the past half-century.

The 'stolen' manuscript may have been the source of this edition. Professor de Lancey Ferguson, however, thinks it was not the 'immediate' source. In any case, the 1800 edition, which I have inspected, is the only reliable printed source, apart from manuscript material which accounts for twenty-one items out of ninety-six in the Auk edition. The 1827 edition, frequently reprinted, included numerous coarse and empty pieces not by Burns, and many of them declaredly and obviously of English and Irish origin.

Two manuscript copies have been made of the 1800 edition, both inaccurate. One by J. C. Ewing, which it was intended to use for a reprint as a pendant to the Henley and Henderson edition: the other, of which fifty copies were taken, by John Farmer in 1903. In 1911, D. McNaught, one of the many so-called Burns 'scholars' who did not consider truth an essential ingredient of scholarship, produced a privately-circulated reprint for the Burns Federation, but indulged in re-writing and falsification in yet another futile attempt to show Burns the author of fewer pieces than he was. The private edition of the Auk Society, edited by Sydney Goodsir Smith and James Barke, with a Preface by Professor Ferguson, issued in an open edition in this country in 1965, and as a paperback the following year, has at last put paid to this nonsense. Professor James Kinsley, in his monumental and definitive *The Poems and Songs of Robert Burns* (1968), disproves some of the attributions of Ferguson, Smith and Barke, and should be consulted.

Michie, Ebenezer (1766–1812)
Schoolmaster first, at Kettle, and then at Cleish, in Fife. Burns was introduced to him by Nicol, and they spent a convivial evening, all three. But Michie fell asleep, and Burns wrote an epitaph for him:

'Here lies Eben Michie's banes;
  O Satan, an ye tak him,
Gie him the schulin' o' your weans,
  For clever deils he'll mak' em!'

Miers, or Myers, John
An artist who was a skilful taker of silhouette portraits. They were both cheap and quickly executed. Burns was one of his sitters, and the poet presented Miers's silhouettes to several of his friends. Clarinda also sat for him.

Miers came from Leeds, but spent two years, 1786–8, in Edinburgh. In the *London Directory* (1792) he is found as Profilist and Jeweller, first at 111 Strand, then at 162. Little is known of his latter years.

He produced his work on cardboard, plaster and ivory, his prices ranging from 6d. to 10s. 6d. 'Ivory was a speciality and might cost 4 guineas.' One branch of his work was in much demand—tiny miniatures suitable for ring, locket or tie-pin. Miers's portrait of Clarinda was used by Burns as a breast pin: 'I thank you for going to Miers. I want it for a breast-pin to wear next my heart. . . .', the poet wrote her.

Miers's outstanding merit seems to have been his accuracy of likeness—particularly valuable in view of the few genuinely good likenesses we have of the poet. Indeed, the artist claimed on the labels to his silhouettes—'Perfect likenesses in miniature profile—with the most exact symmetry and animated expression of the features'; and again, 'Likenesses in a style of superior excellence, with unequalled accuracy'.

Miers, it seems, never lacked work.

Silhouettes were made, of course, long before they were so called. They were named after Etienne de Silhouette (1709–1767), France's Controleur Général des Finances, whose enemies regarded his policies as only outlines!

Royalty, among them George III, George IV, William IV and Queen Victoria, had silhouettes made of themselves; or, as Burns sometimes called them 'shades'.

See Plate 9.

Miller, The Reverend Alexander (d. 1804)

Minister of Kilmaurs parish church, where he was ordained in 1788, much against his parishioners' wishes. According to Burns, Miller professed Auld Licht sentiments, but in reality had leanings the other way. He is the 'Wee Miller' of 'The Holy Fair'.

'Wee Miller neist, the Guard relieves,
                                   [next
An' orthodoxy raibles, [rattles on

Tho' in his heart he weel believes,
   An' thinks it auld wives' fables;
But faith! the birkie wants a manse,
                                   [fellow
So, cannilie he hums them;
Altho' his carnal wit an' sense
   Like hafflins-wise o'ercomes him
                                   [partly
   At times that day.'

Miller later alleged that these derogatory lines had retarded his advancement.

Miller, Betty

Daughter of John Miller. She was one of the 'Mauchline belles', and sister of another, Helen Miller. Betty married a Mauchline merchant, William Templeton. She died at the birth of her first child. 'From thee, Eliza, I must go' was inspired by her. The song appeared in the Kilmarnock Edition, to be sung to the tune 'Gilderoy'. Burns urged Thomson to publish the words to this tune in Select Scottish Airs, but in the volume of 1793, Thomson put it to the wrong tune.

Miller, Helen

One of the 'Mauchline belles', and a daughter of John Miller, who had the Sun Inn at Mauchline. In 1791 she married Burns's friend, Dr Mackenzie, who stayed at the Inn when first he came to Mauchline.

Their son, an antiquarian, John Whitefoord Mackenzie, died in Edinburgh in 1884.

Helen Miller was the Nell of 'A Mauchline Wedding'.

Miller, James

An Edinburgh lawyer who composed the air 'Ye banks and braes o' bonie doon'. See Clarke, Stephen.

Miller, Janet

Eldest daughter and third child of Patrick Miller of Dalswinton. She became the wife of John Thomas Erskine, later twenty-eighth Earl of Mar and thirteenth Lord Erskine, in 1795.

Burns wrote to her from Dumfries on 9th September 1793: 'I have taken the liberty to make you the Heroine of the Song on the foregoing page. Being little in the secret of young ladies' love and lovers—how should I, you know?— I have formed in my fancy a little love-story for you. The air, you know, is excellent, and the verses, I hope and think, are in my best manner.'

The song—not, most readers would agree, at all in his 'best manner'!—was 'Where are the joys I hae met in the morning', and appeared in Thomson's *Scottish Airs*, 1801. The tune, 'Saw ye my father' goes, however, to the splendid song, 'O, saw ye my father, or saw ye my mother' printed in David Herd's first edition of 1769. Herd's folk-words are, for once, undoubtedly superior to Burns's words. The tune first appeared in Stewart's *Scots Songs*, 1772.

Miller of Dalswinton, Patrick (1731–1815)

Son of William Miller of Glenlee and brother of Sir Thomas Miller, President of the Court of session. He started his career as a sailor which stimulated a lasting interest in navigation, then became a banker in Edinburgh. In 1767, he was made a director of the Bank of Scotland. In 1785, he bought Dalswinton estate in the valley of the Nith near Dumfries.

Sixteen years after Burns's death, Miller wrote: 'When I purchased this estate about five and twenty years ago, I had not seen it. It was in the most miserable state of exhaustion and all the tenants in poverty. When I went to view my purchase, I was so much disgusted for eight to ten days that I never meant to return to this county.' Though agriculturally, the estate was run down, Miller started extensive experiments in scientific agriculture, inventing a drill plough and a new threshing machine. He introduced the feeding of cattle on steamed potatoes. His interest in navigation led him to pioneer the building of an unsuccesful catamaran craft with hand-driven paddles. Later, he financed William Symington's pioneer steamboat, which sailed on Dalswinton Loch, and on which it is possible that on one occasion Burns was a passenger. Miller's ideas were sound, but he habitually under-estimated the time necessary to put them into practical operation. Burns himself became a victim of Miller's habit of under-estimating the time ideas take to be turned into realities: for although Ellisland was a farm which ultimately became a profitable one, it did not recover from its exhaustion until several years after Burns had left it.

Miller entered Burns's life in December 1786, when the poet had been in Edinburgh two weeks. On 13th December, Burns wrote to John Ballantine: 'An unknown hand left ten guineas for the Ayrshire Bard in Mr Sibbald's hand, which I got. I have since discovered my generous unknown friend to be Patrick Miller Esq., brother to the Justice Clerk; and drank a glass of claret with him by invitation at his own house yesternight.' A month later, on 14th January, Burns wrote to Ballantine prophetically: 'My generous friend, Mr Peter [*sic*] Miller . . . has been talking with me about the lease of some farm or other in an estate called Dasswinton which he has lately bought near Dumfries. Some life-rented, embittering Recollections whisper to me that I will be happier anywhere than in my old neighbourhood, but Mr Miller is no Judge of land; and though I dare say he means to favour me, yet he may give me, in his opinion, an advantageous bargain that may ruin me.'

Matters rested, however, until the end of September 1787, when Burns indicated his interest in the form of a letter to Miller, and on 20th October, the day the poet returned from his tour of Clackmannanshire with Adair, he wrote again more definitely: 'In two or three days . . . I will take a ride to Dumfries directly . . .

I want to be a farmer in a small farm, about a ploughgang'—i.e. about the size that one 'gang' of two men and four horses could cultivate—'in a pleasant country, under the auspices of a good landlord.'

Meanwhile, he angled for his Excise commission, and indeed, wrote to Clarinda on 23rd February 1788: 'I set off tomorrow for Dumfriesshire. 'Tis merely out of Compliment to Mr Miller, for I know the Excise must be my lot.'

Ten days later he changed his mind, telling her: 'Don't accuse me of being fickle; I have the two plans of life before me, and I wish to adopt the one most likely to procure me an independance.'

He had looked at the farm with his father's old friend John Tennant of Glenconner, who, as Burns told Ainslie on 3rd March 1788, had been 'highly pleased with the bargain, and advised me to accept of it'. By 7th March, Burns had made up his mind, telling Robert Muir: 'I took old Glenconner with me to Mr Millar's farm, and he was so pleased with it that I have wrote an offer to Mr Millar, which, if he accepts, I shall sit down a plain farmer, the happiest of lives when a Man can live by it.'

The arrangement between Miller and Burns was that Miller gave the poet £300 with which to build a farmhouse and fence the fields. The rental was to be fifty pounds annually for three years, and thereafter, seventy pounds during the seventy-six year term. Burns was to take possession on Whitsunday, 25th May 1788. (The lease is printed in full in the appendix **Burns Documents**

The building of the farmhouse took about a year, and was only achieved after numerous and vexating delays.

By September 1788, with his first harvest in, Burns's doubts about Ellisland were already growing. By July 1789, he was 'deliberating whether I had not better give up farming altogether, and go into the Excise wherever I can find employ-

ment'. By 11th January 1790, he had had enough. 'This Farm has undone my enjoyment of myself,' he burst out to his brother, Gilbert: 'It is a ruinous affair on all hands. But let it go to hell! I'll fight it out and be off with it!'

It might not have been so easy for Burns to 'be off with it', had not John Morin, the owner of the adjoining estate of Laggan, offered Miller £1,900 for it. Burns wrote to Peter Hill early in the autumn of 1791: 'I may perhaps see you about Martinmass. I have sold to My Landlord the lease of my farm, and as I roup off everything then, I have a mind to take a week's excursion to see old acquaintances.' There were, in fact, two sales: one in August, and one in early November.

Not unnaturally, relations between Burns and Miller, during the latter part of Burns's Ellisland tenancy, became strained, and Burns told Hill: 'Mr Miller's kindness has been just such another as Creech's was, but this for your private ear.

His meddling vanity, a busy fiend
Still making work his selfish craft
        must mend.'

Once the business relationship was ended, however, Burns and Miller became friendly again.

Miller built himself a new mansion 'almost on Cummin Castle'.

See Plates 12 and 15

Miller, Patrick, Jun. (1769–1845)

The son of Patrick Miller of Dalswinton (see above) and a captain in the Army. With the aid of Queensberry, he was elected Member of Parliament for Dumfries in 1790, and held his seat until 1796. In the ballad of 'The Five Carlins' Burns wrote of him:

'Then neist came in a sodger-boy,
                        [next
   Wha spak wi' modest grace,
   And he wad gae to Lon'on town,
      If sae their pleasure was.

'He wad na hecht them courtly gifts,
                    [*promise*
Nor meikle speech pretend;
But he was hecht an honest heart,
    Wad ne'er desert his friend.'

The burghs, or 'carlins', were Dumfries ('Maggy by the banks o' Nith'); Lochmaben ('Marjory of the many Lochs'); Annan ('Blinkin Bess of Annandale'); Kirkcudbright ('Whisky Jean of Galloway'); and Sanquhar ('Black Joan frae Chrichton-Peel').

Writing to Graham of Fintry on 9th December 1789, Burns described 'Captain Miller, my landlord's son' as: 'a youth by no means above mediocrity in his abilities: and is said to have a huckster-lust for shillings, pence and farthings'.

Writing to Mrs Dunlop from Ellisland on 9th July 1790, Burns reported: 'I have just got a summons to attend with my men-servants armed as well as we can, on Monday, one o'clock in the *morning* to escort Captain Miller from Dalswinton in to Dumfries to be a Candidate for our Boroughs, which chuse their Member that day. The Duke of Queensberry and the Nithsdale Gentlemen who are almost all friends to the Duke's Candidate, the said Captn, are to raise all Nithsdale on the same errand. The Duke of Buccleugh's, Earl of Hopeton's people, in short, the Johnstons, Jardines, and all the Clans of Annandale, are to attend Sir James Johnston, who is the other Candidate, on the same account. This is no exaggeration. On Thursday last, at chusing the Delegate for the boro' of Lochmaben, the Duke and Captn. Miller's friends led a strong party, among others, upwards of two hundred Colliers from Sanquhar Coal-works and Miners from Wanlockhead; but when they appeared on a hill-top, within half a mile of Lochmaben, they found such a superiour host of Annandale warriors drawn out to dispute the Day, that without striking a stroke, they turned their backs and fled with all the precipi-

tation the horrors of blood and murther could inspire. What will be the event, I know not. I shall go to please my Landlord, and to see the Combustion; but instead of trusting to the strength of Man, I shall trust to the heels of my horse, which are among the best in Nithsdale.'

Through Perry of the London *Morning Chronicle*, whom Miller knew, Burns was offered a position on the paper's literary staff in 1794. The poet wrote to Miller declining the position, on the grounds that his political sentiments would endanger the well-being of his family. But he sent Miller a copy of his song, 'Scots wha hae', asking that the paper should publish it anonymously. Miller heired Dalswinton on his father's death, but the estate was later sold. He claimed that his father should 'be held and acknowledged as the real author of the modern system of navigation by means of steam'.

Miller, Sir Thomas (1717–88)

Son of William Miller, of Glenlee, in Kirkcudbright. Educated in Glasgow, he was called to the Bar in 1742, became Lord Justice Clerk with the title Lord Barskimming in 1766, and afterwards Lord Glenlee. In January 1788, he succeeded Sir Robert Dundas as Lord President of the Court of Session, and became a baronet, but died a few months later.

Burns described a scene in Barskimming estate, on the Ayr, in 'The Vision':

'Thro' many a wild, romantic grove,
Near many a hermit-fancied cove,
(Fit haunts for friendship or for love,
    In musing mood),
An aged Judge, I saw him rove
    Dispensing good.'

Sir Thomas's son, Sir William, is mentioned in the Second Heron Election Ballad as 'Barskimming's guid knight'. Sir William became a judge with the title of Lord Glenlee.

Miller, Major William

Second son of Patrick Miller of Dalswinton, and brother of Captain Patrick Miller. He served in the Royal Horse Guards, settled in Dumfriesshire, and was a friend of Burns. The poet wrote several poetic compliments to his wife, Jessie, née Staig.

Mitchell, The Reverend Dr Andrew (1725-1811)

Minister of Monkton from 1775 until his death. Son of Hugh Mitchell, Laird of Dalgair in Ayrshire, he himself was Laird of Avisyard, near Cumnock. He was characterised by an extreme love of money, and eccentric ideas. Praying for the Royal family he referred, according to Chambers, on one occasion to 'His Majesty the Queen—Her Majesty the Prince of Wales'. He pronounced the word 'chemistry', *hemistry, tchemistry,* and *shemistry,* 'but never by any chance in the right way'.

Despite his natural opposition to Burns's religious ideas, he could still laugh at the humour of the poet's verses, and was heard to speak of Burns as 'a droll fellow'.

In 'The Kirk's Alarm', he is called:

'Andrew Gowk, Andrew Gowk, ye
                may slander the book,
And the book nought the waur, let
                me tell ye:
Tho' ye're rich and look big, yet lay
                by hat and wig,
And ye'll hae a *calf's head* o' sma'
                value,
Andrew Gowk! And ye'll hae a
                calf's head o' sma' value.'

Mitchell, The Reverend Andrew (1729 -94)

Minister of Aberlemno, near Forfar, from 1750-94. His father had been minister of this church before him, and his son succeeded him in the charge. Burns met him on his Highland tour, describing him in his *Journal* as 'an honest clergyman'.

Mitchell, Mr

Burns's 'good friend', who owned a printing-works in Carlisle, which employed four or five hundred people, 'many of them women and children'. After visiting the works while on his Border tour, Burns dined with Mitchell and left the town. Mitchell's was the last name to be mentioned in the *Border Journal,* which abruptly terminated.

The City Librarian of Carlisle, Mr Kenneth Smith, has suggested that Mitchell may have been a partner in Messrs Mitchell, Ellwood and Company, one of four printfields operating in Carlisle in 1794. These establishments are described in William Hutchinson's *History and Antiquities of Cumberland:*

'The work in the green or bleachyard found employment for men and stout boys. Apprentices were taken to the several branches of the work, viz. Drawers, Cutters and Calico printers. . . . Little boys were employed as tearing boys to the printers. Women had tables set out for them to pencil the colours into the pieces. Every table employed three or four female children; and even the youngest boys and girls could make near two shillings a week. . . .

'The chief part of the manufacturing business before the year 1761, consisted of a few check and Osnaburg looms, and about a dozen of looms employed in weaving very fine linen. But after the establishment of the manufactory of printed or stamped calicoes, cotton looms were set up. The stamperies had before this been supplied with cottons from Lancashire, at an extraordinary expence in carriage; but now (1794) machinery for carding, roving and spinning of cotton, is erected in different places in the neighbourhood of the city, and they purchase their cottons at a cheaper rate.'

Mitchell, John (1731-1806)

Mitchell was born in Aberdeenshire,

probably the son of a farmer. He studied for the Ministry, but entered the Excise. He worked in the service at Fraserburgh, Kilmarnock and elsewhere, and was appointed Collector at Dumfries in 1788. In 1802 Mitchell became Collector at Haddington, where his name appears in the almanac lists of Excise Officers, until 1804.

Burns presented himself to Mitchell with a letter of introduction from Robert Graham of Fintry. Writing to Graham from Ellisland on 13th May 1789, Burns said: 'I waited on Collector Mitchel with your letter. It happened to be Collection-day, so he was very throng, but he received me with the utmost politeness, and made me promise to call on him soon.' On 31st July Burns told Graham: 'Mr Mitchel did not wait my calling on him, but sent me a kind letter giving me a hint of the business, and on my waiting on him yesterday, he entered with the most friendly ardour into my views and interests.' Just over a fortnight later, Burns seems to have heard of his Excise appointment, though he did not begin work until the beginning of September. By 9th December, Burns was able to tell Graham: 'I have found the Excise business go on a great deal smoother with me than I apprehended; owing a good deal to the generous friendship of Mr Mitchel my Collector, and the kind assistance and instruction of Mr Findlater, my Supervisor.'

A glimpse of Burns's zeal for his duties and of his difficulties in carrying out the law without fear or favour, is to be got from the letter to Mr Mitchell dated September 1790. Burns had reported a farmer, Thomas Johnston of Mirecleugh, for carrying out illicit maltings. The man had been tried and fined five pounds, but petitioned the justices of the peace for Dumfriesshire to give him back his fine, on the grounds that it had been unjust. Fergusson of Craigdarroch and Captain Riddell, both J.P.s, thereupon ordered

Collector Mitchell to stop proceedings until an investigation could be carried through. Burns thereupon submitted an 'answer to the Petition of Thomas Johnston' (published in full by Chambers), detailing the whole fraud case fully. Unfortunately, we do not know how Johnston's case ended, but from Burns's letter to Mitchell, we may guess how he feared it would end: 'I wish and pray that the Goddess of Justice herself would appear tomorrow among our Hon[ble] Gentlemen, merely to give them a word in their ear that, "Mercy to the Thief, is injustice to the Honest Man" . . . I find that every Offender has so many Great Men to espouse his cause, that I shall not be surprised if I am committed to the strong Hold of the Law tomorrow for insolence to the dear friends of the Gentlemen of the Country.'

Writing to Graham from the Globe Inn, Dumfries, on 4th September, Burns told Graham: 'It was in the view of trying for a Port, that I asked Collector Mitchel to get me appointed, which he has done, to a vacant footwalk in Dumfries.' It was to Mitchell that Burns applied on 16th June 1791, for three days' leave of absence to attend his brother Gilbert's wedding: and from Mitchell that Burns heard of the Excise Board's decision to inquire into his loyalties, following a complaint in December 1792. It was no doubt in part due to Mitchell's testimony to the other members of the Board of Inquiry, Corbet and Findlater, that Burns got off with a friendly warning to be more discreet in his political utterances.

Towards the close of 1795, Burns sent a short rhymed epistle 'To Collector Mitchel', asking the return, or possibly even the loan, of a pound, and adding: 'farewell, Folly, hide and hair o't. For ance and aye'.

The relationship between Burns and his immediate Superior seems to have been a warm and friendly one. In a letter addressed to John Leven, General Supervisor, Excise Office, Edinburgh, in March 1792, Burns, after discussing some possibly seizable tea, said; 'Mr Mitchel mentioned to you a ballad, which I composed and sung at one of his Excise Court dinners: here it is.' 'It' was 'The Deil's awa wi' the Exciseman'.

After Mitchell's death, there was found among his papers a sheaf of first copies of poems and songs which Burns had apparently sent him for criticism. Mitchell's family subsequently lost the manuscripts!

Mitchell, The Reverend Thomas (1739 -1811)

Chambers noted that the following epigram was written by Burns about this divine, who was 'an accomplished scholar'. It is entitled 'In Lamington Kirk':

'As cauld a wind as ever blew,
A cauld kirk, and in't but few,
As cauld a minister's ever spak—
Ye'se a' be het or I come back!'

Mitchelson, Samuel (d. 1788)

An Edinburgh Writer to the Signet, who was Ainslie's employer and friend.

Moir, John

An Edinburgh printer who, according to Chambers, claimed that while serving his apprenticeship in a printer's shop in the High Street, he once watched Burns making inquiries about printing a volume of poems from his master. The man is supposed to have thought Burns was some 'poor crack-brained versifier, who might give him a good deal of trouble, but was not likely to yield much solid return in the way of business'. Burns went away offended, having first shown the printer a quantity of money. When the man learnt who had approached him, and what an opportunity he had lost, he resolved to be more careful in future. Accordingly, he printed the works of the

next poet to approach him, an unknown Aberdeenshire versifier, and lost heavily!

Monboddo, Lord. See Burnett.

Monkland Friendly Society

A library society in Dunscore parish, Nithsdale, for the founding of which Robert Burns and Captain Robert Riddell were primarily responsible.

On Riddell's instigation, Burns wrote an account of the Society for Sir John Sinclair's *Statistical Account*. He sent it to Sir John in the autumn of 1791:

'To store the minds of the lower classes with useful knowledge, is certainly of very great consequence, both to them as individuals, and to society at large. Giving them a turn for reading and reflection, is giving them a source of innocent and laudable amusement; and besides, raises them to a more dignified degree in the scale of rationality. Impressed with this idea, a gentleman in this parish, Robert Riddell, Esq. of Glenriddel, set on foot a species of circulating library, on a plan so simple, as to be practicable in any corner of the country; and so useful, as to deserve the notice of every country gentleman, who thinks the improvement of that part of his own species, whom chance has thrown into the humble walks of the peasant and the artisan, a matter of worthy of his attention.

'Mr Riddell got a number of his own tenants, and farming neighbours, to form themselves into a society, for the purpose of having a library among themselves. They entered into a legal engagement, to abide by it for 3 years; with a saving clause or two, in cases of removal to a distance, or of death. Each member, at his entry, paid 5s., and at each of their meetings, which were held every fourth Saturday, 6d. more. With their entry money, and the credit which they took on the faith of their future funds, they laid in a tolerable stock of books at the commencement. What authors they were to purchase, was always to be decided by the majority. At every meeting, all the books, under certain fines and forfeitures, by way of penalty, were to be produced; and the members had their choice of the volumes in rotation. He whose name stood, for that night, first on the list, had his choice of what volume he pleased in the whole collection; the second had his choice after the first; the third after the second, and so on to the last. At the next meeting, he who had been first on the list at the preceding meeting, was last at this; he who had been second, was first; and so on, through the whole 3 years. At the expiration of the engagement, the books were sold by auction, but only among the members themselves; and each man had his share of the common stock, in money or in books, as he chose to be a purchaser or not,

'At the breaking up of this little society, which was formed under Mr Riddell's patronage, what with benefactions of books from him, and what with their own purchases, they had collected upwards of 150 volumes. It will easily be guessed, that a good deal of trash would be bought. Among the books, however, of this little library, were Blair's Sermons, Robertson's History of Scotland, Hume's History of the Stewarts, The Spectator, Idler, Adventurer, Mirror, Lounger, Observer, Man of Feeling, Man of the World, Chrysal, Don Quixotte, Joseph Andrews, and etc. A peasant who can read, and enjoy such books, is certainly a much superior being to his neighbour, who, perhaps, stalks beside his team, very little removed, except in shape, from the brutes he drives.'

Many of the books were bought from Peter Hill of Edinburgh to Burns's order. Sometimes, subterfuge had to be resorted to to overcome the desire of the democrats for 'trash', as in this order to Hill sent on 2nd March 1790: 'At the late meeting of the Monkland friendly Society it was resolved to aug-ment their Library by the following books, which you are to send us as soon as possible—The Mirror—The Lounger—Man of feeling—Man of the World (these for my own sake I wish to have by the first Carrier)—Knox's history of the Reformation—Rae's history of the Rebellion 1715—Any good history of the Rebellion 1745—A display of the Secession Act and Testimony by Mr Gib—Hervey's Meditations—Beveridge's thoughts—and another copy of Watson's body of Divinity. This last heavy Performance is so much admired by many of our Members, that they will not be content with one Copy, so Capt Riddel our President and Patron agreed with me to give you private instructions not to send Watson, but to say that you could not procure a Copy of the book so cheap as the one you sent formerly and therefore you wait further Orders.'

From this, it is clear that Burns, not Riddell, was really the mainspring of the Society's enthusiasm. As Riddell himself put it: 'Mr Burns was so good as to take the whole charge of this small concern. He was treasurer, librarian, and censor to this little society, who will long have a grateful sense of his public spirit and exertions for their improvement and information.'

Monro, Alexander (1733–1817)

In 1754 he succeeded his father, also Alexander Monro (1697–1767), as professor of anatomy and was also the first occupant of the chair of surgery in Edinburgh University (1777). Burns mentioned him in the fragment 'The Poet's Progress'.

'Critics! appall'd, I venture on the
                                    name,
Those cut-throat bandits in the paths
                                    of fame:
Bloody dissectors, worse than ten
                                    Monroes;
He hacks to teach, they mangle to
                                    expose.

Montgomerie, Archibald, eleventh Earl of Eglinton (1726–96)

The Montgomeries, Earls of Eglinton, settled in Scotland in the twelfth century and counted in their number Sir John Montgomerie, who captured Percy at Otterburn in 1388, and Alexander, the sixth Earl, nicknamed Gray-Steel in the Civil War. Archibald, the eleventh Earl, succeeded to the title in 1769. He was known as General Montgomerie, having raised the 77th Regiment of Foot in the Highlands in 1757, of which he was appointed Lieutenant-Colonel in command. He was for a time a Member of Parliament for Ayrshire. In 1776, he was chosen as one of the Sixteen Scottish Representative Peers. He was appointed Governor of Edinburgh Castle in 1782, in which role he was succeeded by his cousin, Colonel Hugh Montgomerie, the 'sodger Hugh' of 'The Poet's Earnest Cry and Prayer'. Eglinton sent ten guineas to Burns on his arrival in Edinburgh as a subscription for two copies of the Edinburgh Edition of his *Poems*. Replying on 11th January 1787, Burns said:

'Your Munificence, my Lord, certainly deserved my very grateful acknowledgements, but your Patronage is a bounty peculiarly suited to my feelings.'

Incidentally, the thirteenth Earl organised the famous Eglinton tournament, which ruined the family, and is described by Disraeli in *Endymion*.

Montgomerie of Coilsfield, Hugh, twelfth Earl of Eglinton (1740–1819)

Hugh Montgomerie served in the Army during the Seven Years War and in America, rising to the rank of colonel of the West Lowland Fencibles in 1793. Burns referred to him as 'Sodger Hugh' in the cancelled stanza of 'The Author's Earnest Cry and Prayer'. He was member of Parliament for Ayrshire from 1784 to 1789, and again in 1796. In the same year he succeeded his cousin, Archibald, and became twelfth Earl of Eglinton.

Montgomerie, James (1735–1829)

A fellow mason of Burns, he became involved in a *cause célèbre* of 1787. Chambers recorded the story: 'A legal point arose between Mr Maxwell Campbell of Skerrington, Cumnock, in Ayrshire, and Captain James Montgomerie, late of the 93rd Foot as to whether the former could prosecute the latter for the dishonour of his wife without previously divorcing her. Mrs Campbell, an heiress in her own right, had left her husband to go with the Captain, to whom she had borne a child.'

Writing to Gavin Hamilton from Edinburgh on 8th March 1787, Burns said: 'Poor Captain Montgomerie is cast . . . their Gravities on the Bench were unanimously of opinion that Maxwell may prosecute for damages directly, and need not divorce his wife at all if he pleases.'

From Burns's obvious sympathy with the Captain and the lady, whom he described as 'the hapless Fair one', it would appear that the decision was not a popular one, and that there were extenuating circumstances. The reason the husband would not divorce his wife was, of course, that in so doing he would lose her estate.

Montgomerie rose to be Lieutenant General James Montgomerie of Wrighthill, and was elected to represent Ayrshire in Parliament in 1818, 1820 and 1826. Train alleges that 'Highland Mary' was his mistress.

Montgomerie's Peggy

She was reputed by the poet's sister, Mrs Isabella Begg, to be the housekeeper at Coilsfield House, where Burns often met her. They sat in the same church, where they: 'contracted an intimacy together'. Burns recorded that he 'began the affair merely in a "gaieté de coeur", and, to tell the truth, a vanity of showing my parts in courtship, particularly my abilities at a "billet-doux", which I always piqued myself upon, made me lay siege to her; and when I had battered myself into a very warm affection for her, she told me one day, in a flag of truce, that her fortress had been for some time before the rightful property of another, but with the greatest friendship and politeness she offered me every alliance, except actual possession'.

Montgomerie's Peggy remains one of the shadowy heroines in Burns's life: but the phrase 'battered myself into a very warm affection' is revealing, since this often seems to be what Burns felt himself obliged to do over any woman to whom he felt even mildly attracted.

The song 'Altho' my bed were in yon muir', sung to the tune 'Orala Water', relates to her.

Montgomery, Major-General Richard (1736–75)

A native of Ireland who soldiered in the British Army. He 'sadly and reluctantly' joined the American side in the War of Independence, and died leading an attack on Quebec. In the 'Address of Beelzebub', Burns wished that the emigrating Highlanders might have 'some Montgomery, fearless (to) lead them'.

Montrose, Duke of. See Graham, James.

Moodie, The Reverend Alexander (1722–99)

Educated at Glasgow University, he started his ministry in Culross in 1759, and moved two years later to Riccarton. Like the Reverend John Russell, he was a staunch member of the 'Auld Licht' party, and, as such, a target for Burns.

But he had a disagreement with Russell over parish boundaries, which inspired Burns's satire 'The Twa Herds' in which Moodie is described as 'Singet Sawnie'.

Moore, Dr John (1729–1802)

Son of the Reverend Charles Moore, and distantly connected with the Mures of Rowallan, John Moore was educated at Glasgow Grammar School and Glasgow University, where he studied medicine under Tobias Smollett's teacher, John Gordon. In 1747, Moore attracted the notice of Colonel Campbell (afterwards fifth Duke of Argyll) of the 54th Regiment, and served with it in the Low Countries as surgeon's mate, until peace was declared the following year. Moore then went to Paris to continue his medical studies. There, he became surgeon to the Earl of Albermarle, the British Ambassador. He received the degree of M.D. from Glasgow University in 1770. From 1772 until 1778, he was tutor and travelling companion to two successive young Dukes of Hamilton. In 1778, he settled in London to practice, and the following year brought out a book based on material he had collected during his years abroad with the Hamilton family, *View of Society and Manners in France, Switzerland and Germany*, a book which had considerable success, and was translated into French, German and Italian. He followed it up with a similar volume on *Italy* in 1781, which was less successful. In 1786, he brought out a volume of *Natural Sketches*, and his first novel *Zeluco*, which, again, had a considerable vogue, and is said to have given Byron suggestions for the character of Childe Harold. Moore then produced *Edward* (1796) and *Mordaunt* (1800), which were less popular.

In 1792 he went to Paris, and there witnessed the rising of 10th August, the dethronement of the king, and the savage massacres of the following month. He recorded his impressions in *A Journal During a Residence in France*, which was praised for its objectivity and humanity, and *A View of the Causes and Progress of the French Revolution*.

He spent his last years at Richmond, and died at his house in Clifford Street, London, leaving five sons, the eldest of whom was Sir John Moore, the hero of Corunna.

In the autumn of 1786, Moore's old friend, Mrs Dunlop, sent him a copy of Burns's Kilmarnock Edition. This aroused Moore's interest, and he wrote to Mrs Dunlop, asking her to tell Burns to write to him. Burns put off doing so, for reasons which he gave Mrs Dunlop on 15th January 1787: 'I will tell you the real truth, for I am miserably awkward at a fib. I wished to have written to Dr Moore before I wrote to you; but though every day since I received yours of December 30th, the idea, the wish to write to him has constantly pressed on my thoughts, yet I could not for my soul set about it. I know his fame and character, and I am one of "the sons of little men". To write him a mere matter-of-fact affair, like a merchant's order, would be disgracing the little character I have; and to write the author of the *View of Society and Manners* a letter of sentiment—I declare every artery runs cold at the thought. . . .'

Burns had, of course, a remarkably inflated idea of Moore's position, though fortunately he paid little attention to the good doctor's literary advice, which was to write in English and concentrate on producing something like Thomson's *Seasons*, only livelier. But Moore was aware of at least some aspects of Burns's genius, for he wrote: 'In my opinion you should plan some larger work than any you have as yet attempted. I know very well you have a mind capable of attaining knowledge by a shorter process than is commonly used, and I am certain you are capable of making a better use of it, when attained, than is generally done.'

After Moore had written to Burns direct, however, the poet replied from Edinburgh on 15th February 1787: 'Not many months ago I knew no other employment than following the plough, nor could boast anything higher than a distant acquaintance with a country clergyman. Mere greatness never embarrasses me: I have nothing to ask from the

Great, and I do not fear their judgement; but genius, polished by learning, and at its proper point of elevation the eye of the world, this of late I frequently meet with, and tremble at its approach. I scorn the affectation of seeming modesty to cover self-conceit. That I have some merit I do not deny; but I see with frequent wringings of heart, that the novelty of my character, and the honest national prejudice of my countrymen, have borne me to a height altogether untenable to my abilities.'

Moore sent Burns a copy of his own *View of Society and Manners*, and, later, of his *Zeluco*. Burns seems to have been delighted with them both. His veneration for Moore did, however, produce one beneficial result. On 2nd August 1787, in Mauchline, Burns took up his pen and told Moore: 'For some months past I have been rambling over the country, partly on account of some little business I have to settle in various places; but of late I have been confined with some lingering complaints originating as I take it in the stomach. To divert my spirits a little in this miserable fog of Ennui, I have taken a whim to give you a history of MYSELF.' What followed was the famous Autobiographical Letter, the original of which is now in the British Museum, and which has formed the basis of all later biographies of Burns. He followed it with a subsequent letter from Ellisland on 4th January 1789, in which the poet brought his story up to that date. He also took a considerable interest in the works of a somewhat indifferent poetess, Miss Williams (*see* **Williams, Helen Maria**), whom Moore was also patronising, and who seems to have acted for a time as his amanuensis.

Only once, towards the end of his life, did Burns criticise Dr Moore, and then in a letter to Mrs Dunlop from Dumfries, dated 20th December 1794. In the *Journal During a Residence in France*, the author deplored the savagery and the bloodshed. At the time his letter was written, Burns's remarks offended the recipient; since then, they have saddened those upholders of the liberal values who are admirers of Burns's work. For words like these, justifying political murder, have become all too familiar in recent years. Wrote Burns: '. . . I must beg leave to say, that he [Moore] has not written this last work in his usual happy manner. Entre nous, you know my Politics; and I cannot approve of the honest Doctor's whining over the deserved fate of a certain pair of Personages. What is there in the delivering over a perjured Blockhead, and an unprincipled Prostitute to the hands of the hangman, that it should arrest, for a moment, attention, in an eventful hour . . .'

Burns's continuing zeal for the Revolution when the idealistic ardour had been replaced merely by a different colour of repression and brutality lost him many friends in the last year and a half of his life. One of those who ceased to correspond with him, and to whom he no longer wrote, was Moore.

Moore, Robert

An offender against the Excise regulations. He received from Burns a note dated 26th October 1789: 'Robt Moore in Dumfries I hereby intimate to you that by decreet of the Justices of the Peace for the County of Dumfries you are fined in the sum of 1£ Ster. for making bricks without entry—and if the said sum be not paid within 14 days from this date you will incur an additional expence of 2d. on each 1 Sh. Ster.'

There is no record of any relationship with Moore, other than this purely business one.

More, Hannah (1745–1833)

An English authoress best known in her own day for *The Search After Happiness*, a pastoral drama, and *Percy* and *The Fatal Secret*, both tragedies. In a letter to Robert Aiken, dated 2nd April 1786, Burns mentioned having inscribed a stanza, beginning 'Thou flat'ring mark of friendship kind' in a 'blank leaf of Miss More's works', presented to the author by a lady. One of the quatrains possibly reflects Burns's opinion of Miss More's qualities:

'She show'd her taste, refin'd and just,
    When she selected thee,
Yet deviating, own I must,
    For so approving me . . .'

Morin, or Morine, John

The Laird of Laggan, which marched with Ellisland. He purchased the farm of Ellisland, when Burns removed to Dumfries, for £1,900. The owner, Patrick Miller of Dalswinton, was willing to sell Ellisland because it was separated by the Nith from the remainder of his estate.

The Rev. Richard Simpson in his book *Ellisland*, quotes Burns's brother-in-law, Adam Armour, as telling 'a curious story about the fate of the window panes at Ellisland on which some of the poet's verses had been engraved'. Evidently Morin had disagreed with Burns over the value of some manure, and had insisted that the fences and offices should all be in proper order. Burns considered he was being hardly treated, in view of the work he had put in on clearing what was virtually waste-ground. On the day of the removal, several things happened to try the poet's temper, and he sent Armour from Dumfries (he had been helping the Burns family to remove) back to Ellisland to smash every pane of glass which carried Burns's hand-writing. According to Armour, these instructions were carried out faithfully.

Syme, in his description of the tour he took with Burns through Galloway, quotes the epigram Burns made on Morin:

'When Morine, deceas'd, to the Devil
                    went down,

'Twas nothing would serve him but
               Satan's own crown:
"Thy fool's head", quoth Satan, "that
               crown shall wear never;
I grant thou'rt as wicked—but not
               quite so clever".'

Morison, Mary (1771-91)

A tombstone in the churchyard at Mauchline maintains she was the daughter of Adjutant John Morison of the 104th Regiment, and that she was the poet's 'bonnie Mary'. Local tradition has it that she met the poet once only. She died of consumption. Her sister was stated by the Reverend Dr Edgar of Mauchline to have said she was the Mary of the poem 'Mary Morison'. Most authorities, however, claim that the name was used by Burns for Alison Begbie, since Burns called the song 'one of my juvenile works', a term he was unlikely to apply to a song written in 1784/5, when the girl would be about fourteen, and twelve years younger than the poet.

Morison, Peter

A Mauchline 'wright'—carpenter and cabinet maker—who made the furniture for Ellisland. He was not, it would seem, a punctual worker, since Burns had to write to him from Isle on 22nd January 1789: 'If ever you wished to deserve the blessing of him that was ready to perish; if ever you were in a situation that a little kindness would have rescued from many evils: if ever you hope to find rest in future states of untryed being; get these matters of mine ready.'

Moro, El

A castle which defended the entrance to the harbour at Santiago, a small island off Cuba. It was stormed in 1762 and taken by the British. Havana surrendered as a result, with a considerable gain in spoil amounting to three million pounds. Burns mentioned the castle in the 'Soldier's Song' from *The Jolly Beggars* Cantata:

'And the Moro low was laid at the
               sound of the drum.'

Morton, Christina

One of the 'Mauchline Belles', whose family was associated with the parish for many years. She married a Mauchline draper, Robert Paterson, in 1788, and bore him four sons and two daughters.

Morton, Hugh

Kept a hostelrie in Mauchline where, the most probable tradition has it, Burns took Jean for his wife before Farquhar-Gray, laird of Gilm:lnscroft and a Justice of the Peace.

Mossgiel

The farm of Mossgiel, or Mossgaville—to give it its old spelling—is in Mauchline parish, about three miles from Lochlea. It has just over a hundred acres. Burns and his brother Gilbert entered into it in March 1784, in circumstances recorded by Gilbert: 'When my father's affairs drew near a crisis, Robert and I took the farm of Mossgiel, consisting of 118 acres, at the rent of ninety pounds per annum, from Mr Hamilton, as an asylum for the family in case of the worst. It was stocked by the property and individual savings of the whole family, and was a joint-concern among us. Every member of the family was allowed ordinary wages for the labour he performed on the farm. My brother's allowance and mine was seven pounds per annum each. The farm lies very high and mostly on a cold wet bottom.' In the Autobiographical Letter, Burns told Dr Moore of his good resolutions on beginning life at Mossgiel: 'I read farming books; I calculated crops; I attended markets; and in short, in spite of "The devil, the world and the flesh," I believe I would have been a wise man; but the first year from unfortunately buying in bad seed, the second from a late harvest, we lost half of both our crops: this overset all my wisdom. . . . My brother wanted my hare brained

I

imagination, as well as my social and amorous madness, but in good sense and every sober qualification he was far my superiour.'

There was another cause of distraction, too. It is only necessary to glance at a list of the poems written by Burns between his arrival at Mossgiel and his departure for Edinburgh to realise that his mind was by no means wholly set on farming. For among the poems were 'The Vision'; the 'Address to the Unco Guid'; the two 'Epistles to Davie'; and the three 'Epistles to J. Lapraik'; 'Hallowe'en'; 'The Jolly Beggars'; 'The Cotter's Saturday Night'; 'The Ordination'; 'The Author's Earnest Cry and Prayer'; the 'Address to the Deil'; 'The Holy Fair'; 'Holy Willie's Prayer'; 'Death and Dr Hornbook'; 'The Braes o' Ballochmyle'; 'Scotch Drink' and 'The Twa Dogs'.

In Burns's day, the farmhouse at Mossgiel was a single storey 'but an' ben' cottage, with a garret containing three small rooms, the centre one of which was occupied by Robert and Gilbert. Burns had a table, where, at the end of the day's work, he wrote out the verses he had composed in the fields. Today, Mossgiel is a two-storey house, and the old thatched roof has long been replaced by a slated roof.

See Plate 4

Mount Oliphant

The farm of Mount Oliphant, on the estate of Doonholm, lies about three miles from Ayr. At Martinmas (11th November) 1765, William Burnes rented Mount Oliphant, and, at Whitsun 1766, moved into it with his family from the 'Auld Clay Biggin' at Alloway. The farm had just over seventy acres at that time, and the rent was to be forty pounds for the first six years, and thereafter, for the remaining six years, forty-five pounds. In order to stock his farm, William Burnes tried, unsuccessfully, to dispose of the lease of his property at Alloway in which his capital

was tied up, so his new landlord, Provost William Fergusson of Ayr, by whom he was still employed as a gardener, lent him one hundred pounds.

Gilbert Burns later said that the soil at Mount Oliphant was almost the poorest that he ever knew of in a state of cultivation. Because of this, William Burnes soon got into difficulties, which were increased by the loss of several of his beasts as a result of accident and disease. The family lived with the utmost economy, and for several years, butcher meat was a rarity on their table. In these difficult times, the family helped in the fields, in the poet's case to such an extent that he overtaxed his strength and probably caused the initial damage to his heart which resulted in his early death. Wrote Gilbert: 'My brother, at the age of thirteen, assisted in threshing the crop of corn, and at fifteen was the principal labourer on the farm, for we had no hired servants male or female. I doubt not, but the hard labour and sorrow of this period of his life, was in a great measure, the cause of that depression of spirits with which Robert was so often afflicted through his whole life afterwards.'

To add to the family's troubles, their landlord died, on 7th November 1769, according to his tombstone in Ayr Auld kirkyard. The estate then passed into the control of a factor, who, in accordance with his duty, took a sterner line over delays in rent. As Burns put it in his Autobiographical Letter: 'My father's generous Master died; the farm proved a ruinous bargain; and, to clench the curse, we fell into the hands of a Factor who sat for the picture I have drawn of one in my Tale of two dogs. There was a freedom in his [Burnes's] lease in two years more, and to weather these two years, we retrenched expenses. We lived very poorly. . . . A Novel-Writer might perhaps have viewed these scenes with some satisfaction, but so did not I: my indignation yet boils at the recollection of the scoundrel tyrant's insolent, threatening epistles, which used to get us all in tears.' If, however, the date on Fergusson's tombstone is correct, Burnes not only did not take advantage of the break in the lease, which occurred in November 1771, but must have endured the factor's 'snash' for almost eight years after Provost Fergusson's death.

In the Autobiographical Letter, however, Burns also related that it was while working at a Mount Oliphant harvest that he fell in love with his first girl—Nellie Kilpatrick—and wrote for her his first song, 'O once I loved a bonnie lass'. He went on: 'My father struggled on till he reached the freedom in his lease, when he entered on a larger farm about ten miles farther in the country.' The larger farm was Lochlea, and the move was made at Whitsun 1777.

See Plate 4.

Muir, Robert (1758–88)

A Kilmarnock wine merchant, whom Burns met in 1786 and apparently found a congenial companion. Muir was one of the first whom Burns informed of the birth of Jean Armour's first twins. Writing to Muir from Mossgiel on 8th September 1786, Burns said: 'You will have heard that poor Armour has repaid my amorous mortgages double. A very fine boy and girl have awakened a thousand feelings that thrill, some with tender pleasure, and some with foreboding anguish, thro' my soul.'

Muir subscribed for seventy-two copies of the Kilmarnock Edition, and for forty of the first Edinburgh Edition.

Burns kept him informed about the people he was meeting in the Capital, and also sent him a kind of letter journal during the Highland tour of 1787.

Though Muir's health was never strong, he appears to have been extremely industrious, clearing the debt with which the estate of Loanfoot was encumbered when he inherited it from his father. On 7th March 1788, Burns wrote hoping that: 'the Spring will renew your shattered frame and make your friends happy'. But less than two months later, on 22nd April 1788, Muir died of consumption.

In the curious 'conscience' letter about Highland Mary which Burns wrote to Mrs Dunlop on 13th December 1789, the poet listed Muir as one of those he hoped to meet if 'there is a world to come . . . Muir, thy weaknesses were the aberration of Human-nature, but thy heart glowed with everything generous, manly and noble; and if ever emanation from the All-good Being animated a human form, it was thine'.

In the same letter, he transcribed for Mrs Dunlop, his rather banal 'Epitaph on R. Muir':

'What Man could esteem, or what
                    Woman could love,
    Was He who lies under this sod:
If Such Thou refusest admittance above,
    Then whom wilt thou favor, Good
                    God!'

It was to Muir, in the last letter he wrote him, dated 7th March 1788, that Burns recorded what was probably his frankest statement of his religious beliefs: 'If we lie down in the grave, the whole man a piece of broke machinery, to moulder with the clods of the valley—be it so; at least there is an end of pain, care, woes and wants: if that part of us called Mind, does survive the apparent destruction of the man— away with old-wife prejudices and tales! Every age and every nation has had a different set of stories; and as the many are always weak, of consequence they have often, perhaps always been deceived: a man, conscious of having acted an honest part among his fellow creatures; even granting that he may have been the sport, at times of passions and instincts; he goes to a great unknown Being who could have no other end in giving him existence but to make him happy; who gave him those passions and instincts, and well knows their force.'

Muir, William (d. 1793)

Owner of Willie's Mill, Tarbolton, which is mentioned in 'Death and Dr Hornbook'. Muir was a friend of the Burns family. He took in Jean Armour when she discovered that, for the second time, Burns had made her pregnant. Here, Burns visited her on 23rd February 1788, riding back to Mossgiel from Dunlop House. Thereafter, he wrote to Clarinda, calling Jean a 'farthing taper beside the cloudless glory of the meridian sun', the 'sun' being, of course, Clarinda.

In his *Second Commonplace Book,* Burns wrote an epitaph on Muir:

'An honest man here lies at rest,
As e'er God with his Image blest:
A friend of man, the friend of truth,
The friend of age and guide of youth;
Few hearts like his—with virtue warm'd,
Few heads with knowledge so
informed:
If there's another world, he lives in
bliss;
If there is none, he made the best of
this.'

Burns was largely responsible for helping Muir's widow, through the good offices of Gavin Hamilton.

Muirhead of Logan, The Reverend Dr James (1742–1805)

Minister of Urr. He was a landed proprietor, and claimed to be chief of Clan Muirhead. According to Young, he was 'a man of considerable humour', but also 'of the *irritable genus,* and nowise disposed to submit to the abuse and sarcastic ballads of Burns, whom he purposed to hunt out of society as a public nuisance.'

Burns described him as being 'as guid as he's true' in the Second Heron Election Ballad. There is an even more pointed reference in the third election ballad:

'And by our banners march'd Muirhead,
And Buittle was na slack,

Whase haly priesthood nane could
stain,
For wha could dye the black?'

Muirhead himself scribbled epigrams and lampoons. As part of his hounding of Burns, he printed a brochure in Edinburgh, which began:

'The ancient poets, all agree,
Sang sweeter far than modern we,
In this, besides, their racy rhymes
Were told in far, far fewer lines. . . .'

Then he quoted Martial's epigram 'In Vacerram', which he paraphrased thus:

'Vacerra, shabby son of whore,
Why do thy patrons keep thee poor?
Bribe-worthy service thou canst boast
At once their bulwark and their post;
Thou art a sycophant, a traitor,
A liar, a calumniator,
Who conscience (hadst thou that)
would'st sell,
Nay, lave the common shores of hell,
For whisky; eke, most precious imp,
Thou art a rhymster, gauger, pimp;
Whence comes it, then, Vacerra, that
Thou still art poor as a church-rat?'

Alexander Young, an Edinburgh lawyer, wrote of Muirhead's verses: 'It consists with my knowledge, that no publication in answer to the scurrilities of Burns ever did him so much harm in public opinion, or made Burns himself feel so sore, as Dr Muirhead's translation of Martial's epigram. When I remonstrated with the doctor against his printing and circulating that translation, I asked him how he proved that Vacerra was a gauger as well as Burns. He answered: "Martial calls him *fellator,* which means *sucker,* or a man who drinks from the cask." '

Mundell, Dr James

A naval surgeon who retired to Dumfries and practised as a doctor. There, he also became a partner in a small cotton-mill, the power for which was provided by an ox on a treadmill.

Burns wrote to him from Isle in October 1788: 'As my symptoms are continuing milder, I have not waited on you; but my liquid drug has failed. You will please send me by my servant the bearer, a recruit of the G—d D—n. I am still using the unction, tho', thank Heaven, not extreme unction.'

Another little domestic note has survived from January 1790: 'The bearer, Janet Nievison, is a neighbour, and occasionally a laborer of mine. She has got some complaint in her shoulder, and wants me to find her out a Doctor that will cure her, so I have sent her to you. You will remember that she is just in the jaws of MATRIMONY so for Heaven's sake, get her "hale and sound" as soon as possible. We are all pretty well; only the little boy's sore mouth has again inflamed Mrs. B—'s Nipples.'

Burns listed Mundell's name as one of eleven subscribers, beside himself, for *The Bee*, when he wrote to its editor, Dr James Anderson, on 1st November 1790.

Writing to Mrs Walter Riddell in November 1793, the poet made a reference to Mundell's Mill: 'There is a species of the Human genus that I call the Gin-horse Class: what enviable dogs they are! Round, and round, and round they go— Mundell's ox that drives his cotton-mill, their exact prototype—without an idea or wish beyond their circle; fat, sleek, stupid, patient, quiet and contented: while here I sit, altogether Novemberish, a damn'd melange of Fretfulness and melancholy; not enough of the one to rouse me to passion, nor of the other to repose me in torpor; my soul flouncing and fluttering round her tenement, like a wild Finch caught amid the horrors of winter and newly thrust into a cage.'

Murdoch, John (1747–1824)

Born at Ayr, Murdoch, when a youth of eighteen, was engaged by William Burnes and some of his neighbours at Alloway, as teacher for their children. When Burnes and his family moved to Mount Oliphant,

Robert and Gilbert went on attending Murdoch's school for a further two years. Murdoch then moved out of the district, but returned to Ayr in 1772, where Burns had some further weeks of instruction from him.

Gilbert Burns later recorded for Dr Currie his memories of the instruction he and his brother received from Murdoch: 'With him we learned to read English tolerably well; and to write a little. He taught us, too, the English grammar; but Robert made some proficiency in it, a circumstance of considerable weight in the unfolding of his genius and character; as he soon became remarkable for the fluency and correctness of his expression, and read the few books that came in his way with much pleasure and improvement; for even then he was a reader when he could get a book. Murdoch, whose library at that time had no great variety in it, lent him the *Life of Hannibal*, which was the first book he read (the school-books excepted), and almost the only one he had an opportunity of reading while he was at school.'

Gilbert also recorded Murdoch's farewell visit, when his school was breaking up because his principal employer had moved: 'Murdoch came to spend the night with us, and to take his leave when he was about to go into Carrick. He brought us a present and memorial of him, a small compendium of English Grammar, and the tragedy of *Titus Andronicus*, and by way of passing the evening, he began to read the play aloud. We were all attention for some time, till presently the whole party was dissolved in tears. A female in the play (I have but a confused recollection of it) had her hands chopt off, and her tongue cut out, and then was insultingly desired to call for water to wash her hands. At this, in an agony of distress, we with one voice desired that he would read no more. My father observed, that if we would not hear it out, it would be needless to leave the play with us. Robert replied that if it was left he would burn it.

My father was going to chide him for this ungrateful return to his tutor's kindness, but Murdoch interposed, declaring that he liked to see so much sensibility; and he left the *School for Love*, a comedy (translated I think from the French) in its place.'

Of Murdoch's subsequent return to Ayr, Gilbert wrote: 'About this time, Murdoch, our former teacher, after having been in different places in the country, and having taught a school some time in Dumfries, came to be the established teacher of the English language in Ayr, a circumstance of considerable consequence to us. The remembrance of my father's former friendship, and his attachment to my brother, made him do everything in his power for our improvement. He sent us Pope's *Works*, and some other poetry, the first that we had an opportunity of reading, excepting what is contained in the *English Collection*, and in the volume of the *Edinburgh Magazine* for 1772 . . .

'The summer after we had been at Dalrymple School, my father sent Robert to Ayr, to revise his English grammar with his former teacher. He had been there only one week, when he was obliged to return, to assist at the harvest. When the harvest was over, he went back to school, where he remained two weeks. . . . During the two last weeks that he was with Murdoch, he himself was engaged in learning French. . . .'

Murdoch later set down his views on the relative abilities of his two pupils: 'Gilbert always appeared to me to possess a more lively imagination, and to be more of a wit, than Robert. I attempted to teach them a little church-music. Here they were left far behind by all the rest of the school. Robert's ear, in particular, was remarkably dull, and his voice untunable. It was long before I could get them to distinguish one tune from another. Robert's countenance was generally grave and expressive of a serious, contemplative and thoughtful mind. Gilbert's face said, "Mirth with thee I mean to live"; and certainly if any person

who knew the two boys had been asked which of them was most likely to court the Muses, he would surely never have guessed that Robert had a propensity of that kind.'

Murdoch's career at Ayr came somewhat abruptly to an end on 14th February 1776. A complaint had been lodged against him that he, in the house of Mrs Tennent, inn-keeper in Ayr, as well as in the house of Patrick Auld, weaver in Ayr: 'did utter the following, or such like, unworthy, base, reproachful and wicked expressions—viz. that he, Dr William Dalrymple, was as revengeful as Hell, and as false as the devil; and that he was a liar, or a damned liar. . . .'

Murdoch thereafter went to London, and for a time did well as a teacher of French. But the French Revolution resulted in a flood of refugees arriving in London, cutting into his income. He seems to have tried to keep a shop. He saw Burns's young brother, William, in London shortly before the youth's death, and assisted in the funeral arrangements, an account of which he sent to Burns, his last communication with his famous pupil.

Murdoch died in extreme poverty.

Murray of Broughton, Alexander (d. 1750)

Husband of Lady Euphemia Stewart, sixth Earl of Galloway. In relation to the conduct of James Murray (see below), Burns refers to the Galloway connection being 'Fast knit in chaste and holy bands/ Wi' Broughton's noble name'.

Murray of Lintrose, Euphemia (b. 1769)

A cousin of Sir William Murray of Ochtertyre, Euphemia Murray was known as 'The Flower of Strathmore'. She was eighteen when Burns stayed with Sir William in 1787, and wrote the song 'Blythe, blythe and merry was she'. Of the song, he recalled: 'I composed these verses while I stayed at Ochtertyre with Sir William Murray. The lady, who was also at Ochtertyre at the same time, was a well-known toast, Miss Euphemia Murray of Lintrose. . . .' The lady, according to tradition, did not appreciate the honour done her by Burns, though one who knew her said that the concluding verse was 'very expressive of her appearance and style of beauty':

'Her bonnie face it was as meek,
  As ony lamb upon a lee; [lea
The evening sun was ne'er sae sweet,
  As was the blink o' Phemie's ee.'

In 1794, she married David Smythe of Methven Castle, later a judge of the Court of Session, by whom she had several children.

The tune, 'Andro and his cutty gun', to which the words are set, goes back to the *Caledonian Pocket Companion*, 1754. Burns's song appeared both in the *Scots Musical Museum* and in Thomson's *Scottish Airs*, 1799.

See Plate 7

Murray of Broughton, James (1727–1799)

Uncle to the Tory candidate Gordon of Balmaghie, who was contesting the Stewartry of Kirkcudbright in February 1795. Murray, who owned the estate of Cally, in Wigtonshire, was M.P. for the county. According to Chambers, Murray had left his wife (his cousin Lady Catherine Stewart, daughter of the Sixth Earl of Galloway) and eloped with Grace Johnston, his niece. Because of his great wealth, he did this with comparative impunity, and did not forfeit his association with his wife's family, one of whose relations he was supporting in the election.

In his Second Heron Election Ballad, Burns wrote:

'An' there'll be Murray commander
  An' Gordon the battle to win:
Like brothers, they'll stan' by each
                  other,
Sae knit in alliance and kin:'

Murray, John, fourth Duke of Athole (1755–1830)

Succeeded his father in the dukedom in 1774. Burns visited the family seat at Blair when he was on his Highland tour. The Duke was absent at the time, but, according to Josiah Walker, the Duchess invited Burns to dinner and to stay at Blair, which he did. The Athole family urged Burns to stay longer, but Nicol, his travelling companion, was anxious to press on. On the Duke's return, he advised the poet to visit the Falls of Bruar. This resulted in the poem 'The Humble Petition of Bruar Water'. Burns met Graham of Fintry at Blair. Had the poet been able to stay a little longer, he would also have met Henry Dundas, 'the uncrowned King of Scotland', a meeting which might have considerably altered Burns's prospects.

The Duke's first wife, whom Burns met, was Jane, daughter of Charles, ninth Lord Cathcart. Burns also met her two sisters at Athole House—Mrs Graham and Miss Cathcart. He described the three of them in a letter to Josiah Walker, from Inverness, 5th September 1787, as: 'the amiable, truly noble Duchess . . . the beautiful Mrs Graham; the lovely, sweet Miss Cathcart'.

Murray, William, first Earl of Mansfield (1705–1793)

Son of the fifth Viscount Stormont, educated at Perth Grammar School, Westminster School and Christ Church, Oxford, he was called to the English bar. He appeared for Edinburgh when it was threatened with disenfranchisement after the Porteous Riots. He was appointed Solicitor General in 1742, Attorney-General in 1754, and Lord Chief Justice in 1756. A member of the Cabinet for fifteen years, he was created Earl of Mansfield in 1776, and acted as Speaker of the House of Lords in 1783. His considerable legal reforms gave rise to some lines attributed to Burns as an answer to his criticism of the Stewarts on a Stirling inn window.

'Rash mortal, and slanderous Poet, thy
name
Shall no longer appear in the records
of fame:
Dost not know that old Mansfield,
who writes like the Bible,
Says the more 'tis a truth, Sir, the
more 'tis a libel?'

Murray of Ochtertyre, Sir William (d. 1800)

Burns visited Sir William and his family in 1787 when he was making his tour in Clackmannanshire with Dr Adair. *See* **Murray, Euphemia**. It was among the Ochtertyre hills that Burns wrote 'On scaring some Waterfowl in Loch Turit'. Sir William was a cousin of Robert Graham of Fintry, to whom Burns, in a letter of 13th May 1798, referred to Sir William as his 'honored friend'.

Music, Burns and

Burns's poems have been set by many composers. The following list contains the more important settings, but otherwise does not claim to be complete. It does not include arrangements, or, in general, unpublished settings.

Settings by German composers
Heinrich Marschner (1795–1861)
    John Anderson
Felix Mendelssohn (1809–1847)
    O wert thou in the cauld blast
J. R. Durner (b. Ausbach 1810–d. Edinburgh 1859)
    John Anderson
Robert Schumann (1810–1856)
    Hey Baloo
    The Independent Man
    John Anderson (two settings)
    The Red, Red Rose
    Out over the Forth
Adolph Jensen (1837–1879)
    John Anderson
Carl Reinecke (1824–1910)
    John Anderson
Alexander Ernst Fesca (1820–1859)
    My heart's in the Highlands

Robert Franz (rea name Knauth) (1815–1892)
    Fourteen songs set to the Poems of Robert Burns

Settings by Russian composers
Dmitri Shostakovitch (b. 1906)
    Six Romances to words by Burns, Shakespeare and Walter Raleigh (1942)
Tikhon Nikolaievitch Khrennikov (b. 1913)
    Five Songs, translated by Marshak, opus II (composed 1942)

Settings by American composers
Edward MacDowell (1861–1908)
    Ye banks and braes

Settings by Finnish composers
Leevi Madetoja (1887–1947)
    Elli Dunbar—male voice choir (1920)

Settings by English composers
Sir W. Sterndale Bennett (1816–75)
    Castle Gordon
    Musing on the Roaring Ocean
    To Chloe
Miles Birket Foster (1851–1921)
    My Heart's in the Highlands
Edward German (1851–1921)
    Charming Chloe
Liza Lehmann (1862–1918)
    Bonnie Wee Thing
Samuel Coleridge-Taylor (1875–1912)
    Here's a Health to Ane I Loe Dear
Freda Swain (b. 1902)
    Five Settings of Poems by Burns (1924)
Phillip Hattey (b. 1911)
    Jean
Benjamin Britten (b. 1913)
    Highland Balou (from a Charm of Lullabies, 1947)
Hugo Cole (b. 1917)
    A Farewell (1961)
Donald Swann (b. 1923)
    O my luve is like a red, red rose—
Alan J. Rideout (b. 1934)
    There's News, Lasses, News (A Cantata on Poems by Burns for female voices and orchestra), 1969
Nicholas Maw (b. 1935)
    Five Epigrams (1961), for mixed voices

Settings by Scottish Composers
Francis George Scott (1880–1952)
  O Steer Her Up
  O Wert Thou in the Cauld Blast
  Robin Shure in Hairst
  The Carles of Dysart
  Ay Waukin O
  Last May a Braw Wooer
  The Wren's Nest
  The Lovely Lass O' Inverness
  Hey' the Dusty Miller
  Wha Will Buy My Troggin?
  O Merry Hae I been Teethin a Heckle
  Mary Morison
  The Weary Pund O' Tow
  Crowdie
  O Were My Love Yon Lilac Fair
  The Tailor Fell Thro the Bed
  O a' the Airts
  My Wife's a Wanton Wee Thing
  O Were I on Parnassus Hill
  O Dear Miny
  Scroggam
  My Love is Like a Red, Red Rose
  Amang the Trees
  Wee Willie Gray
  The Discreet Hint
  O Wha My Babie Clouts Will Buy?
  Wha is That At My Bower Door?
  Landlady, Count the Lawin
  Rattlin', Roarin' Willie
  Scots Wha Hae
W. B. Moonie (b. 1883)
  Bonie Lesley
Ian Whyte (1901–1960)
  Ye Flow'ry Banks
  Auld Lang Syne
Cedric Thorpe Davie (b. 1913)
  A Rosebud By My Early Walk

Settings of Larger Works (and Works 'after' Burns)
Sir Alexander C. Mackenzie (1847–1935)
  The Cotter's Saturday Night—cantata
      for chorus and orchestra (1888)
  The Selkirk Grace and 'O Thou in
      Whom We Live and Move'
      (Two part songs, 1931)
  Tam O' Shanter—Scottish Rhapsody
      No. 3 (1911) Opus 74

G. W. Chadwick (b. Lowell, Mass. 1854–
      d. Boston 1931)
  Tam O' Shanter—Symphonic Ballad
      1917)
F. Learmont Drysdale (1866–1909)
  Ode to Edinburgh—cantata for baritone,
      chorus and orchestra (1890)
  Tam O' Shanter—concert overture
      (1890)
William Howard Glover (1819–75)
  Tam O' Shanter—tenor, chorus, large
      orchestra. (First performed by New
      Philharmonic Society under Berlioz
      on 4th July 1855)
Sir Eugene Goossens (b. 1893)
  Tam O' Shanter—Scherzo
Deryck Cooke (b. 1919)
  Tam O' Shanter—tenor, male chorus,
      piano and orchestra (1958)
Malcolm Arnold (b. 1921)
  Tam O' Shanter—Overture (1955).
Iain Hamilton (b. 1922)
  Sinfonia for two orchestras (Jointly
      commissioned by Edinburgh Festival
      Society and the Burns Federation in
      commemoration of the bicentenary
      of the birth of Burns, and first per-
      formed in the Usher Hall, Edinburgh
      on 18th August 1959)

Mutrie, The Reverend John (d. 1785)
Minister of the Second Charge of Kilmarnock from 1775–85, succeeding the
moderate, William Lindsay. Burns says in
'The Ordination' that Mutrie and his
colleague Robertson 'were just a match,
we never had sic twa drones'.

Mylne, James (d. 1788)
A farmer and poet who died, in early
middle life, of an 'inflammatory fever', at
Loch-hill, near Prestonpans. Among his
papers, he left a considerable number of
plays and poems, one of which, containing
forty-one stanzas, was addressed to
Burns.
  Mylne's son, George, seems to have
communicated with the Reverend Patrick
Carfrae of Morham, Mrs Dunlop's parish.

Carfrae thereupon wrote, on 2nd January 1789, to ask Burns's advice on the publication of Mylne's work: 'It falls to my share who have lived on the most intimate and uninterrupted friendship with him from my youth upwards, to transmit to you the verses he wrote on the publication of your incomparable poems. It is probable they were his last, as they were found in his scrutoire, folded up with the form of a letter, addressed to you, and, I imagine, were only prevented from being sent by himself, by that melancholy dispensation which we still bemoan. The verses themselves I will not pretend to criticise, when writing to a gentleman whom I consider as entirely qualified to judge of their merit. They are the only verses he seems to have attempted in the Scottish style. . . . If it is your opinion they are not unworthy of the author and will be no discredit to you, it is the inclination of Mr Mylne's friends that they should be immediately published in some periodical work, to give the world a specimen of what may be expected from his performances in the poetical line, which,

perhaps, will be afterwards published for the advantage of his family.'

Mrs Dunlop was familiar with Mylne's work, and had no doubt been shown a copy of the poem on Burns by the Reverend Carfrae. At any rate, writing to her from Ellisland on 4th March 1789, Burns said: 'You are right, Madam, in your idea of poor Mylne's poem which he has addressed to me. The piece has a good deal of merit, but it has one damning fault—it is by far too long. Besides, my success has encouraged such a shoal of ill-spawned monsters to crawl into public notice, under the title of Scots Poets, that the very term, Scots Poetry, borders on the burlesque. When I write Mr Carfrae, I shall advise him rather to try one of his deceased friend's English pieces.'

This advice he gave to Mr Carfrae when he wrote to him on 27th April 1789. Mylne's *Poems, consisting of Miscellaneous Pieces and Two Tragedies* was published in Edinburgh in 1790. Burns's name appears on the list of subscribers.

Mc

McAdam, Miss

A daughter of John McAdam of Craigengillan, for whom Burns wrote an epistle. In a letter dated 11th January 1787, to the Mauchline surgeon Dr John Mackenzie, Burns referred to Sir John Whitefoord's son, John, having had 'the good luck to pre-engage the hand of the beauty-famed, and wealth-celebrated Miss McAdam, our Country-woman' for 'the Assembly and Ball of the Caledonian Hunt'.

McAdam of Craigengillan, John

A rich man and an agricultural improver whose lands included Barbeth, Straiton, and Dunaskin, Dalmellington.

McAdam wrote to Burns, who replied with 'To Mr McAdam of Craigengillan, in answer to an obliging letter he sent in the commencement of my poetic career.' The second stanza

> Now deal-ma-care about their jaw, [*chaff*
> The senseless, gawky million. [*foolish*
> I'll cock my nose aboon them a',
> I'm roos'd by Craigengillan!' [*praised*

shows that Burns was by no means always averse from being noticed by the gentry. Writing to Dr Mackenzie from Edinburgh on 11th January 1787, Burns told him that Sir John Whitefoord's son, John: 'who calls very frequently on me, is in a fuss today like a coronation. This is the great day—The Assembly and Ball of the Caledonian Hunt—and John has had the good luck to pre-engage the hand of the beauty-famed and wealth-celebrated Miss McAdam, our Country-woman.' She was Craigengillan's daughter.

McAdam, together with William Chalmers, was also the recipient of a humorous mandate ordering them to have destroyed 'a certain [bawdy], nefarious, abominable and wicked Song or Ballad, a copy whereof We have here inclosed'. The 'Mandate' was dated Mauchline, 20th November 1786.

Burns referred to the McAdam girls as 'loosome kimmers' in the 'Epistle'.

McAdam of Craigengillan, Quinton (d. 1805)

Son of John McAdam of Craigengillan, to whom Burns wrote a rhymed epistle in 1786. Quinton McAdam owned the estate of Dunaskin bought by his father. *See* **McAdam of Craigengillan**. In the Second Heron Election Ballad, Burns describes Quinton as '—o' lads no the warst!' Quinton McAdam committed suicide.

M'Auley, John

Town-clerk of Dumbarton in 1787. He lived in Levengrove House, which no longer exists but stood in what is now Levengrove Park. He secured some subscriptions for the first Edinburgh Edition.

Burns stayed the night of 26th June 1787, at Dumbarton, at the end of his short West Highland tour. M'Auley may well have been his host.

M'Culloch, David (d. 1825)

Son of David M'Culloch of Ardwall and Janet Corsane, David junior was a friend of Burns at Dumfries, and a fellow mason of St Andrew's Lodge. M'Culloch told Lockhart that when on one occasion he rode into Dumfries in 1794, he saw Burns walking alone on one side of the street unrecognised by the gentry on the other. M'Culloch made to cross to the side on which the poet was, but Burns called out, 'Nay, nay, my young friend, that's all over now': then, after a pause, quoted the lines beginning, 'His bonnet stood ance fu' fair on his brow', from 'O, werena my hert licht, I wad die', by Lady Grizel Baillie. Shortly after this episode,

Burns wrote from Dumfries on 21st June 1794, telling M'Culloch he was to visit Galloway, and proposing that M'Culloch should join him and Mr Syme on a visit to Patrick Heron at Kerroughtree.

McDoual, Captain Andrew

At the early age of twenty-five, Captain (afterwards Colonel) McDoual represented Wigtown in Parliament. He seduced Margaret Kennedy (q.v.), who had a daughter by him in 1794. He married the daughter of a Dumfriesshire Laird, and heired his father's estate of Logan in Wigtonshire.

In the Second Heron Election Ballad, among those who would be at Kirkcudbright:

'. . . there'll be Logan McDoual—
Sculdudd'ry an' he will be there'.

and in the 'Epistle from Esopus to Maria (which is possibly not really the work of Burns) he is referred to as:

'The crafty Colonel leaves the tartan'd
lines
For other wars, where he a hero shines.'

Chambers called him 'a noted Lothario', and he was apparently an admirer of Maria Riddell.

McGill, The Reverend William (1732–1807)

The son of William McGill, who farmed in Wigtonshire, the Reverend McGill was educated at Glasgow University, licensed to preach in 1759, and appointed assistant to the minister of Kilwinning. He was ordained to the second charge of Ayr in 1760 and received a doctorate of divinity from Glasgow in 1785. He was a friend of old William Burnes. Father and son both approved of his New Licht doctrines.

McGill, however, was a timid man for all his liberality, 'a mixture of simplicity and stoicism'. When his essay, The Death of Jesus Christ, published in 1786, was denounced as heterodox by Dr William Peebles of Newton-on-Ayr, McGill published a defence, The Benefits of the Revolution, in 1789. The charge was that, while receiving the privileges of the Church, he was at the same time plunging a dagger into her heart. In May 1789, the General Assembly ordered an inquiry into the affair. The Ayr magistrates published in the press their appreciation of McGill's services. McGill brought the proceedings to a close by offering an apology to the court, and the case was dropped.

An explanation of the timidity of one called by Mrs Dunlop 'a poor little white rabbit', is to be found in the letter Burns wrote to Graham of Fintry, in December 1789:

'I think you must have heard of Dr McGill, one of the clergymen of Ayr, and his heretical book. God help him, poor man! though he is one of the worthiest as well as one of the ablest, of the whole priesthood of the Kirk of Scotland, in every sense of that ambiguous term, yet for the blasphemous heresies of squaring Religion by the rules of Common Sense, and attempting to give a decent character to Almighty God and a rational account of his proceedings with the Sons of Men, the poor Doctor and his numerous family are in imminent danger of being thrown out to the mercy of the winter winds.'

To John Logan, 7th August 1789, Burns had written: 'If I could be of any service to Dr McGill, I would do it though it should be at a much greater expence than irritating a few bigotted Priests.'

M'Indoe, Robert

A silk merchant to whom Burns wrote from Mauchline on 5th August 1788, at 'Horn's Land, off Virginia Street, Glasgow', ordering 'fifteen yds. black Lutestring silk, such as they used to make gowns and petticoats of'. No definite facts about M'Indoe seem to be recoverable now.

Maciver, Susanna

Author of Cookery and Pastry, 1787, how

gives the recipe for a haggis, which in Burns's day was a luxury dish.

'Make the haggis-bag perfectly clean; parboil the draught; boil the liver very well, so as it will grate; dry the meal before the fire; mince the draught and a pretty large piece of beef very small; grate about half the liver; mince plenty of suet, and some onions small; mix all these . . . and season them properly with salt and mixed spices; take any of the scraps of beef . . . and some of the water that boiled the draught, and make about a choppin of good stock of it; then put all the haggis-meat into the bag, and that breath in it; then sew up the bag; but be sure to put out all the wind before you sew it quite close . . . If it is a large haggis, it will take at least two hours boiling.'

Mackay, Georgina
A girl whom Burns told Mrs Dunlop had turned his head with 'flattering attentions and artful compliments'. She may have inspired his song 'Tam Glen'.

M'Kenzie of Cassencary, Colonel
Described as 'gay' in the second of Burns's Heron Election Ballads.

Mackenzie, Lady Augusta
Wife of Sir William Murray of Ochtertyre, and youngest daughter of the third Earl of Cromarty, a fervent Jacobite, who just escaped execution on Tower Hill in 1746 where Kilmarnock and Balmerino went to the scaffold. Burns described her in a letter to William Nicol, which he wrote when staying at Ochtertyre, dated 8th October 1787: '. . . a most engaging woman, and very happy in her family, which makes one's outgoings and incomings very agreeable'.

Mackenzie, Henry (1745-1831)
The son of an Edinburgh physician, he was best known as a novelist and writer in his own day. Educated at the High School in Edinburgh, he studied law at Edinburgh University and in London, and in 1768 was practising law in the Scottish Court of Exchequer. He was also a Freemason. In 1771, *The Man of Feeling* was published by him anonymously and achieved wide popularity. In 1773, the year he met Dr Johnson, Mackenzie published, under his own name, *The Man of the World* and, in 1777, *Julia de Roubigné*. He became the editor of, first, *The Mirror*, and then the short-lived *Lounger*. In the copy of the *Lounger* for 9th December 1786, he wrote an article commending the Kilmarnock Edition of Burns's *Poems*, which helped considerably to make Burns's name known among the Edinburgh literati.

'Though I am far from meaning to compare our rustic bard to Shakespeare,' Mackenzie wrote, 'yet whoever will read his lighter and more humourous poems . . . will perceive with what uncommon penetration and sagacity this Heaven-taught ploughman, from his humble and unlettered station, has looked upon men and manners.'

This review established the myth of Burns as the unlettered ploughman. He was not, of course, a ploughman, but a farmer, and much more highly 'lettered' than the kindly though patronising Mackenzie.

Even before the appearance of this review, Burns held an extraordinarily high opinion of Mackenzie. Writing to Murdoch on 15th January 1783, Burns told his old teacher that *The Man of Feeling* was 'a book I prize next to the Bible'.

On 17th April 1787, Mackenzie's professional advice to Burns resulted in the memorandum drawn up between the poet and his Edinburgh publisher, William Creech.

'By advice of friends, Mr Burns having resolved to dispose of the property of his *Poems*, and, having consulted with Mr Henry M'Kenzie upon the subject, Mr Creech met with Mr Burns at Mr M'Kenzie's house upon Tuesday, the 17th April 1787, in the evening, and they three having retired and conversed upon the subject, Mr Burns and Mr Creech referred the sum, to be named by Mr M'Kenzie, as being well acquainted with matters of this kind, when Mr M'Kenzie said he thought Mr Burns should have a hundred guineas for the property of his *Poems* . . .'

Mackenzie has sometimes been criticised for advising Burns to accept what, by modern standards, seems a small sum for so great a work. But by the standards of his day, and having regard to the still limited nature of Burns's fame at the time, it was surely a reasonable settlement.

Mackenzie's friendship with Burns, though it probably never got past the formal stage, resulted in an introduction to Mackenzie's brother-in-law, Sir James Grant of Castle Grant, whom the poet visited during his Highland tour of 1787.

Mackenzie helped found the Royal Society of Edinburgh in 1783, and the Highland and Agricultural Society in 1784. He became Comptroller of Taxes for Scotland in 1799, and held the office till his death. He was the dedicatee of Sir Walter Scott's *Waverley*.

In 1776, he married Penuel, daughter of Sir Ludovic Grant of Grant, by whom he had fourteen children.

Mackenzie is the author of some lines, 'Verses on the Destruction of the Woods near Drumlanrig' once credited to Burns.

Mackenzie, Dr John (d. 1837)

Mackenzie, a native of Ayrshire, studied medicine at Edinburgh University, and, on the invitation of Sir John Whitefoord, set up in practice in Mauchline, where he married Helen Miller, one of the 'Mauchline belles'.

He first met Burns when he attended the poet's father, William Burnes, at Lochlea in the early spring of 1783. Dr Mackenzie later recorded that at first: 'The Poet seemed distant, suspicious, and without any wish to interest or please. He kept himself very silent in a dark corner of the room;

and before he took any part in the conversation, I frequently detected him scrutinising me during my conversation with his father and brother. But afterwards, when the conversation, which was on a medical subject, had taken the turn he wished, he began to engage in it, displaying a dexterity of reasoning, an ingenuity of reflection, and a familiarity with topics apparently beyond his reach, by which his visitor was no less gratified than astonished.'

Mackenzie became a warm friend to Burns, particularly after Burns went to Mossgiel. Depute Master of St James Lodge, Tarbolton, Mackenzie received in 1786 from Burns a rhymed summons to attend: 'a procession celebrating the Festival of the Nativity of the Baptist, Friday first's the day appointed'. In 'The Holy Fair', Dr Mackenzie is personified as 'Commonsense', who left the assembly to keep a dinner appointment with Sir John Whitefoord at the home of the Earl of Dumfries as soon as 'Peebles, frae the water-fit' began to preach.

Mackenzie received from Burns a two-line note, dated 3rd September 1786, enclosing a first draft of 'The Calf'. It was thanks to Mackenzie that Burns was introduced to Professor Dugald Stewart.

When Burns set out for Edinburgh, Mackenzie had already sent off letters of recommendation to Sir John Whitefoord and to the Honourable Andrew Erskine. Whitefoord received Burns with special kindness, as Burns reported to Mackenzie in a letter dated 11th January 1787. On the poet's return from Edinburgh in February 1788, he rented a room in Mackenzie's house for Jean and himself, where Jean's second twins were born. The house is now a museum.

Dr Mackenzie later moved to Irvine, on the invitation of Lord Eglinton, whose family physician he became. He retired in 1827.

Mackenzie of Applecross, Thomas

Told the meeting of the Highland Society

in London in 1786, of the intention of 500 people, from the MacDonald of Glengarry estates, to emigrate. Knox in his *Tour of the Highlands*, mentions MacKenzie's favourable treatment of his people. MacKenzie apparently gave up his feudal rights on their labour, and instead paid them sevenpence or eightpence a day when they worked for him. *See* **Campell, John, Earl of Breadalbane.**

Mackinlay, The Reverend Dr James (1756–1841)

He was inducted to the second charge of Kilmarnock, that of the Laigh Kirk, on the death of the Rev. John Mutrie in 1785. The living belonged to the Earl of Glencairn. Mackinlay was one of the Auld Licht ministers, and the disappointment of the moderates at his being given the charge was considerable. The earl, himself a moderate, appointed Mackinlay, because he believed the majority of the parishioners wanted an Auld Licht man. Mackinlay's induction inspired 'The Ordination'. It sets forth the vigorous treatment that Mackinlay and his colleagues would mete out to 'Curst "Common-Sense"':

'This day M'Kinlay takes the flail,
    An' he's the boy will blaud her!
                                             [*slap*
He'll clap a shangan on her tail,
            [*stick put on the tail of a dog*
An' set the bairns to daud her
                                       [*bespatter*
    Wi' dirt this day.'

Burns sent out a number of manuscript copies of this poem, not all of them in his own name, but some of them signed 'Rob Rhymer'.

Mackinlay became a favourite preacher because of his 'fine manner', and received the degree of D.D. from Glasgow University. He was given a dinner, presided over by the Provost of Kilmarnock, on the fiftieth anniversary of his ministry.

According to a newspaper obituary notice, he was a native of Douglas in Lanarkshire. He tutored the family of Sir William Cunningham of Windyhill, through whose influence with the Earl of Glencairn, he ultimately obtained his Kilmarnock charge.

Writing to James Dalrymple of Orangefield from Edinburgh in February 1787, Burns compared the virtues of Glencairn with '. . . the Wp.full Squire Hugh Logan, or Mass James M'Kindlay'. Said Burns:

'At best they are but ill-digested lumps of Chaos, only one of them strongly tinged with bituminous particles and sulphureous effluvia.' Fairly obviously, the chemical attributes were meant to refer to the Reverend Mackinlay!

McLauchlan, Mrs

Burns noted that his song, 'Musing on the Roaring Ocean', which appeared in the second volume of Johnson's *Museum*, was 'composed . . . out of compliment to a Mrs McLauchlan, whose husband is an officer in the East Indies'.

M'Lauchlan, James

Mentioned in 'The Brigs of Ayr'. Burns called him a 'thairm-inspiring sage', and 'a well-known performer of Scottish music on the violin'.

He was a Highlander who was once footman to Lord John Campbell at Inverary. He came to Ayrshire with a Fencible regiment and was patronised by Hugh Montgomerie of Coilsfield (later Earl of Eglinton), also a player and composer. M'Lauchlan, accompanied by Matthew Hall, travelled over the countryside playing in gentlemen's houses on great occasions, sometimes performing in Glasgow and Edinburgh. Hall said that in one week they '. . . passed twenty-six parish kirks, and returned to Ayr on Friday to a ball, never getting to bed until Saturday night'.

M'Leerie, Duncan

The pseudonym used by Burns in his parody, 'Stanzas of Psalmody'. Thursday,

23rd April 1789, was set aside as a day of thanksgiving for George III's recovery from insanity. Burns considered the 'whole business as a solemn farce of pageant mummery', and composed the 'Stanzas' accordingly, alleging in a prefatory note addressed 'Mr Printer' and dated 'Kilmarnock, 25th April', that the stanzas were composed for and sung in, 'a certain *Chapel* not fifty leagues from the market cross of this good town'. The verses and the note, with the date changed to 'April 30th', were published in the *Morning Star*, London, on 14th May 1789.

The first verse and the last three verses illustrate both the bite of the satire and the brilliance of this parody on the lame-dog style of Scots psalmody:

'O sing a new song to the Lord!
    Make, all and every one,
A joyful noise, ev'n for the King
    His Restoration. . . .

'And now thou hast restor'd our State,
    Pity our kirk also,
For she by tribulations,
    Is now brought very low.

'Consume that High-Place
                    PATRONAGE,
    From off thine holy hill;
And in Thy fury burn the book
    Even of that man M'Gill.

'Now hear our Prayer, accept our Song
    And fight Thy Chosen's battle:
We seek but little, Lord, from Thee,
    Thou kens we get as little.'

The 'book' of 'that man M'Gill' was his *Essay on the Death of Jesus Christ*, which occasioned a clerical controversy. *See* **M'Gill, Reverend William.**

**M'Lehose, Agnes Craig, 'Clarinda'
(1759–1841)**
Agnes Craig—or Nancy as she was known to her friends—was the daughter of a Glasgow surgeon, Andrew Craig. Several of her ancestors had been ministers, and she herself possessed a good deal of some-

what sentimental piety. She also developed a bosomy figure (as may be seen in the Miers silhouette of her), large eyes and a smattering of culture, which put her beyond the ordinary, so far as women were concerned, in an age when it was not thought necessary, or desirable, that women should receive much education.

The first two of these attractions interested a dissolute young Glasgow law agent, James M'Lehose, who was forbidden the house by Mr Craig. But M'Lehose found other ways of seeing Miss Craig, one of them being by making himself the only other occupant of the Glasgow to Edinburgh coach in which Nancy happened to be travelling, he having purchased all the remaining seats. In spite of her father and her uncle, Lord Craig, a Court of Session Judge, Nancy became Mrs M'Lehose at the age of seventeen. She bore her husband four children in four years, one of whom died in infancy. But shortly before the birth of the fourth, she left her husband because of his cruelty to her, and returned to her father. Her father, however, died in 1782, so Nancy came to Edinburgh where she took a small flat in Potter Row, living on an annuity, supplemented from time to time by gifts from Lord Craig.

When Burns became the rage of Edinburgh, Nancy determined to meet him. Her wish was gratified at a tea-party given in the house of Miss Nimmo, a friend of Margaret Chalmers, on 4th December 1787. They were at once attracted to each other. Nancy went home and promptly wrote Burns a note inviting him to drink tea with her the following Thursday. He was unable to come on that day, but said he could, and would, come on Saturday.

But the actions of a drunken coachman caused the poet to fall from a coach, with the result that he was bruised by 'a good, serious agonising, damn'd, hard knock on the knee'. His doctor, 'Lang Sandy Wood', made him lie up. The Saturday party had to be postponed.

Burns wrote explaining the nature of

his mishap on 8th December (if the date may be believed, since many of the dates of Burns's letters were later tampered with by Nancy for some obscure reason of her own). He took up the challenge of the larger invitation which the bright eyes and the plumply-rounded figure of the cultured grass-widow seemed to offer:

'I can say with truth, Madam, that I never met with a person in my life whom I more anxiously wished to meet again than yourself . . . I know not how to account for it. I am strangely taken with some people; nor am I often mistaken, You are a stranger to me; but I am an odd being: some yet unnamed feelings; things, not principles, but better than whims, carry me farther than boasted reason ever did a Philosopher.'

Nancy replied at once:

'I perfectly comprehend. . . . Perhaps *instinct* comes nearer their description than either "Principles" or "Whims". Think ye they have any connection with that "heavenly light which leads astray"? One thing I know, that they have a powerful effect on me, and are delightful when under the check of *reason* and *religion*. . . . Pardon any little freedoms I take with you.'

This must have seemed baffling encouragement, since, on the one hand, he was clearly bidden to go on, while on the other, 'reason'—which has no place in the lover's vocabulary—and 'religion' were pointed out as the ultimate, though perhaps distant, barriers.

Nancy next sent some verses, which Burns acknowledged on 12th December:

'Your lines, I maintain it, are poetry, and good poetry. . . . Friendship . . . had I been so blest as to have met with you *in time*, might have led me—God of love only knows where.'

The word 'love' drew from Nancy the reproof: 'Do you remember that she whom you address is a married woman?'

Burns then fell back upon literary criticism. Professor Gregory had seen Nancy's verses, and pronounced them

good. Nancy was delighted, and wanted to meet Gregory. At Christmas, they exchanged verse, Nancy's poem revealing in the first verse a natural enough reaction to her unhappy marriage, and in the last verse reminding the recipient about those ultimate barriers which were not to be crossed:

'Talk not of Love, it gives me pain,
    For Love has been my foe;
He bound me with an iron chain,
    And plunged me deep in woe. . . .

'Your Friendship much can make me
                              blest,
    O, why that bliss destroy!
Why urge the odious, one request
    You know I must deny!'

Burns said he thought these lines 'worthy of Sappho', and matched them to the tune, 'The Borders of Spey' for the *Scots Musical Museum*. To the man who advised his younger brother to 'try at once for intimacy' that 'one request' was, of course, by no means 'odious'. (*Incidentally,* 'odious' became 'only' in the *Museum* version.) Another mention of love brought reproof again, and counter reproof from Burns, who had agreed with her idea of using the Arcadian names of 'Clarinda' and 'Sylvander':

'I do love you if possible still better for having so fine a taste and turn for Poesy. I have again gone wrong in my usual unguarded way, but you may erase the word and put esteem, respect, or any other tame Dutch expression you please in its place.'

But the 'word' could not now be so easily erased from their relationship. Nancy fell back upon religion, adding: 'I entreat you not to mention our corresponding to anyone on earth. Though I've conscious innocence, my situation is a delicate one.'

It was indeed. Her stern, Calvinistic spiritual adviser, the Reverend John Kemp of the Tolbooth Church, would certainly not have approved of the amorous 'commerce' by letter in which she had got herself entangled. Nor would Lord Craig, whose additions to her income were absolutely necessary to her. Somehow, she had to devise a means of continuing to attract Burns without granting him the physical surrender which he craved. Their relationship moved rapidly to its climax during January 1788.

On 30th December 1787, Burns wrote to his friend Captain Richard Brown, whose ship was then in port at Irvine: 'Almighty Love still "reigns and revels" in my bosom; and I am at this moment ready to hang myself for a young Edin[r]. widow.'

On 5th January 1788, Burns was able to visit Nancy in a sedan chair. During this, the first of six visits this month, he upset Nancy's sensibilities by revealing his admiration for Milton's Satan, soothing them again by explaining that he only admired Satan's 'manly fortitude in supporting what cannot be remedied—in short, the wild broken fragments of a noble mind, exalted in ruins'. He also showed her his Autobiographical Letter to Dr Moore.

After his visit on the twelfth, Nancy wrote:

'I will not deny it, Sylvander, last night was one of the most exquisite I ever experienced. Few such fall to the lot of mortals! Few, extremely few, are formed to relish such refined enjoyment. That it should be so, vindicates the wisdom of Heaven. But though our enjoyment did not lead beyond the limits of virtue, yet to-day's reflections have not been altogether unmixed with regret.'

Burns reassured her: 'I would not purchase the *dearest gratification* on earth, if it must be at your expence in worldly censure; far less, inward peace.'

Nevertheless, he forgot his own words, and after they had been together again on the evening of the twenty-third, Nancy wrote:

'I am neither well nor happy. My heart reproaches me of last night. If you wish Clarinda to regain her peace, determine against everything but what the strictest delicacy warrants.'

'Clarinda, my life, you have wounded my soul,' protested the poet. But there was a further impassioned meeting on the twenty-sixth. 'Perhaps the "line" you had marked was a little infringed,' Nancy wrote, 'but, though I disapprove, I have not been unhappy about it.'

Thereafter, the affair declined. Burns's thwarted physical passion found expression with Jenny Clow, a servant girl about whom little is known, beyond the fact that she later bore him a son. Just before Burns left Edinburgh, on 18th February, there was a hectic exchange of letters between the poet and Nancy. Either the Reverend Kemp or, more probably, Lord Craig had sent a 'haughty dictatorial letter' about the position of his niece's reputation. In impassioned tones, Burns apologised for the 'injury' Sylvander had caused to Clarinda's reputation.

On Saturday, 23rd February, he arrived at Willie's Mill, saw Jean, and wrote to Nancy from Mossgiel:

'Now for a little news that will please you. I, this morning as I came home, called for a certain woman. I am disgusted with her; I cannot endure her! I, while my heart smote me for the prophanity, tried to compare her with my Clarinda; 'twas setting the expiring glimmer of a farthing taper beside the cloudless glory of the meridian sun. Here was tasteless insipidity, vulgarity of soul, and mercenary fawning; there, polished good sense, heaven-born genius, and the most generous, the most delicate, the most tender Passion. I have done with her, and she with me. . . .'

But he had not 'done with her'. Within six weeks he had married her, a fact which he left Robert Ainslie to tell Nancy. For a year 'Clarinda' kept her peace. The letter she then wrote to Burns has been lost. We can guess at its nature from his dignified reply, dated 9th March 1789: 'As I am convinced of my own innocence, and though conscious of high imprudence and egregious folly, can lay my hand on my breast and attest the rectitude of my heart; you will pardon me, Madam, if I do not carry my complaisance so far as humbly to acquiesce in the name of, Villain, merely out of compliment even to YOUR opinion; much as I esteem your judgment, and warmly as I regard your worth. I have already told you, and I again aver it, that at the Period of time alluded to, I was not under the smallest moral tie to Mrs B——; nor did I, nor could I then know, all the powerful circumstances that omnipotent Necessity was busy laying in wait for me.'

(In the interval between the 'farthing taper' letter and his marriage, Burns had had his interview with the Excise authorities, which resulted in his getting his commission. It has been surmised that a possible reason for his *volte face* over Jean may have been a hint, if not an order, from the Excise people that he must regularise his position with Jean if he wished to be appointed.)

Continuing his letter, Burns then told Nancy pretty sharply that the credit for not having taken final advantage of her was his: 'When you call over the scenes that have passed between us, you will survey the conduct of an honest man, struggling successfully with temptations the most powerful that ever beset humanity, and preserving untainted honor in situations where the austerest Virtue would have forgiven a fall. Situations that I will dare to say, not a single individual of all his kind, even with half his sensibility and passion, could have encountered without ruin; and I leave you to guess, Madam, how such a man is likely to digest an accusation of perfidious treachery!'

By 1790, Nancy had sufficiently forgotten about the 'perfidious treachery' for their correspondence to resume something like its former ardour. But she could not resist a further bout of accusation when, in November 1791, she found out that

Jenny Clow was in distress. Burns replied that he had offered to take 'my boy from her long ago, but she would never consent', and asked Nancy to give Jenny five shillings.

On 6th December 1791, these two lovers, on whom later generations have seen fit to pour much patronising scorn, met in Edinburgh for the last time. On 27th December, Burns sent Nancy from Dumfries 'Ae fond kiss', a song so genuine in its resigned passion that it relegates the other nine songs he had written for her, full of 'sensibility' and drawing-room manners, to the realms of the insignificant.

In January, Nancy sailed aboard the *Roselle*, one of the ships Burns himself had once considered sailing upon, to emigrate to Jamaica. Nancy was bound for the same place, to try to bring about a reconciliation with her husband. But her husband was not on the quayside to meet her, and she found, indeed, that her place had been taken by a Negro Mistress Ann Chalon Rivvere, who had borne him a daughter, Ann Lavinia M'Lehose. Pleading an aversion from the climate—according to Grierson, who conversed with her in 1829 'the heat was so excessive and the mosquitos so anoying '[*sic*]—she returned to Scotland when the ship sailed home three months later. A few friendly letters were thereafter exchanged between her and Burns, but Burns's passion was dead.

In her *Journal*, under the date, 6th December 1831, Nancy wrote: 'This day I can never forget. Parted with Burns, in the year 1791, never more to meet in this world. Oh, may we meet in Heaven!'

Sir Walter Scott recorded having seen her at his friend Lord Craig's House, when she was 'old, charmless and devout'. According to her friend Mrs Moodie, among 'Clarinda's' last words were 'I go to Jesus'. On her death, the Clarinda-Sylvander letters in her possession were valued at twenty-five pounds.

The song which celebrates Burns's passion for her, 'Ae fond kiss', first appeared in the *Museum,* 1792. The air, 'Rory Dall's Port', comes from the *Caledonian Pocket Companion, c.* 1756, though it must be much older. Rory Dall was the 'cognomen' of the harpers attached to the M'Leods of Skye. 'Port' is Gaelic for 'air'. *See Plate 9.*

McLeod of Raasay, Flora (d. 1780)

Sister of Isabella McLeod (*see* **McLeod, Isabella**) and eldest daughter of the John McLeod of Raasay who died in 1786. Flora married James Mure Campbell of Rowallan, who became Earl of Loudoun. She herself died in 1780 shortly after giving birth to a daughter, also called Flora, who, at the age of six, on her father's death, became Countess of Loudoun, and was brought up by her aunts, the Misses McLeod.

The Countess married in 1804 Francis Rawdon Hastings, Earl of Moira and Commander-in-Chief of the Forces in Scotland, and subsequently Marquis of Hastings. She died in 1840.

McLeod of Raasay, Isabella

Daughter of the Laird of Raasay who entertained Dr Johnson and died in Edinburgh in 1786, and sister of John McLeod, whose death the following year was commemorated by Burns in 'On Reading in a Newspaper an Account of the Death of John McLeod, Esq.' The poet had probably originally been introduced to the family by Gavin Hamilton. He wrote two poems for Isabella. The first, 'Raving winds around her Blowing', refers to her grief at the loss of her sister, Flora, and her brother-in-law. Burns said of this poem: 'I composed these verses on Miss Isabella McLeod of Raasay, alluding to her feelings on the death of her sister and the still more melancholy death of her sister's husband, the late Earl of Loudoun, who shot himself out of sheer heart-break at some mortifications he suffered owing to the deranged state of his finances.'

Burns's other poem 'To Miss Isabella McLeod', was dated Edinburgh, 16th March 1787:

'The crimson blossom charms the bee,
The summer sun the swallow:
So dear this tuneful gift to me
From lovely Isabella.'

We do not now know what the 'tuneful gift' was.

McLeod, John (d. 1787)

Son of the Laird of Raasay who had once entertained Dr Johnson. The father died in Edinburgh in 1786, the son on 20th July the following year. Burns, who was friendly with the young Laird's daughter, Isabella, sent her from Mossgiel his lines, 'On Reading in a Newspaper an Account of the Death of John McLeod, Esq., brother to a young lady, a Particular Friend of the Author's'.

'Sad thy tale, thou idle page,
And rueful thy alarms:
Death tears the brother of her love
From Isabella's arms.

'Sweetly deckt with pearly dew
The morning rose may blow;
But cold successive noontide blasts
May lay its beauties low.

'Fair on Isabella's morn
The sun propitious smil'd;
But, long ere noon, succeeding clouds
Succeeding hopes beguiled. . . .'

When Burns copied this poem into the Glenriddell Manuscript, he added the note:
'This poetic compliment, what few poetic compliments are, was from the heart.'

McLeod of Raasay, John (d. 1786)

The Laird of Raasay, who entertained Dr Johnson at Raasay House in 1773, when, the carpets being rolled back, that worthy was persuaded to dance. Burns met McLeod at his Edinburgh home a few months before his death. *See* **McLeod,**

Isabella; McLeod, John; McLeod, Flora.

MacLeod of Dunvegan, General Norman (1754-1801)

Laird of Dunvegan, in Skye. He was Member of Parliament for Inverness-shire from 1790 to 1796, and was a supporter of the reforms urged by 'The Friends of the People'. Burns referred to him in 'Here's to them that's awa', as 'Chieftain MacLeod, a chieftain worth gowd'. Chambers stated that when MacLeod succeeded to his estates, there was a debt of £50,000 on them. When he died, the total had reached £70,000.

MacLeod, Sir Roderick (d. 1636)

The heroic MacLeod of MacLeod. Dr Johnson saw at Dunvegan Castle, Skye, 'an ox's horn, hollowed so as to hold perhaps two quarts, which the heir of MacLeod was expected to swallow at one draught before he was permitted to bear arms', which travellers may still see today. Burns refers to him as 'Rorie More' in 'The Whistle'.

McMath, The Reverend John (1755-1825)

'Guid McMath' was assistant to Dr Peter Wodrow at Tarbolton Parish Kirk, and later Dr Wodrow's successor. McMath was a liberal, who supported Gavin Hamilton in that lawyer's conflict with the kirk authorities. In his middle years, however, he took to drink, and had to resign his charge in 1791, when he enlisted as a private soldier. He died in retirement at Rossul, Mull.

On 17th September 1783, Burns sent McMath a copy of 'Holy Willie's Prayer', and with it an 'Epistle' addressed to Mc-Math. The 'Epistle', apart from its intrinsic merit, is important in that it sets out clearly Burns's attitude to sectarianism and to religion. Confessing his own weaknesses frankly, the poet pays homage to Religion, 'maid divine', but says he would rather be

an atheist than use the Gospel as a screen, talking of Mercy, Grace and Truth while at the same time ruining, pitilessly and hard-heartedly in the name of religion, an innocent man. Of such hypocrites the poet tells McMath:

> 'But I gae mad at their grimaces,
> Their sighin', cantin,' grace-proud
>   faces,
> Their three-mile prayers, an' hauf-
>   mile graces,
>   Their raxin conscience,
> Whase greed, revenge, an' pride
>   disgraces
> Waur nor their nonsense.'

M'Morine, The Reverend William (d. 1832)

Minister of Caerlaverock from 1784 until his death. He was the son of the Minister of Kirkpatrick-Durham. In 1811, Edinburgh University gave him the degree of D.D. He was Moderator of the General Assembly in 1812. He baptised Elizabeth Riddell Burns.

M'Murdo, Mrs Jane Blair (1749-1836)

Wife of John M'Murdo, sister of Mrs de Peyster and daughter of Provost Blair of Dumfries. Burns had a great respect for her. He wrote to her from Ellisland on 2nd May 1789, thanking her for her hospitality, and he told her:

'You cannot easily imagine what thin-skinned animals, what sensitive plants, poor Poets are. How do we shrink into the embittered corner of self-abasement, when neglected or condemned by those to whom we look up! and how do we, in erect importance, add another cubit to our stature, on being noticed and applauded by those whom we honor and respect! My late visit to Drumlanrig has, I can tell you, Madam, given me a balloon waft up Parnassus, where on my fancied elevation I regard my Poetic self with no small degree of complacency. Surely, with all their sins, the rhyming tribe are not ungrateful creatures.'

In his 'Election Ballad', 1790, on behalf of the Whigs, Burns refers to:

'M'Murdo and his lovely spouse
(Th' enamour'd laurels kiss her
                                    brows!)
Led on the Loves and Graces:
She won each gaping burgess' heart,
While he, *sub rosâ*, played his part
Among their wives and lasses.'

The M'Murdos had seven sons and seven daughters.

M'Murdo, Jean (1777-1839)

Eldest daughter of John M'Murdo. Burns wrote for her the song beginning: 'There was a lass and she was fair', and sent it to her with a long and rather pompous letter, claiming: 'In the inclosed ballad, I have, I think, hit off a few outlines of your portrait. The personal charms, the purity of mind, the ingenous naivete of heart and manners, in my heroine, are, I flatter myself, a pretty just likeness of Miss McMurdo in a Cottage.' Burns added that the 'dramatic' ending of the ballad 'Young Robie's desertion of Brave Jean' was fiction.

Thomson received part of the song in April 1793, together with a copy of the unprinted air. Burns told Thomson on 2nd July: 'Mr Clarke, who wrote down the air from Mrs Burns's wood-notes wild, is very fond of it; and has given it a celebrity by teaching it to some young ladies of the first fashion here.' He asked Thomson to return the air if he did not like it. Thomson rejected Burns's 'beautiful little air', which is now lost, and published the song to 'Willie was a wanton wag'. 'Bonny Jean' (of Aberdeen), an air in *Orpheus Caledonius*, has been used for this song but, according to Dick, is not, in spite of its title, the air Burns originally intended.

M'Murdo of Drumlanrig, John (1743-1803)

Like his father before him, whom he succeeded in 1780, John M'Murdo was chamberlain to the Duke of Queensberry, until he retired in 1797, settling at Hardriggs, Dumfries.

Burns's first letter to M'Murdo, written when he was 'baiting' on his way to Ayrshire and dated Sanquhar, 26th November 1788, has a warmth and frankness which probably reflected the nature of their friendship. He told M'Murdo: 'I have Philosophy or Pride enough, to support with unwounded indifference against the neglect of my mere dull Superiors, the merely rank and file of Noblesse and Gentry, nay even to keep my vanity quite sober under the larding of their Compliments; but from those who are equally distinguished by their Rank and Character, those who bear the true elegant impressions of the Great Creator, on the richest materials, their little notices and attentions are to me among the first of earthly enjoyments.' M'Murdo, having asked for copies of Burns's 'fugitive Pieces', thus found himself placed by the poet among the select band.

Burns became a welcome guest at M'Murdo's home, and wrote several songs for members of his numerous family—he had seven sons and seven daughters—besides persuading the somewhat indolent musical editor of the *Museum*, Stephen Clarke, to come to Drumlanrig to give some of the young M'Murdos music lessons. Burns enlisted M'Murdo's support for James Clarke, the Moffat schoolmaster threatened with unjust dismissal for alleged cruelty to his pupils. That their friendship had its moments of stress is suggested by an undated letter probably written about February 1792:

'I believe last night that my old enemy, the Devil, taking the advantage of my being in drink (he well knows he has no chance with me in my sober hours) tempted me to be a little turbulent. You have too much humanity to heed the maniac ravings of a poor wretch whom the powers of Hell, and the potency of Port, beset at the same time. In the meantime, allow me to present you with the following Song which I have hammered out this morning.'

Enclosed was 'Lang here awa there awa wandering Willie'.

With a copy of the 1793 Edition, Burns sent a note to M'Murdo, remarking: 'However inferiour now, or afterwards, I may rank as a Poet; one honest virtue, to which few Poets can pretend, I trust I shall ever claim as mine:—to no man, whatever his station in life, or his power to serve me, have I ever paid a compliment at the expence of TRUTH.'

But what was probably a truer self-estimate of his stature as a poet occurs in another letter to M'Murdo, probably written in July 1793: 'Kings give Coronets; Alas, I can only bestow a Ballad. Still however I proudly claim one superiority even over Monarchs: My presents, so far as I am a Poet, are the presents of Genius; and as the gifts of R. BURNS, they are the gifts of respectful gratitude to the WORTHY. I assure you, I am not a little flattered with the idea, when I anticipate children pointing out in future Publications the tribute of respect I have bestowed on their Mothers. The merits of the Scots airs, to which many of my Songs are, and more will be, set, give me this pleasing hope.'

In December 1793, Burns repaid a loan from M'Murdo and sent with it a covering letter accompanying the manuscript of the collection subsequently known as *The Merry Muses*:

'I think I once mentioned something of a collection of Scots songs I have for some years been making: I send you a perusal of what I have got together. I could not conveniently spare them above five or six days, and five or six glances of them will probably more than suffice you. When you are tired of them, please leave them with Mr Clint, of the King's Arms. There is not another copy of the collection in the world; and I should be sorry that any unfortunate negligence should deprive me of what has cost me a good deal of pains. . . .'

M'Murdo, Philadelphia Barbara (1779–1825)

The second daughter of John M'Murdo, and a well-known beauty of the day. She was the subject of several of Burns's songs, notably 'Adown winding Nith I did wander'.

Writing to Thomson in August 1793, Burns said:

'Mr Clarke begs you to give Miss Phillis a corner in your Book, as she is a particular Flame of his, and out of compliment to him, I have made the Song.'

Stephen Clarke had been engaged to give singing lessons to Phillis, and to her sister, Jean. Burns directed that the song should go to 'The Muckin 'o' Geordie's Byre', sung slow with expression. Thomson suggested that the verses should be turned entirely into English. Burns refused, and Thomson did not print the song.

The other song to Phillis, the duologue 'O Philly, happy be that day', to the tune 'The Sow's Tail', from McGlashan's *Scots Measures*, 1781, appeared in Thomson's *Scottish Airs*.

McPherson, James (d. 1700)

A freebooter and the illegitimate son of a member of the Invereshie McPhersons by a gipsy mother. He had great strength and was an excellent violinist. The counties of Aberdeen, Banff and Moray went in fear of him and his gipsy followers, until he was seized by Duff of Braco and tried before the sheriff at Banff. While awaiting execution, he composed a song and air beginning 'I've spent my time in rioting'.

Just before his hanging, which took place in the market-place in Banff in November 1700, he played the tune on his fiddle, asking afterwards if any friend was there to accept his violin. When none came forward, he broke the instrument and threw away the pieces. He was then executed.

Burns rewrote McPherson's song, setting it to the same air, for the second volume of Johnson's *Museum*. Burns's first line reads, 'Farewell, ye dungeons dark and strong'.

MacPherson, Peter

Said to be the husband of a cousin of Mary Campbell's mother, he was a ship-carpenter at Greenock. Mary's younger brother, Robert, was probably apprenticed to MacPherson, although one account says it was to Messrs. Scotts, shipbuilders of Greenock.

It was whilst staying with the Mac-Phersons that Mary Campbell died in the autumn of 1786, and it was in one of his 'lairs', which he had just purchased, or inherited, in the old West Churchyard in Greenock, that she was interred. In 1803, MacPherson gave the Greenock Burns Club permission to erect a memorial tablet on the grave, though in fact the memorial was not erected for another forty years. On 8th November 1920, because of the expansion of Messrs Harland & Wolff's shipyard, the grave was opened. As well as the remains of at least three people, an infant's coffin board was found, strengthening the suspicion, though by no means proving, that while Mary Campbell may in fact have died from a fever contracted from her brother Robert, premature childbirth may at least have been a contributory cause. The remains were transferred to the new Greenock cemetery without, unfortunately, any proper examination of them having been carried out.

M'Quhae, The Reverend William (1736-1823)

Born in Wigtown and educated at Glasgow University, he was ordained minister of St Quivox in 1764. But he declined to become Moderator of the General Assembly when proposed in 1806. He was well known for his business acumen and his conversation. Author of *Difficulties which Attend the Practice of Religion No Just Argument Against It,* he was a prominent member of the New Licht faction.

In 'The Twa Herds', Burns humorously calls him, 'That curs'd rascal ca'd M'Quhae', and mentioned also 'M'Quhae's pathetic manly sense'.

McTaggart, Helen (1742-98)

Wife of Douglas Graham, who farmed Shanter. Douglas and Helen were probably the originals for 'Tam' and 'Kate' in Burns's 'Tam o' Shanter'.

McWhinnie, David (d. 1819)

An Ayr man who secured twenty subscriptions to the Kilmarnock Edition, but about whom almost nothing is now known. De Lancey Ferguson states that McWhinnie was a lawyer.

N

'Nancy', The

A brigantine which sailed with freight and passengers from the Clyde to Savannah-la-Mar, Jamaica, calling at Antigua. Her master was Captain Andrew Smith. It was on this ship that Burns was to have travelled to Jamaica. She was due to sail from Greenock on 10th August 1786, but did not in fact sail until 5th September. Burns never embarked on the *Nancy*, or on any other ship for Jamaica, though he noted the sailing dates of one or two other ships in letters to his friends.

Nanie

Burn's 'My Nanie O'' was a girl called Fleming, according to the poet's brother, Gilbert, and the daughter of a Tarbolton farmer. *See* Fleming, Agnes.

Nasmyth, Alexander (1758-1840)

Son of an Edinburgh architect and housebuilder, Michael Nasmyth, Alexander took an interest in drawing at an early age. He was sent to the Edinburgh Academy of Art and studied under Alexander Runciman. When he was seventeen, he studied under Allan Ramsay in London, and later visited Rome. On his return to Edinburgh, he painted various members of the aristocracy and helped Patrick Miller of Dalswinton as a draughtsman when Miller was carrying out his mechanical and marine experiments. Burns's publisher, Creech, asked Nasmyth to paint a portrait of the poet to illustrate the first Edinburgh Edition, a service which the painter performed gratis. Burns visited Nasmyth frequently at his studio in Wardrop's Court. The portrait was given to John Beugo to engrave, but Nasmyth was displeased with the result, much preferring another engraving done by Walker. The original by Nasmyth was given to Burns,

whose son, Colonel William Nicol Burns, presented it to the Scottish National Gallery, where it now hangs. Nasmyth made two duplicates of it; one is in the National Portrait Gallery, London, the other in Kelvingrove Art Gallery, Glasgow.

Poet and painter frequently went walking together to Arthur's Seat, the Braid Hills and the Pentlands. Forty years after Burns's death, Nasmyth did a full-length portrait of the poet for Lockhart's *Life of Burns*. Writing from Ellisland to Beugo on 9th September 1788, Burns remarked: 'If you see Mr Naesmith, remember me to him most respectfully, as he both loves and deserves respect; tho', if he would pay less respect to the mere Carcase of Greatness, I should think him much nearer perfection.'

Nasmyth latterly gave up portrait-painting in favour of landscape, and scene-painting, which included the stock scenery for Glasgow's Theatre Royal, and in 1820, the scenery for 'The Heart of Midlothian' in the Theatre Royal, Edinburgh. He was also an expert in landscape gardening. The temple of Hygiea at St Bernard's Well was built from his design, and the original design of the Dean Bridge was also his. He was an honorary member of the Royal Scottish Academy, and presided at the dinner given by the Academicians to Sir Henry Raeburn when that distinguished painter was knighted.

Nasmyth's eldest son, Patrick, and his daughter, Anne, were also painters. His youngest child, James, was an inventor, the steam hammer being one of his achievements.

See Plate 1.

National Bard, Scotland's

The title of National Bard, sometimes applied to Burns, is in its usual connotation a creation of nineteenth-century romanticism; but possibly it derives from two references by Burns to himself.

In a letter written from Edinburgh on

14th January 1787, Burns tells John Ballantine: 'I went to a Mason-lodge yesternight where the Most Worshipful Grand Master Charters, and all the Grand lodge of Scotland visited. The meeting was most numerous and elegant; all the different Lodges about town were present, in all their pomp. The Grand Master who presided with great solemnity, and honor to himself as a Gentleman and Mason, among other general toasts gave, "Caledonia, and Caledonia's Bard, brother B—", which rung through the whole Assembly with multiplied honors and repeated acclamations. As I had no idea such a thing would happen, I was downright thunderstruck, and trembling in every nerve, made the best return in my power.' This incident occurred at a meeting of Lodge St Andrew's in Edinburgh.

Writing to Mrs Dunlop from Edinburgh on 22nd March of the same year, Burns told her: 'The appelation of a Scotch Bard, is by far my highest pride; to continue to deserve it is my most exalted ambition.'

Neilson, The Reverend Edward (d. 1824)
Minister of Kirkbean, in the Stewartry of Kirkcudbright, from 1789 until 1824. Burns described him in a letter to Dr Moore from Ellisland, 23rd March 1789, as: 'a worthy clergyman in my neighbourhood and a very particular acquaintance of mine'. The poet went on to ask Dr Moore to tell Neilson how best to travel in France because: 'Mr Neilson is on his way for France, to wait on His Grace of Queensberry, on some little business of a good deal of importance to him'.

According to Chambers, this 'little business' referred to the matter of his presentation. Chambers records that: 'He had been "presented" to the parish of Kirkbean by the Duke of Queensberry, who had, however, forgotten to send "the presentation"—the legal document enabling a Presbytery to proceed with the settlement of a minister—before he left Scotland. Mr Neilson went in pursuit, but failed to find the Duke. Ultimately, a document, signed by the Duke's factor, was accepted by the Presbytery of Dumfries as a legal presentation.'

Neilson, John
See **Thompson, Margaret**

'New Lichts'
See **'Auld Lichts'** and **'New Lichts'**.

Nicol, William (1744-97)
Son of a tailor in Ecclefechan, he was born at Dumbretton, in the parish of Annan. His father died when he was a child, and he received most of his education from a travelling teacher, John Orr. While still a young lad, he opened a school in his mother's house. Later, he attended Annan Grammar School and Edinburgh University, studying first for the ministry, and then medicine. In 1774 he became classical master in the High School, Edinburgh, having won the position in open competition. He remained at the High School until 1795, when, after a violent quarrel with the Rector, Dr Alexander Adam, he opened a school of his own, which he ran until his death two years later.

A man of great talent and ability, his vanity and irascibility made him an embarrassing friend on occasion. In *Memorials of his Times* Lord Cockburn, who had once been Nicol's pupil, thus described his discipline:

'The person to whose uncontrolled discipline I was now subjected, though a good man, an intense student and filled, but rather in the memory than in the head, with knowledge, was as bad a schoolmaster as it is possible to fancy. Unacquainted with the nature of youth, ignorant even of the characters of his own boys, and with not a conception of the art or of the duty of alluring them, he had nothing for it but to drive them: and this he did by constant and indiscriminate harshness.

'The efforts of this were very hurtful to all his pupils. Out of the whole four years of my attendance there were probably not ten days in which I was not flogged, at least once. The beauty of no Roman word, or thought, or action ever occurred to me; nor did I ever fancy that Latin was of any use except to torture boys.'

In spite of his readiness to flare up in anger, Nicol had a fondness for convivial relaxation; and it was probably this which first attracted Burns to him.

No one knows how or when the two men first met. Though a good teacher, Nicol, because of his irascibility, was no favourite in Edinburgh society, and he does not feature among the lists of celebrities and friends whom Burns met at Edinburgh parties and whose names he recounted in his letters. But on 1st June 1787, Burns, on his Border tour, addressed his only surviving letter in Scots to 'Kind honest hearted Willie'. The second half of the letter deals with his travels and 'wi' twa dink quines in particlar'. The first part of the letter is about his mare, Jenny Geddes. Alexander Young, the Edinburgh lawyer, knew Nicol as a client, and considered him 'one of the greatest Latin Scholars of the age ... He had considerable, indeed constant, employment in translating the Medical Law Theses of the graduates at the University, for which he made liberal charges, but was very ill paid. I was employed by him to recover many of these claims.'

Nicol accompanied Burns on his Highland tour when, by Nicol's wish, they travelled in a chaise. He proved a tiresome travelling companion, for when Burns was invited to dine at Castle Gordon, Nicol, piqued at having been kept waiting at Fochabers inn before being invited to join the party, insisted on pressing on with their journey immediately, if necessary alone. Writing to the Duke's librarian and companion, James Hoy, from Edinburgh on 20th October 1787, Burns expressed his feelings on this incident: 'I shall

certainly, among my legacies, leave my latent curse to that unlucky predicament which hurried me, tore me away from Castle Gordon. May that obstinate son of Latin Prose be curst to Scotch-mile periods, and damn'd to seven league paragraphs; while Declension and Conjugation, Gender, Number, and Time, under the ragged banners of Dissonance and Disarrangement eternally rank against him in hostile array! ! ! !'

But the two men remained friends. Burns humoured his touchiness. Writing to Nicol's fellow-master, William Cruikshank, on 3rd March 1788, Burns remarked: 'I would send my compliments to Mr Nicol, but he would be hurt if he knew I wrote to any body and not to him.'

When Burns was farming Ellisland, Nicol loaned him an old bay mare, Peg Nicholson—named after a mad woman, Margaret Nicholson, who tried to assassinate George III in 1776—to use or to sell. Burns reported the position to Nicol on 13th December 1789:

'Now for your unfortunate old mare. I have tried many dealers for her, and I am ashamed to say that the highest offer I have got for her, is fifty shillings. However, I tried her yesterday in the Plough, and I find the poor creature is extremely willing to do what she can, so I hope to make her worth her meat to me, until I can try her at some fair.'

But the poor horse did not survive the winter, and on 9th February 1790, Burns told Nicol: 'That d-mned mare of yours is dead. I would freely have given her price to have saved her; she has vexed me beyond description. Indebted as I was to your goodness beyond what I can ever repay, I eagerly grasped at your offer to have the mare with me. That I might at least shew my readiness in wishing to be grateful, I took every care of her in my power. She was never crossed for riding above half a score of times by me or in my keeping. I drew her in the plough, one of three, for one poor week. I refused fifty-five shillings for her, which was the highest bode I could squeeze for her. I fed her up and had her in fine order for Dumfries fair; when four or five days before the fair, she was seized with an unaccountable disorder in the sinews, or somewhere in the bones of the neck; with a weakness or total want of power in her fillets; and, in short, the whole vertebrae of her spine seemed to be diseased and unhinged; and in eight and forty hours, in spite of the two best farriers in the country, she died and be d-mned to her! . . . While she was with me, she was under my own eye, and I assure you, my much valued friend, everything was done for her that could be done.' He commemorated her in his 'Elegy on Willie Nicol's Mare'.

During the winter of 1792–3, Burns, in difficulties with the Board of Excise, was accused of refusing to rise when the orchestra in the Dumfries theatre played 'God Save the King', and of being concerned in a call for the French Revolutionary song, 'Ça Ira'. Wrote Nicol:

'Dear Christless Bobbie:
    What has become of thee? Has the Devil flown off with thee, as the gled does with a bird? If he should do so there is little matter, if the reports concerning thy *imprudence* are true. What concerns it thee whether the lousy Dumfriesian fiddlers play "Ça Ira" or "God Save the King"? Suppose you had an aversion to the King, you could not, as a gentlemen, wish God to use him worse than he has done. The infliction of idocy is no sign of friendship or love. . . .'

Nicol counselled the behaviour of the Vicar of Bray.

Burns replied on 20th February 1793, with a screed of brilliant fooling, beginning: 'O thou, wisest among the Wise, meridian blaze of Prudence, full moon of Discretion, & Chief of many Counsellors! How infinitely is thy puddle-headed, rattle-headed, wrong-headed, round-headed slave indebted to thy supereminent goodness, that from the luminous path of

thy own right-lined rectitude, thou lookest benignly down on an erring wretch, of whom the zig-zag wanderings defy all the powers of Calculation, from the simple copulation of Units up to the hidden mystery of Fluxions!'

Burns called one of his sons William Nicol, because, as he told George Thomson in a letter of May 1795, of: 'that propensity to witty wickedness and manfu' mischief, which even at twa days auld I foresaw would form the striking features of his disposition. . . .'

Niel, Tom

A noted singer and precentor 'of facetious fame' in Edinburgh, who gave Burns his 'edition' of the song 'Up and warn a' Willie'. It is not known how much Burns altered Niel's version.

Nimmo, Miss Erskine

An acquaintance of Margaret Chalmers and a friend of Clarinda. She lived in Alison's Square, Edinburgh, and it was at Miss Nimmo's house that Burns and Clarinda first met. As Mrs M'Lehose put it in her first letter to the poet of 8th December 1787: 'Miss Nimmo can tell you how earnestly I had long pressed her to make us acquainted. I had a presentiment that we should derive pleasure from the society of each other.' Mrs M'Lehose described Miss Nimmo in a letter eight days later to Burns, as 'lineally descended from "My Uncle Toby"; has hopes of the Devil, and would not hurt a fly'.

Burns saw her on several occasions when he visited Edinburgh for the first time. He told Clarinda: 'I have been with Miss Nimmo. She is, indeed "a good soul", as my Clarinda finely says. She has reconciled me, in a good measure, to the world with her friendly prattle.' Indeed, Burns tried to persuade Miss Nimmo, without success, to accompany him on his visit to Harvieston.

Later, a certain coolness came between Miss Nimmo and Clarinda, probably because of Mrs M'Lehose's friendship with the poet.

Niven, The Reverend Alexander (1760–1833)

Son of Bailie Robert Niven, (d. 1807) who lived in Girvan. He was a day pupil at Hugh Rodger's school in Kirkoswald when Burns was there. While he was tutoring the family of Mr Hamilton of Sundrum in the parish of Coylton, he visited Burns at Mossgiel. He was ordained Minister of Dunkeld in 1793, and St Andrews' University gave him the degree of D.D. in 1816. He married Susanna Stewart in 1794 and had seven children.

Writing to William Niven from Lochlea on 12th June 1781, Burns said: 'Our communion was on Sunday se'en night, I mention this to tell you that I saw your cousin there, with some of Mr Hamilton's sons. You cannot imagine how pleased I was to steal a look at him, and trace the resemblance of my old friend. I was prepossessed in his favor on that account, but still more by that ingenuous modesty (a quality so rare among students, especially in the divinity way) which is so apparent in his air and manner.' William's cousin was, of course, Alexander Niven.

Niven, John, sen.

Father of Robert Niven. John Niven was a blacksmith at Damhouse of Ardlochan, in Kirkoswald parish. He had eight children. He first introduced wheelcarts of his own manufacture into Carrick, replacing the old-fashioned wheelless sledges. He was the smith referred to in 'Tam o' Shanter':

'That ev'ry naig was ca'd a shoe on,
The smith and thee gat roarin' fou' on.'

Niven, John (1754–1822)

Only son of Robert Niven and Margaret Ross, Burns shared Niven's bed at Ballochneil when he was a pupil with him at Hugh Rodger's school in Kirkoswald. He succeeded his father, Robert, at Ballochneil farm, and was known as a benevolent man. He received the Freedom of the burgh of Maybole, because he sold his meal at a time when it was scarce, and other farmers were hoarding theirs to get higher prices. He married Hugh Rodger's daughter, Jean, in 1790.

Niven, Robert

Son of John Niven, sen., and father of John Niven, jun., and tenant of the mill and farm of Ballochneil, near Kirkoswald. He figures in 'Tam o' Shanter':

'That ilka melder wi' the miller,
Thou sat as long as thou had siller.'

Niven, William (1759–1844)

The second son of John Niven by his wife Janet Spear, William Niven was born in Maybole, where he spent almost his whole life. His father, a shopkeeper, also owned the small neighbouring farm of Kirklandhill. William apparently received some assistance up the ladder of fortune from Hugh Hamilton of Pinmore, a director of the bank of Hunters and Company (founded by James Hunter, who had been cashier in Douglas, Heron and Company's bank, whose collapse in 1773 had ruined so many Ayrshire men), though the precise nature of the assistance—'sterling and friendly patronage', Niven later called it— is not clear. At any rate, he became the bank's Maybole agent, and in due course a partner. In 1792, he was co-opted on to the Town Council of Maybole, and a year or two later built himself a new house on the south side of the High Street. In September 1798 he married Isabella Christian Goudie, the daughter of a deceased merchant of Kingston, Jamaica, who, contrary to legend, died a far from rich man. In June 1799 Niven managed to complete the purchase of the farm of Kirkbride, and two other small properties, apparently with something of a struggle, borrowing £3,000 from Hunters and Company with 'the two markland of Kirkbride' as security.

Niven's business in Maybole flourished. He acquired more property, and continued to play a leading part in Town Council affairs.

Sir James Fergusson (in *The White Hind and Other Discoveries*) quotes a contemporary reference to Niven's civic activities:

'The town of Maybole has also of late been much improved. Access to it was formerly inconvenient and difficult, but, by the exertions of Mr Niven of Kirkbride, who has always taken the greatest interest interest in the improvement of his native place, the streets have been opened by spacious roads to and from all quarters.'

Niven became a Deputy Lieutenant for Ayrshire in 1810.

Mrs Niven died in 1841, and Niven died just over three years later. They had no children. His portrait, by an unknown artist, now hangs in Maybole Town House.

The earliest letters from Burns's pen are addressed to Niven, whom Burns had met at Kirkoswald. Niven maintained in later life, against all probability and with no documentary evidence to back up his claim, that Burns's 'Epistle to a young Friend', dedicated to Andrew Hunter Aiken, had originally been dedicated to him.

See Plate 11

North, Frederick, Lord. *See* **Guilford.**

'Notes on Scottish Song' by Robert Burns

The notes written in Robert Riddell's interleaved copy of *The Scots Musical Museum* by Burns and by Riddell himself. J. C. Dick discovered them in the possession of a London owner in 1902, and published them in 1906 under the above title, separating Burns's notes from those of Riddell and those he deemed 'spurious'. All had been published by Cromek in 1808 as genuine.

In 1922, however, David Cuthbertson came upon a manuscript in Burns's handwriting in the library of Edinburgh University. He published the contents in the *Kilmarnock Standard*. This contained most of the 'spurious' notes, more or less as given by Cromek, whose fault in this instance seems to have been that he failed to indicate that he had made use of more than one source.

The interleaved *Museum* was given by Mrs Riddell to her niece, Miss Eliza Bayley of Manchester, who allowed Cromek to see it.

In 1871 John Salkeld, a London bookseller, acquired it as part of a job lot, and catalogued it at £110. It was bought by a book collector, H. F. Nicols, who left it to his housekeeper, Miss Oakshott, with whom Dick found it. It was sold at Sotheby's in 1903 to an American buyer.

Together with Dick's *The Songs of Robert Burns* and Davidson Cook's *Annotations* thereon, it was reissued in a single volume by Folklore Associates, Hatboro, Pennsylvania (1962).

O

Old Rome Forest or Old Room Foord
A house where Jean Brown, an aunt of
Burns on his mother's side, lived with her
husband, James Allan. When Burns had to
go into hiding as a result of James Armour's
warrant for his arrest, the poet stayed at his
aunt's house, which had the additional
advantage of being reasonably near John
Wilson's printing shop in Kilmarnock.
Nothing remains of Old Rome Forest,
and even its location is now largely a matter of conjecture. But according to D.
M'Naught (in an article in the *Burns
Chronicle*, 1893) the house was on the estate
of Fairlie, near Irvine, where Allan was
employed in 1786 as joiner or carpenter.
Incidentally, Allan's son Alexander, bred a
shoemaker, went to sea, and 'became the
progenitor of the proprietors of the "Allan
line"of Atlantic steamers'. *See* **Allan, Jean.**

Oliphant, The Reverend James (1734-1818)
The evangelical Minister of Kilmarnock
High Church from 1764-73, having been
called from the Gorbals Chapel of Ease.
Later, he obtained a charge in Dumbarton.
He was an 'Auld Lichter' with a powerful
voice. Burns referred to him in 'The
Ordination 'as making the church 'yell'. He
wrote *A Mother's Catechism*, and *A Sacra-
mental Catechism*, both of which were
popular in his day.

Orpheus Caledonius
The first important collection of Scots
songs, it was published in London by
William Thomson in 1725. It consisted of
fifty of 'the best Scotch Songs set to music'.
The second edition of 1733 contained a
further fifty songs. Many of the airs to
which Burns later set his own words came
from this collection.

Its editor was the son of Daniel Thomson,
a professional musician in Edinburgh.
Young William spent his boyhood in
Edinburgh, but settled in London as a
youth, and remained there for the rest of
his days.

Orr, Margaret (d. 1837)
A servant of Mrs Stewart of Stair House,
who, having heard one of Burns's songs,
wished to meet the poet. Margaret Orr,
though once engaged to David Sillar, did
not marry him, as is sometimes claimed.
She became the wife of a shoemaker
called John Paton. She is the Meg in the
'First Epistle to Davie'.

Orr, Thomas (d. 1785)
The son of Jean Robinson, who was the
daughter of Julia Robinson of Park Farm,
near Kirkoswald. Julia was supposed to
have been a witch, and was undoubtedly
a reseller of smuggled goods. Burns met
Orr, who was studying navigation, when
he attended Hugh Rodger's School at
Kirkoswald to learn surveying. Orr worked as a harvest hand at Lochlea in 1780 and
1781. He went to sea in 1785 and was
supposed to have drowned during his
first voyage. Burns's three letters to him,
together with those to Niven, are almost
the only survivals of the poet's early
correspondence.

Osnaburg. *See* **York, Frederick Augus-
tus, Duke of.**

Oswald, Mrs Lucy (c. 1760-97)
Daughter of Wayne Johnstone of Hilton,
she married Richard A. Oswald of Auchincruive. She was a celebrated beauty, but
died in Lisbon of pulmonary consumption.
Burns wrote 'O Wat Ye Wha's in Yon
Town' for Jean Lorimer, but, with the
name 'Jean' changed to 'Lucy', sent it
instead to Lucy Oswald, 'that incomparable woman' as he called her, in May 1795.

Writing to Thomson from Ecclefechan
on 7th February, Burns said: 'Do you
know the air—I am sure you must know

it—"We'll gang nae mair to yon town"? I think, in slowish time, it would make an excellent song. I am highly delighted with it, and if you should think it worthy of your attention, I have a fair Dame in my eye to whom I would consecrate it.' The tune comes from Bremner's *Scot's Reels*, 1757, and was also used by Burns for another and superior version of the song, 'There's nane shall ken, there's nane can guess'. The song appeared in Thomson's work with the name Jean, and in Johnson's with the compliment to Lucy.

Lucy Oswald composed the pedestrian air 'Captain Cork's Death', to which Burns's song 'Thou lingering star with lessening ray' (called by Currie 'To Mary in Heaven!') was set. It is now commonly sung to the tune 'Mary's Dream' composed by John Lowe, a Galloway divinity student and minor poet who died in America in 1798.

See Plate 7

Oswald of Auchencruive, Mrs Mary (d. 1788)

Daughter of a wealthy estate owner in Jamaica, Alexander Ramsay, she married Richard Oswald, youngest son of the Reverend George Oswald of Dunnet. Richard Oswald amassed considerable wealth in London as a merchant and contractor during the Seven Years War. Through his wife, he acquired estates in America and the West Indies. In 1764, he bought Auchencruive, St Quivox, the former seat of the Cathcarts, from Lord Cathcart, completed the unfinished mansion, and continued Cathcart's agricultural development. On her husband's death, Mrs Oswald settled in London. It was her funeral cortège which stopped at Sanquhar on its way to St Quivox, where her husband was buried, that so angered Burns. In a letter to Dr Moore from Ellisland, 23rd March 1789, Burns described the incident:

'In January last, on my road to Ayrshire, I had put up at Bailie Whigham's in Sanquhar, the only tolerable inn in the place. The frost was keen, and the grim evening and howling wind were ushering in a night of snow and drift. My horse and I were both much fatigued with the labors of the day, and just as my friend the Bailie and I, were bidding defiance to the storm over a smoking bowl, in wheels the funeral pageantry of the late great Mrs Oswald, and poor I am forced to brave all the horrors of the tempestuous night, and jade my horse, my young favorite horse, whom I had just christened Pegasus, twelve miles farther on, through the wildest moors and hills of Ayrshire, to New Cumnock, the next Inn. The powers of Poesy and Prose sink under me, when I would describe what I felt. Suffice it to say, that when a good fire at New Cumnock had so far recovered my frozen sinews, I sat down and wrote the enclosed Ode.' This was the bitter poem beginning, 'Dweller in yon dungeon dark'.

Earlier, in the same letter to Dr Moore, Burns said of Mrs Oswald: 'I spent my early years in her neighbourhood, and among her servants and tenants I know that she was detested with the most heartfelt cordiality.'

Writing to Peter Stuart, owner of the London *Star*, April 1789, he described her as 'That venerable votary of iron avarice and sordid pride, the late Mrs Oswald of Auchencruive, N——, Ayrshire'.

Under the pseudonym of Tim Nettle, Burns wrote a letter to the *Star* prefacing the 'Ode'.

'Mr Printer—I know not who is the author of the following poem, but I think it contains some equally well-told and just compliments to the memory of a Matron who, a few months ago, much against her private inclinations, left this good world and twice five good thousands *per annum* behind her.

'We are told, by very respectable authority, that "the *righteous* die, and none regardeth"; but as this was by no means the case in point with the departed beldam, for whose memory I have the honour to interest myself, it is not easy guessing why prose and verse have both said so little on the death of the owner of ten thousands a year.

'I dislike partial respect of persons and am hurt to see the public make such a fuss when a poor pennyless gipsey is consigned over to Jack Ketch and yet scarce take any notice when a purse-proud Priestess of Mammon is, by the inexorable hand of death, pinioned in everlasting fetters of ill-gotten gold, and delivered up to that arch-brother among the finishers of the law, emphatically called, by our Bard, the Hangman of Creation.'

The bitterest part of the ode is the strophe:

'View the wither'd beldam's face—
Can thy keen inspection trace
Aught of Humanity's sweet, melting
                             grace?
Note that eye, 'tis rheum o'erflows—
Pity's flood there never rose.
See those hands, ne'er stretched to
                              save,
Hands that took—but never gave.
Keeper of Mammon's iron chest,
Lo, there she goes, unpitied and un-
                             blest

She goes, but not to realms of
                  everlasting rest!'

Wrote Mrs Dunlop on receiving this effusion: 'Are you not a sad wicked creature to send a poor old wife straight to the Devil, because she gave you a ride in a cold night?'

Oswald, Richard A. (1771-1841)

Heir of Mrs Oswald of Auchencruive, whose funeral cortège produced an 'Ode' from Burns. See **Oswald of Auchencruive, Mrs Mary** and **Oswald, Mrs Lucy**. Richard is mentioned by the poet in his Second Heron Election Ballad:

An' there'll be wealthy young Richard,
Dame Fortune should hang by the
                              neck:
But for prodigal thriftless bestowing,
His merit had won him respect. . . .'

In 1793 he married Lucy Johnstone of Hilton-on-Merse, by whom he had two children. She died in 1797, at Lisbon. In 1807, Oswald then married Lady Lilias Montgomerie, daughter of the twelfth Earl of Eglinton and widow of Robert Dundas Macqueen of Braxfield. Oswald was for a time Member of Parliament for Ayrshire.

K

P

Pagan, Isobel or Tibbie (1741-1821)
Born in New Cumnock, she received no
regular education, and throughout most
of her long life supported herself by begging, selling whisky without a licence, and
by singing. She possibly supplied Burns
with the idea for one of his finest songs,
'Ca' the yowes'. Writing to Thomson in
September 1794, Burns said: 'I am flattered
at your adopting, "Ca the yowes to the
knowes", as it was owing to me that ever
it saw the light. About seven years ago, I
was well acquainted with a worthy little
fellow of a clergyman, a Mr Clunzie, who
sang it charmingly; and at my request,
Mr Clarke took it down from his singing.
When I gave it to Johnson, I added some
Stanzas to the song, and mended others,
but still it will not do for *you*.'

There Burns was wrong, or half-way
wrong. The version given to Johnson and
published in the *Museum* in 1790, is the
version which has become popular. The
second version, given to Thomson and
published in *Scottish Airs*, 1805, was
divorced by Thomson from its lovely
modal tune, and put to another air, 'The
maid that tends the goats'.

'Mr Clunzie' was the Reverend John
Clunie (1759-1819), licensed to the Edinburgh Presbytery in 1784 and until 1790
schoolmaster and precentor at Markinch
in Fife, in which year he was ordained to
Ewes, Dumfriesshire. In 1791 he was
presented by Robert Dundas of Arniston
to Borthwick, Midlothian. He had some
reputation as a minor song-writer, and
Kinsley thinks he, and not Pagan, the
probable origin of 'Ca' the Yowes'.

**Park, or Burns, Elizabeth (1791-
1873)**
Illegitimate daughter of Burns and Anna
Park. When she was twenty-one, she
received the sum of £200 from the fund
raised by her father's admirers.

According to an article in the *Burns
Chronicle* of 1916, Betty Burns, as she was
known, married Private John Thomson of
the Stirlingshire Militia, in 1808. The next
day the regiment was ordered to Berwick-
on-Tweed, and remained there for almost
a year. On its being moved again, Thomson sent his wife to his parents in Pollokshaws, Glasgow, where he returned on
leaving the militia in 1814. Thomson took
up the trade of handloom weaving, and he
and his wife both remained in Pollokshaws
until their deaths—Thomson's in 1869, and
Betty Burns's in 1873 at Crossmyloof. They
are both buried in the Old Burgher
churchyard in Pollokshaws once called
the Vennel, and which survives in the
middle of one of Glasgow Corporat-
ion's Comprehensive Redevelopment
Areas.

Of their fairly numerous family, their
second son, Robert Burns Thomson, was
a versifier, and his song 'My Daddy's
Awa' at the war' was popular during the
Crimean War. He was proud of his descent, but made no attempt to 'cash in' on
his grandfather's name, by publishing his
poems in book form. After learning the
trade of handloom weaving he became a
power-loom tenter, and eventually was
appointed manager of Messrs. Scott's
factory in the east end of Glasgow. When
he retired from this position, he founded a
firm of brush manufacturers Messrs R. B.
Thomson & Co., in Stockwell Street,
Glasgow. He died in 1887 aged sixty-nine
and is buried beside his mother.

James Glencairn Thomson, a younger
son of Betty Burns, was the last survivor
of the family. He died in 1911, at the age
of eighty-four, having received at one
time a small Government pension in
recognition of his grandfather's name and
fame. He is also buried in the Vennel. The
two sons, Robert Burns Thomson, and
James Glencairn Thomson, attended the
centenary celebrations of their grand-

father's birth, held in the King's Arms Hall, Trongate, Glasgow, in 1859.

Betty Burns's youngest daughter, Margaret, was second wife of David Wingate the poet, who was born at Cowglen, near Pollokshaws. She died in 1898, aged sixty-three. She was buried in the family burying ground, which also was the burial place of Gilbert Burns Begg, the poet's nephew.

Park, Helen Anne, 'Anna'
Niece of Mrs Hyslop, who kept the Globe Tavern in Dumfries. Very little is known of her, and nothing after the birth of her daughter by Burns. She was Burns's 'Anna of the gowden locks' and the inspiration of his 'Yestreen, I had a pint of wine'—the splendid lovesong Burns considered his best. Anna gave birth to a daughter, Elizabeth, according to Chambers, in Leith. Nine days later, on 31st March 1791, Jean Armour presented Burns with a son, William Nicol. Showing admirable tolerance, Jean brought up the child, Elizabeth, as one of her own family. *See* **Park, Elizabeth.**

Burns's relationship with Anna has usually been supposed to have been purely physical, and there is very little evidence of any sort about their association. One tradition alleges that she 'had other pretty ways to render herself agreeable to the customers at the inn than the serving of wine'. Nothing is known of her later life. De Lancey Ferguson says she died in giving birth to Elizabeth, while another tradition alleges that she obtained a position as a domestic servant in Leith or Edinburgh, where she married a soldier, and died in giving birth to his child.

Parker, Hugh
An early Kilmarnock banker friend, to whom Burns wrote an Epistle bemoaning the smoke in the hut near the tower of Isle, where he was staying waiting for his new but still houseless farm of Ellisland to be completed:

'Here, ambush'd by the Chimla cheek,
Hid in an atmosphere of reek,
I hear a wheel thrum i'the neuk,
I hear it, for in vain I leuk.
The red peat gleams, a fiery kernel,
Enhuskèd by a fog infernal:
Here, for my wonted rhyming raptures,
I sit and count my sins by chapters;
For life and spunk like ither Christians,
I'm dwindled down to mere existence,
Wi' nae converse but Gallowa' bodies,
Wi' nae kend face but Jenny Geddes. . . .'

Parker, Major William
Brother to Hugh, and fellow mason of Burns at the Kilmarnock Lodge, he succeeded to the estate of Assloss, near Kilmarnock, in 1802. He became Right Worshipful Master of the Lodge.

Paterson, Robert
See **Morton, Christina.**

Paton, Elizabeth
During the winter of 1783-4, when Burns's father, William Burnes, lay dying at Lochlea, there was employed as a servant a girl who had a plain face but a good figure, Elizabeth Paton of Lairgieside. Burns's sister, Isabella, had heard of Elizabeth Paton as 'rude and uncultivated to a great degree . . . with a thorough (though unwomanly) contempt for every sort of refinement', though she loved Burns 'with heartfelt devotion'.

After the old man's death, in February 1784, Burns experienced a feeling of emancipation, one result of which was that he seduced Elizabeth Paton, who bore him his first illegitimate child on 22nd May 1785. Burns's mother, who liked Elizabeth Paton, wanted her son to marry the girl. Brother Gilbert more realistically counselled against such a marriage. The child, 'Dear-bought Bess', was also named Elizabeth and baptised when two days old.

The event produced three poems from Burns: some insignificant lines, when 'rough, rude ready-witted Rankine' twitted him over Miss Paton's condition, followed by the brilliant, but somewhat tasteless, outburst of sexual boastfulness of the 'Epistle to John Rankine'. In this poem, Burns describes his seduction in terms of the field. The 'poacher-court' got to hear of the 'paitrick hen' he had brought down with his 'gun', so he had to 'thole the blethers' and pay the fee. However, he is quite unrepentant; for, as soon as her 'clockin'-time is by' and the child is born, he promises himself further 'sportin' by and by' to get value for his guinea. When the child was actually born, however, Burns expressed, not pride in his sexual powers, but warm tenderness, in 'a Poet's welcome to his Love-begotten Daughter' (or, as Burns himself more pithily put it in one of his several versions, to 'his bastard wean'):

'Welcome! my bonie, sweet, wee
dochter,
Tho' ye come here a wee unsought
for,
And tho' your comin' I hae fought
for,
Baith kirk and queir;
Yet, by my faith, ye're no unwrought
for—
That I shall swear! . . .

'Lord grant that thou may ay inherit
Thy mither's person, grace, an' merit,
An' thy poor, worthless daddie's
spirit,
Without his failins,
'Twill please me mair to see thee
heir it,
Than stocket mailens. . . .'

Elizabeth Paton herself inspired no poems directly unless she was in the poet's mind when he wrote the wryly tender song 'The Rantin' Dog': or unless one counts the lines in Burns's first *Commonplace Book* dated September 1784:

'My Girl she's airy, she's buxom and
gay
Her breath is as sweet as the blossoms
in May;
A touch of her lips it ravishes
quite;
She's always good natur'd, good
humor'd and free
She dances, she glances, she smiles
with a glee;
Her eyes are the lightenings of joy
and delight;
Her slender neck, her handsome waist,
Her hair well buckl'd, her stays well-
lac'd,
Her taper white leg, with an et and a c,
For her a, b, c, d, and her c, u, n, t,
And Oh, for the joys of a long
winter night.'

But early in 1784, in the song 'O Tibbie, I hae seen the day', which Burns addressed to the less obliging Isabella Steven or Stein, daughter of a wealthy Tarbolton farmer, Burns told her:

'There lives a lass beside yon park,
I'd rather hae her in her sark,
Than you, wi' a' your thousan mark;
That gars you look sae high.'

Elizabeth Paton's only other appearance in Burns's life was in 1786, when she made a claim on Burns, but accepted a settlement of twenty pounds which the poet paid out of the profits of the Kilmarnock Edition. She married a farm-servant.

The child of Elizabeth Paton and Burns, the poet's first illegitimate daughter, whom he called 'Dear Bought Bess', was born 22nd May 1785. She was baptised two days later. She lived at Mossgiel, under Burns's mother's care, until her father's death. She then returned to her own mother, who was by this time happily married to a farm servant called Andrew.

When Burns meditated flight to Jamaica, he made over his heritable property to his brother, Gilbert Burns, to enable him to bring up the child as one of his own.

When she reached the age of twenty-one, she received two hundred pounds from the money raised for the support of Burns's family.

She married John Bishop, and died on 8th January 1817, one tradition alleges during childbirth.

See also **Burns, Elizabeth.**

Pattison, Alexander

A Paisley manufacturer whom Burns dubbed 'bookseller', because of his success in disposing of a considerable number of copies of the first Edinburgh Edition.

Burns visited Pattison on his return from Edinburgh in February 1788. In a letter to Clarinda from Kilmarnock, dated 22nd February 1788, Burns told her that Pattison —whom, incidentally, she did not know! —had been a 'zealous Anti-burgher; but, during his widowerhood, he has found their strictness incompatible with certain compromises he is often obliged to make with those Powers of darkness, the devil, the world, and the flesh: so he, good, merciful man! talked privately to me, of the absurdity of eternal torments, the liberality of sentiment in indulging the honest instincts of Nature, the mysteries of Concubinage, and etc. He has a son however, that at sixteen has repeatedly minted at certain priviledges,—only proper for sober, staid men, who can use the *good things* of this life without *abusing* them; but the father's paternal vigilance has hitherto hedged him in, amid a corrupt and evil world. His only daughter, who, "if the beast be to the fore, and the branks bide hale", will have seven thousand pound, when her old father steps into the dark Factory-Office of Eternity with his well thrumm'd web of life; has put him again and again in a commendable fit of indignation by requesting a harpsichord—"O, these damn'd boarding-schools!" exclaims my prudent friend; "she was a good spinner and sower, till I was advised by her foes and mine to give her a year of Edin[r]!"

'After two bottles more, my much-respected friend opened up to me a project, a legitimate child of Wisdom and Good-sense: 'twas no less than a long-thought-on and deeply-matur'd design to marry a girl, fully as elegant in her form as the famous Priestess whom Saul consulted in his last hours; and who had been 2[d] maid of honor to his deceased wife. This, you may be sure, I highly applauded; so I hope for a pair of gloves by and by.'

Pattison emigrated to America, where, according to Ferguson, all trace of him is lost.

Paul, The Reverend Hamilton (1773-1854)

He published *The Poems and Songs of Robert Burns, with a Life of the Author,* in 1819.

A broadminded member of the 'New Licht' clergy, he defended Burns's attitude to religion, and his religious satires. He edited *The Ayr Advertiser* for three years. He was an Ayrshire man, who came from the parish of Dailly.

Peacock

According to Burns, 'a scoundrel of the first water, who made money by the mystery of thieving'. Peacock practised flax dressing in Irvine in a shop in the Glasgow Vennel. He may have been a distant relative of Burns's mother, and the poet may have stayed with him when he went to Irvine to learn the flax business. At any rate, the connection ended when the shop was burned out during what the poet called 'a welcome carousal to the New Year'.

Peacock, Mary

A friend of 'Clarinda's', who later became the second wife of James Gray, a master in the High School, Edinburgh. Burns, in a letter to 'Clarinda' of 29th January 1788, referred to Mary as 'a charming girl, and highly worthy of the noblest love'. Burns wrote her several times, the third time being on 6th December 1792, the anniversary of his parting with 'Clarinda'. Writing to 'Clarinda' during March 1793, he mentioned his letters to Mary Peacock: 'There is a fatality attends Miss Peacock's correspondence and mine. Two of my letters, it seems, she never received; and her last, which came when I was in Ayrshire, was unfortunately mislaid, and only found about ten days or a fortnight ago, on removing a desk of drawers.'

Chambers said that Mary Peacock died in India.

Peebles, The Reverend William (1753-1826)

Born at Inchture and educated at Edinburgh, he became minister at Newton-upon-Ayr in 1778, and clerk of the Ayr Presbytery in 1782. A rigid supporter of the 'Auld Lichts', he denounced M'Gill's *Practical Essay on the Death of Jesus Christ*, which led to M'Gill's case being taken up by the General Assembly, and prompted Burns to write 'The Kirk's Alarm'. In the poem, Peebles figures as 'Poet Willie':

'Poet Willie, Poet Willie, gie the
                    Doctor a volley,
Wi' your "liberty's chain" and
                    your wit;
O'er Pegasus' side ye ne'er laid a
                    stride,
Ye only stood by where he sh—,
Poet Willie! Ye only stood by
                    where he sh—.'

Peebles had attracted some ridicule by a line in a poem of his own on the Centenary of the Revolution of 1688:

'And bound in *Liberty's* endearing
                    chain.'

In 'The Twa Herds' he is described as 'Peebles shaul' (shallow). He was the author of several works on religious topics of interest in his own day, and of a poem, *The Crisis*, published in 1803.

In his entertaining yet profound study of Burns, the Christian Rebel, *Bawdy Burns*, Cyril Pearl writes: 'From time to time, of

course, ministers of the kirk, still smarting under the lashes of Burns's satire, repeated their denunciations of the irreverent sinner who had dared to laugh at their imbecilities. In 1811, the Rev. William Peebles . . . showed his real Christian spirit by attacking the dead poet—anonymously—in a turgid work titled *Burnomania; the celebrity of Robert Burns considered in a Discourse addressed to all real Christians of every Denomination.*' In this, Peebles called Burns an 'irreligious profligate' who wrote 'vile scraps of indecent ribaldry'.

Penn, Matthew

The Dumfries solicitor who sent Burns, while he was at Brow, a letter about a bill for seven pounds and four shillings which the poet owed to T. Williamson, a Dumfries draper, for his volunteer uniform. This bill, along with other overdue bills, had been put by Williamson into Penn's hands for collection. Although there was no threat of legal proceedings in Penn's letter, the dying poet interpreted the letter as a threat. Perhaps troubled by dark memories of his father's struggle against debt Burns thereupon wrote two desperate letters for help. To his cousin, James Burness, at Montrose, on 12th July 1796, he wrote: 'A rascal of a Haberdasher to whom I owe a considerable bill taking it into his head that I am dying, has commenced a process against me, & will infallibly put my emaciated body into jail. Will you be so good as to accomodate me, & that by return of post, with ten pound. O James! did you know the pride of my heart, you would feel doubly for me! Alas! I am not used to beg! The worst of it is, my health was coming about finely; you know & my Physician assures me that melancholy & low spirits are half my disease, guess then my horrors since this business began. If I had it settled, I would be I think quite well in a manner. How shall I use the language to you, O do not disappoint me! but strong Necessity's curst command.

'I have been thinking over & over my

brother's affairs & I fear I must cut him up; but on this I will correspond at another time, particularly as I shall [need] your advice.

'Forgive me for once more mention[ing] by return of Post. Save me from the horrors of a jail!

'My Compliments to my friend James, & to all the rest. I do not know what I have written. The subject is so horrible, I dare not look it over again.'

And on the same day, another desperate appeal went to George Thomson:

'After all my boasted independance, curst necessity compels me to implore you for five pounds. A cruel scoundrel of a Haberdasher to whom I owe an account, taking it into his head that I am dying, has commenced a process, & will infallibly put me into jail. Do, for God's sake, send me that sum, & that by return of post. Forgive me this earnestness, but the horrors of a jail have made me half distracted. I do not ask all this gratuitously; for upon returning health, I hereby promise and engage to furnish you with five pounds' worth of the neatest song-genius you have seen. I tryed my hand on Rothiemurchie this morning. The measure is so difficult, that it is impossible to infuse much genius into the lines—they are on the other side. Forgive me!'

With Thomson's note was Burns's last song 'Fairest maid on Devon banks' to the tune 'Rothiemurchie', which first appeared as a song in Thomson's *Scottish Airs,* 1801.

Both men sent the money asked of them. But Thomson wrote on his note: 'This idea is exaggerated—he could not have been in any such danger at Dumfries nor could be in such necessity to implore aid from Edin.'

Perochon, Mrs Joseph Elias (d. 1825)

Agnes Eleanor, eldest of Mrs Dunlop's six daughters, married Joseph Elias Perochon, a French Royalist who fled to London at the time of the Revolution. Perochon set up as a merchant, but he lost his eyesight, and retired to Castlemilk, Dumfries. From there, Mrs Perochon was able to extend to Mrs Burns, the friendship her mother had given the poet. On 20th February 1816, Mrs Burns wrote to Mrs Perochon, agreeing that she might be buried in the grave in St Michael's Churchyard in which Burns had first been interred before the erection of the Mausoleum:

'Much indeed do I already owe to your disinterested friendship; and while a generous public are anxious to do justice to the genius of my husband by building so superb a monument to perpetuate his memory, you have paid the best tribute of your regard by so warmly interesting yourself in behalf of his widow and his children. In this you follow the example of her whose virtues you inherit, and who highly distinguished Mr Burns by a friendship which formed one of his first enjoyments.'

Peterkin, Alexander (1708-1846)

A native of Macduff, Banffshire, where his father was parish minister. In 1785, the Peterkins moved to Leadhills, and later to Ecclesmachan, West Lothian.

Peterkin finished his education at Edinburgh University. He qualified as a solicitor in 1811, and was at one time Sheriff-Substitute of Orkney.

He spent much of his life journalising, editing an edition of Robert Fergusson's *Poems* in 1807, and in 1815 issuing a reprint of Dr Currie's edition of Burns's works, to which he added a critical preface.

His importance lies in the fact that by including in his edition the testimonies of Findlater and Gray, Peterkin struck the first blow against the legend of Burns's perpetual drunkenness which Currie, and others, deliberately foisted upon the public.

de Peyster, Colonel Arent Schuyler (1736-1822)

In spite of his unusual name, de Peyster was a British subject. His family were of

French Protestant descent, and fled to Holland at the Massacre of St Bartholomew in 1572. (The history of the family is traced by John Malcolm Bulloch in the *Burns Chronicle,* 1930.) The Colonel's grandfather, Colonel Abraham de Peyster, married a Dutch kinswoman, Catherine de Peyster, in 1684. Their seventh son, Pierre, married Catherine, daughter of Arent Schuyler, one of the sons of Philip Schuyler. The elder of their two sons was Burns's friend, Arent Schuyler de Peyster. He seems to have spent his boyhood partly in Britain, partly in Holland, though brought up on British traditions. He joined the British Army in 1755. His regiment, the 50th Foot, had been raised in America in 1748, by the Governor of Massachusetts, William Shirley, who, in 1745, had directed the siege of Louisberg with de Peyster's uncle, Colonel Peter Schuyler. Next, de Peyster held a commission in the 51st Foot, also a regiment raised in America and which at one time had three Schuylers in it. Forty-seven years of his service, however, were spent in the 8th Foot, later the King's Liverpool Regiment. With it, de Peyster campaigned in Germany during the Seven Years War. His main service seems to have been in Canada. From 1768 to 1785, he apparently did service as a Military Administrator, handling the Indians with such tact that when he was about to return to England, they sent him a letter, thanking him for all that he had done for them. The last seven years of his service were spent in England and Ireland. He retired to Dumfries in April 1794.

He had married Rebecca Blair, sister of John M'Murdo's wife, Jane, and, like her, a daughter of Provost Blair of Dumfries. On his retirement, de Peyster settled at Mavis Grove, on the Nith, three miles from Dumfries. There, he threw himself eagerly into the Volunteer movement, becoming Major Commandant of the Dumfries Company of which Burns was a member in 1795. Colonel de Peyster must have been physically tough, but 'beneath

a rugged exterior he concealed a warm and affectionate heart', as one Burns editor put it.

In response to an inquiry by de Peyster about Burns's health, in January 1796, Burns wrote:

'My honor'd Colonel, deep I feel
Your interest in the Poet's weal:
Ah! now sma' heart hae I to speel
   The steep Parnassus
Surrounded thus by bolus pill
   And potion glasses.'

At the time of the formation of Dumfries's two companies of volunteers, Burns wrote the patriotic song, 'The Dumfries Volunteers':

'Does haughty Gaul invasion threat?
   Then let the louns beware, Sir!
There's WOODEN WALLS upon our
                              seas,
   And VOLUNTEERS on shore, Sir:
The *Nith* shall run to *Corsincon,*
   The *Criffel* sink in *Solway*
E'er we permit a foreign foe
   On British ground to rally!

Burns is generally considered to be the author of a letter bearing twenty-five signatures, including his own, asking Colonel de Peyster to suspend asking a public subscription 'for defraying the exp[s] of our Association. That our Secretary should have waited on those Gentlemen and others of that rank of life, who from the first, offered pecuniary assistance, meets our idea as highly proper but that the Royal Dumfries Volunteers should go abegging, with the burnt out Cottager and Shipwrecked Sailor, is a measure of which we must disapprove.

'Please then, Sir, to call a meeting as soon as possible, and be so very good also as to put a stop to the degrading business, untill the voice of the Corps be heard.'

De Peyster led his Volunteers on the occasion of Burns's funeral.

In 1813, he published in Dumfries a book of verse, *Miscellanies by an Officer,* only three copies of which are still known to exist, all of them in America. According to Bulloch, this includes 'threnodies on Nelson, Sir John Moore, the Marquis of Cornwallis, and Mrs de Peyster's parrot'. He died as the result of an accident, and was given a large funeral. He is buried in St Michael's Churchyard. His wife died in 1827.

In *Sketches from Nature*, published in 1830, John McDiarmid, who knew de Peyster, wrote: '. . . No man ever possessed more of the principle of vitality. Old age, which had silvered his hair and furrowed his cheeks, made so little impression on his inner man that . . . up to . . . his last illness his mind appeared as active and his intellect as vigorous as they had ever been. When the weather permitted, he still took his accustomed exercise, and walked round the billiard table or bestrode his gigantic charger, apparently with as little difficulty as a man of middle age.'

Pindar, Peter (1738-1819)
The pseudonym used by the English satirist and poet John Wolcot. He was born at Dodbrooke, in Devonshire, and was later apprenticed to his uncle, John Wolcot, a Surgeon. Pindar took his M.D. at Aberdeen in 1767. In 1769, he was ordained, and went to Jamaica with Governor Sir William Trelawny, as incumbent of Vere. On the Governor's death, he returned to England and settled in Cornwall.

He became well known with his series of satires on 'Farmer George' (i.e. George III), one of which may be found in *The Oxford Book of Light Verse,* and was noted for his broad sense of humour and keen eye for the ridiculous. Boswell called him 'a contemptible scribbler [who], having disgraced and deserted the clerical character . . . picks up in London a scanty livelihood by scurilous lampoons under a feigned name'.

Pindar entered the Burns story when George Thomson asked him to provide the English words for the songs in his collec-

tion. Burns was very largely responsible for the Scots ones.

In a letter to George Thomson, dated 26th January 1793, Burns made the comment: 'The very name of Peter Pindar is an acquisition to your work. His "Gregory" is beautiful.' And again in August 1793: 'You may readily trust, my dear Sir, that any exertion in my power, is heartily at your service. But one thing I must hint to you, the very name of Peter Pindar is of great service to your Publication; so, get a verse from him now and then, though I have no objection, as well as I can, to bear the burden of the business.'

Burns evidently received a copy of Pindar's works from Thomson, and his letter of thanks to the editor, dated January 1795, illustrates the extraordinarily high opinion he had of Pindar: 'The Supervisor of Excise here being ill, I have been acting for him, and I assure you I have hardly five minutes to myself to thank you for your elegant present of Pindar. The typography is admirable, and worthy of the truly original Bard.'

Piper, Thomas
He is supposed to have been the 'spunkie youthful' Tammie', to whom Burns sent his 'friendly Compliments' in a letter to William Niven, written from Mossgiel on 30th August 1786. Piper was assistant to Dr Hugh Logan, for many years the only doctor in Maybole.

Pitt, William, the Younger (1759-1806)
In 'The Author's Earnest Cry and Prayer', Burns called him 'Yon Premier youth'. He became Chancellor of the Exchequer in 1784 at the age of twenty-three. (The Government's first minister did not regularly assume the title of Prime Minister until Walpole's day.)

He was the second son of William Pitt, Earl of Chatham, himself a distinguished statesman, who, because of his criticisms of the public school system, educated his son at home under the tutorship of the

Reverend Edward Wilson, of Pembroke Hall, Cambridge. This form of education developed the intellectual abilities of the already precocious child. At the age of ten, William Pitt, junior, was a proficient classical scholar, and when he was thirteen he wrote a political tragedy called *Laurentino, King of Chersonese*.

Pitt went to Cambridge, where his tutor was Dr George Pretyman (later he changed his name to Tomline), to whom Pitt afterwards gave the bishopric of Lincoln, and also bequeathed his papers. Pretyman became Pitt's first biographer.

The young Pitt first entered Parliament as member for the pocket borough of Appleby, although he afterwards always represented Cambridge University. His maiden speech was described by his rival, Lord North, as the best first speech he had ever heard, and Burke went even further by declaring him to be 'not a chip off the old block but the old block itself'. He supported Shelburne's party, and became Chancellor of the Exchequer under his administration.

Pitt's career in Parliament was distinguished by his untiring political warfare with Fox, whom he fought on the Irish question, the India Bill, the Regency question and on France.

On the home front, a Bill he brought forward in April 1785 to suppress thirty-six pocket boroughs, and to transfer their members to increase the representation of certain towns and counties, was defeated. Pitt did not again try to bring in a Reform Bill, though after 1792, when Tom Paine's *Rights of Man* was published, the demand for reform grew. But, alarmed by the turn the French Revolution had taken, Pitt had the *Habeas Corpus Act* suspended, in 1793, and again from 1795 to 1801. There were also the trials of the Friends of the People leaders, Skirving, Margarot, Gerrald and Muir, savagely sentenced for advocating nothing more treasonable than constitutional reform and universal suffrage. To Burns, with his radical sympathies, Pitt thus seemed the tyrannical defender of privilege against reform, a conception, however, which history has hardly sustained.

Because of his Irish policy, Pitt's resignation was at last forced in February 1801, but he returned in 1804, as Chancellor of the Exchequer and First Lord of the Treasury.

He was never really a popular statesman, being considered cold and aloof, though clearly he was an inspired leader.

He was, in a sense, the bridge between the eighteenth and nineteenth centuries, and responsible for the origin of modern financial theory. He approved of the abolition of the slave trade, but did little to advance the social conditions of his workers at home. To quote one biographer, he was 'revered but not loved'.

His debts were so large that he could never bring himself to make a formal declaration for Lord Aukland's daughter, whom he is alleged to have loved. He never married.

Pizarro, Francisco (c. 1478-1541)
The discover and conqueror of Peru. He fell out with his lieutenant, D'Almagro (1475-1538) over territory and had him executed. Burns assigns both a place in Hell in the 'Address of Beelzebub'.

Pleyel, Ignaz Joseph (1757-1831)
Born near Vienna, he became a favourite pupil of Haydn. He settled in Strasbourg as choirmaster of the Cathedral, but during the third year of the French Revolution, when France was faced with considerable foreign opposition, he thought it prudent to leave. Thus it came about that Pleyel was in London at the same time as Haydn, his old master. Stories are sometimes encountered about Haydn's alleged irritation at finding Pleyel giving rival concerts in the British capital. A letter of Haydn's written in December 1791, reads: 'Since his arrival [23rd December] Pleyel has been so modest to me that my old affection has

revived; we are often together and it does him honour to find that he honours the worth of his old father [i.e. Haydn himself]. We shall each take our share of success and go home satisfied.'

Pleyel, however, was not at once able to go home, for he found himself denounced as an enemy of the Republic. Eventually, he settled in Paris, where he founded the famous piano manufactory that still bears his name.

He wrote a considerable quantity of music; symphonies, quintets, and quartets, and several series of sonatas and sonatinas for two violins and for violin and piano which are still widely played by students.

Mozart wrote of him in a letter to his father dated 24th April 1784: 'He is a pupil of Joseph Haydn. If you do not yet know his quartets, try to get them, they are well worth while. . . . What good fortune for music if Pleyel, in his good time, can take Haydn's place for us!'

George Thomson described Pleyel as his 'first Apollo'. The editor probably first wrote to the composer about the time Pleyel was in London. Pleyel provided Thomson with six sonatas based on Scottish airs, and symphonies and accompaniments to thirty-two Scottish songs. For this, he received £131 5s. in 1793. Thomson appears to have had some difficulty with Pleyel, for he told another musician, Kozeluch (who succeeded Mozart as Court Composer to Leopold II), from whom he was insisting on having a signed contract:

'As he is resident in France, I have no means at present of procuring any redress or satisfaction from him. These musicians are generally very incorrect in business and eccentric in their conduct, so that it is the more necessary to be on one's guard in a transaction of this kind.'

Burns regarded Thomson's foreign composers with a measure of suspicion. On 26th April 1793, he cautioned the editor: 'Another hint you will forgive—whatever Mr Pleyel does, let him not alter one iota of the original Scots Air; I mean, in the

Song Department. Our friend Clarke, than whom, you know, there is not a better judge on the subject, complains that in the air "Leerig", the accent is to be altered. But, let our National Music preserve its native features. They are, I own, frequently wild, and unreducable to the modern rules; but on that very eccentricity, perhaps, depends a great part of their effect.'

In May 1794, Burns remarked to Thomson: 'I am quite vexed at Pleyel's being cooped up in France, as it will put an entire stop to our work.' And again, in July: 'Is there no news yet, my dear Sir, of Pleyel? Or is your work to be at a dead stop, untill these glorious Crusaders, the Allies, set our modern Orpheus at liberty from the savage thraldom of Democratic Discords?' By 6th February 1795, Burns was suggesting: 'If you are ultimately frustrated of Pleyel's assistance, what think you of applying to Clarke? This, you will say, would be breaking faith with your Subscribers; but, bating that circumstance, I am confident that Clarke is equal *in Scottish Song* to take up the pen, even after Pleyel.'

Thomson, however, turned to Kozeluch.

Poet, Burns's views on being a
See **Craik, Helen.**

Politics, Burns and
Burns's political allegiance has been claimed by supporters of every political party or faction from extreme right to extreme left. He was, in fact, a good example of Dr Johnson's dictum about the unwisdom of giving one's loyalty of mind to a single party in that his attitude to the political parties of his day changed as he grew older. In any case he was never wholly committed to either.

In a sense, however, Burns's involvement in the wider issues of politics—the values behind politics, of which political parties are necessarily so partial an expression— remained fairly constant, although, like sensitive Scots of his day (and, for that matter, our own) he had to try to balance seemingly irreconcilable opposites. Thus, on the face of it, Burns was at the same time a Jacobite and a Jacobin. But only 'on the face of it'!

His nationalism, his internationalism, and his radicalism never wavered. He believed constantly and passionately in Scotland, in 'the brotherhood of man' and in the rights of the ordinary man.

In his autobiographical letter to John Moore, Burns described his recognition of his feelings for Scotland: '.... the story of Wallace poured a Scottish prejudice in my veins which will boil alang there till the flood-gates of life shut in eternal rest.'

His Jacobitism led him to such songs as 'OKenmure's on and awa'' and 'Scots wha hae'. It could lead him to send to the Editor of the *Edinburgh Evening Courant* a protest when a minister of religion, cele-brating the Revolution of 1688, reviled the Stuarts:

'Bred and educated in revolution principles, the principles of reason and common sense, it could not be any silly political prejudice that made my heart revolt at the harsh abusive manner in which the Reverend Gentleman mentioned the House of Stuart, and which, I am afraid, was too much the language of that day. We may rejoice sufficiently in our deliver-ance from past evils, without cruelly raking up the ashes of those whose mis-fortune it was, perhaps, as much as their crimes, to be the authors of these evils ... The Stuarts have been condemned and laughed at for the folly and impracticabil-ity of their attempts, in 1715 and 1745. That they failed, I bless my God most fervently, but cannot join in the ridicule against them ... Let every man, who has a tear for the many miseries incident to humanity, feel for a family, illustrious as any in Europe, and unfortunate beyond historic precedent; and let every Briton, and particularly every Scotsman, who ever looked with reverential pity on the dotage of a parent, cast a veil over the fatal mistakes of the Kings of his forefathers.'

Whatever his sentimental attachment to the Jacobites, Burns was aware that theirs was a lost cause. In 'Ye Jacobites by name', he advised:

> 'Then let your schemes alone,
>   In the State!
> Then let your schemes alone,
>   Adore the rising sun,
>   And leave a man undone
>   To his fate!'

That he was keenly aware, however, of the inadequacies of the ruling represent-atives of the House of Hanover he showed in 'A Dream'.

> 'Tis very true, my sovereign King,
>   My skill may weel be doubted;
> But facts are chiels that winna ding,
>   [*fellows who'll not be beaten*
> An' downa be disputed: [*can't*
> Your royal nest, beneath your wing,
>   Is e'en right reft and clouted,
>   [*torn and patched*
> And now the third part of the string,
>   [*i.e. The North American colonies had
>   been lost*
> An' less, will gang about it
>   Than did ae day.'

Nor was he under any illusions as to the real nature of the political jobbery which accomplished the unpopular Treaty of Union of 1707:

> 'What force or guile could not subdue
>   Thro' many warlike ages
> Is wrought now by a coward few
>   For hireling traitor's wages.

> 'The English steel we could disdain,
>   Secure in valour's station:
> But English gold has been our bane—
>   Such a parcel of rogues in a nation.'

Which of us today does not echo his protest: 'Nothing can reconcile me to the common terms, "English ambassador, English court, & etc ..."'?

His internationalism and his radicalism were bound up with one another:

'For a that, and a' that,
        It's comin' yet for a' that,
That Man to Man, the world o'er,
        Shall brithers be for a' that.'

What was coming, so far as Burns was concerned, was not only the brotherhood of Man, but changed social conditions where no longer hundreds would have to

        '. . . . labour to support
        A haughty lordling's pride.'

One aspect of his attitude prior to the French Revolution is perhaps summed up in 'The Twa Dogs', in which the manners of the rich are satirised much as Beaumarchais satirised them in *The Marriage of Figaro*. (Incidentally, the kinship between Mozart and Burns, whose short lives coincided within a few years, is not unworthy of comment, since social satire lies behind not only *Figaro,* which appeared the same year as the Kilmarnock *Poems,* but also *Cosi fan Tutte* and *Don Giovanni.*)

Nor are his 'Lines on Meeting with Lord Daer' the toadying contradiction they are sometimes made out to be, for Daer sympathised with the Friends of the People, as did Burns. Besides,

'The fient o' pride, nae pride had he,
        Nor sauce, nor state that I could see,
        Mair than an honest ploughman!'

But after 1793, Burns's sympathy for France seemed to sharpen. Certainly, if 'The Tree of Liberty' is by him, there can be no doubt about his revolutionary sentiments:

'But vicious folk ay hate to see
        The warks o' Virtue thrive, man;
The courtly vermin's bann'd the tree,
        And grat to see it thrive, man!
King Louis thought to cut it down,
        When it was unco sma', man;
For this the watchman crack'd his
                                                crown,
Cut aff his head and a', man.'

This certainly accords with the sentiments in his letter of 12th January 1795 (the month in which 'Is there for honest poverty?' was written) that so offended Mrs Dunlop:

'What is there in the delivering over a perjured Blockhead and an unprincipled Prostitute to the hands of the hangman, that it should arrest for a moment, attention, in an eventful hour, when, as my friend Roscoe of Liverpool gloriously expresses it—

"When the welfare of Millions is hung
                                                in the scale
And the balance yet trembles with
                                                fate!" '

Nor is there much doubt about the significance of the 'Ode on General Washington's Birthday':

'Here's freedom to them that would
                                                read.
        Here's freedom to them that would
                                                write!
There's nane ever fear'd that the
                                truth should be heard
But they wham the truth would
                                                indite!'

So much for Burns's political attitudes. His actual political alignment can be gauged from his various election Ballads. Those written in 1789–90—the 'Election Ballad for Westerha',' 'The Five Carlins', and the 'Election Ballad at Close of the Contest for Representing the Dumfries Burgh, 1790'—are more or less Pittite in sentiment, and therefore pro-Tory. But in 1795, Burns had swung over to the Whigs with his four Ballads in support of Patrick Heron of Kerroughtree, which show, as Thomas Crawford puts it, Burns 'interpreting the French Revolutionary doctrines in terms of the general Whig demands for Parliamentary Reform'. The threat of French invasion may have induced doubts about the intentions of France:

'. . . . For never but by British hands
Maun British wrangs be righted!'

but not about the original principles behind France's revolution: so, said Burns:

'. . . . While we sing *God save the King*
We'll ne'er forget the People!'

Poosie Nansie

Wife of George Gibson, and the owner of
a Mauchline tavern much frequented by
beggars and 'gangrel bodies'. It was this
Inn in the Cowgate which Burns visited,
and where the revels which inspired 'The
Jolly Beggars' took place. Agnes Wilson
was employed as a servant by them. They
had a son, Jock, and a half-witted daughter,
known as 'Racer Jess', because of her speed
in running errands.

Poosie Nansie's is still an Inn.

Portland, third Duke of. *See* Bentinck.

Prentice, Archibald

The farmer of Covington Mains, near
Biggar, in Lanarkshire, whom Burns visited
on 27th November 1786, en route for
Edinburgh. There was 'a most agreeable
little party in the evening'. Burns stayed
the night at Hillhead Farm, with Mr and
Mrs Stodhart—described by Burns as 'a

glorious good fellow with a still more
glorious wife'—and Prentice joined them
for breakfast on the morning of the 28th.

Prentice was an admirer of the poet, and
subscribed for twenty copies of the first
Edinburgh Edition of his *Poems*.

In a letter dated 29th November 1786,
to George Reid, who lent Burns a pony to
ride to Edinburgh, the poet described
Prentice: 'For Mr Prentice, no words can
do him justice. Sound sterling sense and
plain warm hospitality are truly his.'

Pulteney, William, Earl of Bath (d. 1764)

Father of Francis Pulteney, who married
Sir James Johnstone. The Earl was reported
to be one of the richest men in England,
hence Burns's 'Not Pulteney's wealth can
Pulteney save' in the 'Election Epistle to
Robert Graham of Fintry' beginning 'Fintry, my stay in wordly strife'.

Purdie, Andrew

A carpenter in Paisley, and the uncle with
whom Jean Armour was sent to stay by
her parents when she became pregnant for
the first time by Burns.

Q

Queensberry, William Douglas, third Earl of March and fourth Duke of— 'Old Q'. *See* Douglas.

R

Ramsay, Allan (1686-1758)

Son of John Ramsay, superintendent of Lord Hopetoun's lead-mines at Leadhills, Lanarkshire, and his wife, Alice Bower, a native of Derbyshire. The poet's fanciful biographer, George Chalmers, claimed Ramsay's descent from the Ramsays of Cockpen, a younger branch of the Ramsays of Dalhousie; but Burns Martin, in his *Allan Ramsay: A Study of his Life and Works*, has shown this to be quite untrue. Ramsay's father died either just before the poet was born, or very soon after. His mother married again, her second husband being a smallholder called Andrew Crichton. The poet was educated at the parish school of Crawfordmuir. About 1700, his mother died, and his stepfather married again. Following in his elder brother's footsteps, Ramsay went to Edinburgh, where he was apprenticed to a wigmaker. On 19th July 1710, he was admitted a burgess, and soon after he set up his own shop as a master wigmaker. In 1712, he married Christian Ross, the daughter of a deceased lawyer, by whom he had six children, the eldest of whom, born in 1713, became Allan Ramsay, the painter.

It was as a member of the Easy Club that Ramsay seems to have found the first audience for his verse. His first published poem, *A Poem to the Memory of the Famous Archibald Pitcairn, M.D.*, appeared under their patronage. His poems thereafter appeared frequently, among them *Scots Songs* in 1718 and 1719. The quarto edition of his *Poems*, published in 1721, established his reputation throughout literary Scotland. Late in 1722, or early the following year, Ramsay abandoned wigmaking for bookselling, setting up his shop in the High Street, 'on the South-side of the Cross-well', but moving about 1726 to the east end of the Luckenbooths, where

he abandoned his old sign of the 'Mercury' in favour of 'Hawthornden's and Ben Johnson's [*sic*] Heads'. His pastoral opera, *The Gentle Shepherd*, was first published in 1725. Between 1724 and 1737, Ramsay brought out the four volumes of *The Tea-Table Miscellany*, a collection of Scots songs, in Scots and English, made or amended by himself and his friends, including versions of traditional pieces. These anthologies achieved enormous popularity, and ran to many editions. The songs were originally published without the airs, but Ramsay named the airs for which the words were intended, and in 1726, under the editorship of Alexander Stuart, issued *Musick for Allan Ramsay's Collection of Scots Songs*. Other arrangers soon followed Stuart's example.

Another task which Ramsay set himself was to publish modern editions of the Scots Makars (as the 'Scottish Chaucerians' are, more properly, called by the Scots). Two of the four volumes of *The Ever Green*—the last two never appeared—came out in 1724. For all their editorial crudities, they performed a valuable service in keeping the poems of the Makars before a new public.

Ramsay was also interested in the theatre. He may have had a financial interest in the Edinburgh Company of Players, performing between 1733 and 1735: tickets for their performances were certainly sold at his shop. He was undoubtedly managing a Company in the New Theatre in Carrubbers Close in 1736. But the following year, the Edinburgh bailies, under Church pressure, misused the newly passed Licence Act, designed to prevent stage attacks on Walpole, and forced the closure of Ramsay's theatre, at some financial loss to the poet.

In 1733, Ramsay acquired land at Castle Hill, Edinburgh, and, helped by his son, designed and built the grey house (nicknamed 'The Goosedub', or 'Goose Pie', by his contemporaries) which then looked over fields, but now looks out over Princes Street to the north from Ramsay Gardens.

There, he retired in 1740, prosperous, loved and respected. His wife pre-deceased him in 1743. A Jacobite in sentiment, Ramsay nevertheless found it convenient to be at Penicuik when his Prince sent for him to decorate him. The Jacobites seized his house in his absence for use as a vantage-point for firing at the Castle sentries. He died of what was called 'scurvy of the gums', and was buried in Greyfriars' Cemetery. His statue stands at the foot of the mound in Princes Street Gardens, its base housing the works of the cuckoo clock!

Although Ramsay did not actually found the eighteenth century revival in Scots literature—the first brick was laid by James Watson's *Choice Collection of Comic and Serious Scots Poems*, published in Edinburgh between 1706–11—he added to it and popularised it in such a manner as to ensure its success. If Burns drew more from Fergusson in his satires and epistles, where song-work was concerned, Ramsay was his model—Fergusson hardly wrote any songs in his brief life.

As with Fergusson, Burns more than acknowledged his debt to Ramsay, a much less direct one. But he was also aware of the older poet's limitations, referring in a letter of 3rd April 1786, to 'the famous Ramsay of jingling memory'. On 4th June 1789, Burns hoped that John M'Auley, Town clerk of Dumbarton, was, 'in immortal Allan's language', 'Hale, and weel and living.'

In his first *Commonplace Book*, Burns recorded his pleasure in 'the works of our Scotch Poets, particularly the excellent Ramsay, and the still more excellent Ferguson [*sic*]'. In his rhyming letter to William Simson of Ochiltree, Burns's modesty makes us smile now:

> 'My senses wad be in a creel,
>   Should I but dare a hope to speel,
>   Wi' Allan, or wi' Gilbertfield,
>   The braes o' fame. . . .'

'Allan', of course, was Allan Ramsay.

And it was, in part at least, the local patriotism of Ramsay and Fergusson, which stimulated Burns's desire to write about his own part of the country:

> Ramsay an' famous Fergusson
> Gied Forth an' Tay a lift aboon,
> Yarrow an' Tweed, to monie a tune,
>   Owre Scotland rings,
> While Irwin, Lugar, Ayr an' Doon
>   Naebody sings.'—

a position Burns more than remedied!

Ramsay, David

Proprietor in Burns's day of the *Edinburgh Courant*. Under his ownership, the paper was said to have increased its circulation to more than that of any other Scottish paper.

Burns mentioned him humorously in a letter to Peter Hill from Ellisland, 2nd April 1789: 'I beg you will sit down and either compose or borrow a panegyric (If you are going to borrow, apply to our friend, Ramsay, for the assistance of the author of those pretty little buttering paragraphs of eulogiums on your thrice-honored and never-enough-to-be-praised MAGISTRACY—how they hunt down a housebreaker with the sanguinary persev-erance of a bloodhound—how they outdo a terrier in a badger-hole, in unearthing a Resettor of stolen goods—how they steal on a thoughtless troop of Night-nymphs as a spaniel winds the unsuspecting Covey —or how they riot o'er a ravaged B—dy-house as a cat does o'er a plundered Mouse-nest—how they new-vamp old churches, aiming at appearances of Piety—plan Squares & Colledges, to pass for men of taste & learning, etc. etc. etc.—while old Edinburgh, like the doting Mother of a parcel of rakehelly Prodigals, may sing "Hooly & fairly", or cry, "Waes me that e'er I saw ye", but still must put her hand in her pocket & pay whatever scores the young dogs think it proper to contract)— I was going to say, but this d-mn'd Parenthesis has put me out of breath, that you should get that manufacturer of the

tinselled crockery of magistratial reputations, who makes so distinguished & distinguishing a figure in the Ev: Courant to
compose, or rather to compound, something very clever on my remarkable
frugality; that I write to one of my most
esteemed friends on this wretched paper,
which was originally intended for the venal
fist of some drunken Exciseman, to take
dirty notes in a miserable vault of an ale-
cellar.'

In a second undated letter to Peter Hill,
Burns tells him to give Ramsay a piece of
Burns's cheese to help the *Courant's*
proprietor 'digest those damn'd bedaubing
paragraphs with which he is eternally
larding the lean characters of certain great
men in a certain great town'.

Ramsay of Ochtertyre, John (1736–1814)

Son of a Writer to the Signet whose
family had acquired the estate of Ochtertyre, in the parish of Kincardine-in-
Menteith, near Stirling, in 1591. Ramsay
was schooled at Dalkeith, where the
master, a Mr Barclay, had acquired a
reputation for favouring moral rather than
corporal punishment in dealing with his
pupils. Ramsay afterwards related: 'He
seldom whipped but when in a passion,
substituting different degrees of shame
according to the offence,—viz. setting
them on the floor with their breeches
down; making them crawl round the
school, which he called licking the dust; or
putting them naked to bed in a play afternoon, and carrying off their clothes. This
method soon rendered him exceedingly
popular, both with parents and children. . . .'

Ramsay became a good classicist at
Edinburgh University. He then studied
law in his father's office, and passed as an
advocate, though he never practised. His
father died while he was still under age, and
he settled down to live the life of a country
gentleman.

Burns, carrying a letter of introduction

from Dr Blacklock, visited Ramsay during
his ten days' stay at Harvieston, in Clack-
mannshire, in October 1787. Writing to
Cruikshank from the other Ochtertyre, in
Strathearn, home of Sir William Murray,
Burns said: 'I leave this place, I suppose, on
Wednesday, and shall devote a day to Mr
Ramsay at Ochtertyre near Stirling; a
man to whose worth I cannot do justice.'

The second meeting took place, and
Ramsay had Burns to himself. He found
Burns's principles 'abundantly motley, he
being a Jacobite, an Arminian and a
Socinian'. Ramsay supplied information
to Currie, as well as a letter he had addressed to Burns in October 1787, which
Currie published. He transmitted Burns's
alleged statement about the employment
of his grandfather as gardener at Inverugie
Castle, Aberdeenshire, to the Jacobite Earl
Marischal. Ramsay also recorded that he
had asked Burns: 'whether the Edinburgh
Literati had mended his poems, by their
criticisms. "Sir," said he, "the gentlemen
remind me of some spinsters in my country
who spin their thread so fine that it is
neither fit for weft nor woof." He said he
had not changed a word except one, to
please Dr Blair.' This one change was
'salvation' to 'damnation' in 'The Holy
Fair': a change incomparably for the better.

Ramsay's account of what passed between
them also dealt with the impression made
by Burns on the writer, and on the subject
of Burns writing a drama. Said Ramsay:
'I have been in the company of many men
of genius, some of them poets, but never
witnessed such flashes of intellectual bright-
ness as from him, the impulse of the moment, sparks of celestial fire! I never was
more delighted, therefore, than with his
company for two days, *tête-à-tête*. In a
mixed company I should have made little
of him, for in the gamester's phrase, he did
not always know when to play off and
when to play on. . . . I not only proposed
to him the writing of a play similar to *The
Gentle Shepherd,* qualem decet esse soror-
em, but Scottish Georgics, a subject which

Thomson has by no means exhausted in his *Seasons*.

'What beautiful landscape of rural life and manner might not have been expected from a pencil so faithful and so forcible as his, which could have exhibited scenes as familiar and interesting as those in *The Gentle Shepherd* which everyone who knows our swains in their unadulterated state instantly recognises as true to nature! But to have executed either of these plans, steadiness and abstraction from company were wanting, not talents!'

Ramsay related a possible Highland subject which apparently attracted Burns. For further information Ramsay sent the poet a letter of introduction to the Reverend Walter Young of Erskine (*see* **Drama, Burns and the**) and in the covering letter went on: 'I approve of your plan of retiring from din and dissipation to a farm of very moderate size, sufficient to find exercise for mind and body, but not so great as to absorb better things. And if some intellectual pursuit be well chosen and steadily pursued, it will be more lucrative than most farms in this age of rapid improvement. Upon this subject, as your well-wisher and admirer, permit me to go a step further. Let those bright talents which the Almighty has bestowed on you, be henceforth employed to the noble purpose of supporting the cause of truth and virtue. An imagination so varied and forcible as yours may do this in different modes; nor is it necessary to be always serious, which you have been to good purpose; good morals may be recommended in a "comedy", or even in a song.'

From all of which it may be gathered that Ramsay, who had put up 'a Latin inscription over his door, expressing his wish to live in peace and die in joyful hope in the small but pleasant inheritance of his fathers', was an admirer of the Augustan Burns rather than of the virile vernacular poet who needed the Scots tongue to spark fire from his genius.

Ramsay was a good landlord, and an experimenter in the new agricultural techniques then being developed. He was a particular friend of Lord Kames. In 1793, Scott, then recently called to the bar, was a visitor at Ochtertyre. Scott sent a copy of his *Ballads from Bürger* to Ramsay, whose letter of commendation and acknowledgment may be seen in Lockhart's *Life of Scott*. Scott used Ramsay as the prototype for Jonathan Oldbuck, in *The Antiquary*. Ramsay died unmarried. *Letters of John Ramsay, 1799–1812*, edited by Barbara L. H. Horn, were published by the Scottish History Society in 1966.

Rankine, Anne (d. 1843)

She maintained she was the Annie of 'The Rigs o' Barley'. She was the youngest daughter of John Rankine of Adamhill farm. She married John Merry, an innkeeper in Cumnock, and is buried in Cumnock old churchyard.

Rankine, John (d. 1810)

Farmed Adamhill near Tarbolton. A man of coarse good humour, he became friendly with Burns during the later days at Lochlea. He apparently got to know that Elizabeth Paton was expecting a child by Burns—the poet's first—and twitted Burns, who replied with two insignificant stanzas, and then with the clever and technically daring 'Epistle to John Rankine'. The poet describes his successful seduction in terms of the field. The 'poacher-court' got to hear of the 'paitrick hen' he had brought down with his 'gun', so he had to 'thole the blethers an' pay the fee'. He tells Rankine that as soon as her 'clockin'-time' is by, and the child is born, he means to have further 'sportin' by and by', to get value for his guinea.

Burns afterwards sent Rankine a silver-mounted snuff-box. *See* **Rankine, Anne.**

Ratton-Key

Mentioned by Burns in 'The Brigs of Ayr'; he noted that it was 'a small landing-place above the large Key' in Ayr.

Red, Red Rose', 'The
See Urbani, Pietro.

Reid of Kirkennan, Alexander (1747–1823)
Second son of John Reid (1691–1764) of Kirkennan. He got his art-training probably in London and Paris. He did many paintings of people, places and scenes in Galloway and Dumfries. He had a studio in Dumfries, in which he did a miniature of Burns. Writing to Thomson, in a letter dated by Ferguson, May 1795, Burns described Reid's miniature: 'However there is an artist of very considerable merit, just now in this town, who has hit the most remarkable likeness of what I am at this moment, that I think ever was taken of anybody. It is a small miniature; and as it will be in your town getting itself be-crystallised, & etc. I have some thoughts of suggesting to you, to prefix a vignette taken from it to my song, "Contented wi' little and cantie wi' mair", in order that the portrait of my face and the picture of my mind may go down the stream of Time together.'

However, Burns changed his mind about the excellence of Reid's miniature, for he remarked in a letter to Maria Riddell, dated by Ferguson, spring 1795; 'The painter, in my opinion, has spoilt the likeness.'

See Plate 1

Reid, George (1762–1838)
Farmer at Barquharie near Ochiltree, he married Agnes, eldest daughter of John Tennant of Glenconner by his second wife. Burns borrowed Reid's pony to carry him to Edinburgh. See Tennant, Agnes.

Reid, The Reverend Dr Thomas (1710–1796)
Born at Strachan, Kincardineshire, he was descended from a long line of ministers. He studied divinity, and for a time held the living of New Machar, near Aberdeen. In 1751 Reid got a 'regentship' at King's College and later became Professor of Philosophy in Aberdeen University. He was author of An Inquiry into the Human Mind on the Principles of Common Sense (1764) which purported to answer the scepticism of David Hume. Burns referred twice to Reid's common-sense doctrine of philosophy. One reference is in the prologue he wrote for the actor William Woods' Benefit Night:

'Philosophy, no idle pedant dream,
Here hold her search by heaven-
                       taught Reason's beam.'

The other reference is in 'To James Tennant of Glenconner':

'An' Reid, to common sense
                              appealing.'

In 1764, Reid succeeded Adam Smith as Professor of Moral Philosophy at Glasgow University.

Religion, Burns and
Burns's letters and poems have been quoted in support of nearly every variant of religious belief practised in this country since the eighteenth century. He has also been accused of perpetrating fearful sins, notably by the Reverend Dr William Peebles of Newton-on-Ayr—Burns called him 'Peebles fræ the water-fitt' in 'The Holy Fair'—in a work called Burnomania, published in 1811. Peebles alleged that in Burns's life and in his poetry, 'sinfulness, gross immoralities and irreligion' were 'celebrated, extenuated, vindicated: the worst of passions indulged and gratified: the sacred truths of religion treated with levity, and made the song of the drunkard and the abandoned profligate'.

Authority, however intolerant and absurd its behaviour, does not like to be flouted or ridiculed. Peebles, who fancied himself something of a poet, had, in 1788, written verses on the Centenary of the Revolution, containing the line: 'And bound in Liberty's endearing chain'. So, in 'The Kirk's Alarm,' Burns castigated him:

'Poet Willie, Poet Willie, gie the
                              Doctor a volley,
    Wi' your "liberty's chain" and your
                                      wit;
O'er Pegasus' side ye ne'er laid a
                                 stride,
    Ye only stood by where he sh——
    Poet Willie; Ye only stood by
                      where he sh——.,

The feelings behind Dr Peebles's revengeful nonsense can thus easily be understood. Later claimants on Burns's religious allegiance are scarcely less disingenuous. Thus J. R. Campbell, in *Burns the Democrat* (1945), states that 'on one thing Burns never wavered—the existence of a good, benevolent God', while A. B. Jamieson, in *Burns and Religion* (1931), makes the extraordinary claim that Burns was more of a Calvinist than he knew, and that 'Holy Willie's Prayer' was, in fact, 'the ridicule of his own sincerest feelings and profoundest experiences'.

In an age when Christian beliefs no longer hold sway over the majority, it becomes easier to assess what Burns's attitude may have been from his own writings, the only source of evidence that is of any value.

True, William Burnes was a Calvinist of sorts, but one tinged with the new liberalism which was then in the air. This is reflected in the work to which the young Burns was exposed, the *Manual of Religious Belief in the Form of a Dialogue between Father and Son*, compiled, in all probability, by Burnes himself, or by Burns's teacher Murdoch at Burnes's behest.

According to the autobiographical letter to Dr Moore, Burns was a deeply religious boy, for he described his beliefs at this time as 'enthusiastic, idiot piety'.

Quite early on, Burns seems seriously to have begun to question the very foundations of religious belief, for on 21st March 1787, he told his boyhood friend James

Candlish: 'I likewise, since you and I were first acquainted, in the pride of despising old women's stories, ventured in "the daring path Spinoza trod";'—a quotation from John Brown's *Essay on Satire*—'but experience of the weakness, not the strength, of human powers, made me glad to grasp at revealed religion.'

From this, and from other letters, it seems clear that at this time Burns had doubts about religion but wanted to believe in it, though not necessarily in any of the forms purveyed in his day; a point made again in a letter to Clarinda dated 8th January 1788: 'A mind pervaded, actuated, and governed by purity, truth and charity, though it does not *merit* heaven, yet is an absolutely necessary prerequisite, without which heaven can neither be obtained nor enjoyed; and, by Divine promise, such a mind shall never fail of attaining "everlasting life:" hence the impure, the deceiving, and the uncharitable exclude themselves from eternal bliss, by their unfitness for enjoying it. . . . [Christ] will bring us all, through various ways, and by various means, to bliss at last.' Burns added, more specifically: 'My creed is pretty nearly expressed in the last clause of Jamie Deans's grace, an honest weaver in Ayrshire: "Lord, grant that we may lead a gude life; for a gude life makes a gude end; at least, it helps weel!" '

How totally he rejected Calvinism is made plain in his letter to Mrs Dunlop of 2nd August 1788:

'I am in perpetual warfare with that doctrine of our Reverend Priesthood, that "we are born into this world bond slaves of iniquity and heirs of perdition; wholly inclined to that which is evil and wholly disinclined to that which is good untill by a kind of Spiritual Filtration or rectifying process Called effectual Calling & etc.—" The whole business is reversed, and our connections above and below completely change place. I believe in my conscience that the case is just quite contrary. We came into this world with a heart and disposition to do good for it, untill by dashing a large mixture of base Alloy called Prudence alias Selfishness, the too precious Metal of the Soul is brought down to the blackguard Sterling of ordinary currency . . .'

That Burns at times doubted the existence of an after-life, without which Christianity becomes simply an ethical code, is demonstrated in a stoical letter to Robert Muir, dated 7th March 1788:

'The Close of life indeed, to a reasoning eye is, "dark as was chaos, ere the infant son

"Was roll'd together, or had try'd
                                    his beams
Athwart the gloom profound . . ."

But the honest man has nothing to fear. If we lie down in the grave, the whole man a piece of broke machinery, to moulder with the clods of the valley—so be it; at least there is an end of pain, care, woes and wants: if that part of us called Mind, does survive the apparent destruction of the man—away with old-wife prejudices and tales! Every age and every nation has had a different set of stories: and as the many are always weak, of consequence they have often, perhaps always been deceived: a man, conscious of having acted an honest part among his fellow-creatures; even granting that he may have been the sport, at times, of passions and instincts; he goes to a great unknown Being who could have no other end in giving him existence but to make him happy; who gave him those passions and instincts, and well knows their force.

'These, my worthy friend, are my ideas . . . . It becomes a man of sense to think for himself; particularly in a case where all men are equally interested, and where, indeed, all men are equally in the dark.'

How deep was his doubting is shown by a passage in a letter to Mrs Dunlop, dated 13th December 1789:

'Jesus Christ, thou amiablest of characters, I trust thou art no Imposter, and that thy revelation of blissful scenes of existence beyond death and the grave, is not one of the many impositions which time after time have been palmed off on a credulous mankind.'

Burns's poetic references are no more assured—

'Courts for cowards were erected,
Churches built to please the priest.'—

being there to offset—

'An atheist-laugh's a poor exchange
For Deity offended!'

The later references to religion in Burns's letters reveal the same process of questioning still going on. On 21st August 1792, writing to Mrs Dunlop, he declared that 'still the damned dogmas of reasoning Philosophy throw in their doubt'.

His last recorded thoughts on this subject, again set out in a letter to Mrs Dunlop dated 20th and 29th December 1794, eighteen months before his death, do not show him in an orthodox light:

'What a transient business is life! Very lately I was a boy; but t'other day I was a young man; and I already begin to feel the rigid fibre and stiffening joints of Old Age coming fast o'er my frame. With all my follies of youth, and I fear, a few vices of manhood, still I congratulate myself on having had in early days religion strongly impressed on my mind. I have nothing to say to any body, as, to which Sect they belong, or what Creed they believe; but I look on the Man who is firmly persuaded of Infinite Wisdom and Goodness superintending and directing every circumstance that can happen in his lot—I felicitate such a man as having a solid foundation for his mental enjoyment; a firm prop and sure stay, in the hour of difficulty, trouble and distress: and a never-failing anchor of hope, when he looks beyond the grave.'

'Hope', be it noted: not faith. That, as Thomas Crawford has remarked, is not 'either orthodox or atheistic'.

The only fair conclusion to be reached

from studying all Burns's references to religion is surely that his position lay somewhere between these two extremes: that he was, in fact, as C.E.M. Joad once described himself, 'a wistful agnostic'.

Renton, John

Father-in-law of Charles Sharpe of Hoddam, Dumfries. Renton apparently invited Burns to visit him at Mordington House, near Berwick during the poet's Border Tour. Burns accepted the invitation with the line 'Your billet, Sir, I grant receipt,' but did not record such a visit in his Border Journal.

Rhymer, Rob

The name sometimes used by Burns when circulating manuscript copies of 'The Ordination' among his friends.

Richardson, Gabriel (1759-1820)

A popular citizen of Dumfries, born at Kellobank, who became Provost of the town in 1801. He was a brewer, whose brewery Burns surveyed. Richardson complained that he had an unfair amount of tax to pay on his ale by comparison with outside brewers, and Burns took up the matter in a letter to David Staig, the Provost of Dumfries, in January 1793. The position was that there was a 'twa pennies' tax on ale brewed within Dumfries, but no tax on ale brewed in Bridgend and Annan: 'Your brewers here, the Richardsons, one of whom, Gabriel, I survey, pay annually in "twa pennies" about thirty pounds; and they complain, with great justice, of the unfair balance against them in their competition with the Bridgend, Annan and English traders. As they are respectable characters, both as Citizens and men of business, I am sure they will meet with every encouragement from the Magistracy of Dumfries.'

The tax was adjusted evenly, to the satisfaction of the Richardsons, and to the advantage of the town's revenue. Burns wrote a mock-epitaph on Richardson:

'Here brewer Gabriel's fire's extinct,
And empty all his barrels:
He's blest—if, as he brew'd, he drink—
In upright, virtuous morals.'

It was inscribed on a glass goblet, owned by the Richardson family, from which Cunningham printed it.

Sir John Richardson, the Arctic explorer, was the son of Gabriel Richardson.

Richardton

See **Wallace of Riccarton, Adam.**

Richmond, John (1765-1846)

Born at Sorn, he became a clerk in Gavin Hamilton's office and was in this job when Burns met him. Later, Richmond was clerk to an Edinburgh writer. Richmond introduced Burns to James Smith, and the three of them became close friends. They formed the notorious 'Court of Equity' of Burns's poem (see **Court of Equity**) and were also associated in the revelry which led to the writing of 'The Jolly Beggars'. In January 1785 Richmond had to do penance for his fornication with Jenny Surgeoner, who bore him a daughter. He married her six years later.

To Richmond ,Burns wrote on 9th July 1786, telling him that he had: 'waited on Armour since her return home, not by— from any the least view of reconciliation, but merely to ask for her health. . . . The Mother forbade me the house. . . .'

To Richmond, also, Burns told his plans to catch a ship for Jamaica. On 1st September 1786, he trounced Richmond for 'acting very wrong' in the matter of Jenny Surgeoner. See **Surgeoner, Jenny**.

On 27th September he told Richmond: 'I am going perhaps to try a second edition of my book. If I do, it will detain me a little longer in the country; if not, I shall be gone as soon as harvest is over.'

It was Richmond who heard of Burns 'running a drunken race on the side of Loch Lomond with a wild Highlandman' on horseback, in a letter of 7th July 1787, with the result that his 'Bardship' got 'a skinful of bruises and wounds'.

Asking Richmond in a letter, written from Edinburgh on 25th October 1787, how his daughter by Jenny Surgeoner was, Burns made his curiously casual reference to the death of the girl twin of Jean's second set: 'By the way, I hear I am a girl out of pocket . . . which has provoked me and vexed me a good deal.'

When Burns first arrived in Edinburgh, he went to the flat of Mrs Carfrae, in Baxter's Close, Lawnmarket, to share Richmond's room and bed.

After Burns's death, Richmond supplied Grierson with information about the poet and his associates, including Mary Campbell. *See* **Campbell, 'Highland' Mary.**

Riddell, Elizabeth Kennedy (d. 1801) The daughter of William Kennedy, who came from a Galloway family, but settled in Manchester as a fustian merchant. James Currie, Burns's future biographer, was smitten by her charms when a schoolboy at Dumfries. She married Robert Riddell of Glenriddell in 1784. Although Burns's friendship with her husband must often have brought her into contact with the poet, Burns recorded only conventional tributes about her goodness, and never seems to have manifested any of the personal interest he had in her husband and her sister-in-law, Maria.

It now seems beyond dispute that the affair towards the close of 1793 which interrupted Burns's friendship with the Robert Riddells occurred at Friars' Carse, and that the victim was Mrs Robert Riddell. Tradition, wholly unsupported by any first-hand evidence, avers that the male members of the party had been discussing the Rape of the Sabine Women when left alone after dinner, and that on their return to the drawing-room, they staged a somewhat too realistic enactment, Burns's victim being his hostess. The poet, disgraced, was ordered from the house. Next day, he wrote a strange letter which,

De Lancey Ferguson suggests, was to Mrs Robert Riddell, the theatrical tone suggesting that he may well have hoped thereby to talk his way out of the social consequences of the situation:

'I daresay that this is the first epistle you ever received from this nether world. I write you from the regions of Hell, amid the horrors of the damned. The time and manner of my leaving your earth I do not exactly know, as I took my departure in the heat of a fever of intoxication, contracted at your too hospitable mansion; but, on my arrival here, I was fairly tried, and sentenced to endure the purgatorial tortures of this infernal confine for the space of ninety-nine years, eleven months, and twenty-nine days, and all on account of the impropriety of my conduct yester-night under your roof. Here am I, laid on a bed of pityless furze, with my aching head reclined on a pillow of ever-piercing thorn, while an infernal tormentor, wrinkled, and old, and cruel, his name I think is *Recollection*, with a whip of scorpions, forbids peace or rest to approach me, and keeps anguish eternally awake. Still, Madam, if I could in any measure be reinstated in the good opinion of the fair circle whom my conduct last night so much injured, I think it would be an alleviation to my torments. For this reason I trouble you with this letter. To the men of the company I will make no apology. Your husband, who insisted on my drinking more than I chose, has no right to blame me; and the other gentlemen were partakers of my guilt. But to you, Madam, I have much to apologise. Your good opinion I valued as one of the greatest acquisitions I had made on earth, and I was truly a beast to forfeit it. There was a Miss I—— too, a woman of fine sense, gentle and unassuming manners—do make, on my part, a miserable d—mned wretch's best apology to her. A Mrs G——, a charming woman, did me the honor to be prejudiced in my favor; this makes me hope that I have not outraged her beyond all forgiveness.—To all the other ladies please present my humblest contrition for my conduct, and my petition for their gracious pardon. O all ye powers of decency and decorum! whisper to them that my errors, though great, were involuntary—that an intoxicated man is the vilest of beasts—that it was not in my nature to be brutal to any one—that to be rude to a woman, when in my senses, was impossible with me—but——

'Regret! Remorse! Shame! ye three hellhounds that ever dog my steps and bay at my heels, spare me! spare me!

'Forgive the offences, and pity the perdition of, Madam

Your humble Slave,
(Robt. Burns)'

But, the 'humble Slave' was not forgiven, either by Robert Riddell, who died the following April, or by Mrs Robert Riddell. That she was of a narrow and unforgiving nature is further suggested by what happened to Friars' Carse. Under the terms of the will, it could have gone to Walter Riddell, who would have had to pay his widowed sister-in-law an annuity. Writing to an unidentifiable correspondent, called McLeod, from Dumfries on 18th June 1794, Burns said: 'The fate of Carse is determined. A majority of the trustees have fixed its *sale*; our friend John Clarke, whom you will remember to have met with here, opposed the measure with all his might; but he was overruled. He, wishing to serve Walter Riddell, the surviving brother, wanted the widow to take a given annuity, and make over to him the survivancy of the paternal estate; but, luckily, the widow most cordially hates her brother-in-law, and, to my knowledge would rather you had the estate, though five hundred cheaper, than that Wattie should.'

Mrs Robert Riddell removed to Edinburgh, after her husband's death, to live with her father, who had retired there, and

Rachel Kennedy, her unmarried sister. She ended her days at Bath, nursed by Rachel during her last illness. She was buried in St James's Churchyard, Bath, on 24th December 1801.

Riddell, Maria Banks Woodley (1772-1808)

The third and youngest daughter of William Woodley, Governor and Captain-General of the Leeward Islands, and his wife Frances Payne of St Kitts. Maria was born and brought up in England until she was sixteen. In 1788, she accompanied her father to the West Indies. There, she met the dissolute and empty-headed Walter Riddell, younger brother of Robert Riddell of Glenriddell, who lived in Friars' Carse. Walter had married an Antigua sugar-prince's daughter, who, after a few months, had left him a widower and some sugar estates. In 1790, Maria became his second wife. They returned to England the following year. A daughter was born to them in London on 31st August 1791, and a second daughter on 23rd November 1792.

Early in the spring of 1792, they came to Scotland, to look for an estate. Walter put down a thousand pounds as deposit for Colonel Goldie's estate of Goldielea, near Dumfries, renaming it Woodley Park.

Maria, like many young ladies of her time, was a poetess. (Her verses are about equal to Clarinda's in merit.) She was witty, and, as we know from Sir Thomas Lawrence's portrait of her, she was beautiful. Burns probably first met her at Friars' Carse, the home of her brother-in-law, in the latter part of 1791. At any rate, by 22nd January 1792, she had Burns writing an introductory letter to his friend William Smellie, the Edinburgh printer and publisher, about a book she proposed to bring out, *Voyages to the Madeira and Leeward and Caribbee Islands*. Wrote Burns: 'Mrs Riddell who takes this letter to town with her, is a Character that even in your own way, as a Naturalist and a Philosopher, would be an acquisition to your acquaintance. The Lady too, is a votary of the Muses; and as I think I am somewhat of a judge in my own trade, I assure you that her verses, always correct, and often elegant, are very much beyond the common run of the Lady-Poetesses of the day. . . . Lest you should think of a lively West-Indian girl of eighteen, as girls of eighteen too often deserve to be thought of, I should take care to remove that prejudice. To be impartial, however, the Lady has one unlucky failing; a failing which you will easily discover, as she seems rather pleased with indulging it; and a failing which you will as easily pardon, as it is a sin that very much besets yourself; where she dislikes, or despises, she is apt to make no more a secret of it— than where she esteems and respects.' Smellie took to Maria on first sight, and became one of her intimate correspondents. Though not interested in her poems, he published her book on the Leeward Islands.

A month later, when Burns wrote to congratulate Maria on her returning health—she had been to London to get medical advice—he addressed her as 'My dearest Friend'—'God grant that you may live at least while I live, for were I to lose you it would leave a vacuum in my enjoyments that nothing could fill up.' In the autumn, he undertook when visiting Robert Riddell to 'say nothing at all, and listen to nothing at all, in which you are mediately, or immediately concerned'—an indication that there was little love lost between the Riddells of Woodley Park and the Riddells of Friars' Carse. There had been an excursion together to the lead mines at Wanlockhead. Maria had insisted on going down a shaft, and Burns had suffered from claustrophobia.

In April 1793, Maria had become: 'thou first of Friends, and most accomplished of Women; even with all thy little caprices!!!' Songs followed. Sending 'The last time I came o'er the moor', Burns commented: 'On reading over this song, I see it is but a cold, inanimate composition. It will be absolutely necessary for me to get in love, else I shall never be able to make a line worth reading on the subject.'

In June 1793, Walter Riddell had to go out to the West Indies on business, possibly to try to raise the balance of the money due on his Dumfriesshire estate. During his absence, Burns presumably saw Maria at Friars' Carse, and at the theatre in Dumfries, where she was wont to receive friends in her box at the interval. One note from Burns read: 'I meant to have called on you yesternight, but as I edged up to your Box-door, the first object which greeted my view was one of these lobster-coated puppies, sitting, like another dragon, guarding the Hesperian fruit.'

It does not take much reading between the lines to see that Burns's regard for Maria was steadily growing in temperature. Then, towards the close of the year, came the mysterious incident which led to a rupture with the Riddell family, and a temporary interruption in the friendship between Maria and Burns.

Exactly what happened, and exactly where, has puzzled, and still does puzzle, Burns scholars. The facts of the puzzle are most fully set out by Hilton Brown in his book *There was a Lad*, in a chapter called 'The Riddell Quarrel'. All that can be said with certainty is that Burns, egged on by his host, apparently drank too much at a dinner-party, and misconducted himself with his hostess, probably by embracing her in such a way as to give affront and lasting offence. The most probable explanation, though it is by no means completely satisfactory, is that the affair took place at Friars' Carse: that the host was Robert Riddell, and the affronted lady his somewhat prim and colourless English wife, Elizabeth: that Robert Riddell, possibly reluctantly, took his wife's side and ordered Burns out of the house: and that Maria felt obliged, or was persuaded by Robert

Riddell, to teach Burns a severe lesson by withholding her friendship.

True, Mrs Robert Riddell's unmarried Edinburgh sister, Miss Kennedy, wrote a letter to Dr Currie on 20th January 1798, stating categorically that the affair was over: 'improper Conduct of Burns to Mrs Walter Riddell which she represented to Mr [Robert] Riddell and which he thought (in his Brother's absence) he ought to resent and therefore declined taking any further notice of Burns'. This may of course refer to some other incident than the so-called 'Sabine Rape' incident, generally considered the sole cause of the rupture. For if it referred to the 'Sabine Rape', Walter being in the West Indies, Robert Riddell as Burns's host must have seen the affair with his own eyes, and therefore would not need 'representation' from Maria or anyone else.

The reference to 'your husband' makes it fairly certain that the recipient must have been Mrs Robert Riddell. She ignored the letter. Burns probably never much liked her, and would feel the loss of her friendship not at all. Her husband, Robert Riddell, who had been a good friend to Burns, died about four months later, unreconciled to the poet.

What did apparently infuriate Burns, however, was the defection of Maria. On her and, in passing, on her husband, he unleashed the full fury of his pen.

He wrote to Maria, probably in January 1794: 'I have sent you Werther; truly happy to have any, the smallest opportunity of obliging you.

' 'Tis true, Madam, I saw you once since I was at W[oodley] p[ark]; and that once froze the very life-blood of my heart. Your reception of me was such, that a wretch, meeting the eye of his Judge, about to pronounce sentence of death on him, could only have envied my feelings and situation.'

And a few days later: 'I return your Common Place Book. I have perused it with much pleasure, and would have continued my criticisms; but as it seems the Critic has forfeited your esteem, his strictures must lose their value.

'If it is true that "Offences come only from the heart", before you I am guiltless. To admire, esteem, prize and adore you, as the most accomplished of Women, and the first of Friends—if these are crimes, I am the most offending thing alive.

'In a face where I used to meet the kind complacency of friendly confidence, now to find cold neglect and contemptuous scorn—is a wrench that my heart can ill bear. It is however some kind of miserable good luck; that while De-haut-en-bas rigour may depress an unoffending wretch to the ground, it has a tendency to rouse a stubborn something in his bosom, which, though it cannot heal the wounds of his soul, is at least an opiate to blunt their poignancy.'

The reference to seeing Maria once 'since I was at Woodley Park' is puzzling, and the affair is further complicated by the hysterical letter Burns wrote the morning after, unaddressed, but which Ferguson supposes went to Mrs Robert Riddell. *See* **Riddell, Elizabeth Kennedy**.

The 'stubborn something' aroused in Burns was the least pleasant aspect of his character, which found expression in the 'Monody on a Lady Famed for her Caprice' the verses 'Pinned to Mrs Walter Riddell's Carriage', and that cheap and bitter imitation of Pope, 'Epistle from Esopus to Maria' (Professor J. de Lancey Ferguson has gone some way towards demonstrating that possibly they may not, in fact, be by Burns). The 'Monody' closes:

'Here lies now, a prey to insulting
                                              neglect,
Who once was a butterfly gay in life's
                                              beam;
Want only of a Wisdom denied her
                                              respect,
Want only of Goodness denied her
                                              esteem.'

The 'Carriage' lines go:

'If you rattle along like your Mistress's
                                    tongue,
Your speed will outrival the dart;
But a fly for your load, you'll break
                    down on the road,
If your stuff be as rotten's her heart.'

Walter Riddell came in for an even more
unpleasant 'Epitaph':

'So vile was poor Wat, such a
                        miscreant slave
That the worms even damn'd him
                when laid in the grave.
"In his skull there's a famine!" a
                    starved reptile cries;
"And his heart, it is poison!" another
                            replies.'

So far as is known, Burns stopped short
of sending these vulgar trifles to Maria,
though some kind friend would possibly
make sure she was aware of their existence,
after the manner of kind friends. But
Burns did send them to other people: the
'Carriage' lines to Miller, for the *Morning
Chronicle*, where it never appeared; both
the 'Monody' and the 'Carriage' lines to
Clarinda, with the explanation: 'The
subject of the foregoing is a woman of
fashion in this country, with whom, at
one period, I was well acquainted. By
some scandalous conduct to me, and two
or three other gentlemen here as well as
me, she steered so far north of my good
opinion, that I have made her the theme of
several illnatured things.' The 'Monody'
also went to Mrs Dunlop, with the note
that they were about 'a fantastical fine-
fashioned Dame of my acquaintance'.
    If Maria's twenty-one-year-old heart
had really been as rotten as Burns alleged,
her ensuing conduct would have been
different from what it was. She sent him a
book, which he politely acknowledged in
the third person, early in 1795.
    By the spring of 1795, they had so far
become friendly again for Burns to send
her Reid's miniature on loan. By now,
Maria was living, much more humbly,

at Tinwald House, between Dumfries and
Lochmaben. For, on her husband's return
from the West Indies without the balance
of the purchase money, Woodley Park
had been repossessed by its former owner.
In May, the Walter Riddells moved again,
to Hallheaths on the eastern side of Lochmaben. From there, Maria wrote to Burns
asking his advice about getting a job for a
protégé of hers. By the late summer, she
was again sending her verses for Burns's
criticism. In October and November 1795,
Burns told her of 'severe domestic misfortune'—the death of his daughter Elizabeth. He added: 'I am much correspondence in your debt: I shall pay it soon.'
    But he was never able to pay it.
    In June 1796, unaware of the seriousness
of Burns's condition and unwell herself,
Maria apparently invited the poet to
attend the Assembly to be held in honour
of the King's birthday. The last letter she
received from him revealed all too plainly
the state to which he had sunk:

'I am in such miserable health as to be
utterly incapable of showing my loyalty in
any way. Rackt as I am with rheumatisims,
I meet every face with a greeting like that
of Balak to Balaam—"Come, curse me
Jacob; and come, defy me Israel!" So, say
I, Come, curse me that East-wind; and
come, defy me the North! ! ! . . . I may
perhaps see you on Saturday, but I will
not be at the Ball. Why should I? "Man
delights not me, nor woman either!" Can
you supply me with the song "Let us all be
unhappy together". Do, if you can, and
oblige,

                le pauvre miserable,
                        R.B.'

    A month later, when Burns was at Brow,
bathing himself on Dr Maxwell's orders,
under the belief that he was making a last
attempt to regain his health, Maria invited
him to dine with her. She, too, was in
search of health, and living not far away.
She sent her carriage to bring him to her
lodgings. Soon afterwards she recorded

her impressions of this meeting, which must have given deep satisfaction to the dying poet: 'I was struck with his appearance on entering the room. The stamp of death was imprinted on his features. He seemed already touching the brink of eternity. His first salutation was: "Well, madam, have you any commands for the other world?" I replied, that it seemed a doubtful case which of us should be the soonest, and that I hoped he would yet live to write my epitaph. He looked at my face with an air of great kindliness, and expressed his concern at seeing me look so ill. . . . He showed great concern about the care of his literary fame, and particularly the publication of his posthumous works. He said he was well aware that his death would occasion some noise, and that every scrap of his writing would be revived against him to the injury of his future reputation: that letters and verses written with unguarded and improper freedom, and which he earnestly wished to be buried in oblivion, would be handed about by idle vanity or malevolence, when no dread of his resentment would restrain them, or prevent the censures of shrill-tongued malice. . . .

'He commented that he had written many epigrams on persons against whom he entertained no enmity, and whose characters he would be sorry to wound. . . . I had seldom seen his mind greater, or more collected. There was frequently a considerable degree of vivacity in his sallies, and they would probably have had a greater share, had not the concern and dejection I could not disguise damped the spirit of pleasantry he seemed not unwilling to indulge.

'We parted about sunset on the evening of that day [the 5th of July, 1796]. The next day I saw him again, and we parted to meet no more!'

Of all the friends who were dearest to him, she remained the most constant to him after his death. In the Dumfries *Weekly Journal* for August 1796, she wrote

a generous sketch of him, which she later revised for Currie's 1801 Edition. *See* **Riddell, Maria: Memoir by.** Henley and Henderson described it as: 'so admirable in tone, and withal so discerning and impartial in understanding, that it remains the best thing written of him by a contemporary critic'. That ill-natured gossiper Charles Kirkpatrick Sharpe left us his word-portrait of Maria: 'She was an affected-painted-crooked postiche—with a mouth from ear to ear and turned-up nose—bandy legs—which she however thought fit to display—and a flat bosom, rubbed over with pearl powder, a cornelian cross hung artfully as a contrast, which was bared in the evening to her petticoat tyings. This pickled frog. . . . Burns admired and loved. . . . Burns wrote a copy of satirical verses on the Lady—which she afterwards humbly forgave, for a very obvious reason —amid all his bitterness he spared her in the principal point, which made her shunned by her own sex, and despised by the rest of the community.'

Against that estimate, the portrait of Lawrence and her own memoir of the poet speak louder by far.

Maria did not long survive Burns. Her worthless husband died in Antigua in 1802, leaving Maria and one surviving daughter to live as state pensioners at Hampton Court. In 1807, she married a Welsh officer of Dragoons, Philips Lloyd Fletcher, but she died the following year.

See Plate 14

Riddell, Maria: Memoir by

Maria Riddell's *Memoir Concerning Burns* was first published in the *Dumfries Journal,* August 1796. It also appeared in Currie's first edition of 1800. She revised it for his second edition of 1801.

Although it has been reprinted by Chambers and others, it is nowadays not easy for the average reader to come by. As it is, by common consent, the best contemporary comment on Burns, it is given her in full:

'The attention of the public is much

occupied at present with the irreparable loss it has recently sustained in the death of Caledonian poet, Robert Burns. It is not probable that this mournful event, which is likely to be felt severely in the literary world, as well as in the circle of private friendship which surrounded him, shall fail to be attended with the usual profusion of posthumous anecdotes and memoirs that commonly spring up at the death of every rare and celebrated personage. I shall not attempt to enlist with the numerous corps of biographers who may, without possessing a kindred genius, arrogate to themselves the privilege of criticising the character and writings of Burns. An "inspiring mantle" like that thrown over him by the tutelary Muse who first found him "at the plough" has been vouchsafed to few, and may be the portion of fewer still; and if it be true that men of genius have a claim, in their literary capacities, to the legal right of a British citizen in a court of justice—that of "being tried only by his peers" (I borrow here an expression I have frequently heard Burns himself make use of), God forbid I should assume the flattering and peculiar privilege of sitting upon his jury! But the intimacy of our acquaintance for several years past may perhaps justify my presenting to the public a few of those ideas and observations I have had the opportunity of forming, and which to the day that closed for ever the scene of his happy qualities and of his errors, I have never had the smallest cause to deviate in, or to recall.

'It will be an injustice done to Burns's reputation in the records of literature, not only as respects future generations and foreign countries, but even with his native Scotland and some of his contemporaries, that he is generally talked of and considered with reference to his poetical talents *only*. In regarding Burns as something more than a Poet, it must not be supposed that I consider that title as a trivial one; no person can be more penetrated with the respect due to the wreath bestowed by the

Muses than myself; and much certainly is due to the merit of a self-taught bard, deprived of the advantages of classical tuition and the intercourse of congenial minds till that period of life when his native fire had already blazed forth in all its wild graces of genuine simplicity and energetic eloquence of sentiment. But the fact is, that even when all his honours are yielded to him, Burns will perhaps be found to move in a poetical sphere less splendid, less dignified, and less attractive, even in his own pastoral style, than some other writers have done. Nevertheless, I hesitate not to affirm—and in vindication of my opinion I appeal to all who had the advantage of personal acquaintance with him—that Poetry was actually not his *forte*. If others have climbed more successfully the heights of Parnassus, none certainly ever outshone Burns in the charms— the sorcery I would almost call it—of fascinating conversation; the spontaneous eloquence of social argument, or the unstudied poignancy of brilliant repartee. His personal endowments were perfectly correspondent with the qualifications of his mind. His form was manly, his action energy itself, devoid in a great measure, however, of those graces, of that polish acquired only in the refinement of societies where in early life he had not the opportunity to mix; but where—such was the irresistible power of attraction that encircled him—though his appearance and manner were always peculiar, he never failed to delight and to *excel*. His figure certainly bore the authentic impress of his birth and original station in life; it seemed moulded by Nature for the rough exercises of agriculture rather than the gentler cultivation of *belles lettres*. His features were stamped with the hardy character of independence, and the firmness of conscious though not arrogant pre-eminence. I believe no man was ever gifted with a larger portion of the *vivida vis animi*: the animated expressions of his countenance were almost peculiar to himself. The rapid lightnings of his eye were always the harbingers of some flash of genius, whether they darted the fiery glances of insulted and indignant superiority, or beamed with the impassioned sentiment of fervent and impetuous affections. His voice alone could improve upon the magic of his eye; sonorous, replete with the finest modulations, it alternately captivated the ear with the melody of poetic numbers, the perspicuity of nervous reasoning, or the ardent sallies of enthusiastic patriotism.

'I am almost at a loss to say whether the keenness of satire was the *forte* or the foible of Burns; for though Nature had endowed him with a portion of the most pointed excellence in that "perilous gift", he suffered it too often to be the vehicle of personal, and sometimes unfounded animosities. It was not always that sportiveness of humour—that "unwary pleasantry", which Sterne has described to us with touches so conciliatory; but the darts of ridicule were frequently directed as the caprice of the instant suggested, or the altercations of parties or of persons happened to kindle the restlessness of his spirit into interest or aversion. This was not, however, invariably the case; his wit (which is no unusual matter indeed) had always the start of his judgment, and would lead him to the indulgence of raillery uniformly acute, but often unaccompanied with the least desire to wound. The suppression of an arch and full pointed *bon mot*, from dread of injuring its object, the sage of Zurich very properly classes as "a virtue only to be sought for in the Calendar of Saints"; if so, Burns must not be dealt with unconscientiously for being rather deficient in it. He paid the forfeit of his talents as dearly as any one could do. 'Twas no extravagant arithmetic to say of him (as of Yorick), "that for every ten jokes he got a hundred enemies"; but much allowance should be made by a candid mind for the splenetic warmth of a spirit "which distress had often spited with the world", and which, unbounded in its

intellectual sallies and pursuits, continually experienced the curbs imposed by the waywardness of his fortune. His soul was never languid or inactive, and his genius was extinguished only with the last sparks of retreating life; but the vivacity of his wishes and temper was checked by constant disappointments which sat heavy on a heart that acknowledged the ruling passion of independence, without having ever been placed beyond the grasp of penury.

'Burns possessed none of that negative insipidity of character, whose love must be regarded with indifference, or whose resentment could be considered with contempt; so his passions rendered him— according as they disclosed themselves in affection or antipathy—the object of enthusiastic attachment or of decided enmity. In this respect, the temper of his companions seemed to take the tincture from his own; for *he* acknowledged in the universe but two classes of objects—those of adoration the most fervent, or of aversion the most uncontrollable. It has indeed been frequently asserted of him, that, unsusceptible of indifference, and often hating where he ought to have despised, he alternately opened his heart and poured forth the treasures of his understanding to some who were incapable of appreciating the homage; and elevated to the privilege of adversaries those who were unqualified in all respects for the honour of a contest so distinguished.

'It is said that the celebrated Dr Johnson professed to "love a good hater": a temperament that had singularly adapted him to cherish a prepossession in favour of our bard, who perhaps fell but little short even of the surly Doctor in this qualification, so long as his ill-will continued; but the fervour of his passions was fortunately corrected by their versatility. He was seldom—never indeed—implacable in his resentments, and sometimes (it has been alleged) not inviolably steady in his engagements of friendship. Much indeed has been said of his inconsistency and caprice; but I am inclined to believe they originated less in a levity of sentiment, than from an extreme impetuosity of feeling which rendered him prompt to take umbrage; and his sensations of pique, where he fancied he had discovered the traces of unkindness, scorn, or neglect, took their measure of asperity from the overflowings of the opposite sentiment which preceded them, and which seldom failed to regain its ascendency in his bosom, on the return of calmer reflection. He was candid and manly in the avowal of his errors, and *his avowal* was a *reparation*. His native *fierté* never forsaking him for a moment, the value of a frank acknowledgment was enhanced tenfold towards a generous mind from its never being attended with servility. His mind, organised only for the stronger and more acute operation of the passions, was impracticable to the efforts of superciliousness that would have depressed it into humility, and equally superior to the encroachments of venal suggestions that might have led him into the mazes of hypocrisy.

'It has been observed that he was far from averse to the incense of flattery, and could receive it tempered with less delicacy than might have been expected, as he seldom transgressed extravagantly in that way himself; where he paid a compliment it might indeed claim the power of intoxication, as approbation from him was always an honest tribute from the warmth and sincerity of his heart. It has been sometimes represented, by those who, it would seem, had a view to depreciate, though they could not hope wholly to obscure, that native brilliancy which this extraordinary man had invariably bestowed on every thing that came from his lips or pen, that the history of the Ayrshire ploughboy was an ingenious fiction, fabricated for the purposes of obtaining the interests of the great, and enhancing the merits of what in reality required no foil. But had his compositions fallen from a hand more dignified in the ranks of society than that of

a peasant, they had perhaps bestowed as unusual a grace there, as even in the humbler shade of rustic inspiration from whence they really sprung.

'That Burns had received no classical education, and was acquainted with the Greek and Roman authors only through the medium of translations, is a fact that can be indisputably proven. I have seldom seen him at a loss in conversation, unless where the dead languages and their writers were the subjects of discussion. When I have pressed him to tell me why he never took pains to acquire the Latin in particular (a language which his happy memory had so soon enabled him to be master of), he used only to reply with a smile, that he already knew all the Latin he desired to learn, and that was *omnia vincit amor*; a phrase that from his writings and most favourite pursuits, it should undoubtedly seem he was most thoroughly versed in; but I really believe his classical erudition extended little, if any, further.

'The penchant uniformly acknowledged by Burns for the festive pleasures of the table, and towards the fairer and softer objects of Nature's creation, has been the rallying point where the attacks of his censors, both religious and moral, have been directed; and to these, it must be confessed, he showed himself no stoic. His poetical pieces blend, with alternate happiness of description, the frolic spirit of the joy-inspiring bowl, or melt the heart to the tender and impassioned sentiments in which beauty always taught him to pour forth his own. But who would wish to reprove the failings he has consecrated with such lively touches of nature? And where is the rugged moralist who will persuade us so far to "chill the genial current of the soul", as to regret that Ovid ever celebrated his Corinna, or that Anacreon sung beneath his vine?

'I will not, however, undertake to be the apologist of the irregularities even of a man of genius, though I believe it is as certainly understood that genius never *was* free of irregularities, as that their absolution may in great measure be justly claimed, since it is evident that the world must have continued very stationary in its intellectual acquirements, had it never given birth to any but men of plain sense. Evenness of conduct, and a due regard to the decorums of the world, have been so rarely seen to move hand in hand with genius, that some have gone so far as to say (though there I cannot wholly acquiesce), that they are even imcompatible; but, be it remembered, the frailties that cast their shade over the splendour of superior merit are more conspicuously glaring than where they are the attendants of mere mediocrity. It is only on the gem we are disturbed to see the dust; the pebble may be soiled, and we do not regard it. The eccentric intuitions of genius too often yield the soul to the wild effervescence of desires, always unbounded, and sometimes equally dangerous to the repose of others as fatal to its own. No wonder then if Virtue herself be sometimes lost in the blaze of kindling animation, or that the calm admonitions of reason are not found sufficient to fetter an imagination which scorns the narrow limits and restrictions that would chain it to the level of ordinary minds. Burns, the child of nature and sensibility, unbroke to the refrigerative precepts of philosophy, makes his own artless apology in terms more forcible than all the argumentatory vindications in the world could do. This appears in one of his poems, where he delineates, with his usual simplicity, the progress of his mind, and its gradual expansion to the lessons of the tutelary Muse:

"I saw thy pulse's madd'ning play
Wild send thee Pleasure's devious way,
Misled by Fancy's meteor ray,
    By passion driven;
But yet the light that led astray
    Was light from heaven!"

'I have already transgressed far beyond the bounds I had proposed to myself on first committing to paper this sketch, which comprehends what I at least have been led to deem the leading features of Burns's mind and character. A critique, either literary or moral, I cannot aim at; mine is wholly fulfilled if in these paragraphs I have been able to delineate any of those strong traits that distinguish him, of those talents which raised him from the plough—where he passed the bleak morning of his life, weaving his rude wreaths of poesy with the wild field-flowers that sprung around his cottage—to that enviable eminence of literary fame, where Scotland shall long cherish his memory with delight and gratitude. Proudly she will remember that beneath her cold sky, a genius was ripened without care or culture, that would have done honour to climes more favourable to the development of those luxuriances of fancy and colouring in which he so eminently excelled.

'From several paragraphs I have noticed in the public prints, even since the idea was formed of sending this humble effort in the same direction, I find private animosities have not yet subsided, and that envy has not yet exhausted all her shafts. I still trust, however, that honest fame will be permanently affixed to Burns's character—a fame which the candid and impartial of his own countrymen, and his readers everywhere, will find he *has* merited. And whenever a kindred bosom is found that has been taught to glow with the fires that animated Burns, should a recollection of the imprudences that sullied his brighter qualifications interpose, let such an one remember the imperfection of all human excellence,—let him leave those inconsistencies which alternately exalted his nature into the seraph and sunk it again into the man, to the Tribunal which *alone* can investigate the labyrinths of the human heart.

"In vain we seek his merits to disclose,
  Or draw his frailties from their
                              dread abode;

There they alike in trembling hope
                   repose—
The bosom of his Father and his
                   God." '

Riddell, Captain Robert (1755-94)

Robert Riddell was the first son of Walter Riddell of Newhouse—who had been taken captive by Prince Charles Edward Stuart, along with the Provost of Dumfries, as security for the levy laid on the town by the Jacobite army during the retreat to the north in December 1745—and Anne Riddell of Glenriddell. On 1st November 1766, Glenriddell had signed a deed disposing of all his lands to Ann, and then to her son, Robert.

Robert Riddell, their son, was schooled at Dumfries, where his fellow-pupils included Dr James Currie, Burns's future biographer, and the Edinburgh lawyer Alexander Young. Young called him 'the most heavy, dull youth, the least of a Scholar, and the most incorrigible dolt in our class', adding that his greatest success was in marrying 'an excellent and amiable lady . . . whom all his school fellows admired, as much as they under-valued him'. But dolt or no, Riddell went on to study at the Universities of St Andrews and Edinburgh. He joined the Royal Scots as an Ensign, later enlisting in the Eighty-third Regiment, in which he was promoted Captain in 1771. In 1782, he retired on half-pay and made his home at Friars' Carse, on the Glenriddell estate. He heired the estate on the death of his father in 1788, but sold Glenriddell itself and lived on at Friars' Carse.

He seems to have had a lively mind, interesting himself in antiquarian pursuits, and contributing papers on local matters of archaeology to the journal of the London Society of Antiquaries, of which he was a member. He was also a talented musician, composing airs of his own—Burns used Riddell's airs for 'The Whistle', 'Nithsdale's Welcome Home', 'The Blue-eyed Lassie' and 'The Day Returns,'

though, judging by their compass, Riddell must have had the fiddle rather than the voice in his mind's ear: and collecting folk airs—*A Collection of Scotch, Galwegian and Border Tunes for violin and pianoforte* was published in 1794.

On 23rd March 1784, Riddell married Elizabeth Kennedy, the daughter of a wealthy Scots fustian merchant who had settled in Manchester. Burns seems to have respected rather than liked her, although he named his daughter, born on 1st November 1792, Elizabeth Riddell, after her.

Exactly how or when Burns met Riddell is not known. Patrick Miller of Dalswinton, Burns's landlord at Ellisland, may have effected an introduction. In any case, they apparently took to each other quickly, for Burns arrived to take up residence in Ellisland, a mile away, on 13th June 1788, and on the 28th, the poet was composing his 'Lines written in Friars' Carse Hermitage', having already been given a key to the hermitage—an artificial 'link' with the place's monkish past—by Riddell. By September, the friendship seemed secure. Burns sent a poem in honour of the Captain's wedding-anniversary, accompanying it with a request: 'I have seen very few who owe so much to a Wedding-day as Mrs Riddell and you; and my imagination took the hint accordingly. . . . A little gratitude, too, had a pretty large share in firing my Muse; as, amidst all the enjoyment I have in your hospitable Mansion, there is nothing gives me more pleasure than to see the minute, cordial attentions and the sparkling glances of the Lover, while in so many Conjugal scenes in the World, a third person is hourly hurt with the insipid yawn of Satiety, or the malignant squint of Disgust.

'I return you my most grateful thanks for your lad to-day. Dare I ask him for tomorrow? I dare not ask more: I would not ask even that one, did not staring necessity compel me. I have not a person I can command but three; your servant makes a fourth, which is all my forces.'

A pleasant survival of the friendship between Riddell and Burns is the 'Extempore to Captain Riddell on Returning a Newspaper':

'*Ellisland: Monday Even:*

'Your News and Review, Sir, I've
             read through and through, Sir,
With little admiring or blaming:
The Papers are barren of home-news
                         or foreign,
No murders or rapes worth the
                            naming.

'Our friends the Reviewers, those
                    Chippers and Hewers,
Are judges of Mortar and Stone, Sir;
But of MEET OR UNMEET, in a FABRIC
                         complete,
I'll boldly pronounce they are none,
                              Sir.

'My Goose-quill too rude is to tell all
                    your goodness
Bestowed on your servant, The
                         Poet;
Would to God I had one like a beam
                         of the Sun,
And then all the World, (Sir),
                    should know it!'

Riddell and Burns became associated in the communal library scheme known as the Monkland Friendly Society. *See* **Monkland Friendly Society**. Riddell gave 'his infant society a great many of his old books', and Burns bought most of the others from his friend the Edinburgh bookseller, Peter Hill. On Riddell's instigation, Burns wrote an account of the Society for Sinclair's *Statistical Account*.

It was for Riddell that Burns wrote the the two manuscript volumes, one of his poems and the other of his prose, known as the Glenriddell Manuscript. *See* **Glenriddell Manuscript**. Only the volume of poems, however, was ever given to Riddell. The first reference to these documents occurs in a letter possibly written

in May 1789, in which Burns remarked: 'If my Poems which I have transcribed and mean still to transcribe into your Book were equal to the grateful respect and esteem I bear for the Gentleman to whom I present them, they would be the finest Poems in the language.' The Preface to the volume of poetry is dated 27th April 1791, shortly after when, presumably, it was given to Riddell. But work on the prose was slower, for reasons which Burns gave Mrs Dunlop in December 1793; 'I have lately collected, for a friend's perusal, all my letters; I mean, those which I first sketched in a rough draught, and afterwards wrote out fair. On looking over some old musty papers, which, from time to time, I had parcelled by as trash that were scarce worth preserving, and which yet at the same time I did not care to destroy, I discovered many of these rude sketches, and have written, and am writing, them out, in a bound MS for my Friend's Library.'

Riddell was a participant in the drinking contest held at Friars' Carse on 16th October 1789, for 'The Whistle', celebrated in Burns's poem of that name, and of which Fergusson of Craigdarroch was the winner. *See* **Fergusson, of Craigparroch, Alexander**. On the morning of the contest, Burns, who sent over a boy with a request that some letters might be franked by Sir Robert Lawrie, wrote a light-hearted note to Riddell: 'Big with the idea of this important day at Friars Carse, I have watched the elements and skies in the full persuasion that they would announce it to the astonished world by some phenomena of terrific portent. Yesternight until a very late hour did I wait with anxious horror for the appearance of some Comet firing half the sky; or aerial armies of sanguinary Scandinavians, darting athwart the startled heavens, rapid as the ragged lightning, and horrid as those convulsions of Nature that bury nations.

'The elements, however, seem to take the matter very quietly: they did not even usher in this morning with triple suns and a shower of blood, symbolical of the three potent heroes and the mighty claret-shed of the day. For me, as Thomson in his "Winter" says of the storm—I shall "Hear astonish'd, and astonish'd sing".'

The mutual friendship continued happily until the close of 1793. In April Burns sent the Captain a copy of the 1793 Edition of his *Poems* with the inscription: 'When you and I, my dear Sir, have passed that bourne whence no traveller returns, should the volumes survive us, I wish the future Reader of this Page to be informed that they were the pledge of Friendship, ardent and grateful on my part, as it was kind and generous on yours.'

Riddell shared Burns's views on the need for representational reforms, and, at the poet's request, sent 'a Prose Essay signed Cato' to Burns, requesting him to send it to the Editor of the *Gazatteer*, where it appeared.

When, soon afterwards, Burns was in trouble with the Excise Authorities over his loyalty, Erskine of Mar wrote to Riddell, proposing 'a Subscription among the friends of Liberty' for the poet. Riddell showed the letter to Burns, who was deeply touched by Erskine's solicitude.

The friendship with Riddell, which obviously meant a great deal to Burns, was shattered as a result of some sort of drunken incident at Friars' Carse towards the close of December 1793. Mrs Robert Riddell took offence at what was possibly a too-energetic embrace; Burns was ordered from the house; and Maria Riddell, the Captain's sister-in-law, and the poet's close friend, felt bound to 'cut' Burns for a time, in support of the family honour.

In vain did Burns appeal to Mrs Robert Riddell for forgiveness, though the larger-souled Maria eventually forgave him. Nor was there a word from her husband, the Captain, who, a few months later, was dead and buried in Dunscore churchyard.

Burns was deeply distressed by his death. To John Clarke of Locherwoods, to whom he wrote on 21st April 1794, he said: 'This morning's loss I have severely felt. Inclosed is a small heart-felt tribute to the memory of the *man I loved*.' The tribute was the 'Sonnet on the Death of Robert Riddell', which concludes:

'Yes, pour, ye warblers, pour the
notes of woe,
And soothe the Virtues weeping o'er
his bier!
The man of worth—and "hath not
left his peer!"—
Is in his "narrow house" for ever
darkly low.

Thee, Spring, again with joy shall
others greet;
Me, memory of my loss will only
meet.'

To some member of the family, most probably to Miss Elinor Riddell, the Captain's unmarried sister, Burns wrote a few weeks later:

'Nothing short of a kind of absolute necessity could have made me trouble you with this letter. Except my ardent and just esteem for your sense, taste, and worth, every sentiment arising in my breast, as I put pen to paper to you, is painful. The scenes I have passed with the friend of my soul and his amiable connections! the wrench at my heart to think that he is gone, for ever gone from me, never more to meet in the wanderings of a weary world! and the cutting reflection of all, that I had most unfortunately, though most undeservedly lost the confidence of that soul of worth, ere it took its flight!

'These, Madam, are sensations of no ordinary anguish. However, you also may be offended with some *imputed* improprieties of mine; sensibility you know I possess, and sincerity none will deny me.

'To oppose those prejudices which have been raised against me, is not the business of this letter. Indeed it is a warfare I know not how to wage. The powers of positive vice I can in some degree calculate, and against direct malevolence I can be on my guard; but who can estimate the fatuity of giddy caprice, or ward off the unthinking mischief of precipitate folly?

'I have a favor to request of you, Madam; and of your sister Mrs [Riddell], through your means. You know that at the wish of my late friend, I made a collection of all my trifles in verse which I had ever written. They are many of them local, some of them puerile and silly, and all of them unfit for the public eye. As I have some little fame at stake—a fame that I trust may live when the hate of those who "watch for my halting", and the con-tumelious sneer of those whom accident has made my superiors, will, with them-selves, be gone to the regions of oblivion; I am uneasy now for the fate of those manuscripts. Will Mrs [Riddell] have the goodness to destroy them, or return them to me? As a pledge of friendship they were bestowed; and that circumstance indeed was all their merit. Most unhappily for me, that merit they no longer possess; and I hope that Mrs [Riddell's] goodness, which I well know, and ever will revere, will not refuse this favor to a man whom she once held in some degree of estimation.'

Burns's appeal was successful, and the book was duly returned to him.

Riddell has been unjustly sneered at by Burns students from J. C. Dick, who dis-allowed him musical abilities, to Professor Ferguson, who called him a loud and blustering squire. But Burns, who knew and loved the man, recorded his own verdict on Robert Riddell and his wife: 'At their fire-side I have enjoyed more pleasant evenings than at all the houses of fashionable people in this country put together: and to their kindness and hospitality, I am indebted for many of the happiest hours of my life.'

See Plate 14

Riddell, Robert Andrew (fl. 1793)

A minor landscape painter who specialised in topographical views of Scotland. He was a near neighbour of John Murdoch, Burns's schoolmaster, in London. Riddell exhibited a painting at the Royal Academy in 1793. He seems to have presented twelve pictures to Burns. A letter from Burns to Riddell, dated 22nd September 1794, presumably referring to the gift, promises an answer in the form of 'a poetic epistle in one of our Newspapers', as soon as he is able to 'arrange my numbers to please myself'.

The reproductions of Riddell's pictures which have survived do not suggest that the originals can have possessed much merit.

Riddell, Walter (1764-1802)

Younger son of Walter Riddell of Glen-riddell, and brother to Captain Robert Riddell. He married Ann Doig, the daugh-ter of a sugar-prince in Antigua, through whom he inherited estates there when she died a year later. While in the West Indies taking over his estates, he met Maria Banks Woodley, third daughter of William Woodley, Governor and Captain-General of the Leeward Islands. He married her at St Kitts, on 16th September 1790, and soon afterwards returned with her to London. A daughter was born there to them on 31st August 1791, and another on 23rd November 1792.

In the spring of 1792, Walter Riddell acquired the estate of Goldielea from its proprietor, Colonel Goldie, by putting down a small deposit, renaming it Wood-ley Park in his wife's honour. To find the balance of the purchase money, Walter Riddell returned to the West Indies in the summer of 1793, where he remained until the early spring of 1794, being thus out of the country during the 'Sabine Rape' incident at Friars' Carse. But he could not find the necessary money, so Goldie repossessed the estate. At about the same time, Robert Riddell died. Walter had expectations of getting Friars' Carse;

expectations which came to nothing, as Burns explained to an unidentifiable correspondent, McLeod, in a letter of 18th June 1794. McLeod, it seems, hoped to purchase the place himself: 'The fate of Carse is determined. A majority of the trustees have fixed its *sale*. Our friend, John Clarke, whom you remember to have met with here, opposed the measure with all his might; but he was overruled. He, wishing to serve Walter Riddell, the surviving brother, wanted the widow to take a given annuity and make over to him the survivancy of the paternal estate; but, luckily, the widow most cordially hates her brother-in-law, and, to my knowledge, would rather you had the estate, though five hundred cheaper, than that Wattie should. In the meantime, Wattie has sold his Woodley Park to Colon¹ Goldie, the last Proprietor. Wattie gave 16000 £ for it; laid out better than 2000 £ more on it; and has sold it for 15000 £. So much for Master Wattie's sense and management, which, entre nous, are about the same pitch as his worth.'

Burns had a low opinion of Maria's husband, who drew some of his spleen when Maria's support of her sister in the Sabine Rape affair led her temporarily to withhold her friendship, an action which greatly hurt Burns. Burns's epitaph, silly though Walter Riddell may have been, reflects no credit on its author:

'So vile was poor Wat, such a
                                        miscreant slave
That the worms even damn'd him
                                when laid in his grave.
"In his skull there's a famine!" a
                                        starved reptile cries;
"And his heart, it is poison!" another
                                                replies.'

'Poor Wat' seems to have dissipated his estate. The Walter Riddells moved to Tinwald House, between Dumfries and Lochmaben. In May 1795, they moved again, to the smaller house of Hallheaths, on the eastward side of Lochmaben. They were there when Burns died. Walter died in Antigua, apparently penniless, for his widow and surviving daughter had to live at Hampton Court as state pensioners, until Maria remarried in 1807, and died the following year.

Ritson, Joseph (1752–1803)

An English antiquary who published a collection of Scottish songs and airs, entitled *Collection of Scottish Songs*, in two volumes in 1794.

In a letter to Burns from Edinburgh of 14th October 1794, George Thomson said of Ritson: 'He snarls at my publication on the score of Pindar being engaged to write songs for it, uncandidly and unjustly leaving it to be inferred, that the songs of Scottish writers had been sent on packing to make room for Peter's! Of you he speaks with some respect, and gives you a passing hit or two, for daring to dress up a little, some foolish songs for the *Museum*.'

Burns already possessed Ritson's collection of Scots songs, and wrote Thomson to try and get for him, Ritson's collection of English songs. In his 'historical essay on Scottish song' prefixing his *Scottish Songs*, Ritson said of Burns:

'Robert Burns, a natural poet of the first eminence, does not, perhaps, appear to his usual advantage in Song: *non omnia possumus*. The political "fragment", as he calls it (i.e. The verses beginning "When Guilford good our Pilot stood") inserted in the Second Volume of the present collection, has, however, much merit in some of the satirical stanzas, and could it have been concluded with the spirit with which it is commenced, would indisputably have been intitled to great praise; but the character of his favourite minister seems to have operated like the touch of a torpedo; and after vainly attempting something like a panegyric, he seems under the necessity of relinquishing the task. Possibly the bard will one day see occasion to complete his performance as a uniform satire.' And again, in a footnote, Ritson pontificates: 'Mr Burns, as good a poet as Ramsay, is, it must be regretted, an equally licentious unfaithful publisher of the performances of others. Many of the original, old, ancient, genuine songs inserted in Johnson's *Scots musical museum* derive not a little of their merit from passing through the hands of this very ingenious critic.'

Ritson pursued a bitter feud with Bishop Percy, whom he accused of having introduced forgeries in his *Reliques*. He also attacked John Pinkerton's *Select Scottish Ballads* (1783), accusing Pinkerton of using modern forgeries. Pinkerton freely admitted the charge. It was, indeed, to show Pinkerton how a collection should be made, that Ritson issued his collection of *Scottish Songs with the Genuine Music*—or so he said!

Ritson went to Paris, where he was in full sympathy with the French Revolutionary leaders. In 1801, he visited Sir Walter Scott, who had applied to Riston for aid on his proposed work on *Border Minstrelsy*.

Ritson finally went completely insane, and died of 'paralysis of the brain'.

Robertson, The Reverend John (1733-99)

Minister of the first charge at Kilmarnock, and a colleague of the Rev. James Mackinlay. A moderate, he was inducted in 1765.

Burns addressed him in 'The Ordination': 'Now Robertson harangue nae mair, But steek your gab for ever.'

Robertson, The Reverend Dr William (1721-93)

Son of the parish minister of Borthwick, Midlothian, Robertson was educated at Dalkeith Grammar School and Edinburgh University, where John Home, the author of *Douglas*, was one of his friends. He was soon acknowledged to be the leader of the Moderates in the Church of Scotland, and considered the crowning intellectual ornament of the Capital during the first phase

of her late eighteenth- and early nineteenth-century brilliance. In 1743 he became minister of Gladsmuir, near Prestonpans, and in 1745 offered his services as a volunteer to Sir John Cope, an offer which was declined. In 1758 he was called to a church in Edinburgh. He won his reputation in 1759 when his *History of Scotland* was published. This was followed in 1769 by a *History of the Reign of the Emperor Charles V,* and in 1777 by *The History of America*. He was Principal of Edinburgh University from 1761 to 1792, and Moderator of the General Assembly in 1763, in which year he also became Historiographer Royal for Scotland. Although his literary reputation extended to London circles, he remained a modest, honest and friendly man. He retired from the management of Church affairs in 1780, but continued to preach at Greyfriars and to direct the affairs of the University until shortly before his death.

Henry Mackenzie said of him: 'His talents for conversation were remarkable. When introducing strangers to him I often heard him conversing with them on subjects with which they were particularly conversant, and by that means gained their good opinion of him by giving them a good opinion of themselves.' Lord Cockburn has preserved a vivid picture of Robertson as an old man: 'He was a pleasant-looking old man; with an eye of great vivacity and intelligence, a large projecting chin, a small hearing trumpet fastened by a black ribbon to a button-hole of his coat, and a rather large wig, powdered and curled. He struck us boys, even from the side-table, as being evidently fond of a good dinner; at which he sat with his chin near his plate, intent upon the real business of the occasion. This appearance, however, must have been produced partly by his deafness; because, when his eye told him that there was something interesting, it was delightful to observe the animation with which he instantly applied his trumpet, when, having caught the scent, he followed it up, and was the leader of the pack.'

Robertson, who was sixty-five when Burns arrived in Edinburgh, was in ill-health, and does not seem to have taken much notice of the poet. Later, however, through friends, Burns tried to enlist his support in the affair of Clarke, the Moffat schoolmaster threatened with dismissal because of alleged cruelty to his pupils.

But Burns and Robertson certainly met. Robertson recorded that he had: 'scarcely met with any man whose conversation displayed greater vigour than that of Burns'. Burns's poems, he said, had surprised him; the poet's prose had struck him as being finer; but his conversation surpassed both.

Burns refers to Robertson and Hume—rival historians, though good friends—in his 'Prologue Spoken by Mr Woods on his Benefit Night':

'Here history paints with elegance and
                                        force
The tide of Empire's fluctuating
                                        course.'

Robertson, William (d. 1820)

Son of James Robertson of Lude, Perthshire, he succeeded to the estate in 1802. He entered the army when he was only fifteen, and saw service in the American War, in Holland, at the capture of St Lucia, and in other parts of the West Indies. In 1794, he raised an infantry regiment, the Perthshire Fencibles, and in 1804, a corps of Volunteers. He went to Spain with an expedition led by Sir John Murray Pulteney in 1805. Later, he served as staff officer in Scotland, the Channel Islands and various districts of England. He retired with the rank of Lieutenant-General in 1813.

The circumstances of Burns's friendship with him are set out in a letter dated 5th December 1793:

'Heated as I was with wine yesternight, I was perhaps rather seemingly impertinent in my anxious wish to be honored with your acquaintance. You will forgive it: it was the impulse of heart-felt respect. "He is the father of the Scotch County Reform, and is a man who does honor to the business, at the same time that the business does honor to him!" said my worthy friend Glenriddel, to somebody by me, who was talking of your coming to this country with your corps. Then, I replied, I have a woman's longing to take him by the hand and say to him, Sir, I honor you as a man to whom the interests of humanity are dear, and as a Patriot to whom the Rights of your Country are sacred.

'In times such as these, Sir, when our Commoners are barely able, by the glimmer of their own twilight understandings, to scrawl a frank; and when Lords are—what gentlemen would be ashamed to be; to whom shall a sinking country call for help? To the *independant country gentleman*!

'To him who has too deep a stake in his country, not to be in earnest for her welfare; and who, in the honest pride of man, can view with equal contempt, the insolence of office, and the allurements of corruption.

'I mentioned to you a Scots ode or song I had lately composed, and which, I think, has some merit. Allow me to inclose it. When I fall in with you at the Theatre, I shall be glad to have your opinion of it. Accept of it, Sir; as a very humble, but most sincere tribute of respect, from a man, who, dear as he prizes Poetic Fame, yet holds dearer an Independent Mind.'

The song was 'Scots wha hae'. Burns also gave Robertson a copy of 'Wilt Thou be my Dearie'—indeed, two copies, about the second of which there is an amusing note written in February or March 1794: 'Mr Burns presents his most respectful compliments to Major Robertson—begs leave to present him with another copy of the Song—as Mr B—— understands that in a "Treaty of Commerce" with a fair Lady, the little song was among the articles ceded by Major R——.

'Apropos, M^r B——'s most devout wish and earnest prayer for Major Robertson's welfare is,—"That in his commerce with the FAIR, the Balance of Trade may never be against him! Amen!" . . .'

Writing to Cunningham on 3rd March 1794, Burns said of Robertson: 'By the Bye, if you do not know him, let me beg of you, as you would relish a high acquisition to your social happiness, to get acquainted with him.'

Robinson, Jean
Mother of Thomas Orr. See **Orr, Thomas.**

Robinson Julia
See **Orr, Thomas.**

Rockingham, Marquis of
See **Wentworth, Charles.**

Rodger, Hugh (1726-97)
The schoolmaster at Kirkoswald, where Burns was sent to study in the summer of 1775. While there, Burns shared a bed with John Niven. Rodger was well known as a teacher of mathematics, and also functioned as a local surveyor.

Although, as Ferguson suggests, Burns probably did gain some knowledge from Rodger useful later in his Excise duties, mathematics was apparently not his bent. He sums up his own views on the weeks at Kirkoswald in the Autobiographical Letter: 'I spent my seventeenth summer on a smuggling coast a good distance from home at a noted school, to learn Mensuration, Surveying, Dialling, & etc., in which I made a pretty good progress. But I made greater progress in the knowledge of mankind. The contraband trade was at that time very successful; scenes of swaggering riot and roaring dissipation were as yet new to me; and I was no enemy to social life. Here, though I learned to look unconcernedly on a large tavern bill, and mix without fear in a drunken squabble, yet I went on with a high hand in my Geo-

metry; till the sun entered Virgo, a month which is always a carnival in my bosom, a charming Fillette who lived next door to the school overset my Trigonometry and set me off in a tangent from the sphere of my studies. I struggled on with my Sines and Co-sines for a few days more; but stepping out to the garden one charming noon, to take the sun's altitude, I met with my Angel. . . . It was vain to think of doing any more good at school. The remaining week I staid, I did nothing but craze the faculties of my soul about her, or steal out to meet with her; and the two last nights of my stay in the country, had sleep been a mortal sin, I was innocent. I returned home very considerably improved . . .'

The 'charming Fillette' was Peggy Thompson. See **Thompson, Margaret.**

Ronald, John
A carrier between Mauchline and Glasgow, whose uncle, William Ronald, was a ploughman at Lochlea. Burns made use of John's carrier business on several occasions. See **Ronald, William.**

Ronald, William
At one time 'gaudsman' in Lochlea, and later a farmer on his own near Beith in Ayrshire. He claimed that Burns's taking of the family evening prayers after his father's death was 'unequalled'. In 'The Cotter's Saturday Night', Burns described this traditional form of family worship.

Ronald, William
A Mauchline tobacconist, care of whom Burns sent a parcel of two copies of the Edinburgh Edition to George Reid.

Ronalds of the Bennals
The Bennals was a two-hundred-acre farm in Tarbolton parish, owned by William Ronald, a wealthy farmer, and therefore loosely termed a laird. He had two daughters, Jean and Anne, admired by Burns and his brother. Burns's poem 'The

Ronalds of the Bennals' satirises their wealth.

Jean Ronald was baptised in October 1759, and her sister Anne in June 1767. Gilbert wooed the elder, Jean, but she married John Reid, a farmer at Langlands.

William Ronald went bankrupt in 1789. Burns wrote to his brother William in November 1789: 'Mr Ronald is bankrupt. You will easily guess, that from his insolent vanity in his sunshine of life, he will feel a little retaliation from those who thought themselves eclipsed by him, for, poor fellow, I do not think he ever intentionally injured anyone. I might indeed perhaps except his wife, whom he certainly has used very ill. . . .'

Rorie More
See **MacLeod, Sir Roderick.**

'Rosamond', Seizure of

When, in February 1792, Burns was promoted to the Dumfries Third or Port Division, which could be covered entirely on foot, his Excise income was, as he told his 'Dearest Friend' Maria Riddell:

'Cash paid, Seventy pounds a year: and this I hold until I am appointed Supervisor. . . . My Perquisites I hope to make worth 15 or 20 £ more. So rejoice with them that do Rejoice.'

Not long after this promotion, together with a colleague, John Lewars, Burns featured in a dramatic incident which was first of all over-written by Lockhart, and then written off by Snyder.

In the *Edinburgh Evening Courant* of Thursday, 8th March, there appeared an announcement stating that on the previous Wednesday:

'the revenue officer for Dumfries, assisted by a strong party of the 3rd regiment of dragoons, seized a fine large smuggling vessel at Sarkfoot. . . . Upon the officers and the military proceeding towards the vessel, which they did in a martial and determined manner, over a broad space of deep water, the smugglers had the audacity to fire upon them from their swivel guns, loaded with grape shot; but the vessel (owing to her construction) lay in such a situation as prevented their having a direction with effect.'

This, without a doubt, was the brig *Rosamond*, and one of those who advanced in a 'martial and determined manner upon her rebellious crew was Robert Burns.

Amongst the other Revenue Officers who took part was one Walter Crawford, a riding officer at Dumfries. He, it seems, first discovered what was afoot, and attempted to seize the *Rosamond* with a small party he had collected for another purpose. Being unsuccessful, he despatched John Lewars to Dumfries to:

'bring Twenty four more Dragoons, while I went to Ecclefechan for the party there with which I patroled the roads till the arrivall of Mr Lewars with the additional force from Dumfries.'

Crawford's account was given in the *Burns Chronicle*, 1934, in an article 'Burns and the *Rosamond*' by H. W. Meikle. The essentials of Crawford's story are quoted here, with his highly erratic spelling slightly modernised in the interests of intelligibility:

'. . . We approached with . . . Dragoons in all forty four fully accoutered and on horse-back. The vessel having fallen down the Solway Firth about a mile from where she was yesterday, and being about a mile within sea mark, most of which space being covered with water and a very heavy current running between us and the vessel, we deemed it impossible to get at her, either on foot or on horseback, so we agreed to search the coast for boats in which to board her. But the country people, guessing our design, got the start of us and staved every boat on the Coast before we could reach them; the vessel in the mean time keeping up a fire of grape shot and musquetry, we resolved as [a] last resource to attempt the passage on foot, as the quick sands made the ridding on horseback dangerous, or rather impossible.

'We drew up the Military in three divisions, determined to approach and attac[k] her if the s[t]ream was foardable, one part fore and aft, and the third on her broadside, the first party being commanded by Quarter Master Manly, the second by my self, and the third by Mr Burns.

'Our orders to the Military were to reserve their fire till within eight yards of the vessel, then to pour a volley and board her with sword and pistol. The vessel kept on firing, tho without any damage to us, as from the situation of the ship, they could not bring their great guns to bear on us, we in the mean time wading breast high, and in justice to the party under my command I must say with great alacrity; by the time we were within one hundred yeards of the vessel, the crew gave up the cause, got over [the] side towards England, which shore was for a long, long way dry sand. As I still supposed that there were only country people they were putting ashore, and that the crew was keeping under cover to make a more vigorous immediate resistance, we marched up as first concerted, but found the vessel completely evacuated both of crew and every moveable on board, expect as per inventory, the smugglers as their last instance of vengen[c]e having poured a six-pounder Carronade through her broadside. She proved to be the Rosamond of Plymouth, Alexander Patty Master, and about one hundred tons burthern, schooner r[igged].'

The 'Inventory of the Rosamond and Furniture' is apparently in John Lewars's hand, and contains, besides a list of fifty-three items, a draft press advertisement announcing the sale of the ship and its contents by public roup in the Coffee House, Dumfries, on 19th April. This interval between capture and sale was made necessary because the ship had to be repaired. A note in Burns's hand tells us that

two carpenters were employed for eleven days and four seamen for nine days at a cost of £8 18s. and she was then refloated. The sale realised £166 16s. 6d. As the total expenses amounted to £45 15s. 4d. the profit was therefore £121 1s. 2d., part at least of which would presumably have been divided among the Excise Officers.

These papers form part of a bundle of documents relating to the Rosamond given to Joseph Train, antiquary and Supervisor of Excise at Castle Douglas, by John Lewars's widow. In 1825, Train passed the documents to Sir Walter Scott, and Scott showed them to Lockhart, who made use of them to concoct his fanciful account of the whole business, including the absurd tale about Burns's composing 'The De'il's awa' while waiting for Lewars to arrive with his reinforcements! The Train manuscripts came to light in the early 1930s, when the Abbotsford collection was being catalogued by the National Library of Scotland.

Unfortunately, one piece of evidence which Train claimed to have included in the bundle did not come to light, and has not since been traced. This was the document 'detailing the circumstances of Burns having purchased the four carronades at the sale'.

Lockhart avers that Burns paid £4 for these carronades, and the tradition is that he despatched them as a gift to the French Convention to show his sympathy with their cause. According to Train, Sir Walter Scott tried unsuccessfully to trace the receipt of the guns in France, and thereafter 'applied to the Custom House authorities, who, after a considerable search, found that they had been seized at the port of Dover, as stated by Mr Lewars in his memorandum'.

Further researches have failed to enlarge upon Sir Walter's information, though in view of the proven accuracy of the rest of Train's claim, it would be rash to suppose that the carronades were never despatched.

Rose of Kilravock, Mrs Elizabeth (1747-1815)

Born Elizabeth Rose, she married Dr Hugh Rose, who died two years later. Henry MacKenzie, her cousin, gave Burns a letter of introduction to her before the poet set out on his Highland tour in 1787. Her son, Hugh, became the twentieth Laird of Kilravock.

Burns met her at Kilravock, and on hearing her niece, Miss Rose, of Kildrummie, sing two Highland airs, he requested Mrs Rose to send him copies of them. This she did.

Burns, writing to her from Edinburgh on 17th February 1788, thanked her, and added: 'There was something in my reception at Kilravock so different from the cold, obsequious, dancing-school bow of politeness, that it almost got into my head that friendship had occupied her ground without the intermediate march of acquaintance.'

She must indeed have been a remarkable woman, for Cosmo Innes in his *Genealogical Deduction of the Family of Rose of Kilravock* describes her as: 'the choice companion, the leader of all cheerful amusements, the humorous story-teller, the clever mimic, the very soul of society . . . she sung the airs of her own country, and she had learned to take a part in catches and glees, to make up the party with her father and brother. The same motive led her to study the violin. . . . She was enthusiastic and yet steady in her friendships; benevolent, hospitable, kind, and generous beyond her means. . . .'

Burns noted in his *Journal* of the tour that she was 'a true chieftain's wife, a daughter of Clephane'. And again: 'Old Mrs Rose, sterling sense, warm heart, strong passions, honest pride, all in an uncommon degree—Mrs Rose jnr. a little milder than the Mother, this perhaps owing to her being younger.'

She was the recipient of many letters from Ramsay of Ochtertyre. *See* Ramsay, John.

Ross, Alexander (1699-1784)

The most prominent of Ramsay's poetic disciples, Alexander Ross, the son of an Aberdeenshire farmer, took his M.A. degree at Marischal College, Aberdeen, became a schoolteacher, and finally settled in the parish of Lochlee, Forfarshire. In 1768, when in his seventieth year, he published a pastoral modelled on *The Gentle Shepherd* called *Helenore, or The Fortunate Shepherdess*. Under the title *Lindy and Nory*, it achieved immense popularity in Aberdeenshire. Ross's wider and more lasting fame rests on his witty songs, among them 'The Rock and the Wee Pickle Tow', 'Wooed and Married and A'' and 'The Bridal O''.

Burns thought highly of Ross's work, and praised the Aberdeen poet in several letters. Writing to James Hoy, librarian and companion to the Duke of Gordon, on 6th November 1787, Burns said: 'There is I know not what of wild happiness of thought and expression peculiarly beautiful in the old Scottish song style, of which his Grace, old venerable Skinner, the author of Tullochgorum and etc., and the late Ross at Lochlee, of true Scottish poetic memory, are the only modern instances that I recollect, since Ramsay, with his contemporaries, and poor Bob Fergusson, went to the world of deathless existence and truly immortal song.'

Russell, The Reverend John (1740-1817)

A native of Moray, who, after a period of teaching in the Parish School at Cromarty, was ordained minister of the High Church in Kilmarnock in 1744. He was called to Stirling in 1800. He was a staunch supporter of the Auld Licht teaching, and a powerful preacher of the roaring hellfire-threatening sort. Burns was vigorously opposed to his teaching. Russell figures as 'Black Russell' in 'The Holy Fair', and 'wordy Russell' in 'The Twa Herds'. There is a reference to him in 'The Ordination', as being opposed to the common-sense

view of the 'New Licht' party: 'An'
Russell sair misca'd her'. He also appeared
as 'Rumble John' in 'The Kirk's Alarm':

'Rumble John, Rumble John, mount
          the steps with a groan,
Cry, "The Book is with heresy
                    cramm'd";
Then lug out your ladle, deal brim-
          stone like aidle,   [muck-water
And roar every note o' the Damn'd,
Rumble John, and roar every note
                    o' the Damn'd.'

The author of several books and pamphlets
on religion no doubt of interest in his own
day, he became involved in a wordy
doctrinal battle with a fellow 'Auld Licht'
Minister, the Reverend Alexander Moodie
of Riccarton. It was the undignified
spectacle of two members of the 'unco
guid' fighting between themselves that
inspired Burns to write 'The Twa Herds'.
Hugh Miller, the geologist and writer,
was one of Russell's pupils at Cromarty.
Miller recalled Russell as being 'a large,
robust, dark-complexioned man—impert-
urbably grave, and with a sullen expression
seated in the deep folds of his forehead'.
Miller tells the story of a lady, years after
she had left school, who suddenly saw
Russell in a pulpit, and was 'so overcome
with terror that she fainted away'.

Rutherford, Captain
'A polite, soldier-like gentleman', whom
Burns met and dined with, when in
Jedburgh. The Captain, according to
Burns, had been for many years in the
wilds of America, and had been taken
prisoner by the Indians. His wife, Burns
said, was 'exactly a proper matrimonial
second part for him', but his daughter,
although 'her face [was] very fine' was
'too far gone a woman to expose so much
of a fine swelling bosom'.

S

Sackville, Lord George, first Viscount (1716–85)

Son of the Duke of Dorset, he fought with Cumberland at Culloden. He also fought in Flanders, at Dettingen and Fontenoy, and at the battle of Minden was Commander-in-Chief of the British Forces under the full command of Prince Ferdinand of Brunswick. But Sackville failed to carry out the Prince's orders to charge, because he considered they were not clear, and was consequently relieved of the command of his regiment, and court-martialled. He was later restored to favour, became a supporter of Lord North, and under his ministration became Secretary of State for the Colonies. Walpole described him as 'one of the best speakers in the House'. He resigned in 1782, and was created viscount.

Burns referred to him sarcastically in the 'Address of Beelzebub':

'Nae sage North now, nor sager
                                Sackville
To watch and premier o'er the pack
                                vile—'

The poet Churchill, in 'The Candidate', also wisecracked:

'Sackvilles alone anticipate defeat,
And, e'er they dare the battle, sound
                                retreat.

Samson, Thomas (1722–95)

A Kilmarnock friend of Burns, he was 'a seedsman of good credit, a zealous sportsman, and a good fellow'. Burns recalled that when he had been out moorfowling, Samson believed it to be his last such outing, and had expressed a desire to be buried in the moors. On this hint the author composed his 'Elegy and Epitaph'. The epitaph was:

'Tam Samson's weel-worn clay here
                                lies,
Ye canting Zealots, spare him!
If Honest Worth in Heaven rise,
Ye'll mend or ye win near him.'

Burns was said to have often met Samson in the 'Bowling-green House', an inn which Alexander Patrick, the nurseryman's son-in-law, kept. It was here, at a convivial party, that Burns read 'Tam Samson's Elegy' to the company. Samson kept reiterating that he wasn't dead. So, after Burns had finished reading, he went out and returned with the additional 'per contra' stanza:

'Go, Fame, an' canter like a filly,
Thro' a' the streets an' neuks o' *Killie*,
Tell ev'ry social, honest billie
    To cease his grievin',
For yet, unskaithed by Death's gleg
        gullie,   [*unharmed, sharp knife
    Tam Samson's livin*'!'

Along with the Ministers Robertson and Mackinlay, mentioned in the first stanza, Samson lies buried in the Laigh Kirkyard, Kilmarnock, beneath Burns's epitaph. The firm was still in business in Kilmarnock in 1969.

Sancho, Ignatius (1729–80)

A Negro of 'extraordinary character', whose letters are mentioned in a letter from 'Clarinda'. *The Letters of the late Ignatius Sancho, an African*, were published in two volumes in London in 1782. They were said to possess 'great originality and display strong powers of intellect'. There is a full article on him in the Dictionary of National Biography.

Sanquhar

A town in Upper Nithsdale, about twenty-six miles from Dumfries. Burns had to pass through Sanquhar when riding between the Isle and Mauchline. He stayed at 'the only tolerable inn in the place', which was kept by Bailie Edward Wigham. It was here that the arrival of Mrs Oswald of Auchencruive's funeral cortège forced the poet to ride twelve miles further on to New Cumnock. *See* **Oswald, Mrs Lucy.**

Schetky, Johann Georg (1740-1824)

Born at Darmstadt, he was intended for the law, but was determined to make music his career. He studied under Filtz and became 'cellist at the court of Hesse. In 1773, he was engaged for the St Cecilia Concerts in Edinburgh, where he afterwards settled permanently as a music teacher. John Christian Schetky, his son, became a successful painter.

Burns met Schetky when he was in Edinburgh, and remarked in a letter of 24th January 1788, to 'Clarinda' that he had been drinking with 'Mr Schetki, the musician, and he has set the song finely'. The song was 'Clarinda, mistress of my soul'.

Schoolbooks, Burns's

The earliest schoolbooks which the poet used seem to have been those prescribed by John Murdoch, whom William Burnes and four other families brought to Alloway to teach their children in May 1765. Wrote Murdoch: 'The books most commonly used in the school were, the *Spelling Book,* the *New Testament,* the *Bible,* Masson's *Collection of Prose and Verse,* and Fisher's *English Grammar.*'

Of these, by far the most important influence on Burns's style was Arthur Masson's *Collection of Prose and Verse,* an anthology which included no Scots-writing authors, but selections from the works of Thomson, Gray, Shenstone, Shakespeare, Milton, Dryden, Addison, and Elizabeth Rowe, whose *Letters Moral and Entertaining* was represented. To this last work may be attributed the awkward formality of Burns's earlier letters.

Murdoch, on his farewell visit to the Burnes household, left 'a small compendium of English grammar', read *Titus*

Andronicus, but on finding that it provoked the future poet's distress, left instead the translation of a French novel *The School for Love,* which has not been certainly identified. The Murdoch influence was thus entirely on the side of gentility and the Augustan English tradition.

Fortunately, however, the poet came under other influences: the folk-tales of Betty Davidson and, as he related in his Autobiographical Letter, a life of Hannibal (probably a chapbook) and a history of Sir William Wallace: 'Hannibal gave my young ideas such a turn that I used to strut in raptures up and down after the recruiting drum and bagpipe, and wish myself tall enough to be a soldier; while the story of Wallace poured a Scottish prejudice in my veins which will boil along there till the flood-gates of life shut in eternal rest.' *The History of Sir William Wallace* was William Hamilton of Gilbertfield's eighteenth-century modernisation of the late fifteenth-century poem by 'Blind Harry'.

There were also those strange works which William Burnes bought for his children to study during the Mount Oliphant days: Salmon's *Geographical Grammar,* William Derham's *Physico- and Astro-Theology,* both of which endeavoured to prove the existence of God by the teleological argument from design popular at the time: and John Ray's *The Wisdom of God Manifested in the Works of the Creation,* and Thomas Stackhouse's *New History of the Bible.* To augment this store Mrs Burnes's brother brought home 'a small collection of letters by the most eminent writers, with a few sensible directions for attaining an easy epistolary style', to quote Gilbert. The poet described the book as 'a collection of letters by the Wits of Queen Anne's reign', which his uncle had bought by mistake instead of a *Complete Letter-Writer.*

The final stage in the poet's boyhood reading, taken when he was 'about thirteen or fourteen', was two volumes of Richardson's *Pamela,* borrowed from 'a bookish acquaintance of my father's'. Gilbert tells us that these two volumes were: 'the only part of Richardson's works my brother was acquainted with till towards the period of his commencing author. Till that time, too, he remained unacquainted with Fielding, with Smollet (two volumes of *Ferdinand Count Fathom*, and two volumes of *Peregrine Pickle* excepted) with Hume, with Robertson, and almost all our authors of eminence.' Gilbert completed the list of books the future poet read with the volume of the *Edinburgh Magazine* for 1772 and 'those *Excellent new songs* that are hawked about the country in baskets, or exposed on stalls in the streets'.

From the age of seventeen, when Shenstone's works were added to Burns's store, his reading was wide-ranging. Indeed, the 'unlettered ploughman' became one of the best-read Scots of his day.

Scotland, Capital of

Edinburgh, Scotland's capital, grew up along the rocky spine which was originally a path between the Castle on the summit and the Abbey of Holyrood at the foot. Fortifications of some sort have been sited on the Castle rock since the earliest times, and the present Castle must have been preceded by other, less durable fortresses. The oldest surviving part of Edinburgh Castle is St Margaret's Chapel, built for the wife of Malcolm Ceannmor, the first sovereign to rule a more or less unified Scotland. Queen Margaret heard mass in this tiny chapel on 16th November 1093, the day before her death. Apart from David II's tower, begun in 1357, most of the Castle as it stands today dates from the sixteenth century.

The Abbey of Holyrood is traditionally supposed to have been founded by David I, in thankfulness for a 'holy rude' or shining cross which miraculously saved him from a vicious stag while he was out hunting near Salisbury Crags on Rude-Day.

The Canons of Holyrood for long enjoyed the privilege of having their own burgh, granted to them by their founder. Thus, the Canons' Gait, or Canongate as the lower part of the Royal Mile is called, came into being. The splendid palace of Holyrood House is a creation of the later Stuart monarchs, the earliest tower being built by James IV. Prince Charles Edward Stuart held court in Holyrood House before he marched south in 1745.

The first stone houses between the Castle and Holyrood went up about the middle of the sixteenth century. For more than two hundred years, although it became more crowded, Edinburgh remained confined within its medieval bounds.

The Edinburgh into which Burns thus temporarily settled in 1786, was a bewildering panorama of ancient vernacular colour and smelling squalor. A few pigs still roamed the streets, nosing amongst the litter in the gutters. At ten o'clock every night, the windows of the 'lands' were still wont to open for servants to pour the day's household slops (including the contents of the chamber-stools) and rubbish into the streets, to be collected by half-hearted and inefficient scavengers with wheel-barrows at seven o'clock the next morning. The French cry *'Gardez l'eau'*, Scotified by the servants of the rich into 'Gardy loo', was shouted with a similar disregard of probable consequences resulting from any neglect of their warning, as a golfer's vain cry of 'Fore' after the ball has been struck! True, by 1769, seventeen years before Burns arrived in the capital, the English journalist Thomas Pennant had noted that while:

'. . . in the closes or alleys the inhabitants are very apt to fling out their filth, etc., without regarding who passes . . . the sufferer may call every inhabitant of the house it came from to account, and make them prove the delinquent, who is always punished with a heavy fine.'

Yet when Boswell brought Dr Samuel

Johnson to Edinburgh in 1773, he records that he could not prevent his distinguished visitor from:

'. . . being assailed by the evening effluvia of Edinburgh. I heard a late baronet, of some distinction in the political world in the beginning of the present reign, observe that "walking in the streets of Edinburgh at night was pretty perilous, and a good deal odoriferous". The peril is much abated, by the care which the magistrates have taken to enforce the city laws against throwing foul water from the windows; but, from the structure of the houses in the Old Town, which consist of many stories, in each of which a different family lives, and there being no covered sewers, the odour still continues. A zealous Scotsman would have wished Mr Johnson to be without one of his five senses upon this occasion. As we marched slowly along, he grumbled in my ear, "I can smell you in the dark!" But he acknowledged that the breadth of the street and the loftiness of the buildings on each side, made a noble appearance.'

The loftiness of the buildings—some of the 'lands' had as many as fourteen storeys —made necessary by the cramping of the eighteenth-century city into more or less its medieval bounds, resulted in a shortage of water. Along the High Street would be seen the tribe of Water Caddies, bent under the weight of the casks on their backs as they carried water from the public wells which, Lord Cockburn tells us, 'were then pretty thickly planted in the principal street'. Up the narrow turnpike stairs to the six-roomed apartments of people of quality, or the two- or three-roomed flats of the lower gentility, these Caddies bore their kegs.

Because of the 'evening effluvia'— referred to locally as 'the flowers of Edinburgh'—the 'best' people chose to live in the middle flats of the lands. Poorly-paid clerical workers, runners and scavengers occupied the lower flats: aristocrats, professional men and ladies of independent means had their houses in the middle floors; above them might be the shopkeepers, the merchants, and the dancing and music-masters: on top of them all, in the garrets and attics, were to be found the artisans and labourers. Inevitably, all social classes met from time to time—if nowhere else, on the winding stairs, which could not carry two-way traffic, and must have been something of a trial to a behooped countess—and although social distinctions were rigidly observed on public occasions, there developed a feeling of communal friendliness among the occupants of this squeezed-up town. Everyone knew what everyone else was doing. So robberies were less frequent than they became in the 1780s, when the wealthier people had started to depart, and the tone of the Old Town had taken its first downward turn.

Edinburgh's later reputation for the cold aloofness of its middle and upper classes was a product of the social revolution which occurred when the Old Town at last spilled over its banks, and moneyed folk began to abandon their cosy, clarty, ancestral 'lands' for the spacious graces and formalities of the New Town. The first move in this direction had been made as early as 1765, when speculative builders constructed George Square and Brown Square. These squares were at first considered to be hopelessly out of the way, and the real overspill did not begin until 1772, when the first bridge leapt its arch over the gulf between the hump-backed ridge of the Old Town and the gentler ridge of the New, between which lay a swampy marsh called the Nor' Loch. In Burns's day, Princes Street, George Street and Queen Street were already developing westwards. Sedan chairs, carried by Highland characters noted for the volubility of their Gaelic execrations whenever their swift passage was hindered, began to give place to still swifter hackney carriages. The Town Guard, that band of aged and infirm ex-soldiers who did duty as policemen when almost the only crime to be dealt with in quantity was drunkenness, and whom Robert Fergusson ridiculed so mercilessly, were becoming unable to cope with their enlarging responsibilities. The seven-year-long criminal career of the notorious Deacon Brodie—highly respected merchant by day, key-forger and thief by night—was drawing towards its climax, which resulted in his flight to Holland, his arrest and trial, and his execution on the drop gallows, himself the first victim of this new manner of death-dealing, which he had invented as being more humane than the old method of turning off a criminal from a ladder. There was much talk, too, about balloon ascents, and a so-called 'Learned Pig', which was being exhibited in the Grassmarket.

Burns spent a total of almost sixty weeks in the capital. These were made up of seven stays. From 28th November 1786, to 5th May 1787, he stayed with John Richmond in Baxter's Close, behind the Lawnmarket, in a 'land' demolished at the construction of Bank Street in 1798. The poet left Baxter's Close to make his Border Tour with Ainslie. From 7th to 25th August 1787, Burns stayed with William Nicol in Buccleugh Street above the Buccleugh Pend. This property was demolished in 1949. Burns and Nicol set out from Buccleugh Street on the Highland Tour. From 16th September to 4th October 1787, Burns again stayed with Nicol. He left with Dr Adair to visit Harvieston and the Ochtertyres. From 20th October 1787, Burns stayed with Nicol's teaching colleague at the High School, William Cruikshank at number 2 (later 30) St James Square. Burns occupied the attic. From 11th to 22nd March 1788, Burns again stayed at Buccleugh Street. From 16th to 28th February 1789, Burns was back at St James Square. On his final visit to Edinburgh from 9th November to 6th December 1791, Burns lived at 'Mr Mackay's White Hart inn, Grassmarket', then one of the most celebrated inns in Edinburgh.

Scots Musical Museum, The

A publication whose six volumes appeared between 1787 and 1803, produced by James Johnson (see **Johnson, James**), but of which Burns was the virtual editor and principal contributor, Stephen Clarke (see **Clarke, Stephen**) was the musical editor. The melodies were printed above a thorough bass. The *Museum* has never been surpassed as the finest of all collections of Scottish Song. It was re-issued by Folklore Associates, Hatboro, Pennsylvania, in 1962.

'Scots Wha Hae'

Syme said the poet had composed this song during the Galloway tour on the way to Kenmure, and on returning from St Mary's Isle, where he had dined with Lord Selkirk and his family; but Burns's letter to Thomson, dated by Ferguson about 30th August 1793, contradicts this story:

'You know that my pretensions to musical taste, are merely a few of Nature's instincts, untaught and untutored by Art. For this reason, many musical compositions, particularly where much of the merit lies in Counterpoint, however they may transport and ravish the ears of you Connoisseurs, affect my simple lug no otherwise than merely as melodious Din. On the other hand, by way of amends, I am delighted with many little melodies, which the learned Musician despises as silly and insipid. I do not know whether the old air, "Hey tutti tatie", may rank among its number; but well I know that, with Fraser's Hautboy, it has often filled my eyes with tears. There is a tradition, which I have met with in many places of Scotland, that it was Robert Bruce's March at the battle of Bannockburn. This thought, in my yesternight's evening walk, warned me to a pitch of enthusiasm on the theme of Liberty and Independence, which I threw into a kind of Scots Ode, fitted to the Air, that one might suppose to be the gallant ROYAL SCOT's address to his heroic followers on that eventful morning.'

Then followed the poem. In a postscript,

Burns told Thomson that he had shown the air to Urbani, who was also at Lord Selkirk's and that Urbani had begged him: 'to make soft verses for it: but I had no idea of giving myself any trouble on the subject, till the accidental recollection of that glorious struggle for Freedom, associated with the glowing ideas of some other struggles of the same nature, *not quite so ancient*, roused my rhyming Mania'.

The air, with other words, had already appeared in the *Museum*. Words and air together first appeared in Thomson's *Scottish Airs*, 1799.

Scott of Wauchope, Mr

Husband of the authoress, Mrs Elizabeth Scott (q.v.). Burns noted in his *Border Journal* that Mr Scott had 'exactly the figure and face commonly given to Sancho Panza—very shrewd in his farming matters, and not unfrequently stumbles on what may be called a strong thing rather than a good thing, but in other respects a compleat Hottentot.'

Scott, Mrs Elizabeth, née Rutherford (1729–1789)

A niece of Mrs Alison Cockburn, she married Walter Scott of Wauchope House, near Jedburgh, Roxburghshire, where Burns visited them during his Border tour. Mrs Scott had sent the poet a long verse epistle, offering him 'a marled plaid', in token of her admiration of his work. Burns replied with his lively verse epistle, 'I mind it weel in early date'. Burns noted in his *Border Journal* that Mrs Scott had all the sense, taste, intrepidity of face, and bold, critical decision, which usually distinguish female Authors'.

Her relations published her collected poems in 1801, under the title of *Alonza and Cora*. Most of the poems are in the vapid Augustan manner of minor eighteenth-century versifiers. Three are in Scots, one of them the address to Burns. They are by far the most spirited pieces in the book.

Scott, Francis George (1880–1958)

Scottish composer, born in Hawick, Roxburghshire, son of a supplier of mill-engineering parts. Educated at Hawick, and at the universities of Edinburgh and Durham, he studied composition under Roger-Ducasse. In 1925, he became Lecturer in Music at Jordanhill Training College for Teachers, Glasgow, a post he held for more than twenty-five years.

He wrote more than three hundred songs, including many settings of Burns's poems. He believed that the strophic treatment, inevitable where folk-settings are employed, ignores the drama so often implied by Burns's lyrics. Because of the strong folk-element in his own nevertheless thoroughly contemporary style, his best settings give the impression of arising out of a long tradition of Scottish art-music which does not, in fact, exist. He succeeded in providing superb versions even of such masterpieces among the original Burns marryings of music and verse as 'The Red, Red Rose' and 'Of a' the airts'.

Scott, Jeany

According to a local tradition, the daughter of the Ecclefechan postmaster, whom Burns set eyes on when snow-bound in what he called that 'unfortunate, wicked little village'. He is said to have written his lines 'To Miss J. Scott, of Ayr'—

'Oh! had each Scot of ancient times
  Been, Jeany Scott, as thou art,
The bravest heart on English ground
  Had yielded like a coward'—

on a window.

Scrimgeour, John, third Viscount Dudhope (1620–1668)

Fought with Charles II at Worcester. Made Earl of Dundee at the Restoration. On his death, the title became dormant, until proved by the eleventh Earl.

Burns called him 'bold Scrimgeour' in his 'Second Epistle' to Graham of Fintry on the Dumfries Burgh Elections.

Selkirk

A royal burgh, standing on a hill over-looking Ettrick Water, and a town at the centre of the Anglo-Scottish wars that raged on the Borders for three centuries. It was the birthplace of Mungo Park, the explorer. A statue of Sir Walter Scott in the triangular market-place commemorates the years from 1799 to 1832 when he was sheriff of the county.

Once a shoe-making town, it now depends for its livelihood on the manufacture of tweed and other woollen goods.

Burns, in company with Ainslie, arrived in the town on Sunday, 13th May 1787, during the Border tour. It had been raining hard, and the two were soaked when they put up for the night at Veitch's Inn. James Hogg tells us in his edition of Burns's work that a Dr Clarkson was sitting in the inn over a drink, with two friends, when the travellers arrived. When asked by the inn-keeper if the strangers could join them, the doctor refused on the grounds that the new arrivals did not look like gentlemen. Three days later, he learnt that it was Burns who had asked to join him and, to quote Hogg, 'that refusal hangs about the doctor's heart like a dead weight to this day, and will do till the day of his death, for the bard had not a more enthusiastic admirer'.

Selkirk, Earl of
See **Douglas, Dunbar.**

Sharpe of Hoddam, Charles (1750–1813)
Born Charles Kirkpatrick, he assumed the name of Sharpe when his kinsman, Matthew Sharpe, bequeathed him Hoddam estate, in Dumfriesshire. Charles was a grandson of Sir Thomas Kirkpatrick, Second Baronet of Closeburn. He was said to be a good violinist, and composed both music and verse. He was trained for the law, but did not practise.

His third son was Charles Kirkpatrick Sharpe (1781–1851), the so-called 'Scottish

Walpole', more aptly described by the literary historian J. H. Millar as being a 'singular character with an unusual appetite for all manner of scandal past and present, and also with a really sound knowledge of the antiquarian side of some periods of Scottish history'. It was clearly the first of these talents he exercised on Maria Riddell (q.v.).

Burns wrote to Charles Sharpe under the fictitious name of Johnny Faa, enclosing a ballad of three stanzas. What the stanzas told is not now known.

Burns's letter, which was addressed to Sharpe as a member of the same family as himself 'the Family of the Muses', told Sharpe: 'Fortune has so much forsaken me, that she has taught me to live without her; and amid my ragged poverty, I am as independent, and much more huffy, than a monarch of the world. According to the hackneyed metaphor, I value the several Actors in the great Drama of Life, simply as they perform their parts. I can look on a worthless fellow of a Duke with unqualified contempt, and can regard an honest Scavenger with sincere respect.'

Sharpe married Eleanora, the youngest daughter of John Renton of Lamerton in 1770. She was a granddaughter of Susanna, Countess of Eglinton.

Shaw, The Reverend Andrew (1741–1805)
One of the two Shaws of 'The Twa Herds', he was the son of the Reverend Andrew Shaw of Edenkillie, later Professor of Divinity at St Andrew's University. He was ordained at Craigie in 1765, St Andrews University giving him his Doctorate of Divinity in 1795. He had the reputation of being a good speaker and scholar, but was very shy.

Shaw, The Reverend David (1719–1810)
Brother-in-law to the Rev. William Dalrymple, Shaw is mentioned along with the Rev. Dr Andrew Shaw in 'The Twa Herds'.

329

He was minister at Coylton from 1749 until 1810. It was not until the last year of his ministry, at the age of ninety-one, that he employed an assistant. St Andrews University made him a Doctor of Divinity in 1749. He was Moderator of the General Assembly in 1776, and allegedly never wore glasses for reading, wrote neatly until the end of his life, and had no wrinkles or furrows.

Shenstone, William (1714-63)
English poet, son of Thomas Shenstone and Anne, daughter of William Penn of Harborough Hall, Hagley. Shenstone was born at the Leasowes, in the parish of Halesowen, which was then in Shropshire, but is now in Worcestershire. At school, he began his life-long friendship with Richard Jago. His other life-long friendship, with Richard Graves, began at Pembroke College, Oxford.

Shenstone inherited the Leasowes, his father's property, and, in 1745, retired there and spent the rest of his life and all his inheritance beautifying it into a marvel of landscape gardening. He was visited by many famous people at the Leasowes. Among his literary correspondents was Bishop Percy. It was from Shenstone that the idea of the collection of the *Reliques* first came.

In 1742, Shenstone published, anonymously, the revised version of his most famous poem, 'The Schoolmistress', based on his own former teacher, Sarah Lloyd. His collected works were published after his death by his friend, Richard Dodsley. Dr Johnson wrote a short 'Life of Shenstone' for Chalmer's *British Poets*.

Burns had a higher opinion of Shenstone's poetic abilities than the verdict of posterity has sustained. Reporting his progress in educating himself, to Murdoch from Lochlea on 15th January 1783, Burns wrote: 'In the matter of books, indeed, I am very profuse. My favourite authors are of the sentim'l kind, such as Shenstone, particularly his Elegies, Thomson, Man of

Feeling, a book I prize next to the Bible, Man of the World, Sterne, especially his Sentimental journey, Macpherson's Ossian, & etc.; these are the glorious models after which I endeavour to form my conduct, and 'tis incongrous, 'tis absurd to suppose that the man whose mind glows with sentiments lighted up at their sacred flame —the man whose heart distends with benevolence to all the human race—he "who can soar above this little scene of things"—can he descend to mind the paultry conccerns [sic] about which the terrae-fillial race fret, and fume, and vex themselves?'

Burns was fond of using quotations from Shenstone, notably, 'When proud fortune's ebbing tide recedes' (from 'Elegy VII'), which formed the text of the reviews of his own position as a newly-established poet sent to Greenfield and Mrs Dunlop in December 1786, and January 1787. To Margaret Chalmers, on 16th September 1788, Burns wrote: 'When I may have an opportunity of sending this, Heaven only knows. Shenstone said "When one is confined idle within doors by bad weather, the best antidote against ennui is to read the letters of, or write to one's friends": in that case, then, if the weather continues thus, I may scrawl you half a quire.'

In his first *Common-Place Book,* Burns noted down two quotations from Shenstone, which provide some insight of his attitude to the purpose of poetry before he had publicly 'commenced poet':

'There are numbers in the world, who do not want sense, to make a figure; so much as an opinion of their own abilities, to put them upon recording their observations, and allowing them the same importance which they do to those which appear in print.'

'Pleasing when youth is long expir'd
to trace
The form our pencil or our pen
design'd!

Such was our youthful air and shape
and face!
Such the soft image of our youthful mind.'

In 'The Vision', Coila, Burns's Muse,
tells him that though she has followed his
career with interest, and taught him his
'manners-painting strains', yet for all that,
he can neither learn, nor can she teach him:

'To paint with Thomson's landscape
glow;
Or wake the bosom-melting throe,
With Shenstone's art;
Or pour, with Gray, the moving flow
Warm on the heart.'

There can be few instances of more
fantastic literary modesty; for, with or
without the aid of Coila, Burns poured a
warmer flow on the heart than Thomson's,
Shenstone's and Gray's libations put together.

The garden of Leasowes is now a golf-
course.

Shepherd, The Reverend John (1741-99)

Son of the minister of Newbattle, educated
at Edinburgh, translated from Hemel
Hempstead to Muirkirk in 1775, he
contributed a well-written account of
Muirkirk to Sir John Sinclair's *Statistical
Account*. He had an unfortunate habit of
saying rude things in the mistaken idea
that they were funny, thus provoking
Burns's satire.

In 'The Kirk's Alarm' Burns called him:

'Muirlan' Jock, Muirlan' Jock, whom
the Lord gave a stock
Would set up a tinkler in brass;
If ill manners were wit, there's no
mortal so fit
To prove the poor Doctor an ass,
Muirlan' Jock! To prove the poor
Doctor an ass.'

Sheriff, Mr

Burns dined at his house, when on his

Border tour with Ainslie. He described
him in his *Journal* as 'talkative and conceited', and in a letter to Ainslie from
Newcastle, 29th May 1787, remarked that
Mr Sheriff tired me to death'.

He was a tenant of Sir James Hall of
Dunglass, whom Burns also met.

Shirrefs, Andrew (1762-1807?)

Scottish poet. A son of David Shirrefs, an
Aberdeen carpenter. Two of his brothers
achieved distinction, James becoming minister of St Nicholas Church in 1778, while
Alexander was sheriff-clerk-depute, and
latterly President of the Society of Advocates.

Andrew was educated at Aberdeen
Grammar School, and at Marischal College, where he graduated Master of Arts
in 1783. The development of a crippling
infirmity made him abandon his intention
of following a learned profession, and he
set up in business in Aberdeen as a bookseller. With others, he helped found in
1787 the short-lived *Aberdeen Chronicle*
(which re-started under different auspices
in 1806) and became owner and joint
editor of the *Caledonian Magazine*. When
this magazine ceased publication in 1790,
he went to Edinburgh as a bookseller and
printer. In 1798 he left for London, where
all trace of him was lost. As his name does
not appear along with those of his brothers
in the will of a cousin who died in 1801, he
may have been dead by then, although
1807 is usually given as the unconfirmable
date of his death.

Shirrefs corresponded with both 'Tullochgorum' Skinner and James Beattie.
Burns met him on his northern tour, and
called him 'a little decrepid body with some
abilities'. Shirrefs wrote a pastoral comedy,
Jamie and Bess (in imitation of Ross's
Helenore, or The Fortunate Shepherdess),
which was performed in Aberdeen in 1787,
and in Edinburgh in 1796, at which benefit performance he himself appeared, singing his splendid song 'A cogie o' yill and
a pickle aitmeal' which Burns put in the

Scots Musical Museum. Shirrefs' *Poems, chiefly in the Scottish Dialect* appeared in Edinburgh in 1790, with a portrait by Beugo.

Sibbald, James (1745-1803)

Born in Roxburghshire, the son of a farmer, he began life as a farm labourer. Then he went to Edinburgh, where he was employed in the shop of Charles Elliot, bookseller. Later, Sibbald set up in business on his own account. In 1783, he founded the *Edinburgh Magazine*, and in 1792 became editor of the *Edinburgh Herald*. He wrote numerous articles on subjects of antiquarian interest, and in 1802 published a literary history, *Chronicle of the Poetry of Scotland.*

The October 1786 number of the *Edinburgh Magazine*, published on 3rd November, carried the first review of the Kilmarnock Edition to be published. It forestalled Henry Mackenzie's review in *The Lounger* by five weeks. Sibbald was thirled to the polite standards of his day. Even so, he realised that Burns was 'a striking example of native genius bursting through the obscurity of poverty and the obstructions of a laborious life'. He went on: 'To those who admire the creations of untutored fancy, and are blind to many faults for the sake of numberless beauties, his poems will yield singular gratification. His observations on human character are acute and sagacious, and his descriptions are lively and just. Of rustic pleasantry he has a rich fund, and some of his softer scenes are touched with inimitable delicacy. . . .' Extracts from the poems appeared in subsequent issues.

Burns, delighted, wrote to Sibbald the following January: 'The warmth with which you have befriended an obscure man, and young Author, in your three last Magazines—I can only say, Sir, I feel the weight of the obligation, and wish I could express my sense of it.'

When Patrick Miller of Dalswinton left his anonymous ten guineas for Burns on the poet's arrival in Edinburgh, he deposited it, we learn from a letter to Ballantine of 13th December 1786, 'in Mr Sibbald's hand'.

Siddons, Mrs Sarah (1755-1831)

The famous actress made her début in Edinburgh 22nd May 1784, in *Venice Preserved* by Thomas Otway. For this performance, and for her performance the following year, the Capital was in a state of considerable excitement. According to the *Edinburgh Weekly Magazine*: 'The manager took the precaution after the first night to have an officer and Guard of Soldiers at the principal door. But several scuffles having ensued through the eagerness of the people to get places, and the soldiers having been rash enough to use their bayonets, it was thought advisable to withdraw the guards on the third night, lest any accident had happened from the pressure of the crowd, who began to assemble round the doors at 11 in the forenoon.' In 1788, she played again in Edinburgh. This time in the role of Lady Randolph in John Home's *Douglas*. Burns mentioned her in the Prologue which he wrote for the actor William Woods' Benefit Night:

'It needs no Siddons' powers in Southern's song.' The reference is to *The Fatal Marriage* by Thomas Southerne (1660-1746), in which Mrs Siddons was celebrated for the part of Isabella.

She was a sister of John Kemble, and her son, Henry, was the manager of Edinburgh's Theatre Royal.

Henry Mackenzie said that: 'She could not untragedise herself . . . She promised Scots *oatmeal porridge* in terms that might have applied to *nectar* or *ambrosia*'.

Sillar, David (1760-1830)

The third of the four sons of Patrick Sillar, farmer at Spittalside, near Lochlea, Sillar was largely self-educated. He became interim teacher in the parish school, but failed to get the permanent appointment, which went to John Wilson of Dr Hornbook fame. Sillar then set up his own school, which was unsuccessful. He became a member of Tarbolton Bachelors Club in 1781, of which Burns was a founder member, and of the Mauchline Debating Society, of which Gilbert Burns was a member.

Sillar later recorded the circumstances in which he came to meet the poet:

'Mr Robert Burns was some time in the parish of Tarbolton prior to my acquaintance with him. His social disposition easily procured him acquaintance; but a certain satirical seasoning, with which he and all poetical geniuses are in some degree influenced, while it set the rustic circle in a roar, was not unaccompanied by its kindred attendant—suspicious fear. I recollect hearing his neighbours observe he had a great deal to say for himself, and that they suspected his *principles*. He wore the only tied hair in the parish; and in the church, his plaid, which was of a particular colour, I think *fillemot*, he wrapped in a particular manner round his shoulders. These surmises, and his exterior, had such a magical influence on my curiosity, as made me particularly solicitious of his acquaintance. Whether my acquaintance with Gilbert was casual or premeditated, I am not now certain. By him I was introduced not only to his brother, but to the whole of that family, where, in a short time, I became a frequent, and, I believe, not unwelcome visitant.

'After the commencement of my acquaintance with the bard, we frequently met on Sundays at church, when, between sermons, instead of going with our friends or lassies to the inn, we often took a walk in the fields. In these walks I have frequently been struck by his facility in addressing the fair sex; and many times, when I have been bashfully anxious how to express myself, he would have entered into conversation with them with the greatest ease and freedom; and it was generally a death-blow to our conversation, however

agreeable, to meet a female acquaintance.'

Burns and Sillar became firm friends. They both played the fiddle, although Sillar was reported to be a better fiddler than the poet. Burns is reputed to have played 'blackfoot' to Sillar when Sillar was wooing Peggy Orr, the nurse-maid at Stair House. Sillar was the recipient of two verse-epistles from Burns. In the first, which carries the title 'An Epistle to Davy, a Brother-Poet, Lover, Ploughman and Fiddler', Burns wrote:

'There's a' the pleasures o' the heart,
　The lover an' the frien',
Ye hae your Meg, your dearest part,
　An' I my darling Jean.'

Sillar did become engaged to Peggy Orr, but she broke the engagement and married John Paton, an Edinburgh shoemaker. Sillar also married another.

In 1783, he removed to Irvine, where he tried his hand in business as a grocer. He failed again, possibly partly because he was devoting too much time to versifying. Burns, who found the literary companionship of Sillar and Lapraik necessary for the development of his own poetic gifts, seems to have thought highly of Sillar's talents, and in the 'Second Epistle to Davie' wrote:

'Hale be your heart, hale be your fiddle;
Lang may your elbuck jink an' diddle,
　　　　　　　　　　[elbow
Tae cheer you thro' the weary widdle
　　　　　　　　　　[struggle
　O' war'ly cares,
Till bairns' bairns kindly cuddle
　Your auld, gray hairs.

'But, Davie, lad, I'm red ye're glaikit;
　　　　　　　　　　[foolish
I'm tauld the Muse ye hae negleckit;
　　　　　　　　　　[told
An' gif it's sae, ye sud be licket [beaten
　Until ye fyke;　　　[move uneasily
Sic hauns as you sud ne'er be faikit,
　　　　　　　　　　[spared
　Be hain't wha like.'
　　　　　　　　[saved from exertion

Inspired by the success of Burns's *Poems*, Sillar persuaded Wilson of Kilmarnock to bring out his own *Poems* in 1789, prefacing it with Burns's 'Second Epistle'. The volume was, however, a failure, the reason why being perhaps suggested by his 'Epistle to the Critics':

'Then know when I these pieces made,
Was toiling for my daily bread;
A scanty learning I enjoy'd,
Sae judge how I hae it employed.
I ne'er depended for my knowledge
On school, academy, nor college;
I gat my learnin' at the flail,
An' some I catch'd at the plough-tail;
Amang the brutes I own I'm bred,
Since herding was my native trade.

'Some twa-three books I read wi' care,
Which I had borrow'd here an' there.
The actions an' the ways o' men,
I took great pains an' care to ken;
Frae them, their manners, an' their
                                    looks,
Their words, their actions, an' frae
                                    books;
On these for knowledge I relied,
Without anither for my guide.
Latin an' Greek I never knew sic,
An' sae how can my works be classic?'

Soon after his book was published, Sillar became bankrupt. Eventually, he founded a school for navigation, and came into wealth on the death of his uncle, a partner in the Liverpool mercantile house of Sillar and Henderson. Prosperous at the last, he served for some years on Irvine Town Council.

Contrary to a frequently repeated allegation, Sillar's name was among one of the first of the subscribers to the Burns Monument at Alloway. In 1827, he helped to found the Irvine Burns Club.

Simpson's

Burns tells us that this was 'a noted tavern at the Auld Brig End'. It is mentioned in the poem, 'The Brigs of Ayr'.

Simson, John

Farmer of Ochiltree, and father of William and Patrick, both at one time schoolmasters of Ochiltree parish school.

Simson, Johnie

Believed to have been a dancing master. Burns in his 'Epistle to James Tennant of Glenconner', asked Tennant to 'assist poor Simson a' ye can'.

According to tradition, Tennant was to introduce Simson to possible patrons. The result was said to be 'the biggest dancing-class ever known in Ochiltree'.

Simson, Patrick (1765–1848)

Son of John Simson of Ochiltree, and brother of William. *See* **Simson, William**.

Patrick was session clerk at Ochiltree, and did much to sort out the confused parish register. He was an expert scholar, particularly of the classics. He was responsible for correcting the proofs of the reprints issued by the Auchinleck Press, by permission of Sir Alexander Boswell.

Simson, William (1758–1815)

Burns's 'winsome Willie', William Simson, was the elder of John Simson's two sons. William studied at Glasgow University, and was intended for the Church, but he became instead schoolmaster at his native Ochiltree in 1780. In 1788 he became Cumnock's schoolmaster, and remained there until he died. He was succeeded at Ochiltree by his brother Patrick. William was a rhymer, and wrote an epistle in verse to Burns, who retorted with his 'Epistle to William Simson', which describes his psychology of composition, and is one of the highlights of the Kilmarnock Edition:

'The Muse, nae poet ever fand her,
                                    [*found*
Till by himsel he learn'd to wander,
Adown some trotting burn's meander,

An' no think lang:
>   [*not find time tedious*
> O, sweet to stray, an' pensive ponder,
>   A heart-felt sang!'

Simson's friend Thomas Walker, a tailor at Poole, near Ochiltree, encouraged by Simson's receipt of Burns's epistle, and perhaps aided by Simson, himself wrote a verse epistle to Burns, beginning: 'What woefu' news is this I hear?', dealing with the Jean Armour affair and the rumours of the poet's intention to flee the country. The answer, bearing Burns's name, 'What ails ye now, ye lousie b——h,' though severe, was much treasured by Walker, who believed it to be by Burns, though no manuscript of 'What ails ye now' has ever been found to justify this claim. (Kinsley, however, accepts it as genuine.) During the lifetime of Patrick Simson, James Paterson's book *Contemporaries of Burns* appeared, containing the information that William had told Burns of the hoax played on Walker. 'Happening to meet Burns not long after this', Paterson wrote, 'Simson informed him of the liberty he had taken with his name. "You did well," said the Poet, laughing, "you thrashed the tailor much better than I would have done".' Paterson's story, of course, proves nothing. But it adds strength to the belief, based on stylistic evidence, that the poem in question may not be by Burns.

Sinclair of Ulbster, Sir John, Bart. (1754–1835)

Born at Thurso Castle, he was Member of Parliament for Caithness in 1780; for Lostwithiel in 1784; and for Petersfield from 1796 to 1811. He was the first president of the Board of Agriculture. He died in Edinburgh. His chief works were his *History of the Revenue of the British Empire*, 1784, and, by far the most important, his *Statistical Account of Scotland*, in twenty-one Volumes, published between 1791 and 1799. The first systematic attempt to compile social and economic statistics for the whole country, it was written largely by ministers of the various parishes, and has preserved for us a vivid record of life in Scotland at the close of the eighteenth century.

Burns's friend, Robert Riddell, was highly dissatisfied with the account of the parish of Dunscore, sent in by the parish minister (and with some cause!); so he persuaded Burns to send Sir John an additional article on the Monkland Friendly Society, which he and the poet founded. Burns despatched his contributions from Ellisland in August or September 1791, and it duly appeared. *See* **Monkland Friendly Society**.

Skinner, The Reverend John (1721–1807)

The author of the song 'Tullochgorum' was born at Balfour, Aberdeenshire, the son of the schoolmaster of Birse. He was educated at Marischal College, Aberdeen, became assistant schoolmaster at Monymusk, took orders in the Scottish Episcopal Church in 1742, spent two years in Shetland as preceptor in the family of the Sinclairs of Scalloway, then, returning to Aberdeen, ministered at Longside, near Linshart, for the rest of his life.

He was the author of an *Ecclesiastical History of Scotland* and many other theological works, as well as 'Tullochgorum' and other Scots songs which included 'John o' Badenyon' and 'Ewie wi' the Crookit Horn'.

Although he was willing to subscribe the oath of allegiance, Skinner's church was wrecked after the '45 rising by the Duke of Cumberland's men, and Skinner was imprisoned for six months in Aberdeen because he preached to an assembly of more than four people.

His song 'Tullochgorum', which Burns described as 'the best Scotch Song ever Scotland saw', was suggested by Mrs Montgomery, wife of the Inland Revenue Officer in Ellon. She thought Skinner might provide for the air, 'The Reel o' Tullochgorum', a set of decorous words, which were sadly lacking for many Scottish airs at that time.

Burns was disappointed that he did not meet Skinner on his Highland tour, having unwittingly passed only four miles from the minister's home; but Burns did meet Skinner's son in Aberdeen—he had previously been introduced to him in Edinburgh—and suggested that his father might write him. The Reverend John Skinner senior wrote Burns a long verse epistle—'by far the finest poetic compliment I ever got'—and Burns answered on 25th October 1787, 'in plain dull prose'. Burns asked Skinner to send him any songs he had suitable for inclusion in the Museum, telling him that 'Tullochgorum', 'John of Badenyon' and 'Ewie wi' the Crookit Horn, were going into the second volume. Burns duly sent Skinner the second volume of the *Museum* from Edinburgh on 14th February 1788: 'as a mark of the veneration I have long had, and shall ever have, for your character. . . .' Among Skinner's other correspondents were John Ramsay of Ochtertyre, and Dr Gleig, Bishop of Brechin.

Skinner lost his wife in 1799, and when his son met with a similar misfortune some years later, he retired from his duties and went to live with his son at Aberdeen. The old man died quietly in his chair, having just dined happily with three generations of his descendants.
See Plate 8

Skinner, The Reverend John (1744–1816)
Son of the Reverend John Skinner, author of 'Tullochgorum'. Skinner junior became primus of the Scottish Episcopal Church. He met Burns in Edinburgh, and again at Aberdeen, during the poet's Highland tour.

Sloan, Thomas
According to Chambers, Sloan was 'understood' to have been a native of Wanlockhead. Burns is supposed to have made his acquaintance when travelling between Ellisland and Ayrshire, during the first year of his occupation of Ellisland.

From a note, conjecturally dated by Ferguson May 1789, it appears that Sloan and Burns intended to pay a joint call on Captain Riddell at Friars' Carse. Sloan was one of those listed by Burns to subscribe to Dr Anderson's magazine, *The Bee*. He may have been the recipient of an unaddressed invitation to spend New Year Day, 1791, with Burns.

The last two letters of Burns to Sloan are to a Manchester address. From a note of 1st September 1791, it would seem that Sloan was in some kind of business embarrassment and had asked Burns to try to enlist the assistance of 'Mr Ballantine'. Burns regretted: 'that Mr Ballantine does not chuse to interfere more in the business. I am truly sorry for it, but cannot help it'.

Sloan, William
The 'Haverel Will' of 'Hallowe'en', he acted as gaudsman or plough-guide to Burns when he leased Mossgiel. Sloan returned later to Kirkoswald, where he had been born, and became apprenticed to the shoemaker John Davidson ('Souter Johnnie'). He finally settled in Dalmellington.

Smeaton, or Smytane, The Reverend David
He was ordained to the Burgher Pastorate of Kilmaurs in 1740, having previously been an itinerant Dissenting (Whig or Cameronian) Minister in Ayrshire.

Burns alluded to him in a letter to Miss Chalmers from Edinburgh, October 1787. 'The whining cant of love, except in real passion, and by a masterly hand, is to me as insufferable as the preaching cant of old Father Smeaton, Whig-minister at Kilmaurs.'

Smellie, William (1740-95)

'Shrewd Willie Smellie to Crochallan
came:
The old cock'd hat, the brown sur-
tout, the same;
His grisly beard just bristling in its
might,
('Twas four long nights and days to
shaving night;)
His uncomb'd hoary locks, wild-
staring, thatched
A head for thought profound and
clear unmatch'd;
Yet tho' his caustic wit was biting
rude,
His heart was warm, benevolent and
good.'

Thus Burns described, in 'The Poet's Progress', the man who printed the Edinburgh editions of his poems, and who was Creech's partner. Burns further described him in a letter to Peter Hill from Ellisland, dated 2nd February 1790, as 'that old Veteran in Genius, Wit and B— dry, Smellie'.

It was in Smellie's untidy office in Anchor Close, off the High Street of Edinburgh, that the poet corrected his proofs, sitting on a certain stool, which, according to Smellie's son, Alexander, came to be known as Burns's Stool.

Son of a Duddingston mason, Smellie was trained as a printer, having been previously educated at Duddingston Parish School, and Edinburgh High School. He had a wide knowledge of literature and science, and became the editor and principal author of the first edition of the *Encyclopaedia Britannica*. He translated Buffon, and wrote a *Philosophy of Natural History* highly regarded in his day. He knew all the eminent literary and philosophical figures in the Capital, and was described by Sir John Dalrymple to Edmund Burke as 'one of the most learned men in Scotland'. He had printed the works of many of them, including Gilbert Stuart (with whom he started the *Edinburgh Magazine*), Robert Fergusson, William Robertson, Hugo Arnot, and Adam Smith.

It was Smellie who founded the Crochallan Fencibles (*see* **Crochallan Fencibles,**) and introduced Burns to that convivial club, whose recorder of proceedings and 'hangman' the naturalist was. It was the custom of the Club to submit any new entrant to a barrage of raillery to test his temper, and the contest between Smellie and Burns was said to have been remarkable. Burns said on his installation that he was 'thrashed' beyond anything he had formerly experienced.

Burns was the means of introducing his friend Maria Riddell to Smellie. Mrs Riddell had written an account of a voyage to Madeira and the Leeward Isles, with some notes on their natural history, on which she thought Smellie might give an opinion. Burns was clearly somewhat taken aback at the thought of introducing a lady of quality to the uncouth and rather boorish Smellie. However, he gave her a letter of introduction, which began: 'I sit down, my dear Sir, to introduce a young Lady to you, and a Lady in the first ranks of fashion, too. What a task! You, who care no more for the herd of animals called young Ladies than you do for the herd of animals called young Gentlemen. You, who despise and detest the groupings and combinations of Fashion: an idiot Painter that seems industrious to place staring Fools and unprincipled Knaves in the foreground of his pictures, while Men of Sense and Honesty are thrown in the dimmest shades. . . . She has one unlucky failing—a failing which you will easily discover—as she seems rather pleased with indulging in it; and a failing that you will as easily pardon, as it is a sin which very much besets yourself: Where she dislikes or despises, she is apt to make no more a secret of it than where she esteems and respects.'

But Smellie and Maria Riddell took an instant liking for each other, and remained on terms of close friendship until Smellie died. He was much impressed with her book, and advised publication and sale, as opposed to a subscription list, which had originally been proposed. He wrote to her on 27th March 1792: 'When I consider your youth [she was only eighteen], and still more, your sex, the perusal of your ingenious and judicial work, if I had not previously had the pleasure of your conversation, the devil himself could not have frightened me into the belief that a female human creature could, in the bloom of youth, beauty and, consequently, of giddiness, have produced a performance so much out of line of your ladies' work. Smart little poems, flippant romances, are not uncommon. But science, minute observation, accurate description and excellent composition are qualities seldom to be met with in the female world.'

Her book was duly published under the title of *Voyages to the Madeira and Leeward Caribbee Islands, with Sketches of the Natural History of these Islands*, and enjoyed some little success.

Later, in the summer of 1792, Smellie visited Maria Riddell and Burns in Dumfries, where the lady induced Smellie to go to one of the Assemblies. According to Chambers, there was a tradition that Burns and Smellie received some sort of public entertainment from the Dumfries Magistrates.

Unfortunately, most of the records of the friendship between Burns and Smellie have been destroyed, because, according to Smellie's biographer, Robert Kerr: 'Many letters of Burns to Mr Smellie which remained, being totally unfit for publication, and several of them containing severe reflections on many respectable people still in life, have been burnt'.

Some of the pieces which form *The Merry Muses* were probably given an airing at the meeting of the Crochallan Fencibles which Burns attended.

See Plate 10

Smith, Adam (1723–90)

The famous economist, and author of *The Wealth of Nations*. His name appears for four copies on Burns's subscription list for his First Edinburgh Edition. Although possibly the most distinguished Scot in Edinburgh when Burns arrived there, the two men never met.

From Mrs Dunlop's letter to Burns of 29th March 1787, Smith's views on Burns emerge: 'Indeed, first when your Book reached Edr., Mr Smith, Commissioner of the Customs, suggested a thing which he thought might be procured, and which he said was just what he would have wished for himself had he been in narrow circumstances—being a Salt Officer. Their income is from £30 to £40, their duty easie, independent, and free from that odium or oppression attached to the Excise. He has through life been a friend to unfriended merit, has great fame in the world as an author, both his *Theory of Moral Sentiment* and *Wealth of Nations* being much applauded. He was one of those first held forth your name forcibly to the public at Edr. when very few had seen your book, and my son told me was the person he heard take the most interest in your future prospects, wishing to procure you leisure to write, which he said was all you wanted to insure your figure and fortune. He lately complained that he had asked it, but could not get a sight of you.

'I have a favor to beg you that you will deliver the enclosed out of your own hand with my compts. to Mr Smith, and at same time thank him for the will he exprest towards you. Excuse me giving you this trouble. I would not had I not believed him one of the best, and found him one of the most agreeable men in the world. . . . Should this Salt plan, mentioned before the world's opinions could be known, still have wherewithal to please you, you may introduce it, and beg Mr Smith would be so good as instruct you in the proper forms of application. . . .'

Burns, however, was not destined to

see Smith, who had been seriously ill with chronic obstruction of the bowel during the winter of 1786-7, and who, immediately he was well enough to travel, set out for London to consult his friend John Hunter, the famous Scots surgeon. So, on 15th April 1787, Burns wrote to Mrs Dunlop: 'Dr Smith was just gone to London the morning before I received your letter to him.'

Smith, The Reverend Andrew (1741-89)

Burns met him at Duns, on his Border tour. He described him in his *Journal* as 'a famous punster'. He was minister of Langton, in the Presbytery of Duns, from 1766 until his death. He married Ann Drummond, heiress of Concraig, to which estate he ultimately succeeded, and took the name of Drummond.

Smith, The Reverend George (1748-1823)

Minister at Galston from 1778 until his death. In 'The Holy Fair', Burns apparently meant to compliment him for the rationalism of his preaching though his friends regarded the lines in question as having injured his popularity:

'Smith opens out his cauld harangues,
   On practice and on morals;
An' aff the godly pour in thrangs,
                              [*crowds*
   To gie the jars an' barrels
      A lift that day.

'What signifies his barren shine,
   Of moral pow'rs an' reason?
His English style, an' gesture fine,
   Are a' clean out o' season. . . .'

In 'The Twa Herds', Burns suggested that while pretending 'New Licht' sympathies, he was not to be trusted:

'An monie a ane that I could tell,
   Wha fain would openly rebel,
   Forby turn-coats amang oursel;
      There's Smith for ane—

      I doubt he's but a grey neck still
         An' that ye'll fin'.'

Angered by the criticism of his lines on Smith in 'The Holy Fair', Burns did not spare him in 'The Kirk's Alarm'.

'Cessnock-side, Cessnock-side, wi'
                  your turkey-cock pride,
O' manhood but sma' is your share;
Ye've the figure, 'tis true, even your
                        faes maun allow,
   And your friends daurna say ye
                              hae mair,
Cessnock-side! And your friends
            daurna say ye hae mair.'

Smith was great-grandfather of R. L. Stevenson.

Smith, James (1765-c. 1823)

The son of a Mauchline merchant who was killed in an accident when the boy was ten years old. Smith was brother to one of 'the Mauchline belles', Jean. He was strictly brought up by a step-father, a Mr Lamie, but revolted against his upbringing when a youth. Snyder describes Richmond, Smith and Burns as 'forming a happy triumvirate in village revelry', which, in view of the fact that two of them were responsible for putting local unmarried girls in the family way, is perhaps something of an understatement. *See* **'Court of Equity'**.

Smith had a draper's shop in Mauchline, almost opposite Nanse Tinnock's, but he later went into partnership with a Linlithgow calico-printer. When this business failed, Smith emigrated to St Louis, Jamaica, and died there at an early age. (Cromek speaks of him as being dead in 1808.)

Burns favoured Smith with a number of letters revealing his unguarded thoughts on sex and marriage. When the poet was distracted on the supposed desertion of Jean, it was through Smith, in a letter tentatively dated by Ferguson 1st August 1786, that Burns indicated he would meet her: 'So help me Heaven in my hour of need.' It was to Smith, too, that, on 30th June the following year, Burns gloated on his skill as a seducer: 'I am an old hawk at the sport, and wrote her such a cool, deliberate, prudent reply, as brought my bird from her aerial towerings, pop, down at my foot, like Corporal Trim's hat.'

It was also to Smith, in a letter of 28th April 1788, that Burns first announced unequivocally that he had married Jean: 'There is, you must know, a certain clean-limbed, handsome, bewitching young hussy of your acquaintance, to whom I have lately and privately given a matrimonial title to my corpus. . . . I intend to present Mrs Burns with a printed shawl, an article of which I daresay you have variety: 'tis my first present to her since I have *irrevocably* called her mine. . . .'

Smith was also the recipient of the 'Epistle to James Smith' in which Burns calls him: 'the slee'st, pawkie thief, That e'er attempted stealth or rief'. It is in this poem that Burns works up to his glorious denunciation of hypocritical, censorious, and cold-blooded people in the powerful closing stanzas, beginning:

'O ye douce folk that live by rule,
Grave, tideless-blooded, calm an'
                                        cool,
Compar'd wi' you—O fool! fool!
                                        fool!
  How much unlike!
Your hearts are just a standing pool,
  Your lives, a dyke! . . .'

Smith, Jean (1768–1854)

The witty one of the 'Mauchline belles', and the sister of Burns's youthful friend James Smith. She married James Candlish, an Edinburgh lecturer in medicine, and an early friend of Burns. She died in Edinburgh, and was buried in the Old Calton Churchyard, where there is a tablet erected to her memory by her son, who became a Free Church theologian, the Reverend Dr R. S. Candlish.

Sneddon, David

In his *Burns Holograph Manuscripts in the Kilmarnock Monument Museum*, Sneddon printed full reproductions, verbatim and literatim, of Burns's manuscripts in the Burns Monument Museum. His book was published in Kilmarnock by D. Brown and Company in 1889.

Somerville, John (d. 1810?)

An Edinburgh lawyer and 'a particular friend' of Burns. He subscribed for four copies of the first Edinburgh Edition. In 1793, Somerville appears to have been living at 67, Princes Street.

In a letter to Peter Hill from Ellisland, dated by Ferguson March 1791, Burns described 'honest John Somerville' as: '. . . Such a contented happy man that I know not what can annoy him, except perhaps he may not have got the better of a parcel of modest anecdotes which a certain Poet gave him one night at supper, the last time the said Poet was in town.'

When John ('Dr Hornbook') Wilson appealed to Burns for help in becoming 'an Edinburgh Quill-driver at twopence a page', Burns advised Wilson against such a course; but on 11th September 1790, sent him a letter of introduction to Somerville, lest this advice should be disregarded. (It was, in fact, taken.)

Somerville, The Reverend Dr Thomas (1741–1830)

Minister at Jedburgh and author of a *History of Great Britain during the Reign of Queen Anne* (1798). His niece and daughter-in-law was the mathematician and physicist, Mrs Mary Somerville. Burns met Dr Somerville at Jedburgh on his tour. He recorded in his *Journal*: 'Mr Somerville, the clergyman of the place, a man, and a gentleman, but sadly addicted to punning.'

It is said that Somerville gave up the punning habit when he read this extract in Dr Currie's memoir of Burns.

Somerville's *My Own Life and Times*, his most important book, is a valuable and interesting journal of local and national affairs covering the period 1741 to 1814.

Staig, David (1740–1824)

He became Provost of Dumfries in 1783, and frequently thereafter, occupying the office for a total of twenty years. The Provost's daughter, Jessie, married Major William Miller, a son of Patrick Miller of Dalswinton. During the later part of his life, Staig became Collector of Customs for Dumfries.

He was a popular and energetic public figure. Among the benefits he secured for his town were an academy, a new quay, a new bridge, and a regular mail-coach service between Edinburgh, Dumfries and Portpatrick, then the link with Ireland.

Two letters from Burns to Staig survived. One accompanied a copy of a Prologue for Mrs Sutherland. The other dated by Ferguson provisionally January 1793, contained a suggestion to the Provost and Magistrates of Dumfries as to how they could remedy a defect in their 'twa pennies' tax levied on ale brewed within the town, but not on ale brewed elsewhere and imported. Burns's suggestion was adopted.

Staig, Jessie (1775–1801)

Daughter of Provost David Staig of Dumfries, she became the wife of Major William Miller, a son of the landlord of Ellisland. Burns wrote for her: 'Truehearted was he, the sad swain o' the Yarrow,' which contains the lines:

'To equal young Jessie, seek Scotland
all over;
To equal young Jessie you seek it
in vain:
Grace, beauty, and elegance, fetter
her lover,
And maidenly modesty fixes the
chain.'

The song appeared in Thomson's *Scottish Airs*, 1798, after an unsuccessful effort on the part of the editor to get what

he felt to be a stiff line altered. Burns, while agreeing about the stiffness, declined to make any alteration, saying 'it would spoil the likeness, so the picture must stand'.

Writing to Mrs Dunlop in September 1794, Burns said: 'I sympathised much, the other day, with a father, a man whom I highly respect. He is a Mr Staig, the leading man in our Borough. A girl of his, a lovely creature of sixteen, was given over by the Physician, who openly said that she had but few hours to live. A gentleman who also lives in town, and who had studied medicine in the first schools— the Dr Maxwell whom Burke mentioned in the House of Commons about the affair of the daggers—he was at last called in; and his prescriptions in a few hours altered her situation, and have now cured her. . . . I addressed the following epigram to him on the occasion:

"Maxwell, if merit here you crave,
   That merit I deny:
You save fair Jessie from the grave!
   An Angel could not die."

But the 'angel' did die a few years later— at the age of twenty-six! And Dr Maxwell's 'prescription' for Burns's own heart ailment hastened the poet's end.

Stair Manuscript

A collection of eight of his early songs and poems which Burns compiled for Mrs Alexander Stewart of Stair in 1786. It was sent to her under cover of a somewhat inflated letter dated September. It included 'The Lass of Ballochmyle', 'My Nannie O', 'Handsome Nell' and 'The Vision'.

The collection was heired by Mrs Stewart's grandson, Allason Cunningham of Logan, who sold it in 1850 to an Ayr bookseller called Dick. It is now part of the Burns Cottage Collection.

'Standard Habbie'

The stanza form characteristic of the eighteenth-century Revival of Scots poetry, and particularly associated with Burns. But it was also used by Ramsay and Fergusson, and by almost every minor poet who employed Scots.

Ramsay called it 'Standard Habbie', because the earliest use of it known to him was in 'Habbie Simpson, the Piper of Kilbarchan', by Robert Sempill of Beltrees (*c*.1595–*c*.1659). Lamenting the death of the piper, Sempill wrote:

'Now who shall play, The day it
                                    daws?
Or Hunt up when the cock he craws?
Or who can for our Kirk-town-cause,
    Stand us in stead?
On Bagpipes (now) nobody blaws
    Sen Habbie's dead.'

'Standard Habbie' is an easy stanza to write, and was particularly suited for the fast-moving social comment which was a major preoccupation with the writers of the Revival. Burns varied the form by substituting half-rhymes for full rhymes, especially at the ends of the four long lines. He, of course, made use of many verse forms, including the 'bob-wheel' stanza of the later Makars, and over all of them showed his easy technical mastery.

Stanhope, Philip Dormer, fourth Earl of Chesterfield (1694–1773)
Succeeded his father to the earldom in 1726. An accomplished orator in the House of Lords, he became a friend of Walpole, but was opposed to the Premier's Excise Bill. After that, he tried to bring about Walpole's downfall by signing the protest for the Prime Minister's dismissal. When the new government was formed, it did not include Chesterfield, who continued in opposition, distinguishing himself by the courtly bitterness of his attacks on George II, who came to hate him violently.

Because of his experience of the Continent, Chesterfield was sent as ambassador to the Hague, to negotiate with the Dutch with a view to their joining in the war of the Austrian Succession. His mission was successful, and he was awarded the lord-lieutenancy of Ireland. It was on his brilliant administration of Ireland that his reputation as a statesman rested.

He was a clever and witty essayist and epigrammatist, but is most famous for his *Letters to his Son* and his *Letters to his God-son*. He had no children by his wife, Melusina von Schulemberg, illegitimate daughter of George I, but Mademoiselle du Bouchet bore him a son, Philip Stanhope, to whom the famous letters were written. Philip died at the age of thirty-six and his death was an overwhelming grief to Chesterfield.

In a letter to Mrs Dunlop from Ellisland, dated 10th April 1790, Burns described Chesterfield as:
'. . . one of the ablest judges of men, and himself one of the ablest men that ever lived. . . . In fact, a man who could thoroughly control his vices whenever they interfered with his interests, and who could completely put on the appearance of every virtue as often as it suited his purposes is, on the Stanhopian plan, the *perfect man*: a man to lead nations.' Burns added: 'But are great abilities, compleat without a flaw, and polished without a blemish, the standard of human excellence? This is certainly the staunch opinion of men of the world; but I call on honor, virtue and worth, to give the Stygian doctrine a loud negative.'

Steuart, James
Invited Burns to celebrate the birthday of Prince Charles Edward along with some other Jacobites at 'Cleland Gardens', his ale-house that stood at the east end of Edinburgh.

Burns, who relished outbursts of what Hilton Brown calls 'Stewarting', eagerly accepted the invitation on 26th December 1787: 'Monday next is a day of the year with me as hallowed as the ceremonies of Religion and sacred to the memory of the sufferings of my King and my Fore-

M

fathers.' Then follows eight lines of verse, beginning with what is surely the worst line Burns ever wrote: 'Tho' something like moisture conglobes in my eye'. It is not known whether he recited, or merely wrote for the occasion, his 'Birthday Ode for 31st December 1787'. He was still suffering from his bruised leg, and in a letter to 'Clarinda' of 3rd January 1788, he mentioned that 'Monday, for the first time, I dine in a neighbour's, next door'.

Steven, Alexander

The mason who built the New bridge mentioned in the poem 'The Brigs of Ayr'. Local tradition has it that he was also the architect. See **Adam, Robert.**

Steven, Isabella

'Tibbie' of Burns's song 'O Tibbie I hae seen the day' was identified by Burns's sister Mrs Begg as being Isabella Steven of Littlehill, by Lochlea. Burns was eighteen when the song was written, and farming Lochlea with his father.

Steven, The Reverend James (1761–1824)

A native of Kilmarnock, Steven was assistant to the Reverend Robert Dow of Ardrossan when Burns heard him preach, probably on exchange with Auld at Mauchline. His text, Malachi iv, 2, 'And Ye shall go forth, and grow up, as Calves of the Stall', prompted Burns to write his poem 'The Calf', winning with it a wager made with Gavin Hamilton that he 'would not produce a poem on the subject in a given time'.

Steven moved to London in 1787 and became a founder of the London Missionary Society.

In March 1790, Burns's brother William heard Steven preach in London, and reported 'the Calf' to be 'grown very fat, and . . . as boisterous as ever'.

He returned to Ayrshire as minister of Kilwinning in 1803.

Steven, Katie

According to dubious local tradition the 'winsome wench and waly' in 'Tam o' Shanter', who 'cou'd put on her claiths fu' brawly'; a fortune-teller of Laighpark, Kirkoswald, said also to have been a smuggler's accomplice, a receiver of stolen goods, and a witch.

Stewart, Anne

Daughter of John Stewart of East Craigs. Alexander Cunningham, Burns's friend, was very much in love with her, but she married instead an Edinburgh surgeon called Forrest Dewar, and in doing so, according to Burns's ridiculous phrase, 'prostituted her character'. Cunningham himself married some four years later, though it has been said, somewhat absurdly, that he never recovered from the blow of Anne Stewart marrying his rival.

Burns referred to Cunningham's attachment for Anne in a letter to Cunningham from Ellisland, dated 27th July 1788, part of which is in verse:

'And is thy Ardour still the same?
    And kindled still at Anna?
Others may boast a partial flame,
    But thou art a Volcano. . . .
'Sweet Anna has an air, a grace,
    Divine, magnetic, touching!
She takes, she charms—but who can
                                    trace,
    The process of BEWITCHING?'

In another letter to Cunningham from Ellisland, dated 24th January 1789, Burns, who had noticed the announcement in the newspaper of Anne's marriage to Dewar, condoled with his friend: '. . . I am certain that a disappointment in the tender passion must, to you, be a very serious matter . . . to your scanty tribe of mankind, whose souls bear, on the richest materials, the most elegant impress of the Great Creator, Love enters deeply into their existence, and is entwined with their very thread of life.'

Stewart of Stair, Mrs Catherine (d. 1818)

The daughter of Thomas Gordon of Afton, she married in 1770 a grandson of the Earl of Galloway, Alexander Stewart of Stair, on the banks of the Ayr, three miles below Barskimming. Stewart became a Major-General, and Member of Parliament for Kirkcudbrightshire from 1786. Stewart was interested in agricultural improvement, and in mining. He died in 1795, his death causing the bye-election in which Burns supported the Whig, Heron of Kerroughtree. In 1796, Mrs Stewart sold Stair House and built a new house on the Enterkine estate, which she named Afton Lodge, where she died. Enterkine was the property of her son-in-law, William Cunningham, who, in 1794, had married the eldest of her four daughters. Mrs Stewart is buried in Stair churchyard.

In September 1786, Burns wrote to Mrs Stewart, enclosing a parcel of his songs (the Stair Manuscript): 'One feature of your character I shall ever with grateful pleasure remember, the reception I got when I had the honor of waiting on you at Stair. I am little acquainted with Politeness, but I know a good deal of benevolence of temper and goodness of heart. Surely, did those in exalted stations know how happy they could make some classes of their Inferiours by condescension and affability, they would never stand so high, measuring out with every look the height of their elevation, but condescend as sweetly as Mrs Stewart of Stair.'

In 1787, her sixteen-year-old son, Alexander Gordon Stewart, died 'at a Military Academy at Strasburgh', and Burns made the lines: 'Fate gave the word, the arrow sped' do double duty, having already applied them to the son of Mrs Fergusson of Craigdarroch, who had died on 19th November. In 1791, Burns prepared for Mrs Stewart the Manuscript Collection known as the *Afton Manuscript*, which is now in the Cottage Museum, Alloway.

Dr Currie claimed that Burns's song 'Flow Gently Sweet Afton' was composed in Mrs Stewart's honour, though Gilbert Burns said it was inspired by Highland Mary. Burns certainly sent Mrs Stewart a copy of it. Mary Murdoch of Laight, by the other Afton, which joins the Nith near New Cumnock, has also been said to be the heroine of the song, which first appeared in the *Museum*, 1792. Burns himself communicated this beautiful air to Johnson, and the frequent substitution of inferior later airs to his words is much to be deplored.

It was at Stair House, a century before Burns visited it, that the tragedy described by Scott in *The Bride of Lammermoor* took place.

Stewart, Professor Dugald (1753–1828)

An eighteenth century metaphysician who, in his nineteenth year, became assistant to his father, Professor Matthew Stewart (1717–85), who held the Chair of Mathematics in the University of Edinburgh. Dugald was elected to succeed him. But in 1785, Professor Dugald Stewart exchanged his Chair for that of Moral Philosophy. He attained a considerable reputation in his day as a metaphysician, a reputation which later philosophers have not, however, endorsed.

In August 1786, Dr Mackenzie of Mauchline sent a copy of the Kilmarnock Edition to Dugald Stewart, then in vacation at his country seat, Catrine Bank, Catrine, near Mauchline. Stewart was much impressed by Burns's genius, and on 23rd October, had Burns to dinner with him at Catrine. Among the guests was Lord Daer, and although Burns had expressed sentiments hardly flattering to the aristocracy in the past—'You see you birkie ca'd a lord'—he changed his tune in 'Lines on Meeting with Lord Daer' to:

'This wot ye all whom it concerns:
I, Rhymer Rab, alias Burns,
    October twenty-third,

A ne'er to be forgotten day,
Sae far I sprachled up the brae,
                              [*clambered*
I dinner'd wi' a Lord.'

During the following winter in Edinburgh, Burns was given a good deal of attention and hospitality by Stewart. Of Stewart's lectures, Lord Cockburn said: 'Stewart supplied both young and old with philosophical ideas on what they had scarcely been accustomed to think philosophical subjects, unfolded the elements and the ends of that noble science, and so recommended it by the graces of his eloquence that even his idler hearers retained a permanent taste for it.'

The Professor died in Edinburgh on 11th June 1828. A Monument to his memory by W. H. Playfair was put up on the Calton Hill in 1832.

Stewart, John, seventh Earl of Galloway (1736–1806)

Succeeded to the Earldom in 1773, and from 1774 to 1790 he was a Representative Peer for Scotland in Parliament. He supported Gordon of Balmaghie when he contested the Stewartry of Kirkcudbright in 1795. See **Gordon of Balmaghie**. He was a Tory and Burns disliked both him and his politics. The Earl is rigorously satirised in Burns's Third Election Ballad, 'John Bushby's Lamentation.' The poet also wrote some bitter verses 'On the Earl of Galloway':

'What dost thou in that mansion fair?
    Flit, Galloway, and find
Some narrow, dirty, dungeon cave,
    The picture of thy mind!'

When he heard, erroneously or otherwise, that the Earl resented this, Burns retorted with:

'Spare me thy vengeance, Galloway!
    In quiet let me live:
I ask no kindness at thy hand,
    For thou hast none to give.'

The other side of the coin is shown in a newspaper obituary notice on the Earl's death: 'His loss will be extensively and deeply felt; his numerous friends and connections profited by his advice and assistance; his active frame and mind he never spared; he did nothing by halves. As a husband and father he was exemplary; as a friend, indefatigable; he adored the Supreme Being; he loved his king; his affairs prospered. He was admired for his taste in music; and had great skill in agricultural pursuits.'

He married, first, Charlotte Mary, a daughter of the first Earl Brooke and Earl of Warwick. Two sons died in infancy. Galloway then married Anne, second daughter of Sir James Dashwood, second Baronet of Kirtlington. By her he had sixteen children.

Stewart, Mary or 'Polly' (1775–1847)

Daughter of the factor at Closeburn, William Stewart. She is the subject of the song 'The flower it blows, it fades, it fa's', which was published in 1796 in the *Museum*. According to Scott Douglas, Polly had a somewhat erratic life. She married her cousin, by whom she had three sons. But because of some scrape, he was compelled to abscond. Later, she contracted a 'quasi-matrimonial alliance' with a farmer called George Welsh, a grand-uncle of Jane Welsh Carlyle. But as they found that they could not agree, they separated. In 1806, she came to live with her father at Maxwelton, and there formed another association, this time with a Swiss soldier called Fleitz, with whom she went abroad. After many wanderings, she died at Florence.

Burns's wish for her in the first stanza of the song may possibly have been granted, if not the wish in the second stanza:

'The flower it blows, it fades, it fa's,
    And art can ne'er renew it;
But worth and truth eternal youth
    Will gie to Polly Stewart!

'May he whase arms shall fauld thy
                                       charms
Possess a leal and true heart!
To him be given to ken the Heaven
He grasps in Polly Stewart!'

Stewart, Dr Matthew (1717–85)

Professor of Mathematics at Edinburgh
University, and father of Professor Dugald Stewart. 'The learned Sire and Son'
were mentioned by Burns in 'The Vision'.

Stewart, Montgomery

A younger son of the fourth Earl of
Galloway, and Patrick Heron's opponent
for the Kirkcudbright seat in 1786, which
gave rise to the 'Fourth Election Ballad'.

Stewart, Polly. See Stewart, Mary.

Stewart, Thomas

A Glasgow publisher, who, in 1801 and
1802, produced a series of pamphlets which
included many of Burns's songs and poems,
and several miscellaneous letters, including
twenty-five addressed by the poet to
Clarinda. The Clarinda letters were obtained by fraud, and were printed by
Stewart without her consent. She thereupon took legal action to stay the publication, and succeeded in driving it out of the
British market. Clandestine reprints, however, appeared in Ireland and America
during her lifetime.

Stewart, William (1749?–1812)

The son of a publican in Closeburn. When
Burns knew him he was the factor of the
Closeburn estate of the Rev. James Stuart
Menteith of Barrowby, Lincolnshire. He
was also the father of 'lovely Polly Stewart'.
When on Excise business, Burns frequently
visited him, and cut the song 'You're
welcome Willie Stewart' for him on a
crystal tumbler, later acquired by Sir
Walter Scott and now preserved at Abbotsford.

His sister, Catherine, was the wife of
the owner of Brownhill Inn, Mr Bacon, a

few miles south of Ellisland, from where
on a 'Monday even' in 1789, Burns sent
Stewart a rhymed epistle beginning:

'In honest Bacon's ingle-neuk,
                                      [chimney corner
Here maun I sit and think;   [must
Sick o' the world and world's folk,
And sick, d—mn'd sick o' drink. . . .'

When Friars' Carse, the home of
Captain Riddell, was to be put up for sale,
Burns wrote to an unidentified Mr
McLeod, who apparently thought of pur-
chasing the place, from Dumfries on 18th
June 1794, telling him: 'The trustees have
appointed a gentleman to make out an
estimate of the value of the terra firma in
the estate. . . . The gentleman they have
pitched on, is a Mr Wm Stewart, factor
and manager for Mr Menteath of Closeburn. Stewart is my most intimate friend;
and has promised me a copy of his estimate
—but please let this be a dead secret. . . . I
have in a manner beset and waylaid my
friend Stewart, until I have prevailed on
him.' Burns then undertook to supply
McLeod with Stewart's estimate of the
'exact value of every stick on the property'.

On 15th January 1795, Burns wrote a
'painful, disagreeable letter' to Stewart
from Dumfries, asking for 'three or four
guineas' because: 'These acursed times, by
stopping up Importation, have for the last
year lopt off a full third part of my
income.' Beneath the letter is a note in
Stewart's hand, dated 16th January: 'This
day forwarded and enclosed in a letter to
Mr Burns £3 3s. str and for which I
hold no security in writing.'

It is obvious from another of Burns's
letters to the factor of Closeburn that
Stewart shared with Cleghorn Burns's
fondness for bawdy verse.

Stewart spent his retirement at Maxwelton, Dumfries.

According to Stewart's will he 'possessed
the lands of Bilbow and the houses built
thereon lying in the parish of Troqueer;

he was tenant of three farms belonging to the Duke of Queensberry, and joint-tenant of Kelhead Limeworks; and he held one-fourth share of the woollen manufactury carried on at Cample under the firm of Stewart, Mathison & Co.'

Stirling

The royal burgh and university town of Stirling, Sir David Lyndsay's 'Fair Snow-doun', and the county town of Stirling-shire, was probably a natural stronghold in Pictish times, or earlier. From the thirteenth century to the seventeenth, its castle was a seat of the Scottish kings, and the decisive battle in the War of Independence was fought almost within sight of its ramparts, at Bannockburn. Its old town, like that of Edinburgh, struggled up a hilly spine towards the castle on the summit. The tides of Scottish history have surged around its walls.

Burns paid his first visit to Stirling on his way to Inverness. In company with Nicol, he arrived on the evening of Sun-day, 26th August 1787. On the Monday, Burns left Nicol to pay a visit to Harvie-ston. On the 28th, they left Stirling for Crieff.

On the Sunday night, Burns wrote to Robert Muir, describing his day's travel-ling: '. . . just now, from Stirling Castle, I have seen by the setting sun the glorious prospect of the windings of Forth through the rich carse of Stirling, and skirting the equally rich carse of Falkirk.'

The then ruined state of the former home of Scotland's kings aroused Burns's Jacobitism, and with a diamond pen he had recently acquired, he is said to have scrawled on the window of his room:

'Here Stewarts once in glory reigned,
And laws for Scotland's weal ordained;
But now unroofed their palace stands,
Their sceptre's swayed by other hands;
Fallen, indeed, and to the earth
Whence grovelling reptiles take their
birth,

The injured Stewart line is gone,
A race outlandish fills their throne;
An idiot race, to honour lost;
Who knows them best despise them
most.'

On the evening of Monday, Burns recorded: 'Supper—Messrs Doig (the schoolmaster) and Bell; Captain Forrester of the Castle—Doig a queerish figure and something of a pedant—Bell a joyous, vacant fellow who sings a good song—Forrester a merry, swearing kind of man, with a dash of the Sodger.' They had 'breakfast with Captain Forrester' before leaving on the 28th.

Burns visited Stirling again, in company with Adair, in October. Adair later recounted to Dr Currie: 'At Stirling the prospects from the Castle strongly inter-ested him; in a former visit to which, his national feelings had been powerfully excited by the ruinous and roofless state of the hall in which the Scottish parliaments had been frequently been held. His indig-nation had vented itself in some imprudent, but not unpoetical, lines, which had given much offence, and which he took this opportunity of erasing by breaking the pane of window at the inn in which they were written. At Stirling, we met with a company of travellers from Edinburgh, among whom was a character in many respects congenial with Burns. This was Nicol, one of the teachers of the High-Grammar-school at Edinburgh—the same wit and power of conversation; the same fondness for convivial society and thought-lessness of to-morrow, characterised both.'

Later, at the inn: 'Many songs were sung; which I mention for the sake of observing, that when Burns was called on in his turn, he was accustomed, instead of singing, to recite one or other of his own shorter poems, with a tone and emphasis which, though not correct or harmonious, were impressive and pathetic. This he did on the present occasion.'

Next day, Burns and Adair went on to

Harvieston in Clackmannanshire, where they stayed ten days.

A statue of Burns by Albert H. Hodge was put up in Stirling in 1914.

Strathallan, Viscount
See **Drummond, William.**

Stuart, Charlotte, Duchess of Albany (1753-1789)
Daughter of Prince Charles Edward by his mistress Clementina Walkinshaw, herself the daughter of a Lanarkshire laird, John Walkinshaw of Barrowfield. He had fought at Sherriffmur for the Pretender, and had been his secret agent in Europe. Clementina and Charles had been playmates in Rome when his mother had acted as godmother to Clementina. They met again at Bannockburn during the '45, after the battle of Falkirk, and Clementina followed the Prince to the Continent, where she bore him a daughter, Charlotte, in 1753. She left him in 1760, however, because of ill-usage. Owing to the Prince's having no family by his wife Louise, Princess of Stolberg and mistress of the poet Alfieri, his daughter by Clementina was legitimated under the title of Duchess of Albany, by a deed registered by the Parliament of Paris in 1784.

The Duchess is the subject of Burns's poem 'The Bonnie Lass of Albanie'. He may have been inspired to write it as a result of his recent Highland tour through Stuart country. There is, however, another tradition, that it was the death of the young Pretender on 31st January 1788, which induced Burns to write this poem. After she had been legitimised, the Duchess of Albany went to live with her father, whom she heired, but did not long survive.

Stuart, Peter (fl. 1788-1805)
The second son of three brothers, descendants from the Stuarts of Loch Rannoch, Perthshire, who claimed to have stemmed from the Royal House of Stuart. They all went from Edinburgh to London early in the seventies to take up journalism. Charles, the eldest, who had been a schoolfellow of Robert Fergusson, became a playwright. Daniel, the youngest, joined the other two in 1778, and Peter and Daniel took over the printing of the *Morning Post*. They acquired, first, *The Oracle*, and, in 1788, the *Post* itself. Daniel, then twenty-nine, became its editor, and built it up into one of the great newspapers of the day, attracting writers like Lamb, Southey, Wordsworth and Coleridge, and increasing its circulation from 350 to 4,500 copies.

In 1788, Peter Stuart, who edited *The Oracle*, resigned from the *Morning Post* to undertake the issuing of the first regular London evening paper, *The Star*. He had seen in the improved mail coach facilities of Palmer a new means of circulation. For editor, he chose a brother Scot, Andrew Macdonald. Under the title *The Star and Evening Advertiser*, the first issue of what was to become the leading Whig evening paper appeared on 3rd May 1788, and appeared regularly until 1831, when it was incorporated in *The Albion*. But on 13th February 1789, Peter Stuart quarrelled with the other proprietors, the reason he gave being his refusal to 'support Mr Pitt through thick and thin'.

Peter Stuart seems to have become an admirer of Burns's poems, through the Kilmarnock Edition. With this new 'evening' on his hands, he was eager to find contributors, so he wrote to Burns, offering him 'for communications to the paper, a small salary quite as large as his Excise office emoluments'. Burns, however, did not wish to become a regular contributor to any paper, though he agreed to make occasional contributions; in return for which, Stuart put him on the free list of the paper. Burns wrote to thank him in May 1789. He told Stuart: 'Any alterations you think necessary in my trifles, make them and welcome. In political principles, I promise you I shall be seldom out of the way; as I could lay down my life for that amiable, gallant, generous fellow, our heir-apparent. Allow me to correct the address you give me:— I am not R.B. Esq. No Poet, by statute of Parnassus, has a right, as an author, to assume Esquire, except he has had the honor to dedicate, "by permission", to a Prince, if not to a King; so I am as yet simply Mr. ROBERT BURNS, at your service. . . . I must beg of you never to put my name to any thing I send, except where I myself set it down at the head or foot of the piece. I am charmed with your paper. I wish it was more in my power to contribute to it; but over and above a comfortable stock of laziness of which, or rather *by* which, I am possessed, the regions of my fancy are dreadfully subject to baleful east-winds, which, at times, for months together, wither every bud and blossom, and turn the whole into an avid [*sic*] waste.'

Enclosed on this occasion was the 'Ode Sacred to the Memory of Mrs Oswald of Auchencruive', ostensibly submitted by one, Tim Nettle.

The offer of Peter Stuart was repeated a year later, and again declined. But among the other pieces of Burns published in *The Star*, were the lines 'Kind Sir, I've read your paper through', the 'Address of the Scottish Distillers', the 'Ode to the Departed Regency Bill', and, cleverest of all of them, the burlesque, 'A New Psalm'. When the gratuitous paper failed to arrive as regularly as it might have done, Burns remonstrated in verse:

'Dear Peter, dear Peter,
    We poor sons of metre
Are often negleckit, ye ken.
    For instance, your sheet, man,
    (Though glad I'm to see't man)
I get it no ae day in ten.—R.B.'

When *The Star* published some uncomplimentary verses about the Duchess of Gordon, allegedly by 'Burns, the ploughing poet', and *The Gazatteer* reprinted them, Burns, who saw them first in the latter publication, remonstrated to its editor, and then to the editor of *The Star*, on 13th April 1789.

After disowning the two sets of spurious verses Burns went on: 'I beg of you, Sir, that in your very first paper, you will do justice to my injured character with respect to those verses, falsely said to be mine; and please mention farther that in The Gazetteer and New Daily Advertiser of March 28th, another forgery of the like nature was committed on me in publishing a disrespectful stanza on the Duchess of Gordon. I have written to the Conductor of that Paper, remonstrating on the injury he has done me; but lest from some motive or other, he should decline giving me that redress I crave, if you will undeceive the Public, by letting them know through the channel of your universally known paper, that I am guiltless of either the one or the other miserable pieces of rhyme, you will much oblige. . . .'

'Mr Printer' printed the letter with some flattering editorial observation on the 'very ingenious Poet' from whose pen it came. The letter is, of course, mainly of interest for what it reveals of Burns's attitude to his reputation, and his loyalty to his patrons.

Stuart and Burns also corresponded over the stone on the grave of the poet Robert Fergusson, the cost of which Burns paid. *See* **Fergusson, Robert**.

The last trace of Stuart's career was his appearance before the bar of the House of Commons in 1805, when he was reprimanded for the remarks he had made in *The Oracle* in defence of the recently impeached Henry Dundas, Lord Melville.

Surgeoner, Jenny

A Mauchline girl who was seduced by Burns's close friend John Richmond, which led to his having to do public penance for his misdeeds. Although she bore a child to Richmond, he disowned her. Burns wrote to Richmond on 1st September 1786: 'I saw Jenny Surgeoner of late, and she complains bitterly against you. You are acting very wrong. My friend; her happiness or misery is bound up in your affection or unkindness. Poor girl! she told me with tears in her eyes that she had been at great pains since she went to Paisley, learning to write better; just on purpose to be able to correspond with you; and had promised herself great pleasure in your letters. Richmond, I know you to be a man of honour, but this conduct of yours to a poor girl who distractedly loves you, and whom you have ruined—forgive me, my friend, when I say it is highly inconsistent with the manly Integrity that I know your bosom glows with.'

Five years later Richmond, who had settled again in Mauchline, married Jenny.

Sutherland, George S.

A 'Mr Sutherland' was named as a member of John Jackson's company in the winter of 1781-2, at the Theatre Royal, Edinburgh. He was not named as outstanding in the list of talent which Jackson had been responsible for bringing to the Theatre Royal.

Sutherland's company, which included his wife, acted in Glover's Hall Theatre, Perth, in 1792.

At the theatre in Dumfries, where he seems to have been in charge of the company, Burns wrote a prologue for him and one for his wife, both spoken in the 1789/90 season—'No song nor dance I bring from yon great city', and 'What needs this din about the town o' Lon'on'.

On 11th January 1790, Burns wrote to his brother Gilbert: 'We have gotten a set of very decent Players here just now. I have seen them an evening or two. David Campbell in Ayr wrote me by the Manager of the Company, a Mr Sutherland, who is indeed a man of genius and apparent worth.'

Burns was on the free list for the theatre, and appears to have been on cordial terms with both Sutherland and his wife.

M*

Swan, James

Elected a bailie of Dumfries when John M'Murdo was elected Provost in 1794, and at the ensuing entertainment, Burns scribbled:

'Baillie Swan, Baillie Swan,
    Let you do what you can,
God ha' mercy on honest Dumfries
    But e'er the year's done,
    Good Lord! Provost John
Will find that his *Swans* are but
                                    Geese.'

Burns's prophecy proved correct. Swan was 'voted off Council' by 1796.

Syme, John (1755-1831)

Son of the Laird of Barncailzie, Kirkcudbrightshire, and, like his father, a Writer to the Signet, young Syme spent some years in the Army, as an ensign in the 72nd Regiment. He then retired to his father's estate, where he experimented with farming improvements. But his father lost heavily as a result of the Ayr Bank failure, and Syme was no longer able to live at Barncailzie. Appointed to the Sinecure of Collector of Stamps for the District, Syme moved to Dumfries in 1791. His office was on the ground floor of a house in what is now Bank Street. When Burns, a few months later, moved from Ellisland to Ryedale, Dumfries, he became a tenant of Captain John Hamilton, on the floor immediately above Syme's office.

Syme, a few years older than Burns, found Dumfries society dull, and welcomed in the poet a kindred convivial spirit. Burns was a frequent guest at Syme's villa, Ryedale, on the west side of the Nith. Of Syme as a host, Burns wrote, in an impromptu verse:

'Who is proof to thy personal con-
                                verse and wit,
Is proof to all other temptation.'

In the summer of 1794, Syme accompanied Burns on a tour through Galloway. The poet, smarting from the restrictions on his Jacobin sympathies placed on him by the Commissioners of the Excise, apparently raged against the rich at the mere sight of a mansion. According to Syme's remembered recollection of the trip, they rode to Kenmure the first day, then on to Gatehouse-of-Fleet, Kirkcudbright and St Mary's Isle, where they were happily entertained by Lord Selkirk. Again, according to Syme: 'The poet was delighted with his company, and acquitted himself to admiration. . . .'

Syme visited Burns at Brow on 15th July 1796, and again a few days later, when Burns had returned to Dumfries. He was horrified at the poet's deteriorated condition.

After Burns's death, Syme organised the funeral, and, with Alexander Cunningham, worked unsparingly raising money to help the poet's widow and children. He was one of those who urged Dr Currie to undertake his edition of Burns's work, and along with Gilbert Burns spent three weeks staying with Currie at his Liverpool home.

Syme left some highly-coloured, though valuable, reminiscences of Burns. His correspondence with Cunningham came to light a few years ago.

Of Burns's features, Syme wrote: 'The poet's expression varied perpetually, according to the idea that predominated in his mind: and it was beautiful to mark how well the play of his lips indicated the sentiment he was about to utter. His eyes and lips, the first remarkable for fire, and the second for flexibility, formed at all times an index to his mind, and as sunshine or shade predominated, you might have told, *a priori*, whether the company was to be favoured with a scintillation of wit, or a sentiment of benevolence, or a burst of fiery indignation. . . . I cordially concur with what Sir Walter Scott says of the poet's eyes. In his animated moments, and particularly when his anger was aroused by instances of tergiversation, meanness, or tyranny, they were actually like coals of living fire.'

See Plate 11

T

Tait, Alexander ('Saunders')

An eccentric tailor in Tarbolton, well advanced in years when Burns first became known as a poet. He seems to have been born in Peebleshire. Burns and his friend David Sillar annoyed Tait. Sillar, it seems, had called Tait's muse 'a tumbling cart, Gaun wantin' shoon.' Tait made much play with the common weakness which Burns and Sillar shared, addressing Sillar in verse:

'Search Scotland all around by Lorn,
Next round by Leith and Abercorn,
Through a' Ayrshire, by the Sorn,
    Tak merry turns,
There's nane can sound the *bawdy*
                                    horn
    Like you and Burns.'

Addressing Burns next, Tait undertook to

'. . . trace his pedigree
Because he made a sang on me.'

And this Tait did, in scabrous, doggerel pieces with titles like 'Burns in his Infancy,' 'Burns in Lochly' and 'Burns's Hen clockin' in Mauchline'.

In his early days, Tait practised mantua-making, which was then a regular part of the tailor's trade. Having sold his gown-piece to a lady, he would make-up the dress in the house of the customer. Latterly, he gave up this travelling trade and settled in Tarbolton, where he eventually owned several houses in the village, and where he also held several offices, as he recounts with pride in one of his verses:

'I'm Patron to the Burgher folks,
I'm Cornal to the Farmer's Box,
And Bailie to guid hearty cocks,
    That are a' grand—
Has heaps o' houses built on rocks,
    Wi' lime and sand.'

Tait published a volume of poems, 280 pages of octavo, in 1790, and sold it at one shilling and sixpence the copy. It was printed in Paisley, where he seems once to have lived.

In 1794, a future Earl of Eglinton, then Major Montgomerie, raised his regiment of West Lowland Fencibles, and Tait, though elderly, was one of the first to enrol. A note under the memoir on the Earl of Eglinton in *Kay's Edinburgh Portraits* had this to say of Tait:

'Among others who "followed in the field" was an eccentric personage of the name of Tait. He was a tailor, and in stature somewhat beneath the military stature; but he was a poet, and zealous in the cause of loyalty. He had sung the deeds of the Montgomeries in many a couplet; and, having animated the villagers with his loyal strains, resolved, like a second Tyrtaeus, to encourage his companions in arms to victory by the fire and vigour of his verses. It is said he could not write; nevertheless, he actually published a small volume of poems. These have long sunk into oblivion. Still "Sawney Tait, the tailor" is well remembered. He was a bachelor; and like a true son of genius, occupied an attic of very small dimensions. At the "June fair", when the village was crowded, Saunders . . . annually converted his "poet's corner" into a temple for the worship of Bacchus, and became a publican in a small way. . . . His apartment was always well frequented, especially by the younger portion of the country people, who were amused with his oddities.'

Tait, Crawford or Crauford (1765?–1832)

Son of John Tait of Harvieston, and a Writer to the Signet in Edinburgh. Crawford Tait heired his father's estate in 1800. His father had entertained Burns at Harvieston in 1787.

Burns wrote to Tait from Ellisland on 15th October 1790, on behalf of 'the bearer, Mr. Willm Duncan, a friend of mine whom I have long known and loved', and whose father, owner of 'a decent little property in Ayrshire', had 'bred the young man to the Law'. Tait was asked to 'assist him in the, to him, important consideration of getting a place'.

Tait married a daughter of Sir Ilay Campbell, the Lord President. Their son, Archibald Campbell Tait, was Archbishop of Canterbury from 1869 until his death in 1882.

Tait, John (1729–1800)

A Writer to the Signet in Edinburgh, he purchased the estate of Harvieston. He met Burns on the introduction of his sister-in-law, Mrs John Chalmers, and invited him to Harvieston. This visit lasted only one day, 27th August 1787— but the poet, at the family's insistence, made a second visit to Harvieston with Dr James Adair in October, when he stayed ten days. John Tait's son, Crawford Tait, was also a friend of Burns.

'Tam O' Shanter'

A narrative poem by Burns which first appeared in the Edinburgh Magazine for March 1791, a month before it appeared in the second volume of Francis Grose's Antiquities of Scotland, for which it was primarily written. Robert Riddell introduced Burns to Grose. According to Gilbert Burns, the poet asked the antiquarian to include a drawing of Alloway Kirk when he came to Ayrshire, and Grose agreed, provided Burns would give him something to print with it.

Writing to Grose in June 1790, Burns gave three witch stories associated with Alloway Kirk, two of which he says are 'authentic,' the third, 'though equally true, being not so well identified as the two former with regard to the scene'. The second of the stories was, in fact, 'Tam o' Shanter'. This is Burns's prose version of it to Grose:

'On a market-day, in the town of Ayr, a farmer from Carrick, and consequently whose way lay by the very gate of Aloway kirk-yard, in order to cross the river Doon, at the old bridge, which is almost two or three hundred yards farther on than the said old gate, had been detained by his business till by the time he reached Aloway it was the wizard hour, between night and morning.

'Though he was terrified with a blaze streaming from the kirk, yet as it is a well known fact, that to turn back on these occasions is running by far the greatest risk of mischief, he prudently advanced on his road. When he had reached the gate of the kirk-yard, he was surprised and entertained, through the ribs and arches of an old gothic window which still faces the highway, to see a dance of witches merrily footing it round their old sooty blackguard master, who was keeping them all alive with the power of his bagpipe. The farmer stopping his horse to observe them a little, could plainly desern the faces of many old women of his acquaintance and neighbourhood. How the gentleman was dressed, tradition does not say; but the ladies were all in their smocks; and one of them happening unluckily to have a smock which was considerably too short to answer all the purpose of that piece of dress, our farmer was so tickled that he involuntarily burst out, with a loud laugh, "Weel luppen, Maggy wi' the short sark!" and recollecting himself, instantly spurred his horse to the top of his speed. I need not mention the universally known fact, that no diabolical power can pursue you beyond the middle of a running stream. Lucky it was for the poor farmer that the river Doon was so near, for notwithstanding the speed of his horse, which was a good one, against he reached the middle of the arch of the bridge and consequently the middle of the stream, the pursuing, vengeful hags were so close at his heels, that one of them actually sprung to seize him: but it was too late; nothing was on her side of the stream but the horse's tail, which immediately gave way to her infernal grip, as if blasted by a stroke of lightning; but the farmer was beyond her reach. However, the unsightly, tailless condition of the vigorous steed was to the last hours of the noble creature's life, an awful warning to the Carrick farmers, not to stay too late in Ayr markets.'

Thus began what was to be Burns's most sustained poetic effort, and by common consent, one of the first narrative poems in a European tongue.

The story that the poem was written in one day was put about by Lockhart, aided by Allan Cunningham. Its subtle nuances of tempo, pace and tone suggest that it had, indeed, been given, as Burns told Mrs Dunlop on 11th April 1791, 'a finishing polish that I despair of ever excelling'.

Tarbolton Lassies', 'The

A sarcastic early song by Burns about some of the girls in the parish. They included Peggy, daughter of the Laird; Sophy who had a fortune; Mysie the obstinate who lived down by the Faile, senseless Jenny, her sister, and conceited Bessy:

'There's few sae bonie, nane sae guid,
    In a' King George' dominion;
If ye should doubt the truth o' this—
    It's Bessy's ain opinion!'

Taylor, John

Apparently a man of influence in Wanlockhead. When Burns arrived at the forge there on a frosty day, the smith was too busy to frost his horse's shoes, so Burns wrote a verse on the spot to Taylor. When Taylor heard what was the matter, he spoke to the smith who attended to the poet's horse at once.

'Poor slip-shod, giddy Pegasus
Was but a sorry walker,
To Vulcan then Apollo gaes
To get a frosty caulker.

'Obliging Vulcan fen to wark,
Threw by his coat and bonnet

And did Sol's business in a crack,
Sol pay'd him with a sonnet.'

Chambers explained that a horse was: 'said in Scotland to be "frosted" or "sharpened" when it is rough shod for frosty weather, by having the edges at the front of the shoes—the calks, calkins, calkens, or caulkers—turned over so as to grip on the slippery ground.'

Taylor, The Reverend Dr John (1694–1761)

A Norwich divine whose *Scripture Doctrine of Original Sin*, published in 1740, argued that in biblical interpretation, nothing should be admitted that was contrary to common-sense and human understanding. His book became popular with New Light supporters.

Burns mentioned him in his 'Epistle to John Goldie'. Addressing Orthodoxy satirically, he said:

'It's you and *Taylor* are the chief
To blame for a' this black mischief. . . .'

Telford, Thomas (1757–1834)

Scottish architect and civil engineer, born at Westerkirk, in Eskdale, Dumfriesshire. The son of a shepherd who died while Telford was an infant, the boy was brought up by his mother, and served his apprenticeship as a stonemason. In 1780, he went to Edinburgh, and afterwards to London, where he was employed in the building of houses—in London, on Somerset House. His first big appointment was as Surveyor to the County of Salop, an appointment procured for him by William Pulteney. *See* **Pulteney, William**. His first major project was the Ellesmere Canal, to which he was engineer, and for which he built the mighty viaducts of Chirk and Ponty-Cysyllte.

Thereafter, Telford built the Caledonian Canal, many miles of road (including the Glasgow-Carlisle road) and numerous bridges in Scotland, the Conway and Menai Straits bridges in Wales, the Dean

Bridge, Edinburgh, and the Broomielaw Bridge, Glasgow. He also advised on the construction of the Gotha Canal.

Telford never married. He made one of his numerous tours of his Scottish works in company with the Poet Laureate, Robert Southey, who left a fascinating *Journal of a Tour in Scotland*, 1819, valuable for its portrait of the great engineer himself, as well as for its observations on Highland social conditions at the time.

From his earliest days, Telford wrote verse himself, and was keenly interested in the literary developments of his day. He regarded Burns's entry into the Excise as something of a degradation, and on the poet's death wrote a poem denouncing the officials who had so great a man in their power. It reaches this climax:

'The Muses shall that fatal hour
   To Lethe's streams consign,
Which gave the little slaves of pow'r,
   To scoff at worth like thine.

'But thy fair fame shall rise and spread,
   Thy name be dear to all,
When down to their oblivious bed,
   Official insects fall.'

Templeton, William
A merchant of Mauchline who married Betty Miller, one of the 'Mauchline belles'.

Tennant, Agnes (1764–87)
Eldest daughter of John Tennant of Glenconner, by his second marriage. She is Burns's 'auld acquaintance, Nancy' in the 'Epistle to James Tennant'. She married George Reid, a farmer at Barquharie, who loaned Burns the pony on which to ride to Edinburgh in 1786. Burns wrote to thank him immediately on arriving in the capital, and sent Agnes a copy of the Kilmarnock Edition.

Tennant, Charles (1768–1838)
Fourth son of John Tennant of Glenconner by his second marriage. He went to Kilbarchan to learn weaving and is

'wabster Charlie', in the 'Epistle to James Tennant'.

He started bleaching near Barrhead, and obtained a patent for the manufacture of chloride of lime, by the hand process; two years later he got a patent for the dry process, or bleaching powder.

He formed the company of Tennant, Knox & Co., for bleaching with these inventions, and built the works in St Rollox, Glasgow.

Tennant, David (1762–1839)
Third son of John Tennant of Glenconner by his second wife. After a spell of schoolmastering at Ayr Academy, he became a sailor in the merchant service, finally obtaining command of a ship. He was privateering during the French wars. Burns refers to him in the 'Epistle to James Tennant', as 'the manly tar, my mason-billie'.

David Tennant lost his right hand during a naval battle. He was offered a knighthood, which he refused.

Tennant, James (1755–1835)
Eldest son of John Tennant of Glenconner, Burns wrote for him the 'Epistle to James Tennant', which contains references to many of Tennant's numerous relations and expresses the hope that James himself will have:

'Mony a laugh, and mony a drink,
And aye enough o' needfu' clink.'

He also was Burns's 'auld comrade dear and brither sinner'. He was known familiarly as 'The miller' because he had Ochiltree Mill. A neighbour is said to have described him as 'a dungeon of wit'.

Tennant of Auchenbay, John (1760–1853)
Second son of John Tennant of Glenconner by his second wife. He was Burns's fellow boarder for three weeks during the summer of 1773 with John Murdoch, then master at the English school in Ayr.

Tennant's business attempts, first as a ship-builder and then as a distiller, were unsuccessful, so he turned to farming and rented Auchenbay, in the parish of Ochiltree, where he prospered.

Tennant the younger married Margaret Colville in 1785.

Burns, referring to the expected birth of Tennant's first child, in the 'Epistle to James Tennant', wrote:

'An' Auchenbay, I wish him joy,
If he's a parent, lass or boy,
May he be *Dad*, and Meg be *mither*,
Just five-and-forty years thegither.'

Tennant was a skilled farmer, and gave evidence about the state of Scottish agriculture before a Committee of the House of Commons. He purchased the estate of Creoch for £9,000, the reputed profits of one year from his farming.

Tennant of Glenconner, John (1725–1810)

'A worthy, intelligent farmer, my father's friend and my own', was how Burns described the prolific John Tennant of Glenconner in a letter to Clarinda, dated 2nd March 1788. He accompanied the poet on an inspection of Ellisland, and somewhat injudiciously, as things turned out, advised him to take it from Miller. He was factor to the Countess of Glencairn at Ochiltree for eleven years, and rented the farm of Glenconner. Previously, he had been Willian Burnes's neighbour, at which time he was renting the farm of Laigh Corton, near Bridgend. He was one of the witnesses at Robert's baptism and is the 'guid auld Glen, The ace an wale of honest men', of the 'Epistle to James Tennant', which Burns addressed to John Tennant's eldest son.

John had five sons, all of whom are noted separately, as is his daughter.

Tennant, Katherine

Daughter of Alexander Tennant, a younger brother of John Tennant of Glenconner.

She was the 'Cousin Kate' referred to by Burns in his 'Epistle to James Tennant'.

Tennant, Robert (1774–1841)

Youngest son of John Tennant of Glenconner by his second wife. He is the 'Singing Sannock' of the 'Epistle to James Tennant.' He settled as a bleacher in Ireland, where he died.

Tennant, William (1758–1813)

Eldest son of John Tennant of Glenconner, by his second wife. He is described in the 'Epistle to James Tennant' as 'Preacher Willie'. He was Chaplain to the Forces in India, and on his retirement settled at Glenconner. He was strictly Evangelical in views, and wrote two books on India.

Glasgow University gave him an honorary doctorate.

Thompson, Margaret

The poet had met her at Kirkoswald, when very young, and his poem 'Composed in August', is said to have been inspired when he met her again later. In his Autobiographical Letter, Burns refers to her as: 'a charming Fillette, who lived next door to the school, over-set my trigonometry, and set me off in a Tangent from the sphere of my studies'.

Burns presented Margaret, who was by then married to John Neilson of Monyfee, with a copy of the Kilmarnock volume with the inscription 'Once fondly lov'd, and still remembered dear'.

These lines are in the first volume of the Glenriddell Manuscript, with a note in Burns's hand:

'. . . Poor Peggy! Her husband is an old acquaintance and a most worthy fellow. When I was taking leave of my Carrick relations, intending to go to the West Indies, when I took farewell of her, neither she nor I could speak a syllable. —Her husband escorted me three miles on my road, and we both parted with tears.'

Thomson, George (1757–1851)
Son of the schoolmaster at Limekilns, Dunfermline, he was given some legal training. In 1780, John Home, the author of *Douglas*, recommended Thomson for a clerical appointment with the Board of Trustees for the Encouragement of Art and Manufacture in Scotland, a body set up under the terms of the Treaty of Union, to promote Scottish trade with money given by Parliament in compensation for losses in the Darien scheme, and for assuming a share of England's national debt. He remained with the Board throughout his long and uneventful career, eventually becoming Chief Clerk.

Thomson's absorbing passion was music. He played in the orchestra of the St Cecilia Concerts, and enjoyed the Italianate renderings of Scots songs, which castrati, like Tenducci, indulged in when they visited Scotland. Thomson's general musical taste seems to have led him to prefer the rather colourless music of Haydn's pupil Pleyel to that of Haydn himself, or the music of of Beethoven.

It was the singing of Pietro Urbani which gave Thomson the idea of marrying Scots songs to accompaniments to the leading masters of the day. During the summer of 1792, Thomson interested Andrew Erskine, younger brother of the composing Earl of Kellie, in bringing out a collection along these lines, and with words strictly respectable. Erskine, however, was by then becoming heavily involved in gambling debts, and although he took some hand in the project at the beginning, going over some of the songs composed for inclusion, he ended his life in the autumn of the following year by jumping into the Forth. So Thomson went on alone. In September 1792, he asked Alexander Cunningham for a letter of introduction to the poet, which he sent to Burns in mid-September, accompanied by an explanation of his requirements and ideals:

'For some years past, I have, with a friend or two, employed many leisure hours in collating and collecting the most favourite of our national melodies, for publication. We have engaged Pleyel, the most agreeable composer living, to put accompaniments to these, and also to compose an instrumental prelude and conclusion to each air. . . . To render this work perfect, we are desirous to have the poetry improved wherever it seems unworthy of the music. . . . Some charming melodies are united to mere nonsense and doggerel, while others are accommodated with rhymes so loose and indelicate as cannot be sung in decent company. To remove this reproach would be an easy task to the author of "The Cotter's Saturday Night".'

It was as the author of one of his weakest poems that Thomson, like the Edinburgh patricians, thought of Burns. Having set forth the general scheme, he then came down to practical terms:

'We shall esteem your poetical assistance a particular favour, besides paying any reasonable price you shall please to demand for it . . . tell me frankly, then, whether you will devote your leisure to writing twenty or twenty-five songs, suitable to the particular melodies which I am prepared to send you. A few Songs exceptionable only in some of their verses, I will likewise submit to your consideration; leaving it to you either to mend these or make new songs in their stead.'

Burns told him frankly, replying by return. He would cheerfully do the work, so long as he was not to be hurried.

'As to any remuneration, you may think my Songs either *above,* or *below* price; for they shall absolutely be the one or the other. In the honest enthusiasm with which I embark in your undertaking, to talk of money, wages, fee, hire, and etc. could be downright Sodomy of Soul! A proof of each of the Songs that I compose or amend, I shall receive as a favor.'

When Thomson sent Currie that letter after Burns's death, Currie revealed a nice sense of moral distinction by substituting the word 'Prostitution' for 'Sodomy'.

The idea of contributing to a better-printed and more lavishly produced publication than the *Museum*, probably appealed to Burns, who at that time could have had little idea of the dangers into which Thomson was running with Pleyel and the other foreign composers whom he was to employ to provide the accompaniments.

From the start, Burns made it plain to Thomson, as he had done earlier to Johnson, that he intended to abide by the editorial decision—an unfortunate admission as things turned out, for Thomson had neither Johnson's sturdy literary sense nor his humility. By the end of the year, Burns had sent Thomson half a dozen songs, including 'The Lea Rig', 'My Wife's a Winsom Wee Thing' and 'Duncan Gray'.

In June 1793, Thomson brought out the first part of his *Select Scottish Airs*. It contained the twenty-five songs originally promised by Burns. The editor sent the poet a copy, enclosing a five-pound note, accompanied by the explanation:

'I cannot express to you how much I am obliged to you for the exquisite new songs you are sending me; but thanks, my friend, are a poor return for what you have done. As I shall benefit by the publication, you must suffer me to enclose a small mark of my gratitude, and to repeat it afterwards when I find it convenient. Do not return it, for, by Heaven! if you do, our correspondence is at an end.'

By then, Burns was already beginning to feel the first privations of the French war, caused, so far as he was concerned, by the cutting down of imports and consequent loss of his duty perquisites—indeed, only a few weeks before he had been lamenting the fact that a friend of his had 'fallen a sacrifice to these accursed times'! In spite of this, Thomson's payment roused him to indignation.

'I assure you, my dear Sir, that you truly hurt me with your pecuniary parcel. It degrades me in my own eyes. However, to return it would savour of bombast affectation; But, as to any more traffic of that D^r and C^r kind, I swear, by that HONOUR which crowns the upright Statue of ROB^t BURNS'S INTEGRITY! On the least notion of it, I will indignantly spurn the by-past transaction, and from that moment commence entire Stranger to you! BURN'S character for Generosity of Sentiment, and Independance of Mind, will, I trust, long outlive any of his wants which the cold, unfeeling, dirty Ore can supply: at least, I shall take care that such a Character he shall deserve.'

Thomson never tried to repeat his gesture, until a few days before the end when, in an agony of desperation, the dying poet begged him for a further five pounds.

It has been argued that had Thomson known better how to cope with Burns's pride, or had someone like Henry Mackenzie drawn up a proper settlement as in the affair with Creech, the difficulty of song-payment need never have arisen. Possibly so. But at that time the value of literary property was considerably less than it is now, and Burns reaped so much vexation from the Creech transaction that it might not have been easy to bring him to the point of signing another contract.

In any case, his position reasserted, he then went on to congratulate Thomson on the elegant appearance of his book. It was, indeed, the only volume of Thomson's which came out during the poet's lifetime. But the Editor, taking the measure of Burns's enthusiasm, soon decided to widen the scheme so that he could make still more use of his willing collaborator by including 'every Scottish air and song worth singing'.

Burns therefore went on supplying Thomson with songs until a few days before his death. Because Thomson freely put forward counter-suggestions, Burns had, perforce, to carry on a fairly extensive correspondence with him. Often, the poet found it necessary to justify his reasons for what he had done to an old song, or for setting a new song to a particular tune. Because of this, Burns's correspondence with Thomson gives us a fuller insight into his attitude to Scots song than even the notes in the interleaved *Museum*. Once Burns had stated his wishes—or rebutted Thomson's—the wily Editor rarely argued back. That would have risked an interruption in the correspondence, for there were obvious limits to Burns's patience. So Thomson altered, where it suited him, without consulting the poet, who, in any case, was dead by the time the results appeared. Many of the songs sent to Thomson, Burns asked to be returned to him if unsuitable, so that Johnson might have them. So jealous was Thomson of the engraver, however, that he made a practice of retaining even what he had no intention of using, merely so that Johnson would be deprived!

Writing to Thomson in April 1793, Burns cleared up the question of the ownership of the songs:

'Though I give Johnson one edition of my songs, that does not give away the copy-right; so you may take "Thou lingering star, with lessening ray", to the tune of Hughie Graham, or other songs, of mine. . . .'

The point is of particular interest, because Thomson later tried (unsuccessfully) to secure the copyright of the songs Burns provided for *Select Scottish Airs*.

In August 1793, when 'Peter Pindar' (the pen-name of the English minor poet John Wolcott) withdrew his dilatory services from Thomson's project, the editor asked Burns if, in addition to the Scots verses he was already providing, he would also provide some of the alternative English words, which Thomson had undertaken to publish with each air. Forgetting that he had originally told Thomson he would have nothing to do with English words, Burns replied:

'You may readily trust, my dear Sir, that any exertion in my power, is heartily

at your service. But one thing I must hint to you, the very name of Peter Pindar is of great Service to your Publication; so, get a verse from him now and then, though I have no objection, as well as I can, to bear the burden of the business.'

Thus Burns committed himself with Thomson still further, though, as he had truly remarked the previous April:

'I have not that command of the language that I have of my native tongue. In fact, I think my ideas are more barren in English than in Scottish.'

A few months later, he added:

'You must not, my dear Sir, expect all your English songs to have superlative merit. 'Tis enough if they are passable.'

The correspondence went on, Thomson suggesting niggling 'improvements', most of which Burns very properly rejected, sometimes almost bluntly:

'I cannot alter the disputed lines in the "Mill Mill O". What you think a defect, I esteem as a positive beauty: so you see how Doctors differ.'

Thomson's gravest error of judgment occurred over one of Burns's most stirring songs. The shameful trial of the Friends of the People took place during August 1793. The fact that the frightened Government chose to make its examples in Scotland—perhaps with the 1715 and 1745 risings still in mind—rather than in England, where Reform supporters were numerically greater, may have helped to turn Burns's mind towards the historical parallel through which he chose to declare his unshaken belief in 'Liberty and Independance'. [*sic*] Thomson came upon the song after an epistolary introduction in which the poet explained the limitations of his musical taste:

'You know that my pretensions to musical taste, are merely a few of Nature's instincts, untaught and untutored by Art. For this reason, many musical compositions, particularly where much of the merit lies in Counterpoint, however they may transport and ravish the ears of you

Connoisseurs, affect my simple lug no otherwise than merely as melodious Din. On the other hand, by way of amends, I am delighted with many little melodies, which the learned Musician despises as silly and insipid. I do not know whether the old air "Hey, tutti, tatie", may rank among this number; but well I know that, with Fraser's Hautboy, it has often filled my eyes with tears. There is a tradition, which I have met with in many places of Scotland, that it was Robert Bruce's March at the battle of Bannock-burn. This thought, in my yesternight's evening walk, warmed me to a pitch of enthusiasm on the theme of Liberty and Independance, which I threw into a kind of Scots Ode, fitted to the Air, that one might suppose to be the gallant ROYAL SCOT's address to his heroic followers on that eventful morning.'

Then followed 'Scots, wha hae wi' Wallace bled'. The first four verses clearly refer to the English menace which Robert the Bruce encountered and broke. The last two verses, and the accompanying comment, could also be held to refer to contemporary events:

'By Oppression's woes and pains!
By your Sons in servile chains!
We will drain our dearest veins,
     But they *shall* be free!

'Lay the proud Usurpers low!
Tyrants fall in every foe!
LIBERTY's in ev'ry blow!
     Let us DO—or DIE!!

'So may God defend the cause of Trust and Liberty, as he did that day!—Amen.'
The postscript, too, is revealing:
'P.S. I shewed the air to Urbani, who was highly pleased with it, and begged me to make soft verses for it; but I had no idea of giving myself any trouble on the subject, till the accidental recollection of that glorious struggle for Freedom, associated with the glowing idea of some other struggles, of the same nature, *not quite so*

ancient, roused my rhyming Mania. . . .
Thomson liked the words, but not the tune. He suggested to Burns that the poem ought to go to the tune 'Lewie Gordon'. This necessitated a weakening addition to every fourth line: i.e. 'But they shall be, shall be free'. Thomson's Edinburgh 'advisers' took a similar view. Reluctantly, Burns agreed, though he came nearer to losing his temper with Thomson over this than over any other matter. Dr Currie, however, printed the original words in his life and edition of Burns's works, and told the story of the controversy. Thomson thereupon tacitly admitted his error of judgment by reprinting in his volume of 1802 the correct words to 'Hey, tuttie tatti', the sixteenth-century tune for the old popular song 'Hey, now the day dawes'.

However tiresome Thomson may have been, and however wrong-headed over the matter of his accompaniments, he undoubtedly stimulated Burns's muse at a time when some such stimulation was probably essential to keep him going at all.

In a letter dated September 1793, wherein the poet reviews a long list of songs that Thomson had sent him, Burns explained his method of song composition:
'Laddie, lie near me—must *lie by me*, for some time. I do not know the air; and until I am compleat master of a tune, in my own singing, (such as it is) I never can compose for it. My way is: I consider the poetic Sentiment, correspondent to my idea of the musical expression; then chuse my theme; begin one Stanza; when that is composed, which is generally the most difficult part of the business, I walk out, sit down now and then, look out for objects in Nature around me that are in unison or harmony with the cogitations of my fancy and workings of my bosom; humming every now and then the air with the verses I have framed: when I feel my Muse beginning to jade, I retire to the solitary fireside of my study, and there commit my effusions to paper; swinging, at intervals, on the hind-legs of my elbow-

chair, by way of calling forth my own critical strictures, as my pen goes.

'Seriously, this, at home, is almost invariably my way.'

That song-writing was essential to him, he had revealed in a letter sent to Thomson the previous April:

'You cannot imagine how much this business of composing for your publication had added to my enjoyments. What with my early attachments to ballads, Johnson's Museum, with your book, and etc. Ballad-making is now as compleatly my hobby-horse, as ever Fortifications was Uncle Toby's; so I'll e'en canter it away till I come to the limit of my race (God grant that I may take the right side of the winning post!) and then chearfully looking back on the honest folks with whom I have been happy, I shall say, or sing, "Sae merry as we a' hae been".'

Burns did, indeed, 'canter' his 'hobby-horse' till he came to the limit of his race. As late as February 1796, when the last fatal decline in his health had already set in, he was promising Thomson verses for twenty-five Irish airs which the editor now wanted to include in his collection.

At the end of April, Burns wrote:

'Alas! my dear Thomson, I fear it will be some time ere I tune my lyre again! "By Babel streams" and etc. Almost ever since I wrote you last, I have only known Existence by the pressure of the heavy hand of Sickness; and have counted time by the repercussions of PAIN! Rheumatism, Cold, and Fever have formed, to me, a terrible Trinity in Unity, which makes me close my eyes in misery, and open them without hope.'

In May, he was a little more hopeful, writing to thank Thomson for the present of a new seal made on a 'Highland Pebble', and incorporating his own unregistered Arms design:

'On a field, azure, a holly-bush, seeded, proper, in base; a Shepherd's pipe and crook, Saltier-wise, also proper, in chief. On a wreath of the colors, a woodlark perching on a sprig of bay-tree, proper, for Crest. Two mottoes: Round the top of the Crest "Wood-notes wild". At the bottom of the shield, in the usual place, "Better a wee bush than nae bield".'

This design, which he had worked out with Maria Riddell, shows something of his knowledge of the science of Heraldry. 'Beautiful seal' though it was, he was not to have much opportunity of using it. At the same time, he wisely refused to assign the whole copyright of his songs to the editor, altering the agreement drawn up by Thomson's lawyer in favour of a more limited agreement of his own, which Thomson never publicly produced, and is now lost. On 18th May 1796 Burns made his own intentions regarding his songs clear:

'When your Publication is finished, I intend publishing a Collection on a cheap plan, of all the songs I have written for you, the Museum, and etc.—at least of all the songs of which I wish to be called the Author. I do not propose this so much in the way of emolument, as to do justice to my Muse, lest I should be blamed for trash I never saw, or be defrauded by other claimants of what is justly my own.'

To the last, pathetic letter of 12th July, begging twelve pounds by return, Thomson responded promptly.

According to Stationers' Hall, Thomson's six Scottish volumes appeared in 1793, 1798 (vol. 1), 1799 (vol. 2), 1802 (vol. 3), 1818–26 (vol. 5), and 1841 (vol. 6). The Welsh volumes appeared between 1809 and 1814, the Irish between 1814 and 1816. In 1822, he published a six-volume selected edition, drawn from them all. This, and the first part of the first Scottish volume, published separately in 1793, sold reasonably well. The rest were more or less complete failures financially. Haydn, Beethoven, Weber and Hummel replaced Pleyel on the musical side: Scott, Moore, Byron, Campbell and Sir Alexander Boswell replaced Burns as the providers of the words. Haydn's accompaniments are, on the whole, the best of the set. (Curiously enough, he set some value on them!) None of the other poems is of much account, since none of the poets other than Burns found it easy to fit words to existing tunes.

For Thomson's volumes, Burns provided about a hundred and fourteen songs; for Johnson about a hundred and sixty. In neither case can any exact figure be given, because in many instances songs by other people which Burns merely claimed to have polished, he so subtly and surely transformed that he clearly deserves the main share of the credit for their immortality.

Although, after Burns's death, Thomson did his share of falsifying and suppressing in the true Currie tradition, he fiercely resented any suggestion that he had not treated Burns justly. When Professor John Wilson ('Christopher North') published a scathing attack on Thomson in his *Land of Burns* in 1838, which Thomson did not see for some years, he vigorously rebutted Wilson's charges. Writing from hearsay, in a letter to the publisher Blackie, dated 30th June 1843, he said:

'Perhaps the professor thinks I was to blame in not sending *more* than the sum asked. If this has provoked his ire I would merely say that I was not then burdened with money, and had to borrow of a friend the £5 I sent. And on consulting two of the poet's most intimate friends whether I should enlarge the sum, they both were of opinion that if I sent more than the poet asked there would be a greater risk of offending than of pleasing him in the excited and nervous state in which the altered character of his handwriting showed him to be. What the professor may have chosen to say of me I know not, but this I say, that if my conduct in regard to Burns, from beginning to end, be investigated fairly and candidly, with the utmost strictness, I have not the slightest fear of the result.'

In 1845, Thomson came upon a copy of

Wilson's book lying on a table in the house of one of Burns's sons. Thomson then sent a letter rebutting the charges to *Tait's Magazine*:

'I felt anxious to show him my sense of his great liberality, by sending him a few presents such as I thought he could not well refuse. Accordingly I got the ingenious artist David Allan to paint for him *con amore* the interesting scene of family worship from *The Cotter's Saturday Night*, which he thankfully received. I also sent him a Scoto-Indian shawl for Mrs Burns, and a gold seal with his coat of arms engraved on it from his own curious heraldic design. These cost me but five and twenty guineas, and I freely confess were more suited to my means than to the poet's deserts. But if the prosperous critic himself'—this of course refers to Wilson— 'had stood in my situation with a small income and a large family, who knows whether his own largesses would have exceeded mine? Well did my friends know how gladly I would have tried a race of generosity even with him, if the power had been brother to the will. But Wilson knew me not, as in these evil times an ultra Tory held little communion with a Whig, and he and I were and are strangers to each other.'

Thomson was a member of the committee formed to deal with the question of a Burns memorial in Edinburgh, so played a considerable part in raising money for the erection of the Calton Hill Memorial. He remained jealous of all rival collections of Scots songs to his own; of Urbani's and of Johnson's during Burns's lifetime, and of several later editors thereafter.

Thomson retired from his official duties in 1839, and soon afterwards went to London, in order to be near his two sons and their families. His wife, Katherine Miller of Kelso, whom he had married in 1781, died in London in 1841, while visiting her daughter, Mrs Hogarth. Thomson had two sons and six daughters, one of whom married George Hogarth, an Edinburgh W.S., historian and music critic. A daughter of the Hogarths became the wife of Charles Dickens in 1836. In his lonely old age, Thomson returned to Edinburgh for a public dinner which was held in Gibb's Royal Hotel on 3rd March 1847, one day before Thomson completed his ninetieth year. Lord Cockburn was in the chair, and presented Thomson with an inscribed vase. He finally settled at 1 Vanbrugh Place, Leith, where he died on 18th February 1851. He was buried beside his wife in Kensal Green Cemetery. The inscription on his tombstone was written by Dickens. Raeburn painted his portrait.

See Plate 12

Thomson, Mrs John
See **Lewars, Jessy.**

Thriepland of Fingask, Sir Stewart (1716–1805)
He joined the Rising of 1745, then escaped to France, was attainted and had his estate forfeited. When the Act of Indemnity was passed he returned to Scotland and repurchased his paternal estates near Castle Huntly, in 1782. Burns made a note of his name in his Journal of his Highland tour, possibly signifying that he had met him when visiting Huntly Castle.

A member of the Royal College of Physicians in Edinburgh, Sir Stewart was elected its President in 1766.

Thurlow, Edward, first Baron (1731–1806)
Born at Bracon Ash, Norfolk, eldest son of the Reverend Thomas Thurlow, and educated at Canterbury Grammar School and Caius College, Cambridge, he left without a degree, but took silk in 1761. In 1768, he became Member of Parliament for Tavistock, and in 1770 was made Solicitor General. In 1778, he became Lord Chancellor and received a peerage. He was thus Lord Chancellor at the time of the Regency Bill, which proposed giving the Prince of Wales full monarchic powers because of George III's insanity. Pitt and Thurlow strongly opposed the bill.

In his 'Stanzas of Psalmody', Burns refers to Thurlow as:

'. . . him among the Princes chief
  In our Jerusalem,
The Judge that's mighty in Thy Law
  The Man that fears Thy Name.'

He had an awe-inspiring presence. Dr Johnson said of him: 'I would prepare myself for no man in England but Lord Thurlow. When I am to meet with him I should wish to know a day before.'

Tibbie
See **Steven, Isabella**

Tinnock, Nanse
Burns said she was one of his Mauchline hostesses, where he studied politics over a 'glass of gude auld "Scotch Drink"'. Nanse, when she read the poem, 'The Author's Earnest Cry and Prayer', where Burns mentions drinking a health in her house, said he was only there once or twice. 'Auld Nanse Tinnock's', known before Burns's time as 'The Sorn Inn', stands in Castle Street, almost opposite the house of Dr John Mackenzie. It is supposed to date from 1712. It overlooks the parish church, and once had a stairway leading down to the churchyard, made well known by Burns as the setting of 'The Holy Fair'. It is now the property of the Glasgow and District Burns Association, having been donated, along with Dr Mackenzie's House and the one known as the 'Burns House', by Charles Rennie Cowie between 1915 and 1924. It was once occupied by old people, free of rent. But in 1958 they were moved to a row of new cottages opposite Mossgiel. The old houses have been preserved and made into a Museum.

'Tootie'
According to Cromek, a Mauchline cattle dealer of doubtful reputation, Burns refers

to him in 'To Gavin Hamilton Esq. Mauchline (Recommending a Boy)', dated 'Mosgaville, 3rd May, 1786'. The poem begins:

'I hold it, Sir, my bounden duty
To warn you how that Master Tootie,
    Alias Laird M'Gaun,
Was here to hire yon lad away
'Bout whom ye spak the tither
                         day. . . . ,

'Tootie,' it seems, tried to hire the boy, about whom Burns had already spoken to Gavin Hamilton.

Train, Joseph (1779–1852)

His father was land-steward to John Farquhar-Gray of Gilmilnscroft. Joseph, after a weaver's apprenticeship and service in the army, where he attracted the notice of Sir David Hunter Blair, joined the Ayr District of the Excise, as an officer, thanks to the influence of his titled patron. Later, he took over from John Lewars as Supervisor of Dumfries.

Train was a keen antiquarian, and Scott drew on his knowledge for several of the 'Waverley' novels. The two kept up a steady correspondence. According to an article in the *Glasgow Herald* of 22nd February 1896, by Dr W. Wallace, Train supplied Lockhart with information for his book on Burns, including a story of Richmond's which reflected on the character of a Mary Campbell, supposed to be 'Highland Mary': Lockhart did not use the story, but at the same time did not destroy Train's manuscript.

Train's gossip has come in for a certain amount of criticism, particularly from those who have tried sentimentally to whitewash Burns. Doubtless much of it is idle chatter. But some of it seems to ring true.

Translation, Burns in

Burns's poems have been translated into most European tongues, and into English. In *Robert Burns In Other Tongues* (1896) William Jack has made a critical comparison of several poems in various languages. The English translations of William Kean Seymour, however, suggest that to translate the colloquial speed and texture of Burns's Scots satires is virtually an impossibility, and that often the content removed in this way from its proper context either seems thin or so different from the original as hardly to reflect the spirit of Burns at all.

The translations which have achieved the widest circulation are, of course, the Russian translations of Samuel Marshak.

Turnbull, Gavin

Employed in a carpet factory at Kilmarnock, Turnbull wrote verses which included an ode to David Sillar, based on the style of Burns's 'Epistle to Davie'. Later, he accompanied his family to Glasgow, where he worked as a labourer. In 1789, he published from the press of David Niven, a Glasgow publisher, his *Poetical Essays*. This book included a poem, 'The Bard', inscribed to Mr R(obert) B(urns). Burns, incidentally, had some difficulty in transmitting the money for five of the six copies he distributed of the book by his 'brother Poet'.

Turnbull abandoned labouring and turned to the stage, becoming a member of Sutherland's Company at Dumfries. Burns was a frequent visitor to the theatre, and writing to George Thomson in October 1793, commended to him Turnbull's songs—'O condescend, dear Charming Maid' to the air 'John Anderson, My Jo', 'The Nightingale' and 'Laura'. The opening stanzas of 'The Nightingale' give a fair idea of Turnbull's entirely conventional Augustan style:

'Thou sweetest minstrel of the grove
    That ever tried the plaintive strain,
Awake thy tender tale of love,
    And soothe a poor forsaken swain;
Who though the Muses deign to aid,
    And teach him smoothly to
                              complain;

Yet Delia, charming, cruel maid
  Is deaf to her forsaken swain.'

Thomson replied: 'Your friend Mr
Turnbull's songs have doubtless considerable merit, and, as you have the command
of his manuscripts, I hope you will find
some that will answer as English songs, to
the airs yet unprovided.'

Turnbull married an actress, and with
her emigrated to America, where all
trace of them has been lost.

Turner, Andrew (b. 1749)
'A vain coxcomb of an English commercial
traveller', who had the ambition to be
known as a poet. He tried to patronise
the 'ploughman' poet over a bottle of
wine in the King's Arms, Dumfries. Burns
was asked by his friends, whose party had
been interrupted by Turner, to give an
example of his impromptu versifying. On
hearing the traveller's name and age,
Burns immediately produced the following
epitaph:

'In Se'enteen Hunder'n Forty-nine
The Deil gat stuff to mak a swine,
  An' coost it in a corner;
But wilily he chang'd his plan,
An' shap'd it something like a man,
  An' ca'd it Andrew Turner.'

Tytler, Alexander Fraser (1747–1813)
Eldest son of William Tytler of Woodhouselee. He was educated at Edinburgh
High School and Edinburgh University,
where he studied law. He was called to the
bar in 1770. He became Joint Professor of
Universal History in his Alma Mater with
John Pringle, and six years later, sole
Professor. Like his father, he was very
interested in Burns's work, and when
'Tam o' Shanter' appeared in the *Edinburgh
Magazine*, and in Grose's *Antiquities*, he
wrote to the poet offering him several
suggestions, including that of removing
the lines beginning, 'Three lawyers' tongues turn'd inside out', which Burns
agreed to do.

Tytler also gave Burns some excellent
advice. 'Go on,' he urged, 'write more
tales in the same style—you will eclipse
Prior and La Fontaine; for with equal wit,
equal power of numbers and equal naivete
of expression, you have a bolder and more
vigorous imagination.'

Burns replied from Ellisland in April
1791, the first letter he had written since he
broke his right arm in a fall from his horse:

'Your approbation, Sir, has given me
such additional spirits to persevere in this
species of poetic composition, that I am
already resolving two or three stories in
my fancy. If I can bring these floating
ideas to bear any kind of embodied form,
it will give me an additional opportunity
of assuring you much I have the honor to
be, and etc.'

Unfortunately, circumstances, and an
apparent decline in Burns's capacity for
sustained creative effort, prevented these
dreams from being realised.

Tytler appears to have corrected the
proofs of the two volumes of the Edinburgh Edition of 1793. Burns, thanking
him in a letter of 6th December 1792,
said: 'I am much indebted to you for
taking the trouble of correcting the Press-
work', when he sent 'another, and my
last, parcel of manuscript'.

Tytler became Judge-Advocate in 1790.
Two years later, he succeeded to his father's
estate, and in 1802, became a Lord of
Session, with the title of Lord Woodhouselee.

An occasional versifier, he was also the
author of several books, among them
*Decisions of the Court of Session, Elements
of German History* and *The Life of Lord
Kames*.

Tytler, James (1747–1805)
Son of the Reverend George Tytler, he
studied medicine but was unsuccessful in
setting up a practice. He got himself into
debt, and only escaped being arrested by
taking sanctuary at Holyrood Abbey,
where he wrote a ballad called 'The

Pleasures of the Abbey'. He edited the second and third editions of the *Encyclopaedia Britannica* for some years, and Burns made use of him in compiling the *Scots Musical Museum*. Tytler himself contributed several songs to this collection, including 'The Young Man's Dream', and two others, based on older songs, 'I hae laid a herring in saut', and 'The Bonnie Brucket Lassie'. Like Burns, too, Tytler clearly had access to the manuscript collection of David Herd. Burns wrote in his Commonplace Book about 'The Bonnie Brucket Lass'; 'The two first lines of this song are all of it that is old. The rest of the song, as well as those songs in the *Museum* marked T, are the works of an obscure, tippling, but extraordinary body of the name of Tytler, commonly known by the name of "Balloon Tytler", from his having projected a balloon, a mortal who, though he drudges about Edinburgh as a common printer, with leaky shoes, a sky-lighted hat, and knee-buckles as unlike as George-by-the-Grace-of-God and Solomon-the-Son-of-David; yet that same unknown drunken mortal is author and compiler of three-fourths of Elliot's pompous *Encyclopaedia Britannica*, which he composed at half-a-guinea a week.'

Tytler was accidentally drowned in a clay-pit near Salem.

Tytler of Woodhouselee, William (1711-92)

Son of a Writer to the Signet and himself a W.S. The Laird of Woodhouselee, he helped Johnson with the first volumes of the *Museum*, and afterwards assisted Burns to collect the verses for later volumes. Burns sent him a copy of the Miers silhouette portrait of himself, with his Jacobite verses, beginning, 'Reverend defender of beauteous Stuart'. Besides being a Jacobite, Tytler was an enthusiastic supporter of Scottish music, and also encouraged George Thomson to begin his collection. A historian and antiquary, he contributed papers to *The Antiquarian Transactions*, but is best known for his *An Historical and Critical Enquiry into the evidence . . . against Mary Queen of Scots* (1760), a defence of the Queen against the attacks of Tytler's contemporaries, Robertson and Hume. He also edited *The Poetical Remains of James I of Scotland*, and was thus largely responsible for bringing to eighteenth-century notice the merits of *The King's Quair*. His son, Alexander Fraser Tytler, was also an admirer of Burns.

U

Urbani, Pietro (1749–1816)

Born in Milan, he came to London as a young man. He went to Glasgow in 1780, and to Edinburgh in 1784, singing Scots songs, teaching and composing. In 1785, an opera of his, *The Siege of Gibraltar*, was produced in Edinburgh. Between 1792 and 1794, Urbani published his *Selection of Scots Songs . . . Improved and with Simple and Adapted Graces*, which Henry Farmer, in his *History of Music in Scotland*, calls 'a highly meritorious piece of work, which was, in addition, scored for strings'. George Thomson, his rival editor, called it 'a water-gruel collection'. In 1795, Urbani went into the music publishing business in earnest, with a partner, as Urbani and Liston, at 10 Princes Street, Edinburgh. But between 1806 and 1809, the business failed, and Urbani, who had already lost money trying unsuccessfully to promote the oratorios of Handel in Edinburgh, went to Dublin, where he died destitute.

Burns seems first to have met Urbani in 1793, and again at Lord Selkirk's estate at St Mary's Isle, during the Galloway Tour of 1794. (The poet must certainly have heard of him during his winter in Edinburgh.) At any rate, in April 1793, Burns was sending to Maria Riddell 'a new Song, which I have this moment rec^d. from Urbani'. Thomson was asked: 'Is, Whistle and I'll come to you, my lad, one of your airs? I admire it much; and yesterday, I set the following verses to it. Urbani, whom I have met with here, begged them of me, as he admires the air much; but as I understand that he looks with rather an evil eye on your WORK, I did not chuse to comply. However, if the song does not suit your taste, I may possibly send it him. He is, entre nous, a narrow, contracted creature; but he sings so delightfully, that

whatever he introduces at your concert, must have immediate celebrity.' On 28th August 1793, when Burns sent Thomson 'Scots Wha Hae', he put a postscript to the letter: 'I shewed the air to Urbani, who was highly pleased with it, and begged me to make soft verses for it; but I had no idea of giving myself any trouble on the subject, till the accidental recollection of that glorious struggle for Freedom, associated with the glowing ideas of some other struggles *not quite so ancient*, roused my rhyming mania.'

'Soft verses', indeed!

In a long letter written to Thomson in September, Burns said, of 'Todlin Hame': 'Urbani mentioned an idea of his, which has long been mine; that this air is highly susceptible of pathos. . . . I pointed out some verses that were unknown to him, to give them a trial for celebrity. Clarke told me what a creature he is, but if he will bring any more of our tunes from darkness into light, I would be pleased.'

Johnson was more accommodating to Urbani than was Thomson. Burns wrote to Johnson on 29th June 1794; 'Pray, will you let me know how many, and what are the songs Urbani has borrowed from your Museum.'

The friendship between Burns and Urbani came to an end a few months later. Urbani, encouraged, no doubt, by his borrowings from the *Museum*, apparently told Alexander Cunningham that he had got the poet to collaborate fully with him. From Dumfries, Burns wrote angrily to Cunningham in the autumn of 1794: 'Urbani has told a damned falsehood. I made no engagements or connections with him whatever—after he and I had met at L^d. Selkirk's, we lived together three or four days in this town, and had a great deal of converse about our Scots Songs. I translated a verse of an *Italian* song for him, or rather made an English verse to suit his rhythm, and added two verses which had been already published in Johnson's Museum. I likewise gave him a simple old Scots song which I had pickt up in this country, which he had promised to set in a suitable manner. I would not even have given him this, had there been any of Mr Thomson's airs, *suitable to it*, unoccupied. I shall give you the song on the other page. Urbani requested me to lend him a hand now and then in his work —I told him, and told him truly, that such was my enthusiasm for the subject, had I met with him previous to my acquaintance with Mr Thomson, I would most gladly have lent him any assistance in my power, but that now, untill Mr T——'s publication was finished, I could not promise anything: however, that at a future period, when the humour was on me, I would chearfully write a song for him. He hinted, I remember, something about using my name in an advertisement, which I *expressly* forbade. One thing he may mean; Johnson, I know, has given him full permission to anything I have written in the Museum. Beyond that, he had no right to expect, and for his impudence, shall never receive any assistance from me.'

So ended Burns's friendship with Urbani. The song 'on the other page' was 'O my Love's like the red, red rose', which, Burns told Cunningham, was the only 'species' of song about which he and Thomson disagreed: 'What to me appears the simple and the wild, to him, and I suspect to you likewise, will be looked on as the ludicrous and the absurd.'

The song first appeared in Urbani's *Scots Songs*, 1794, to an original tune. In his publication, Urbani explained that: '. . . the words of the RED, RED ROSE were obligingly given to him by a celebrated Scots Poet, who was so struck with them when sung by a country girl that he wrote them down, and, not being pleased with the air, begged the Author to set them to Music in the style of a Scots Tune, which he has done accordingly.'

The first three stanzas of the song appeared in the *Museum*, 1797, to the Gow tune, 'Major Graham', the tune Burns himself specified. It also appeared in Thomson's *Original Scottish Airs*, 1799, 'improved' by that insensitive editor to fit Marshall's 'Wishaw's Favorite', a tune of double measure (i.e. 'And fare thee weel awhile' became 'And fare thee weel a little while'!)

The 'Red, Red Rose', however, only achieved popularity when matched to 'Low down in the Broom', an air which first appeared in the *Caledonian Pocket Companion*. Burns's words and the air 'Low down in the Broom' were first brought together by the Paisley composer and editor, Robert Archibald Smith, in his *Scottish Minstrel*, published in 1821.

W

Walker, Josiah (1761–1831)
Josiah was the youngest son of the Reverend Thomas Walker, minister of Dundonald, Ayrshire, by his third wife, Anne Shaw. He graduated at Edinburgh University, and was for seven years a private tutor in Edinburgh. In 1787, he became tutor to the fifth Duke of Athole's nine-year-old son, the Marquis of Tulibardine, accompanying the boy to Eton, where the Marquis died in 1796.

A friend in Edinburgh wrote to Walker about: '. . . the sensation then created in that city by a bard of my native country, and promised to bring me his volume on a subsequent visit. By his praise of its contents my expectations were very moderately excited, as in my own mind I instantly classed the poetical ploughman with the poetical milkmaids and thrashers of England, of whose productions I was no violent admirer . . . thus prepared, the poems were put into my hands and before finishing a page I experienced emotions of surprise and delight of which I had never been so conscious before. The language that I had begun to despise, as fit for nothing but colloquial vulgarity, seemed to be transfigured by the sorcery of genius into the genuine language of poetry. It expressed every idea with a brevity and force, and bent itself to every subject with a pliancy in which the most of languages too often fail. Every line awakened a train of associations; every phrase struck a note which led the mind to perform the accompaniment. On every page the stamp of genius was impressed.'

Walker was introduced to Burns in Edinburgh by Dr Blacklock, and met the poet again at Athole House, in 1787, the latter visit producing the only two extant letters from the poet to the tutor. In one of them, Burns politely rejects a piece of Walker's criticism.

Walker visited Burns at Dumfries for a couple of days in November 1795, just before the poet entered the six-months decline which ended in his death from heart disease.

In 1811, Walker wrote a critical memoir of Burns as prefix to an edition of his poems. It is not without some penetrating observations, but the general tone employed by the author is one of condescension. Walker's tale of taking Burns to the Globe Inn at Dumfries, and of the poet firing off epigrams and laying down the law in between intervals of calling for more drink, could be explained either by the state of Burns's health then, or merely by Walker. Ferguson goes so far as to say: '. . . one may surmise that Burns's abrupt and decisive manner was due to irritation at being patronised by an ass.'

In 1796, on the death of his pupil, Walker became Collector of Customs at Perth, and later edited the *Perth Courier*. In 1815, he became Professor of Humanity at Glasgow University. He died in Glasgow.

Walker's recollection of Burns is as follows:

'I was not much struck with his first appearance, as I had previously heard it described. His person, though strong and well knit, and much superior to what might be expected in a ploughman, was still rather coarse in its outline. His stature, from want of setting up, appeared to be only of the middle size, but was rather above it. His motions were firm and decided, and though without any pretensions to grace, were at the same time so free from clownish constraint, as to shew that he had not always been confined to the society of his profession. His countenance was not of that elegant cast which is most frequent among the upper ranks, but it was manly and intelligent, and marked by a thoughtful gravity which shaded at times into sternness. In his large dark eye the most striking index of his genius resided. It was full of mind, and would have been singularly expressive, under the management of one who could employ it with more art, for the purpose of expression.

'He was plainly, but properly dressed, in a style midway between the holiday costume of a farmer and that of the company with which he now associated. His black hair, without powder, at a time when it was very generally worn, was tied behind, and spread upon his forehead. Upon the whole, from his person, physiognomy, and dress, had I met him near a seaport, and been required to guess his condition, I should have probably conjectured him to be the master of a merchant vessel of the most respectable class.

'In no part of his manner was there the slightest degree of affectation; nor could a stranger have suspected, from anything in his behaviour or conversation, that he had been for some months the favourite of all the fashionable circles of a metropolis.

'In conversation he was powerful. His conceptions and expression were of corresponding vigour, and on all subjects were as remote as possible from commonplaces. Though somewhat authoritative, it was in a way which gave little offence, and was readily imputed to his inexperience in those modes of smoothing dissent and softening assertion which are important characteristics of polished manners. After breakfast I requested him to communicate some of his unpublished pieces . . . I paid particular attention to his recitation, which was plain, slow, articulate, and forcible, but without any eloquence or art. He did not always lay the emphasis with propriety, nor did he humour the sentiment by the variations of his voice. He was standing, during the time, with his face towards the window, to which, and not to his auditors, he directed his eye; thus depriving himself of any additional effect which the language of his composition might have borrowed from the language of his countenance. In this he resembled the generality of singers in ordinary company, who, to shun any charge of affectation, withdraw all meaning from their features, and lose the advantage by which vocal performers on the stage augment the impression and give energy to the sentiment of the song.

'The day after my first introduction to Burns, I supped in company with him at Dr Blair's. The other guests were very few, and as each had been invited chiefly to have an opportunity of meeting with the poet, the doctor endeavoured to draw him out, and to make him the central figure of the group.

'Though he therefore furnished the greatest proportion of the conversation, he did no more than what he saw evidently was expected. Men of genius have often been taxed with a proneness to commit blunders in company, from that ignorance or negligence of the laws of conversation which must be imputed to the absorption of their thoughts in a favourite subject, or to the want of that daily practice in attending to the petty modes of behaviour which is incompatible with a studious life. From singularities of this sort Burns was unusually free; yet on the present occasion he made a more awkward slip than any that are reported of the poets or mathematicians most noted for absence. Being asked from which of the public places he had received the greatest gratification, he named the High Church, but gave the preference as a preacher to the colleague of our worthy entertainer, whose celebrity rested on his pulpit eloquence, in a tone so pointed and decisive, as to throw the whole company into the most foolish embarrassment. The doctor, indeed, with becoming self-command, endeavoured to relieve the rest by cordially seconding the encomium so injudiciously introduced; but this did not prevent the conversation from labouring under that compulsory effort which was unavoidable, while the thoughts of all were full of the only subject on which it was improper to speak. Of this blunder he shewed the return of good sense by making no attempt to repair it. His secret mortification was indeed so great, that he never mentioned the circumstance until many years after, when he told me that his silence had proceeded from the pain which he felt in recalling it to his memory.

'About the end of October, I called for him at the house of a friend, whose daughter, though not more than twelve, was a considerable proficient in music. I found him seated by the harpsichord of this young lady, listening with the keenest interest to his own verses, which she sung and accompanied, and adjusting them to the music by repeated trials of the effect. In this occupation he was so totally absorbed, that it was difficult to draw his attention from it for a moment; and it is to the enthusiasm which the nature of his undertaking inspired, that the excellence of its execution must be ascribed.'

Walker, Thomas (d. c. 1812)

A tailor who lived at Pool, near Ochiltree, and a friend of the schoolmaster William Simson. Walker wrote verses, and sent a long rhyming epistle to Burns hoping to elicit an epistle in reply. But the poet took no notice of him, so, when the Kilmarnock Edition appeared, Walker wrote Burns again, this time attacking his morals. Burns responded with the 'Reply to a Triming Epistle, received from a Tailor'. The manuscript of Walker's verses, which were printed by Stewart, shows that Simson had a hand in its composition. The authenticity of Burns's reply has also been questioned, and by some attributed to Simson; but it is now generally accepted as genuine and printed in collected editions of Burns's work.

Wallace of Riccarton, Adam

Son of Sir Richard Wallace and a cousin of William Wallace, the preserver of Scottish independence.

In 'The Vision', Burns described him as 'bold Richardton'.

Wallace, Mr

A young lawyer in Dumfries, who admired Burns greatly, and who did much to help the poet's family after Burns's death.

Wallace, Sir John, Laird of Craigie

Called by Burns in 'The Vision': 'the chief, on Sark, who glorious fell in high command.' This Wallace was said to be second-in-command under Douglas, Earl of Ormond, at the battle of 1448, fought on the banks of the Sark. The victory over the English which ensued was largely due to the bravery of the Laird of Craigie, who three months later died of his wounds, at Craigie Castle.

He represented the Riccarton line of Wallace.

Wallace, Sir William (c. 1270–1305)

Second son of Sir Malcolm Wallace of Elderslie and Auchinbothie, in Renfrewshire. He was probably educated by an uncle, who may have been a parson, at Dunipace, in Stirlingshire, and later at Dundee. Here, the killing of an Englishman named Selby, in response to an insult, is said to have caused Wallace to be outlawed, and so driven into rebellion against the English. Wallace gathered a band of followers around him, including Sir Andrew Moray, Sir John de Graham, Douglas the Hardy and others, and they attacked the English justiciar, who was holding court at Scone. In revenge for the slaughter by the English of Wallace's uncle, Sir Ronald Crawford, Wallace and his followers burned the Barns of Ayr, the quarters of the English soldiers.

Edward I then sent a force under Sir Henry Percy and Sir Robert Clifford against Wallace. All the nobles except Sir Andrew Moray then deserted Wallace, signing the Treaty of Irvine. Wallace retired north, and in spite of the barons' desertion was soon at the head of a large army which recovered nearly all the fortresses the English then held north of the Forth. While besieging Dundee, Wallace learned that an English army, led by Surrey and Cressingham, was marching northwards. Wallace moved south to meet it, and descended on it crossing the bridge over the Forth by Stirling on 11th September 1297. When the English troops were half over, Wallace attacked, routing his opponents and killing many, among them Cressingham. Sir Andrew Moray was killed on the Scots side, but the Scots pursued the English to Berwick and virtually drove them out of Scotland.

Wallace had by now been given the title of Guardian of Scotland. Edward, in Flanders at the time, hurried back home, and in July 1290, entered Scotland at the head of a great army. The untrustworthy Scots nobles again deserted Wallace's standard, and on 22nd July 1298, after a vigorous battle, the Scots were defeated near Falkirk, Sir John de Graham being among the slain.

Wallace resigned his Guardianship, returned to predatory war against the English, paid a visit to France, and on 5th April 1325 was taken by the English at Robroyston, aided by the treachery of Sir John Menteith. Wallace was sent through Dumbarton south to London, where, on 22nd August, he was impeached as a traitor to a king to whom, as Wallace pointed out, he had never sworn allegiance, and the same day barbarously executed.

However, Wallace did not die in vain, for his actions and his fate played some part in moving Robert the Bruce to end his vacillations, and thereby set in course the train of events which ended at Bannock-burn, and the freeing of the Scots from forcible English domination.

Wallace's Dundee friend, John Blair is said to have written a life of this national hero of Scotland. The life by Blair was apparently used by the Lothian writer Henry the Minstrel (d. 1492), often styled 'Blind Harry', whose poem The Actis and Deidis of . . . Schir William Wallace collected all the facts and legends by then surrounding Wallace's exploits, magnifying and mythifying them over some twelve thousand lines of somewhat pedestrian heroic couplets.

In 1722 William Hamilton of Gilbert-field (1665?–1751), one of the minor poets of the Eighteenth Century Revival, put Blind Harry's Wallace into English. This was the version of the poem with which Burns was familiar.

In his autobiographical letter to Dr Moore, Burns said 'The two first books I ever read in private, and which gave me more pleasure than any two books I ever read again, were, the life of Hannibal and the history of Sir William Wallace . . . The story of Wallace poured a Scottish prejudice in my veins which will boil along there till the flood-gates of life shut in eternal rest.'

Mrs Dunlop, daughter of Sir Thomas Wallace of Craigie, touched Burns's 'darling heart-chord' by taking note of his praise of her ancestor. Thereafter, the patriot was for Burns 'GLORIOUS WALLACE, the SAVIOUR of his Country', the scenes of whose exploits he longed to visit.

He wrote to Robert Muir from Stirling on 26th August 1787:

'I knelt at the tomb of Sir John the Graham, the gallant friend of the immortal Wallace; and two hours ago I said a fervent prayer for Old Caledonia over the hole in the blue whinstone, where Robert de Bruce fixed his royal standard on the banks of Bannockburn.'

His reverence for Wallace's share of the War of Independence no doubt helped to inspire 'Scots Wha Hae'. It also produced Burns's versifications of an episode from Wallace, the ballad-like song 'Gude Wallace', based on a chap-book version of about 1750. The air to which it is set in the Museum, 1796, has not been traced else-where.

Wallace Tower, Ayr
It was an old baronial tower at the corner

of High Street and Mill Vennel, which contained a clock. The clock is referred to in Burns's poem 'The Brigs of Ayr'. The original tower was owned by the Cathcarts of Corbieston, but was acquired by the Town Council in 1673. It is not known how it came to be called the Wallace Tower. In 1834 the first tower was replaced by the present Gothic one, 113 feet high with a statue of Wallace in front of it.

Warton, Thomas (1728–90)

Son of the Vicar of Basingstoke, he graduated at Trinity College Oxford, and became a fellow. He also entered the Church and held various livings, but did not take his clerical duties very seriously. In 1757, he became Professor of Poetry at Oxford, a post he held for ten years. In 1785, he became Camden Professor of History and Poet Laureate. In this latter capacity, he wrote an Ode beginning:

'When freedom nursed her native fire
In ancient Greece and ruled the lyre,
Her bards, disdainful, from the
                                   tyrants brow,
The tinsel gifts of flattery tore
But paid to guiltless power their
                          willing vow. . . . ,

for 4th June 1786, George III's birthday. This prompted Burns to write 'A Dream'. Warton is best known now for the first three volumes of his *History of English Poetry* (which he never completed), and his critical edition of Milton's early works. His verse appealed to a considerable audience in his day. Wordsworth, Coleridge, Hazlitt, and Charles Lamb have all gone on record with favourable encomiums. But nowadays we might be more inclined to agree with Christopher North, who said of Warton that 'the gods had made him poetical, but not a poet'.

Washington, George (1732–99)

In his 'Address of Beelzebub', Burns refers to the emigrating Highlanders as perhaps

having 'Some Washington' to 'head them'.

George Washington was general in command of the American forces in the War of Independence. Unlike some generals, he was also a fine statesman. He became the first President of the United States after the American War of Independence, and was largely responsible for the American Constitution. Burns's specifications for a Highland leader were thus nothing if not ambitious!

Watson Manuscript

A collection of Burns's holograph poems and letters, now part of the collection in the National Library of Scotland.

Watt, David (1756 1823)

Miller of Doon-foot Mill, a school-fellow of Burns at Alloway, and the last person to be baptised in Alloway Kirk.

Webster, The Reverend Dr

An Edinburgh clergyman in the Scottish Episcopal Church from whom Burns borrowed a Latin publication by the Rev. John Skinner, for his host in Edinburgh, William Cruikshank, in February 1788.

Welsh

Mentioned by Burns in his 'Second Epistle to Robert Graham Esq. of Fintry, on the Election for the Dumfries string of Boroughs, Anno 1790'. He was the man 'who never flinch'd his ground'. A footnote in the Chambers-Wallace edition claims him to have been 'Sheriff of the County'. According to Sir James Fergusson, however, there was no Sheriff of Dumfriesshire of that name.

Wentworth, Charles Watson, Marquis of Rockingham (1730–82)

Opposed North's colonial policy and succeeded him as Prime Minister in 1782, but died on 1st July that year, hence Burns's reference to him in 'A Fragment' as taking 'up the game, Till Death did on him ca', man'.

Whigham, Edward (1750–1823)

Keeper of the Queensberry Arms Inn at Sanquhar, a Bailie when Burns met him on the poet's first journey into Nithsdale, and Provost of the town from 1793 to 1800. Burns described 'the landlord and landlady' as 'my particular acquaintances'. He certainly gave Mrs Whigham copies of one or two of his poems.

It was with Whigham that Burns was drinking at the Queensberry Arms on a Saturday in January 1789, when the cortège of Mrs Oswald of Auchencruive arrived, and Burns was forced to ride on a further twelve miles to the next inn.

It may well have been Whigham who was responsible for Burns being made an honorary burgess and freeman of Sanquhar on 23rd December 1794.

Whigham, on at least one occasion, was asked by Burns to procure him copies of some airs he wanted.

Whistle', 'The

See Fergusson, Alexander.

White, The Reverend Hugh

Burns referred to him in his letter to his cousin in Montrose of 3rd August 1784 (see Buchanites). He was a member of the 'Relief' sect of Presbyterians, and a preacher in Irvine. In 1782, he gave a service near Glasgow, which Mrs Elspat Buchan attended, and from this sprang his association with the Buchanites. In 1783 he was deposed by his Presbytery, after a charge of heresy had been brought against him. He published a Divine Dictionary which set forth the beliefs of the sect. When Mrs Buchan left Irvine, he accompanied her to the farm of New Cample in Galloway. In 1792, after her death, he gave up his beliefs, and emigrated along with some other followers, to America, where he became a teacher in Virginia, preaching to a few Universalists, but without mentioning 'any of his former whimsical doctrines'. The last Buchanite died in 1848.

White, Thomas (1758–1825)

A Hexham, Northumberland man, who taught in Dumfries Academy for forty years, first as mathematics master, and then as rector. He was a second lieutenant in the Dumfriesshire Volunteers. Burns presented him with a copy of the 1793 Edinburgh Edition of his Poems, and with a copy of Voltaire's La Pucelle, which is still extant.

White is supposed to have testified to the interest Burns took in his children's schooling. In White's family, there ran the tradition that Burns was a guest at White's house every Saturday. He did much to promote interest in Burns's work, and remained a friend even in the last months when the poet's revolutionary opinions had alienated many of his other friends. On Burns's death, White produced in verse 'A Tribute to the Memory of Burns'. He himself lies buried in St Michael's Churchyard, Dumfries, not far from Burns's grave. A contemporary described him as 'This excellent man and profound mathematician . . . as a man, he has not left an honester behind him'.

White corresponded regularly with another mathematician, Dr Olinthus Gregory, who said of him: 'His abilities, both as a speculative and as a practical mathematician, were of no common order.'

Whitefoord Arms

An inn in Mauchline, whose proprietor was John Dove or Dow, nicknamed by his patrons 'Johnnie Doo'. It was situated on the Cowgate, which is now Castle Street, opposite the parish church. It was the meeting place of 'The Court of Equity', a secret bachelors' club which met: 'to search out, report, and discuss the merits and demerits of the many scandals that crop up from time to time in the village', and of which Burns was 'Perpetual President'. See Court of Equity.

The old inn has been replaced by a later building bearing the legend:

'This is the house, though built anew
Where Burns cam' weary frae the
                              pleugh
To hae a crack wi' Johnnie Doo
  On nights at e'en,
And whiles to taste the mountain dew
  Wi' bonnie Jean.'

Whitefoord, Sir John (1734–1803)

Third Baronet of Blairquhan, an agricultural improver, master of St James's Masonic Lodge, Tarbolton, and a friend of the Earl of Glencairn. John Kay described him as 'a remarkably smart, active little man'. He heired the estate of Ballochmyle, but owing to his heavy losses as a shareholder in the Douglas, Heron and Company Bank disaster, he was forced to sell to the Alexander family in 1788.

Writing to Whitefoord on 1st December 1786, soon after he arrived in Edinburgh, Burns said, apropos his own position: 'the situation of poets is generally such, to a proverb, as may, in some measure, palliate that prostitution of heart and talents they have at times been guilty of. I do not think prodigality is, by any means, a necessary concomitant of a poetic turn, but I believe a careless, indolent attention to economy is almost inseparable from it; then there must be in the heart of every bard of Nature's making, a certain modest sensibility, mixed with a kind of pride, that will ever keep him out of the way of those windfalls of fortune which frequently light on hardy impudence and foot-licking servility. It is not easy to imagine a more helpless state than his whose poetic fancy unfits him for the world, and whose character as a scholar gives him some pretensions to the politesse of life—yet is as poor as I am.'

The advice he got from Whitefoord was that 'your character as a man (forgive my reversing your order) as well as a poet, entitles you, I think, to the assistance of every inhabitant of Ayrshire . . . If a sum could be raised by subscription for a second edition of your poems . . . lay it out in the stocking of a small farm,' advice which, of course, Burns took.

'Farewell to Ballochmyle' was written by the poet when the estate was sold. He Enclosed his 'Lament for James, Earl of Glencairn' with the 'Lines to Sir John Whitefoord Bart', Whitefoord having been a friend of the Earl of Glencairn. The Whitefoord family moved to Edinburgh after Ballochmyle was sold, and there Burns also visited them. Mary Anne Whitefoord, Whitefoord's eldest daughter, was the Maria the of 'Farewell to Ballochmyle'. Burns was also friendly with Mary's brother, John.

Sir John's brother Caleb was a once well-known wit and satiric versifier, whom Goldsmith described in 'The Retaliation' as 'the best natured man with the worst-natured muse'.

Incidentally, a predecessor of Sir John's, Colonel Allan Whitefoord, is supposed to have provided Sir Walter Scott with the prototype of Colonel Talbot in *Waverley*.

Whitefoord, Mary Anne

The Maria of the autumn song 'Farewell to Ballochmyle', and the eldest of Sir John Whitefoord's four daughters. She married the grandson of the fifth Lord Cranstoun, Henry Kerr Cranstoun. Her sister-in-law, Helen D'Arcy, married Professor Dugald Stewart, who owned the 'Catrine Woods' and the 'Catrine Lea' mentioned in the song. They marched with the estate of Ballochmyle, which had for many years been owned by the Whitefoord family until 1785, when the consequences of the failure of the Ayr Bank, of which Whitefoord was a partner, forced him to sell them.

The song appeared in the *Scots Musical Museum* to the tune 'The Braes O'Ballochmyle,' composed by Allan Masterton.

Whyte, James (1732–1822)

A retired Jamaican planter who owned Over Stroguhan, about two miles from

Dunscore parish church. Before that he lived in Glaisnock, near Cumnock, and may well be the Mr Whyte referred to in Burns's letter to 'Mons. James Smith, Mauchline', dated 'Mosgiel, Monday morning, 1786'. The passage reads: 'I found the doctor with a Mr and Mrs White, both Jamaicans, and they have deranged my plans altogether'. 'The doctor' was Dr Douglas of Ayr, and what the Jamaican Whytes had apparently done was to express horror at Burns's intention to land at a port from which he would have to make an extra two-hundred-mile journey across disease-ridden country to reach the estate in Jamaica where he proposed to take employment as book-keeper. They advised Burns not to sail on the *Nancy* from Greenock, but on the *Bell*, due to leave Greenock later, bound for Kingston.

Burns, of course, soon afterwards abandoned all intention of emigrating to Jamaica.

William Henry, Prince, Duke of Clarence, later William IV (1765–1837)

Third son of George III, he was educated for the Navy. He 'formed a connection' with Mrs Jordan, an actress, to whom he remained faithful for twenty years. Burns referred to them both in 'A Dream':

'Young, royal "tarry-breeks", I learn
Ye've lately come athwart her;
A glorious galley, stem and stern,
Weel rigg'd for Venus' barter.'

The death of Princess Charlotte, heiress to the throne, forced him to break with Mrs Jordan, and marry Adelaide of Saxe-Meiningen in 1818. In 1793, when war was declared against Republican France, Prince William was unable to get a command, so he turned to politics and support-ed the Prince of Wales and the Duke of York, in opposition to the King, his father. He became William IV in 1830.

N*

Williams, Helen Maria (1762–1827)

An English authoress, born in London, who spent her early years in Berwick. She served Dr Moore for a time as an aman-uensis. On reading Burns's 'To a Mountain Daisy', she composed a sonnet in the poet's honour. On 25th June 1787, Dr Moore forwarded the sonnet, which contains the injunction:

'Scotia! from rude afflictions shield
                                      thy Bard,
His Heav'n taught numbers Fame
                             herself will guard.'

On hearing of Burns's approval of it, she replied that 'a much less portion of applause' from him would have been 'gratifying'.

In 1790 she settled in Paris. Like Burns an early supporter of the French Revolut-ion, she upheld the Girondists, and was imprisoned from the fall of the Girondists until the death of Robespierre. She later condemned the Revolutionaries, and up-held the Bourbon cause.

She published *Julia*, a novel, in 1790, and translated *Paul and Virginia*. Her poem *The Slave Trade*, appeared in 1788. Burns read this poem and sent her a long letter of criticism from Ellisland in August 1789. She also wrote several books on France.

She died in Paris.

Williamson, The Reverend David (c. 1630–1706)

A Covenanting minister denounced as a rebel on 6th July 1674 for holding con-venticles, and intercommuned on 6th August the following year. After a final indulgence granted to the Church in 1687, he returned to Edinburgh where a meeting-house was erected for him in the village then known as Water of Leith. However, he was arrested again the following February, his name having been discovered in papers belonging to the Covenanting leader Renwick, though released in a fort-night, the date of the reference being found to be within the period covered by his indemnity. Some time afterwards, he was arrested for refusing to pray for the Prince of Wales, but again released. He was restored to his Lothian parish by the General Assembly of 1690, the first to meet after what Burns called 'the glorious Revolution,' and was one of the Commissioners sent to London to congratulate William of Orange on his accession to the throne. He became Moderator to the General Assembly in March 1702, but died the following August.

His matrimonial adventures were no less robust than his professional career. He was married seven times and had at least nine children.

The manner of his wooing of his second wife, Jean, daughter of the Kerrs of Cherrytrees, was celebrated in a song 'Dainty Davy'. The event occurred about 1690, and in Burns's words in his *Notes on Scots Song*, Williamson 'begat the daughter of Lady Cherrytrees with child, while a party of dragoons was searching her house to apprehend him for being an adherent of the Solemn League and Covenant. The pious woman had put a lady's night-cap on him . . . and passed him to the soldiery as . . . her daughter's bed-fellow.'

Burns's reference to the fiddler in 'The Jolly Beggars' 'shoring' (or offering) 'Dainty Davie' is thus a reference to Williamson's sexual member, the prowess of which is also commemorated in numerous lampoons to be found in Maidment's *A Packet of Pestilent Pasquils* (1688).

Williamson, James or John Brown (d. 1802)

The leading actor in the dramatic company which occasionally played behind the George Inn in Dumfries. The *Burns Chronicle* for 1948 alleges that the man's name was John Brown (not James as Chambers says), 'that he married Louisa Fontenelle (d. 1800) (*see* **Fontenelle, Louisa**), and that both emigrated to America. Like Burns, he had been admitted to the Riddell social circle at Woodley Park. When the company

were playing at Whitehaven, the 'bad Earl of Lonsdale' imprisoned the entire company as vagrants. Burns—if the author of the piece was indeed Burns—took the opportunity of hitting back at Maria Riddell, who had broken off her friendship with him, and at the Earl, whom he disliked, by writing his 'Epistle from Esopus to Maria' (Aesopus was the most famous tragic actor in Cicero's Rome):

'Why Lonsdale, thus thy wrath on
                              vagrants pour?
Must earth no rascal save thyself
                              endure?
Must thou alone in guilt immortal
                              swell
And make a vast monopoly of Hell?
Thou know'st the Virtues cannot hate
                              thee worse:
The vices also, must they club their
                              curse?
Or must no tiny sin to others fall,
Because thy guilt's supreme enough
                              for all?

'Maria, send me, too, thy griefs and
                              cares,
In all of thee sure thy Esopus shares;
As thou at all mankind the flag
                              unfurls,
Who on my fair one Satire's ven-
                              geance hurls!
Who calls thee pert, affected, vain
                              coquette,
A wit in folly and a fool in wit!
Who says that "fool" alone is not thy
                              due,
And quotes thy treacheries to prove
                              it true?'

Wilson, Agnes

Dr A. Edgar in his social history, *Old Church Life in Scotland*, alleged that Agnes Wilson was a vagrant woman, and the 'tozie drab' referred to in 'The Jolly Beggars'. She had a bad reputation, and there is a reference to her in a Mauchline Kirk-Session minute dated 6th March 1786 'as being of lewd and immoral practices'

and being 'haunted and entertained by . . .
George Gibson', the landlord of Poosie
Nansie's. Dr Edgar also alleged that she was
the 'jurr' referred to in 'Adam Armour's
Prayer'.

Wilson, Mrs David
Chambers records that after a night of
jollification in a tavern in the High Street
of Edinburgh, Burns and the painter
Nasmyth walked to Roslin, where they
breakfasted at Mrs Wilson's inn. In gratitude for their meal, Burns wrote two verses
on the reverse side of a wooden plate:

'My blessings on you, sonsy wife;
    I ne'er was here before;
You've gi'en us walth for horn and
                knife, [*wealth, spoon*
Nae heart could wish for more.

'Heaven keep you free frae care and
                                    strife,
Till far ayont fourscore;
And while I toddle on thro' life,
I'll ne'er gang by your door.'

Wilson, John (c. 1751–1839)
Burns's 'Dr Hornbook' was the son of a
Glasgow weaver. He was at Glasgow
University in 1769, taught first at Craigie,
Ayrshire, and in 1781 was appointed
schoolmaster at Tarbolton. (A 'hornbook'
—a sheet of paper carrying the alphabet,
digits, the Lord's Prayer, and elements of
spelling, mounted on wood and covered
by a protective plate of transparent horn—
was in common use in primary schools
until the close of the eighteenth century.)
Gilbert Burns recorded that to eke out a
scanty living, Wilson opened up a grocer's
shop, where he also sold a few medicines,
and offered advice 'in common disorders'
gratis. It was this diversification of his
interests, indeed, that ultimately led the
parishioners to accuse him of neglect, and
to demand his replacement. Because of
this and also because, while Clerk to the
Kirk Session, Wilson quarrelled with his
superior the Reverend Dr Patrick Wod-

row, he left Tarbolton in 1792. When
Burns and his family moved to Lochlea in
1784, it was Wilson who, as Session Clerk,
signed the 'certificate of character' required
by the church law of the time.

Burns obtained the inspiration for 'Death
and Dr Hornbook' upon listening to
Wilson airing his medical knowledge at a
meeting of Tarbolton Masonic Lodge, of
which Wilson was Secretary from 1782 to
1787. The satire, however, was not written
until after Burns had left Tarbolton.
Though Wilson had no reason to feel
kindly towards Burns, he seems to have
borne the poet no ill-will. (Lockhart's story
of the poem forcing Wilson to close his
shop seems to be pure fiction!) When in
1790 Wilson wanted to change his employment, it was to his former satirist that he
wrote. Wilson sought employment as a
clerk or copyist in an Edinburgh office,
possibly with the Excise. Burns advised
him: '. . . for Mrs Wilson's sake, and your
sweet little flock, not to quit the Present,
poor as it is, until you be pretty sure of
your hold of the Future.' The letter, written
from Ellisland on 11th September 1790,
enclosed a note of recommendation to the
lawyer, John Sommerville. But Wilson
heeded the warning that 'the life of an
Edinburgh Quill-driver at twopence a
page' was no life. 'I should be very sorry
any friend of mine should ever try it,'
Burns added. Wilson abandoned his
dreams of going to the Capital, and went
instead to Glasgow, where he taught for a
time in High Street. Later, he opened a
'Commercial Academy' in Buchan Street.
He became Session Clerk of Gorbals
Parish, Glasgow, an appointment he held
for thirty years. He was buried in Gorbals
cemetery.
See Plate 13

Wilson, John (1759–1821)
Born in Kilmarnock, John Wilson, along
with his brother Peter, founded the
earliest Ayrshire newspaper, the *Ayr
Advertiser*. They also carried on business

as printers and publishers, specialising in editions of the classics. Wilson published the poems of John Lapraik, Burns's friend; but it was his earlier venture, the first edition of Burns's *Poems Chiefly in the Scottish Dialect*, published from his press situated probably in the Star Inn Close (now demolished), which brought him fame.

It is not known how Burns got in touch with Wilson, though doubtless the poet had many Kilmarnock friends who would have introduced him to the printer. On 17th April 1786, there appeared:

'Proposals for Publishing by subscription, Scottish Poems, by Robert Burns.' 'The work to be elegantly printed, in one volume, octavo. Price, stitched, three shillings. As the author has not the most distant mercenary view in publishing, as soon as so many subscribers appear as will defray the necessary expense, the work will be sent to the press.'

After a quotation from Ramsay, came the undertaking: 'We, the undersubscribers, engage to take the above-mentioned work on the conditions specified.'

The subscribers who assured the success of the venture were not so much the purchasers of single copies (the poet himself took three), but friends of Burns such as the Ayr attorney McWhinnie, who took twenty copies; John Kennedy of Dumfries House, near Cumnock, who took another twenty copies; John Logan of Knockshinnoch, who also took twenty, 'Orator Bob' Aiken, with his hundred and forty-five subscriptions; Robert Muir of Kilmarnock, with his seventy copies; Gavin Hamilton, who took forty copies; and Gilbert, the poet's brother, who, like Wilson himself, disposed of seventy copies.

The actual work of printing began on 13th July, and on 31st July, the edition of six hundred and twelve copies was ready for distribution. The book, costing three shillings per copy, sold far beyond the list of three hundred and fifty advance sub-

scribers. By 28th August, Wilson had only thirteen copies left. In October, the cautious Wilson offered to print a second edition of a thousand copies, but required Burns to pay about twenty-seven pounds for the paper and fifteen or sixteen pounds for the printing, which Burns was unable to do. Wilson's timidity thus in a sense drove Burns from a local to a national publisher for his next edition. So far as can be ascertained, the receipts totalled about £90. Wilson's note of the cost of production brings the amount spent to thirty-five pounds seventeen shillings, which should have left Burns about fifty-four pounds. Burns, however, stated that the venture only brought in about twenty pounds.

Wilson prospered, became a magistrate and left money which for many years provided local bursaries for poor children. He was buried in Kilmarnock.

Wilson, Robert

A young weaver who was a native of Mauchline, and who knew Jean Armour there. He later moved to Paisley. When Jean's parents discovered that she was pregnant by Burns, they sent their daughter to relatives in Paisley, apparently hoping that Wilson's interest in their daughter would be rekindled. A rumour that Wilson and Jean Armour were likely to be married contributed to Burns's sense of resentment at Jean's alleged 'desertion'.

Wilson, William (d. 1787)

A Writer to the Signet, who employed John Richmond. Burns, on hearing of his death, referred to him in a letter to Richmond, from Mossgiel, dated 7th July 1787, as: 'the old confounder of right and wrong. . . . His chicane, his left-handed wisdom, which stood so firmly by him, to such good purpose, here, like other accomplices in robbery and plunder, will, now the piratical business is blown, in all probability turn king's evidence, and then the devil's bagpiper will touch him off "Bundle and go"!'

Wodrow, The Reverend Dr Patrick (1713–93)
The second of the three sons of the Reverend Robert Wodrow, the Church Historian, and Minister at Eastwood, all of whose sons were ministers—Dr Patrick at Tarbolton; Robert at his father's charge of Eastwood; and James at Stevenston.

Dr Patrick Wodrow was ordained at Tarbolton in 1738. He features in 'The Twa Herds'.

Wood, Alexander (1725–1807)
An Edinburgh surgeon and 'character', who was nicknamed 'Lang Sandy' Wood, because of his lanky figure. Burns greatly liked the warmth and generosity of Wood's nature. He had a high reputation as a doctor in Edinburgh, and attended Burns when he badly hurt his leg falling from his coach. For his part, Wood admired Burns's genius and recommended him for a post to the Excise Commissioners. He was the first man in Edinburgh, Henry Mackenzie tells us, to own an umbrella, about 1780. When he was seized one night by a rioting mob, he cried: 'I'm lang Sandy Wood; tak me to the licht and ye'll see.' He was at once released.

Wood, Alexander
A tailor in Tarbolton who made Burns a mason there.

Woods, William (1751–1802)
An English actor who began his career in Southampton, and settled in Edinburgh early in the 1770s. Robert Burns probably met Woods at the Cannongate Kilwinning Lodge. He appeared first at the Haymarket Theatre, Edinburgh (or the Haymarket, London, according to two different biographers!). The greatest part of his career, however, was spent in Edinburgh, where he was a member of the Edinburgh Company of players for thirty-one years.

He was a close friend of Robert Fer-gusson, the poet, and is said to have given him regular free seats at the theatre. On his retiral he taught elocution. He is buried in Calton cemetery.

Burns wrote a prologue for him for his benefit night, beginning, 'When by a generous Public's kind acclaim'. The play was Shakespeare's *Merry Wives of Windsor*.

Woolwich Hulks
Burns' expression for the transportation ships used to transport such Scottish Friends of the People as the lawyer Thomas Muir, the minister Thomas Palmer, and others sentenced by the savage Lord Bradfield, who took the line that: 'The constitution was perfect. Therefore anyone proposing change was *prima facie* an enemy of the State.'

Wycombe, William Petty, Earl of (1737–1805)
Better known as Lord Shelburne, he was also Marquis of Lansdowne, and a supporter of parliamentary reform. On Rockingham's death while Prime Minister in 1782, George III sent for Shelburne, a more amenable politician to the king's way of thinking. Thus Burns in 'A Fragment':

> Then R–ck–ngh–m took up the game;
> Till Death did on him ca', man;
> When Sh–lb–rne meek held up his cheek,
> Conform to Gospel law, man . . .'

He is also mentioned in Burns's 'Here's to them that's awa'—a political peom in favour of the 'Buff and Blue'; i.e. Fox's party.

Wyndham, William, Lord Grenville (1759–1834)
William Wyndham, Lord Grenville, was Pitt's cousin, and later as his Foreign Minister along with Dundas, he carried weight in the Commons; hence Burns's reference to Grenville having 'a secret word or twa' behind the throne, in 'A Fragment' ('When Guilford good').

Y

'Ye Banks and Braes'
See **Doon, River.**

York, Frederick Augustus, Duke of (1763-1827)
The second son of George III. As an infant of seven months, he was in 1764 elected by his father titular bishop of Osnaburg, in Westphalia. This 'secular dignity with an ecclesiastical designation worth £20,000 a year' was 'a favourite topic of ridicule' according to P. Fitzgerald in *The Royal Dukes . . . of the Family of George III*: hence Burns's reference to him as 'right reverend Osnaburg' in 'A Dream'. His character was certainly not 'right reverend', his most famous mistress having been Mary Ann Clarke whose use of him to sell military commissions led to a parliamentary inquiry and his resignation as Commander-in-Chief of the army. Although he was to be commemorated by the Duke of York's column in London, he had been also involved in a series of disasters as commander in the field, and even the height of the column was popularly ascribed to the need to put him out of the way of his creditors. He married the Princess Royal of Prussia.

Thirty-two years after 'A Dream' was written, the Duke took the chair at a dinner held in London to raise funds for the erection of a monument to Burns on the Banks of Doon. Three leaves torn from the memoirs of Rush, 'Envoy Extraordinary and Minister Plenipotentiary from the U.S.A. to Court of St James' in 1817, describe the scene at the dinner, at which he was present. The leaves are in the Public Reference Library in Ayr:

'The leading person was Mr [Alexander] Boswell, son of the biographer of Johnson; and a Member of Parliament. He made a speech on the genius of Burns, and urged the propriety of erecting a monument on the site of the cottage where he was born. A son of the Poet was present. On "Success to the Fame of Burns" being given as a toast, he thanked the company in a modest, feeling manner. The punch-bowl that had belonged to Burns and of which it is known that he was too fond was handed round as a relic. A full band was in the orchestra . . . . Several hundred pounds [five hundred] were collected towards the monument.'

Young of Harben, Alexander
A prim Tory Writer to the Signet who, in 1834, drafted his own *Memoir* of Burns, which is published in Fitzhugh's *Robert Burns, his Associates and Contemporaries* (1943). The manuscript is in the library of the University of Edinburgh. Young's recollections were continued by the Right Honourable Charles Hope, later Lord Granton, also published by Fitzhugh.

Young, The Reverend Edward (1683-1765)
English poet, born at Upham, new Winchester, the son of Edward Young, rector of Upham and fellow of Winchester, later Dean of Salisbury and chaplain to William and Mary. The poet was schooled at Winchester. In 1702 he matriculated as a commoner at New College, but later the same year entered Corpus College as a gentleman commoner.

In 1708, he was appointed to a law fellowship at All Souls by Archbishop Teneson, out of regard for his father. But although, to begin with, Young may have been, in Pope's words, 'a foolish youth, the sport of peers and poets', Young graduated D.C.L. on 10th June 1719, and thereafter entered Addison's literary circle. Young was given an annuity by the Duke of Wharton, though Young became involved in a lawsuit over the non-payment of it, and won.

In 1728 he took orders, and was appointed chaplain to the King, and in 1730 received the rectory of Welwyn, Hertford-shire, from All Souls. The following year, he married Elizabeth, daughter of the Earl of Lichfield, who had a daughter by a former marriage. Young and his wife had one son.

Young's first play, *Busiris*, was produced at Drury Lane in 1719, and earned Field-ing's ridicule. Later plays were no more successful. Satires and epistles flowed from his pen, but it was with his series of meditations, called *Night Thoughts*, the first of which appeared in 1742, that he achieved fame. Though *Night Thoughts* gained him a literary reputation, he never achieved preferment. But he led a rich and dignified retirement at Welwyn, number-ing Samuel Richardson and Colley Cibber among his friends. He became addicted to melancholy in his closing years.

Among later editions of *Night Thoughts*, of which there were many, was a folio edition, published in 1797, with designs by Blake.

Burns was fond of quoting Young, his favourite quotation being from *Night Thoughts*:

'On reason build resolve,
That column of true majesty in man!'

Having twice quoted it earlier to 'Clarinda', Burns described it to Mrs Dunlop, on 26th March 1788, as 'my favourite quotation now'. On 10th August, Mrs Dunlop heard of it as 'my most favourite Quotation'. It was also used to Ainslie, William Burns and Thomas Sloan. Another of the quotations Burns took from Young was:

'What Truth on earth so precious as
the Lie!'

from *Night Thoughts*, and again, from the same book:

' 'Tis nonsense destin'd to be future
sense.'

On one or two occasions, Burns para-phrased quotations of Young's from memory.

Young, The Reverend James (1711-95)

The son of a Falkirk cooper, he was or-dained minister of New Cumnock in 1758. Burns called him 'Jamie Goose' in 'The Kirk's Alarm':

'Jamie Goose! Jamie Goose, ye hae
    made but toom roose [*empty boast*
O' hunting the wicked Lieutenant;
But the Doctor's your mark, for the
                    L—d's holy ark,
He has cooper'd and ca'd a wrang
                    pin in't, [*driven*
Jamie Goose! He has cooper'd and
            ca'd a wrang pin in't.'

The reference is to Young's 'ecclesiatic persecution' in 'the houghmagandie pack'.

Young, The Reverend Stephen (1745-1819)

Educated at Glasgow, he was an assistant minister at Ochiltree until 1780, then minister of Barr till 1819. Burns called him 'Barr Steenie' in 'The Kirk's Alarm':

'Barr Steenie! Barr Steenie, what
            mean ye? what mean ye?
If ye'll meddle nae mair wi' the
                            matter,
Ye may hae some pretence, man, to
    havins and sense, man, [*manners*
Wi' people that ken you nae better,
Barr Steenie! wi' people that ken
                ye nae better.'

Young, The Reverend Walter (1745-1814)

Minister of Erskine Parish Church, Ren-frewshire, from 1771–1814. He was said to have been the most accomplished private musician of his day. Ramsay of Ochtertyre gave Burns a letter of introduction to Young, when the poet was anxious to learn more about Highland music, and collect Highland airs.

BURNS DOCUMENTS

Burns' Lease on the Farm at Ellisland

The Burns Lease was first printed by Snyder, who saw it in the possession of its then owner, Mr O. R. Barrett. Snyder tells us that it 'occupies three and a half pages of a folio of stamped paper. At the bottom of each page the two principals signed their names as well as at the conclusion of the document. The last half of page 4 is occupied by Burns's renunciation of the lease written in his own hand.'

The text is as follows:

'It is contracted and agreed between the parties following viz. Patrick Miller of Dalswinton Esqr. on the one part, and Robert Burns late in Mossgavill in the parish of Mauchline in Airshire on the other part in manner and to the effect underwritten; that is to say, the said Patrick Miller by these presents sets and in tack and assedation Lets to the said Robert Burns, his heirs and assignees whatsoever but secluding subtenants in all events, and also secluding assignees during the natural life of the said Robert Burns, but reserving to him power to assign by any deed to take effect after his death, all and whole that part of the lands of Elliesland lying on the South side of the river Nith in the parish of Dunscore and Sheriffdom of Dumfries, and that for the space of four nineteen years and crops from and after his entry thereto which is hereby declared in every respect to commence at the term of Martinmas next seventeen hundred and eighty eight; Reserving expressly from the lands above mentioned two acres of any part or parts thereof which the said Patrick Miller pleases, for the purpose of planting, the planting and inclosing which two acres to be at the said Patrick Miller's sole expence, and reseruing also to be planted and inclosed a Belt of twenty yards in breadth along the march which divides the aboue mentioned lands from those of Captain Riddel of the Carse, the expence of planting the said belt to be defrayed by the said Patrick Miller, but the expence of inclosing the same to be disbursed by the tenant out of the three hundred pounds after mentioned. And reserving further for planting the Bank along the riuer side, the expence of planting which shall be defrayed by the said Patrick Miller. And, In respect that it is agreed upon between the said parties that the said Robert Burns shall build a dwelling house, Barn, byre and stable on the said farm, on a plan to be approuen of by the said Patrick Miller, and shall inclose the said lands. For these purposes the said Patrick Miller Binds and obliges him and his heirs and successors to pay to the said Robert Burns the sum of Three hundred pounds Sterling; of which sum he is, in the course of the ensuing summer, to advance him

(signed)	PATRICK MILLER
(signed)	ROBERT BURNS

(page second)

him one hundred and fifty pounds Sterling, on condition of at least building a dwelling in the course of the said summer; and to pay to him the remaining one hundred and fifty pounds afterwards in whole or in parts as the said Robert Burns shall find it necessary to receive it, upon the said Robert Burns always giuing the said Patrick Miller euidence that he has expended, in carrying on the building and inclosing, sums equal to those which he shall from time to time ask and claim; and also vouching to him that he has laid out one hundred pounds of the sum first stipulated for the purposes for which he received it. And it is also prouided that, should the said Robert Burns get the building and inclosures completed for less than three hundred pounds, then the remainder of the said sum given to the said Robert Burns shall be laid out by him in the improvement of the farm as to him shall seem most expedient; Which tack aboue written, with and under the reservations foresaid the said Patrick Miller binds and obliges himself and his foresaids to warrant to the said Robert Burns and his aboue written at all hands and against all deadly (?) as his will. For which causes and on the other part The said Robert Burns Binds and obliges himself and his heirs, Executors and successors whomsoeuer to content and pay to the said Patrick Miller and his heirs or assignees the sum of Seuenty pounds Sterling yearly in name of tack duty, but to be restricted for the first three years and crops to fifty pounds Sterling yearly payable at two terms in the year Whitsunday and Martinmas by equal portions, beginning the first payment of the said tack duty at the term of Whitsunday seventeen hundred and eighty nine and the next term's payment at Martinmas thereafter for the first crop and year of his said possession, and so on thereafter during the currency of this lease, with a fifth part or more of each of said termly payments in liquidate penalty in case of faillie and the legal interest thereof from the respective terms when the same became due and during the not payment of the same. And further, as it is agreed by the said parties that the

(signed)   PATRICK MILLER
(signed)   ROBERT BURNS

(page third)

the said Robert Burns shall be allowed to make use of the houses and pasture the grass of the said farm from Whitsunday to the said term of Martinmas next, which is aboue declared to be the commencement of this lease, therefore the said Robert Burns hereby Binds and obliges him and his foresaids to pay to the said Patrick Miller and his foresaids, for the said houses and grass, so to be used by him, such a sum as shall at the time be agreed upon by the said parties, and, failing such agreement, then the said Robert Burns and his foresaids shall pay for the same such sum as shall be fixed upon by an Arbiter mutually chosen by the parties. And also the said Robert Burns Binds and obliges him and his foresaids to labour and manure the lands hereby let in a proper manner during the currency of this lease; and, during the last six years thereof, not to keep more than one third of the said lands in crop each year, and during that period to use a sufficient quantity of manure with whatever crop he lays down the lands. Moreouer he binds and obliges himself and his foresaids to build and complete the aforesaid dwelling house and the other buildings and execute the inclosing on this said farm in manner aboue mentioned, and particularly of the Belt of planting aboue specified, Declaring always that the inclosures to be made on said farm shall consist of Six—in number, or of any other number which the said parties shall afterwards agree upon, the said Robert Burns and his foresaids being always obliged to make the said inclosures sufficient and to leaue the same in that state at the issue of the lease; and which dwelling house the said Robert Burns becomes bound to finish and complete during the course of the ensuing summer. And further that he or his foresaids shall make no encroachments on the said riuer Nith, by making any Caul, pier, or embankment, throwing in stones or rubbish, or by driuing piles or in any other manner of way whateuer. And the said Robert Burns Binds and obliges himself and his foresaids to remoue himself, his family, servants, goods and gear forth of the

(signed)   PATRICK MILLER
(signed)   ROBERT BURNS

(page fourth)

the said lands at the expiry of this lease without any previous warning or process of remouing to that effect, and leaue the houses and offices in a tenantable condition at his said remoual; And further, Both parties Bind and oblige themselves and their foresaids to implement and perform their respective parts of the premises to each other under the penalty of one hundred pounds Sterling to be paid by the party failing to the party performing or willing to perform ouer and above performance, And they consent to the registration hereof in the books of Council and session or any other Competent that letters of horning on six days charge and other necessary execution may pass on evidence to be Interponed hereto in form as others and to that effect they Constitute their pro [manuscript illegible] &c.

In witness thereof they haue subscribed these presents consisting of this and the three preceding pages and likewise a duplicate hereof all written on stampt paper by Thomas Walker Baird Clerk to John Gordon writer to the Signet at Edinburgh this Eighteenth day of March one thousand seven hundred and eighty eight years before these witnesses the said Thomas Walker Baird and John Murray one of the Clerks in the Bank of Scotland's office.

(signed) John Murray Witness   (signed) PATRICK MILLER
(signed) Thos. W. Baird Witness   (signed) ROBERT BURNS

Whereas, I have paid the rents of the farm of Ellisland to the term of Martinmas first, & settled my accounts relating thereto with Mr Miller of Dalswinton the proprietor of said farm, & have agreed to give up my tack of the said farm at Martinmas first I accordingly hereby give up and renounce for ever the said Tack; in witness whereof I write and subscribe these presents at Dalswinton, this tenth of September, in the year one thousand, seven hundred and ninety one—'

                                                           ROBERT BURNS

Burns's Excise Commission

Burns's Excise Commission, first printed by Snyder, was seen by him in the possession of its then owner, Mr John Gribbel. Snyder comments:

'The signatures of the three Commissioners appear in the left-hand margin; each was originally accompanied by a seal. These seals, and the great seal,

o

which appeared in the upper left-hand corner, have been removed. The date is of interest—14th July 1788, an indication that the machinery of the Board moved slowly, for Burns had qualified for the commission some time before.'

The text is as follows:

'TO ALL TO WHOM these Presents shall come, Greeting. Know Ye, That we, whose Hands and Seals are hereunto set, being the major part of the chief Commissioners and Governors for the Management of the Receipt of the Excise; that is to say, the Duties upon making and importing Beer, Ale, Spirits, and other Excisable Liquors, in that Part of Great Britain called Scotland, and in all and every of the Islands and Territories thereunto belonging; and of the Duties upon making Candles, and of the Duties upon Hops growing, and to grow, within the Limits aforesaid: And we also, being the major Part of the Commissioners and Governors for the Receipt and Management of the several and respective Duties hereinafter mentioned within the Limits aforesaid; that is to say, of the several and respective Duties upon making of Soap, Paper, Pasteboard, Millboard and Scaleboard, respectively; and upon printing, painting, or staining of Paper; and upon printing, painting, staining, or dying of Silks, Callicoes, Linens, and Stuffs respectively; and upon the making of Starch, and of Gilt and Silver Wire respectively; and upon tanning, tawing, or dressing of Hides and Skins, and Pieces of Hides and Skins; and upon the making of Vellum and Parchment respectively; and of the Inland Duties upon Coffee, Tea and Chocolate respectively; and upon making Malt, and making and importing Mum, Cyder and Perry respectively; and of the Duties upon Glass, and all the Materials or Metal, or other Preparations made use of in the making of Glass; and upon every Coach, Berlin, Landau, Chariot, Calash, Chaise-marine, Chaise, Chair, and Caravan, or by what Name soever such Wheel Carriages now are or hereafter may be called or known, that shall be kept by or for any Person for his or her own Use, or to be let out to hire respectively; and of the Duties payable by all persons and Bodies Politick or Corporate, owning, using, having or keeping, certain Quantities of Silverplate, arisen or accrued, or to arise or accrue in SCOTLAND aforesaid, and in all and every of the Islands and Territories thereunto belonging, reposing especial Trust and Confidence in the Knowledge, Skill, Industry, Integrity, Fidelity, and Circumspection of Robert Burns Gentleman [written] HAVE (pursuant to the several and respective Powers to us given and granted, in and by the several and respective Statutes relating to the said several and respective Duties, and in and by our several and respective Commissions, Constitutions and Appointments) nominated, constituted and appointed, and, for His Majesty's Service, DO nominate, constitute, and appoint him, the said Robert Burns [written] to be One of the Surveyors, Messengers, Gaugers, and Officers, of and for the said several and respective Duties before mentioned, all and every one of them respectively; and of all other Duties that shall or may be put under the Management of us the said present Commissioners, or of the like Commissioners for the Time being; and of the measuring and attending Malt that shall be shipped for Exportation; and for the seizing of all Brandy, Arrack, Rum, Spirits, Strong Waters, Coffee, Tea, Chocolate, and Cocoa Nuts, which shall be unlawfully imported or carried within the Limits aforesaid: AND do hereby impower and require him, the said Robert Burns [written] that, pursuant to the Powers and Authorities in and by the said several and respective

Statutes relating to the said several and respective Duties, he shall and do, from Time to Time, by gauging, weighing, Measuring and otherwise take, and also do enter into a Book and Books, to be from Time to Time delivered to him for that Purpose, full and true Accounts of the Quantities, Qualities, Natures and Kinds, of all and every the several and respective Goods, Commodities, and Manufactures respectively, chargeable with, and liable to, the said several and respective Duties, which he, from Time to Time, shall or may find out or discover; and thereof respectively shall and do, from Time to Time, make and deliver to us the present Commissioners, and to the Commissioners for the said Duties for the Time being, or to the major Part of us or them respectively, or to such as we, or the Major part of us, have appointed, or as we, or the Commissioners for the said Duties for the Time being, or the major Part of us or them respectively shall nominate and appoint for such purpose, full and true Returns, Reports, Registers, Vouchers and Accounts in Writing, of the full and true Quantities, Qualities, Natures and Kinds of all and every the said several and respective Goods, Commodities, and Manufactures before mentioned, chargeable with or liable to the said several and respective Duties, by him from Time to Time found out or discovered; and that he shall and do exercise, execute, and perform, all and every the Powers and Authorities in and by the several and respective Statutes given and granted, or enacted to be done, exercised, executed, and performed by such Surveyor, Messenger, Gauger, or Officer, according to the true Intent and Meaning of such Statutes respectively; TO HOLD, exercise, execute, and perform, the said Office of such Surveyor, or Messenger, Gauger, and Officer, as aforesaid, during the Pleasure of us the said present Commissioners, and during the like Pleasure of the Commissioners for the said Duties for the Time being, or of the major Part of us or them respectively. AND all Sheriffs, Bailies, Justices of the Peace, Magistrates of Burghs, Constables, and other Officers of the Peace, and all and every other Person and Persons whatsoever, is and are hereby prayed and required to be aiding and assisting unto him the said Robt. Burns [written] in the due Execution hereof, as he or they will answer the Contrary at his or their utmost Peril. GIVEN under our Hands and Seals at the Chief Office of Excise, and for the said Duties, in EDINBURGH, this Fourteenth [written] Day of July [written] in the Twenty eighth [written] Year of the Reign of our Sovereign Lord George the Third [written] by the Grace of GOD, of Great Britain, France and Ireland, KING, Defender of the Faith, and so forth; and in the Year of our Lord One thousand seven hundred and Eighty eight [written].'

(Signatures)

J. WHARTON,

GEO. BROWN,

JAS. STODDARD.

Narrative by Gilbert Burns of his Brother's Life

(Originally written as a letter to Mrs. Dunlop)

I have often heard my father describe the anguish of mind he felt when he parted with his elder brother Robert on the top of a hill, on the confines of their native place, each going off his several way in search of new adventures, and scarcely knowing whither he went. My Father undertook to act as a gardener and shaped his course to Edinburgh, where he wrought hard when he could get work, passing through a variety of difficulties. Still, however, he endeavoured to spare something for the support of an aged parent, and I recollect hearing him mention his having sent a bank-note for this purpose, when money of that kind was so scarce in Kincardineshire, that they hardly knew how to employ it when it arrived.

Passing from Edinburgh into Ayrshire, he lived for two years as gardener to the laird of Fairly in Dundonald parish, and then changed his service for that of Mr Crawford of Doonside in the parish of Alloway. At length, being desirous to settle in life, he took a perpetual lease of some acres of land from Dr Campbell, physician in Ayr, with a view to cultivate it as a nursery and meal-garden. With his own hands he built a house on part of this ground, and in December 1757, married Agnes Brown, belonging to respectable connexions near Maybole in Carrick. The first fruit of the marriage was the subject of this memoir, born on 25th January 1759. The education of my brother and myself was in common, there being only twenty months between us, in respect of age. Under Mr John Murdoch we learned to read English tolerably well, and to write a little. He taught us too the English grammar. I was too young to profit much from his lessons in grammar, but Robert made some proficiency in it, a circumstance of considerable weight in the unfolding of his genius and character; as he soon became remarkable for the fluency and correctness of his expression, and read the few books that came in his way with much pleasure and improvement; for even then he was a reader when he could get a book. Murdoch, whose library at that time had no great variety in it, lent him *The Life of Hannibal,* which was the first book he read (the school books excepted) and almost the only one he had an opportunity of reading while he was at school; for the *Life of Wallace* which he classes with it in one of his letters, he did not see for some years afterwards, when he borrowed it from the blacksmith who shod our horses.

At Whitsunday 1766 we removed to Mount Oliphant, a farm of seventy acres (between 80 and 90 English statute measure) the rent of which was to be forty pounds annually for the first six years, and afterwards forty-five pounds. My father endeavoured to sell the leasehold property in Alloway, for the purpose of stocking his farm, but at that time he was unable, and Mr Fergusson lent him a hundred pounds for that purpose. It was I think not above two years after this that Murdoch, our tutor and friend, left this part of the country, and there being no school near us, and our little services being useful on the farm, my Father undertook to teach us arithmetic in the winter evenings by candlelight, and in this way my two elder sisters got all the education they received. I remember a circumstance that happened at this time, which, though trifling in itself, is fresh on my memory, and may serve to illustrate the early character of my brother. Murdoch came to spend a night with us, and to take his leave when he was about to go into Carrick. He brought us a present and memorial of him, a small compendium of English Grammar, and the tragedy of *Titus Andronicus,* and by way of passing the evening, he began to read the play aloud. We were all attention for some time, till presently the whole party was dissolved in tears. A female in the play (I have but a confused recollection of it) had her hands chopt off, her tongue cut out, and then was insultingly desired to call for water to wash her hands. At this, in an agony of distress, we with one voice desired he would read no more. My father observed that if we would not hear it out, it would be needless to leave the play with us. Robert replied that if it was left he would burn it. My father was going to chide him for this ungrateful return to his tutor's kindness; but Murdoch interposed, declaring that he liked to see so much sensibility; and he left the *School for Love* a comedy (translated I think from the French) in its place.

Nothing could be more retired than our general manner of living at Mount Oliphant; we rarely saw any body but the members of our own family. There were no boys of our own age, or near it, in the neighbourhood. Indeed the greater part of the land in the vicinity was at that time possessed by shopkeepers, and people of that stamp, who had retired from business, or who kept their farm in the country at the same time that they followed business in the town. My father was for some time almost the only companion we had. He conversed familiarly on all subjects with us as if we had been men, and was at great pains, while we accompanied him in the labours of the farm, to lead the conversation to such subjects as might tend to increase our knowledge, or confirm our virtuous habits. He borrowed Salmon's *Geographical Grammar* for us, and endeavoured to make us acquainted with the situation and history of the different countries in the world; while, from a book-society in Ayr, he procured for us Durham's *Phisico and Astro-Theology*, and Ray's *Wisdom of God in Creation,* to give us some idea of astronomy and natural history. Robert read all these books with an avidity and industry scarcely to be equalled. My Father had been a subscriber to Stackhouse's *History of the Bible,* then lately published by John Meuros in Kilmarnock: from this Robert collected a pretty competent knowledge of ancient history: for no book was so voluminous as to slacken his industry, or so antiquated as to damp his researches. A brother of my mother who had lived with us some time, and had learned some arithmetic by our winter evening's candle, went into a bookseller's shop in Ayr, to purchase *The Ready Reckoner, or Tradesman's sure Guide,* and a book to teach him to write letters. Luckily, in place of *The Complete Letter-Writer,* he got by mistake a small collection of Letters by the most Eminent Writers, with a few sensible directions for attaining an easy epistolary style. This book was to Robert of the greatest consequence. It inspired him with a strong desire to excel in letter-writing, while it furnished him with models by some of the first writers in our language.

My brother was about thirteen or fourteen, when my father, regretting that we wrote so ill, sent us week about during a summer quarter, to the parish school of Dalrymple, which, though between two and three miles distant, was the nearest to us, that we might have an opportunity of remedying this defect. About this time a bookish acquaintance of my father's procured us a reading of two volumes of Richardson's *Pamela,* which was the first novel we read, and the only part of Richardson's works my brother was acquainted with till towards the period of his commencing author. Till that time too he remained unacquainted with Fielding, with Smollett (two volumes of *Ferdinand Count Fathom,* and two volumes of *Peregrine Pickle* excepted), with Hume, with Robertson, and almost all our authors of eminence of the later times. I recollect indeed my father borrowed a volume of English history from Mr Hamilton of Bourtree-hill's gardener. It treated of the reign of James the First, and his unfortunate son, Charles, but I do not know who was the author; all that I remember of it is something of Charles's conversation with his children. About this time (1772) Murdoch, our former teacher, after having been in different places in the country, and having taught a school some time in Dumfries, came to be the established teacher of the English language in Ayr, a circumstance of considerable consequence to us. The remembrance of my father's former friendship, and his attachment to my brother, made him do every thing in his power for our improvement. He sent us Pope's works, and some other poetry, the first that we had an opportunity of reading, excepting what is contained in *The English Collection,* and in the volume of *The Edinburgh Magazine* for 1772; excepting also *those excellent new songs* that are hawked about the country in baskets, or exposed on stalls in the streets.

The summer after we had been at Dalrymple school, my father sent Robert to Ayr, to revise his English grammar, with his former teacher. He had been there only one week, when he was obliged to return, to assist at the harvest. When the harvest was over, he went back to school, where he remained two weeks; and this completes the account of his school education, excepting one summer quarter, some time afterwards, that he attended the parish school of Kirk-Oswald (where he lived with a brother of my mother's), to learn surveying.

During the two last weeks that he was with Murdoch, he himself was engaged in learning French, and he communicated the instructions he received to my brother, who, when he returned, brought home with him a French dictionary and grammar, and the *Adventures of Telemachus* in the original. In a little while, by the assistance of these books, he had acquired such a knowledge of the language, as to read and understand any French author in prose. This was considered as a sort of prodigy, and, through the medium of Murdoch, procured him the acquaintance of several lads in Ayr, who were at that time gabbling French, and the notice of some families, particularly that of Dr Malcolm, where a knowledge of French was a recommendation.

Observing the facility with which he had acquired the French language, Mr Robinson, the established writing-master in Ayr, and Mr Murdoch's particular friend, having himself acquired a considerable knowledge of the Latin language by his own industry, without ever having learnt it at school, advised Robert to make the same attempt, promising him every assistance in his power. Agreeably to this advice, he purchased *The Rudiments of the Latin Tongue,* but finding this study dry and uninteresting, it was quickly laid aside. He frequently returned to his *Rudiments* on any little chagrin or disappointment, particularly in his love affairs; but the Latin seldom predominated more than a day or two at a time, or a week at most. Observing himself the ridicule that would attach to this sort of conduct if it were known, he made two or three humorous stanzas on the subject, which I cannot now recollect, but they all ended,

'So I'll to my Latin again.'

Thus you see Mr Murdoch was a principal means of my brother's improvement. Worthy man! though foreign to my present purpose, I cannot take leave of him without tracing his future history. He continued for some years a respected and useful teacher at Ayr, till one evening that he had been overtaken in liquor, he happened to speak somewhat disrespectfully of Dr Dalrymple, the parish minister, who had not paid him that attention to which he thought himself entitled. In Ayr he might as well have spoken blasphemy. He found it proper to give up his appointment. He went to London, where he still lives, a private teacher of French. He has been a considerable time married, and keeps a shop of stationery wares.

The father of Dr Paterson, now physician at Ayr, was, I believe, a native of Aberdeenshire, and was one of the established teachers in Ayr when my father settled in the neighbourhood. He early recognised my father as a fellow native of the north of Scotland, and a certain degree of intimacy subsisted between them during Mr Paterson's life. After his death, his widow, who is a very genteel woman, and of great worth, delighted in doing what she thought her husband would have wished to have done, and assiduously kept up her attentions to all his acquaintance. She kept alive the intimacy with our family, by frequently inviting my father and mother to her house on Sundays, when she met them at church.

When she came to know my brother's passion for books, she kindly offered us the use of her husband's library, and from her we got the *Spectator, Pope's Translation of Homer,* and several other books that were of use to us. Mount Oliphant, the farm my father possessed in the parish of Ayr, is almost the very poorest soil I know of in a state of cultivation. A stronger proof of this I cannot give, than that, notwithstanding the extraordinary rise in the value of lands in Scotland, it was, after a considerable sum laid out in improving it by the proprietor, let a few years ago five pounds per annum lower than the rent paid for it by my father thirty years ago. My father, in consequence of this, soon came into difficulties, which were increased by the loss of several of his cattle by accidents and disease. To the buffettings of misfortune, we could only oppose hard labour and the most rigid economy. We lived very sparingly. For several years butcher's meat was a stranger in the house, while all the members of the family exerted themselves to the utmost of their strength, and rather beyond it, in the labours of the farm. My brother, at the age of thirteen, assisted in threshing the crop of corn, and at fifteen was the principal labourer on the farm, for we had no hired servant, male or female. The anguish of mind we felt at our tender years under these straits and difficulties was very great. To think of our father growing old (for he was now above fifty) broken down with the long continued fatigues of his life, with a wife and five other children, and in a declining state of circumstances, these reflections produced in my brothers' mind and mine sensations of the deepest distress. I doubt not but the hard labour and sorrow of this period of his life, was in a great measure the cause of that depression of spirits, with which Robert was so often afflicted through his whole life afterwards. At this time he was almost constantly afflicted in the evenings with a dull headache, which, at a future period of his life, was exchanged for a palpitation of the heart, and a threatening of fainting and suffocation in his bed, in the night time.

By a stipulation in my father's lease, he had a right to throw it up, if he thought proper, at the end of every sixth year. He attempted to fix himself in a better farm at the end of the first six years, but failing in that attempt, he continued where he was for six years more. He then took the farm of Lochlea, of 130 acres, at the rent of twenty shillings an acre, in the parish of Tarbolton, of Mr ——, then a merchant in Ayr, and now (1797) a merchant in Liverpool. He removed to this farm at Whitsunday 1777, and possessed it only seven years.

No writing had ever been made out of the conditions of the lease; a misunderstanding took place respecting them; the subjects in dispute were submitted to arbitration, and the decision involved my father's affairs in ruin. He lived to know of this decision, but not to see any execution in consequence of it. He died on the 13th of February, 1784.

The seven years we lived in Tarbolton parish (extending from the nineteenth to the twenty-sixth of my brother's age) were not marked by much literary improvement; but, during this time, the foundation was laid of certain habits in my brother's character, which afterwards became but too prominent, and which malice and envy have taken delight to enlarge on. Though when young he was bashful and awkward in his intercourse with women, yet when he approached manhood, his attachment to their society became very strong, and he was constantly the victim of some fair enslaver. The symptoms of his passion were often such as nearly to equal those of the celebrated Sappho. I never indeed knew that he *fainted, sunk, and died away*: but the agitation of his mind and body exceeded anything of the kind I ever knew in real life. He had always a particular jealousy of people who were richer than himself, or who had more consequence in life. His love, therefore, rarely settled on persons of this description. When he selected any one out of the sovereignty of his good pleasure to whom he should pay his particular attention, she was instantly invested with a sufficient stock of charms, out of the plentiful stores of his own imagination; and there was often a great disparity between his fair captivator, and her attributes. One generally reigned paramount in his affections; but as Yorick's affections flowed out toward Madame de L—— at the remise door, while the eternal vows of Eliza were upon him, so Robert was frequently encountering other attractions, which formed so many under-plots in the drama of his love. As these connexions were governed by the strictest rules of virtue and modesty (from which he never deviated till he reached his twenty-third year), he became anxious to be in a situation to marry. This was not likely to be soon the case while he remained a farmer, as the stocking of a farm required a sum of money he had no probability of being master of for a great while. He began, therefore, to think of trying some other line of life. He and I had for several years taken land of my father for the purpose of raising flax on our own account. In the course of selling it, Robert began to think of turning flax-dresser, both as being suitable to his grand view of settling in life, and as subservient to the flax raising. He accordingly wrought at the business of a flax-dresser in Irvine for six months, but abandoned it at that period, as neither agreeing with his health nor inclination. In Irvine he had contracted some acquaintance of a freer manner of thinking and living than he had been used to, whose society prepared him for over-leaping the bounds of rigid virtue which had hitherto restrained him. Towards the end of the period under review (in his twenty-sixth year), and soon after his father's death, he was furnished with the subject of his Epistle to John Rankin. During this period also he became a freemason, which was his first introduction to the life of a boon companion. Yet, notwithstanding these circumstances, and the praise he has bestowed on Scotch drink (which seems to have misled his historians), I do not recollect, during these seven years, nor till towards the end of his commencing author, (when his growing celebrity occasioned his being often in company) to have ever seen him intoxicated; nor was he at all given to drinking. A stronger proof of the general sobriety of his conduct need not be required, than what I am about to give. During the whole of the time we lived in the farm of Lochlea with my father, he allowed my brother and me such wages for our labour as he gave to other labourers, as a part of which, every article of our clothing manufactured in the family was regularly accounted for. When my father's affairs grew near a crisis, Robert and I took the farm of Mossgiel, consisting of 118 acres, at the rent of £90 per annum (the farm on which I live at present), from Mr Gavin Hamilton, as an asylum for the family in case of the worst. It was stocked by the property and individual savings of the whole family, and was a joint concern among us. Every member of the family was allowed ordinary wages for the labour he performed on the farm. My brother's allowance and mine was seven pounds per annum each. And during the whole time this family concern lasted, which was four years, as well as during the preceding period at Lochlea, his expenses never in any one year exceeded his slender income. As I was intrusted with the keeping of the family accounts, it is not possible that there can be any fallacy in this statement in my brother's favour. His temperance and frugality were everything that could be wished.

The farm of Mossgiel lies very high, and mostly on a cold wet bottom. The first two years that we were on the farm were very frosty, and the spring was very late. Our crops in consequence were very unprofitable, and notwithstanding our utmost diligence and economy, we found ourselves obliged to give up our bargain, with the loss of a considerable part of our original stock. It was during these two years that Robert formed his connexion with Jean Armour, afterwards Mrs Burns. This connexion could no longer be concealed, about the time we came to a final determination to quit the farm. Robert durst not engage with a family in his poor unsettled state, but was anxious to shield his partner by every means in his power from the consequences of their imprudence. It was agreed therefore between them that they should make a legal acknowledgement of an irregular and private marriage, that he should go to Jamaica to push his fortune, and that she should remain with her father till it might please Providence to put the means of supporting a family in his power.

Mrs Burns was a great favourite of her father's. The intimation of a marriage was the first suggestion he received of her real situation. He was in the greatest distress, and fainted away. The marriage did not appear to him to make the matter any better. A husband in Jamaica seemed to him and to his wife little better than none, and an effectual bar to any other prospects of a settlement in life that their daughter might have. They therefore expressed a wish to her that the written papers which respected the marriage should be cancelled, and thus the marriage rendered void. In her melancholy state, she felt the deepest remorse at having brought such heavy affliction on parents that loved her so tenderly, and she submitted to their entreaties. This wish was mentioned to Robert, he felt the deepest anguish of mind. He offered to stay at home and provide for his wife and family in the best manner that his daily labours could provide for them; that being the only means in his power. Even this offer they did not approve of; for humble as Miss Armour's station was, and great though her imprudence had been, she still, in the eyes of her partial parents, might look to a better connexion than with my friendless and unhappy brother, at that time without house or hiding-place. Robert at length consented to their wishes, but his feelings on this occasion were of the most distracting nature, and the impression of sorrow was not effaced, till by a regular marriage they were indissolubly united. In the state of mind which the separation produced, he wished to leave the country as soon as possible, and agreed with Dr Douglas to go out to Jamaica, as an assistant over-seer, or as I believe it is called, a book-keeper, on his estate. As he had not sufficient money to pay his passage, and the vessel in which Dr Douglas was to procure a passage for him was not expected to sail for some time, Mr Hamilton advised him to publish his poems in the meantime by subscription, as a likely way of getting a little money to provide him more liberally in necessaries for Jamaica. Agreeably to this advice, subscription bills were printed immediately, and the printing was commenced in Kilmarnock, his preparations going on at the same time for his voyage. The reception however which his poems met with in the world, and the friends they procured him, made him change his resolution of going to Jamaica, and he was advised to go to Edinburgh to publish a second edition. On his return in happier circumstances, he renewed his connexion with Mrs Burns, and rendered it permanent by an union for life.

NOTES ON THE ILLUSTRATIONS

1. B. C. Skinner in his *Burns, authentic likenesses* (Oliver & Boyd, 1963) writes 'One . . . transposition of the Nasmyth portrait is the red-chalk head by Archibald Skirving . . . in one letter to his brother he [i.e. Skirving] refers to this head of Burns as "taken from a picture, for him I never saw".' The date assigned to the Skirving portrait by Skinner is 1796–8.

The three-inch miniature on an ivory dome by Alexander Reid of Dumfries, done in 1795–6, was thought by the poet himself to be the best likeness.

The Swinton portrait, a bad picture by an anonymous artist, yet catches the sturdy quality also recorded by Reid and was once owned by Burns's mother.

The oil painting by Peter Taylor is claimed to have been painted from the life in 1786–7, but is more probably of Gilbert, the poet's brother.

The portrait by Alexander Nasmyth was painted in Edinburgh during the winter of 1786.

2. The view of Lochlie is from a somewhat romanticised print of c. 1840, and the print of the birthplace is the earliest known picture, taken from James Storer and John Grieg, *Views in North Britain illustrative of the works of Robert Burns* (1805).

3. The portrait of Jean Armour, later Mrs Robert Burns, was engraved by W. Holl from a painting by Samuel Mackenzie, R.A., and the photograph of Robert Burns the Younger is reproduced from the *Memorial Catalogue of the Burns Exhibition* (1898).

5 and 6. The view of Ayr c. 1800 is taken from James Fittler and John Claude Nattes *Scotia Depicta*; and those of Irvine, Kilmarnock, Tarbolton, Mauchline, Edinburgh Castle from Greyfriars Churchyard, the Banks of Doon and Glenafton, are all from paintings by David Octavius Hill in the 1830s for 'Christopher North's' *Land of Burns*.

7. The engraving of Euphemia Murray is by H. Robinson from a miniature by Anthony Stewart; of Jessie Lewars, later Mrs James Thomson, from a painting by J. Irvine, A.R.S.A.; of Lucy Johnstone, later Mrs Lucy Oswald, by H. T. Ryall from a painting by Sir Henry Raeburn, R.S.A.; of Elizabeth Burnett by H. Robinson; and of Margaret Chalmers, later Mrs Lewis Hay, by H. Cook from a drawing by J. Irvine, A.R.S.A.

8. The engraving of the Rev. John Skinner is by T. Woolnoth from 'North's' *Land of Burns*; of Dr John Moore by J. Cochran from a painting by Cochrane of Rome; of Robert Ainslie by J. Cochran, and of Captain Francis Grose, F.S.A., by H. B. Hall from a painting by N. Dance, R.A. The cartoon of Dr James Gregory is by Kay and dated 1797.

9. The engravings of the Rev. John Kemp, D.D., 'Clarinda's' minister, and of

Lord Craig, are both from portraits by John Kay, and the silhouette of 'Clarinda' is by J. Miers.

10. The portrait of William Inglis is by an unknown artist (photo by Archie Stirling); the engraving of Lord Glencairn is by H. Robinson; of the Rev. Thomas Blacklock by W. F. Holl; and of William Smellie, F.S.A., by H. B. Hall from a drawing by G. Watson, P.S.A. The miniature of John Ballantine is possibly by one of the brothers Plimer.

11. The engraving of Mrs Catherine Bruce of Clackmannan is by H. Robinson from a painting by G. Chalmers; of Mrs Frances Dunlop of Dunlop by H. Robinson; of William Niven from Fergusson's *White Hind*; and of John Syme by J. T. Kelly. The portrait of Alexander Cunningham is by Sir Henry Raeburn, R.S.A.

12. The portrait of Alexander Findlater is by R. Forbes. The engraving of the Rev. George Lawrie, D.D., is by W. F. Holl from a painting by W. Bonnar, R.S.A., and of George Thomson by J. Cochran from a painting by Sir Henry Raeburn, R.S.A.

13. 'The Cotter's Saturday Night' is an engraving by T. G. Flowers from a drawing by David Allan.

14. The portrait of Robert Riddell is from a frontispiece drawing in a manuscript volume in the library of the Society of Antiquaries, and Friar's Carse is reproduced from Francis Grose's *Antiquities of Scotland* (1789–91).

15. Dumfries in the 1830s is from 'North's' *Land of Burns*.

16. The room in which Burns died is from a print dated 1859.

INDEX

397